THE ST. MARTIN'S
GUIDE TO
TEACHING WRITING

Third Edition

THE ST. MARTIN'S GUIDE TO TEACHING WRITING

Robert Connors

UNIVERSITY OF NEW HAMPSHIRE

Cheryl Glenn

OREGON STATE UNIVERSITY

ST. MARTIN'S PRESS

NEW YORK

Senior English editor: Karen Allanson
Development editor: Kristin Bowen
Managing editor: Patricia Mansfield Phelan
Project editor: Amy Horowitz
Cover design: Sheree Goodman

Library of Congress Catalog Card Number: 94-65182

Manufactured in the United States of America.

9 8 7
f e d

For information, write:
St. Martin's Press, Inc.
175 Fifth Avenue
New York, NY 10010

ISBN: 0-312-10349-2

Acknowledgments

Classical Rhetoric for the Modern Student, Edward P. J. Corbett. From pages 450-58 © 1971 by Oxford University Press.
    "The ESL Student in the Freshman Composition Class," William G. Clark. *Teaching English in the Two-Year College.* February 1986. Copyright 1986 by the National Council of Teachers of English. Reprinted with permission.
    "Frequency of Formal Errors in Current College Writing, or Ma and Pa Kettle Do Research," Robert J. Connors and Andrea A. Lunsford. *College Composition and Communication.* December 1988. Copyright 1988 by the National Council of Teachers of English. Reprinted with permission.
    "Grammar, Grammars, and the Teaching of Grammar," Patrick Hartwell. *College English.* February 1985. Copyright 1985 by the National Council of Teachers of English. Reprinted with permission.
    "Inventing the University," David Bartholomae. *When a Writer Can't Write: Studies in Writer's Block and Other Composing Process Problems.* Ed. Mike Rose. Reprinted with permission of the author and Guilford Press.
    "One-to-One: Tutorial Instruction in Freshman Composition," Roger H. Garrison. *New Directions for Community Colleges* 5. 1974.
    "Problem-Solving, Composing, and Liberal Education," Richard Larson. *College English,* March 1972. Copyright 1972 by the National Council of Teachers of English. Reprinted with permission.
    "Responding to Student Writing," Nancy Sommers. *College Composition and Communication.* May 1982. Copyright 1982 by the National Council of Teachers of English. Reprinted with permission.

Acknowledgments and copyrights are continued at the back of the book on page 467, which constitutes an extension of the copyright page. It is a violation of the law to reproduce these selections by any means whatsoever without the written permission of the copyright holder.

PREFACE

There it is in black and white. You've been assigned to teach a college writing course: first-year composition. Sentences, paragraphs, essays. "Me—teach writing? I never took a writing course in my life, except freshman English, which I barely remember. What am I going to do?"

That last question, the central concern of every new writing teacher, is the question explored in this book, which was written to help you plan and teach your writing classes and to help your students become better writers. The theories, techniques, and methods in the following chapters are based on our own teaching practice; all have been classroom-tested; and as a whole, they represent the greater part of our current knowledge—both theory and practice—about teaching writing.

The contents of *The St. Martin's Guide to Teaching Writing* are informed by a three-part thesis. First, writing is teachable; it is an art that can be learned rather than a mysterious ability that one either has or does not have. Second, students learn to write from continual trial-and-error writing and almost never profit from lectures, from teacher-centered classes, or from studying and memorizing isolated rules. Third, the theories and methods included here were selected according to what works. This is not a complete introduction to composition studies; some important composition and education theories are not covered in the following chapters for the simple reason that they don't immediately lend themselves to classroom use.

This book is divided into three parts: "Practical Issues in Teaching Writing," "Theoretical Issues in Teaching Writing," and "An Anthology of Essays." Aimed at the first-time teacher of writing, Part I offers the nuts and bolts of teaching composition, with chapters ranging from "Preparing for the First Class" to "Responding to and Evaluating Student Essays." If you are a new teacher, you may want to begin with Part I and become familiar with the framework: how to prepare for, set up, and teach your first writing course.

More experienced teachers may want to begin with Part II, theoretical background and application, which covers the three most important areas of traditional rhetoric (invention, arrangement, and style) and the three most important elements of composition (the sentence, the paragraph, and the sustained piece of discourse). Each of the five chapters in Part II consists of an introduction followed by discrete units describing specific theories and classroom activities. The classroom activities are structured according to Richard Graves's important teaching model, CEHAE—Concept, Example, Highlighting, Activity, Evaluation. These activities have been successful for us and for other teachers. We hope they work for you—and that you will help to improve them.

Part III presents a set of essays that explicitly attempt to link theory and practice, beginning with articles that explore the teaching and learning of writing, cover classroom practices, and conclude with larger theory and research questions. It ends with two articles on the research that informs *The St. Martin's Handbook* itself. We hope these beginning readings will lead users of this book to conduct their own research in their own classrooms.

Acknowledgments

Many people have helped us write this book. At St. Martin's we wish to thank Karen Allanson, Marilyn Moller, Barbara Heinssen, Kristin Bowen, Amy Horowitz, Steven Kutz, and Susan Cottenden. Special thanks go to the reviewers for the third edition: Anita Anger, University of Massachusetts, Boston; Bruce Appleby, Southern Illinois University; Michael Moran, University of Georgia; Nell Ann Pickett, Hinds Community College; and Lucy Schultz, University of Cincinnati. The materials in Part I, "Practical Issues in Teaching Writing," have been updated and improved with help from three master teachers at the University of New Hampshire, and we want to thank Rebecca Rule for her work on the sections on workshopping and conferencing, Bruce Ballenger for his contribution to the section on teaching the research paper, and Donald Jones, whose admirable research and writing richly contributes to the chapter on teaching the composing process. We thank also the teacher-researchers whose work constitutes Part III of this book for their kind permission to reprint their articles. We are grateful, finally, to Danielle Mitchell at Oregon State University for her assistance and clerical support.

As the preceding paragraph suggests, teaching writing is always collaborative. There are few teaching methods that can really be said to belong to any one person. We are a large and far-flung community, but writing teachers *are* a community. We're all in this together, and one of the most satisfying parts of teaching writing is in the ways we all help one another out. We want to welcome you to our community, and we hope this book helps you out as you get ready for your first—or your twentieth—adventure in the writing classroom.

Robert Connors
Cheryl Glenn

Work Cited

Graves, Richard. "CEHAE: Five Steps for Teaching Writing." *English Journal* 62 (1972): 696–701.

CONTENTS

Practical Issues in Teaching Writing

1

Practical Issues in Teaching Writing

1 PREPARING FOR THE FIRST CLASS

FINDING OUT ABOUT THE COURSE

The first thing any new teacher must do is gather information. You have been assigned to teach a writing course, but writing courses, even first-year (FY) writing courses, come in many varieties. Before you can make intelligent and useful plans, you need to find out some of the definitions and vital statistics concerning your course. Such information may be presented in the form of an orientation session for new teachers. Indeed, some departments organize special practicums or colloquia for new teaching assistants, and new instructors are usually welcome to sit in. Such an introduction will provide you with all the information you need. If your program does not present an orientation session, the course director, the director of composition, or the chair of the department can undoubtedly answer most of the questions raised here. Some of your most important questions concerning unwritten practices may be answered by experienced teachers, and at many schools, their wisdom is a vital element of the program; but your writing-program administrator (WPA) is the most reliable source for official departmental policy.

The first things you should find out are the number of credit hours the course carries and the number of times each week the class meets. A three-credit course that meets three hours a week provides far less time for reading and writing than does a five-credit, five-hour course; students willing to write ten essays and fifty journal entries for five credits may object to doing the same amount of work for three credits. So as you plan your syllabus, adjust the number of writing assignments according to the number of credit hours.

Second, ask how many sections you will be teaching and how many students you should expect to have in each class. The National Council of Teachers of English (NCTE) recommends that each graduate student teach only one undergraduate section and that the maximum number of students in a class be twenty (or fifteen in a basic writing course). Most English departments try to adhere to these recommendations, keeping the numbers within reasonable limits (from twenty to twenty-five students). Of course, the fewer students you have, the fewer papers you must read and evaluate and the fewer conferences you must conduct; and the fewer students you have, the more time you will have for each student and for class preparation. If you are willing to teach at 8:00 A.M. or 5:00 P.M., you may get a smaller class than if you teach at a popular time slot, say late morning or early afternoon. Nonetheless, you should count on having the maximum allowable number of students in your class. This information about the student load will help you organize assignments and plan a syllabus.

Third, find out whether there is a standardized departmental structure for the course. Many departments have official policies that new teachers must adhere to strictly, and such standards will inform your own course arrangement. Are there a certain number of essays each student has to write? Must a journal be kept? Is there a departmental policy on revisions, workshops, conferences, or evaluation?

Finally, make inquiries about the academic level of the students you will be teaching. If your college or university has open admissions, then the range of their abilities will be wide. Some FY students may be "basic writers," with reading and writing abilities far below those of other students, while other students may be strong writers, accomplished and sophisticated products of hard-driving college-prep programs. Naturally, you must gear your preparation—from textbook selection to syllabus design—to the abilities of your students. If you are teaching at an open-admissions school, find out whether incoming students write English placement essays and whether the school has a basic writing (BW) program, an English as a second language (ESL) program, or a Writing Center. You will also want to know whether there are different levels of FY courses—an honors section, perhaps, or special-interest sections—or whether all FY students are placed in the same course. Try to find out whether students from all years and levels can be placed in FY English; if so, you may have some more experienced students in your class.

Try at this point to find out all you can about the backgrounds of the students you are likely to encounter. For most of our history, teachers of writing have treated all students as if they were pretty much alike, but that convenient fiction is no longer feasible to maintain. Our students have different native tongues and different levels of fluency in Edited American English; they come from different socioeconomic classes and different sectors of society. And now more than ever before, there is a huge range in their ages and life experiences. The entrance of such a diverse student body into the academy has made us aware of our past inattention to these differences; it has led us to recognize how we had neglected to devise curricula that would address the differences and the political—or apolitical—agendas of our institutions. Find out what you can about your students' gender, ethnicity, age, and so on. You'll find that planning a course aimed mainly at Euro-American eighteen-year-old males from suburban high schools is very different from planning one for a group that includes urban African-Americans, Hispanics, or older students. Especially if your course meets in the late afternoon or evening—after the workday—be prepared for more diversity in your students—and, correspondingly, more diverse demands on you.

If your school has a BW or an ESL program, you might want to find out its entrance and exit requirements and its relations with the standard FY writing course. And while you are discussing these things, try to find out about other adjunct writing programs on campus. Not only will you have a better picture of the entire writing program, but you will know where to send your students for help. You may be surprised at the number of support systems your school offers. Some schools have Writing Labs or Writing Centers that provide students with tutorial help with particular problems and send representatives into classrooms to give minilessons on such topics as process writing, writer's block, and essay exams. In addition, some schools have set up Reading Centers, where reading and comprehension problems can be diagnosed and helped. Often affiliated with the Communications Department, the College of Education, or the College of Allied Medicine may be a Learning Disabilities Center, where dyslexia, dysgraphia, and Attention Deficit Disorder (ADD) can be diagnosed and treated. By asking questions and talking to representatives of the various reading- and writing-related programs, you will be much better prepared to guide your students through their writing course. When they have problems you cannot solve, you will be ready to send them to the specialists who can help.

CHOOSING THE TEXTBOOKS

After you have discovered all you can about the nature of the courses you are to teach and the kinds of students you can expect, the next step is to investigate the available textbooks. Since the textbook you use will serve to structure a number of important elements in your course, you will undoubtedly want to make your use of it as well-informed as possible. Many writing programs require that all teachers use certain texts; others specify a primary text and allow teachers to choose the supplementary ones; and still others allow teachers to choose from a list of approved texts. The freedom you have in choosing textbooks will depend on your school and its program and on the needs and interests of your students. In general, you may choose from among four types of textbooks: (1) *rhetorics*, the large, general textbooks that explain the techniques of writing; (2) *readers*, or *anthologies*, which provide selections of readings and are usually accompanied by exercises; (3) *handbooks*, which give guidance about process writing, and the rules and conventions of the written language; and (4) *workbooks*, which provide drills and exercises. Some textbooks combine two or more of these purposes, of course, and you will seldom be asked to use all four types.

Begin your consideration of textbooks by finding out what texts others have used and examining them carefully. Most departments that allow teachers some freedom in textbook selection maintain a small library of texts for teachers to examine. In order to make sense of the books you find there, you may wish to do some background reading on textbooks; several review articles and bibliographies provide an overview of the world of textbooks.[1] Brochures and catalogs are another source of information about a text's approach and contents. Book fairs, if your department or school organizes them, provide opportunities to see and compare a range of texts from different publishers.

---

[1] For a discussion of composition textbooks, see Woods. See also Lindemann, *CCCC Bibliography*, for current essays on, and reviews of, textbooks. In addition, the February issue of *College Composition and Communication* (*CCC*) often carries textbook reviews.

When examining textbooks, keep in mind the question of structure. How much do you want the structure of the text or texts to inform the structure of the course? If the order of topics is invention, organization, diction, style, and paragraphs, will you design your course around that structure and plan to spend a week or two weeks on each chapter? Or will you structure your course differently and organize textbook readings according to a theme or some other plan? Perhaps you will find a book whose organizational schema is congenial to you; on the other hand, you may decide to re-order the topics in your text or to use only certain sections of the book.

Talking with experienced teachers in your program about textbooks can be helpful at this point. Get several people's ideas about a book before you make your choice, and don't decide hastily. Remember, for the next ten or fifteen weeks, you will live with your decision (or the decisions of a textbook selection committee). Make sure you're comfortable with the texts you use and with your plan for teaching from them.

Finally, be aware that there is no substitute for personal experience with a textbook. After teaching from a text, you may or may not want to continue to use it. Have your students evaluate each textbook; their responses will make your future choices easier. In any case, choose your first text carefully, and make certain you get a free desk copy.

PLANNING THE FIRST TWO WEEKS

Leading a class of college-level writers may be a daunting prospect. You may have heard composition referred to as a content-less course, and every new teacher fears (at least secretly) the prospect of running out of material. Therefore, it is best to prepare your classroom time for the first two weeks with extra thoroughness. Carefully think through the structure for each class; it is always better to carry some of your plans over to the next class than to take the chance of coming to the end of your prepared notes and gazing around helplessly with half an hour of class time left.

Though with experience, you will find that the classroom offers more teaching possibilities than you can take advantage of, by dipping into the following chapters, you can get a quick idea of some options. As you'll see, teaching writing is so activity–oriented that with a little preparation, you'll never run out of material. For course structure as a whole, unless you plan to be guided by a text or have some specific schema of your own, you may want to speak to an experienced teacher and adapt a course structure that has proved successful. After your first term of teaching, you will probably want to revise and experiment with your structure. Before you confront such possibilities, however, you will want to work on a basic strategy for planning and teaching the individual lessons.

When drawing up lesson plans, make sure each lesson contains a section detailing the *goal*, or *object*, you want to address. If the lesson involves the explanation and exemplification of a method of essay organization, then the goal would be stated like this: "To familiarize students with basics of three-part organization and show them the rudimentary forms of introduction and conclusion. Examples: one on a handout; two from the reader." If the lesson involves activities, spell out the purpose of the activities: "To practice introductions and conclusions for three-part arrangement and enable students to write thesis statements." Without such statements of your goals, it is easy to get away from the point of the lesson.

The amount of other material you include in a lesson plan is up to you. Some teachers at the beginning of their careers prepare full paragraphs and short essays, while experienced teachers often work from notes made up of only key words. Make certain that you add to your notes cross-references to pages in any textbook or reader you are using.

Examples 1-1 and 1-2 show two kinds of daily lesson plans. Example 1-1 outlines an inquiry activity, one that asks students to respond to pictures and then write, share, and rewrite drafts. Notice how the teacher has written the objective in the first sentence: "Look over the rough drafts; see what problems and successes students have had, making brief comments on their drafts where appropriate." Her objective drives her carefully ordered and carefully timed classroom activities.

Example 1-2 is based on an assigned reading, "The Price of Reading Is Eternal Vigilance," by Anatole Broyard (*New York Times Book Review*, 10 April 1988: 11–12). If, like this teacher, you are using a reader in your writing course, you will naturally want to draft lesson plans that incorporate material from the reader. In preparation for an upcoming writing assignment, this teacher wanted her students to master the art of writing objective summaries, starting with one on "The Price of Reading."

But before her students began writing, she wanted to talk with them about the genre and the trouble they might encounter with the word *objective*. So she outlined important points she wanted to hear her students talk about: the central issue of the essay, the writer's point of view, how the progression of the essay relates to the purpose of the essay, and the assumptions on which a writer's views are based.

Then the class was to turn to another essay, "Frisbee Golf," and talk through the same points, discussing the problems with any claim to objectivity. Only toward the end of class would the teacher specify the practical elements of the assignment: "Use only the information in the essay. Try hard not to color your summary with your opinions or with extra information. An objective summary means you are conveying information and not opinion."

Example 1-1 SAMPLE LESSON PLAN 1: INQUIRY ACTIVITY

English 110

Inquiry Activity 1

Day 2 [Day 1 was "responding to pictures"]

Before class, look over the rough drafts; see what problems and successes students have had, making brief comments on their drafts where appropriate. (See the trouble-shooting sheets for a list of criteria.) Select one or two examples from students' writing for class discussion, or use examples provided by the writing staff. Run these samples off for use in class.

1. Have students read the sample narration-description(s). Ask students from the other groups (groups that haven't written on this particular illustration) to identify the dominant impression they get from the written description. Ask them to identify the aspects of the writing that make it easy or difficult to get a picture of what is in the illustration. Discuss.

2. Show the illustration. Discuss how the description could have been improved to give a better picture of what is in the illustration. As a part of the discussion, examine the roles that establishing a context, using details, and organizing descriptions play in narrative-descriptive writing. (15–20 minutes)

3. Have students rewrite their drafts. (25–30 minutes)

4. Collect the revised drafts. Make brief comments on them, especially on their use of details to picture and support the dominant impression. Assign each draft a check, a check plus, or a check minus. Return the drafts.

Example 1-2 SAMPLE LESSON PLAN 2: OBJECTIVE SUMMARY WRITING

Students should come to class having already read "The Price of Reading Is Eternal Vigilance" by Anatole Broyard (cf. SMH p. 9, 3rd ed.). They should be prepared to write an objective summary of the piece, and, to that end, they should have read the article to gather information for their writing assignment. Ask them to consider the following as they read: (1) the title of the piece, (2) what they already know about the topic of reading, and (3) the main point of the text. Also, as they read, they should mark places in the text that are confusing to them, that identify key points and terms, and that they question.

In class, ask students to identify in writing (1) the central issue of the essay, (2) the writer's point of view, (3) the progression of the essay and its connection to the purpose of the essay, and (4) the assumptions on which the writer's views are based.

Encourage students to compare their responses and to talk among themselves about "The Price of Reading." After they have compared notes for five minutes or so, ask them each to write an objective summary of the essay.

Students should aim to write an objective summary that

1. is one-third the length of the original essay.
2. foregrounds the main idea (the thesis statement),
   a. includes key words and phrases
   b. mentions the supports for the author's main point or argument.
3. is in their own words, avoiding plagiarism.
4. follows the author's pattern of organization.
5. uses only the information in the original essay.
6. tries hard not to color the information with personal opinion.
7. lists the source of the original essay.

Remind students that an objective summary conveys information, not opinion.

Until you know how well your examples will go over and how much time you will devote to each item on your lesson plan, for every concept you introduce and exemplify (plagiarism, for instance), have two or three other examples in your notes and ready to use. It's always better to be slightly overprepared with examples.

While working out your classroom strategies and preparing your lesson plans, you may wish to annotate your textbooks, noting material you plan to key to classwork. Don't feel that annotating of books is a messy business best avoided. Instead, inhabit the book; underline and mark in it—if doing so will make your teaching life easier. Textbooks are a raw material, and they may be with you for years. Make sure they serve you and save you from repetitious work in the future. Annotate any part of the rhetoric that you feel may need more explanation, and mark the exercises you plan to use. If any exercises fail, note the problem and the potential reasons for it. Your marks need be no more than checks or underlines, so long as they are meaningful to you. You should be able to open the book to a page and know immediately what you wish to accomplish with it.

But before you prepare your class notes or lesson plans and your textbook annotations, you will need an overview of, and a plan for, the entire course: the forms your classes will take, the sorts of writing assignments you will require, the order of the material you plan to teach, and so forth. After you have read through this book, talked with your colleagues, and carefully looked over your chosen texts, you should be ready to make a rough draft of your plan. Formalized, this draft will be the basis for the central document of your course, the syllabus. Writing the syllabus is your next major task.

CREATING A SYLLABUS

The syllabus for college courses originated as a list of the books for which every student was to be held responsible; in our day, though, it is usually more encompassing. In writing courses, the syllabus, for all intents and purposes, is a contract between teacher and student. It states the responsibilities of the teacher and the students as well as the standards for the course. Everyone concerned, from your department administrators to the parents of incoming students, may want to know your exact plans and expectations. Such a written contract has other uses: it shows a student who feels ill-used or wants special privileges your position on the issue in question, whether it be your attendance policy or your due-date policy. To protect yourself and your students from potential misunderstanding, then, a detailed syllabus that clearly spells out your purposes and policies is best.

The syllabus also publicly informs the structure of the class, explaining what the course will cover, when it will be covered, and what your qualitative and quantitative expectations are. With a copy in each student's hands, the syllabus saves you from having to repeat explanations of course policies, goals, and dates. It is also the first written expression of your personality that you will present to your students.

Syllabi for writing courses need to be longer and more detailed than those for literature courses because most students do not have developed a set of expectations and intentions for composition courses as they have for their literature courses. If you follow the outline below, you should be able to create a syllabus that fills all your major needs and answers all your students' major questions. This outline will not lead you to produce an exhaustive syllabus, but it is a good model for first-time teachers because of its simplicity and its schematic development. Keep in mind that although few teachers adhere unconditionally to their syllabi, fewer still depart from them seriously.

1. *Your name, the course number, your office address, classroom location, your office hours, and your office telephone number.* Office hours are those periods when you must be in your office so that students may drop by without an appointment. If your department does not require a minimum number of office hours, a rule of thumb is that you should schedule as many office hours as your course has contact hours—hours you are in the classroom with your students. So if your class meets five hours a week, you might want to set aside five hours a week for your office hours. (In a conferencing system,[2] these would include hours spent in conference.) Teachers can generally choose their office hours, but immediately before or after class are the most usual times. Try to schedule office hours on two successive days so that students who come in only on Mondays, Wednesdays, and Fridays or only on Tuesdays and Thursdays have a chance of seeing you. If you include a phone number, specify the hours during which students may call you.

2. *Information about the textbook.* This includes the author, title, edition, and publication information for each text. If you wish students to purchase any supplementary materials, details should be included.

3. *Course policy.* Include in this section your policies on the following:
   a. Attendance—how many absences you allow for each student and what you will do if that number is exceeded. You'll need to see whether the department has a policy on this before making your own.
   b. Tardiness—what you will do about students who consistently come to class late.
   c. Participation—how much, if any, of the final course grade will depend on classroom participation.
   d. Late papers—whether and under what conditions you will accept written assignments after their due dates.
   e. Style of papers—what you will demand by way of the physical format for graded assignments: whether they may be handwritten or must be typewritten, or word-processed, whether they may be single-spaced or must be double-spaced and so forth.

4. *Course requirements.* Discuss the following aspects of written work:
   a. The number and length of essays to be submitted for grading; your policy on revision.

---

[2]For more information on conferences, see pages 37–43.

    b. The requirements for keeping a journal and an explanation of the journal policy and how or whether the journal will be applied to the final grade (optional).

    c. Any explanation of policy on ungraded homework, in-class writing assignments, drafts, and so forth and how or whether ungraded work will apply to the final grade.

5. *Grading procedures.* Here you set forth the procedures you will follow in evaluating and grading written work. You do not have to discuss the standards that will be applied; you may merely detail how you will deal with assignments in order to arrive at final grades. Include a listing of the percentage value of each piece of written work as it applies to the final grade and, if you are using a revision option, a detailed review of how it works.[3] The statement needs to be spelled out in detail; otherwise, students may be confused and may not do the required amount of work.

6. *Grading standards.* This section is optional; many teachers do not like to spell out the standards they will use in any quantitative or prescriptive way. On the other hand, many departments have created grading standards that must be used by all teachers, and they may require that these standards be published in the syllabus. If a section on grading standards is included, it can contain the following:

    a. Standards of content—the levels of semantic and organizational expertise (a clear thesis, support of assertions, coherently developed paragraphs and arguments, and so forth) that must be apparent in a passing essay.

    b. Standards of form—the impact of serious syntactic errors (sentence fragments, comma splices, run-ons, and so forth) and of lesser errors (for example, in spelling, punctuation, and usage) on "acceptable" essays.

7. *Meetings.* Specify how many days per week the course will meet, on which days, and any special information about specific events—for instance, workshop meetings, in-class writing assignments, or sentence-combining lessons that will always fall on specific days of the week.

8. *Course calendar.* Course calendars may be simple or complex. The only essential element is a listing of the due dates for written assignments and, if part of the syllabus, journal reviews. The calendar can also contain detailed information on lessons to be prepared, reading to be done, skills to be worked on, goals to be met, and a host of other things. Whether or not you include this more detailed material will depend on the degree to which you wish to structure your course beforehand. Our advice is not to overstructure your calendar at first—allow yourself the freedom to change your plans if the methods you originally meant to use seem not to be working well.

---

[3] For information on using a revision option, see Chapter 3, "Everyday Activities."

9. *Course goals.* Whether this is a departmental statement that must be included in the syllabus or a personal definition of your objectives for the course, some statement of goals should be included. It should mention the number of graded assignments, the basic skills that will be expected of each student by the end of the course, the question of student participation, and the level of competency each student will have to demonstrate in writing in order to pass the course. You can also include a personal message about the course and its expectations.

10. *English Department information.* Your department may have special provisions—a Director of Writing or an Ombud—for handling students' questions and complaints. If so, you may be required to list the pertinent information on your syllabus: names, office numbers, office hours, official capacity, policy on confidentiality, and so forth.

The preceding ten points comprise the main elements of a composition syllabus. Other sections can be added, of course, but these are the ones needed for your protection and for your students' understanding of the course.

To have your syllabus ready for distribution on the first day of class, avoid the inevitable rush and get your photocopying done as early as possible. Make more copies than there are students on your roster; a rule of thumb is to increase the number by one-third: if you have twenty-four students on your roster, make thirty-two copies of the syllabus. Students who drop the class will carry off their copies, and students who join the class late will need copies; others will lose theirs and ask for new ones.

We have provided examples on the following pages of two syllabi. Both focus on the writing process, but the first shows a more traditional structure, and the second relies strongly on individual choice and student-teacher conferences.

Example 1-3 SAMPLE SYLLABUS 1
TRADITIONAL COURSE STRUCTURE

English 110

Roger Graves
Section 03
Room 238 Denney Hall
M, T, W, Th, F; 12:00 noon
Office: Denney Hall, Room 515; M and W; 1:00–3:00 P.M.; Th
3:00–4:00 P.M.
Textbook: Lunsford and Connors, <u>The St. Martin's Handbook</u>,
3rd ed. (1995)

<u>Structure of the Course</u>

One of the best ways to learn to write is by writing, and
for this reason you will be asked to do a great deal of
inventing, drafting, and revising—that's what writing is. Sharing
work with others, whether in peer-response sessions, writing
groups, or collaborative efforts, promotes learning about writing
by widening the response to their work that writers receive.
Finally, guidance from texts constitutes another important
component of learning to write, by answering questions you may
have or by suggesting ways of going about the business of
writing. Because these three approaches—writing, collaborat-
ing with peers, and reading the text—operate powerfully in the
classroom, they form the basis of the course schedule outlined
below.

Class meetings will often be devoted to writing workshops. These workshops will give you the chance to draft
essays, to see how other students handle writing assignments,
and to practice the skills of editing by helping others edit
their work. Many class meetings will involve discussion of a
student's essay that demonstrates how a writing assignment
might best be handled. In addition, many meetings will open
with a short writing assignment, a freewriting period, or a
journal-writing period. Each week you will read sections from
<u>The St. Martin's Handbook</u> that address issues about writing,
guide your understanding of those issues, and suggest ways to
broaden your knowledge and apply that knowledge to your writing. The goal for this course is for you to demonstrate confidence and competency in your writing.

Written Assignments

You will write five essays, the due dates for which are listed below. An "acceptable" draft of each essay must be turned in by its due date. At least one week before the end of the term, you must turn in final drafts of the first four essays for final evaluation. Before the last day of class, you must turn in the fifth essay for a final grade. At any time during the term, however, I will assign a grade to the draft of an essay that you judge to be your final effort on that essay.

Since you can suspend final evaluation of your progress until the end of the semester, this grading system provides you with the opportunity to have your best work evaluated. All work to be graded must be double-spaced in letter-quality print. Each essay should be 2-4 pages long, minimum.

Attendance

Because much of your most important work will be done in class, attendance is mandatory. Late students will be warned once; thereafter, each late appearance will be counted as an absence. If you miss more than two classes, your grade could be affected.

Final Course Grades

Final course grades will be arrived at by combining grades for the five essays, class attendance, class participation, and conferences with the teacher in the following manner:

Final graded essays (4 × 15%)	60%
Research essay (the fourth essay)	20%
Attendance and class participation	10%
Conferences, writing-process journals	10%

SAMPLE COURSE SCHEDULE[4]

Topics and Focus

Week 1.   Introduction. Briefly outline the course; identify
           learning objectives from your perspective, and ask
           students to add some of their own; present guidelines
           for grading, plagiarism, late essays, attendance.
               Assign diagnostic writing sample.
               Present introduction to The St. Martin's Handbook.
               Introduce the writing process (Chapter 1, "Writ-
           ing, Reading, and Research," and Chapter 2, "Consid-
           ering Purpose and Audience"). Have students rewrite
           their diagnostic samples to demonstrate drafting and
           learning through writing.
               Assign the first essay. Clearly identify the task
           and criteria for evaluation; provide models of suc-
           cessful attempts; link the assignment to learning
           objectives; suggest ways for students to use the as-
           signment to learn about something that interests them.

Week 2.   Introduce invention techniques: mapping and brain-
           storming (Chapter 3, "Exploring, Planning, and Draft-
           ing"); cover "Becoming a Researcher" (Chapter 40).
           Apply invention methods to the first assignment.
               Draft of first essay is due. Conduct in-class
           peer-response session. Evaluate essays for overall
           direction, scope, and suitability for the course and
           the assignment.
               Discuss "Revising and Editing" (Chapter 4).
               Compare writing-process log entries.

Week 3.   Second draft of first essay is due. Conduct in-class
           peer-response session. Discuss "Constructing Para-
           graphs" (Chapter 6).
               Confer with students individually during office
           hours or classroom writing workshops.
               Identify specific patterns of errors; conduct
           minilectures for students who share error patterns
           (specific chapters to be determined by the needs of
           the class; see Chapters 7–18 and 30–39); for more
           guidance, see "Thinking Critically about Your Own
           Writing."

Week 4.   Acceptable draft of first essay is due.
               Assign the second essay. Identify the task clearly;

---

[4] This course schedule is for the instructor's use; however, it can be modified and handed out to
   students as well.

provide models of successful attempts; link the assignment to learning objectives, suggest ways for students to use the assignment.

Repeat invention techniques used for the first essay; add Burke's dramatistic pentad.

Assign freewriting; repeat freewriting sessions, and have students exchange their work to share ideas and approaches to the assignment.

Week 5. Draft of the second essay is due. Conduct in-class peer-response session. Respond to focus and questions to promote further research or development.

Discuss "Creating Memorable Prose" (Chapter 23) and "Creating Coordinate and Subordinate Structures" (Chapter 20).

Hold writing workshops and/or individual conferences.

Second draft of second essay is due.

Week 6. Discuss "Considering Diction" (Chapter 27) and "Enriching Vocabulary" (Chapter 26).

Confer with students individually during office hours or in classroom workshops.

Identify specific patterns of errors; conduct minilectures for students who share error patterns (specific chapters to be determined by the needs of the class; see Chapters 7–18 and 30–39).

Week 7. Acceptable draft of second essay is due.

Assign the third essay. Identify the task clearly; provide models of successful attempts; link the assignment to learning objectives; suggest ways for students to use the assignment.

Repeat invention techniques (heuristics) used for the second essay; add tagmemics or clustering.

Discuss "Thinking Critically: Constructing and Analyzing Arguments" (Chapter 5).

Week 8. Draft of the third essay is due. Conduct in-class peer-response session. Respond to focus and questions to spur research or development. Discuss "Creating and Maintaining Parallel Structures" (Chapter 21) and "Varying Sentence Structures" (Chapter 22).

Confer with students individually in class or during office hours.

Week 9. Identify specific patterns of errors; conduct minilectures for students who share error patterns (specific chapters to be determined by the needs of the class; see Chapters 7–18 and 30–39).

Week 10. Third essay is due.
Assign the fourth essay, a research paper. Identify the task clearly; provide models of successful attempts; link the assignment to learning objectives; suggest ways for students to use the assignment.
Discuss "Becoming a Researcher" (Chapter 40), "Conducting Research" (Chapter 41), and "Using Dictionaries" (Chapter 25).

Week 11. Research file due: list of all sources consulted so far; notes; photocopies of relevant readings; summaries; quotations.
Discuss choosing, evaluating, and using source materials "Using Sources" (Chapter 42) and "Writing a Research Essay" (Chapter 43).

Week 12. Draft of research essay is due. Confer individually with students; devote class time to writing workshops.
Discuss "Considering Diction" (Chapter 27) and "Creating Memorable Prose" (Chapter 23).

Week 13. Second draft of research essay is due. Conduct in-class peer-response session.
Discuss "Documenting Sources" (Chapters 44–45).

Week 14. Final acceptable draft of research essay is due.
<u>Fifth assignment.</u> Rewrite or revise an essay from (1) a course in your major, (2) a discipline that interests you, or (3) this course.
Discuss "Understanding Disciplinary Discourse" (Chapter 46) and "Writing in the Disciplines (Chapter 47).
Description of the conventions of the appropriate discipline and description of the style of chosen field are due.
Typed, final drafts of first four papers are due for final grading.

Week 15. Draft of the fifth assignment is due. Conduct in-class peer-response sessions. Hold individual conferences in class or during office hours to respond to the fifth assignment. Conduct workshops in class.
Final draft of fifth essay is due.
Conduct course evaluations.

Example 1-4 SAMPLE SYLLABUS 2:
CONFERENCING-BASED COURSE STRUCTURE

Professor Connors
English 401
Office: Hamilton Smith, Room 51A; T and Th 3:30-5:00 P.M.
Phone number: 555-1212
Class meets: M and W; 2:00-3:30 P.M.

Textbooks

Rise B. Axelrod and Charles R. Cooper, The St. Martin's Guide
   to Writing, 4th ed. (New York: St. Martin's Press, 1994).
Andrea Lunsford and Robert Connors, The St. Martin's Handbook,
   3rd ed. (New York: St. Martin's Press, 1995).

Schedule

Readings and Assignments in The St. Martin's Guide to
Writing, 4th ed.

Sept. 5	Introduction to the course
Sept. 7	Ch. 1, Ch. 11, pp. 68-95; begin Assignment 1
Sept. 12	pp. 95-97, Ch. 15
Sept. 14	pp. 97-99; Assignment 1 draft due; workshop day
Sept. 19	pp. 99-107
Sept. 21	pp. 114-143; begin Assignment 2
Sept. 26	pp. 143-146
Sept. 28	pp. 146-151; Assignment 2 draft due; workshop day
Oct. 3	pp. 152-193; begin Assignment 3
Oct. 5	pp. 193-195, Ch. 20
Oct. 10	pp. 195-197; Assignment 3 draft due; workshop day
Oct. 12	pp. 197-208
Oct. 17	pp. 340-366; begin Assignment 4
Oct. 19	pp. 366-369, Ch. 21; final drafts of Assignments 1-3 must be submitted by this date.
Oct. 24	pp. 369-375; Assignment 4 draft due; workshop day
Oct. 26	pp. 375-381
Oct. 31	pp. 300-324; begin writing Assignment 5
Nov. 2	pp. 324-326, Ch. 22
Nov. 7	pp. 326-327; Assignment 5 draft due; workshop day
Nov. 9	pp. 327-338
Nov. 14	pp. 210-238; begin writing Assignment 6

Nov. 16   pp. 238-242; Assignment 6 draft due;
               workshop day
Nov. 21   pp. 243-299; Debate 1
Nov. 23   Ch. 19; Debate 2
Nov. 28   pp. 491-502; Debate 3
Nov. 30   Conferences; final paper 1 due; Assignments
               4-6 <u>must</u> be submitted by this date.
Dec. 5   Conferences; final paper 2 due
Dec. 7   Conferences; final paper 3 due

Structure of the Course

This course is based on two simple but powerful ideas: first, that you learn to write by writing and revising under the guidance of sympathetic readers and editors—your classmates and your teacher; and second, that examining and discussing writing is more helpful than trying to master abstract theory about composition. The course is therefore structured to provide a great deal of freedom for each writer while guaranteeing help and support throughout the semester. The largest part of most classes will be spent in writing and revising your work and in individual conferences with the teacher. On most class days, there will also be a class discussion of a student's essay that demonstrates how the sort of writing currently being done might be handled. Six days in the semester will be set aside for workshops. These are extremely important, since they will give you the chance to see how other students have handled writing assignments, to practice editing, and to help other writers by editing their work.

In addition, each class will open with a ten-minute writing assignment, which will be created by a class member. Every class member, including the teacher, will write a response to this assignment. These papers will be collected and evaluated by the person who created the assignment. More information on this process will be given during the first few days of class.

Written Assignments

There will be six written assignments (of 3-5 pages each) due during the semester. Except for Assignments 1 and 6, you may choose your own paper type from the nine essay types covered in Chapters 2-10 of Axelrod and Cooper. The readings on the schedule represent the sequence that will inform our class discussion, but <u>this sequence is not mandatory</u>. You may write an essay on any type of writing covered in the book and in any order. But no essay type may be used more than once.

Each assignment is to be begun on the dates noted above, and each is due in complete—neatly handwritten or typewritten—form on the appropriate workshop day. The schedule lists two deadlines for paper Acceptability. These exist to prevent you from becoming jammed up with work at the end of the course. Beyond that, however, no written assignment has to be turned in until the very end of the course, when you will choose *three* of the six written assignments you have completed and turn those three papers in for your final course grade.

NOTE CAREFULLY: *Two* specific requirements for each of the six assignments must be met *before* the end of the semester. Failure to fulfill both requirements can affect your grade, so please take them seriously:

1. You *must* have a complete draft of each assignment ready on the assigned workshop day or your final grade on that paper will be lowered by one full point.
2. Each of your six papers must be evaluated by the teacher during conferences in or outside of class and must be found Acceptable. Guidelines for Acceptability are essentially those for a grade of D or above. Papers may be revised any number of times and can be evaluated again and again, but each paper must finally be revised in an Acceptable state. Please take responsibility for making the necessary conference arrangements for talking about your revisions, conferences that fall outside the regular weekly or bi-weekly office conference times. If your paper is not found Acceptable by the date listed in the schedule, it will receive a lowered final grade at the end of the course.

Not fulfilling either one of these requirements can hurt your grade.

At the end of the semester, you will choose three of your six Acceptable papers to be typed and turned in for a final grade. The dates listed in the schedule for final submission of papers are the *last* days that papers can be turned in for grades; I will be glad to give any paper a final grade at any time during the course if you wish. Be aware, though, that only three papers will be graded, and that once a grade has been assigned, it cannot be revoked. It is clearly to your advantage to see which of your papers look best as the course proceeds.

Obviously, this system puts responsibility on you. It is up to you and to confer with the teacher often, to keep up with assignments, and to make certain that each of your papers is examined and declared Acceptable in good time. If you fall behind during the early part of the course, it may be difficult to catch up. Staying in touch with the teacher by holding frequent conferences to discuss your papers will be essential.

Class Periods and Attendance

Following each in-class writing assignment and the reading of successful responses to previous assignments (see above), there will be a discussion of the assigned reading and its relation to your current writing task. Finally, the last thirty minutes of class will often be devoted to student-teacher conferences and to the writing and revising of the assignments. Conferences are optional, but regular contact with the teacher has proved extremely important to final grades, mainly because conferences give you clear ideas about what the teacher regards as criteria for paper Acceptability. Conferences also can help you clarify topics, better understand problems with revisions, and deal with patterns of errors and questions of how best to proceed with a writing assignment. Whether or not you wish to speak to the teacher, every student will be expected to remain until the end of the class period.

At the end of the semester, the class will conduct three debates on issues you choose. Each of you will be a member of one of the six teams. The debating topics will be linked to Assignment 6, an argumentative research paper. The research you do for this paper will be the basis of your debate presentation. More on this assignment will be forthcoming after midsemester.

The procedures for workshop days will be discussed during the first few days of class.

Attendance in class is mandatory. You will be allowed two cuts (or one week), after which each absence will begin to affect the grades of your final papers. Avoid being late. But if you must be late, please come in to class quietly.

Final Course Grades

Final course grades will be arrived at on the basis of the three final graded papers, class attendance and participation, performance in workshops, and frequency and seriousness of conferences with the teacher. In general, the percentages look like this:

Each final graded paper (3 x 25%)   75%
Class participation   10%
Conference participation   10%
Debate performance   5%

A Final Word

The key in this course is your participation. You will want to keep up with the work and take advantage of the feedback you receive from the teacher and your readers.

WORKS CITED

Connors, Robert J. "Textbooks and the Evolution of the Discipline." *CCC* 37 (1986): 178-94.

Lindemann, Erika. *Longman Bibliography of Composition and Rhetoric.* 2 vols. White Plains, N.Y.: Longman, 1984-85, 1986.

——. *CCCC Bibliography of Composition and Rhetoric.* 7 vols. to date. Carbondale: Southern Illinois UP, 1987-1993.

Woods, William F. "Composition Textbooks and Pedagogical Theory 1960-1980." *CE* 43 (1981): 393-409.

2 THE FIRST FEW DAYS OF CLASSES

THE FIRST CLASS

As the time approaches for you to walk into your first class meeting, you will find yourself getting a little anxious. Every new teacher does. There is nothing like the prospect of teaching your first college class to make you wonder about your own image and how you are perceived by others. Be aware that the nervousness you feel is natural and that every good teacher feels something of it on the first day of every new class. The teaching act is a performance in the full sense of that word; the teacher is instructor, coordinator, actor, facilitator, announcer, pedagogue, ringmaster. For the time that you are "on the air," the show is your responsibility, especially if you want your students to participate fully and actively in the course.

Teaching style, the way you carry off your performance, is partially determined by conscious decisions that you make and partially determined by personality factors over which you have little control. It is difficult to control completely the manner and tone with which you naturally address the class as a whole, the way you react to individual students on an intuitive level, the quick responses you make to classroom situations as they come up, and the general public self you exhibit in front of the class. You cannot really change who you are, nor should you try.

This is not to say, however, that a teacher has no control at all over how he or she appears. Although your essential personality style may not be amenable to change, you can consciously modify the other variables. You can control what the class does with its time, the order in which it tackles lessons, the sorts of skills it concentrates on—all the content-oriented material that is at the heart of every class. You can make an effort to control those aspects of your personal style that you want specifically to change or suppress—an unthinking tendency toward sarcasm, for instance, which can turn a bright, outgoing student into a sullen lump. If your personality tends toward condescension or intimidation, you can carefully and consciously wrestle your comments around so that they come out as encouragement; if you tend toward too much modesty or passivity, you can work toward speaking up more and taking a more active approach.

More important than anything else, you should try to evince the two most important traits of a good teacher: humanity and competence. If students believe you to be kind and to know your stuff (and in a writing class, part of your job will be showing them that there is stuff to know), they will put themselves in your hands and give you a chance to be their teacher. Few who want to be teachers possess neither element; many strike a successful balance between the two. Humanity and competence, however, cannot be demonstrated in a first-day lecture. They show themselves over time, not by how many jokes you tell or how hard you grade but by the total picture of who you are and how you feel about your students and their struggles as beginning writers. If you are humane and know your subject, you and your students will, over time, build a common ethos, one characterized by mutual respect and trust.

It is the first day of classes, an important day for writing classes. Teachers of other classes often do little more than distribute syllabi and show the texts; writing teachers, however, have a good deal to get done on the first day. In your office, prepare everything you will take to class with you. Gather your books, notes, handouts, the class roster, and the pile of syllabi. (For moving materials from floor to floor or room to room, a briefcase or satchel is no affectation.) If your throat tends to get dry, get water, a coffee, or a soda—such a prop can help you through the first day.

There's the bell. Having scouted it out, you know where your classroom is. Grab your materials and your drink, and enter the river of students passing through the corridor. There is your classroom. As you open the door, twenty pairs of eyes follow you to the front of the room. You look out at your students for the first time.

Bureaucratic Tasks

It is your good fortune that the school requires you to spend the first ten minutes of the first class—nearly always the hardest—in an undemanding routine. Put your materials down at the front desk and greet those students present. Students will continue to come in, even well into the class hour.

Write your name, office number, and office hours on the blackboard, and then arrange your books, notes, and handouts so they are within easy reach. Look up every few seconds, trying to maintain eye contact with the students— it is natural to avoid their eyes until you speak to them in an official capacity, but eye contact establishes a friendly connection. Since you will probably want to begin teaching standing up, check to see that the classroom has a lectern that you can use, or set up your satchel or briefcase so that it will hold your papers.

Your students are learning their way around campus, so some of them will almost certainly continue to drift in during the first fifteen minutes. Give most of the stragglers a chance to come in before you call the roll. Introduce yourself, the course, your office number and hours. These first few announcements, routine though they are, are the most difficult. Speak slowly, and remember that you have everything planned, that you are in your element, that you will perform well. Meet the students' eyes as you speak, and try to develop the ability to take in large groups of students as you move your gaze about the classroom. You may be surprised at how young some of them look. This may be their first day in college, and depending on the time of day, you may be their first college teacher.

Describe the add-drop policy of your college or university. There may be specific school or departmental policies you are expected to announce; it usually pays to repeat the add-drop policy at least once. Finally, call the names on your class roster, marking absences. You will want your students to raise their hands if present and to tell you if you have mispronounced their names. A good system is to call only the last name of each student on the roster, asking that students tell you what they prefer to be called in class. Note the preferred name and pronunciation on your roster, and try to make eye contact with each student as you call the roll. Try to connect names with faces as soon as possible.

After you have called the roll, ask for a show of hands of those whose names you did not call. There will always be a few, usually students who have shown up hoping they can add the class. It usually pays to repeat the add-drop policy, and now is the time to announce that after class, you will talk to those students who wish to add or drop the course. After class, then, you can attend to them and decide whether you can handle more students in your class. Often there is a maximum number of students established by the department, and only the director of the Writing Program or an advisor or scheduler can give permission for an overload. If the ultimate decision about accepting more students is yours, keep in mind that each student whom you accept over the limit means that less of your time and energy will be available for the rest of the students. If the decision is not yours do not make it. Send the student to the appropriate person.

The Syllabus

Hand out copies of the syllabus. After everyone has one, read through the important parts of it aloud. On this first reading, stress the textbooks—bring your copies to class, and display them so your students will know what to look for at the bookstore. Discuss attendance and lateness policies, the form for written assignments (typed or handwritten, double-spaced or single-spaced, and so forth), the number and length of required papers, the policy on keeping a journal (or writing-process log). If you are using a revision policy, go over it in detail, giving examples of how it is to be used. It is in this explanation of the syllabus that you will actually start to teach students what revision is. Some students will initially think of revision as punishment or as simply editing for a cleaner copy. There is inevitably confusion about a revision policy and how it works, and you will be explaining revision for the first few weeks of the course. Go over the calendar of due dates, and mention the grading standards you will be applying.

It is important as you explain the syllabus not to back away from or undercut any of the policies it states. Sometimes you will sound harsh to yourself as you explain the penalties for absence, lateness, or failure to do work on time, but do not apologize. You will find that it is far simpler to ease up on harshly stated policies than to tighten up lax policies. After you have gone through it, ask whether there are any questions about the syllabus. Finally, you will want to tell students about the diagnostic essay that you have scheduled for the second day of class.

Dismissal

There is little left that must be done on the first day. You might try to get to know your students a little—ask them to answer a few questions about their general goals, their academic likes and dislikes, what they most want to learn, and so forth. Then ask them to write down any questions about course policies that they think of and want to talk about during the next class. Make your assignments, including the reading of the syllabus. If there are no final questions, dismiss the class.

You will undoubtedly be surrounded by a postclass swirl of students wishing to talk to you—students who only a moment ago had no questions. Some will want to add the course: tell them whether they have a chance, and send them to the appropriate office. Some will have completed add or change-of-section forms: add those students' names to your roster. Some will have questions that they were too shy to ask in class: speak to them. As you resolve each situation, the crowd will diminish, and eventually the last petitioner will leave. You will be alone. This first day of class is over.

THE SECOND CLASS

On the second day, there are still some bureaucratic tasks to be cleared away—you will need to call the roll again (make eye contact, and see whether you can begin to remember students' names), and perhaps you will want to make a short speech about the add-drop policy. If new students have joined the class, as will probably happen on the second, and perhaps the third day, give them copies of the syllabus and ask them to speak to you after class—or better yet, ask other students to volunteer to explain the syllabus to them, one volunteer for each newcomer. Ask the class for the questions they wrote down about the syllabus and course policies and go over one more time those questions and any others that may be confusing.

Because you want to find out as quickly as possible your students' strengths and weaknesses as writers, you will want to assign the diagnostic essay today. If your school offers a BW or an ESL program, the diagnostic essay serves to alert you to students who might best be helped by these particular programs. If your school has a Writing Center or a Learning Disabilities Center, you have backup resources. Writers are helped most when they receive an evaluation early. And the diagnostic essay allows you to gauge immediately the level of writing each student is capable of as the course begins and to calculate your own pace in teaching each student and the class as a whole.

As its name suggests, this exercise gives you an idea of how "healthy" or prepared your students are as writers. Very simply, you ask them to take out paper and pen and to write for twenty to thirty minutes on a topic that allows for narrative or descriptive responses. (You can bring paper with you and pass it out if you object to the appearance of paper torn from notebooks.) The best topics for the diagnostic exercise are those that can be answered in a short essay and that ask students to rely on their own experiences. Master diagnostician Edward White offers the following option in his *Teaching and Assessing Writing:*

> Describe as clearly as you can a person you knew well when you were a child. Your object is to use enough detail so that we as readers can picture him or her clearly from the child's perspective and, at the same time, to make us understand from the tone of your description the way you felt about the person you describe. (252)

Here are two other options.

> In a short essay, discuss the reasons why your best (or worst) high school teacher was effective (or ineffective).
> In a short essay, discuss the best, most worthwhile, and most valid advice you received about adjusting to college life so far. What advice stands out to you in your first week?

Introduce the diagnostic essay to the class for what it is—an exercise that will give you an idea of how well students are writing now. Stress that the essay will not be given a letter grade and will have no effect on the final class grade. But remind students that you will be looking at form and content, at their ability to organize a piece of writing and develop it with specific examples. You might want to spend a few moments talking with them to help them see the difference between general assertion and specific detail.

Ask students to try to write as finished a piece of work as possible in the time allowed. Make certain that they put their names on the papers and that they note whether they have already taken BW or ESL courses. Write the diagnostic assignment on the board, and then give the class the rest of the hour to think and write. Announce the amount of time remaining once or twice so that no one runs short of time. At the end of class, collect the essays.

After the Second Class

You will have several tasks to accomplish after class or that evening, the most important of which is marking and evaluating the diagnostic essays. But even before you look at the pile of papers, you must prepare yourself psychologically for what you will find. Unless you are teaching at a selective school, some beginning writers may seem to you to write at an appallingly low level. If you plunge into a set of diagnostic essays cold, you may be brought up short by the apparently overwhelming number of formal usage errors and mechanical problems you see. As Mina Shaughnessy points out, some teachers of underprepared students initially cannot help feeling that their students might be deficient in some organic sense; certain pervasive error patterns are so severe and look so damaging on a paper that they can be shocking (2-3). This problem is particularly likely if you are teaching at a two-year or an open-admissions college without a BW program. With luck, your students' essays will not evidence any irreparable problems. Be prepared, however, and recall that even large numbers of errors usually fall into just a few patterns.[1]

Having prepared yourself, plunge into the pile of essays. Most will be short—two or three pages. Aside from some nearly illegible handwriting and inventive spellings, most essays should be readable. It is a good idea to scan each essay quickly, trying to get a sense of the writing as a purposeful whole. Then, in a second reading, mark the paper, looking for the following three specific areas of skill (listed in order of importance):

1. Knowledge of and ability to use paragraph form, including topic sentences, specific details and examples, a well-supported and well-developed controlling idea
2. Ability to write a variety of grammatically correct and interesting sentences
3. Ability to use language—including grammar, usage, punctuation, and spelling—in a relatively standard fashion

To get a sense of how these three skills are demonstrated in an essay, you may have to read the essay two or three times—but since each one is not very long, this task is not as time-consuming as it sounds. By the time you reach the bottom of the pile, you should be spending about ten minutes on each diagnostic, noting the mechanical problems and writing a short comment at the end.

Whether or not you decide to use some form of portfolio evaluation,[2] you may want to purchase a small notebook or a card file in which to keep semester-long records, with a page or a card for each student. With such a record, you can chart each student's strengths and weaknesses as they appear in each major piece of writing. The first entry would cover the diagnostic exercise. Note whether the student grasps organization, can use sentences, has control of usage, and so forth. A short, three- to five-sentence description of each student's strengths and problems, consulted and added to as you evaluate each new writing assignment, can be of great help in setting individualized goals for students and in discovering the particular kind of practice writing each student needs. These notes on students' progress will also help you when you confer individually with your students.

As you read the diagnostics, look especially for patterns of errors—a continual inability to use commas correctly, a continual confusion about verb endings, a continual tendency to begin fragments with relative pronouns. Chart such patterns carefully, for they will be your concern in the future, and they can provide important information for tutors at the Writing Center or the Learning Disabilities Center.

---

[1]For more on patterns of formal errors, see Shaughnessy. For details on formal errors and the frequency with which they are found in student writing, see Connors and Lunsford, "Frequency of Formal Errors in Current College Writing," on p. 430 in Part III of this *Guide*.

[2]See Chapter 5, pages 77–81, for a discussion of portfolio evaluation.

The diagnostic essays and the way you respond to them will shape your students' perceptions of you as much as your classroom attitude will. As always in grading and evaluating, take the time to consider how the students will feel upon reading your comments. Will they come away thinking they have problems they can deal with, or will they be overwhelmed? Try to balance critique with encouragement; see whether you can find something to praise, and treat errors and problems as signposts pointing to needed work, not as dead-end signs.

Before the next class, you must decide whether any of your students might benefit from switching to another course or working at a tutoring center. If you feel that a student should be enrolled in the BW or ESL program instead of FY writing, now is the time to make the necessary arrangements, through either the director of composition or the director of one of these other programs. Do not feel you are betraying a student by recommending BW or ESL; you want your students to thrive under your guidance, not merely survive.

If you think a student would benefit from the services of the Writing Center or the Learning Disabilities Center, you may decide to talk to a consultant at the appropriate center and find out how the student can enroll and how you can work with the Writing Assistant to best help the student.

For especially good students, the diagnostic essay may provide pleasant news: some schools provide for strong writers to be exempted from FY writing courses. If that is the case at your school and you have a student who deserves to be exempted, make the necessary arrangements.

After you have read the diagnostics, marked them, and recorded the marks and your comments, you can put them aside and turn to the other task of the evening: planning the next class. The third class will be your first real class, the first class that demands a prepared lesson plan. Be certain that you know what you want to introduce and accomplish.

THE THIRD CLASS

Announce that you will talk about the diagnostic essays at the end of the class. This is a good way to introduce the policy of not returning assignments until the end of a period. Such a policy keeps attention on the day's lesson and keeps students' reactions to their grades and your comments from coloring the class period.

So, you will begin your first day of actual teaching. You will want to state the goals of, and introduce, the first lesson.[3] You may or may not decide to connect the work you begin today with the first writing assignment. You are the teacher; the choice is yours. Because students may not yet have been able to get their textbooks, you may want to begin with a handout. Remember, you are there to lead the class but not to do all the work. Get students talking, even this early in the course, to you, in small groups, or in pairs.

---

[3] You may wish to base your first lesson on material from Chapters 6–10 of this book.

Fifteen minutes or so before the end of class, make your assignments for reading and homework exercises, and return the diagnostic essays. Before you dismiss the class, call out the names of the students with whom you wish to speak after dismissal. Dismiss the class at least ten minutes early.

Students whose writing is so advanced that they may be exempted from your course should be congratulated, and arrangements should be made for their transferrals. Students who need to work at the Writing Center while they take your course should be encouraged to schedule an appointment with a Writing Assistant and instructed to show their diagnostic essays to the Assistant. Students who look as if they could not do the level of work required in your course should be moved to BW or ESL. (You should speak to these students privately. Ask them to come back to your office during the remaining class time, and explain the situation to them there.)

You're an experienced teacher by now and starting to get used to the role. Enjoy it, but don't allow yourself to get too comfortable. There's still plenty left to learn.

WORKS CITED

Shaughnessy, Mina. *Errors & Expectations: A Guide for the Teacher of Basic Writing.* New York: Oxford UP, 1977.

White, Edward M. *Teaching and Assessing Writing.* 2nd ed. San Francisco: Jossey-Bass, 1994.

3 EVERYDAY ACTIVITIES

CLASSROOM MANAGEMENT

Absenteeism

In writing courses, the most common classroom-management problem has nothing to do with classroom order. It is absenteeism. The temptation to skip classes can be great for FY students, who may for the first time in their lives be in a situation in which no one is forcing them to go to school. In dealing with absenteeism, teachers must first consider that this is college, not high school, and that they have no "big stick" with which to compel attendance.

Even before the term begins, you should be familiar with your school's policy on class attendance, and you should work with it as best you can. In general, unless your department has a specific written policy, teachers may be forbidden or discouraged from using grades to compel attendance in writing courses. Some schools will not allow you to fail a student who never comes to class but writes the assigned papers. Still, you have options. You can, of course, make class participation and groupwork a part of the final grade so that the grades of those students who do not attend class will suffer. In addition, brief in-class writing assignments and group projects will encourage steady attendance.

Often the best way to deal with absenteeism is to plan the course so as to discourage it. Try this: give information about graded assignments on one class day, hold editing workshops on another class day, have graded papers due on yet another class day. In other words, fill up the week with requests for specific actions, and provide meaningful progress toward a goal. If a student misses a class, the goal becomes harder to attain and the tasks at hand become more difficult. If a student skips a peer-editing session and then receives a poor grade on an essay because the support for her thesis is vague, and if she realizes her editing group would have pointed out this shortcoming, she will quickly become aware of the concrete advantages of attending class.

You may also encounter students who consistently show up for class five, ten, even fifteen minutes late. Here again, your school may have a policy, but usually this matter is best settled privately. Speak to the student after class or in conference, and find out whether there is a valid reason for the lateness. Surprisingly often, students do have good excuses—a long walk across campus between classes, an inconsiderate teacher in a previous class, personal responsibilities of different sorts—but just as often the lateness is a result of late rising, poor planning, or careless habits.

If the student's reasons for lateness do not seem valid, state politely but seriously that students who are late will be marked absent. If you take attendance at the start of each class, students will quickly realize that latecomers are marked absent. Treating students as responsible adults and showing an interest in them can have a good deal of effect; after such discussions, tardy students most often begin to appear on time.

Late Essays

Late essays—written assignments handed in (often slipped surreptitiously under your office door or into your office mailbox) after their due date—can be another problem, but only if you allow them to be. State in your syllabus that you will not accept late essays: "No late papers. Period." Then when the inevitable requests for extensions appear or when the late papers show up, you can adjust the policy as seems fit and humane. It is often better to announce an unyielding policy initially and then adjust it than to announce a liberal policy, see it abused, and then try to establish a harder line. If you do receive a late essay that has not been explained in advance, one common way of dealing with it is to note the time and date when it came into your hands, write "late essay" on it, and lower the grade. You can also give it credit without reading it, which will keep the student from being penalized for not turning in the essay but will not add to her grade average. And you can, of course, also choose not to accept it.

Plagiarism

Plagiarism in the classroom—students' presenting the work of others as their own—is sometimes a serious problem for writing teachers. Plagiarism ranges in severity from a single, uncited magazine quotation to a carefully retyped fraternity-file version of an A research essay. It can be as crude as a long passage from Bertrand Russell amidst a jumble of sentence fragments and misspellings, or it can be as sophisticated as an artfully worked-in introduction lifted directly from a sociology text. Whatever the degree, it is bad news for both student and teacher. Hence, you will want to approach the problem with subtlety and caution.

Some departments have completely worked-out plagiarism policies that you must explain to the class, adhere to, and enforce. If your department does have a set of rules or a statement on plagiarism, be sure to read it aloud and discuss it with your class early on. After that, however, you will still need to make your own peace with the issue. Instead of railing against the evils of plagiarism, you might better serve your students by explaining the ethical and professional advantages of giving full credit to their sources—especially in American culture.[1] Try to make clear that crediting sources fully is an important and expected element in establishing one as a participant in the academic community.

---

[1] See, for instance, Barry Kroll's essay "How College Freshmen View Plagiarism," which shows that FY students' view of plagiarism is often very different from their teachers' view. Also, see chapter 42 of *The St. Martin's Handbook*, 3rd edition.

First, stress that by acknowledging their sources, students will be better able to examine their own research and thinking critically. Suggest that they ask themselves these questions: "How timely and reliable are my sources?" "Are they at the right level for my audience?" "Have I used them accurately?" Second, make clear that crediting sources places each writer's work in a *context* of other thinking and writing; it shows readers that the writer's work is part of a textual conversation and allows them to see the writer's precise contribution to that conversation. Finally, suggest that crediting sources allows a writer to thank those whose work he or she has built on. In sum, crediting sources fully and generously provides a means of establishing *ethos* as a writer; failure to credit sources corrupts the textual conversation, misleads readers, and destroys the credibility of the writer and the work. By raising these issues, you'll provide a forum for discussing the ethical and cultural dimensions of citing, paraphrasing, and quoting sources.

In addition, the best policy for dealing with plagiarism is by not inviting it. Avoid writing assignments that lend themselves to easy answers found in readily available sources; eschew topics that have been around your department for years. Instead, use topics that must be personalized in some way. And if you make certain that all students' essays have gone through several revisions and that all early drafts are turned in with the typed final versions, you can be pretty sure your students have written their own papers. Good assignment planning and classroom management can make plagiarism difficult—more difficult, in fact, than writing the paper.

If you do find indisputable evidence of plagiarism, you need to determine how to proceed. Consider whether the student intended dishonesty and whether the uncited material is a result of ignorance, carelessness, or turpitude. Most teachers would rather not set the wheels of institutional punishment going unless they are sure the student intended dishonesty. Instead, they will try to deal with the student's failure in the context of the class, by asking the student to rewrite the paper or by giving that one paper a failing grade. Pressing plagiarism cases publicly is time-consuming and unpleasant, and only where the intent to deceive is clear and the case is obvious and provable is it usual for a teacher to invoke the full majesty of the academic code against a plagiarist.

Classroom Order

The final management issue is that of classroom order. Order, of course, is a relative term; very often an orderly writing class is abuzz with discussions of rhetorical choices, editing and correctness. Order does not mean silence. It does, though, signify a progression of meaningful activities, one that can be disrupted in a number of ways. Whether students are taking part in a class-wide discussion, listening to you lecture, or working in small groups, certain protocols should be observed. One of your functions is to demonstrate these protocols by accepting the responsibility for running the class, for making the progression of activities possible. But students can also demonstrate these protocols.

By the end of the first week, ask students to advise you on classroom order, and write their suggestions on the board for all to see. Students usually have clear and strong ideas about how they want their class to be ordered. They will tell you that when one person is talking, everyone else should listen; that no one person should dominate the class discussion; that when one person speaks, the next person should respond to that speaker before adding new information to the discussion; and that they want their classmates to address them by name.

Rare is the problem with classroom order that cannot be solved by serious words to the right person—in private. College students are anxious to prove their maturity and usually will not continue behavior that they have been made to understand is undesirable, particularly if they realize their peers also disapprove. Ask to see disruptive students and speak plainly to them about the problem they are causing for you and for the whole class. They will nearly always help you out.

Occasionally a truly disturbed student may resist all rationality, every effort to keep order and even to help. If such a student ends up in one of your classes, seek immediate assistance from your program or department, and if the disruptive behavior continues, get the student out of your class. You owe it to the other students in the class—as well as to yourself.

CLASSROOM ROUTINES

Most new teachers of writing are used to certain classroom routines: those they grew up with—lecture by the teacher or teacher-directed classroom discussion. These are the routines we know best, and we all are tempted to rely on them in writing classes as completely as we have in literature classes. Unfortunately, however, they cannot be used successfully as the only methods of classroom instruction in a writing course; in fact, they cannot even hold center stage. The writing teacher must use a much larger array of classroom activities, an array that brings students' writing—not their talking, listening, or note-taking—to center stage.

Let's deal first with the old standbys. Classroom discussion is probably the teaching method most congenial to new writing teachers. The teacher does not "lead" the class in any authoritarian way; instead, she guides the discussion, and everyone has a chance to contribute. Inexperienced teachers of composition usually envision themselves as using classroom discussion, but the essential component of discussion—content—is not available in a composition course in the same way it is in history, biology, or psychology courses. The content of a composition class is often theoretical, yet teaching abstract theory has not been shown to help students learn to write better. The theory is best discussed in practical terms, as it applies to a student's piece of writing or to a short story, a poem, or any other piece of literature.

This is the hard truth about discussion in writing classes: it cannot be practiced without content, and the content should be that of the students' own writing. Otherwise, the writing class will concern itself with form, which is easy to isolate but hard to discuss enthusiastically. Students don't want to talk about sentence fragments or three-part organization unless the fragments and the organization are in their own writing.

Therefore, to be useful and interesting, classroom discussions must be carefully planned and directed.[2] A teacher can, of course, assign essays in a reader and then spend the class time discussing the content of the essays: ecology and bigotry and love and death—all fascinating subjects. Such use of class time is appropriate to a course in the appreciation of nonfiction, but not to a writing course—unless the teacher successfully manages to connect the reading of the literature to the students' work on their own essays.

Discussion in writing classrooms, then, should not be the central routine that it is in literature classrooms. It does have a place in the teaching of composition, however, and can be used for two main purposes. The first is relatively traditional: classroom discussion of an object, an idea, or a situation is a prewriting activity that can give students ideas about content that they might wish to use in their writing. Fifteen minutes of discussion on different kinds of computers, for instance, might allow students access to ideas for their own papers about using computers at college. Such discussion needs to be limited and carefully directed, however, because it can easily take up more class time than it is worth.[3]

The second valid use of discussion in a composition course involves classroom conversations about different stylistic and organizational options available in the construction of sentences and paragraphs.[4] Such discussion can be a valuable element in helping students make formal and stylistic choices about their writing. Any discussion of form, however, must focus on concrete examples of stylistic choices; otherwise, students may try to engage in arguments over abstract concepts but will not be able to apply their ideas to their work. Examples printed on handouts, drawn on a blackboard, or projected overhead often successfully supplement this kind of discussion by making the concepts concrete.

The other old standby of classroom routines, one with which most new teachers are familiar, is the lecture. Many of us have admired teachers who delivered brilliant lectures in literature courses. Lectures in writing classes, however, are not likely to be brilliant. They must consist of the application of abstract rhetorical principles; and as the thesis of this book has suggested, students simply do not learn to write—do not learn to control any art—by studying abstract principles. As the philosopher Michael Polanyi writes,

> The aim of a skillful performance is achieved by the observance of a set of rules which are not known as such to the person following them. . . . Rules of art can be useful, but they do not determine the practice of art; they are maxims, which can serve as a guide to an art only if they can be integrated into the practical knowledge of the art. (49-50)

---

[2] See the descriptions in Chapters 6-10.

[3] It should not be used in place of the invention activities described in Chapter 7, but as a supplement to them.

[4] This use of classroom discussion is described in Chapters 8, 9, and 10.

In this case, the "practical knowledge" of writing cannot be gained by listening to lectures on the rules and protocols of writing but can be gained only by actually writing and performing writing-based activities.

This is not meant to suggest that you cannot tell your students anything or that a teacher explaining material to students is somehow invalid. The very act of teaching is predicated, as rhetorician Richard Weaver says, on the idea that one person can know more than another and that knowledge or skill can be transmitted. Every chapter of this book contains material that must be explained to students. Such explanations, though, are but the preludes to writing or to a writing-based activity. After explaining, exemplifying, and pointing out the major components of a skill, you as the teacher must set up a learning situation and let the students practice the skill. Rather than announcing rules, you will be describing behavior; and when the students practice that behavior enough, they will inductively come to grasp the rules that govern it. Only in this way are "lectures" in a writing class truly beneficial.

Other classroom routines peculiar to the writing classroom take different forms, but all have one thing in common: they involve students' practicing the skill of planning, writing, or editing. You want your students to spend the larger part of their classroom time writing and talking, to you and to other students, about the choices and options that make up process writing. Most of the classroom material in the following chapters is based on this sort of activity-based classroom approach, according to which students may work alone, with one other student, or in a group. At first, the writing-centered classroom may seem appallingly disorienting, accustomed as we are to the teacher-centered atmosphere—especially in the literature classes—of our own education. It may take you some time to get used to the meaningful chaos of a writing classroom, but as you do, you will begin to see how discoveries take place within the busy buzz.

In-class writing assignments, an important part of the writing-centered classroom, can take the form of writing short essays based on the instructions of the teacher, freewriting in response to a prompt, practicing sentence or paragraph patterns, or editing drafts according to specific guidelines. What use you make of writing-based activities will depend on the skills you are trying to teach. There are, though, some activities not based in any one specific pedagogy that can be used with excellent results.

David Jones has developed one such successful activity, the daily in-class essay. On the first day of the course, inform the class that each student will be responsible for assigning and grading a short essay. Send around a sign-up sheet, and have students pick the date on which they will present a short writing assignment to the rest of the class. The only stipulation is that the topic must be simple enough for students to write coherent essays in ten minutes. On the chosen day, each student puts the assignment on the blackboard at the beginning of class. For the first ten minutes, the rest of the class writes in silence. (You might write the assignments, too, thereby showing solidarity with the class and allowing students to see the task as dignified.)

Each student usually produces three-quarters of a page to a full page of longhand. At the end of ten minutes, collect the essays and give them to the student who created the assignment and who then has one week in which to evaluate and grade them—yours included. Ask the assigner to read aloud to the class a favorite response to the assignment. This gives the writer of the "winning" essay satisfaction and allows other students to hear their peers' work. The essays should then be returned to you. Check them, and return to the students their essays. Although not necessarily brilliant, those essays represent valuable practice.

Evaluation of these short essays can be a problem. Because students are such tentative graders, peer evaluation usually produces a disproportionate number of B's and bland, generally approving comments. ("I can relate to this, and it flows well.") A guided evaluation procedure is more helpful to the student readers and writers. You may want to implement the following five questions that the grader must address for each paper. Under this system, each evaluation must include a sentence in response to each of the following questions:

1. What idea in the essay is handled most successfully?
2. What idea is handled least successfully?
3. What is the main idea, and is it well supported?
4. If you see a formal or mechanical problem, what is it?
5. How well did this essay answer the assignment, and why?

Then instruct the reader to give the paper a grade of A, C, or F, using an evaluation system described on the syllabus or in class. The grades do not, of course, count toward the students' final grades, but they do give class members an idea of how their writing is perceived by their peer group and what a particular grade "means" to the class. Evaluating these essays also gives students some small idea of what we as teachers have to go through in order to evaluate their papers.

STUDENT CONFERENCES

The student-teacher conference has a number of functions, but the primary ones have to do with getting to know your students better as writers, intervening more immediately in their composing processes, and letting them know you care about how they are doing. The student conference allows you the opportunity to explain writing strategies, discuss the strengths and weaknesses of a student's work, plan and examine future work with the student, and in general establish the coach-athlete or editor-author relationship that is our ideal of teacher-student interaction. Most important, though, the conference allows the student to talk about her writing, ideas, and plans.

Unfortunately, in spite of all these desirable goals and possibilities, you usually can't rely solely on your office hours for fostering contact with your students, especially if you teach at a commuter institution, where many students are juggling work, school, and responsibilities at home. Probably the best way to ensure personal contact and effect useful help with revisions, then, is by instituting a system of conferences held in either the office or the classroom. Mandatory conferences need to be specified as such from the beginning of the course, preferably on the syllabus. The number of conferences you schedule with your students is up to you. Some teachers specify only three conferences per term; others ask their students to meet with them weekly or biweekly.

To arrange conferences, specify a range of possible times on a sign-up sheet, and send the sheet around the class during the week preceding the first conferences. Make the hours broad enough (usually covering two consecutive days) to allow most students to find a time. Depending on what is to be discussed, allow ten or fifteen minutes per conference. If some students need more time than that, you can make separate appointments with them or book double appointments.

There are two schools of thought about student-teacher conferences: with Donald Murray's approach, students come to the teacher's office; with Roger Garrison's approach, all conferences take place in the classroom. Garrison's method is an encompassing system in which all classroom activity revolves around short, specific, and frequent in-class student-teacher conferences. It has proved to work well, especially in two-year-college settings and for teachers with heavy student loads.[5] The rest of this section will be devoted to the more common Murray-style conference, which is held in the teacher's office and functions as a support to the regular classroom activities.

Using a Conference-Based System

Handling office conferences requires forethought and planning. If you try to "wing" it, your students will quickly know you have nothing specific to tell or ask them and will lose interest. The whole purpose of a student-teacher conference is to establish an understanding about work to be done, ideas to be developed, or problems to be solved, and you should make your plans with those tasks in mind. Your talk may draw on the past, but it should be oriented to the future. If a conference becomes a postmortem on an unsuccessful paper, the student will (understandably) want to escape as soon as possible. (Besides, the student should do most of the talking—it's her paper, her conference.)

Conferences work best when they have one of the following purposes:

- Discussion of a plan or draft for a new assignment
- Discussion of the content or structural revisions of a draft in progress
- Discussion of the progress of any long-term ongoing project (a research paper, for instance)
- Discussion of a process, particularly changes in a student's writing process, and the sharing of anecdotes about writing (since you, the teacher, are a writer, too, with your own blocks, ruts, successes)
- Discussion of activities meant to deal with specific and identified patterns of formal problems: syntactic errors, verb endings, and so forth

[5] For more information, see Garrison's article "One-to-One," which is reprinted in Part III of this book.

Student-teacher office conferences, then, are always conversations about writing. Through one-on-one discussion of students' work—previous, in hand, or planned—you get to know your students, demonstrate your interest in their work, and provide a responsive audience complete with individualized instruction. The students, meanwhile, get to talk about their intentions and their work to an interested and expert mentor.

Using a regular conference system means your teaching will be more interactive than presentational, and your students' learning will be more collaborative and active. If students view writing as a complex, long-term, interactive process of prewriting, drafting, receiving feedback, revising, and so forth, they will seek responses from you and from one another. When students are excited about writing, they want to talk about it—before class, during class, after class. Regularly scheduled conferences are simply an extension of this process: writers talk themselves through their drafts, over the rough spots, into new territories, and you, the reader-teacher, provide a knowledgeable, supportive audience.

If you decide to use a conferencing system, you may decide to schedule ten- or fifteen-minute conferences every week or every other week. Some teachers schedule conferences for several weeks in a row at the beginning of the course and then gradually decrease the frequency of the conferences as students gain confidence and independence. During the last three or four weeks, if conferences are optional, you can allot more time to those students motivated to seek extra help and let the others work on their own or in groups, perhaps providing brief written feedback. Whatever pattern you choose, timely response to any work students submit is important, whether the response comes from you in conference or in writing or from their peers in a small-group or whole-class workshop. Students (all writers, for that matter) are encouraged when they know somebody cares enough to read and respond to what they write.

However you decide to structure your course, let your students know your reasons, and establish a schedule as early in the semester as possible so they know what kind of feedback to expect and when. They should understand that yours is not the only word, and that feedback from their peers individually, in writing groups, and in whole-class workshops are useful alternatives to a conference.

Letting Students Lead the Way

In a conference, you can tailor instruction to individual needs and learning styles, particularly if you take your cues from the students themselves. When given the opportunity, students will lead the way. They will help determine the content and the direction of a conference through their questions and comments about the work or the course. When students reveal what they are ready to learn, then your few minutes together can result in progress. For example, a student who is concerned about hooking the reader in an introduction is ready to hear suggestions about drawing the reader in or clarifying the theme early on. The following week that same student might be ready for some serious line-by-line editing. But to impose line editing when the student's mind is on creating a lively introduction is to miss an opportunity.

If your purpose in a conference is to respond only to the student's text, you might as well take the papers home and leave the student out of the process altogether. Instead, you should be making room for students to articulate what they know or sense, allowing them to realize what they know. Usually conversation focuses on a draft the student has submitted. Each conference draws on past work and past discussions but looks to and stimulates future work.

Ideally, you respond to the student's response to the text. You respond fully and immediately, not only to what is on the page but to what isn't on the page: intention, process, ideas for revision, and so forth. In conference, your text-specific comments will assure students you have read with care. Gradually, your students will begin to see you as an interested and knowledgeable reader rather than as a nitpicking critic or a grammar enforcer. When students accept you as reader, their work is transformed from putting words on a page in order to fulfill the assignment to real communication.

Getting students to lead the way in conferences is not easy. Most are more than willing to let the teacher dominate any discussion, particularly a one-on-one conference. Some students are intimidated by the very idea of meeting alone with a teacher, of having the teacher's complete attention. To students used to blending into the crowd of the classroom, the potential for miscommunication or misjudgment may seem high. But as soon as they realize that the direction of the conference belongs to them, not to you, they will be more comfortable meeting and talking about their work.

Students sometimes perceive a role reversal in conferences, and that can also make them uncomfortable. If you ask, "Where do you want to go with this paper?" the answer may be silence or "Where do you think I should go?" Some students have come to expect teachers simply to tell them what is wrong with their writing and how to fix it. Some may hope, in fact, you will tell them what to think about their own work. Getting students to ask questions and then to try new answers in their writing pushes them toward self-evaluation and independence; it helps them develop as their own best critics.

One way to ensure student leadership in a conference is to ask students to write questions in advance and to submit them with their papers. The questions should be specific: not "What did you think of this paper?" but "Do you think I stray from my main point in the long paragraph on page 3?" or "What do you see as my main point?" or "Should this closing story be my opening hook?" Early in the semester, work with the class to generate a list of model questions, and then hand out copies of the printed list.

A paragraph describing the process of writing a paper is also a useful accompaniment, providing you with further context. You might ask students to write a half-page letter about the paper, including their questions, or you might even provide a formal covering sheet with space for students to answer questions like "Where did you get the idea for this paper? What do you want to accomplish with this paper? What surprised you in writing this paper?" This preparatory information serves many purposes.

1. It helps you monitor the progress of the students' critical abilities. As the semester progresses, their questions and answers inevitably become sharper and more interesting.
2. It provides structure for at least part of the conference, ensuring that the meeting deals with issues the student is ready to talk about.
3. It provides an opening for your agenda. A student's question may lead to a subject you believe the student ought to explore. It may allow you to help students see their work in an objective light. For example, a student might ask, "Does the middle drag? Do I include too much information there?" This question about content could easily lead to a discussion of focus: Why did you include this section at all? How does it relate to your main point? What is your main point?
4. It provides the basis for a record of the conference. You and the student may add notes to it during the conference.
5. On weeks when no conference is scheduled, it can provide a format for your written response, serving as the voice of the absent student. It can also guide group writing or even a full-class workshop.

Whether you take notes yourself, ask your students to take notes, or keep a formal record, it is important that someone keep track of each conference. Tracking expectations and related tasks allows you and the student to track progress and then to come to a mutual understanding of what you are accomplishing together.

In a conference, it is a good idea to assume the writer knows the work better than you do. The student wrote the paper and knows the kind of effort that went into it, what was hard and what was easy. The writer may also have thought about purpose, audience, and possibilities for revision. Your questions and responses will help the student see the draft in a fresh or less subjective way. In conferences then, you use your experience as a reader to teach students how to read their own work.

When you open a conference with "How can I help you? What is your purpose in this piece of writing?" you hit the ball into the student's court. Other open-ended questions that may help students get going include the following:

What are the stronger sections? the weaker? Why?
Who is your audience?
What are you pleased with? What are you not so happy with?
What did you learn in writing this?
Is this finished? If not, what would you like to change?
What surprised you in this paper?
What did you discover while writing this?
What is the key line or passage? Why is it so important?

Often it is helpful to let students know exactly what you understand from the reading. Tell them what you think they are getting at in their essays so that they can compare your reading, your understanding, with what they hoped the reader would understand. If you missed the point, the student will see the need for appropriate revision.

If you can teach a student to use the conference as a chance to communicate with a supportive, informed reader, you will both relax a little and become two writers, or perhaps a writer and a writing coach, working together to push a draft forward and, ultimately, to improve the student's overall writing and reading skills.

Supporting Student Responsibility

Student leadership and investment in a conference ensure student "ownership" of the paper that is discussed. It is all too easy for teachers to appropriate students' work by being too much the director, by revising for students instead of helping them choose the course of the revision. Some teachers write all over papers, before or during a conference; some keep their pencils in the desk drawer, encouraging students to make their own marks. The issue is not who marks up the paper or whether it is marked up at all. The issue is responsibility, and responsibility depends entirely on the nature of the discussion and the spirit in which advice is given and received.

For example, a student who questions the introduction of her essay does so because she suspects there is a better place to begin. And with her question, she opens the door for you to point to a spot (or two or three) that might work as a better beginning. You might give a minilesson in audience, tension, tone, even argumentation—depending on the nature of the paper—as you discuss introductions and what they can do. It is always left to the students to evaluate your advice, to weigh what they have learned in the conference, and to consider their own instincts before deciding what to do in the next draft. A discussion initiated by the student of possible leads differs considerably from the teacher's saying that the introduction should be replaced by the third paragraph. In the second case the student's responsibility (and initiative) for the paper is lost. When a paper improves as the result of a revision, the student should "own" the improvement.

Conversely, too much praise early in the process can also usurp a student's responsibility. A teacher can bring the revision process to a halt by proclaiming a draft "wonderful," particularly if the student has doubts about it. The teacher-approved draft becomes the final draft, and the essay that might have been is lost. You can avoid this early closure by listening to your students. Look at their drafts, hear what they say, and respond accordingly.

During a conference, you may wish to introduce your own agenda at times. You may have ready specific questions and bits of advice, and you may want to refer to an index card or file where you've recorded the student's progress. Although you may say things that begin to seem repetitive to you, remember that to each student, your advice is always personal.

A successful conference should end with at least a tacit "task assignment," in which you and the student agree on your expectations for the next stage of work (Arbur 338-42). When the conference ends, both you and the student should have a clear sense of what has been accomplished. You should know what expectations have been raised, what task comes next, and why.

Conferences about drafts and papers may be demanding, but they are a much more efficient way to help students understand content and questions of organization than is the marking up of papers. Conferences are *dialogic*: Students can ask questions, explain themselves, react to suggestions. The bond between writer and reader becomes real and personal. The more conferences you hold with your students, the better they will come to understand the concept of an audience and the responsibilities of a writer.

WORKSHOPS

Workshops are expanded conferences, with writers still in control of their work but with the benefit of more than one reader. In a sense, workshops are quickly assembled discourse communities. Students are exposed to the feedback of an audience in addition to the (relatively) rarefied judgment of the teacher. The conflicting judgments pronounced in a workshop must be studied and analyzed; when a workshop ends, writers will choose to accept only the advice that makes sense to them. In the revision that follows, they choose among possibilities that they might not have generated on their own. Workshops, like conferences, allow writers to see their work through the eyes of their readers and help them gain distance so they can evaluate the work for themselves.

In practical terms, writing groups may consist of as few as three students or as many as the whole class. Small groups, initially chosen and assembled by the teacher, meet during class to accomplish specific tasks.[6] These tasks can include a brainstorming discussion of an essay topic, analysis of an upcoming assignment, editorial work on one another's drafts, advice about one another's problem areas, division of a research project, and other mutual-aid endeavors.

Smaller workshop groups can provide a peer group for each student, a group that is intimate and whose members may come to look on one another over the course of a term as familiar and trustworthy. But whether workshops take place in small groups or with the whole class, students take on the role of conference moderator or coach, offering oral and written response to the work of their peers. Their experience with conferences—asking questions to evoke the reader's response, taking responsibility for the primary focus of the conference, concentrating on developing the potential of an essay—will carry over into workshop. Like conferences, workshops will evolve over the term as students learn to be better readers, to ask better questions, and to find the help they need to improve their drafts.

---

[6] When most students live on or near the campus, teachers can often ask the groups to meet outside of class. Students at "commuter" schools will usually need to meet during scheduled class times.

Whole-Class Workshops

The whole class can act as an effective workshop group. Before setting up small groups, some teachers prefer to run several whole-class workshops in order to train students in the process and to get to know them as readers. In whole-class sessions, you may choose to let students take the lead as they do in conferences, but you will, no doubt, provide guidance through your questions and comments.

The following practices will help make whole-class workshops positive learning experiences:

1. Present strong work so the students can easily recognize its strengths. Readers will learn the techniques that work for their peers; writers gain confidence from well-deserved praise and from recognizing what in their drafts is working.

2. A day or two ahead of time, hand out copies of the paper to be discussed to give students a chance to read it at their own pace. Ask them to write comments in the margins as they read, indicating points of confusion and strength. Finally, have them write a note to the writer giving their reaction to the overall content, describing the work's strengths, and offering one or two specific suggestions for improvement. And ask them to sign their name to their comments.

3. Begin the workshop by asking the writer to read aloud from the draft. This helps students focus on the paper and remember it. After the writer asks for and receives specific guidance, the readers should be prepared to ask about the background of the piece: "How long have you been working on this?" "What are your concerns?" "Do you already have plans for revision?" In this process, students will get some idea about the kind of feedback that is helpful.

4. At the end of the workshop, have readers hand the writer their signed comments. Let the class know that when the writer has finished reading the comments, you will also read them (in order to record your students' progress as readers).

Writing Groups

If you use whole-class workshops as a training ground for talking constructively about writing, then your students may be able to move directly into small writing groups without much further preparation. Many teachers, though, prefer to use small groups from the beginning since beginning writers, whose self-confidence may not be high, tend to be more comfortable in writing groups. In addition, with several writing groups meeting simultaneously, more papers will be discussed in a given period of time. A final advantage of small writing groups is that they often evolve into teams or support groups, especially if their members make contact outside the scheduled meetings.

Because you can't be there to lead the way as each group meets, it is important that you let your students know what they are expected to do for one another. In the beginning, you will need to offer detailed instructions, and these may change from session to session as you train students to take on increasingly sophisticated tasks. For example, the first workshop might be a simple exercise in reading aloud: each group member will read a draft to the others, who simply listen, concentrating on the work. Through reading aloud, writers gain distance: they hear strengths and weaknesses they hadn't noticed before; they hear the draft with new objectivity, as though someone else had written it. Just as important, group members get to know what others are working on, gain a sense of how their work compares, and learn to give the most useful advice.

In subsequent sessions, the groups might be asked to work on these tasks:

1. Without rereading, recall the most memorable points. ("This is what struck me as I listened/read.")
2. Jot down ideas or questions they want to raise.
3. Summarize the writer's point. ("This is what I think you're trying to say.")
4. Respond honestly and thoroughly to the writer's specific questions.
5. Talk through ideas for essays.

Assigning tasks to writing groups early in the term shows students what kinds of activities might be useful, gives groups a shared set of goals and objectives (a repertoire), and builds camaraderie. Later in the semester little instruction is needed: students who are working well in their groups will use their shared repertoires and respond naturally and in a variety of useful and supportive ways to one another's needs.

Should you assign students to writing groups, or should they form their own? How many students should there be in a group? Should membership rotate or remain intact week after week? Should groups deal with one paper in depth during a session, or should each student receive feedback each time? Should you drop in on the groups (even those held outside of class), participate actively, or stay away? The answers depend on you, your students, the dynamics of your class and the groups, and the task at hand. The answers will also change as the semester progresses and the class changes, but some general guidelines are provided here.

The size of the groups—and they should be created by the second week if possible—depends on the amount of time you have and the complexity of the tasks to be accomplished. After all, the more group members, the longer it will take the group to go through the written work. Asking a group of four people to share thesis ideas in twenty minutes is realistic; asking a group of six is not. Keep in mind that groups seem to work best (more inclusively) when there are no more than five students in each. Allowing students to form their own "affinity workshop groups" of friends almost guarantees that exclusion of other students will take place. The best writing groups are usually made up of students who don't know one another well enough initially to talk about anything but the writing assignment. In fact, by waiting until the second week of class to form groups, you will have had the opportunity to see who is friends with whom and then assign friends to different groups.

When forming writing groups, try to include in each group at least one student who writes well and try to balance the groups in terms of race, age, and gender. Then encourage the members in each group to swap names, addresses, and phone numbers so that they can continue their support system after class.

Membership in groups can be rotated during the semester, to allow students to make contact with new peers, but some rotation will occur naturally if you move students around to replace absentees. How often you want or need to reconstitute your groups is up to you, of course. Rotating the makeup of groups every three weeks or so allows members a chance to move beyond introductions and to trust one another, but not to become so predictable in their behaviors as to be unhelpful. Often, though, a group will work so well that the students will ask to remain together. Most teachers will respect such a request.

The key to the success of a writing group is student motivation: the more motivated the students, the more apt they are to enjoy the work of their writing group, and the more work they will do. For this reason, some teachers will not allow students to revise their essays, for instance, unless they have worked in a group. Other teachers count group participation as part of students' final grades. Decisions about how to run small groups—or whether to use them at all—will depend on how motivated you and your students are, and on whether the class comes to rely on such groups. The following model has proved successful. But if you choose to experiment with it you may decide that for your next course, you will modify it as your teaching style, your goals, and, particularly, your students demand.

The Model

Divide the class into groups of three or four. Have students bring copies of their papers to class the day before the workshop and distribute them to the other group members, who will read them ahead of time, write their comments on them, and come to class prepared to discuss them. Devote about an hour each week to the group meeting and ask that the groups divide their time equally among the papers. Writers are responsible for posing questions to keep the discussions going.

During the group meetings, as during in-class writing activities, drift from group to group, sitting in on each for a few minutes. Be ready to answer questions, to guide debates on conventions, to read entire papers or passages. You can best serve your students not as the judge but, rather, as someone who can help them find their own way. Your presence will change the group dynamics, so you may want to stay clear at first, letting each group establish itself and letting the students learn to work with one another. Even then, however, your presence in the room, the impression you give of paying attention—even from a distance—will help students stay with their task. Let them know you are available to join them upon request. Act as a resource person, who can pose friendly and informal questions that move along the group more. Try to draw into the life of the group students who seem shy or withdrawn. Most important, be supportive of the activity; if you show your enthusiasm for writing group work, students will show theirs.

For many teachers, the hardest part of group work is dealing with the concern that without direct guidance, not enough work will get done. It is important to remember, therefore, that the *kind* of work that gets done is as important as the *amount* of work that gets done. And for most students, writing groups allow for a new kind of shared responsibility. Students need your support and encouragement as they learn how to work in, contribute to, and profit from writing groups. But small groups by nature are hard to monitor—and that's good. Too much monitoring is a sure way to impair them.

After one or two sessions, try asking for a brief, written evaluation of the group's effectiveness:

What does your writing group do well?
What has helped you as a writer? What has helped you as a reader?
Suggest one thing your group could do differently to improve its effectiveness. Complete this statement: Next time let's try. . . .
What are you contributing to the group?
What would you like to do better?

Have students discuss their evaluations at a subsequent group meeting and implement some of their own suggestions. Later have them evaluate the groups again:

What has the group accomplished so far?
What has it been most helpful with? What has it been least helpful with? Explain.
What has each of us, as an individual, contributed?
How can we make our group more effective?

In this way, especially if you use these questions as the basis of whole-class analysis and discussion, you can keep loose tabs on each group's work and reinforce the idea that students are responsible for the success of their groups. Groups will learn from the successes and trials of other groups as well as from the finest contributions of the individual group members.

TASKS FOR WRITING GROUPS

The ideal writing group—a number of motivated students who know how, and are willing, to talk about writing in progress—simply responds to the questions of the writer honestly, tactfully, specifically, and more successfully than a teacher could on his or her own. But just as you expect students' writing to improve during the course, so you can expect their reading and critical skills to improve along with their ability to articulate their observations. Your students may not be confident or acute readers at first, but they will grow in their knowledge of what is effective and what is not. The tasks you assign will help them learn how to read and how to respond. Once they have learned these lessons and techniques, once they know what is expected, all you have to say is, "Writing groups, one hour, go to it," and they will.

Writing groups of this sort work because they provide a forum for supportive peer editing and evaluation of written work. Initially, students may be unwilling to critique one another's work because they don't know what sorts of constructive criticism are appropriate. But as they develop their editing and reading skills, as well as their reliance on one another, they will become serious about assessing one another's work. Since you are modeling the techniques involved in reading and evaluation, they will come to see that every comment, or notation the group makes on a rough draft is one the teacher will not have to make on the final version. By seeing different stages in one another's essays, students will develop a sense of the plasticity of prose and how changes can really help. Finally, peer judgments make the teacher's evaluation seem less arbitrary.

Though writing groups are capable of performing many tasks, their primary use lies in providing advice about revising and practice in editing. Several days or a week before a written assignment is due, have students meet in groups to discuss rough drafts of the assignment. Have them pass around, edit, and critique their peers' work. Better than the system of "buddy editing," in which two students trade drafts, the system of writing-group revision allows each draft to be critiqued by at least two readers. Problems not spotted by one member of the group are usually caught by others, and every writer may hear a variety of responses to a piece of writing. In addition, better writers are given the opportunity to assist poorer ones; weaker writers are witnessing the behaviors of stronger writers. And all students get an idea of how others are approaching an assignment.

To support students in their work, you may want to specify an editing process or a specific area on which students should concentrate. For instance, you might ask them to evaluate the introductions or develop and support theses, or you might ask them to concentrate on the variety or structure of sentences. Such direction gives structure to critiques. The following list of questions, compiled by Mary Beaven, provides a general structure for students' critiques:

1. Identify the best section of the composition and describe what makes it effective.
2. Identify a sentence, a group of sentences, or a paragraph that needs revision, and revise it as a group, writing the final version on the back of the paper.
3. Identify one (or two) things the writer can do to improve his or her next piece of writing. Write these goals on the first page at the top.
4. (After the first evaluation, the following question should come first.) What were the goals the writer was working on? Were they reached? If not, identify those passages that need improvement and as a group revise those sections, writing final versions on the back of the paper. If revisions are necessary, set up the same goals for the next paper and delete question 3. (149)

Students can write on their copies of the draft, or they can write on a separate sheet of paper and clip it to the draft. Each writer should have several written evaluations by the end of the meeting.

More comprehensive advice on revising can be derived from the following questions from Chapter 4 of Lunsford and Connors's *St. Martin's Handbook*, which give students a range of topics appropriate for group discussion. The descriptive rather than directly evaluative nature of the responses elicited provides a comfort zone for students who are reluctant to criticize. In addition, students can use the questions to respond to their own drafts. One indirect but significant benefit of writing groups, however, is that what students see in others' drafts they soon learn to look for in their own. The payoff for responding generously but demandingly to their peers' work is that they become better critics of their own work.

Responses to workshop questions like the following are more useful if they are written down and clipped to the original draft than if they are just discussed. When these questions are used as a work sheet, eliciting written answers, students may initially take twenty-five or thirty minutes to work through them while reviewing a paper. But as the term progresses, they will work more quickly.

Questions for Reviewing a Draft

1. *The assignment:* Does the draft carry out the assignment? What could the writer do to better fulfill the assignment?
2. *The title and introduction:* Does the title tell the reader what the draft is about? Does it catch the reader's interest? How? What does the opening accomplish? How else might the writer begin?
3. *The thesis and purpose:* Paraphrase the thesis as a promise: "In this paper, I will . . ." Does the draft fulfill that promise? Why, or why not? Does it fulfill the writer's major purposes?
4. *The audience:* How does the draft capture the interest of and appeal to the intended audience?
5. *The rhetorical stance.* Where does the writer stand on the issues involved in the topic? Is the writer an advocate or a critic? What words or phrases in the draft indicate the stance? Where does the writer's stance come from — that is, what influences have likely contributed to that stance?
6. *The supporting points:* List the main points, in order of presentation. Then number them in order of interest to you. Review them one by one. Do any need to be explained more fully or less fully? Should any be eliminated? Do any seem confusing or boring? Do any make you want to know more? How well are the main points supported by evidence, examples, or details?
7. *The organization:* What kind of overall organization plan is used—spatial, chronological, logical, or some other plan? Are the points presented in the most useful order? What, if anything, might be moved? Can you suggest ways to make connections between paragraphs clearer and easier to follow?
8. *The paragraphs:* Which paragraphs are clearest and most interesting to read, and why? Which ones are well developed? How are they developed? Which paragraphs need further development? What kind of information seems to be missing?
9. *The sentences:* Number each sentence. Then reread the draft, and choose three sentences you consider the most interesting or the best written

—stylistically effective, entertaining, or otherwise memorable. Then choose three sentences you see as weak—confusing, awkward, or uninspired. Are sentences varied in length, structure, and openings?

10. *The words:* Mark words that are particularly effective, that draw vivid pictures or provoke strong responses. Then mark words that are weak, vague, or unclear. Do any words need to be defined? Are verbs active and vivid? Are any words potentially offensive, to the intended audience or to anyone else?

11. *The tone:* What dominant impression does the draft create—serious, humorous, satiric, persuasive, passionately committed, highly objective? Mark specific places where the writer's voice comes through most clearly. Is the tone appropriate to the topic and the audience? Is it consistent throughout? If not, is there a reason for its being varied?

12. *The conclusion:* Does the draft conclude in a memorable way, or does it seem to end abruptly or trail off into vagueness? If you like the conclusion, tell why. How else might it end?

13. *Final thoughts:* What are the main strengths and weaknesses in the draft? What surprised you and why? What was the single most important thing said? What do you want to know more about? (58-59)

Another activity that writing groups can engage in is the selection and reading aloud of final versions of essays. You may want to spend half a period every several weeks on this. On the day that final versions are due, give each group five minutes to meet and choose an essay and a reader. Because no one reads his or her own essay, you can critique the work without publicly embarrassing the writer, who may choose to remain anonymous. After each reading (and there are usually four essays read, one from each group), try to make a comment or two in which you point out the strengths or the potential of the essay. In general, try to say only positive things, and then ask for the impressions of others in the class. If you see severe problems in an essay, deal with them in the context of the essay's strengths. The stipulation about this in-class reading is that the choice of reader and essay must rotate each week, so that by the end of the course, every student will have had his or her essay read and will have been a reader.

Benefits for Readers and Writers

The hope is, and experience suggests, that after working with assigned questions and with issues of effectiveness like those discussed in this chapter, students will begin to deal with these matters on their own—in conferences, in whole-class workshops, and in their writing groups. Early on you provide the scaffolding; later on—when students have learned how to read a draft, what to look for, what kinds of comments help writers, what to think about when they are revising or editing their own drafts—you can take down the scaffolding.

Workshops benefit readers and writers simultaneously. Readers find ideas for their own work, both topics and techniques. Watching other writers struggle with the process, they become aware that they are not alone, that their problems are not unique, that good writing is not magic but, usually, the result of hard work. In helping others solve writing problems, they practice using a writer's vocabulary. They develop standards for good writing as they are exposed to the standards of others.

When these readers assume the role of writer—when their work is on the table—they benefit additionally by seeing their audience brought to life, by listening to what their readers have to say. They learn exactly what their written words communicate. They get advice about what is working and what isn't working, and they begin to see their work from a distance. They learn how to tell the difference between what they intended or wished to write and what they have written. Finally, and perhaps most important, when the writing works, they see its effect on readers and understand the power of their own well-chosen words.

WORKS CITED

Arbur, Rosemarie. "The Student-Teacher Conference." *CCC* 28 (1977): 338–42.

Beaven, Mary H. "Individualized Goal Setting, Self Evaluation, and Peer Evaluation."
Evaluating Writing: Describing, Measuring, Judging. Ed. Charles R. Cooper and Lee Odell. Urbana, IL: NCTE, 1977. 135–56.

Garrison, Roger. "One-to-One: Tutorial Instruction in Freshman Composition." *New Directions for Community Colleges* 2 (1974): 55–84.

Jones, David. "The Five-Minute Writing." *CCC* 28 (1977): 194–96.

Kroll, Barry. "How College Freshmen View Plagiarism." *Written Communication* 5 (Apr. 1988): 203–27.

Lunsford, Andrea, and Robert Connors. *The St. Martin's Handbook.* 3rd ed. New York: St. Martin's, 1995.

Murray, Donald. "The Listening Eye: Reflections on the Writing Conference." *College English* 41 (1979): 13–18.

Polanyi, Michael. *Personal Knowledge: Towards a Post-Critical Philosophy.* New York: Harper, 1964.

Weaver, Richard. *Language Is Sermonic.* Ed. Richard L. Johannesen, Rennard Strickland, and Ralph T. Eubanks. Baton Rouge: Louisiana State UP, 1970.

4 SUCCESSFUL WRITING ASSIGNMENTS

ASSIGNMENTS

Initiating student writing and evaluating writing assignments are at the heart of a composition teacher's job, and the life of a writing teacher has often been described as a perpetual search for effective topics, writing prompts, and assignments. All good writing teachers, no matter how finished their courses seem, are on the lookout for more fruitful ways to get students writing.

We make the assumption in this book that the course you are teaching is "straight composition"—a course in which the *content* of literature plays at most a minor role. Therefore, the assignments discussed in this chapter do not include the genre of assignments that asks writers to respond to literature. This is not to say that such literary topics are insignificant; they are, however, more applicable to literature courses, which have a critical-semantic emphasis, than to composition courses, which have a generative-formal emphasis.[1]

The first question you need to ask yourself is whether you will give your students a free choice of topics. The possibilities range from complete student choice of form and content of all topics through complete teacher specifications for all aspects of every assignment. Your program may have conditions you must meet, but most programs give teachers considerable leeway in determining how much control to exert over students' choice of topics. There are arguments for and against free choice. When students determine all the elements in their assignments, they can feel more emotionally invested in their writing than they do when responding to a teacher's specifications. And a benefit for you is that you are likely to get essays on a variety of topics, and so you won't have to spend an evening reading twenty papers on the same subject. On the other hand, given free choice, some students may feel as if they have been set adrift. In addition, some students may tend to respond to free choice by writing personal narratives, and you may wish to encourage your students to try other kinds of writing. For a first-time teacher, relying on some of the carefully developed writing topics found in almost any rhetoric textbook is not a bad idea, and the following discussion will assume you are providing specifications for writing assignments.

---

[1] If you find yourself teaching a course with an emphasis on responding to literature, the best source for writing assignments will be your colleagues or the director of the course. For specific suggestions on writing assignments for responding to literature, see Edward M. White's *Assigning, Responding, Evaluating*.

First, you will need to establish the number and length of essays you will require. Second, you will want to decide whether you will make the assignments in a sequence of some kind or correlate the written assignments with the classwork in any given week. The detailed correlation of assignments and lessons has both good and bad aspects. On the one hand, students may become more involved in the lesson and its related activities; on the other hand, your class can become completely grade directed, with students wanting you to spend the time teaching nothing except "how to do this week's assignment." Such activity will not make students better writers, and for this reason alone, you may not want to link graded assignments closely to classwork. Correlations can be made in the students' own minds rather than in the plan for the course.

The best sequence for writing assignments is probably one loosely based on the work of nineteenth-century Scottish logician Alexander Bain. Bain divided all writing into four modes of discourse: narration, description, exposition, and argumentation (118–21). The first two, which are the more concrete, serve as the bases for initial course assignments; they allow students to draw on their own experiences and observations for subject matter, seldom forcing any higher-level generalizations or deductions. The second two modes, which are the more abstract, are left for later assignments, when students will presumably be better able to manipulate nonpersonal ideas and concepts in expository or persuasive fashion.

The supposition of this sequence of assignments is that students gain confidence in their writing by first using the more concrete and personal modes of narration and description and are then better able to use the abstract modes. Unfortunately, skill with narration and description does not seem to carry over easily to exposition and argumentation; students who are confident and even entertaining when narrating experiences and describing known quantities sometimes flounder when asked to generalize, organize, or argue for abstract concepts.[2] Bain's modes of discourse are far from the realities of the writing process. As James Kinneavy and James Moffett, among others, have pointed out, modes are not aims, and teachers using the modes must be aware of their limitations. In *Teaching the Universe of Discourse*, Moffett posits a highly schematic, centrifugal representation of the spectrum of discourse, one that acknowledges the limitations of beginners. Beginners build on "interior dialogue" to move on to "conversation," "correspondence," "public narrative," and, finally, "public generalization or inference."[3] Similarly, Kinneavy's *Theory of Discourse* talks about increasingly complex communicative acts. Kinneavy would have students begin with *expressive* discourse before moving to *reference* (or informative), *literary*, and *persuasive* discourse.

However you decide to design your course, one thing is certain: when structuring the sequence of assignments, it is important to connect each assignment to the others, always asking that your students expand their repertoire. In cre-

---

[2] See, for example, the research described in Crowhurst and Piche.

[3] For more information on Moffett's sequence, see Chapter 6.

ating the sequence, you must always consider "the activities and operations of mind in which the student must engage if he is to cope with the assignment," as Richard Larson says, and arrange assignments so that they inform one another (212). It makes sense to proceed only from assignments that are cognitively less demanding to those that are more complex. Asking a student for a "five-part argument" between a "comparison-contrast essay" and a personal narrative is not logical because the progression is unclear. Connect each assignment to skills that have been practiced previously and to skills that will follow.[4]

If you will be assigning a research paper, another sequence of assignments hinges on preparation for it. Research writing is not, as some students seem to think, some unnatural creation distinct from all other writing, and it should build on earlier assignments. A composition course that teaches research may be structured around the four sources of information that feed nonfiction writing: memory, observation, interviews, and research. Students first look within themselves for material and then cast a progressively wider net. Their work culminates in the research essay, which may incorporate all four sources of information. A series of assignments—narrative or descriptive essays, then profiles based on interviews (perhaps with one another), and then a critical essay that brings together and discusses several readings—will move students naturally toward a research essay. In this sequence, the research paper encourages students to look at the world in the widest sense, often examining topics that affect a great many people and listening to what diverse voices have to say about them. This approach may demand that students—and their instructors—alter the way they have viewed research: it is not just going to the library and reading books and articles, but rather using a growing grasp of all other sorts of writing and planning skills to build to a new kind of complexity. (The research assignment will be discussed more fully later in this chapter.)

After you have decided on the length, the number, and the sequence of assignments, you can get down to the business of creating each one. You will want to write down all assignments beforehand and pass out copies of them to your students rather than writing them on the board or reading them aloud. This not only allows you to be as specific as you wish to be but also helps to prevent any misunderstandings by the students. Each word in an assignment, no matter how small, is extremely important: the wording is the seed from which the oak—or the dandelion—will grow. When you distribute an assignment, ask your students to pay close attention to the wording, to what is being asked, before all else.

You may, in fact, want to take some time to go over the wording of the assignment and the general issue of wording. Students need to know, for all their classes, that words like *analyze, describe,* and *explain* tell them the strategy to use and often determine the form of their response. The following list, adapted from Chapters 3 and 6 of Lunsford and Connors' *St. Martin's Handbook,* defines the most commonly used strategy terms:

---

[4] There are larger issues in sequencing assignments that are too complex to be handled effectively here. For detailed discussions of different philosophies of assignment sequencing, see Coles; see also Bartholomae and Petrosky, whose sequencing approach is currently very popular.

Analyze. Divide an event, idea, or theory into its component elements, and examine each one in turn. *Example:* Analyze the American way of death, according to Jessica Mitford.

Compare and/or contrast. Demonstrate similarities or dissimilarities between two or more events or topics. *Example:* Compare the portrayal of women in "In Search of Our Mothers' Gardens" and "I Want a Wife."

Define. Identify and state the essential traits or characteristics of something, differentiating them clearly from other things. *Example:* Define "FY student."

Describe. Tell about an event, a person, or a process in detail, creating a clear and vivid image of it. *Example:* Describe the dress of the "typical" college professor.

Evaluate. Assess the value or significance of the topic. *Example:* Evaluate the contributions of African American musicians to the development of the American tradition of music in the nineteenth century.

Explain. Make a topic as clear and understandable as possible by offering reasons, examples, and so forth. *Example:* Explain the responsibilities of resident advisors in dormitories.

Summarize. State the major points concisely and comprehensively. *Example:* Summarize the major arguments against surrogate parenthood.

"Strategy" words give students important clues for determining the thesis of their essays. Once they understand what such a word asks of them, they need only understand the meaning of all the other words in the assignment.

Discussing strategy words with students is a good way to begin your larger discussion of the criteria that will be used to evaluate their drafts and essays. In a sense, of course, criteria for the evaluation of essays are the theoretical heart of any course in rhetoric or writing, but you need to boil them all down to specifics for each new assignment. For each type of assignment, a slightly different kind of invention works best, a slightly different group of forms or genres is appropriate, as are different levels of descriptive detail or narration and different methods of logical development. In a new assignment to a class, you need to describe thoroughly what you want to see, from specific thesis statements to levels of support, formal structure, use of personal pronouns, use of dialogue, various conventions, and so forth. Some of these criteria will be spelled out in the wording of the assignment, but some you should present and discuss in class.

As you continue teaching, it is a good idea to ask students whose essays are particularly effective whether you can make photocopies of their work for use in subsequent semesters. Such models of successful responses to assignments can help students immensely by letting them see concretely what your necessarily abstract criteria can produce.

So what *is* a good assignment? Edmund J. Farrell tells us what a good assignment is *not* (220-24):

A good assignment is *not* an assignment that can be answered with a simple true/false or yes/no answer: "Do the SAT exams have too much power over students' lives?" Such assignments do not offer a writer enough purpose or give enough direction, and students are often at a loss for a place to go after they have formulated their simple answers.

A good assignment is not one that leads to unfocused or too-short answers. For example, "How do you feel about the ozone layer?" does not give students enough direction, and to ask "Is the national debt a serious problem?" encourages a brief, affirmative response. A good assignment is also not one that assumes too much student knowledge. "What are the good and bad points of U.S. foreign policy?" or "Is America decaying as the Roman Empire did?" is far too broad, and even a minimal answer would require students to do a considerable amount of reading and research.

Nor is a good assignment one that poses too many questions in its attempt to elicit a specific response: "In the popular television show *Star Trek: Deep Space Nine*, what do the writers and producers wish to suggest about society? Do the different races of aliens have analogous groups in our contemporary society? What image does the show provide of law enforcement? Of racial tendencies? Of moral leadership? What ethical message does the show give its viewers?" This sort of assignment means to help students by supplying them with many possibilities, but it can provoke panic as inexperienced writers scramble to deal with each question discretely.

A good assignment, finally, is not one that asks students for too personal an answer: "Has there ever been a time in your life when you just couldn't go on?" or "What was the most exciting thing that ever happened to you?" Though you might sometimes get powerful writing in response to such visceral topics, some students will be put off and not wish to answer them, while others will revel in the chance to advertise their angst or detail their road trip to Daytona Beach. Either way, you are likely to get some bad writing, replete with evasions or clichés.

If good assignments are not any of these things, then what are they? In *Teaching Expository Writing*, William Irmscher lists a number of useful criteria (69-71). Foremost, a good assignment has to have a purpose. If you ask students to write a meaningless exercise, that is what you will get. An assignment like "Describe your dorm room in specific detail" has no purpose but to make students write; the response to such an assignment is meaningless as communication. If the assignment is extended, though, to "Describe your dorm room, and explain how various details in it reflect your personality and habits," it becomes a rhetorical problem. The answer to the assignment now has a purpose, a reason for saying what it says.

Irmscher tells us that a good assignment is also meaningful within students' experience. *Meaningful* here does not necessarily mean "completely personal," but keep in mind that your students do not usually have access to as wide a world of opinion, fact, or experience as you do. Though you can perhaps talk coherently about the recession during the Reagan era or the civil rights struggle of the sixties, for seventeen- and eighteen-year-olds, these subjects are probably topics for research. The subjects that students can be expected to write about well without doing research are those that fall within their own range of experience—the civil rights issue as it relates to the busing program at their high school, or the drug problem as it relates to their circle of acquaintances.

A good assignment, says Irmscher, also asks for writing about specific and immediate situations rather than abstract and theoretical ones. "Discuss the problem of sexism" will not elicit the good, specific writing that an assignment tied to concrete reality will: "Discuss how you first became aware of sexism and how it has affected the way you deal with men and women." If you pose a hypothetical situation in an assignment, make certain it is one students can conceptualize. "If you had been Abraham Lincoln in 1861 . . ." is the sort of assignment that will only invite wearying and uninformed fantasy, whereas "Write a letter to the board of trustees explaining why it should reconsider its decision to raise tuition by three hundred dollars per year" is a hypothetical situation (or perhaps it is not) that students can approach in an informed and realistic manner.

A good assignment should suggest a single major question to which the thesis statement of the essay is the answer. "Is smoking tobacco harmful, and should the tobacco laws be changed?" asks for several different, though related, theses. It is better to stay with a single question whose ramifications can then be explored: "Discuss why tobacco should or should not be legal, supporting your argument with details from your own experience or the experiences of people you know."

The assignment itself should be neither too long nor too short. It should certainly be no longer than a single paragraph unless it includes content information, such as a table, a graph, a quotation, or evidence of some sort that must be responded to in the essay. Too long and too complex an assignment will frustrate and confuse students. Too short an assignment, on the other hand, will fail to give sufficient guidance.

A good assignment, then, must be many things. Ideally, it should help students practice specific stylistic and organizational skills. It should furnish enough data to give students an idea of where to start, and it should evoke a response that is the product of discovering more about those data. It should encourage students to do their best writing and should give the teacher her best chance to help.

A final word on assignments: do not be reluctant to change or jettison assignments that do not work out. As mentioned earlier, every writing teacher is always on the lookout for new and better topics, not because the old ones are necessarily bad but because good teachers constantly search for better ways of teaching. You may also find that you get tired of reading students' responses, even good responses, to an old assignment. When you find boredom setting in, it is time to change assignments, as much for your students' sake as for your own.

REVISION

As the sample syllabi in Chapter 1 suggest, the revision of students' essays before the essays are finally graded should be an important element in college writing courses. The inclusion of a revision option is up to you, of course (unless your department requires or forbids one), but most experienced writing teachers are committed supporters of such an option. Their experience has shown them that the reasons for allowing revision seem to outweigh by far any inconveniences.

The revision of essays allows teachers to escape from having to grade all the writing students do. At the same time, it removes from the writing situation the constant pressure of working for a grade and thus allows students to concentrate on their writing. In other words, it provides a less judgmental relationship between teacher and student, one in which the teacher can be a writing coach rather than a judge whose only function is to give grades.

Revision allows students an insight into the editing process that is difficult to achieve if all work is graded and then filed away without the writers having any chance to change or reexamine it. Studies of the composing process have shown that many students write a paper with little planning, make no notes, grind out the minimum number of words, and make few changes as they type up what they have written. They see writing as a one-shot, make-or-break process. Because the very idea of large-scale revision is alien to these students, providing a revision option allows them to approach the task of editing as a means of re-seeing their writing. They need to learn that in producing quality writing, self-evaluation and self-correction are important elements.

A revision option can work in several different ways, but all of them involve the same general idea: the teacher collects and evaluates students' essays and then returns them to the writers, who have the option of rewriting them for a higher grade. The mechanics of turning in essays and of grading them differ from system to system, but all have in common this "second-chance" element.

Revisions are usually the focus of conferences and workshop sessions, but you needn't use either of these systems. According to another system using a revision routine, students must turn in essay A on the day it is due. They will either mark the essay DRAFT, which indicates that the writer wants the paper evaluated but not graded, or they will leave it unmarked, which indicates that the paper is to be evaluated and graded.

You evaluate all the essays but grade only those considered final efforts. The drafts are approached differently. On a draft, your task is to provide guidance in revising, not merely in editing. You are looking not for a neater or more "correct" copy of an essay but for a re-envisioned essay. Thus your terminal, or closing comments will contain far more specific suggestions and criticisms than will those on a graded essay. The terminal comments on a preliminary draft must serve as blueprints or suggestions for revision, whereas those on a final essay must, by the very nature of the grading process, be more concerned with justifying the grade and giving closure to the assignment.

The next week, you return the students' papers, and give those students who had turned in drafts a week or ten days in which to revise their papers, which must then be turned in for a final grade. If a draft is very good, as occasionally one is, the student may just return it unchanged; but most students rewrite their papers. When the final versions are handed in, ask that the original draft be clipped to the revision so that the changes will be evident. You also ask that any comments from workshop members be attached as well. On this second sweep through essay A, you will read the essays, write comments in the margins, note any remaining formal errors (usually with a check mark), write a short comment on the success of the revision and the general quality of the essay, and return it to the writer for the last time.

In the week before the final drafts of essay A are due, rough drafts of the next assignment, essay B, will have come in and perhaps a few early revisions of essay A will have arrived as well. By the time you get all the final versions of essay A, you will be seeing the rough drafts of essay C. During any given week, therefore, you may be evaluating or grading as many as three assignments. It is not so confusing as it sounds. Here is a diagram:

Week 2

Monday

Friday
Drafts of essay A due

Week 3

Monday
Drafts of essay A returned
Some final drafts of essay A turned in this week

Friday
Drafts of essay B due

Week 4

Monday
Final drafts of essay A due
Drafts of essay B returned
Some final drafts of essay B turned in this week

Friday
Drafts of essay C due

Week 5

Monday
Final drafts of essay A returned
Final drafts of essay B due
Drafts of essay C returned
Some final drafts of essay C turned in this week

Friday

Other permutations of the revision system work better for some teachers. For example, they may permit students to submit multiple versions of an essay, especially if the class is working in writing groups. Other teachers may allow only one or two revisions during the term. Still others will allow students to submit their revisions during a "revision week" at the end of the quarter or the semester. This allows students more time in which to revise, but it also results in a great influx of papers to be read and graded during that final, hectic week. Teachers who grade all papers as they come in and then re-grade those that students choose to revise give students a clear idea of how they are doing in terms of grades. In such a system, however, the grading process is burdensome for the teacher, especially since the terminal comment on a graded paper is expected to justify the letter grade rather than provide suggestions for revision.

The most common objection to the revision option is that it creates more work for the teacher. And in some ways, it does. In a class of 24 students that demands 6 graded essays from each student, the teacher must read and evaluate 144 essays. If revision is allowed, the number of papers to be evaluated naturally increases.

But there is not as much extra work for the teacher as there might seem to be at first. The revision option places more of the added responsibility on the student. Reading for evaluation takes less time than the combined effort of reading for evaluation, assigning a grade, and justifying the grade; and the final reading and grading of the revision take less time than reading for evaluation and justifying the grade. Once you get the system down, you should be able to read for evaluation and write a terminal comment in about five to seven minutes. Grading the revised version takes only about five minutes because you already know the writer's purpose. In neither reading should you give small, formal errors the amount of attention that you would give such errors in a single reading. In the first reading, in fact, you mark no errors at all, although you may mention serious error patterns in your terminal comment. In the second reading, errors get only a check mark. The act of revision generally means that the final essay will have fewer formal problems.

This paean to the revision option should not obscure the problems the revision option can present. The most obvious one is the students' temptation to use the teacher only as an editor. If you mark all the formal errors on each rough draft, you will lead your students to believe that their revision need be no more than a simple reprinting of the essay with the formal errors corrected. If you want to mark errors in drafts, do so with a simple check mark over the error, which the writer must then identify and correct. Encourage students to rely on one another as editors and proofreaders before submitting drafts. Don't hesitate to say, "This draft isn't ready for me."

The second problem that revision presents is psychological: students tend to believe that a paper that has been revised in a formal process will automatically receive a higher grade than one the teacher sees only once—the A-for-effort misconception. If a draft merits a D and the revision raises the grade to a C, the student often has a hard time understanding why, with all the changes she made, the paper is not worth an A or a B. Students may see any paper without serious formal errors as worthy of an A or a B, not realizing that its content is vacuous or its organization incoherent. Such issues make for useful classroom discussion and exploration. After an assignment has been graded, the class can analyze the criteria for evaluation and grading. Some students, used to grade inflation, simply cannot get used to receiving C's and even lower grades, especially if the work is formally perfect or they received high grades in high school. One way around this expectation is to assign a paper no grade at all until after at least one revision has been submitted or until you can declare the essay "acceptable" (usually the equivalent of a passing grade or a C).

As you evaluate the merits of a revision option, keep in mind that revision of written work is immensely useful to students. No longer is an essay a one-shot deal, submitted in fear or resignation because it must soar or crash on its maiden voyage. The opportunity for revision can foster commitment to the assignment and real intellectual growth. By allowing students to reflect on and improve their writing, a teacher allows them to see writing for what it is: a process of re-seeing a subject, a process that isn't completed until the writer is ready to say, "I can do no more."

RESEARCH PAPERS

More than 80 percent of college writing programs require a specific writing assignment: the research paper. The research paper is an extended essay, usually of at least one thousand words. It makes all the usual demands on students, but in addition, it demands that they master more extended essay-writing skills together with the skills involved in library research and documentation. Research papers are generally written in response to topics assigned by the teacher and are often worth a larger percentage of the final grade than is any one of the shorter essays written for the course. They tend to be long-range tasks, requiring from three to five weeks, and may work better in a semester-long course than in a quarter-long course.

This assignment carries heavy baggage and is sometimes seen as meaningless drudgery for both student and teacher. Students often think of a research essay as a certain number of quotations in a certain number of pages on a certain topic. They often concentrate more on stringing quotations together than on developing an opinion or a thesis, and they may be more aware of the conventions of bibliographies and footnotes than of the need to place their position in context. Many FY students walk into class having spent years preparing for the college research paper. What they are prepared for is a kind of ritualized boredom.

Some college instructors come prepared for the same—for enduring seven to ten pages of lifeless "research" prose, even though they may believe, at least in theory, that the assignment is important. It does, after all, teach practical library skills; and it encourages analysis, synthesis, and interpretation of outside sources, skills that are key to critical thinking and scholarly work. As a writing task, the research paper requires students to work from an abundance of information, a challenge they don't encounter with shorter essays. But does the assignment have to be so tedious?

No, it doesn't. In fact, it can be the most important and the most interesting assignment in a composition course, building powerfully on everything that came before it. One great failure of the research-paper assignment is that it is often presented as a separate activity, as generically different from the essays and all the other work students do in a writing course (Larson 814). In the first half of the course, much of the writing students do—narratives, descriptions, profiles—may strike them as creative. The work in the second half, however, consisting of the research paper in the form they know from high school, is likely to seem antithetical to creativity.

The research-paper assignment thus provides the teacher with a chance to take on a form that students may think inviolable and to demonstrate that the shape of every piece of writing is a servant to the writer's purpose. This assignment can also show students that finding information from outside sources is not a specialized activity but something all writers do to find out what they want or need to know. The research paper even promises students as great a chance for discovery as did the personal essay they wrote the third week of class, and it is every bit as creative.

The Less Formal Research Paper

To begin, a short introductory lecture or classroom discussion should help students understand what a college research essay is not. It is not a research report or an extended summary of what is known about a topic—it is not a recycled encyclopedia entry. Like any other essay they have written for your class, this essay must have a purpose, and part of the challenge of writing a research-paper is discovering that purpose. To discover the purpose, students must look beyond their own experiences, find out what they want to know, and explore their interests openly. Their reactions to this process are as important to the research paper as they were to the personal essays they wrote at the beginning of the course.

Not enforcing all the drab protocols of the "formal" FY composition-course research paper may not be an option in your program; but if you can, modify the assignment, turning it into a research essay. Though it is important that students learn to document sources and build all their papers around a controlling idea, or thesis, they should be given some freedom in choosing the form in which to express what they've discovered. They may want to use first-person pronouns and to include personal experiences and observations. In the future, whenever students are asked to write a formal research paper, they will be expected to follow the specific conventions of the discipline in which they are working. They will conduct research in the discipline and write scholarly papers for those best equipped to guide them: the faculty members in their discipline. The best that the instructor of an FY writing course can do is give students a feel for the excitement of research, impress upon them the ethics of honest reporting, and stress the importance of following discipline-specific guidelines.

What must drive the research assignment, then, is not a desire to "get it right" formally but the student's curiosity and desire to explore. This motivation is best served by an open, or at least democratically structured, choice of topics. As early as the first few weeks of the semester, challenge students to think about experiences they have had that raised questions research can help answer. Some of the best research topics (and essay topics, too) grow out of the writer's experiences. For example, one of our students survived an abusive relationship with her boyfriend and wondered why she had stayed with him as long as she did. She wrote a paper that focused on the paradox in which many victims of abuse feel dependent on their abusers. Another student visited graveyards on Cape Cod, searching for the headstone of an ancestor. He noticed certain recurring designs on the older headstones and wondered about their significance. Thus he had a topic. And when a class got into a discussion of political correctness on campus, some students wanted to explore and debate the subject; there was a topic for a whole group of students.

Sometimes, too, research topics grow out of essay topics that were discarded because they seemed to demand more background than could be handled in a short work. Other topics may stem from class discussion, newspaper articles or editorials, lectures by visiting speakers, late-night conversations, and even a reference work's subject index, as when a student looks up a general area of interest (for example, advertising) and then focuses on narrower subject headings (advertising—effects on children).

The following exercise might get your students thinking about what makes them curious:

1. Brainstorm for five minutes to generate a list of things about which you know something but would like to know more. Make the list as long as you can. Whenever possible, be specific, and don't censor yourself.
2. Brainstorm for another five minutes, making a list of things about which you don't know much but would like to learn more. Write down whatever comes to mind.
3. Look at both lists, and circle the one item that piques your curiosity more than any other does.
4. Now take another five minutes, and build a list of questions about the item you chose. If that topic goes nowhere, if you can't come up with a strong list of questions that you'd like to learn the answers to, try another topic from the brainstormed list.

Students who have the freedom to act on their own curiosity can't dismiss unsuccessful papers with the excuse that the assigned topics were boring. More important, such freedom fosters conditions that can make research genuinely rewarding—for example, late-night moments in the library when students stumble on a source that suddenly opens a door to their topic. In doing research, students can experience, often for the first time, the same joy of discovery they may have experienced when they wrote personal essays. The key is that they are in command of the journey.

If your program demands that all students in a class choose from just a few topics, however, you might devote a class period to brainstorming and sharpening the topic or a small number of topics that the class will tackle. Ask each student to bring in two research topics they would be interested in writing about. Then assign the students to workshop groups, charging the members of each group to discuss their various suggestions for ten minutes and come up with a group-sponsored list of four or five subjects. As the groups report on their subjects, write them down in a numbered list on the blackboard. This should give you twelve to twenty possible subjects. Students may then vote on how much they like the subjects, using a numerical system—four points for "really want to write on this one" down to one point for "have no interest at all in this." Using a process of elimination, you can reduce your twenty topics to two or three within a relatively short time, and your students may then feel that they had a stake in the selection of their topic.

The risk of an open-ended approach to the research paper is that students may choose less intellectually challenging or more general topics than those you would assign. Though you'll be amazed at the range of topics students will come up with when they are allowed to act on their own interests, many of the topics won't be scholarly. If a topic has little promise, a student might best be steered away from it. A student might think that *Melrose Place* is a fascinating research topic, for example, but since few sources on this new program will be available (and many will be repetitive and one-sided), the topic is likely to be a dud.

The rewards of allowing students to choose their topics can be great: when allowed to find out for themselves whether a topic is fruitful or fruitless, most students overcome their alienation from research and come to approach all research papers with more confidence. They also come to see that through research, they can become authorities capable of interpreting and analyzing information and that what they think matters.

A Model Five-Week Assignment

Though there are many variations on the research-paper assignment, typically it is an eight- to ten-page documented paper, researched and written in just over a month. By providing a structure within the course that supports students' activities, you can smooth the tasks of conducting research and writing an essay based on it.[5]

Although all agree that procrastination is the enemy of good research writing, many students have never researched and written a paper more than twenty-four hours before it was due. The following model incorporates short weekly assignments that allow you to supervise students' progression toward the completion of interesting research papers.

---

[5] The chapters on conducting and writing research in *The St. Martin's Handbook* can be a useful accompaniment to students during the various stages of the process.

Week 1 At the beginning of the semester, encourage students to begin collecting possible research-paper topics. Ask, for example, "What have you seen or experienced or read that raises questions that research might help answer?" They might want to know about trends in university housing, the historical arguments for and against the Greek system of fraternities and sororities, the major areas of study that lead to the best chances of employment and to the most lucrative job offers, the effects of stepfamilies on student achievement, or the best preparation for transferring from a community college to a university. Several weeks before you begin the assignment, remind students to consider their tentative topics, including those that promise the possibility of interviews. The key is to stress the extent to which the success of their projects depends on their curiosity about the topics. Providing examples of successful papers and topics also greatly helps students to think about their own ideas; in fact, you may want to provide them with an opportunity to discuss their potential topics in their writing groups.

Despite your emphasis on curiosity, many students will continue to hold some stale assumptions about research and research papers being only form and facts. Begin the week, therefore, by bringing these assumptions into the open. Ask students to complete the following freewriting exercises:

1. Write *research* and *research papers* at the top of a page in your notebook, and spend five minutes freewriting about any initial thoughts, preconceived notions, or prejudices that come to mind when you focus on these words.
2. Skip a few lines, and freewrite for another five minutes, this time focusing on people, anecdotes, situations, and specific experiences that come to mind when you think of these words.
3. Now spend five minutes making a list of sayings, clichés, rules, principles, and ideas about research and research papers that you've heard, including those you believe to be untrue.

This exercise is the means for launching a class discussion about how this research assignment may differ from assignments students have done in the past. Take pains to make the distinction between a research essay and a college research paper: the point is not simply to collect and document information on a topic but to do something with the information. Usually a controlling question will inform and guide the research and writing.

Students must also be helped to discover that research, in the hands of a good writer, is lively as well as informative. You may want to provide the class with copies of a strong research-based essay or article that will challenge any assumption that facts "kill" writing. Popular magazines that value good writing—*The New Yorker, Harper's, The New Republic, Rolling Stone, Sports Illustrated*—are a good source. Or look to the work of some of the best essayists who also happen to be first-rate researchers: Barry Lopez, Joan Didion, Lewis Thomas, Barbara Tuchman, and John McPhee. A successful student research paper, either from your files or a real student's work in a textbook, like Danny Taffe's research essay on Frida Kahlo in *The St. Martin's Handbook*, will work as well. Any research-based essay, student or professional, that features lively writing and an engaging treatment will challenge the prejudice that writing based on research must be boring.

Suggest that students read the essay looking for devices that hold their interest, and follow up with a discussion about what a research-based essay shares with any other essay: a distinct voice, a point of view, concrete information, a discrete focus, and perhaps even the telling of a story. Most important, though, help students see that the writer of the research essay has the same motivation as the writer of the personal essay: the desire to make sense of something. Both writers share their discoveries with their readers.

This first week you'll need to confront one final problem: library-phobia. Even students who feel as though they mastered their hometown or local libraries may find the campus library an intimidating wilderness, especially now that computer terminals have replaced most bound indexes and card catalogs. Most university libraries offer orientation programs, ranging from tours to in-class presentations. We have often found it useful, however, to accompany our classes to the library and give over a large part of one class to a library tour. When students are ready to begin their research, they're ready to learn about the appropriate sources, and they are often more comfortable asking their teacher specific questions than they are asking a reference librarian, whom they do not know.

For many students, this tour may be the first introduction to the world of the college library, with its computerized searches, card catalogs, serial files, reference room or section and staff of librarians. You will want, at the least, to explain the basics of the research procedure: how to search a subject index, how to use indexes and bibliographies to expand a search, how to use note cards, what sorts of notes are most useful, and so forth. Suggest that when students are ready to begin their research, those who have chosen similar topics work together and share their findings, so that no student is left without help or a place from which to begin. Suggest, too, that those who find particularly useful sources note their names and location in the library and share the information with the class.

You may find, as you give your library tour, that some students are completely unfamiliar with the increasingly important computerized research tools now found in up-to-date libraries. Some may take to the CD-ROM and networked indexes immediately, but others may be overwhelmed by the idea of mastering new software while learning the other research skills. (In fact, unless you update your knowledge every year you may yourself not even be completely up-to-date on what computer resources the library offers.) Take a few minutes after the main tour to work at several of the computer terminals with students who want to practice running a few searches. Often this minimal introduction is all uncertain students need to feel more comfortable.

Tours can be supplemented with library exercises that encourage hands-on experience with key college reference sources. One approach is a kind of scavenger hunt. Before leaving the library, hand out slips of paper with specific questions ("How and when did Virginia Woolf die?"). Better yet, ask each student to write down one question related to his or her research. Students will then exchange questions and spend at least twenty-five minutes searching for the answers to one another's questions. When the library session is over and everyone returns to class, students may announce the answers they discovered and discuss any issues that came up during their brief research experience.

A more comprehensive exercise may be assigned as homework. For example, devise or use a work sheet that requires students to consult increasingly specialized reference materials, from the card catalog and magazine, newspaper, and government-document indexes to general academic indexes, and indexes to discipline-specific journals. Have students jot down answers to specific questions about each reference work they consult. This can be especially effective if the exercise is designed to get students started on their own topics. Ask the librarian whether any such work sheets are available, or assign exercises such as those found in *The St. Martin's Handbook* (chapters 40–42).

If you are meeting with students in conferences, urge them to talk about the research topics they are considering. Always challenge their curiosity. Ask, for example, "Why are you interested in that?" Ask that every student come to class the following week ready to discuss their tentative topics.

Week 2 When your students walk in this week with a tentative topic, be prepared for generality. Many students will begin with the big picture: "My topic is advertising," or "I want to write about whales." These general topics are not necessarily a bad place to begin. They give researchers plenty of room in which to roam until they discover what they are really interested in. But a lack of focus plagues college research papers (and most other essays), and the sooner students narrow the field, the better. Among other things, a narrower focus makes the research process more efficient; instead of being compelled to glance at forty articles on the depletion of rain forests a student can choose the five articles that deal with its impact on native peoples. A narrow focus also means that the writer is more likely to reveal less obvious aspects of her subject. At this point, your job is to help students narrow their focus to the point where they are making a specific comment, or asking a specific question, about their chosen topic.

All writing answers questions. That's especially true of the research paper. Students simply need to decide which question they are most interested in exploring. Try this focusing exercise at the beginning of the second week.

1. Ask students to bring a tentative topic idea and a felt-tipped marker to class. Give every student a large piece of newsprint (or other kind of paper), and have them tape it to a convenient place on the wall.
2. Have them write their topic idea in a few words at the top of the paper (for example, "Child Abuse," "Steroid Use," and so forth).
3. Have them take a few minutes to state why they chose the topic. (Did they read something about it? discuss it in class? Is it based on personal experience?)

4. Ask each student to spend about five minutes listing what he or she knows about the topic. Some students may know very little, whereas others may know some striking statistics, something about the extent of the problem, the names of important persons involved, pertinent schools of thought, some common misconceptions, or some facts they have observed on their own.

5. Ask students to spend fifteen or twenty minutes building a list of questions about their topic that they would like to learn the answers to.

6. As the students are finishing up, encourage them to move around the room and look at the gallery of topics. Now they can help one another. Ask them to stop at each sheet of paper and do two things: add a question they would like answered about the stated topic, and check the one question (it could be their own) they find most interesting.

This exercise rarely fails to impress students with the range of interesting topics their peers have chosen. And the list of questions helps each student see the many angles on her chosen topic. The one question that will provide the focus for the student's paper may even be somewhere on that sheet of paper. By taking the exercise a few steps further, you can challenge each student to find that question.

7. Ask the students to look over their lists of questions and circle the one they find most interesting. Urge them to choose a specific "focusing" question rather than a general one. They should write this question at the top of a fresh sheet of paper.

8. Ask that they build a new list of questions in response to this question: "What do I need to find out in order to answer my focusing question?" For example, if a student's focusing question is "Why do many college students abuse alcohol?" she might wish to find out about the consumption patterns among college students. "Do they differ from those in the general population?" "Do drinking patterns vary by gender?" "How frequently do college students seek treatment?" "How often does abuse end in tragedy?" "Have efforts by colleges to curtail abuse succeeded anywhere?" "Why, or why not?" Many of these questions may also have appeared on the first sheet of paper. Urge students to cull the first list as they build their new list.

If the exercise is successful, students will leave the class with a clear sense of the direction they want their research to take. In conferences, help the undecided students settle on a tentative focus (or two). They can change their minds later, but for now they need a discrete trail to follow.

A follow-up class discussion of the library exercise would also be useful. Ask students where they ran into problems and what references proved to be gold mines. Spend some time discussing how to evaluate sources. Most students will be unfamiliar with college-level indexes. Their favorite sources for high school research papers were probably the *Encyclopaedia Britannica*, the *Readers' Guide to Periodical Literature*, and the library card catalog. They should be pushed to dig more deeply and to turn to more authoritative sources. Encourage them to work toward the bottom of an inverted pyramid of sources (see Diagram A). There they are most likely to find more surprising, more specific, and more reliable information. Explain what makes an article in the *Journal of Alcohol Studies* more authoritative than one in *Good Housekeeping* (even if it isn't better written). Insist that they consult at least the two key general indexes to journal articles, the *Humanities Index* and the *Social Sciences Index*.[6]

In conferences, discuss research strategies. Ask students where they will begin looking. Suggest indexes that may be appropriate to their subjects. Handbooks on writing college research papers often have useful appendixes that list sources by discipline. Encourage students to consider live sources and fieldwork as well. Could they interview an expert on their topic or someone affected by it in some way?

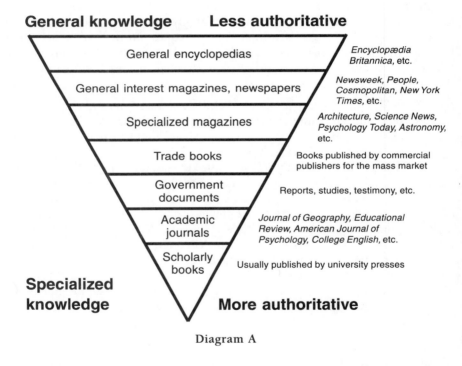

Diagram A

Week 3 Begin the week with a discussion of note-taking. It is, unfortunately, a skill that has suffered from the wide availability of photocopiers. Students think, "Why do any writing from a source when I can make a copy and bring it home?" The answer is simple. By taking the time to write about sources as they research, students are in effect starting to write their papers. Note-taking is a kind of prewriting. Taking time to make good notes has another effect, too: it

[6] See Chapter 41 of *The St. Martin's Handbook* for more sources.

helps the researcher make the information her own. Every experienced researcher knows that a stack of carefully accumulated note cards can lead almost effortlessly to suggestions for organizing material, whereas a stack of photocopies leads to more work. Soon your students will themselves be experienced researchers.

Students struggle with their material to gain control of it. If students are swamped with information, their own voices may get lost in the chorus of experts. But by paraphrasing, summarizing, and analyzing their sources as they encounter them, students will begin to reassert their own voices and reestablish their authority over the paper.

Despite their experience, many students aren't sure what distinguishes a paraphrase from a summary or even what constitutes plagiarism. Some students have never used notes to synthesize or analyze source material—let alone to support their opinions. In class, hand out a page from a research source. Then show two paraphrases of a passage from the source, one of which is plagiarized. Use these two passages as a basis for discussing the improper use of a source. Then ask that each student paraphrase another passage from the source. In pairs, students can check each other's work for plagiarism. Their questions can be the basis for further discussion.

Ask students to summarize in their own words the central ideas in a larger source. Then talk about what seems worth quoting from the sample passage and what constitutes a strong quote.[7] Finally, introduce another type of note-taking—analysis or commentary, in which the writer essentially reflects on what the source says and how it relates to the purpose of her paper. This kind of writing is probably most important of all, since it encourages students to make active use of the information, shaving it and shaping it.

Though many students are familiar with using note cards in the research process—and note cards do have advantages—you can also suggest the double-entry journal technique made popular by Ann Berthoff. According to this method, students divide each page of a notebook vertically (or write only on every other page), using the left side for quotes, paraphrases, or facts and the right side for reflections on these notes—that is, for freewriting that the students can do when they finish note-taking (41-47). The chief advantage of this approach is the right column, which challenges students to read more actively, to analyze their sources and determine why—or if—they are important.

The discussion about note-taking inevitably segues into another about citation conventions. At this point, you can review the basics of the Modern Language Association (MLA) format for parenthetical citation.[8]

In conferences, keep pressing students to narrow the focus on their subjects even if they are not sure they can find enough information. Encourage them to

---

[7] Chapter 42, section C of *The St. Martin's Handbook* provides helpful directions for note-taking, paraphrasing, and summarizing.

[8] Chapter 44, section A of *The St. Martin's Handbook* can be a useful resource for your students in this demanding area.

deepen their library searches by checking more specialized indexes and to broaden the scope of their hunt by considering nonlibrary sources—interviews, informal surveys, campus lectures, films, and so forth. Though some students may have started their research with a clear thesis in mind, most others will not yet be sure what they want to write about. Challenge these students to consider some tentative ideas, to articulate a trial thesis, to pose a controlling question.

Week 4 Some students will feel ready to attempt a draft; others will be immersed in collecting information; still others may decide to abandon their topics altogether. Here is where you can help move the process along. Because research, like writing, is a recursive process, you'll want to use assignments and discussion this week to prod your students to complete a first draft.

Try beginning the week with the following in-class exercise on voice. Students, as one once wrote, often think research papers are supposed to sound as though they were "generated by individuals who can facilitate and implement effective word usage at a level that far surpasses themselves." In other words, research papers should sound as though they weren't written by human beings. With the following exercise, you can inspire a critical discussion of the reasons—good and bad—why much scholarly writing adopts an impersonal, detached voice, as well as why these reasons may not apply to less formal research papers. At the very least, students should understand that the voice for this paper should be appropriate to their purpose, subject, audience, and most important, who they are.

1. Assume that you're a fashion-conscious person with imported leather shoes and exquisitely tasteful designer clothes. Today as you were getting out of a taxicab, another taxi whizzed by you, splashing you with a wave of muddy water. Spend ten minutes composing a letter to a friend, describing the incident.
2. Now assume you're the driver of the first taxicab. Spend ten minutes composing a story to tell your friends over lunch, describing the same incident.

After listening to several examples of each version read aloud in class, students may recognize that they can write effectively in more than one voice. You might point out the voices they have used—in their college admission essays, in letters to their parents, and especially in their research papers. Reinforce the point that no single voice is appropriate to research writing; as with any piece of writing, the writer of a research paper assumes a voice that serves his or her purpose. Urge students not to abandon the "real" voices they discovered in their personal essays but to adapt these voices to this new rhetorical situation.

You might follow up this discussion with an assignment that asks students to write three distinctly different one- or two-paragraph leads for their papers, paying special attention to voice. Consider providing examples of published or student work, with different kinds of introductions—introductions that use, for example, a scene, a quote, a description, an anecdote, a profile, a question, a case study, or a comparison. Beginnings have an enormous influence over the direction of a piece of writing, and finding three different ways in which to start their papers may point students in some useful directions. This exercise also reintroduces the idea of writing for an audience; each lead may well be aimed at a different audience.

Ask your students to share their three introductions with the class, and ask the readers to mark the lead that most encourages them to read on and to explain why it does.

As students begin their drafts, they should try to nail down the controlling idea around which they will build the paper. It is not easy. Swamped with expert information, much of it contradictory, they may be unsure of what they think—let alone what they want to argue. Careful note-taking should have helped them overcome the feeling that they are in over their heads. Just as important, however, is for them to tune out the voices of their sources and take some time to listen to their own voices. Assign the following freewriting exercise to help students reflect on the purpose of their papers and perhaps come up with a thesis statement:

1. Quickly read over your notes, and review your most important sources. Your head may be swimming with information. Now clear off your desk. Begin freewriting a narrative of how your thinking about your topic has developed since you began your research paper. What did you think when you started? What did you discover? What did you think then? What do you think now? Write fast for ten minutes.

2. Skip a few lines, and freewrite for another ten minutes, focusing on specific stories, anecdotes, people, case studies, observations, and so forth that really stick with you when you reflect on what you've learned. Describe them in as much detail as you can.

3. Spend another ten minutes writing a dialogue between you and someone you imagine you are talking to about your topic (your instructor, your roommate, a friend). Begin by trying to answer the question you think they would be most likely to ask about your topic, and go on from there.

4. Finally, spend five minutes composing a one- or two-sentence answer to this question about your topic: "So what?"

When this exercise works, several things happen. First, when students are freed from the chorus of experts that they have drowned out and can write in their own voices, they establish their authority over the material. Second, they produce writing that they can use in their drafts. The dialogue in step 3 can help them determine how to structure the paper, whereas the final question challenges them to state their point succinctly.

In conferences this week, discuss the two preceding exercises. Also be prepared for a great many technical questions about citations, the library, and the format of the paper.

Week 5 The drafts are due at the end of this week. With the five-week approach, any revisions are made subsequently. But students have probably never revised a research paper, and they put an enormous effort into producing a strong first draft. No matter how curious they are about the topic, they are looking forward to being done with it.

You may want to provide exercises and class discussion this week that will assist students with their writing. You might showcase some research papers from previous terms that demonstrate inventive approaches. You can also introduce the more conventional ways of structuring a paper: by posing a question and proposing an answer; by describing cause and effect or effect and cause; by narrating events chronologically; by posing a problem and proposing a solution; by comparing and contrasting; by treating the known and then the unknown; by discussing the simple and then the complex, the specific and then the general, or the general and then the specific.[9] And you might show how successful papers often effectively mix these conventions.

You'll undoubtedly also need to discuss in some detail the format of the paper, especially that of the works-cited section.[10] Suggest the visual devices that make a paper more readable: block quotations, bulleted lists, subheadings or subtitles, and diagrams. Briefly discuss methods of weaving quotations into the text, and reiterate the importance of attribution.

Also remind students of the devices writers use to make a work engaging to a reader. It might be helpful to list some of these on the board:

People on the page. Ultimately, what makes a subject interesting is its effect on people. Demonstrate this by pointing out profiles, case studies, or the use of quotations from interviews.

Strong openings and conclusions. Students should recognize the limitations of bland introductions and conclusions.

Voice. Discuss what the voice of a work reveals about the writer's relationship to the subject.

Active voice. Remind students to avoid passive-voice constructions, a bane of research writing. Find examples and discuss the reasons the passive voice is so often lifeless.

Stories. People love stories: they bring a point to life, and they arouse a reader's curiosity about what will happen next. Research papers can make use of anecdotes or can even tell the story of what the writer learned—they can serve as a kind of narrative of thought.

Detail. The meat of strong writing is specific, concrete information. In a research paper, details aren't just sensory; they can be statistics, unusual facts, strong quotations—any sort of memorable, convincing detail.

Surprise. Readers like to be surprised. Ask students to consider what they can tell their audience that might be surprising. Ask what surprised them and whether they can use a surprise to hook their readers early on.

---

[9] See Chapters 42 and 43 in *The St. Martin's Handbook* for more detail on these forms.

[10] Again, the research section of *The St. Martin's Handbook* can be helpful.

At the end of the week, when your students bring in their carefully typed papers, they will feel as if they were finished. Having labored over their papers for five weeks, they are likely to find the prospect of revision difficult to face. Because they may have difficulty seeing the possibilities for further development, you may want to end the week with an exercise in essay resuscitation. Ask students to bring a photocopy of their draft (printed on one side only), a pair of scissors, and tape. Don't tell them until they have arrived with their supplies that they are going to cut their carefully composed research papers to pieces. Here are the instructions.

1. Take the copy of your paper, and cut each paragraph apart. Shuffle the paragraphs.
2. Go through the paragraphs, and look for the core paragraph, the one that most clearly reveals the purpose of the essay. It may be the paragraph that contains the thesis. Set it aside.
3. Go through the remaining stack, and make two piles: paragraphs that are relevant to the core in some way, and those that seem to have little to do with it. You may find that part of a paragraph seems unimportant and the rest is useful. Cut away what is unimportant, and set it aside.
4. Take the pile of relevant paragraphs and your core paragraph, and rebuild the paper. Try new beginnings, new conclusions, and new middles. Don't worry about transitions. You can add those later. Look especially for gaps, places where you should add information. Splice in your ideas for new material. Tape the pieces of paper together when you have an order that seems promising, even if it is the same one you started with.

In conferences or in class, discuss what the cut-and-paste exercise may have suggested about where to go next. This exercise is most useful in helping students conduct a "purpose test" on their drafts, encouraging them to ask, "Is every piece of information contributing to a convincing thesis?" They should not consider it a setback that their work ended up in pieces, but as a chance to take another, fresher look.

Alternative Assignments

The five-week schedule described above works well in helping students produce eight- to ten-page research essays that rely heavily on library work. It can be adapted for the production of shorter or even longer papers. There are also many other approaches based on the notion that the writer's curiosity should drive the process. The collaborative research project, in which students work in small groups on subjects of shared interest, each finding their own angle, is an example of one such approach. In some cases, students even collaborate on writing the paper. Ken Macrorie's "I-Search Paper" encourages students to choose a topic that is not only relevant but even practical. (Students may want to investigate the best personal computer for their needs and budget or the best used car, camera, or CD player.) Such papers are often narratives describing the writer's experience learning about the topic, and they often rely more heavily on "live" sources than on traditional library sources.

You can also assign an argumentative research paper, asking students to use research to support a central argumentative position. This "argumentative edge" gives a point to the assignment that it might not otherwise have. Some successful topics we have used include these:

> What are the effects of the "political correctness" movement on our campus?
>
> Should the Greek system be banned? Why or why not?
>
> Single-payer national health care—are you in favor of it or opposed to it?
>
> How prevalent is acquaintance rape on this campus?

Political events in your state or on your campus might well be conducive to topics that students wish to choose. In assigning sides for the argument, always let students choose the side they feel more strongly about once they have done their research; one always argues better for truly held beliefs.

When designing your research assignment, consider how much time you want to devote to it and how it can build on the things about writing your students already know as well as on what you hope to teach. When your students discover that good research leads to good writing, you may find that the research paper is your students' favorite assignment.

WORKS CITED

Bain, Alexander. *English Composition and Rhetoric.* London: Longmans, 1877.

Bartholomae, David, and Anthony R. Petrosky. *Facts, Artifacts, and Counterfacts.* Portsmouth, NH: Boynton/Cook, 1986.

Berthoff, Ann E. *The Making of Meaning.* Portsmouth, NH: Boynton/Cook, 1981.

Coles, William E., Jr. *The Plural I: The Teaching of Writing.* New York: Holt, 1978.

Crowhurst, Marion, and Gene L. Piche. "Audience and Mode of Discourse Effects on Syntactic Complexity in Writing at Two Grade Levels." *Research in the Teaching of English* 13 (1979): 101-19.

Farrell, Edmund J. "The Beginning Begets: Making Composition Assignments." *Rhetoric and Composition: A Sourcebook for Teachers.* Ed. Richard L. Graves. Rochelle Park, NJ: Hayden, 1976. 220-24.

Irmscher, William F. *Teaching Expository Writing.* New York: Holt, 1979.

Kinneavy, James L. *A Theory of Discourse.* New York: Norton, 1980.

Larson, Richard. "Teaching before We Judge: Planning Assignments in Composition." *Teaching High-School Composition.* Ed. Gary Tate and Edward P. J. Corbett. New York: Oxford UP, 1970. 207-18.

Lunsford, Andrea, and Robert Connors. *The St. Martin's Handbook.* 3rd ed. New York: St. Martin's, 1995.

Macrorie, Ken. *The I-Search Paper.* Portsmouth, NH: Boynton/Cook, 1988.

Moffett, James. *Teaching the Universe of Discourse.* Portsmouth, NH: Boynton/Cook, 1983.

White, Edward M. *Assigning, Responding, Evaluating: A Writing Teacher's Guide.* 3rd ed. New York: St. Martin's, 1995.

5 RESPONDING TO AND EVALUATING STUDENT ESSAYS

In a sense, it is unfortunate that we have to grade student papers at all, for too often a grade halts further work on and thought about a piece of writing. If we could limit our responses to advice for revision and evaluation of progress, we could create a supportive rather than a competitive or a judgmental atmosphere in our classrooms. If approached cautiously and thoughtfully, evaluating and marking students' papers can serve as an encouraging record of student progress—but only if we supply students with useful information.

PORTFOLIOS

The last ten years have seen a great deal of interest in moving from the evaluation of individual student papers to a larger consideration of the student's overall writing ability. In practical terms, this means considering a portfolio of the student's writing. The term *portfolio* comes from Latin words meaning "to carry" and "sheets, or leaves, of paper," and until recently the word was usually associated with the large, flat cases in which artists carry samples of their work. Writing teachers have begun to use the term in a similar way, to indicate a folder, case, or notebook in which is stored the whole range of writing a student does during a term.

Much of the conversation surrounding portfolio evaluation has had to do with using the process in whole-writing programs, either to determine a student's placement in the program or to determine exit standards from basic writing courses.[1] Your program may indeed use some version of portfolio assessment, in which case you will be trained in the appropriate methods. In this section, however, we will discuss ways in which you as an individual teacher can use portfolios to work with your students and evaluate their work.

Why should you consider using portfolios? Many teachers who use them had been dissatisfied with the system of evaluating individual papers. Grading papers separately provides snapshots of what students are doing on particular topics in a given week, but the aggregate may not be a coherent album of the students' progress or abilities. Assigning a grade a week moves the course along in a linear way, but often a teacher has difficulty envisioning progress because she remembers each assignment largely in the form of a letter in a grade book.

[1] For information on portfolio assessment in whole programs, see Belanoff and Elbow; Hamp-Lyons and Condon; and Roemer, Schultz, and Durst.

Teachers are left with thin data to go on when summing up their students' abilities at the end of the term.

Portfolios, on the other hand, provide a physical record of where students began, where they went during the term, and where their writing abilities seem to be heading as the course ends. Rather than showing a series of letter-grade snapshots, a portfolio demonstrates the kind of progress a student has made, the ways in which the student used successive drafts to work through the writing process, the student's strengths and weaknesses in choosing topics and working on different types of assignments, and the themes in the student's work. The portfolio serves students and teachers as a continual source of material for conversation, documenting where things have been and where they are going in their editorial relationship. For teachers, portfolios encourage what Bonnie Sunstein and Joseph Potts call "reflexive theorizing" about their teaching and expectations in a writing course (9). And, finally, the portfolio gives students exactly what it has always given artists: a place to put work and a place to store, and from which to show, their best work.

Portfolios usually contain examples of several different kinds of writing, and they may contain different drafts of each assignment. Often students are asked to write a cover description for each assignment in a portfolio. In their descriptions, they discuss the rhetorical techniques and moves they made in the essay, its strengths and weaknesses, how it relates to the readings in the course, and the progress it shows in the student's movement toward more skillful writing.

There are several ways in which you can use portfolios in your course, and you should check with your writing program administrator (WPA) for advice on which ones are appropriate for your program. The least elaborate writing portfolio is a simple folder for storing assignments. As each assignment is graded and completed, the student adds it to the portfolio, along with notes, drafts, and workshop comments. The teacher continues to keep a grade book, but at the end of the term she calls for each student's portfolio. The portfolio, then, is evidence the teacher can examine for information about the student's development during the semester, perhaps using it to determine part of the final grade.

Even such a simple use of portfolios has advantages, especially if the course involves student-teacher conferences. The portfolio is brought to every conference and provides the basis for a discussion of the student's progress. Such longitudinal conferences are greatly enhanced by the inclusion of a table of contents that shows exactly what the folder contains. Notes, drafts, and final versions are marked with number-letter designations, keyed to the table of contents, and placed in the portfolio in sequential order. Example 5-1 shows a typical table of contents:

Example 5-1 SAMPLE PORTFOLIO TABLE OF CONTENTS

This folder contains important material. If found, please return to

Owner   _____

Address _____

Telephone _____

Assignment 1

Topic:

    1a. First draft; length and date:
    1b. Workshop evaluations; names of readers and date(s):
    1c. Conference(s); notes and date(s):
    1d. Final draft; length and date:
        Final grade:

Student's comment on grade and teacher's evaluation:

Assignment 2

Topic:

    2a. First draft; length and date:
    2b. Workshop evaluations; names of readers and date(s):
    2c. Conference(s); notes and date(s):
    2d. Final draft; length and date:
        Final grade:

Student's comment on grade and teacher's evaluation:

Assignment 3

Topic:

    3a. First draft; length and date:
    3b. Workshop evaluations; names of readers and date(s):
    3c. Conference(s); notes and date(s):
    3d. Final draft; length and date:
        Final grade:

Student's comment on grade and teacher's evaluation:

Assignment 4

Topic:

>   4a. First draft; length and date:
>   4b. Workshop evaluations; names of readers and date(s):
>   4c. Conference(s); notes and date(s):
>   4d. Final draft; length and date:
>   Final grade:

Student's comment on grade and teacher's evaluation:

Assignment 5

Topic:

>   5a. First draft; length and date:
>   5b. Workshop evaluations; names of readers and date(s):
>   5c. Conference(s); notes and date(s):
>   5d. Final draft; length and date:
>   Final grade:

Student's comment on grade and teacher's evaluation:

A more comprehensive portfolio plays a central role in determining the final grade, though it does not completely leave the evaluation of papers until the end of the course. In this system, students keep a portfolio like the one described above; but instead of assigning each essay a final grade within a few weeks of its submission, the teacher reads work submitted during the semester for Acceptability. *Acceptability*, which may correspond to a grade of C or higher, merely indicates that a draft is finished enough to be left for a time while the student goes on to new work.[2] The drafts and notes go into the portfolio, and the student drafts the next paper. The table of contents for this sort of portfolio uses slightly different notations:

```
Assignment 1
Topic:

    1a. First draft; length and date:
    1b. Workshop evaluations; names of readers and dates:
    1c. Conference(s); notes and date(s):
    1d. Second draft; length and date:
    1e. Third draft; length and date (if needed):
Date of Acceptability:
Students comment on accepted draft:



Revision intention:
```

At the end of the semester, the teacher asks students to choose a specified number of accepted drafts for final revision and grading. These are placed in a separate portfolio, which is due at the end of the term. Each paper in it is graded separately.

In addition to acting as a physical storage system, the portfolio acts as a mental "cold storage" system. As all writers know, revising work too soon after drafting it is not easy; a writer has a hard time getting emotional distance from something just created. So by storing "Acceptable" essays in a portfolio, students are assured of having basically workable drafts and the time and distance that make final revisions fruitful.

The final system using portfolios is probably the most rarely used, at least by individual teachers. In it, the portfolio itself, rather than individual papers, is the focus of the course. As with the systems described above, all notes and drafts are kept in the portfolio. Unlike the other systems, however, no essay is ever graded individually. Students work on assignments or topics

---

[2] This is the system used in the conferencing-based syllabus described in Chapter 1

until they wish to move on to the next one, and they may be asked to write evaluations of their essays or reflections on how their work is developing.

The teacher may or may not use this system in conjunction with some version of the Acceptability system. At the end of the semester, the teacher looks through the entire portfolio, usually in conference with the student, and grades it as a whole, taking into consideration effort, progress, the work of peers, and the quality of each piece of writing. This is a significant departure from the standard methods involved in teacher oversight, and you should make certain your program allows it before you institute this most thorough of portfolio systems.

HOLISTIC RATING VERSUS PERSONAL EVALUATION

There are two major methods of evaluating individual student papers: personal and group. We all know about personal evaluation: the system in which the teacher sits down alone and carefully reads, marks, evaluates, and grades a piece of student writing. Group evaluation, on the other hand, usually involves *holistic marking,* in which groups of trained "raters" meet in organized sessions and quickly read many pieces of student writing. Charles R. Cooper, a leading theorist of holistic evaluation, describes it thus:

> Holistic evaluation of writing is a guided procedure for sorting or ranking written pieces. The rater takes the piece of writing and either (1) matches it with another piece in a graded series of pieces or (2) scores it for the prominence of certain features important to that kind of writing or (3) assigns it a letter or number grade. The placing, scoring, or grading occurs quickly, impressionistically, after the rater has practiced the procedure with other raters. The rater does not make corrections or revisions in the paper. Holistic evaluation is usually guided by a holistic scoring guide which describes each feature and identifies high, middle, and low levels for each feature. (3)

Which method of evaluation is better, holistic or personal? If the desired end of evaluation is to let students know how well they write in a general cultural sense, the evaluation must be *reliable*; that is, it must eliminate random personal biases and somehow stabilize measurement. Personal grading cannot do this with any degree of success. More than thirty years ago, for example, the Educational Testing Service of Princeton, New Jersey, conducted a study in which 300 student papers were rated on a scale of 1 to 9 by fifty-three professionals—editors, lawyers, teachers. Of the 300 papers, 101 received every grade from 1 to 9, and no paper received fewer than five different grades—a pathetic testament to the reliability of personal grading (Diederich 3). Even assuming that the sense of intuitive agreement about grading among teachers of FY writing would lead to more agreement than is found among professionals in general, this test shows that in the assignment of grades, the degree of variation due to personal bias is huge. Teachers simply do not share values about what constitutes good writing to the degree necessary for them to achieve a respectable consensus; as a result, personal grading, which produces a rate of agreement ranging from 30 to 50 percent, is not reliable.

Holistic rating by trained raters, on the other hand, can produce an agreement rate of more than 90 percent and can cut down appreciably on the amount of time teachers spend evaluating papers. Holistic grading is more reliable than personal grading, promotes better student-teacher relations, takes less time to accomplish, and relieves students of the pressure of being graded weekly. It requires a level of organization, coordination, and training, however, that is not generally available to new teachers of composition or, for that matter, to many teachers at any level.

In addition, for holistic grading to succeed, all essays to be rated must have been written for the same assignment and must share a certain physical format. Raters must assemble at a neutral location at a certain time and agree on the analytic scale they will use. They must be trained, directed, and checked by persons familiar with holistic analysis.

Unless the decision to use holistic ratings is made and enforced by the WPA or the chair of a department, such a system can be difficult to organize, especially when so many writing teachers want to maintain close contact with their students and their students' progress. Nevertheless, if you are interested in working with other teachers to establish a holistic rating scheme for your program or part of it, speak to your composition director, find out the department's stance on rating procedures, and find out what resources are available to you. There are several good books and programs you can use as models (Cooper; White, for instance).

Chances are, however, that you will be using the most common method, personal evaluation. If so, in preparing to grade and evaluate your first stack of essays, you must consider some questions. First, are you expected to enforce departmental grading standards? If your department has such standards, you must be prepared to grade accordingly; for in all probability they were instituted in a serious attempt to reduce grade inflation and standardize grades within the composition program.

Whether or not you have to follow departmental guidelines, the question of enforcing standards usually comes down to practical questions you will have to answer for yourself. Will you assume that every paper can be, or must be, revised to meet a higher standard? Will you assume that every paper starts out as a potential A and with each flaw discredits itself, gradually becoming a B, a C, and so forth? Or will you assume that each paper begins as a C—an average, competent paper—and then rises above or falls below that middle ground? To great degree, the answers to these questions will depend on the ethos of the program in which you're teaching.

Teachers who begin the work of evaluation with the assumption that all papers are A's until proved otherwise tend to see only what is wrong with a student's essay. On the other hand, those who start from the position that all papers are C's are perhaps overly willing to see all work as average and to be grudging with their A's. Whichever position you start from, you will have to reach some decision about one other question: will improvement—presumably the goal of a writing course—be taken into consideration during final grading? Should a student who starts out writing at C level and works up to B level be given a B even if her mathematical average is only a C plus? This question can be answered in two ways, assuming you do want to make improvement a consideration.

One method of treating improvement is to set up your schedule of written assignments so that later assignments are worth a larger percentage of the grade for the course, thus weighting the final grade in favor of improvement late in the course. The other method is to use the concept of "degree of difficulty," assigning more cognitively demanding topics as the course progresses. Thus a paper that would be creditable in the second week would seem simplistic in the eighth week. The first method works better for newer teachers since the process of establishing degrees of difficulty in assignments is learned only with experience.

Finally, you'll want to think carefully about how to address your students. The written comments you make on a student's paper will often be the basis of your relationship with that student. It is important that you consider this relationship as you comment and grade and that your responses to students' writing be part of what is called a conversation of respect. That is, we expect students to respect our knowledge of the subject and our good intentions toward them; and in return, we must respect their attempts to fulfill our expectations and to move forward in their learning. You may encounter a wide range of abilities and motivations as you evaluate papers, but you must consider each student's work separately because comparisons are inherently invidious.

Your students may constitute a diverse group in terms of age, background, and ethnicity. To all of them, however, you represent—though you may not always feel comfortable with it—the academic community; they see you as a sort of gatekeeper of discourse. Although many of them will hesitate to join in the conversation of what they see as your community, you should assume and respect their desire to be part of it, and you should take responsibility for helping them become part of it. Remember, as you write your comments and suggestions, that some of your students' backgrounds may be far different from yours and far different from that of the academic community. You will want, therefore, to represent academic conventions to them with a sympathetic, as well as a judicious, eye.

GENERAL ROUTINES FOR EVALUATION

If you are not using a multidraft evaluation process, an efficient general procedure for handling papers is that suggested by Richard Larson (152-55). First, read over the paper quickly, making no marks but instead trying to get a sense of the organization and the general nature of the work. Try to decide during this reading what you like about the paper and what elements need work. Next, reread the paper more slowly, marking it for errors and writing marginal comments. You may read it paragraph by paragraph this time, thinking less about overall organization. Finally, reread the paper quickly, this time taking into consideration the overall purpose of the paper, its good and bad features, the number of formal errors it shows, and your marginal notes and comments. After this reading, you will write your terminal comment and grade the paper.

Next, make a note of the paper in your student file. Compare its successes and failures with those of the student's past papers, and note any improvement or decline. You might at this point add to your terminal comment a sentence or two concerning the paper's success compared with previous efforts. Finally, you can put the paper in your out basket and take up another one. This general routine seems time-consuming at first; but with experience, you should be able to evaluate a two- or three-page paper in about ten minutes.

There are other evaluation procedures, of course. Some teachers use evaluation sheets detailing areas of content, organization, and style. The teacher fills out a sheet for each paper and clips it to the essay instead of making comments directly on the paper. The evaluation sheets can be formatted so that each student submits the same sheet for all assignments, providing an easy way for both student and teacher to track progress, particularly with regard to trouble spots. Other teachers have experimented successfully with tape-recording their comments and returning each student's paper along with a cassette containing the comments. Both of these methods are useful but require more setup than does the Larson procedure; and in most ways, they are merely permutations of it.

The final act, of course, is to return the students' papers (at the *end* of a class). You should return student papers as quickly as possible—no doubt you can remember the anxiety of waiting for your own teachers to get papers back to you. Some students will rush to your desk, asking to speak with you immediately about their grades. You may want to ask them to look carefully at their papers and your comments before speaking to you and to write a brief summary of your comments and their responses. Such a procedure helps diffuse immediate emotional reactions to a grade and allows a student to prepare for a more productive meeting with you.

MARGINAL COMMENTS

A good number of the marks you make on students' papers will be marginal comments about specific words, sentences, and paragraphs. Making marginal comments allows you to be specific in your praise or questioning—you can call attention to strengths or weaknesses where they occur. Marginal comments may deal with substantive matters, arrangement, tone, support, and style. Especially effective are notes that make the student aware of other options she has in particular places.[3]

In writing marginal comments, you will want to balance advice and criticism with praise. Try to avoid the temptation to comment only on form and to point out only errors. You can and should use conventional editing symbols, but do not let them be your only marginal effort. Nor should you use a mere question

---

[3] For a more thorough discussion of marginal and terminal comments, see "Teachers' Rhetorical Comments on Student Papers" in Part III of this book.

mark if you do not understand a section; instead, spell out your question. If reasoning is faulty, do not merely write "logic" or "coh?"; let the student know what is wrong, and try to give them some direction for revision.

What sorts of marginal comments are effective? Remember that praise is always welcome. If students say something or make stylistic points that seem effective or appealing, do not be afraid to tell them. A simple "Good!" or "Yes!" next to a sentence can mean a great deal to a struggling writer, as you may recall from your own voyages on seas of red ink. In addition, simple questions like "Evidence?" or "Does this follow?" or "Proof of this?" or "How did you make this move?" or "Seems obvious. Is it true?" can lead a student to question an assertion more effectively than will a page of rhetorical injunctions.

Mary Beaven mentions three sorts of marginal comments that she has found particularly helpful:

1. Asking for more information on a point that the student has made.
2. Mirroring, reflecting, or rephrasing the student's ideas, perceptions, or feelings in a non-judgmental way.
3. Sharing personal information about times when you, the teacher, have felt or thought similarly. (139)

All of these sorts of comments, you will note, are text specific; they will make students feel as if the teacher were genuinely interested in what they have written.

Marginal comments are nearly always short—single sentences or phrases. As Nancy Sommers has noted, marginal comments tend to "freeze" students in the current draft, whereas terminal comments often invite a new draft (151). It is best, therefore, to limit your marginal comments when evaluating first drafts. If you write a response to every aspect of a paper, you will put in a tremendous amount of work, and your students are likely to be put off. For many good reasons, students tend to believe that the more a teacher comments on their work, (even when the commentary is in the form of praise), the worse the work is. So consider three or four marginal comments per page an upper limit, at least for substantive comments.

Purely formal marginal or interlinear comments on errors are another area entirely. You must decide for yourself on a system for noting such errors. (See the discussion of "Formal Standards" below.) Much will depend on your philosophy.

Two teachers are likely to see a page of writing in two completely different ways: one might mark a fragment, a comma splice, and three misspellings, while another might mark those errors plus four misuses of the comma, three awkward phrasings, a misplaced modifier, and five questionable word choices. A great deal depends on the stage of the composing process the student is concentrating on. ESL teachers, for instance, have long concentrated on global errors, those that obstruct meaning, and only later on will they point out errors that merely violate the conventions of Edited American English.

Members of the minimalist school of marking errors leave minor faults alone unless they are the only errors in a paper. In "Minimal Marking," Richard Haswell explains this method: "All surface mistakes in a student's paper are left totally unmarked within the text. These are unquestionable errors in spelling, punctuation, capitalization and grammar. . . . Each of these mistakes is indicated only with a check in the margin by the line in which it occurs" (601). Haswell's method may seem radical, but recall that the sight of a paper whose margins are completely filled with criticism can make any writer despair.

Certainly after the term has run for a few weeks and students have become aware of their individual error patterns, you may find that simply placing a check mark over an error is effective. This system asks students to discover for themselves the cause and solution of their errors and saves you from having to continue as editor. Because check marks are also considerably faster to apply, you can devote your time, instead, to a more attentive rhetorical reading of the paper and thus to providing fuller and more substantive comments.

TERMINAL COMMENTS

Terminal, or general, comments are probably the most important message you give students about their papers, even more important than the grades you assign.[4] Students turn first to their grades and then to your comments, which they interpret as a justification of the grade. Therefore, terminal comments must do a great deal in a short space: they must document the strengths and weaknesses of a paper, let students know whether they responded well to your assignment, help create a psychological environment in which the students are willing to revise or write again, encourage and discourage specific writing behaviors, and set specific goals that you think the student can meet.

The type of terminal comment you make will depend on your purpose—on whether, for example, you are justifying an irrevocable grade or making suggestions for revision. The task of justifying a grade often forces a teacher to focus the terminal comment in a closed way on the successes and problems of the paper. It is a kind of autopsy report on a moribund paper, one that will not see further development. Advice on revision, on the other hand, can focus on the future and build on an analysis of error patterns and the student's ongoing writing experience. Both sorts of terminal comments share certain components, though, and more than anything else the difference between them is a matter of the percentages of these components that each contains.

Extensive research by Robert Connors and Andrea Lunsford has shown that the most common kind of terminal comment that composition teachers put on students' papers—42 percent of all terminal comments—opened with praise for some aspect of the paper and then made suggestions for other areas of the paper that needed work. Terminal comments most commonly began with rhetorical issues—content, organization, general effectiveness—and then discussed the smaller-scale issues of form and mechanics; thus, teachers moved from global to local concerns. More than 75 percent of the comments dealt with the

---

[4] We are calling all general comments *terminal* comments here because research (Connors and Lunsford) indicates that 84 percent of all teachers place their longer comments at the end of a student paper rather than at the beginning.

large-scale rhetorical issues in the students' papers. The average length of terminal comments in the sample studied was about thirty-one words, but the more effective comments were somewhat longer. After analyzing the most effective comments, Connors and Lunsford derived the following characteristics of a good terminal comment.

Every terminal comment should focus on general qualities, presenting the teacher's impression of the paper as a whole. A good terminal comment devotes a large part of its content to an evaluation of the paper's thesis and how well the thesis is supported. It answers the question, How well does the thesis respond to the assignment? If a thesis is thought of as a promise of what the paper will include, the terminal comment should evaluate how well the paper keeps this promise. The evaluation must take in content, organization, and style, concentrating all of this information in a short space.

The teacher should maintain a serious yet interested tone—don't risk humor at the writer's expense unless the paper has earned an A. The teacher's comment should include praise for the effective elements of the paper as well as mention of the elements that need work. It should point out improvements made since previous efforts and encourage more. Except perhaps to mention one or two of the most important error patterns, time need not be spent pointing out formal errors. Nor is there need to summarize or review material covered in the marginal comments. In general, a terminal comment need not ever contain more than 150 words and seldom more than 100.

Meeting these goals is not as difficult as you might think. After an entire afternoon of grading, you will have gained a sense of your class as a continuum of writing abilities. Even when fatigue sets in and your critical apparatus gets creaky, you will see how each paper compares with the ones that came before and with those of the rest of the class this time. But if you are still uncertain about your ability to write good comments or want to look at examples of comments that good teachers make, your colleagues are a natural resource. Ask around about teachers in the department who are highly respected *as* teachers, and ask them whether they would check your annotations and show you theirs. Colleagues constantly help one another with revisions of their own scholarly writing, so it is natural to seek help in the same way when wishing to improve your teacherly writing of terminal comments. Also consider the most worthwhile and helpful comments you have received on your own papers.

A final word: terminal comments should show students that you have read their work carefully, that you care about helping them improve their writing, and that you know enough about your subject to be able to help them effectively. As in all aspects of teaching, your terminal comments will be useful to students only if they demonstrate humanity and competence.

THE GRADE

The comments you make in the margins and at the end of a paper are the truly important responses that a student gets from you about her writing, but the grade, the simple letter, remains the first thing a student looks for. Although personal grading can be difficult, it can be made easier for you and for all new teachers if you can organize or attend a departmental grading seminar. Such a seminar will bring together new and experienced teachers to discuss and practice grading. This group need not meet more than once or twice and need not be large, but in one afternoon, the experienced teachers can share many of their techniques and standards with the new teachers—and everyone can learn from one another.

Such a seminar works best if each participant brings copies of several unmarked essays, enough so that everyone present receives one of each. Each teacher should mark and grade her copy of the essay separately and contribute to the discussion following the marking session. Out of this discussion of the problems and strengths of each paper will come a stronger sense of context and unity for both new teachers and old.

Though they can be difficult to organize, such seminars are extremely useful—they are better able than this or any other book or any one teacher to give new teachers a sense of how to grade papers, and they introduce teachers to the philosophy and practice of holistic grading.

If you have to proceed alone, however, make certain that your grading system corresponds to that used by your school, lest you find out at the end of the term that you must adapt your system to some other one. Before you grade your first paper, find out whether your school uses a four-point system or a five-point system and whether or not you can give plus/minus grades. If your department, your program, or even those with whom you share an office have devised standards of grading that you agree to follow, you can avoid many anxieties about grading.

As you grade, be on the alert for the B fallacy: the temptation to overuse the B. This grade does, after all, seem like a nice compromise: a paper is not A quality, but a C is so. . . *average*. To many teachers, new and experienced alike, a C seems such a condemnation. Why not a B? If you think you are assigning too many B's and are vaguely dissatisfied with and confused by your practice, try to get back on track by asking yourself what elements in the essay deserve that grade. What, in short, makes this paper better than average? Is it word choice? organization? expression of ideas? If you can honestly point to a specific area in which the paper is better than most others you've seen, it may deserve the B. If you can find no specific area in which the paper excels, you can be fairly certain it is indeed average.

FORMAL STANDARDS

As all experienced writing teachers are aware, formal standards of Edited American English are by far the easiest to mark, recognize, and enforce. They are largely standards of convention and correctness, and you will find that marking formal errors in a paper is an easy and rather mechanical job. You mark a spelling error here, a sentence fragment there. There is a natural feeling after having marked formal errors that you have done a solid, creditable job of reading a student's paper, when you may not have responded to content issues at all.

That false sense of having completed a job makes formal evaluation seductive. Because of it, teachers are often tempted to base most of their grade on the formal qualities of the paper and not enough on the content. One can easily see why: formal evaluation is concrete and quantitative; it demands few complex judgment calls and ignores content evaluation. When teachers fill a student essay with red marks, they may think they've done a thorough reading of it—so why do more? Justifying a D on the basis of three fragments and nine misspelled words is easier than dealing with the complex, sometimes arbitrary world of content: thesis statements, patterns of development, assertions, and support.

A piece of writing consists of far more than its grammar and punctuation, however. If we stress nothing but formal grading, we quickly become pedants, obsessed with correctness to the detriment of meaning. We do have a responsibility to evaluate formal errors, for as Mina Shaughnessy says, they are "unintentional and unprofitable intrusions upon the consciousness of the reader" that "demand energy without giving any return" (12). We must mark them, but we should not give them more than their due.

To this end, Robert Connors and Andrea Lunsford surveyed over twenty-one thousand essays and identified the twenty errors most often made by students today. Here, in order of occurrence, is their list of the twenty most common error patterns.

1. Missing comma after an introductory element
2. Vague pronoun reference
3. Missing comma in a compound sentence
4. Wrong word
5. Missing comma(s) with a nonrestrictive element
6. Wrong or missing verb ending
7. Wrong or missing preposition
8. Comma splice
9. Missing or misplaced possessive apostrophe
10. Unnecessary shift in tense
11. Unnecessary shift in pronoun
12. Sentence fragment
13. Wrong tense or verb form
14. Lack of agreement between subject and verb
15. Missing comma in a series
16. Lack of agreement between pronoun and antecedent
17. Unnecessary comma(s) with a restrictive element
18. Fused sentence
19. Dangling or misplaced modifier
20. *Its/it's* confusion

You will need to determine, of course, how much you will emphasize each kind of formal error. Within any group of serious errors, many teachers distinguish between *syntactic errors* (sentence fragments, fused sentences, comma splices), which take place on the sentence level, and *word-level errors* (spelling, verb forms, agreement). Syntactic errors are considered much more serious than word-level errors because these more global errors often present the reader with a situation in which it is impossible to know what the writer meant. When teachers quantitatively count errors, they nearly always count syntactic errors and word-level errors separately.

Once again, looking at a paper in terms of its formal and mechanical problems is an important part of our task but only a small part of it. Read your students' writing with an eye to discerning their error patterns. By seeing these patterns rather than their individual mistakes, students can work on breaking their patterns one at a time, concentrating on a series of single goals in a way that does not overwhelm them.

STANDARDS OF CONTENT

Unlike formal correctness, in which conventions are so completely agreed upon (a comma splice is, after all, a comma splice), content is a much more abstract business. And despite the fact that content is every bit as important as form, writing teachers in general are less confident about their ability to judge ideas and organization and therefore may be tempted to give these aspects of composition less than their due when grading.

In response to content, teachers must make serious judgments that inform the evaluation or the final grade of a paper. Usually grades for content are assigned on the basis of how successful the paper seems to be in four specific areas, which Paul Diederich calls *ideas, organization, wording,* and *flavor* (55–57).

Connors and Lunsford's research shows that more teachers commented on *ideas* than on any other single area. More than 56 percent of the papers they examined contained teachers' comments on ideas and their support. In general, comments on ideas are based on the following questions:

1. How well does the essay respond to the assignment?
2. How novel, original, or well presented is the thesis of the essay?
3. Are the arguments or main points of the essay well supported by explanatory or exemplary material?
4. Is the thesis carried to its logical conclusion?

After comments on supporting evidence and examples, Connors and Lunsford's study revealed that teachers were most likely to comment on a paper's *organization.* Comments on organization are based on questions such as the following:

1. Does the essay have a coherent plan?
2. Is the plan followed out completely and logically?
3. Is the plan balanced, and does it serve the purpose of the essay?
4. Are the paragraphs within the essay well developed?

Issues of *wording* can impinge on the formal standards of a work; but with respect to content, comments on wording are more concerned with word choice than with grammatical correctness. Addressed are such questions as the following:

1. Does the essay use words precisely?
2. Does the essay use words in any delightful or original fashion?

Finally, there is the level of *flavor,* the term Diederich uses for what others might call style. More than 33 percent of the papers analyzed contained comments on issues of flavor, or style, in response to the following questions:

1. Is the writing pleasing to the reader?
2. Does the writer come across as someone the reader might like and trust?
3. Does the writer sound intelligent and knowledgeable?
4. Are the sentence structures effective?

These guidelines may help you as you grade content, but it is you who must ultimately decide whether an essay says something significant, has a strong central idea, adheres to standards of logic in development, and supports its contentions with facts. All teachers know the uncomfortable sense of final responsibility that goes with the territory of teaching, so don't hesitate to share your problems, solutions, and evaluation questions with your colleagues. Neither should you hesitate to participate in the common and useful practice of reading and responding to the student writing of your colleagues' classes.

WORKS CITED

Beaven, Mary H. "Individualized Goal Setting, Self Evaluation, and Peer Evaluation." Cooper and Odell 135-56.

Belanoff, Pat, and Peter Elbow. "Using Portfolios to Increase Collaboration and Community in a Writing Program." *Journal of Writing Program Administration* 9 (1986): 27-39.

Connors, Robert J., and Andrea Lunsford. "Teachers' Rhetorical Comments on Student Papers." *CCC* 44 (1993): 200-23.

Cooper, Charles R. "Holistic Evaluation of Writing." Cooper and Odell 3-32.

Cooper, Charles R., and Lee Odell, eds. *Evaluating Writing: Describing, Measuring, Judging.* Urbana, IL: NCTE, 1977.

Diederich, Paul B. *Measuring Growth in English.* Urbana, IL: NCTE, 1974.

Hamp-Lyons, Liz, and William Condon. "Questioning Assumptions about Portfolio-Based Assessment." *CCC* 44 (1993): 176-90.

Haswell, Richard. "Minimal Marking." *CE* 45 (1983): 600-04.

Larson, Richard. "Training New Teachers of Composition in the Writing of Comments on Themes." *CCC* 17 (1966): 152-55.

Lunsford, Andrea, and Robert Connors. *The St. Martin's Handbook,* 3rd ed. New York: St. Martin's, 1995.

Roemer, Marjorie, Lucille M. Schultz, and Russel K. Durst. "Portfolios and the Process of Change." *CCC* 42 (1991): 455-69.

Shaughnessy, Mina P. *Errors and Expectations: A Guide for the Teacher of Basic Writing.* New York: Oxford UP, 1977.

Sommers, Nancy. "Responding to Student Writing." *CCC* 33 (1982): 148-56.

Sunstein, Bonnie S., and Joseph P. Potts. "Teachers' Portfolios: A Cultural Site for Literacy." *Council Chronicle* 3 (1993): 9.

White, Edward M. *Teaching and Assessing Writing.* San Francisco: Jossey-Bass, 1986.

APPENDIX TO
CHAPTER

5 | THE END OF THE TERM

FINAL GRADES

That final grade next to a student's name represents your ultimate judgment on that student, usually the only judgment she will carry away from your class. It is both a difficult task and a relief, a closure, to mark down that letter.

You have, of course, since before the first day been preparing a system that would allow you to judge each student's performance. In front of you are the following factors:

1. Grades for each written essay
2. Weight of each assignment (by percentage)
3. Test grades, if any
4. Amount of class participation
5. Faithfulness of homework and journal, if required
6. Amount of perceived improvement in writing ability

Of these six factors, the first three are easily amenable to a mathematical solution, and many teachers have devised ways to quantify the last three as well. To arrive at a mathematical "raw score" for a student is a bit time-consuming but not difficult. If each essay and test is weighted alike, you need only convert the letter grade to its numerical equivalent, add the numbers, divide by the number of assignments, and then convert the result back to a letter grade.

Consider the example of student X, whose grades are B-, C, B+, D, C+, C+, B-, and C-. The following example assumes a four-point system:

Conversion chart: The student's grades thus convert to

A	= 4.0	2.7
A-	= 3.7	2.0
B+	= 3.3	3.3
B	= 3.0	1.0
B-	= 2.7	2.3
C+	= 2.3	2.3
C	= 2.0	2.7
C-	= 1.7	1.7
D+	= 1.3	———
D	= 1.0	18.0
F	= 0	

The next step is to divide the sum by the number of assignments.

$$18 \div 8 = 2.25$$

The result can then be converted back into a grade or left in the form of a grade point average. If you convert to a grade, you must establish your own cutoff points. In this case, a 2.25 GPA is closer to a C+ than to a C. The grade becomes more difficult to decide when the GPA is 2.5 or 2.85. In such cases, you must apply other criteria in deciding whether to lower the grade or raise it.

If your assignments are not all weighted the same, working out the raw score is a more complex process. Let's assume, for instance, that you are considering nine grades, which are weighted as follows (percentages refer to the percentage of the raw score):

Assignment 1.   5%
Assignment 2.   10%
Assignment 3.   15%
Assignment 4.   5%
Assignment 5.   10%
Assignment 6.   10%
Assignment 7.   15%
Assignment 8.   10%
Assignment 9.   20%
            —————
            100%

The following table can help you figure the weighting of each assignment:

	5%	10%	15%	20%	25%
A	5.00	10.00	15.00	20.00	25.00
A-	4.75	9.50	14.25	18.40	23.75
B+	4.50	9.00	13.50	17.60	23.00
B	4.25	8.50	12.75	17.00	21.25
B-	4.10	8.20	12.30	16.40	20.50
C+	3.90	7.80	11.70	15.60	19.50
C	3.75	7.50	11.25	15.00	18.75
C-	3.60	7.20	10.80	14.40	18.00
D+	3.40	6.80	10.20	13.60	17.00
D	3.25	6.50	9.75	13.00	16.25
D-	3.00	6.20	9.30	12.40	15.50
F	2.50	5.00	7.50	10.00	12.50

Using the table is not difficult. Simply find the value of each grade indicated at the left according to the percentage value indicated at the top of each column, and add up the values for all assignments. The score for assignments that are all A's would be 100; that for all F's, 50. If you wish to convert the final numerical score to a grade, you can use this chart:

A	= 96–100	C	= 75–77
A-	= 92–95	C-	= 72–74
B+	= 88–91	D+	= 68–71
B	= 85–87	D	= 65–67
B-	= 82–84	D-	= 62–64
C+	= 78–81	F	= 50–61

To give an example of this system in action, let us evaluate student Y's nine grades. They are, respectively, C+, D+, B-, A-, C-, C-, B, C+, and C-.

Given the weighting of the grades previously mentioned, Student Y's grades would be as follows:

Assignment 1.	(5%)	C+ = 3.90	Assignment 6.	(10%)	C- = 7.20
Assignment 2.	(10%)	D+ = 6.80	Assignment 7.	(15%)	B = 12.75
Assignment 3.	(15%)	B- = 12.30	Assignment 8.	(10%)	C+ = 7.80
Assignment 4.	(5%)	A- = 4.75	Assignment 9.	(20%)	C- = 14.40
Assignment 5.	(10%)	C- = 7.20			Total Score: 77.10

The score of 77.1 equals either a C or a C+ on the grade scale. Once again, you will have to establish your own cutoff points. To simplify, you might move scores of half a point and greater to the next higher number and scores of less than half a point to the next lower number. Thus a rating of 77.1 would mean a raw score of C.

Mathematical systems can aid us in figuring a final grade, but they are not all that goes into it. The raw score based on the graded assignments will certainly be the most important element determining a final grade, but if we haven't already made allowances for them, we must add in our judgments of many subtle qualities that fall under the heading "class participation." Did the student attend classes and conferences faithfully? How serious was she about making revisions? How hard did the student try? How willing was she to help others? How was her performance in workshops? How much time did the student give to journal entries? These and other considerations must eventually go into the process of turning the raw mathematical score into a final grade. And ultimately, as with grades on individual papers, this decision is one that you, the teacher, must make alone.

The question of failing a student is painful, especially if you know the student has been trying hard to pass—it is less difficult to write down the F for a student who has given up coming to class or who has not written many assignments. But that desperate, struggling one is hard to fail.

No one wants to fail such students. If a student looks as if she is in danger of failing, you may want to recommend that she drop the course, seek outside help, and pick it up again when she is able to pass. Most do drop a class if they see there is no hope, but sometimes no amount of advice helps; the student cannot or does not drop out, and you are left with no alternative but writing down that damning F.

STUDENT EVALUATIONS OF COURSE AND TEACHER

The teacher has to make final judgments about her students in the form of grades, but students' judgments about the teacher and the course, important as they are, are often optional. Not all departments demand that teachers ask their students to fill out teacher- or course-evaluation forms. Even if yours does not, however, you will learn a great deal about your course and your teaching by developing an evaluation form or using a departmental or school form and asking students to complete it. Evaluation forms should be filled out anonymously either as homework or during one of the last days of classes. You may want to seal them—unread—in an envelope and ask one of your students to keep them until after you have turned in your grades.

If you don't have a departmental form to work from, you may want to use or adapt the following questions:

An Evaluation Form

(Be sure to space questions to leave room for student responses.)

1. How would you improve the content of the course?
2. What was the most useful assignment in the course? Explain.
3. What was the least useful assignment? Explain.
4. In what particular way was/were the textbook(s) helpful? for which assignment? What are the weaknesses of the textbook(s)? Do you recommend that it/they be used again?
5. What in the way of the teacher's responses to and comments on your written work seemed helpful or useless? What specific advice do you have for the teacher?
6. How has the revision policy affected the way you do your writing? Do you have any suggestions that might improve this policy?
7. Do you believe the course requirements are fair? Why or why not?
8. Did your writing group sessions help you edit and improve your work? How might the group structure be improved?
9. Did you know what the teacher's objectives for the course were? If so, did the instructor accomplish these objectives?
10. How might the teacher make her in-class presentations more effective?
11. What did you gain from completing the research-paper assignment? Did you gain the ability to do research? to marshal evidence? to work in a group?
12. How did the grading policy compare to those in other courses in terms of clarity and fairness?
13. How helpful were the conferences? Would more or fewer be better?
14. What general comments do you have?

After you have turned in your grades, you can take some time to read these evaluations. We have found that they are more easily understood and applied if you let a few days or even several weeks go by before reading them. As you do, note in writing any elements that surprised you and any changes you plan to make on the basis of the evaluations. Sometimes you will be transported by your evaluations; sometimes you will be chagrined. But they are always important input for your teaching life, and they are worth your attention.

AFTERWORD

Your evaluations have been read and digested; your grade sheets have been marked, signed, and turned in. Nothing remains but the stack of students' theme folders (or portfolios) and your faithful grade book, filled with red and black hieroglyphics where previously only blank squares existed. Your first writing course is a memory; you are now a seasoned veteran, a resource for the nervous new teachers of next year. You will be able to help them by telling them what helped you and to welcome them to the conversation that is always going on among teachers of writing.

Theoretical Issues in Teaching Writing

CHAPTER

TEACHING
COMPOSING PROCESSES

With some solid teaching experience behind you, you are ready to explore more fully the discipline of composition and rhetoric. The following chapters will guide you in an exploration of how some important contemporary theories can be translated into practice.

Historically, many teachers of writing ignored the process of composing: they assumed that their essential task was educating students to write correct sentences with few formal errors. The idea that mental processes could be broken into their components and that students should be taught how experienced writers accomplish their task was not seriously considered. Not until this century, when psychology began to come under serious scrutiny, were the writing processes—the mental and physical activities undertaken by experienced writers—considered vital to the teaching of writing. Thus, after World War II, a new generation of writing teachers began to analyze and value the processes inherent to the act of writing. Since then, teachers and researchers have worked continually to learn more about the physical, emotional, and intellectual elements that make up the composing process. Knowledge of the composing process (or process writing) is now considered fundamental information for writing teachers, and integral to their teaching. For these reasons, we will begin our discussion of putting theory into practice here.

STAGE-MODEL THEORY

The first modern theory of the composing process to be discussed in detail was the simple three-part concept that we now call *stage-model theory*. Stage-model theory breaks down the composing process into linear stages, which follow one another in a sequence. The stages were sometimes called *planning, drafting,* and *revision*, but today they are usually called *prewriting, writing,* and *rewriting*.

It may be difficult to imagine that so simple and so self-evident a concept as breaking up the writing process into these linear steps was not always a central part of the teaching of composition. Indeed, few teachers of composition would ever have denied that writers plan first, then write, and then rewrite. Thus the rise of stage-model theory was not so much a result of new ideas about writing coming to the fore as it was the result of a new emphasis being given to accepted ideas. Textbooks and English journals from the 1940s mention planning and revision, but in only a page or two and never as the pivot of a discussion. Before the 1960s, few texts—or teachers—considered in any depth what makes up the processes of planning and revising. Instead, those textbooks and

101

the teachers who used them took what we now refer to as a *product approach*, emphasizing the final product of the writing process—especially its formal correctness.

The real breakthrough for understanding the importance of teaching the composing processes came in the early 1960s as a result of what is now often referred to as the "New Education" movement. Often associated with the ideas of Jerome Bruner, the New Education movement took the position that it was not enough to teach students that something was as it was; education should teach the processes of discovering how and why things were as they were. The best-known offshoot of this movement was the so-called "new math," by which students learned not just mathematical techniques—addition, division, and so forth—but learned (or were to learn) how and why these techniques had been arrived at.

In composition, the New Education movement influenced the work of D. Gordon Rohman and Albert O. Wlecke at Michigan State University in the early 1960s. Rohman and Wlecke developed prewriting as a theory of invention and teaching, and they and other teachers modified this theory over the next ten years. Their emphasis on prewriting aimed to promote student self-actualization by providing models of *how* writing is done. In "Pre-Writing: The Stage of Discovery in the Writing Process," Rohman critiques traditional approaches to composition.

> A failure to make a proper distinction between "thinking" and writing has led to a fundamental misconception which undermines so many of our best efforts in teaching writing: if we train students how to recognize an example of good prose ("the rhetoric of the finished word"), we have not given them a basis on which to build their own writing abilities. All we have done, in fact, is to give them standards to judge the goodness or badness of their finished effort. *We haven't really taught them how to make that effort.* . . . Unless we can somehow introduce students to the dynamics of creation, we too often simply discourage their hopes of ever writing well at all. (106–07)

As we will see in the next chapter, the prewriting theorists were concerned primarily with invention, which they referred to as "Pre-Writing." And yet integral to their theories was the stage model of composition: the description of a process in which prewriting is followed by writing, which in turn is followed by rewriting. With the great interest in invention that was the mark of the composition theory of the 1960s, the stage model, as it was first stressed by Rohman, quickly became the preferred model of the composing process. Through the 1960s and into the early 1970s, teachers adopted it, and textbooks picked it up; it became conventional wisdom in early "process" writing courses.

Of course, no one would deny that the stage model is an accurate description of how writing is done. But through the 1970s, researchers who wanted to look at the composing process in more detail came to criticize the stage model with increasing vehemence. Not only were the stages so simply described as to be reductive, these critics said, but they suggested that composing is a completely linear process, starting at one place and chugging unstoppably in a straight line to its destination. Nancy Sommers made the case against the stage model most strongly in her 1979 article "The Need for Theory in Composition Research":

> A linear system, according to systems theory, demands that we must be able to recover past states and predict future states of the system, as when we develop a photograph or when we follow a prescribed recipe. If composing was only such a linear activity, then we should be able to construct a behavioral checklist in which we predict that at a given point a writer should be in the thinking stage of the process, then he/she will gather information, then he/she will write, then he/she will rewrite. And then, if these stages were reliable and valid junctures, then we should have completion criteria for each stage, so that we could tell when one stage is terminated and another begins. Each stage must be mutually exclusive, or else it becomes trivial and counterproductive to refer to these junctures as stages.
>
> With our present state of knowledge, however, we lack a finite set of criteria by which we could judge where one stage of the process begins and the other ends, and it seems neither useful nor accurate to describe composing only as a linear sequence of stages. (47)

Since we can see significant recurring patterns in composing, Sommers says, "we can hypothesize that the composing process is both linear and recursive. Thus it is possible to view the composing process not just as a linear series of stages but rather as a hierarchical set of sub-processes." Most research on the composing process, as we will see in the next section, takes this position as a starting point.

Using the Stage-Model Theory in the Classroom

The idea that planning precedes writing, which precedes revising, does not at first seem impressively original. Like Aristotle's claim that every complete whole has a beginning, a middle, and an end, it seems self-evident—until you realize how easily forgotten it is. Although critics have made strong claims about the lack of deep descriptive power in the stage model of writing, this model remains a cornerstone of teaching process writing. To many students, the idea that writing is made up of discrete stages of planning, drafting, and, especially, revising is entirely new. Thus it is a good idea to introduce the simple stage model early in the course, to structure some parts of the course around each stage, and then to ask students to reflect and report on how these stages occur in their writing.

It is not at all uncommon for FY students to appear in your class without any experience in writing a long or complex piece of prose. Nor is it uncommon for them to think of planning as writing an ironclad outline or just chewing a pencil for fifteen seconds before blasting off, or to think of revising as running their essays through a computer spell checker or grammar checker. Where traditional writing courses have emphasized a one-shot product, they have trained students to crank out a hasty draft the night before a deadline, hand it in, and go on to the next assignment in a continuing series of one-chance writing tasks. By emphasizing the stage model, and especially the depth and importance of each step, you are asking your students to pay close attention to what they do when they compose. So you'll want to ask your class to take some time with prewriting, with drafting, and with revision.

The prewriting, or invention, stage is covered thoroughly in the next chapter, so for now the best advice is to start students off with the idea that planning, or prewriting, is an essential and expected part of the work they will do for every required essay. Also note that at some point in the writing process, they will be expected to submit evidence of their prewriting, proof that they have not just thought about their papers but have written down and tried out some part of the plan.

In discussions of the stage model, the drafting stage of composition is often addressed less thoroughly than either of the other stages. "Then you write a draft" was all many teachers could say about it before the 1970s. Now, however, the topic is frequently given more attention.[1]

Each student's drafting habits are different, of course, and can never really be standardized because they are aspects of the student's personality. Nonetheless, by keeping writing inventories, students can learn to take advantage of their individual styles and behaviors. Ask your students, therefore, to pay attention to the way they take up the task of writing. And when they have trouble with their writing or when they succeed, you can use their writing inventories as the basis for a discussion of what habits and behaviors work best for them.

The rewriting stage is where your role as editor-coach can really help your students. Often students have the least experience with revision or have only the cursory experience of checking for mechanical correctness. Yet knowledge about how students most effectively learn to write suggests that revision should be an important component of any writing assignment. As we've discussed in Chapters 1–4, you can include revision in the course structure by asking students to include multiple drafts when they turn in their papers or by setting up workshops, writing groups, or conferences for discussing work in progress.

In any case, if you teach any sort of process-oriented class—and most composition teachers now do—the stage model will tacitly or obviously inform many of your practical expectations of your students. If you wish to leave students with one strong idea about writing, you might choose to impress upon them the concept that writing is a process that *always* consists of drafting and revising toward the finished version.

RECURSIVE AND COGNITIVE-PROCESS THEORIES

With the 1971 publication of Janet Emig's *Composing Processes of Twelfth Graders*, the idea of three linear stages as the absolute model of all writing was called into question. Originally written in 1969 as her doctoral dissertation, Emig's innovative description of composing as a recursive process—that is, one with

[1] For example, for a discussion of organizing a draft, discovering one's most successful writing habits, and reflecting on the writing process, you can direct students to Chapter 3 of *The St. Martin's Handbook*. Just as useful is the writing inventory discussed in Chapter 1 of this guide.

complex, recurring subprocesses—specifically opposed Rohman and Wlecke's theory of prewriting, writing, and rewriting, which emphasized the importance of the prewriting stage. Through her observation of eight twelfth-grade writers, Emig notes that students did not create outlines before composing and that their writing did not "occur as a left-to-right, solid, uninterrupted activity with an even pace" (84), as contemporary textbooks proposed. Instead of smoothly striding up three flights of a wooden composing staircase, writers had to stroll up, down, and around a sand dune of composing, on which a step forward to revision might leave them two steps back, again engaged in the planning process.

Using the case-study approach and the think-aloud methodology of psychology, Emig met with her subjects four times. During three of these sessions, the students were asked to articulate all of their thoughts as they simultaneously composed and wrote a short piece on an impromptu or a planned topic. Although Emig admitted that composing aloud is a "difficult, artificial, and at times distracting procedure" (5), she insisted it was one of the most important features of her research because her goal was to examine the mental activities of the writer rather than the visible text created. Emig focused on one subject, named Lynn, and in a case study sought to describe Lynn's composing processes by analyzing her notes and texts, her comments about composing, her behavior, and her responses to questions during the tape-recorded sessions.

On the basis of her research, Emig warned that the oversimplified depiction of composing given by most textbooks underconceptualized the rigors of writing so that "planning degenerate[d] into outlining; reformulating [became] the correction" of minor errors (*Web* 94). She attacked the then-current method of writing instruction which taught students to analyze models by professional writers in order to learn to recognize and reproduce categories of rhetoric, modes of discourse, and features of the preferred style. Such analysis of the desired product, said Emig, mystified the actual processes of composing. Rather than merely assigning and evaluating writing, instructors should be involved in helping students initiate and sustain the composing process. Emig proclaimed the demise of "teacher-centered presentation of composition" as "pedagogically, developmentally, and politically an anachronism" (*Web* 95).

Although this report of the death of presentational teaching was greatly exaggerated, a new era was dawning in the study of composition, an era focusing on the writing process and on empirical research methodology. Even while critical of Emig's empirical study, Ralph Voss acknowledged her creation of a "science consciousness" in the field (278). The publication of Emig's study inspired numerous observational studies, but more important, it set into motion a great wave of research on the writing process. Thus, the 1970s saw the development of the case-study approach and think-aloud cognitive protocols based on psychological research. In addition, Emig's research stimulated studies of pausing during composing, by Ann Matsuhashi ("Pausing and Planning" 1981) and Linda Flower and John Hayes ("Cognitive Process Theory" 1981); of revision, by Sondra Perl ("Understanding Composing" 1980), Lillian Bridwell

(1980), and Lester Faigley and Stephen Witte (1981); and of writers of different ages and abilities, by Charles Stallard (1974), Richard Beach (1976), Sondra Perl (1979), Sharon Pianko (1979), and Nancy Sommers (1980). Emig also called for longitudinal studies that would not only contrast various writing abilities but also trace their development, hence the work of Donald Graves (1978–1980) and Glenda Bissex (1980).

These diverse research topics are united by the essential assumption underpinning cognitive psychology: that to understand observable behavior, one must comprehend the mental structures that determine the manifested actions. Basing their work on the ideas of Jean Piaget, Lev Vygotsky, and the later Jerome Bruner, cognitive researchers have asserted that the mind consists of structures, such as language and thought, that develop as the individual interacts with the world. As these mental structures are altered to make sense of the world, learning occurs in a process of ever more organized and differentiated schemes. Learning is thus a process of *cognitive development.* Since this learning process is chronological, the sequential development of various mental structures can be traced through the stages of children's acquisition of knowledge and can be used to help understand the mature mind.

Although cognitivists believe that an adult's linguistic and intellectual capacities develop in a natural sequence, they also believe that the development depends on certain "fostering" experiences that must occur at appropriate times. In this regard, Emig distinguishes between the formal, or "extensive," writing sponsored by the teacher and the personal, or "reflexive," writing initiated by the student, and she critiques the overuse of extensive writing, which she says, too often asks students to convey to the teacher, however blandly, literary or public topics. To further students' cognitive development, she advocated more use of reflexive writing, which focuses on personal feelings and experiences and prompts more planning, exploratory writing, and revision by student writers.

Using Emig's Cognitive Research in the Classroom

As suggested by her study's title, *The Composing Processes of Twelfth Graders,* and as exemplified by her research methodology, Emig was concerned with the mental processes of students as they compose. Her interest was a sharp departure from the long-held obsession with the ideal compositions that students *should* write. She challenged teachers to be writers themselves so that they can begin to consider their own writing process rather than merely repeating prescriptive textbook formulae. Robert Zoellner and others have followed Emig in advocating that instructors demonstrate writing to their students by composing aloud while writing on the blackboard (an idea you may want to explore). Although time constraints won't always allow you to write a full blackboard draft with your students, you may want to try composing a draft of an assignment at least once and discussing your writing process with the class for fifteen to twenty minutes.

To begin this task, give each student a copy of your draft (which should be a manageable length—a maximum of two pages). Your draft should reveal your composing process, including your methods for invention, your false starts, and your crossed out and revised phrases. Talk about the problems you faced, your success in solving them, and the colleagues you spoke to or asked to comment on your draft. Encourage students to comment on and offer revisions of your writing as well. If students are working in writing groups, they will need experience and confidence in critiquing one another's writing, and your simple modeling of the process will help them with this. A teacher who matter-of-factly explains the difficulties she faced in writing an assignment reveals the process of composing and the problems with it in a way students remember.

Most teachers are anxious about their class presentations, and you, too, may be uncomfortable with the idea of exposing possible hesitations and weaknesses in your own work. But an occasional failure on your part is instructive to students because it shows them that even experienced writers do not compose by some automatic, flawless process. Teachers can also compose with their students during their individual conferences by asking open-ended questions that will help students consider composing and content issues of their writing.[2]

As a teacher writes with her students, the students participate in what the psychologist Lev Vygotsky calls the "zone of proximal development." There students stretch their mental abilities and can succeed at imitating the behaviors the teacher models. Although students may not yet be capable of independently performing the processes they are practicing, they will internalize and later use this guided and appropriate interaction.

According to Emig, teachers can successfully initiate and sustain their students' writing if they also foster the students' awareness of their own composing process. Few FY students have been asked to reflect on their composing process, so asking them to do so may, at first, elicit many formulae learned for writing the five-paragraph theme or the research paper. To prompt your students to attend to their composing process, ask them occasionally to turn in their Writing Logs[3] or to bring the logs with them to their conferences. You can help them start a Writing Log by offering several open-ended questions that will stimulate reflections on their writing. For example, for the reflective essay suggested below, ask your students to write a page in response to some of the following questions:

How did you generate the details of your experience? Which details did you recall with ease? Which did you recall with difficulty?

Which detail(s) suggested the significance of the experience? How did your understanding of the significance develop and change?

How did you organize the "sea" of details into a significant and coherent experience? What information had to be excluded or elaborated for the reader to understand the event and your reflections on it?

[2] For more on conferencing, see Chapter 3.

[3] See Chapter 1 in *The St. Martin's Handbook.*

Ask your students to discuss some of their notes on their composing process. If you have previously discussed your own writing, students will have already begun to feel comfortable talking about, and reflecting on, their composing processes. These conversations about composing do not have to be very long; a mere ten to fifteen minutes can provide ample opportunity for instructive comments.

Assigning a reflective narrative near the beginning of the course is a common and effective way to encourage students to engage in personal, exploratory writing. Ask students to describe a memorable experience that significantly altered their thoughts, feelings, and/or actions and stress that the key to this assignment is not only to narrate the experience but also to reflect on its significance. An effective metaphor to teach the twofold requirements of a reflective narrative is to invite your students to plunge into the "sea of experience" and follow the currents of their memory. Suggest that students keep this metaphor in mind as they experiment with several of the invention techniques suggested in Chapter 7. Finally, to analyze this experience in which they have been immersed, suggest that they climb the "mountain of reflection."

Students can also learn more about composing processes by reading published authors' accounts of the act of writing. Frequently anthologized essays, such as Joan Didion's "Why I Write," excerpts of Anais Nin's "The Personal Life Deeply Lived," William Zinsser's "Style," William Stafford's "A Way of Writing," and Donald Murray's "The Feel of Writing—And Teaching Writing," can stimulate fruitful discussions. As students respond to these essays, it is important that they not seek a "correct" way to write but discover, instead, similarities and differences between the authors' and their own composing processes.

You can also challenge students to create their own theories and depictions of the writing process. One student, for example, compared the layering of various meanings and the shifting emphases that result from revision to the recording and mixing of music. To foster an awareness of composing as a series of processes, begin with the simple prompt of "Writing is like . . . ," which encourages students to compare writing to an ongoing action. (Don't be discouraged if some students come up with negative analogies; everything is grist for the mill.)

Another activity to focus students' attention on composing processes is to have them interview skilled and/or published writers. Most college communities are teeming with talented writers—historians, scientists, poets, journalists, and music theorists—to match any interest. These face-to-face conversations with professionals often help students appreciate the labor that goes into writing and the diversity of processes writers employ.

This diversity of writing processes is something all teachers must keep in mind as they teach composing. There is simply no one paradigmatic process, no uniform sequence. Jack Selzer contends that teachers must offer a variety of composing options, in addition to a variety of writing assignments, instead of prescribing specific tactics for planning, inventing, and revising every composing experience. He suggests, too, that teachers acknowledge that not every writing task requires the same composing tactics; if they acknowledge a number of effective overall composing styles—as well as operations for performing each composing activity—they will be more likely to produce flexible, resourceful writers (276-77).

Emig's pedagogical legacy, then, has been twofold. She has shown us that we cannot be rigid in our assignments and in our expectations of students, and she has encouraged us to study carefully what our students do—and what we do when we teach them.

COGNITIVE AND DEVELOPMENTAL RESEARCH

Much of the work done in studying the composing process over the last three decades has rested on the studies of the Russian psychologist Lev Vygotsky, who died in 1936. Emig is clearly indebted to Vygotsky's notions of inner speech (subvocalizing; the mental transformation of thought into words) and the development of language. In the 1960s and 1970s, other researchers were equally influenced by the work of Vygotsky and that of the Swiss developmental psychologist Jean Piaget, who died in 1980. Tying these theorists together is their interest in the processes of human development, especially the development of language skills.

One way in which these developmental schemata found a place in composition studies was through proposals for curricular change. Those who had put together the older curricula made little provision for the processes of growing and learning because their concepts of those processes were undeveloped. When theoreticians proposed new ways of teaching writing and new ways in which learning to write takes place, they based some of their most influential ideas on the ideas of development first introduced by Vygotsky and Piaget. Three names often associated with these curricular changes are James Moffett, James Britton, and Mina Shaughnessy.

James Moffett offered comprehensive curricular reform based on Piaget's principles of cognitive development. In his groundbreaking *Teaching the Universe of Discourse*, he provided a thorough rationale for his proposed curriculum. Like Emig, Moffett criticized standard textbooks and their presentation of skills and modes of discourse, a presentation based on product analysis (analyzing one final written product). Derived from Piaget's theory of cognitive development, Moffett's theory, and its practical presentation in his textbook *A Student-Centered Language Arts Curriculum*, progressed "from the personal to the impersonal, from low to high abstraction, from undifferentiated to finely discriminated modes of discourse" to enable students to overcome their egocentrism and literal thinking (12). Moffett's theory is based on the idea of two continua, or horizontal scales, along which the kinds of writing may be categorized. Moffett's first scale is the *audience* scale, and the second is the *subject* scale. Together, they give us a developmental schema of writing tasks.

The audience continuum categorizes discourses by the distance between the speaker/writer and her audience. Moffett proposes four main "stops" on this continuum:

Reflection: Intrapersonal communication between two parts of one nervous system.

Conversation: Interpersonal communication between people in vocal range.

Correspondence: interpersonal communication among remote individuals or small groups with some personal knowledge of one another.

Publication: impersonal communication to a large, anonymous group extended over space and/or time. (*Universe of Discourse* 33)

The subject continuum categorizes discourse by the distance between the speaker/writer and her chosen subject, ranging from "I am here now" reportage to the most distanced and abstract treatment. Moffett uses the example of sitting in a cafeteria eating lunch: a speaker may discourse on *what is happening* in the scene around her at the moment; she can later report on *what happened* in the cafeteria at lunch, with inevitable selections and compressions; she can generalize about *what happens* in the cafeteria typically; or she can discourse predictively or argumentatively about *what may or should happen* in the cafeteria in the future. Each stop on this continuum can correspond to a kind of discourse:

what is happening — drama — recording

what happened — narrative — reporting

what happens — exposition — generalizing

what may happen — logical argumentation — theorizing
(*Universe of Discourse* 35)

Putting these two continua together, Moffett evolved what he calls the spectrum of discourse, which runs from the speaker/writer's being closest to subject and the audience to her being most distanced from each.

Interior Dialogue (egocentric speech)

Vocal Dialogue (socialized speech)

Correspondence

Personal Journal

Autobiography

Memoir

Biography

Chronicle

History

Science

Metaphysics (*Universe of Discourse* 47)

This sequence was designed to teach students to render experience in words—to produce discourse, not linguistic or literary analysis. Therefore, Moffett asserted, "Most profoundly considered, a course in language learning is a course in thinking" (*Universe of Discourse* 11).

In a British study done slightly later, James Britton, Tony Burgess, Nancy Martin, Alex McLeod, and Harold Rosen also critiqued traditional categories of discourse and the cognitive impact of school writing. Having analyzed a sample of approximately two thousand papers written by students aged eleven to eighteen, they argued that the teaching of narration, description, exposition, and argument is prescriptive, concerned "with how people should write, rather than how they do. It can scarcely, therefore, be helpful in studying the emergence of mature writers from young writers" (4). Instead, these researchers sought to "create a model which would enable [them] to characterize all mature written utterances and then go on to trace the developmental steps that led to them" (6).

Britton and his colleagues used a continuum structure to explain their findings. In *The Development of Writing Abilities (11-18)*, they divided students' writing into three functional categories: *transactional*, *expressive*, and *poetic*. Expressive writing, like speaking, is the most natural type of writing, meant to express ideas to a known audience, and it tends to be the type out of which the other two emerge. Poetic writing is a complex discourse between the self and a subject and deals with audience only peripherally. Most school writing was classified as transactional: it communicates information, but it places the writer in a passive role and engages her in a complex relationship with the audience (82-85).

Like Emig, these British researchers urge that students write expressively more often because the student writer assumes an active, participatory role when exploring her ideas in relation to feelings, knowledge, and intentions. Thus, they argued, expressive writing stimulates learning. Despite the warning of Britton and his colleagues that "we classify at our peril" (1), their descriptive categories, nonetheless, frequently became prescriptive assignments.

The curricular reforms suggested by Moffett and Britton et al. reflect two concerns of research on cognitive development. The first of these involves the differences between speaking and writing; although both processes represent communication through language, they differ in several significant ways. Vygotsky states, for example, that oral speech differs from written language both structurally and functionally. Writing lacks an immediate audience and an obvious context and employs its own medium of communication. Writing must be more functionally self-sufficient than speech, and it must be comprehensible over time. Thus writing is a storage technology. Whereas oral language can linger only in a listener's memory, a text can be read repeatedly and at a great distance from its author. Writers must therefore master awareness of audience and presentation styles without the benefit of immediate feedback—which can be difficult.

The ability to communicate through writing develops at a much slower rate than does the ability to communicate through speech and requires much more formal instruction. For most children, the expression of ideas through spoken language becomes a much more fluent process than does the expression of ideas through writing. Even for skilled writers, the ability to invent ideas often outstrips the ability to organize them and present them in written form (Barritt and Kroll 51–52). The developing writer must master the ability to hold sentences in memory and then revise them as if they were a slowed-down version of inner speech.

The second concern of Moffett and Britton's work involves ways of addressing audiences that are connected with the writer's cognitive growth from egocentrism to outreach. Although younger children may be familiar with a subject, they often cannot adequately communicate their grasp of it to a listener. From this observation, Piaget formulated the concept of the egocentric nature of children, hypothesizing that because children cannot conceive of the listener's perspective, they do not adapt their message to their audience's needs. Cognitive researchers have wondered how young children, who have difficulty communicating ideas orally to listeners in their presence, ever learn to address an imagined audience in writing. And by extension, how does a skilled adult writer ever learn to shape written discourse according to the needs of her audience?

This question has been taken up most usefully by Linda Flower in "Writer-Based Prose: A Cognitive Basis for Problems in Writing."[4] Flower distinguishes between what she calls "writer-based" prose and "reader-based" prose—discourse that is churning along in the mental process and discourse that has been prepared for an audience. She says,

> In function, Writer-Based Prose is a verbal expression written by a writer to himself and for himself. It is the record and the working of his own verbal thought. In its structure, Writer-Based Prose reflects the associative, narrative paths of the writer's own confrontation with her subject. In its language, it reveals her use of privately loaded terms and shifting but unexpressed contexts for her statements. (19)

In other words, writer-based prose represents a failure to fulfill the interpretive needs of the reader. This egocentric text is marked by a narrative or survey structure that replicates the way it is generated, and by the writer's internal associational relationships, tacit contexts, and personal—even idiosyncratic—diction. Writer-based prose represents an ineffective balancing of the demands of composing, which, Flower suggests, results from a novice writer's not knowing quite how to juggle complex cognitive constraints.

The abilities of novice writers to handle the shifting goals and constraints of composing lead to an important question for teachers of writing: are there developmental stages that students must attain if they are to effectively write certain kinds of discourse; and if so, can these stages be "pushed" by certain kinds of teaching? Using Piaget's and Vygotsky's theories of development, Andrea Lunsford, in "Cognitive Development and the Basic Writer," (1979) sug-

[4] See Part III.

gested that basic writers "have not attained the level of cognitive development which would allow them to form abstractions" because even though they "may have little difficulty in dealing with familiar everyday problems requiring abstract thought . . . they are not aware of the processes they are using" (38, 39). Sharon Pianko (1979) also asserted that basic writers engage in abbreviated composing processes and reflect less on their writing than do more mature writers.

Lunsford argues that to stimulate the abstract thought processes of analysis and synthesis, basic writers should participate in active workshops where they can group concepts of writing inductively. Active workshops offer a rich alternative to teacher-centered lectures, during which students listen and memorize the precepts delivered. To foster active thinking involving analysis and synthesis, Lunsford advocates activities for practicing grammatical conventions, sentence-combining, essay writing, and workshop discussions.

Mike Rose (1983) also stressed that basic writers' "narrow, ossified conceptions" of composing cannot be remedied by mechanical drills and memorization of rules ("Remedial" 128). Rather, basic writers need "opportunities so they can alter those conceptions for themselves . . . be ambitious and . . . err" (128); furthermore, BW courses should approximate the intellectual challenge of academic studies. While the jury is still out on the question of cognitive stages, everyone seems to agree that students can be helped to break through to new plateaus of ability.

Using Theories of Cognitive Development in the Classroom

Theories of cognitive development usually find immediate (and reductive) applications as sequenced assignments. Starting with the assumption that mental abilities grow organically, designers of curricula try to fashion assignments that will make them grow faster or more inclusively. James Moffett's continua of subject and audience have been used, for example, as the starting point for an entire sequence of assignments based on the abilities of students to learn a more complex task only after they have mastered a simpler one. Moffett's own college textbook, *Active Voice*, is a well-explained series of assignments. If you are interested in Moffett's theory and his assignment sequence, you may want to follow his order for assignments. The following is a mere skeleton of his text:

Group 1: Revising inner speech

1. Stream of consciousness
2. Spontaneous sensory monologue
3. Composed observation
4. Spontaneous memory monologue
5. Composed memory
6. Spontaneous reflection monologue
7. Composed reflection

Group 2: Dialogues and monologues

1. Dialogue
2. Exterior monologue
3. Interior monologue
4. One-act play
5. Dialogue of ideas
6. Dialogue converted to essay

Group 3: Narrative into essay

1. Correspondence	11. Parable
2. Diary	12. Fable
3. Diary summary	13. Proverb and saying
4. Autobiography: Incident	14. Directions
5. Autobiography: Phase	15. Narrative illustrating a generality
6. Eyewitness memoir: Human subject	16. Thematic collection of incidents
7. Eyewitness memoir: Nature	17. Generalization supported by instances
8. Reporter-at-large	18. Research
9. Biography: Phase	19. Theory
10. Chronicle	

Moffett insists that these assignments do not represent a linear sequence, and he argues that any of them can be approached with varying levels of expertise and ability (*Active Voice* 8–9). Even so, he continues to believe that this sequence mirrors growing cognitive abilities more effectively than any other developmental sequence.

How can you use Moffett's sequence? Rather than adhering slavishly to it, you will probably be better served by choosing among the assignments in the sequence and paying attention to the gradually increasing cognitive demands they place on a writer.

Moffett himself suggests that his assignments should never be used as topics for the whole class at once since the development that the sequence mirrors always takes place on an individual basis. Instead, he'd advise you to offer an array of assignments and let students choose their own point of entry. Since each one can be done at many different levels of ability, you may want to allow students to find their own challenge and try their hands at their own choice. After a student has satisfactorily completed one kind of writing, she can be encouraged to proceed to a more demanding assignment.

Studies of cognitive development have also influenced our approach to formal errors. Throughout most of the history of the teaching of composition, errors were considered the result of carelessness or ignorance. There was little study of the reasons they were made—until Mina Shaughnessy's groundbreaking *Errors and Expectations* (1977) and Barry Kroll and John Schafer's oft-cited article, "Error Analysis and the Teaching of Composition" (1978). Both studies pursued the cognitivist question of why a student makes a particular kind of error. These inquiries helped reorient teachers' evaluation of errors, especially those common in the work of basic writers, bilingual students, and speakers of nonstandard dialects. It was found that as understandable phenomena, errors reveal a writer's mental processes rather than merely indicating a student's apathy or incapability.

As a result of this new understanding, cognitive researchers have hammered away at the uselessness of mechanical drills aimed at teaching correctness—even though this practice still dominates much of composition instruction. When we view errors as a normal and necessary part of learning, we can see that they are not best remedied by punishment or by assigning a particular exercise in a workbook. The central message of Shaughnessy's work is that teachers should not deal with errors individually; they should seek, instead, to determine the patterns that formal errors fall into. When you see that a student is repeating a certain kind of error, you can try to discern the cognitive structures of the pattern. Rather than giving a student an F because of five comma splices in a paper, see what the splices have in common. What do the splices tell you about the student's understanding of sentence boundaries? What kinds of structures appear around them? What assumptions underlie the error pattern? The student may have conscious answers to some of these questions, so you might discuss the issue with her before you attempt to clarify the conventions of so-called Edited American English. Errors are opportunities for instruction, not censure.

Once you can distinguish deliberate errors—that is, wrong choices—from unintentional slips, you can better address the way such errors vary from conventions of standard dialect. David Bartholomae's research technique of asking students to edit (or fix) errors and explain their corrections as they read aloud allows both researchers and teachers to note the etiologies of various mistakes. In "The Study of Error," Bartholomae found that students unconsciously correct many errors during oral editing without noting the presence of the errors in the text. By focusing the student's attention on these unnoticed corrections, a teacher can discuss the conventions that underlie them as well as advise students on practicing and continuing to apply these conventions.

A large part of working on developmental issues is guiding students away from their own concerns and awarenesses to a concern for and an awareness of their audience. Kroll's study of egocentrism and audience awareness suggests that the ability to adapt to meet the needs of one's audience develops more slowly in writing than in speech. Yet the ability to assume the audience's perspective, or to "decenter," can be stimulated when writers are asked to rewrite their writer-based prose as reader-based prose. Such practice in revision is essential because many inexperienced writers assume "the reader understands what is going on in the writer's mind and needs therefore no introduction or transitions or exploration" (Shaughnessy 240).

For example, ask your students to write two accounts of the following scene: A weary college student working as a waiter is bringing an elegantly dressed woman her order of chicken Marbella. Just as the waiter is setting the plate before her, the fashion plate raises her wineglass to propose a toast, knocking the chicken into her lap. Ask your students to describe the event first as if they were the exasperated diner blaming the waiter and then as if they were the fretful student worried about losing necessary employment. Attention to audience can be fostered by pointing out students routine adaptation of speech to each situation. Asking reflective questions—Who are the members of the intended audience? What do they need to know and in what order? What tone will best affect the audience?—and assigning writing tasks with credible purposes and conceivable audiences—such as the student waiter responding to the diner's complaint—can help stimulate awareness of audience.

FLOWER AND HAYES'S
COGNITIVE MODELS OF COMPOSING

The cognitive research of Linda Flower and John Hayes has probably been the most influential psychology-based research in composition studies in the last three decades. Flower and Hayes and those whose research followed theirs have set out to do nothing less than map the strategies of the mind engaged in writing.

Flower, an English professor involved in studying technical communication, and Hayes, a psychologist trained in the cognitive tradition of studying human activity by asking subjects to give verbal "protocols" of behavior, teamed up in the 1970s. They combined composition questions with the cognitive-psychology research technique of protocol analysis, proposing to use this "unusual condition of thinking out loud" (Flower, "Construction of Purpose" 528) to "capture in rich detail the moment to moment thinking of a writer in action" (Flower, Hayes, and Swarts, "Designing" 53).

Verbal protocols are essentially records of a person talking aloud while completing a task, giving present-tense explanations of why she is doing what she is doing. When a writer is asked to verbalize everything in her mind while writing—including false starts, fragmentary thoughts, and stray ideas—a protocol offers both a "unique window" to the mind and a "wealth of unsorted information" (Flower, Hayes, and Swarts, "Designing" 53). The tape-recording of a thinking-aloud protocol is transcribed and numbered by lines, clauses, or sentences, according to the research topic.

The researchers, using the protocol transcript, their notes regarding observations of the writer, the writer's notes and text, and their knowledge of the tasks performed and of human capabilities, then attempt to formulate a hypothesis concerning the research topic. From this hypothesis, the researchers create a coding scheme by which to interpret and categorize the various statements of the transcript according to the mental activities involved, checking their discriminations using inter-rater reliability. Verbal protocols of writing can be used to explore new topics, to suggest the structure of a problem, to compare performances by writers of different ages or abilities, and to create a model of the cognitive processes of writing.

Like Emig, Flower and Hayes usually admitted the incompleteness of verbal protocols, which they likened to the brief surfacings of a porpoise, from which they must infer its unseen underwater directions ("Identifying the Organization" 9-10), but they claimed that their present-tense protocols were more accurate than retrospective accounts of writing. For over two years, this research team analyzed the "rich set of traces of cognition" (Flower, "Construction of Purpose" 533) in numerous verbal protocols to infer a tentative model of the cognitive processes of composition. Their model is elegant in its simplicity (see Figure 1, p.118). Their model consists of the task environment, the writer's long-term memory, and the various processes within the writing process. The *task environment* includes "everything outside the writer's skin that influences" the writing (Flower and Hayes, "Identifying the Organization" 12): the writing assignment, the writer's motivation, and as the composing proceeds, the existing text. The *writer's long-term memory* involves her knowledge of the topic and the audience and previous writing strategies and experiences.

This process model proposes that writing entails three major cognitive operations: *planning*, which consists of generating information, organizing ideas, and setting various goals; *translating*, which expresses the planned material in the visible language of acceptably written language; and *reviewing*, which involves evaluating and revising the written text to improve its quality. These three major cognitive operations also interact with what Flower and Hayes call the *monitor*, which is described below.

Although the cognitive-process model was not created as a pedagogical tool (and we know no one who tries to teach it directly), its multidirectional arrows and boxes within boxes provide an insightful explanation of composing as a recursive process. Rather than illustrating a linear sequence of distinct stages, such as Rohman and Wlecke's prewriting, writing, and rewriting, Flower and Hayes's model can account for the intriguing complexity of a writer's mind engaged in composing processes. A recursive model can describe looped and embedded behaviors—action that moves from generating to organizing to translating to monitoring the produced draft and then to revising, generating again, comparing the product with different levels of desired goals, reorganizing, and so on. This embedding of one component or subcomponent within another distinguishes Flower and Hayes's model from the tidy sequence of stage theory and accounts for the recursive patterns of cognition that Emig observed in her watershed study of the composing process.

The preceding example, in which the revising process is interrupted by another cycle of generating, is not the only possible instance of embedding one subcomponent of the process within another. Throughout the verbal protocols Flower and Hayes examined, they located frequent and widely distributed interruptions of other subcomponents, especially by the process of revising and generating. Writers, they found, are continually creating hierarchies of short- and long-term goals in which one goal becomes the paramount concern while the others are relegated to subordinate positions; then all shift places as the writer seeks an answer to another problem that has arisen. In this sense, all composing is a constant stream of problem recognition and solution. Although the first third of most protocols generally demonstrates planning and the latter third primarily demonstrates reviewing, any subcomponent is capable of interrupting the process and embedding itself within another. Thus the model's multidirectional arrows and its boxes within boxes represent the interrupted, recursive nature and the shifting, hierarchical attention of the writer's mind at work.

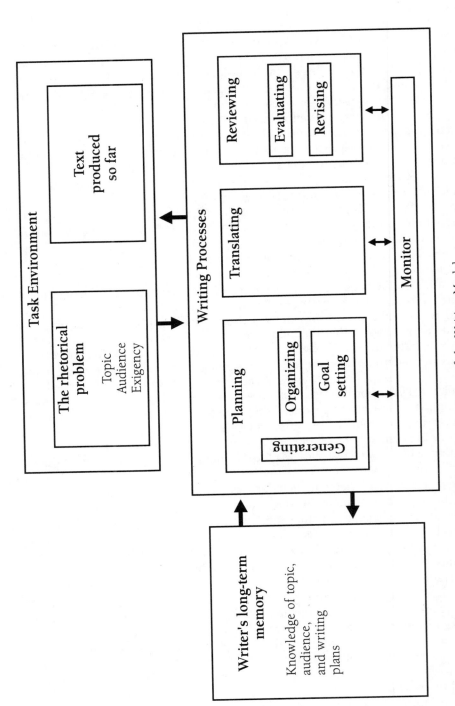

Figure 1 Structure of the Writing Model

As the task environment, the writer's long-term memory, and the writing process interact, the writer may, for example, begin planning by setting goals based on the assigned topic, continue planning by generating information from long-term memory, shift to translating these ideas into visible language, and return to planning for organization by numbering the items on a brainstorming list. The writer might then jump to evaluating and revising some of the brainstorming items, then continue to generate material before noticing a previously written sentence and revising it, and then switch to goal setting by considering the audience of the assignment in relation to recollected strategies for addressing a similar audience of a previously written text. The constantly changing hierarchies of the writer's attention and the embedding of one component or subcomponent within another suggest that a linear sequence would involve each of the subcomponents in dynamic permutations guided by the writer's conscious and unconscious creation of goals that parallel the development of the evolving text.

Flower and Hayes have continued to refine and develop their cognitive-process model of composing since the late 1970s, when they first developed it. In particular, since the rise of the social construction movement of the late 1980s, they have been working on a "social-cognitive" version of their model that takes the task environment into greater consideration. Still, the version of their model presented here is the best known, and social critiques of the cognitive movement have not resulted in its replacement by another model.

Using Flower and Hayes's Cognitive Theory in the Classroom

Though Flower and Hayes's model is an important one with which to become familiar, it is seldom taught directly. The real significance of Flower and Hayes's research lies in its explanations of, and its potential solutions for, the problems with composing that students face daily.

The first significant implication of their research is that writers, especially inexperienced ones, must confront a possibly overwhelming number of writing concerns as they compose. Consciously trying to juggle all these concerns simultaneously is almost impossible for most writers; short-term memory simply cannot attend to so many items at once. The great difference between experienced writers and novice writers seems to be in how much automaticity is available—how many issues can be put on automatic pilot. Experienced writers can, for instance, pay little attention to issues of spelling, syntax, punctuation, and paragraph structure, since their trained "writing mechanism" takes care of those issues. They can concentrate on solving higher-level problems, like addressing their audience, ordering the presentation, choosing examples, and structuring the argument. But novice writers face all those issues in addition to the formal and mechanical issues that experienced writers hardly think about, thus their task is so much harder.

The monitor in Flower and Hayes's model regulates the attention that the writer pays to the subcomponent atop the hierarchy of the writing process, determines the length of time to devote to a particular subcomponent, and decides which subcomponent to attend to next. A successful performance requires that some items are intentionally and temporarily ignored until they can be integrated into the complete writing process. It is from the monitor, then, that we can draw a major lesson for teaching composition, which is that student writers need to learn to reduce their cognitive loads; they need to choose to ignore some issues at some points in the writing process.

There are several ways writers can deal with this constant round of demands. First, like an overburdened juggler, a writer can simply let one or two items drop from her attention and concentrate on the paramount concern(s). Invention strategies such as brainstorming, freewriting, and clustering demonstrate this principle,[5] for they allow a writer to concentrate on generating and translating while delaying goal setting, organizing, evaluating, revising, and editing. You may want to suggest that students draft their papers without worrying at all about spelling and grammar, so that they keep editing-level concerns from interfering with the flow of translating ideas into written language. If students just write, they can go back later and fix anything they don't like. The beauty of writing as compared with speech is that one gets the chance to say exactly the right thing.

Second, student writers can learn to create a network of goals that prevents both cognitive overload and the omission of important composing concerns. Flower stresses the idea that goal setting, like the complete composing process, is a dynamic, hierarchical, "continuing, unpredictable, and often opportunistic process" ("Construction of Purpose" 535). Therefore, writers create and assign priorities to a network of goals before and during the writing process. These goals involve not only the abstract outline of what to say but also—and just as important—solutions to a continuous stream of rhetorical problems, the often obscured consideration of *how* to compose. Student writers must decide on ways to generate information and translate these ideas into acceptably written language. Marlene Scardamalia and her colleagues, Carl Bereiter and Hillel Goelman, have shown that because young writers have difficulty establishing these goals, they frequently fail to switch among subcomponents and/or to sustain a subcomponent (generating, for example) long enough to reach a necessary level of fruition.

A good way to try to teach students about juggling the complex demands of writing is to model them yourself for the class. Ask students to give you an assignment that specifies a subject and an audience, and then write out your response, talking all the time about what you are doing and why you are doing it. This modeling can be done on the blackboard, but blackboard composing, if it goes on for long, can be physically tiring. It may be easier for you to compose on a piece of clear plastic on an overhead projector.

Begin by brainstorming the assignment aloud, writing down any notes you want (the blackboard is good for this). Then begin to compose while talking about what you're doing. Don't be afraid to make mistakes, admit you have

---

[5] See Chapter 7.

gone down a wrong path, or to cross out whole sections—doing these things will demonstrate the composing process much more effectively than will your writing out a perfect essay. After you have completed at least three full paragraphs, ask for questions and comments as you continue. You needn't finish the essay for students to draw the lesson. Your purpose here is to show students your shifting network of goals and how it develops as you write.

Since Flower and Hayes view writing as problem solving, they urge students to try to set goal-based plans rather than topic-based plans. Goal-based plans have to do with the desired effect on the audience, possible strategies for writing the paper, and information about the topic itself. These threefold concerns can be sketched out using a brainstorming list, a clusterlike tree of issues, or freewriting—for example, "I'm going to show my readers . . . how noise affects their mood and productivity. . . . That means I'll want to start with a vivid demonstration of how noise affects us" (Flower, *Problem-Solving Strategies in Writing* 59).

Another easy way to teach composition students to consider all three concerns—the rhetorical problem, the desired product, and the possible writing strategies—is blocking or chunking, an alternative to the traditional outline. This tentative plan for a draft asks the writer to consider her material, audience, and purpose. "What do I know about my topic?" "What effect do I want to have on my audience?" "How many blocks/chunks of material will I need?" "What belongs in each chunk?" and "How do I want to develop each chunk?" are questions that guide the writer to consider not only the desired product but also the rhetorical problem and the processes of composing (Lindemann 163-66).

Flower and Hayes also recommend that teachers demonstrate the use of heuristic strategies so that inexperienced writers don't have to resort to prescriptive formulas, a passive (and often disappointing) search for inspiration, or inefficient attempts at trial and error. Heuristic problem-solving strategies offer writers a greater repertoire of "alternatives and the power of choices" while they are engaged "in the struggle with words" ("Problem-Solving Strategies and the Writing Process" 453). In the third edition of *Problem-Solving Strategies for Writing*, Flower has effectively combined theory and practice to enable students to manage the myriad problems posed by composing. Although all of her suggested strategies cannot be summarized here, Flower's insightful advice for generating ideas includes the following:

1. Turn off the editor, and brainstorm. Brainstorm rather than freewrite because brainstorming is more goal-directed than freewriting.
2. Imagine talking to your reader. This simulates a face-to-face discussion and prompts you to clarify opinions and anticipate possible objections.
3. Systematically explore your topic using Aristotelian topoi, tagmemic invention, and/or analogies that tap as yet undiscovered relevant knowledge and language.
4. Rest and incubate after formulating the next unsolved problem so that it can actively simmer. When inspiration strikes, write it down.

The danger of overly elaborate heuristics is that instead of making explicit the efficient, intuitive methods of thinking, they can recast them in the same prescriptive formulas they were intended to replace.[6]

Limiting the cognitive load for student writers also means teaching them about the different kinds of revision, from local revisions such as crossing out a word and replacing it with another while writing a sentence to global issues of moving of text and recomposing entire sections. As Sommers finds in contrasting student writers and experienced adult writers ("Revision Strategies" 1980), for students to engage in the various levels of revision, many first need to be disabused of the notion that revision is merely the act of eliminating redundancy and superfluity.

To teach that revision can involve global or semantic as well as local or lexical alterations, return to one of the examples of writer-based prose, and work with the class to revise it. Provide each student with a copy of the anonymous paragraph(s), and write it on the blackboard as well. As students suggest and vote on proposed changes, they are participating in Vygotsky's "zone of proximal development": they learn to re-see this egocentric prose from the audience's perspective. This activity also models Flower and Hayes's "pregnant pause" of planning, in which writers rescan the existing text, compare the actual text with their desired meanings, and adopt the reader's perspective ("Pregnant Pause").

FURTHER COGNITIVE RESEARCH

A recent and controversial elaboration of Flower and Hayes's research has been Stephen Witte's formulation of a writer's pretext, which he defines as a writer's "trial locution that is produced in the mind, stored in the writer's memory, and sometimes manipulated mentally prior to being transcribed as written text" (397). Witte concluded that a writer's pretext may have an immediate or delayed effect on written or rewritten text, is evaluated and revised while stored in memory according to the same criteria as written text, and can "function as a critical link among planning written text, translating ideas into linguistic form, and transcribing ideas into visible language" (417). These multiple functions of pretext, he advises, "should warn against a Procrustean process of fitting the activities of composing into discrete cubbyholes, however necessary such categorization may seem" for theoretical or pedagogical purposes (416).

Likewise, the danger of any of these cognitive models of composing or sequences of cognitive development lies in their potential misuse such that they set rigid standards. The essential theoretical and pedagogical insight of cognitive research is that investigators and teachers should focus on the actual ways students write rather than measuring their writing against an ideal product or even measuring their composing process against a perfect process.

Another specific area of cognitive research has focused on writer's block. Led by Mike Rose's research, this problem has been defined as the inability to

---

[6] For several well-tested composing heuristics, you can refer students to Chapter 3 of *The St. Martin's Handbook.*

begin or continue writing when the reasons are not related to a lack of skill or commitment. In *Writer's Block: The Cognitive Dimension*, Rose proposes these as some reasons for writer's block.

1. Rigid, inappropriately invoked, or incorrect rules for composing
2. Misleading assumptions about composing
3. Premature editing during composing
4. Conflicting rules, assumptions, plans, or strategies
5. Insufficient, inappropriate, or inflexible planning and discourse strategies
6. Ineffective evaluation due to inappropriate or misunderstood criteria (4)

As with the cognitive approach to error analysis, a teacher should respond to writer's block by trying to discern its causes before suggesting solutions. By discussing an episode of writer's block as soon after its occurrence as possible, a teacher can try to comprehend and enhance a student's concept of the writing processes.[7]

Writer's block is often associated with writing apprehension, but these two problems do not always correlate with each other. Apprehension does not always prevent the production of discourse, but the anxiety that highly apprehensive writers feel for writing often causes them to avoid whenever possible courses and careers dependent on writing. John Daly and Michael Miller have designed a twenty-six item survey to measure writing apprehension. Daly and his many co-researchers have found that misconceptions about writing processes, negative attitudes toward writing, and unrealistic expectations about the quantity of writing required by many professions all correlate with writing apprehension, although a causal link has not been established. They suggest that addressing the correlated factors can help alleviate writing apprehension.[8]

SOCIAL CONSTRUCTION AND THE CRITIQUE OF COGNITIVE RESEARCH

The years 1977–87 have been called "The Cognitive Decade" because the work of cognitive researchers was so important and influential at this time. Carnegie-Mellon University, where Flower and Hayes did their work, was the central node of a psychology- and social science–based network of researchers. Around the middle part of the 1980s, however, a countermovement began, one that strongly critiqued certain elements of the cognitive research movement.

In "Cognition, Convention, and Certainty: What We Need to Know about Writing," Patricia Bizzell asserts that for many readers, the composing model of

---

[7] Rose's numerous strategies for coping with writer's block are detailed in his research. See the Works Cited at the end of this chapter.

[8] For an introduction to the theory of, and instructional practices for, writing apprehension, see Michael Smith's NCTE publication and Daly's research, also listed under Works Cited.

the leading cognitive researchers, Flower and Hayes, offers a "surprising mix of daunting complexity and disappointing familiarity" (222). For example, says Bizzell, the model's "monitor" uses a computer-programming term to identify a writer's decisions concerning planning, translating, and reviewing, but this elaborate nomenclature fails to account for *why* a writer decides, for instance, to translate and then to review. Like the computer flowchart on which it was based, Flower and Hayes's model does provide a useful theoretical description of *how* writing occurs. Bizzell warns, however, that it does not enable teachers of composition to "advise students on difficult questions of practice" ("Cognition" 222), such as why and when to shift from translating back to planning and how long to spend with each component of the process.

Martin Nystrand has objected that Flower and Hayes relegate composing's essential decision-making to a "mysterious black box" (69) without revealing the monitor's inner workings. Bizzell, Nystrand, and others have also criticized Flower and Hayes's distinction between planning and translating because it implies that writers first consider meaning and then seek the words with which to express their ideas.

Although writers are capable of generating ideas using nonverbal images, such visual planning does not mean that thought always precedes language, as Flower and Hayes's model suggests. Critics of cognitive research believe that Flower, Hayes, and their colleagues have inaccurately viewed Jean Piaget and Lev Vygotsky as complementary theorists instead of as thinkers who differed significantly on the relationship between thought and language. Unlike Piaget, Vygotsky did not view language as the medium through which pre-existing thoughts are communicated. Instead, he asserted that as a young child talks aloud while playing a game alone or while performing a task (which Piaget termed egocentric speech), she is beginning to employ language not only to name objects and ideas but also to develop and evaluate thoughts. This instrumental speech is gradually internalized; and then—when it occurs in the child's head, rather than on her lips—thought becomes inseparable from language. This inner speech, however, is bound to the particular language the child has learned; so for Vygotsky, the nature of a child's cognitive development has changed from Piaget's biological basis to a "historical-cultural process" with "specific properties and laws" (qtd. in Bizzell "Cognition" 223).

This concept of discourse and thought as being socially and culturally constructed, and not merely the product of some abstract cognition lacking context, lies at the heart of the social-construction movement. That there is a diversity of languages and dialects, each one inseparable from thought, means that there are multiple ways of thinking, all historically and culturally bound. One of Vygotsky's students, A. R. Luria, demonstrated the effect of language and culture on perception and understanding in his study of Uzbek peasants. More recently, Shirley Brice Heath also has described the differences in language and thought patterns among three communities in North and South Carolina.

Nevertheless, when cognitivists promote problem-solving strategies as guides to internalizing fundamental structures of thought and language or when tagmemic theorists characterize their particle-wave-field heuristic as based on "universal invariants that underlie all human experience" (Richard Young qtd. in Bizzell "Cognition" 240), they fail to acknowledge linguistic, social, and intellectual diversity. When cognitive researchers assume that universal and fundamental mental structures exist for all individuals, Bizzell cautions, the standard form of English is usually treated as socially privileged and intellectually superior to other ways of speaking, writing, and thinking.

This position, known in philosophy as *constructivism* and in composition studies as *social constructionism*, denies that an individual directly observes reality and contemplates what she observes to ascertain truth. As opposed to what cognitivists and most Western thinkers since Descartes have assumed, social constructionists assert that a child is born into a world of objects and motions and into a particular society of words which constantly mediates each individual's knowledge.

The continuing underlying critique of cognitivism that has been made by the social-construction movement is that it strips cognition of its contexts, reducing huge varieties of social and cultural motives to a box that is marked *task environment* and is never much investigated. As a result, say the social constructionists, cognitive research is loath to leave the laboratory, loath to look at nonacademic writing or at the countless variables that real-world writing is subject to. Therefore, they say, cognitivism can tell us only a few things about a few carefully controlled situations. As an explanatory theory, it is severely limited.

BRUFFEE AND BIZZELL'S ADVOCACY OF SOCIAL CONSTRUCTIONISM

Kenneth Bruffee, Patricia Bizzell, James Berlin, David Bartholomae, and other social theorists reject the cognitivist conception—tacit but genuine—of a writer as a solitary individual scribbling businesslike in a laboratory or romantically in a garret, engaged in universal mental processes to turn thoughts that she has already generated into language. By overemphasizing the individual, cognitivists conceive of a writer as entering a social context only when the verbalized message is cast in "its most persuasive form to accommodate the audience" (Bizzell "Cognition" 217). In practice, social constructionists are also suspicious of the tenets of "writing-process" pedagogies such as those advocated by Donald Murray and Peter Elbow. Critiquing these pedagogies as "romantic" and "expressivist," social constructionists see in them another example of the unexamined individualist bias found in theoretical form in cognitive theory.

Bruffee and Bizzell argue that a writer never composes as an autonomous individual because even when one writes in isolation, one is mentally composing according to Vygotsky's internalized speech, which has become thought (Bruffee "Writing and Reading" 167). Even when a writer seems to be just trying to get down some ideas, seemingly heedless of any audience, she is functioning within a social context. While cognitivists acknowledge its importance only during audience analysis, Bizzell counters that the social context helps explain the reasons for decisions made by the otherwise mysterious monitor of Flower and Hayes's model. The social context operates not only in public discourse but also during reflective thought—Vygotsky's inner speech—so a writer composes according to a particular culture's inseparably linked patterns of language and thought.

From the philosopher Michael Oakeshott, Bruffee borrows a phrase to conceive of each individual as born into "the conversation of mankind," and it is this conversation, in its various forms of discourse, that "gives place and character to every human activity and utterance" (qtd. in Bruffee "Collaborative Learning" 639). Bruffee contends that "we draw on the accepted values, metaphors, signs, and institutional commitments of our community of knowledgeable peers to give meaning and value to our actions" ("Liberal Education" 101). Since there are diverse ways of speaking, writing, thinking, and knowing, as demonstrated by Luria's and Heath's studies, then thought is not a natural, universal structure of all human minds, as cognitivists assume. Rather, it is an intellectual artifact constructed by social interaction within a particular community of discourse. Or as Bruffee explains, "We can think because we can talk, and we think in the ways we learned to talk" ("Collaborative Learning" 640). Because thought is internalized speech and writing is a re-externalization of this conversation, one must participate in the community that generates and maintains a discourse if one is to learn its ways of speaking, writing, thinking, and knowing—be it the discourse of scientists, anthropologists, literary critics, or composition scholars.

Bruffee ("Social Construction") and Bizzell ("Thomas Kuhn") cite Thomas Kuhn's controversial *Structure of Scientific Revolutions*, which explains change in scientific knowledge in terms of its social construction. Kuhn, as a philosopher and historian of science, observes that scientific change is not produced by the incremental, evolutionary process of "normal science"; rather, changes in scientific knowledge occur through drastic, revolutionary shifts in interpretive frameworks, or "paradigms," of the scientific community's conversations. Kuhn offers many examples, including the change from an earth-centered universe to a sun-centered one when the knowledge of physicists—culminating in Galileo—could no longer be accounted for by an earth-centered paradigm. Scientific knowledge, says Kuhn, depends on the interpretive paradigms common to a community of knowledgeable peers—sixteenth- and seventeenth-century physicists in the case of Copernicus and Galileo.

Bruffee's and Bizzell's advocacy of social constructionism also depends on the pragmatic philosophy of Richard Rorty. In *Philosophy and the Mirror of Nature*, Rorty argues that all knowledge is constructed by a community of like-minded peers. Synthesizing the ideas of John Dewey, Martin Heidegger, and Ludwig Wittgenstein, Rorty asserts that knowledge is "socially justified belief" (qtd. in Bruffee "Social Construction" 774), an idea that jibes with the indeterminacy of scientific knowledge that has been demonstrated most strikingly in modern physics by the Heisenberg Uncertainty Principle. Although this principle asserts that an observer's perspective affects the result of the observation, social constructionism rejects both an absolute relativism of knowledge as anything an individual chooses to believe and the positivism of objective truth directly discerned from reality. Social constructionists such as Bruffee and Bizzell believe that individuals experience the world according to the shared beliefs or paradigms of one or more communities of knowledgeable peers to which they belong.

Writers in the fields of history and ethnography have long been making this point. Greg Myers and Charles Bazerman, for example, have demonstrated that the knowledge and the writing of scientists are sanctioned by the consensus of their community. In *Local Knowledge*, the anthropologist Clifford Geertz concludes that modern consciousness is an "enormous multiplicity" of cultural values (qtd. in Bruffee "Social Construction" 775), and Bruffee offers the diversity of students now entering composition classrooms and the current debate over the literary canon as illustrations of the multiple paradigms of modernity. In literature, Stanley Fish has proposed that reading and writing depend on interpretive communities that socially construct conventions of language use. Because they reflect the ongoing activity of knowledgeable members, a community's interpretive standards are not arbitrary; and because a literate person can participate in more than one interpretive community, they do not totally determine individual behavior. These groups of like-minded peers do, however, sanction certain topics, methods, and styles of reading and writing (Bizzell "Cognition" 226).

Collaborative learning has always been associated with social construction in composition, though this pedagogical approach predates the theories of social constructionism. In "Collaborative Learning and the 'Conversation of Mankind,'" Bruffee, with whose work collaborative learning is most often associated, traces the history of collaborative learning only to the 1950s and M. L. J. Abercrombie's teaching of medical students through group diagnosis (637). Anne Ruggles Gere, however, stresses that the practices of collaborative learning have "a much greater history" (56) than the coining of the term by several British educators, one of whom, Edwin Mason, gave the movement a name when he published *Collaborative Learning* in 1970. For example, in 1917, during the early progressive education movement, Sterling Leonard proposed that students should "be knit into a social group organized for mutual help, and aided to move steadily forward in an arduous way of attaining effective expression" (qtd. in DeCiccio 5), and Dewey advocated that instead of learning that is imposed by a teacher, learning should be motivated by the "moving spirit of the whole group" as a class is "held together by participation in common activities" (qtd. in Trimbur 92).

Collaborative learning as a practice developed more from social and educational challenges than from theoretical foundations, such as progressive education or social constructionism. In particular, it arose in response to new challenges for which American educators were unprepared. In the 1970s, open-admission policies and student bodies more diverse in age, ethnicity, and academic preparation, brought disadvantaged and nontraditional students into colleges and universities; these previously excluded students seemed to lack not the necessary intelligence but the familiarity with academic discourse(s) they needed to succeed. Teachers found it easier to let students learn these conventions together than to attempt to teach each student individually. As Bruffee states, "For American college teachers, the roots of collaborative learning lie neither in radical politics nor in research . . . [but in] a pressing educational need" ("Collaborative Learning" 637).

Since collaborative learning developed from the insights of practitioners rather than from theoretical implications, John Trimbur correctly labels it a "generic term" (87), covering an amalgam of associated practices that include small-group work, joint writing projects, peer response, peer tutoring, and writing across the curriculum. The unifying precept of this association is the redistribution of power arrangements between teacher and students to engage students in their own learning. In Bruffee's words, it is "a form of indirect teaching" that early proponents of writing as a process promoted ("Collaborative Learning" 637): Peter Elbow suggested the use of "teacherless writing groups"; Donald Murray recommended that students should be taught to respond to their peers' drafts; and Ken Macrorie advocated the value of creating a "helping circle" (qtd. in Hermann).

Collaborative learning has not been without its critics. Thomas Newkirk has explored the potential conflict between students reading as an audience of peers and a teacher reading according to the standards of an academic community, and Diana George has studied the problems of group dynamics, such as gender differences, in attitudes toward and involvement in collaborative learning. Beyond these practical problems, other scholars in the field of composition have examined theoretical difficulties of collaborative learning. One critic, Greg Myers, has suggested that "the rhetoric of collaborative learning seems to suggest that there is something inherently good and innocent about agreement, persuasion, compromise, and a deliberative procedure" (212). Collaboration may be an effective writing strategy, but as the Marxist scholar Terry Eagleton has warned, "language is power, conflict, and struggle—weapon as much as medium, poison as well as cure, the bars of the prison-house as well as a possible way out" (qtd. in Ede "What Is Social" 9). In addition, Joseph Harris has urged advocates of collaborative learning and social constructionism to investigate the largely unexamined term *community*. And even one leading proponent of collaborative learning, Lisa Ede, has grown skeptical of social constructionism's rapid challenge of cognitivist and expressivist paradigms of writing; she now advocates using the theory of social constructionism not only to justify, but also to better understand and further explore collaborative learning. Such rigorous examination is necessary so that collaborative learning does not become, as Ede warns, "just another pedagogical fad" ("Case for Collaboration" 10).

Social construction takes many forms, ranging from abstrusely philosophical writing to the most pragmatic classroom-oriented advice, from the most overtly radical liberationist pedagogies to the most inflexible cultural conservatism. Generally, however, it is defined in opposition to both the positivist assertion that the world is composed of inarguable, observable "facts" and the pure relativism of romantic individualism. We are social creatures, say these constructionist theorists, and we are inevitably created by the action of social and cultural forces on whatever physical or genetic matrix we may have.

The Pedagogical Implications of Social Constructionism

The application of social constructionism by a teacher of composition cannot simply be listed under the heading "Using the Theories of Social Constructionism in the Classroom." The possible pedagogical implications of this melange of theories are as varied as their scientific and philosophical origins in the work of Thomas Kuhn, Richard Rorty, Paulo Freire, and others. Although most purveyors of social construction would identify themselves with the academic left, the theory itself is amenable to many different points of view. Even E. D. Hirsch's *Cultural Literacy*—usually identified with right-wing cultural critique—can be considered as a pedagogical application of social constructionism. At the base of Hirsch's theory of cultural literacy is the idea that coherence in a culture is created by all members knowing certain things in common.[9]

The concept of discourse communities is perhaps the central idea in social construction as it appears in composition studies. According to their belief that all knowledge is socially constructed, Bruffee, Bizzell, and Bartholomae have asserted that the academic disciplines of the university can be viewed as particular discourse communities whose knowledgeable peers, through their consensus, sanction the topics and the methods of inquiry, the resulting knowledge, and the appropriate forms of its presentation. When a student speaks, reads, or writes within the university, Bartholomae asserts she is expected to

> invent the university . . . or a branch of it, like history or anthropology or economics or English. The student has to learn to speak [academic] language . . . to try on the peculiar ways of knowing, selecting, evaluating, reporting, concluding, and arguing that define . . . the various discourses of [the university] community. ("Inventing the University" 134)

How do we learn to interact in any community? By observing the conventions of discourse within that group. According to Bizzell, teachers of composition can initiate students into academic discourses by organizing students' participation in the collaborative exchanges of academic discourse and/or by training them to analyze the rhetorical features of a particular academic discourse ("Academic Discourse" 1). In practical terms, this refers to two specific

---

[9] Hirsch's compilation of significant names, phrases, dates, and concepts is supposed to represent the expected knowledge of a literate person as defined by American society. Critics object that Hirsch has "only one past in mind," which "is not so easily recoverable as [he] makes it seem" (George, "Politics" 5) and that "to be culturally literate involves more than knowing key referents; it requires the ability to employ certain patterns of discourse" (Newkirk, *More than Stories* 198). In composition, most social constructionists would reject any divorce of form from content, since particular forms are considered to be constructed from specific social contexts that also guide content. Hirsch, however, has specifically rejected formalism in teaching—the idea that forms can be taught without content. Even if a writing teacher wished to use Hirsch's ideas, she would be forced to give up teaching writing skills in favor of trying to teach issues of content.

features that nearly always appear in constructivist classrooms: (1) group work of various kinds, with its need for collaboration and intellectual sharing, and (2) analytic reading, especially of the kinds of writing that the academic-discourse community values.

Bartholomae in "Inventing the University," and Bruffee, in *A Short Course in Writing*, advocate engaging students in scholarly projects "that allow students to act as though they were colleagues in an academic enterprise" (Bartholomae, "Inventing the University" 144). Students participating in Bruffee's conversation in a scholarly community learn to produce academic discourse by functioning within a discourse community rather than by reporting on the discipline's knowledge as an outsider to the community's discourse and its conventions. For example, instead of asking students to summarize an article on some event or topic in history, Bartholomae proposes that students should be encouraged to "think (by learning to write) as a historian" ("Inventing the University" 145).

In *Facts, Artifacts, and Counterfacts*, a book on pedagogy that has been influential in introducing teachers to the social construction movement, Bartholomae and Anthony Petrosky present a theoretical overview and a practical description for establishing these collaborative projects of academic enterprise. Briefly, the course for basic writers that Bartholomae and Petrosky designed at the University of Pittsburgh consists of a sequence of twelve writing assignments and revisions, a corresponding reading sequence, the requirement that each student keep a journal of responses to the reading, and a reading list individually designed for each student. Taught as a small-group seminar, the class focuses on a single issue, such as "Growth and Change in Adolescence," for the entire term. Students begin by writing personal essays on a relevant experience, and each week, two or three students' papers are duplicated and distributed. The class then discusses the writers' experiences, their reflections on them, and their presentations in prose.

The important movement in this pedagogy is outward, from self to group. The discussions gradually lead to generalizing, conceptualizing, and theorizing about the theme of the semester. In essence, the students become members of a research team, in this example, on adolescent experience. They learn to define a subject, consider matters of relevance and authority, form concepts, use jargon, and function within the constraints of a discourse community. The corresponding reading sequence stimulates them to envision themselves as textual interpreters negotiating meaning with a writer rather than as decoders trying to discern an author's intended meaning. By requiring students to read published academic studies on the research topic later in the term, Bartholomae and Petrosky ask their students to begin to appreciate the interpretive framework that academic discourse provides and that enables the members of the discourse community to construct knowledge.

The academic enterprises proposed by Bartholomae and Petrosky and by Bruffee encourage teachers to create situations in which students work collaboratively. As we discuss in Chapter 7, the teaching of invention strategies also offers opportunities for small groups or the entire class to work collaboratively. In addition, collaborative learning can be implemented in peer-response groups, or writing groups, in which students give, seek, and react to other students' oral and written comments as they write.

Students need guidance, however, for their collaborations to be beneficial. A composition teacher cannot simply assign students to peer-writing groups and expect them to function successfully. To ask one student to read another's essay and respond to it is to invite the disappointment of noncommittal comments such as "I really liked it" or "It flows really well." Given the traditional emphasis on individual effort and the enforcement of student passivity in many secondary-school classrooms, FY writers are often unprepared and initially ill at ease when placed in collaborative learning situations. For collaborative learning to succeed, it must be gradually cultivated and always supported.[10]

To begin implementing writing groups, you may want to ask your students to select a satisfying passage from one of their essays (fifty to one hundred words) and to read it aloud to another student. Because the intended audience in the traditional classroom has usually been the teacher, this practice may seem unusual to many students. The students who are to listen should be instructed to offer no comments, for they will best learn to practice effective listening by suppressing both vacuous praise and harsh criticism. Using your intuition and students' suggestions, organize ongoing groups of two or three students (response partners), and begin using more involved response techniques.

After the simple shared reading described above, Peter Elbow and Pat Belanoff suggest that the listeners (the response group) employ the "sayback" technique: after listening to or reading the writer's draft, the response group tries to restate the effect of the text on the audience in the form of a question. Responses like "Do you mean. . . ?" and "Are you trying to show. . . ?" serve as invitations for the writer to continue developing or even inventing ideas (13). When the writer replies, "Yes, I was trying to explain . . ." and expresses the text's ideas with newfound clarity, then Bruffee's conversational model of writing has been enacted. Benjamin Glassner and Kenneth Kantor have found that audience awareness and revision improve as writing is fostered within these small communities. And Nina Ziv has found that the initial comments in peer-response groups tend to be primarily positive, but as collaborative groups stabilize and members begin to trust one another, more critical comments are made and heeded.

In *Sharing and Responding*, Elbow and Belanoff offer several more-demanding response techniques. Descriptive responding consists of "pointing" to memorable or striking features of a text; "summarizing," which restates the main meaning, suggesting ideas "almost said" but undeveloped or even unstated; and locating the "center of gravity," the point that seems to generate the writing (15-16). For more persuasive or argumentative writing, analytic responding

---

[10] See Chapter 3 of this book and Chapters 1, 3, and 4 of *The St. Martin's Handbook* for information that can help your students work fruitfully in writing groups.

involves noticing how the writer initially gets the reader "listening" and interested in the subject; identifying the main claim, the reasons provided, and additional or counter supports; and considering the intended audience, the tone of the text, and the assumed attitude of the audience. Both of these response techniques are designed to encourage peer comments on broader issues of form and style and the content of the text rather than a premature concentration on mechanical correctness; consequently, peer response should not be confused with "peer editing," which involves proofreading. Many variations on peer response are possible, such as submitting a student's draft for comments by the entire class and having the class respond in writing as well as orally in response groups during class, at conferences, or outside class at mutually convenient times.

In addition to supporting students' writing with guided-response techniques, writing teachers are also paying attention to the importance of allowing students to develop their own language with which to discuss their writing (Trimbur 104). Especially for minority and nontraditional students, collaborative learning and writing groups can provide a transitional social unit that eases students' access to the new discourse community by assisting their competency in the language of the community, whose discourse and knowledge they want or need to master (DeCiccio 4). By participating in these transitional, collaborative groups, students develop what Eleanor Kutz has termed "interlanguage," a jargon mixing students' everyday language and academic discourse, before internalizing the conventions and the content of the desired discourse—in our case, FY writing.

Such transitions are often problematic and arduous, as is collaborative learning in general. Learning the details and conventions of a new discourse is demanding and may not come quickly. You and your students will have to work hard to identify and use correctly even some of the more obvious conventions of academic and intellectual discourse. And you will need to model effective collaboration for your students all the time. Peer workshops and writing groups are effective means of introducing students to the discourse community,[11] but you must provide additional support as students evolve for themselves an understanding of the criteria for good writing.

Leslie Moore and Linda Peterson, in "Convention as Connection," and Elaine Maimon and her coauthors in *Writing in the Arts and Sciences*, have proposed using rhetorical analysis, also known as discourse analysis, to initiate students into academic discourse. Moore and Peterson claim that rhetorical analysis quickly and effectively helps students understand both obvious and subtle requirements of a particular academic discourse. By increasing students' comprehension of the various academic discourses and their attendant conventions, it also helps students begin to realize how they, too, have been socially constructed.

Rhetorical analysis treats convention not as "merely" superficial rules of style: according to the social constructionists' insistent marriage of form and con-

[11] See Chapter 3.

tent, conventions are inseparably linked to the epistemological assumptions of an academic discipline. For example, Moore and Peterson ask their students to discern the conventions of a laboratory report, such as its seven-part structure, the use of the past tense to present data in the results section, the use of the present tense to present the interpretation of data in the discussion section, and the frequent use of the passive voice to de-emphasize the role of the experimenter and to highlight the data. They then encourage students to speculate on what these discourse conventions reveal about "what the discipline believes constitutes evidence, about what it considers [to be] a legitimate presentation of evidence, [and] the stance of the researcher in relation to evidence" (469). To implement this initiation into academic discourse through rhetorical analysis, Moore and Peterson ask colleagues in other departments to suggest well-written scholarly essays that exemplify the conventions of their academic disciplines. These extradepartmental colleagues are also asked to help devise realistic assignments resembling those given in the introductory courses of their departments and to participate in a class discussion on their academic discipline and its conventions.

Moore and Peterson also train their students in invention techniques, rhetorical analysis, and strategies for collaborative revision. They generally devote two to three weeks to analyzing a particular academic discourse. To begin, students read and analyze the sample essays, each time using the same questions: "What do we notice about structure? What do we notice about style? What do we notice about the strategies for presenting evidence? the kinds of evidence that are allowed, the kinds of presentations of evidence that are missing?" (472). Then, with a professor representing the academic discipline, they discuss their conclusions about the discourse conventions of the discipline, and examine the problems of composing that are created by the inseparable epistemological assumptions and discourse conventions.

Such assignments illustrate the clear relationship between social-constructionist pedagogy and the important and growing writing-across-the-curriculum movement, particularly in terms of their constructive effects on the teaching of composition. For instance, both affirm the importance of the teacher as an essential member of an academic discipline who helps to perpetuate and revitalize the enabling conventions of the discourse community and as an initiator of new members who empowers students by supplementing—not supplanting—their familial and communal discourse conventions. Bartholomae warns that when a student appropriates an academic discourse, she can also be appropriated by that discourse, as Richard Rodriguez has depicted in his autobiography, *Hunger of Memory*. But almost every person belongs to more than one discourse community already and can learn to operate biculturally.

Many advocates of social-constructionist pedagogy in composition hope that the mastery of academic discourse will ultimately foster in students the "critical consciousness" of Paulo Freire's liberation pedagogy. For Freire, the context of socially constructed knowledge includes the social forces and power relationships of a community of like-minded peers, and the discourse replicates these cultural and political structures. Mastery of several forms of discourse can culminate in Freire's critical consciousness, which empowers students by making them aware that a discourse community's language and thought patterns (and its corresponding cultural and political structures) are neither fundamental nor universal. They are all socially constructed and, therefore, alterable.

The politics implicit in social construction also affects pedagogy. Bruffee contends that although memories of subject matter may fade, students "do not easily forget the experience of learning it and the values implicit in the conventions by which it is taught" (qtd. in Trimbur 94). This "hidden curriculum" represents the content of a course as much as its formal subject matter, for it shapes students' assumptions about knowledge, learning, and power relations. The practices of collaborative learning, validated by the theory of social constructionism, can reveal this hidden curriculum and engage students in Bruffee's conversational pedagogy.

Social construction and collaborative learning are currently much more a philosophical and political mindset than a completely developed pedagogy. The debate they raise about the purpose and uses of learning is ongoing, however, and crucial to our understanding of what it means to teach about communication. This debate has been serving to make us aware of the larger questions that always loom behind the seemingly simple pedagogical decisions we make whenever we presume to teach anyone how to write.

WORKS CITED

Abercrombie, M. L. J. *Anatomy of Judgment.* Harmondsworth, England: Penguin, 1960.

Barritt, Loren, and Barry Kroll. "Some Implications of Cognitive-Developmental Psychology for Research in Composing." *Research on Composing: Points of Departure.* Ed. Charles Cooper and Lee Odell. Urbana, IL: NCTE, 1978.

Bartholomae, David. "Inventing the University." *When a Writer Can't Write: Research on Writer's Block and Other Writing Process Problems.* Ed. Mike Rose. New York: Guilford, 1986.

———. "The Study of Error." *CCC* 31 (1980): 253–69.

Bartholomae, David, and Anthony Petrosky. *Facts, Artifacts, and Counterfacts.* Portsmouth, NH: Heinemann, 1986.

Bazerman, Charles. "What Written Knowledge Does: Three Examples of Academic Discourse." *Philosophy of the Social Sciences* 11 (1981): 361–87.

Beach, Richard. "Self-Evaluation Strategies of Extensive Revisers and Non-Revisers." *CCC* 27 (1976): 160–64.

Bissex, Glenda. *Gnys at Wrk: A Child Learns to Write and Read.* Cambridge, MA: Harvard UP, 1980.

Bizzell, Patricia. "Academic Discourse: Taxonomy of Conventions or Collaborative Practice?" *CCCC* paper (1986): ERIC ED270806.

———."Cognition, Convention, and Certainty: What We Need to Know about Writing." *PRETEXT* 3 (1983): 213–43.

———. "Thomas Kuhn, Scientism, and English Studies." *CE* 40 (1979): 764–71.

Bridwell, Lillian. "Revising Strategies in Twelfth-Grade Students' Transactional Writing." *Research in Teaching of English* 14 (1980): 197–222.

Britton, James, Tony Burgess, Nancy Martin, Alex McLeod, and Harold Rosen. *The Development of Writing Abilities (11–18).* Basingstoke, England: Macmillan Education, 1975.

Bruffee, Kenneth. "Collaborative Learning and 'The Conversation of Mankind.' " *CE* 46 (1984): 635-52.

——."Liberal Education and the Social Justification of Belief." *Liberal Education* 68 (1982): 95-114.

——. *A Short Course in Writing*. 3rd ed. Boston: Little, 1985.

——. "Social Construction, Language, and the Authority of Knowledge." *CE* 48 (1986): 773-90.

——. "Writing and Reading as Collaborative or Social Act." *The Writer's Mind: Writing as a Mode of Thinking*. Eds. Janice Hays, Phyllis Roth, Jon Ramsey, and Robert Foulke. Urbana, IL: NCTE, 1983. 159-70.

Bruner, Jerome. *The Process of Education*. Cambridge, MA: Harvard UP, 1960.

Daly, John. "Writing Apprehension and Writing Competency." *Journal of Educational Research* 72 (1978): 10-14.

DeCiccio, Albert. "Social Constructionism and Collaborative Learning: Recommendations for Teaching Writing." *CCCC* paper (1988): ERIC ED294201.

Ede, Lisa. "The Case for Collaboration." *CCCC* paper (1987): ERIC ED282212.

——."What Is Social about Writing as a Social Process?" *CCCC* paper (1988): ERIC ED293151.

Elbow, Peter. "Reflections on Academic Discourse." *CE* 53 (1991): 135-55.

——. *Writing without Teachers*. New York: Oxford UP, 1973.

——. *Writing with Power*. New York: Oxford UP, 1981.

Elbow, Peter, and Pat Belanoff. *Sharing and Responding*. New York: Random, 1989.

Emig, Janet. *The Composing Processes of Twelfth Graders*. Urbana, IL: NCTE, 1971.

——. *The Web of Meaning*. Portsmouth, NH: Boynton/Cook, 1983.

Faigley, Lester, and Stephen Witte. "Analyzing Revision." *CCC* 32 (Dec. 1981): 400-14.

Fish, Stanley. *Is There a Text in This Class? The Authority of Interpretive Communities*. Cambridge, MA: Harvard UP, 1980.

Flower, Linda."The Construction of Purpose in Writing and Reading." *CE* 50 (1988): 528-50.

——. *Problem-Solving Strategies for Writing*. New York: Harcourt, 1981.

——. "Writer-Based Prose: A Cognitive Basis for Problems in Writing." *CE* 41 (1979): 19-37.

Flower, Linda, and John Hayes. "A Cognitive Process Theory of Writing." *CCC* 32 (1981): 365-87.

——."The Dynamics of Composing: Making Plans and Juggling Constraints." Gregg and Steinberg 31-50.

——."Problem-Solving Strategies and the Writing Process." *CE* 39 (1977): 449-62.

——."The Pregnant Pause: An Inquiry into the Nature of Planning." *Research in the Teaching of English* 15 (1981): 229-44.

Flower, Linda, John Hayes, and Heidi Swarts. "Designing Protocol Studies of the Writing Process." *New Directions in Composition Research*. Ed. Richard Beach and Lillian Bridwell. New York: Guilford, 1984. 53-71.

Freire, Paulo. *Pedagogy of the Oppressed*. New York: Seabury, 1968.

Geertz, Clifford. *The Interpretation of Cultures*. New York: Basic, 1973.

——. *Local Knowledge*. New York: Basic, 1983.

George, Diana. "Working with Peer Groups in the Composition Classroom." *CCC* 35 (1984): 320-26.

Gere, Anne Ruggles. *Writing Groups*. Carbondale: Southern Illinois UP, 1987.

Glassner, Benjamin. "Discovering Audience/Inventing Purpose." *CCCC* paper (1983): ERIC ED227513.

Graves, Donald. "How Children Change in the Writing Process." National Institute of Education Study. Periodic reports appear in the "Research Update" section of *Language Arts* (1978-80).

Gregg, Lee, and Erwin Steinberg, eds. *Cognitive Processes in Writing: An Interdisciplinary Approach*. Hillsdale, NJ: Erlbaum, 1980.

Harris, Joseph. "The Idea of Community in the Study of Writing." *CCC* 40 (1989): 11-22.

Heath, Shirley Brice. *Ways with Words*. Cambridge: Cambridge UP, 1983.

Hermann, Andrea. "Teaching Writing with Peer Response Groups." ERIC ED307616.

Hirsch, E.D. *Cultural Literacy*. Boston: Houghton, 1987.

Kantor, Kenneth. "Classroom Contexts and the Development of Writing Intuitions." *New Directions in Composition Research*. Ed. Richard Beach and Lillian Bridwell Bowles. New York: Guilford, 1984.

Knoblauch, C. H., and Lil Brannon. *Rhetorical Traditions and the Teaching of Writing*. Upper Montclair, NJ: Boynton/Cook, 1984.

Kroll, Barry. "Writing for Readers." *CCC* 35 (1984): 112-85.

Kroll, Barry, and John Schafer. "Error Analysis and the Teaching of Composition." *CCC* 29 (1978): 242-48.

Kuhn, Thomas. *The Structure of Scientific Revolutions*. 2nd ed. Chicago: U. of Chicago, 1970.

Kutz, Eleanor. "Between Students' Language and Academic Discourse." *CE* 48 (1986): 385-96.

LeFevre, Karen Burke. *Invention as a Social Act*. Carbondale: Southern Illinois UP, 1987.

Leonard, Sterling. *English Composition as a Social Problem*. Boston: Houghton, 1917.

Lindemann, Erika. *A Rhetoric for Writing Teachers,* 2nd ed. New York: Oxford UP, 1987.

Lunsford, Andrea. "Cognitive Development and the Basic Writer." *CE* 41 (1979): 38-46.

——. "Cognitive Studies and Teaching Writing." McClelland and Donovan 145-61.

Lunsford, Andrea, and Lisa Ede. "Why Write . . . Together?" *Rhetoric Review* 1 (1983): 150-58.

Luria, A. R. *Cognitive Development: Its Cultural and Social Foundations*. Cambridge, MA: Harvard UP, 1976.

McClelland, Ben, and Tim Donovan, eds. *Perspectives on Research and Scholarship in Composition*. New York: MLA, 1985.

Macrorie, Ken. *Writing to Be Read*. Rochelle, NJ: Hayden, 1968.

Maimon, Elaine, et al. *Writing in the Arts and Sciences*. Boston: Winthrop/Little, 1981.

Mason, Edwin. *Collaborative Learning*. London: Ward, 1970.

Matsuhashi, Ann. "Pausing and Planning: The Tempo of Written Discourse Production." *Research in the Teaching of English* 15 (1981): 113-34.

Moffett, James. *Active Voice: A Writing Program across the Curriculum*. Portsmouth, NH: Boynton/Cook, 1981.

——. *A Student-Centered Language Arts Curriculum*. Boston: Houghton, 1968.

——. *Teaching the Universe of Discourse*. 1968. Portsmouth, NH: Boynton/Cook, 1983.

Moore, Leslie, and Linda Peterson. "Convention as Connection: Linking the Composition Course to the English and College Curriculum." *CCC* 37 (1986): 466-77.

Murray, Donald. *A Writer Teaches Writing*. Boston: Houghton, 1968.

Myers, Greg. "Comment and Response." *CE* 49 (1987): 211-14.

Newkirk, Thomas. "Direction and Misdirection in Peer Response." *CCC* 35 (1984): 301-11.

Nystrand, Martin. "A Social-Interactive Model of Writing." *Written Communication* 6 (1989): 66-85.

Perl, Sondra. "The Composing Process of Unskilled College Writers." *Research in the Teaching of English* 13 (1979): 317-36.

——. "Understanding Composing." *CCC* 31 (1980): 363-69.

Piaget, Jean. *The Language and Thought of the Child*. New York: World 1926/55.

Pianko, Sharon. "A Description of the Composing Processes of College Freshmen Writers." *Research in the Teaching of English* 13 (1979): 5-22.

Reither, James. "Academic Discourse Communities, Invention, and Learning to Write." *CCCC* paper (1986).

Rohman, D. Gordon. "Pre-Writing: The Stage of Discovery in the Writing Process." *CCC* 16 (1965): 106-12.

Rorty, Richard. *Philosophy and the Mirror of Nature*. Princeton, NJ: Princeton UP, 1979.

Rose, Mike. "Rigid Rules, Inflexible Plans, and the Stifling of Language: A Cognitivist Analysis of Writer's Block." *CCC* 39 (1980): 389-400.

——. "Remedial Writing Courses: A Critique and a Proposal." *CE* 45 (1983): 109-28.

——. *When A Writer Can't Write: Studies in Writer's Block and Other Composing Problems.* New York: Guilford, 1985.

——. *Writer's Block: The Cognitive Dimension.* Carbondale: Southern Illinois UP, 1984.

Scardamalia, Marlene, Carl Bereiter, and Hillel Goelman. "The Role of Production Factors in Writing Ability." *What Writers Know: The Language, Process, and Structures of Academic Discourse.* Ed. Martin Nystrand. New York: Academic, 1982. 173-210.

Selzer, Jack. "Exploring Options in Composing." *CCC* 35 (1984): 276-84.

Shaughnessy, Mina. *Errors & Expectations: A Guide for Teachers of Basic Writing.* New York: Oxford UP, 1977.

Smith, Michael. *Reducing Writing Apprehension.* Urbana, IL: NCTE, 1984.

Sommers, Nancy I. "The Need for Theory in Composition Research." *CCC* 30 (1979): 46-49.

——. "Revision Strategies of Student Writers and Experienced Adult Writers." *CCC* 31 (1980): 378-88.

Stallard, Charles. "An Analysis of the Writing Behavior of Good Student Writers." *Research in the Teaching of English* 8 (1974): 206-18.

Trimbur, John. "Collaborative Learning and Teaching Writing." McClelland and Donovan. 87-109.

Voss, Ralph. "Reassessment of Janet Emig's Composing Processes of Twelfth Graders." *CCC* 34 (1983): 278-83.

Vygotsky, Lev. *Mind in Society.* Ed. Michael Cole. Cambridge, MA: Harvard UP, 1978.

——. *Thought and Language.* Cambridge, MA: MIT, 1962.

Witte, Stephen. "Pre-Text and Composing." *CCC* 38 (1987): 397-425.

Zoellner, Robert, "Talk-Write: A Behavioral Pedagogy for Composition." *CE* 30 (1969): 267-320.

7 TEACHING INVENTION

Invention, the central, indispensable canon of rhetoric, traditionally meant a systematic search for arguments. In composition classes, it has become a much broader term: it has become the writer's search for the *thesis,* the central informing idea of a piece of writing, and for all the *supporting material* that will illustrate, exemplify, or prove the validity of that thesis. Without content, there can be no effective communication, and invention is the process that supplies writers and speakers with their content material.

Invention is particularly important in college writing courses because it helps students *generate* and *select from* material they will write about (Lauer, *Invention* 3). This process is often difficult, especially for students who have had little practice at it. When faced with a writing assignment, many students are troubled not by the lack of a subject or topic (often one is supplied) but by a seeming lack of anything important or coherent to say about it. Invention comes into play here, providing processes by which the student can analyze the assigned or chosen subject in order to discover things to say.

Most serious and experienced writers have incorporated into their habits some system of invention that they use to plan and carry out their writing. For many this is a subconscious process, and to them, theories of, and suggestions for, teaching invention as a conscious activity may seem artificial.

Such discomfort with artificial systems is not new. The history of rhetoric is characterized by a continuing disagreement about the usefulness of systems and topics.[1] On the one hand are the idealists, rhetorical theorists who believe there can be no meaningful communication unless the speaker or writer is broadly educated, trained in philosophy, morals, ethics, and politics, and possessed of natural intellectual ability. For a person of this order, systems and topics might be secondarily useful, for subject matter flows primarily from individual meditations and wisdom rather than from any artificial system of discovery. On the other hand are the realists, whose greatest spokesman is Aristotle. The realists are aware that not everyone who needs to communicate possesses the broad educational background necessary to produce subject matter from personal resources: many people need an external system to consult in order to probe their subjects and discover subject matter and arguments.

The systems of invention presented in this chapter will provide that assistance. Most FY students have had little opportunity to practice serious, ex-

---

[1] For a useful survey of rhetorical invention through history, see Harrington.

tended, coherent writing, and (a no longer surprising) few of them have read even two books in the past year. Clearly, many of our students are in need of training in invention; without some introduction to the techniques of discovering subject matter and arguments, they might flounder all term in a morass of vague assertions and unsupported, ill-thought-out papers. They need a system that will buoy them until they can swim by themselves.

The revival of rhetorical theory witnessed since the early 1960s has reacquainted teachers with the primary elements of the rhetorical tradition—*ethos*/writer; *pathos*/audience; *logos*/text—and with the way these elements of the rhetorical triangle have been played out in the canon of rhetoric. Close attention to the writer has resulted in much important work that attempts essentially to answer this twofold question: Where do a writer's ideas come from, and how are they formulated in writing? Such a question demands a new focus on invention, the first canon of rhetoric, and has led in two provocative and profitable directions.

The first, represented in the work of Richard Young and Janice Lauer (to name only two), aims at deriving heuristic procedures or systematic strategies that will aid students in discovering and generating ideas about which they might write. Such strategies may be as simple as asking students about a subject: *who? what? when? where? why?* and *how?*—the traditional journalistic formula. Or they can be as complex as the nine-cell matrix presented in Young, Becker, and Pike's *Rhetoric: Discovery and Change*. Essentially this heuristic asks students to look at any subject from different perspectives. For example, a student writing about a campus demonstration might look at it as a "happening" frozen in time and space, as the result of a complex set of causes, as a cause of certain effects, or as one tiny part of a larger economic pattern. Looking at a subject in such different ways loosens up the mind and jogs writers out of a unidimensional, or tunnel-vision, view of a subject.

We see the interest in procedural heuristics as related theoretically to the work of researchers interested in cognition. Co-authors Linda Flower and John Hayes are best known for their studies of writers' talk-aloud protocols, tape-recorded documents that catch a writer's thoughts about writing while the writing is actually in progress.[2] In "Interpretive Acts," Flower and Hayes discuss a schema of discourse construction comprising social context, discourse conventions, language purposes and goals, and the activated knowledge of both the reader and the writer. The writer and the reader balance these elements in order to create and recreate a text.

Stephen Witte has recently built on the work of Flower and Hayes in order to study what he calls a writer's *pretext*, a writer's "trial locution that is produced in the mind, stored in the writer's memory, and sometimes manipulated mentally prior to being transcribed as written text" (397). Other researchers have attempted to map the relationship of affective factors to a writer's invention: John Daly has done so in terms of writing apprehension ("Message En-

---

[2] See Chapter 6.

coding" and "Writing Competency"); Mike Rose has done so in terms of writer's block. All of this research aims to help teachers understand the rich, diverse, complex, and largely invisible processes students go through in their writing.

The second direction in which the interest in invention has led is characterized most notably by the work of Ken Macrorie and, more pervasively, Peter Elbow. Elbow is interested in how writers establish unique voices, in how they realize individual selves in discourse, and his work with students presents dramatic evidence of such activity. In a series of influential books (*Writing without Teachers, Writing with Power,* and *Embracing Contraries*), he focuses on how writers come to know themselves and then share those selves with others.

The researchers and teachers surveyed in this chapter differ from one another in many ways, but they are alike in that their work is aimed primarily at that point of the rhetorical triangle that focuses on the writer's powers of invention. They want to know what makes writers tick and how teachers can help writers "tick" most effectively.

In this chapter, *invention* will deal with the development and expansion of three different but closely related elements: the *thesis statement,* a declarative sentence that serves as the backbone of an essay; the *subject matter,* which fills out, expands, and amplifies the thesis; and the *argument,* a specialized form of subject matter consisting of persuasive demonstrations of points the writer wishes to prove. Some of the techniques discussed here will work best for one or two of these elements, some for all three. You will easily see the characteristics of each technique, and you can choose those you wish to adapt according to what you want your students to learn. Before reviewing the techniques of invention, though, you should be aware of a few facts about invention as a whole.

Nearly all the systems of invention covered in this chapter can be called *heuristic,* or questioning, systems.[3] In her important study of invention, contemporary rhetorical theorist Lauer defines heuristic procedure

> as a conscious and non-rigorous search model which explores a creative problem for seminal elements of a solution. The exploratory function of the procedure includes generative and evaluative powers: the model generously proposes solutions but also efficiently evaluates these solutions so that a decision can be made. Heuristic procedures must be distinguished from trial-and-error methods which are non-systematic and, hence, inefficient, and from rule-governed procedures which are rigorous and exhaustive processes involving a finite number of steps which infallibly produce the right solution. ("Invention" 4)

Although the systems described here differ widely in their approaches, with few exceptions they fit Lauer's definition.

In "Heuristics and Composition" (1970), Lauer asserted that composition needed to appropriate theories from other fields if this emerging discipline is ever to establish a respectable theoretical foundation. She suggests that com-

---

[3] The Greek word *heuresis* means "finding" and is related to Archimedes' cry of *Eureka!* "I have found it!".

position researchers and teachers should consult the extensive bibliography of psychological research on heuristics, which comprises most of her eight-page article. The works she cites include pioneering studies and contemporary research, such as Herbert Simon, Cliff Shaw, and Allen Newell's cognitive investigations which greatly influenced Flower and Hayes's composition research.

Lauer's suggestion sparked a lively exchange between her and Ann Berthoff, in which the two debated the benefits, the drawbacks, and the philosophical and political basis of heuristics. In her 1971 response, aptly entitled "The Problem of Problem Solving," Berthoff condemned heuristics as an indoctrination of mechanical procedures that serve a bureaucratic and technological society, and she critiqued the researcher's failure to consider adequately the relationship between language and the world. In her "Response," Lauer replied that problem-solving strategies were not a dictatorial procedure to find "the right solution, the correct answer," using "a finite number of steps governed by explicit rules" (209). She defined heuristics as open-ended, "systematic, yet flexible guides to effective guessing" that seek reasonable answers (209).

In her 1979 "Towards a Metatheory of Heuristic Procedures," Lauer proposes that the best invention techniques need to be applicable to a wide variety of writing situations so that they will transcend a particular topic and can be internalized by the student. They also should be flexible in their direction so that a thinker can return to a previous step or skip to an inviting one as the evolving idea suggests. Finally, they should be highly generative, by involving the writer in various operations—such as visualizing, classifying, defining, rearranging, and dividing—that are known to stimulate insights.

In "Piaget, Problem-Solving, and Freshmen Composition," Lee Odell asserts the need for, and the limitation of, teaching problem-solving strategies—because writing is "an aspect of a person's general intellectual development and cannot be fostered apart from that development," but "there can be no quick and painless way to develop a well-stocked mind, a disciplined intelligence, and a discriminating taste in language and fluency in its use" (36, 42). Heuristics can help fill the gap between the knowledge of all and everything that the ideal writer possesses and practical inability to use all of those resources.

In judging the heuristic procedures that this chapter discusses, you can run each one through the set of questions Lauer has developed to test heuristics. The three characteristics possessed by the best heuristic procedures, she says, are *transcendency*, *flexible order*, and *generative capacity*. Put into question form, the test of a heuristic model looks like this.

1. Can writers transfer this model's questions or operations from one subject to another?
2. Does this model offer writers a direction of movement which is flexible and sensitive to the rhetorical situation?
3. Does this model engage writers in diverse kinds of heuristic procedures? ("Toward a Methodology" 269)

Before you choose a system, you might try applying this test to it.

All seven systems described in this chapter are discrete. You can choose one and ignore the others; you can use several concurrently or at different times. Since invention is a central skill in composition, you will want to introduce some system near the beginning of the course; otherwise, you may not have a coherent framework on which to hang the other elements you teach. Your students can practice some of these methods (for example, prewriting, freewriting, and brainstorming) with you in class. They can use the other methods at home, after you have introduced them in classroom exercises. Ideally, your students will gradually assimilate these systems of invention into their subconscious, recalling them when needed.

The goal, then, is to make these artificial systems of discovery so much a part of the way students think about problems that the systems become second nature. Truly efficient writing is almost always done intuitively and then, at the revision stage, checked against models for completeness and correctness. We cannot expect that the process of subconscious assimilation will be completed in ten or fifteen weeks, but if a system of invention is conscientiously taught and practiced for that period of time, it will at least become a useful tool for students to fall back on in other classes, and eventually it may become part of their thought process.

CLASSICAL TOPICAL INVENTION

The tradition of classical rhetoric, as it developed from Aristotle and Cicero and then was codified by Quintilian, is the only complete system that we will deal with in this book, and it remains one of the most definitive methodologies ever evolved by the Western mind. The rhetoric of the Renaissance was largely informed by it. Even the epistemological rhetoric of the eighteenth century is far less coherent as a system than is classical rhetoric in its finished form. In contrast to classical rhetoric, the "New Rhetoric" of the twentieth century is in its infancy, with many workable techniques but no informing paradigmatic structure. Many books have been devoted to analyzing and explaining the structure and usefulness of the classical rhetorical tradition, but for our purposes, only a few elements of classical theory are useful.

The classical technique that we will concentrate on as an aid to invention is that of the *topics*, or seats of argument. This technique can be used to conceptualize and formulate the single-sentence declarative thesis that usually constitutes the backbone of a FY essay, and it can also be used to invent subject matter and arguments. Remember, though, that all classical techniques were originally devoted to the creation of persuasive discourse and that classical invention works most naturally in an argumentative mode; it should not be expected to work as well for nonexpository prose.

Aristotle is responsible for our first introduction to the *topics* or "seats of argument," but his doctrine was continued and amplified by the other classical rhetoricians. The topics were conceived of as actual mental "places" (the term itself comes from geography) to which the rhetorician could go to find arguments.

The system of topics described here is a modern arrangement of classical topical invention adapted from the work of Edward P. J. Corbett, Richard P. Hughes, P. Albert Duhamel, and other teachers at the University of Chicago (including Bilsky et al.). These topics are not so much places to go for ready-made arguments as they are ways of probing one's subject in order to find the means to develop that subject. The four common topics that are most useful to students are *definition, analogy, consequence,* and *testimony.*

Definition The topic of definition involves the creation of a thesis by taking a fact or an idea and expanding on it by precisely identifying its nature. The subject can be referred to its class, or *genus,* and the argument made that whatever is true of the genus is true of the species: "A single-payer national health plan is a socialist policy—and should therefore be classed with other socialist policies." A far less powerful and less sophisticated form of definition is "the argument from the word"—the use of dictionary or etymological meanings to define things or ideas. For many beginning writers, the dictionary definition is the easiest place to begin.

Analogy The topic of analogy is concerned with discovering resemblances or differences between two or more things, proceeding from known to unknown. It should always be kept in mind that no analogy is perfect and that all deal in probabilities. Nonetheless, analogy is a useful tool for investigating comparisons and contrasts: "The first week of college is like the first week of boot camp." Another type of analogical reasoning is the argument from contraries, or *negative analogy:* "The marijuana laws are unlike Prohibition." Although analogy is often thought of only as a figure of speech, it is an important tool of demonstration as well.

Consequence The topic of consequence investigates phenomena in a cause-to-effect or effect-to-cause pattern. The best use of consequence is in the prediction of probabilities from patterns that have previously occurred: "Inability to prevent clan warfare led to the failure of the United Nations peacekeeping effort in Somalia." The topic of consequence is prone to two fallacies. The first is the fallacy of *post hoc, ergo propter hoc,* "after this, therefore because of this." Just because one element precedes another element does not mean that the former is the cause of the latter. An extreme example of this fallacy might be "The first human-powered flight led to the failure of the United Nations peacekeeping effort in Somalia." The second fallacy, *a priori,* claims but does not demonstrate a cause-and-effect relationship between two phenomena.

Testimony The topic of testimony relies on appeals to an authority, some external source of argumentation. For example, the authority could be an expert opinion, statistics, or the law. This topic is not as useful today as it once may have been: our controversial age produced so many authorities whose views are in conflict with one another that all too often they cancel one another out, and celebrities often give paid—and therefore untrustworthy—testimony, in the form of advertising. Still, testimony can be a good starting place for an argument, especially when students have a familiarity with, and an understanding of, the source of the testimony.

Let us look first at teaching the use of the topics in general and then at the task of familiarizing students with their use in generating theses, subject matter, and arguments.

Using Classical Topical Invention in the Classroom

Classical invention takes just a short time to teach because it is elegantly simple. Students are often impressed when they learn the background of the technique—at last, a high-level classical skill!—and use it with enthusiasm once they have learned to apply the different terms.

Ultimately, a thesis or an argument must say something about the real world. In teaching the topics, this means using examples. Good examples are to be had by applying each topic to a definite subject and coming up with several thesis statements. You may want to pass out examples for students to have in front of them as they begin to create their own theses. You won't find that drawing theses from the topic is difficult for you. In the following discussion of the siege of Sarajevo and "political correctness," run through the topical-thesis mechanism.

Definition   Definition always answers the question, "What is/was it?" asked in a variety of contexts. The subject can be defined in its immediate context, in a larger context, in different settings, in space, in time, or in a moral continuum. Here are some examples.

The siege of Sarajevo was the longest battle of the Bosnian war.

The siege of Sarajevo was a damaging defeat for the Serbians.

The siege of Sarajevo was a tragedy of errors in command on both sides.

The siege of Sarajevo was a rallying point for the Bosnians.

"Political Correctness" is a scourge sweeping our campuses.

"Political Correctness" is a fiction created by right-wingers.

"Political Correctness" is supported by Teachers for a Democratic Culture.

"Political Correctness" is becoming increasingly widespread.

Analogy   Analogy always asks the question "What is it like or unlike?" and the topic of the analogy usually answers the question by explaining a lesser-known element in the context of a better-known element. Because of its explanatory nature, at least one side of the analogical topic statement is often historical or general, as in these examples.

Sarajevo was a Pyrrhic victory for the Bosnians.

The siege of Sarajevo was for Milosevic what Waterloo was for Napoleon.

In tactics, the siege of Sarajevo was completely unlike the siege of Stalingrad. [negative analogy]

The U.N. airlift of supplies to Sarajevo was the post-Cold War version of the Berlin airlift of the 1960s.

"Political Correctness" is the new McCarthyism.

"Political Correctness" is a slogan used by the same people who called the Nicaraguan contras "freedom fighters."

The "Political Correctness" uproar is much like that created by Swift's "Modest Proposal."

People in favor of "Political Correctness" are not at all similar to the anti-communist witch-hunters of the 1950s. [negative analogy]

Consequence   Consequence always answers the question, "What caused/ causes/will cause it?" or "What did it cause/is it causing/will it cause?" It is not a topic to be taken lightly because, even in a thesis statement, it demands that the writer trace the chains of consequence to the end. Consequence can be either explanatory or predictive.

The siege of Sarajevo lost the Serbians much territory in eastern Bosnia.

Superior military stockpiles allowed the Serbian army to carry on the siege of Sarajevo even as the Serbian economy melted down.

If the Serbs had taken Sarajevo, the Bosnian Muslims would have been driven into Croatia.

If the airlift had been interrupted for long, the Bosnians would have been forced out of Sarajevo.

If "Political Correctness" candidates are elected to the student senate, the Greek system will be abolished.

If the outcry about "Political Correctness" continues unquestioned, all progressive gains on campus will be in danger.

The demand for "Political Correctness" arose when feminists and gay-rights activists first got into positions of power.

The controversy over "Political Correctness" is the result of a sophisticated PR campaign started by the Heritage Foundation in 1989.

Testimony   Testimony always answers the question "What does an author-ity say about it?" Authorities can range from experts and statistics to eyewit-nesses and accepted wisdom.

Radovan Karajic considers the siege of Sarajevo to be the most important battle of the Bosnian war.

With three Bosnian casualties for every Serb casualty, the siege of Sarajevo was more crippling to the defenders than to the attackers. [reliance on statistics]

Lord Owen, the UN negotiator, called Sarajevo the pivot of the entire Bosnian war.

The Serbian tactics were indefensible, for common sense demands that a besieged city not be resupplied. [accepted wisdom]

Former president Reagan says that "Political Correctness" is the most dangerous cultural movement since the New Left.

At universities known for their "Political Correctness," claims of sexual harassment have gone up by 35 percent. [reliance on statistics]

Everyone agrees that "Political Correctness" has been overexposed in the popular media. [accepted wisdom]

Susan Faludi has written that "political correctness charges are just another tactic of the far right to roll back the rights of women."

These are just a few of the theses available for each topic. Using the topics to create theses demands some immediate knowledge of the subject, but students will derive theses and argumentative lines that are very specific. You can also see that some topics will be more fruitful than others. The topics of definition, analogy, and consequence are the most useful for creating theses, whereas testimony is most naturally suited to the buttressing of already created theses.

The topics are not magic formulas that can make something out of nothing, but they are useful in organizing masses of information. Students need not have more than a layperson's knowledge of the siege of Sarajevo or "Political Correctness" to come up with the thesis statements above, but after having created these theses, they will know more clearly what they do know. They will also have a much better idea of where they need to go to look up information they do not have at hand.

As you work through the topics in class, spend enough time on each of the first three (testimony is more specialized) to allow your students to digest the examples you have provided and to see the process by which you arrived at the statements under each topic. You may want to pass out a photocopied sheet with the examples of the topics in action on a particular subject. This process takes only a couple of days. After you have explained the examples and shown how they derive from the topics, assign a few subjects, and ask students to use the topical system to come up with at least three theses for each topic (perhaps nine theses in all). After this assignment has been written, either in class or as homework, ask students to volunteer to read their theses aloud in class. If the class has been successful, the next step is to ask students to come up with ideas for an essay on a topic relevant to one of the other classes they are currently enrolled in and to apply classical topical invention to that subject. They should be comfortable enough with the system at this point—perhaps even openly pleased with it—to be able to reel off theses for other subjects without much trouble.

Once students have successfully used the topics to produce theses, they will readily see how they can use them to generate supporting subject matter. After they have chosen their thesis from among the myriad possibilities that the topical system offers, they are left with many other statements that are at least indicators of other informational lodes. Very often after choosing a thesis, students can structure their essays around other thesis statements that they need change only slightly to make them subordinate to the main purpose of their essays.

If you have the time in class, ask your students to put together a rough topic outline of a projected essay by arranging as many of the theses they have generated as possible in an order that could be used to structure an essay (remind them that often they may have to change the direction of the theses slightly to subordinate them to the main thesis). Here is an example of such a rough list-outline using some of the theses generated about "Political Correctness."

Main thesis: "Political Correctness" is a fiction created by right-wingers.

Subordinate thesis 1:	The "Political Correctness" controversy is the result of a sophisticated PR campaign started by the Heritage Foundation in 1989.
Subordinate thesis 2:	"Political Correctness" is a slogan used by the same people who called the Nicaraguan contras "freedom fighters."
Minor thesis:	Former president Reagan says that "Political Correctness" is the most dangerous cultural movement since the New Left.
Subordinate thesis 3:	If the outcry about "Political Correctness" continues unquestioned, all progressive gains on campus will be in danger.
Minor thesis:	Susan Faludi has written that "political correctness charges are just another tactic of the far right to roll back the rights of women."
Subordinate thesis 4:	People in favor of "Political Correctness" are not at all similar to the anti-Communist witch-hunters of the 1950s.

This is more structured than the lists that many students will come up with, but it exemplifies how such a topic list can be constructed.

The preceding description shows a deductive use of the topics, in which the thesis statement is decided on and then subject matter is arranged according to the perceived needs of the thesis. The topics can, of course, also be used inductively, to explore the subject and gather a mass of potential material, with the student creating a thesis only after the subject material has been grouped or categorized. With this inductive use of the topics, it is necessary for students to leave the whole area of thesis creation until after they have used the topical system to gather subject matter. You may well find that students often cannot wait to begin to arrange the material under a thesis and so greet the stage of thesis creation with enthusiasm.

Thus far, we have discussed fairly simple uses of the topics; using the topical system to support argumentation is a somewhat more complicated task. The best description of using topical argumentation in the classroom is found in "Looking for an Argument" by the aforementioned Bilsky and a group of rhetoricians at the University of Chicago. The method that follows is adapted from the system they describe (Bilsky et al. 215-16).

Before you begin to teach argument, your students should be comfortable with the idea of topics and should be able to manipulate them fairly well. In introducing Bilsky's topical arguments, it is necessary to provide examples of their use. You can usually find several good examples of arguments based on definition, analogy, and so forth in any of the widely used FY readers. Classify the passages by topic, and hand them out so that students can see the new angle from which they will have to view the use of the topics. When you have gone over the handouts, try the following exercise.

Choose three propositions that are simple, fairly clear, and controversial, at least to some degree. These can most often be chosen from current news events and can involve political opinions. As homework, ask your students to use the topics to write short supporting statements—no more than one or two sentences—for each proposition, and during the next class convene writing groups or have students exchange papers with one another, and ask that they try to identify the use of specific topics in one another's work.

The next steps are optional. After simple manipulation of topical arguments, expose the class to writing that makes use of complex and combined argument. Try classic persuasive pieces, such as *The Federalist*, no. 10, "Civil Disobedience," or "A Modest Proposal," or more contemporary pieces, such as "I Have a Dream," "College Is a Waste of Time and Money," "Motherhood: Who Needs It?" or "Letter from Birmingham Jail." Only after students have been exposed to topical argumentation in its most developed form should they be given the long persuasive assignments that are the goal of topical argumentation.

Classical invention in its simplified form can be satisfying to teach. As you teach it, you are aware of a tradition of education that is as old as any in Western culture. And since it is easy enough for students to memorize, they can carry it with them and use it in other classes. It is neither the simplest nor the most complex heuristic system, but it has a charm and a comprehensiveness that make it one of the most attractive.

BURKE'S PENTAD

In his long life, the late Kenneth Burke was a poet, a short story writer, a music critic, a book reviewer, a translator, a novelist, a literary critic, a magazine editor, a social commentator, an essayist, a researcher, a teacher at at least fourteen colleges and universities, and foremost, a rhetorician. He was one of those rare authors whose analytic work was as brilliant as his synthetic work.

Beginning in the early 1950s, Burke's ideas penetrated universities' Departments of Communication (or Speech Departments, as they were called), for his analysis of literature had meaning for the study of rhetoric. Gradually, his influence and reputation spread to practitioners of rhetoric and composition in English Departments, where Burke had previously been known only as a brilliant but somewhat obscure literary critic. For some years now, Burke's analytic invention, the *Pentad*, has been used by specialists in the teaching of writing.

Burke calls his central method of analysis "dramatism." The Pentad is sometimes called "the dramatistic Pentad" because "it invites one to consider the matter of motives in a perspective that, being developed from the analysis of drama, treats language and thought primarily as modes of action" (*Grammar* xvi). The idea of "language as symbolic action" runs throughout Burke's critical and rhetorical work, leading to a method of literary analysis that concentrates on what a work does to its audience and to a rhetorical outlook that is far from idealistic or rarefied—Burke refers to social communicative situations as "the Human Barnyard" full of action.

Burke's rhetoric is like Aristotle's in many ways, particularly in its insistence on awareness of the nature and needs of the audience. Burke has said that "wherever there is persuasion, there is rhetoric. And whenever there is 'meaning' there is 'persuasion'" (*Rhetoric* 172). If this seems to enlarge the field of rhetoric to include all human actions, that is exactly what Burke means it to do; his investigation of linguistic phenomena ranges from Shakespeare's *Venus and Adonis*, to Hitler's *Mein Kampf*, to advertising jingles and to the Ten Commandments, all of which he considers rhetoric: "the use of language in such a way as to produce a desired impression on the reader or hearer" (*Counter-Statement* 165).

Kenneth Burke's contributions to rhetorical metatheory are many, but his primary—although indirect and unintended—contribution to invention is his Pentad, first introduced in *A Grammar of Motives* as a device for the analysis of literature. Simply put, it is a list of five terms that can be used as principles of invention.

Act

Scene

Agent

Agency

Purpose

Burke explains the genesis of these terms in the Introduction to *A Grammar of Motives*:

In any statement about motives, you must have some work that names the act (names what took place, in thought or deed), and another that names the scene (the background of the act, the situation in which it occurred); also you must indicate what person or kind of instruments he used (agency) and the purpose.

As William Rueckert has suggested, Burke feels that the stress on *act* characterizes the realists; the stress on *scene*, the materialists; the stress on *agent*, the idealists; the stress on *agency*, the pragmatists; and the stress on *purpose*, the mystics, with whom Burke identifies (93–96).

The most immediately obvious quality of the Pentad is its resemblance to the journalistic formula of *what?*, *where?*, *who?*, *how?* and *why?* It has, however, become accepted wisdom that the Pentad differs from the journalistic formula because of a further development of Burke's, the "ratios" between elements in the Pentad. "Simple as it appears," says Richard Young,

> Burke's procedure is capable of far more complex analyses. The terms and their references can be combined in various ratios (e.g., act-scene, act-purpose, act-agency), ten ratios in all being possible. The relationships revealed in analyses using the ratios often provide original and important insights into behavior. (13)

Not intended as a heuristic that aids discovery or invention, Burke's Pentad nonetheless supplies writers and readers with a method for establishing the focus of a written (or spoken) text. His theory of dramatism, focusing on the ratios between the elements in the Pentad, calls attention to the ways these representative terms link up.

Dramatism is a theory of action that breathes life into a text, humanizing the action. And the key term of Burke's Pentad is *act*, for it is the starting point for textual analysis. When a person's acts are to be interpreted in terms of the circumstances—that is, when action is to be interpreted according to the context in which it takes place (as in *Robinson Crusoe, Lord of the Flies*, or *Riddley Walker*, for example)—behavior would fall under the heading of a *scene-act ratio*. In *Lord of the Flies*, both Ralph and Jack, leaders of opposing factions, act in reaction to the *scene*: they are stranded on a desert island without the traditional protection of society. Yet within the *scene-act ratio* falls a range of behaviors that must be evaluated according to the *agent-act ratio*—the correspondence between a person's character and his action. Well-adjusted, optimistic, and athletic, Ralph "naturally" acts out the desire for civilization, while Jack, the cruel and ugly bully, acts out the feral desire for mastery by intimidation and violence.

Once students begin to understand the concept of "dramatism," they can analyze Romeo's *act* in response to the *scene* of his apparently dead Juliet or Charles Barkley's *act* in response to his *scene*, the seventh game of the NBA finals. An awareness of this ratio can help students develop actions in their own texts: the actions taken in response to sexism, for example, or the acts of violence in sports or the actions that constitute dormitory life.

Texts such as *Madame Bovary, Anna Karenina*, and *The Portrait of a Lady* reflect a prominent *agency-act ratio* between each character and the character of her behavior. And in *The Adventures of Huckleberry Finn*, the *agency-act ratio* explains the effect of Emmeline Grangerford's maudlin character on her poetry and the effect of Widow Douglas's high-mindedness on her treatment of Huck.

Once students begin to understand these concepts, they can then apply their understanding to their own subjects, such as their reasons for commuting to school or their parents' philosophy of upbringing. And other dynamic relationships, other ratios, disclose still other features of human relations, behavior, and motives. It remains true, however, that the ratios of the Burkean system are most easily applicable to literary texts.

Using Burke's Pentad in the Classroom

Not intended as an isolated heuristic technique, the Pentad can be useful in the writing classroom, for it is one of the easiest heuristics to teach and to remember. The Pentad can form the basis for several different sorts of invention activities, each of which must be carefully described. Until students are taught how to manipulate it, however, the Pentad is nothing more than a collection of terms.

For a relatively limited sort of invention that is best used in classes discussing works of literature, W. Ross Winterowd has evolved a use of Burke's terms that can be helpful in the analysis of a piece of writing. Here is his adaptation of the terms of the Pentad.

What does it say? (Act)

Who wrote it? (Agent)

In what source was it published? (Agency)

Where and when was it published? (Scene)

What is its purpose? (Purpose)

(82–89)

The most complete adaptation of Burke's terms for use in general invention was by William Irmscher, who in *The Holt Guide to English* compiled fifteen questions, which he places in Burke's five categories. Irmscher's use of Burke is not a method of inventing thesis statements or single declarative statements; it is best used for "accumulating a mass of material" on subjects, gathering subject matter in the form of supporting propositions or kernel thoughts (28).

Irmscher's questions are these.

Action: To generate thought about an action, ask

1. What happened?

2. What is happening?

3. What will happen?

4. What is it?

Actor-agent: To generate thoughts about an agent, ask

   1. Who did it? Who is doing it?

   2. What did it?

   3. What kind of agent is it?

Scene: To generate thoughts about a scene, ask

   1. Where did it happen? Where is it happening?

   2. When did it happen?

   3. What is the background?

Means-agency: To generate thoughts about an agency, ask

   1. How was it done?

   2. What means were used?

Purpose:

   1. Why?

You may want to make copies of these questions for your students. Not the only possible approach to the Pentad, Irmscher's is representative of the methods writing teachers use to put the code words of the Pentad into a form that students work with. Unlike other techniques of invention, this one is so simple and schematic that it takes little teaching. Once students are exposed to the terms and the questions, they can work on their own. You will want to assist your students in distinguishing which of the terms of the Pentad will be most useful when applied to the subject at hand.

If students submit a subject to all the questions suggested by the Pentad, faithfully jotting down an answer to each one, they will generate much information that they can use well in a coherent essay. The subject of subliminal advertising, for instance, can be put into the perspective of any of the five terms and thus be seen primarily as an action, or in terms of who does it or where it is done, or according to the technical means by which it is accomplished or the purpose behind it. Your task as a teacher of the Pentad is to assist students in figuring out how much information they need for an essay and what questions will best assist them in generating that information.

When you are teaching invention, make sure to use the blackboard so your students can watch the Pentad technique in action. Demonstrate how it works with a few subjects before you ask students to try manipulating it themselves. You may find that students can use the Pentad well to provide subject-based questions and material but that they do not find other important elements of rhetorical purpose—such as considerations of audience and arrangement of material—to be natural parts of the inventive system of the Pentad. It is likely, therefore, that your students will need your help to determine the purpose of their essays and to arrange the material into a coherent form.

PREWRITING

The term *prewriting* applies to all forms of activity that precede actually beginning the first draft. What many people do not know is that the term evolved from a theory of invention and teaching developed at Michigan State University in the early sixties by D. Gordon Rohman and Albert O. Wlecke and was modified by them and other teachers over the next ten years.[4]

Prewriting as a theory seeks to promote the process of self-actualization in the student. In "Pre-Writing," Rohman defines "good writing" as "the discovery by a responsible person of his uniqueness within his subject"; Rohman's definition of a responsible person is "one who stands at the center of his thoughts and feelings with the sense that they begin in him. He is concerned to make things happen . . . he seeks to dominate his circumstances with words or actions" (106).

Prewriting suggests that writing in general consists of two contexts: the *subject* and the *personal*. The subject context is made up of objective material that can be discovered through research, the sort of factual material that is found in encyclopedias, is inert, and is manipulable by a writer. The personal context, on the other hand, has to do with the writer's personality; and it is within the personal context, says Rohman, that a writer finds "that combination of words that make an essay his" (108). The prewriting theorists were convinced that much student writing is dull because students are fearful of tapping their personal contexts. Prewriting techniques were designed, therefore, to allow students to do just that. As a result, prewriting diverges in some important ways from other heuristic techniques: not only can it be used to generate material, but it also prompts students to respond personally to the material.

Rohman tested his theories and techniques in a sophomore-level writing course and found that prewriting classes produced writing that "showed a statistically significant superiority to essays produced in control sections" (112). It is an open question, though, whether techniques of self-actualization that worked for elective sophomore classes in the 1960s can work for required FY classes in the 1990s. Prewriting assumes an interest in written self-expression that is often hard to find among students in FY composition classes. Nonetheless, its techniques have much to offer a teacher willing to experiment with them. In using prewriting, our task as writing teachers is to encourage that middle ground between self-indulgent personalizing and an unimaginative commitment to rules and product.

Using Prewriting Techniques in the Classroom

It's useful to look critically for a moment at the philosophical position that prewriting theories occupy in order to understand the nature and tendencies of their classroom-based techniques. Prewriting theorists take an existential

---

[4] See also the discussion of Rohman and Wlecke in Chapter 6.

approach to composition. They seek an image of an individual within the problem-solving process. This focus on the existential self as an important part of the writing act leads to emphases on the process of thought and on personal writing. These emphases are useful: they point out the sterility of any rule-based system that concentrates only on the product and ignores the composing process, which is so vital to the writer. The problem, however, is that prewriting concentrates on personal writing to such a degree that it often ignores the needs of the audience. Prewriting can easily be used to produce informal essays, but it must undergo adaptation to be useful in the assigned, subject-based discourse demanded by college and the professions.

Because of its emphasis on personal experience, prewriting runs the risk of shortchanging the context. Composition teachers today must turn out students who can write on assigned subjects and demonstrate their engagement with a topic. As Dixie Goswami and Lee Odell's study shows, actual writing in the professional world is indeed done in response to assignments rather than out of choice. Nevertheless, prewriting techniques can be adapted in many ways and can be extremely helpful in teaching invention.

The journal Over the last twenty years, journal writing has become an intrinsic part of many English classes. Teachers and students genuinely like using journals as a repository of material and concepts that can lead to more formal essays; journal-writing does not impose systematic techniques of invention and thus can have a salutary effect on students' feelings about writing (Gannett).

For students to get the most from journal-writing, however, it is necessary to introduce them to the art of keeping a journal. First, acquaint your students with a definition of a journal: it is a record of reactions, not actions. A journal is not a diary, nor is it a record of events. If you fail to be specific about this, students may end up writing diary entries—"Got up at 7:30, went to Commons for breakfast, saw Diane." Students need to be shown, and then convinced, that a journal is a record of a mind and its thoughts rather than a record of a body and its movements. One good way of demonstrating this is by showing students excerpts from the journals of established writers, like Thoreau, Pepys, Woolf, Hawthorne, and Nin, or from student writing submitted in previous classes. Compared to keeping a journal, keeping a diary will soon seem to most of your students like a lame activity.

Along with familiarizing students with good examples of journal-writing, you may want to provide a list like that shown in Example 7-1.

Provide just enough prompts that students will occasionally have to grope for a sense of their own will to write something; too many questions and suggestions can be a crutch. Encourage students to move beyond each prompt to more self-directed writing.

One problem with journal-writing for FY students is the tendency to rely on ready-made opinions, premanufactured wisdom, and clichés. Because some students have not yet begun to question their parents' or their friends' norms, they will repeat the most appalling prejudices as if they had invented them. A

Example 7-1 IDEAS FOR JOURNAL ENTRIES

Any idea you wish to grapple with is suitable, whether it's from a text you're reading or from a conversation you've had with friends or with yourself. If you're stuck for something to write about, try responding to one of these suggestions.

1. Does the way you dress affect your mood?
2. Children often suffer injustice at the hands of adults.
3. Who has been a hero?
4. What book has affected your thinking? What movie?
5. How does your life differ from that of your parents or your siblings?
6. What Americans do you admire? Explain.
7. What Americans don't you admire? Explain.
8. Are you interested in U.S. politics? Why, or why not?
9. Do you know anything about the concerns of nations other than the United States? Why, or why not?
10. What judgments do we make about people based on the appearance of something they own (cars, clothes, pets, houses)?
11. Why do you think it is often said that you spend your second year in college getting rid of the friends you made your first year?
12. What courses would you never take while in college?
13. Many students are smarter than their grades indicate.
14. Whom do you dislike? Why? Is it because of jealousy, resentment, hurt, outrage, or disapproval?
15. What is the most interesting thing in your hometown?
16. How do you go about writing a paper? Do you watch television? stand on your head? cry? spend an hour looking for your favorite pen? Describe everything you do and how you feel during the writing process.
17. Why is watching television a waste of time?

---

ready-made challenge to such secondhand thought is the requirement that students be as concrete in their entries as possible. Discourage generalizing and opining unless the opinion can be tied to some actual experience in the student's life. (This is, after all, just good argumentation—no assertions should be made without concrete support.)

The question of whether to grade or evaluate journals is simple to answer: don't. Instead, assign a grade based on the number of pages a student turns in; four a week for ten weeks might earn an A; three a week, a B; and so on. Students are expected to write sincerely, presumably for themselves, yet they know that the instructor will see everything in the journal (everything, that is, except parts labeled "Please Don't Read"). While some teachers put no marks on journals except for a date after the last entry, others initiate a written conversation with the students and still others write on separate sheets of paper, which they insert into the journal. At times, you may find an entry directed to you—an invitation to reply.

Journals, then, shouldn't be judged by the standards you might bring to a student essay. The fact that students' journals do have an audience, however—namely, the teacher—means that they "do not speak privately," as Ken Macrorie puts it in *Telling Writing* (130). Macrorie insists that journals

> can be read with profit by other persons than the writer. They may be personal or even intimate, but if the writer wants an entry to be seen by others, it will be such that they can understand, enjoy, be moved by. (131)

Macrorie suggests that students write journal entries on the same topic over a period of time, from "different and developing viewpoints" (137). Such writing gives students the distance they need to reflect on, deepen, and enrich their perceptions and thus make their stories more moving and effective. But most important, Macrorie tells us, journals are the best starting place and the best storehouse for ideas: "A journal is a place for confusion and certainty, for the half-formed and the completed" (141).

Peter Elbow, too, would have students keep a journal, what he calls a "freewriting diary." He warns that it is "*not* a complete account of your day; just a brief mind sample from each day" (*Writing without Teachers* 9). Like Macrorie, Elbow sees the "freewriting diary" as the motherlode of ideas for essays. Elbow writes that "freewriting helps you to think of topics to write about. Just keep writing," he tells his readers; "follow threads where they lead and you will get the ideas, experiences, feelings, or people that are just asking to be written about" (*Writing with Power* 15).

Most students enjoy keeping and learning from a journal and will continue writing in their journals after the course is over. You, too, should join your students in the journal-keeping practice, recording your own classroom experiences and your responses to your students' journals and essays. Nancy Comley, director of FY writing at Queens College, City University of New York, encourages her teaching assistants to keep their own journals. Comley writes that

> through the journal one comes to know oneself better as a teacher, and in the discipline of keeping a journal the teacher can experience what students experience when they are told to write and do not really feel like it. As part of the journal, I suggest that each teacher keep a folder of the progress (or lack of it) of two of his or her students, noting the students' interaction with the class and the teacher as well as evaluating their written work. Such data can form the basis for a seminar paper presenting these case histories, augmenting journal observations with student conferences and with research done into special problems or strengths the students had as writers. (55-56)

That teachers and students alike should keep journals underpins Comley's sage pedagogical advice: never give an assignment you have not tried yourself.

Brainstorming   Brainstorming is the method used by most professional and academic writers. It is not in the canon of official prewriting techniques (if there is one), but it fits most naturally in this area of invention theory.

The technique of brainstorming is simple. The writer decides on a subject, sits down in a quiet place with pen and paper, and writes down everything that comes to mind about the subject. Alex Osborne codified the main rules of brainstorming in the late 1950s:

1. Don't criticize or evaluate any ideas during the session. Simply write down every idea that emerges. Save the criticism and evaluation until later.
2. Use your imagination for "free wheeling." The wilder the idea the better, because it might lead to some valuable insights later.
3. Strive for quantity. The more ideas, the better chance for a winner to emerge.
4. Combine and improve ideas as you proceed. (84)

The writer, in other words, free-associates, writing down ideas until the motherlode is exhausted. (Invariably, the lode is not really mined out, and new aspects, arguments, or ideas pop up throughout the writing process.)

At this point, the writer either tries to structure the information in some way—by recopying it in a different order or by numbering the items, crossing some out, adding to others—or she finds the list suggestive enough as it stands and begins to work.

Brainstorming is extremely simple—and effective. The most widely used inventive technique, brainstorming moves in naturally to fill the void if no structured method is ever taught. Research suggests that if an inventive system is not internalized by around age twenty, brainstorming is adopted, probably because it represents the natural way the mind grapples with the storage and retrieval of information. Most professional and academic writers were never taught systematic invention and therefore turned to brainstorming.

Sometimes, young, self-conscious writers who have little specialized educational experience are initially stymied by brainstorming, for their stores of knowledge and general intellectual resources aren't as developed as those of experienced writers. Hence, they go dry when confronted with the task of listing ideas about an abstract topic. You may want to walk such writers through the brainstorming system by doing a sample exercise on the board before you turn them loose with their own ideas.

Mapping or clustering In *Writing the Natural Way*, Gabriele Lusser Rico describes *clustering,* a prewriting technique she credits as similar to Tony Buzan's *mapping* techniques. Based on theories of the brain's hemispheric specialization, Rico's creative-search process taps the right hemisphere of the brain, the hemisphere sensitive "to wholeness, image, and the unforced rhythms of language" (12). Usually, Rico tells us, beginning writers rely solely on the left hemisphere, the hemisphere of reason, linearity, logic. By clustering, they can learn to tap the other hemisphere as well and produce writings that demonstrate

a coherence, unity, and sense of wholeness; a recurrence of words and phrases, ideas, or images that [reflect] a pattern sensitivity; an awareness of the nuances of language rhythms; a significant and natural use of images and meta-

phors; and a powerful "creative tension." Another by-product of clustering
seem[s] to be a significant drop in errors of punctuation, awkward phrasing,
even spelling. (11)

Clustering is an easy-to-use prewriting activity because there is no right or
wrong way to cluster. And Rico guarantees that the words will come and that
writing eventually takes over. You may want to try clustering with your students, perhaps ending up with a cluster like the one in Example 7-2, which
uses *risk* as its nucleus, as its storm center of meaning. The following are Rico's
simple directions:

1.   Write the word *afraid* in the upper third of the page, leaving the lower
     two-thirds of the page for writing, and circle it. We'll start with this
     word because even the most hesitant of us will discover many associa-
     tions triggered by it.

2.   Now get comfortable with the process of clustering by letting your play-
     ful, creative . . . mind make connections. Keep the childlike attitude of
     newness and wonder and spill whatever associations come to you onto
     paper. What comes to mind when you think of the word? Avoid judging
     or choosing. Simply let go and write. Let the words or phrases radiate
     outward from the nucleus word, and draw a circle around each of them.
     Connect those associations that seem related with lines. Add arrows to
     indicate direction, if you wish, but don't think too long or analyze.
     There is an "unthinking" quality to this process that suspends time.

3.   Continue jotting down associations and ideas triggered by the word
     "afraid" for a minute or two, immersing yourself in the process. Since
     there is no *one* way to let the cluster spill onto the page, let yourself be
     guided by the patterning . . . [abilities of your] mind, connecting each
     association as you see fit without worrying about it. Let clustering hap-
     pen naturally. It will, if you don't inhibit it with objections from your
     censoring . . . mind. If you reach a plateau where nothing spills out,
     "doodle" a bit by putting arrows on your existing cluster.

4.   You will know when to stop clustering through a sudden, strong urge
     to write, usually after one or two minutes, when you feel a shift that
     says "Aha! I think I know what I want to say." If it doesn't happen
     suddenly, this awareness of a direction will creep up on you more gradu-
     ally, as though someone were slowly unveiling a sculpture. . . . Just know
     you will experience a mental shift characterized by the certain, satisfy-
     ing feeling that you have something to write about.

5.   You're ready to write. Scan [your] clustered perceptions and insights. . . .
     Something therein will suggest your first sentence to you, and you're off.
     Students rarely, if ever, report difficulty writing that first sentence; on
     the contrary, they report it as being effortless. Should you feel stuck,
     however, write about anything from the cluster to get you started.
     The next thing and the next thing after that will come because your
     [right hemisphere] has already perceived a pattern of meaning. Trust it.
     (36–37)

Even if prewriting seems idealistic or naive to you, the techniques can be
used fruitfully to help students find something to say. And perhaps if we can

Example 7-2 **CLUSTERING**

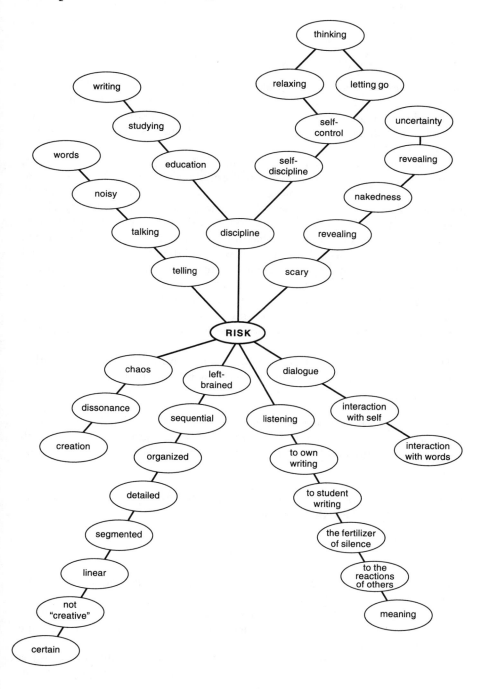

imitate the attitudes of Rohman and his disciples, the originators of prewriting, we might see a student whose goal is to be self-actualizing, who feels that her creativity is repressed by convention, who is waiting to be freed to explore her own humanity through writing.

TAGMEMIC INVENTION

For years, composition scholars hoped that the sophisticated, complex work being done in linguistics would yield a new approach to the teaching of writing. But the fields had little successful crossover until Kenneth L. Pike, at the University of Michigan, began applying terms from his theory of *tagmemic linguistics* to composition.

The ultimate goal of contemporary linguistic theory is essentially explanatory, not prescriptive. Noam Chomsky's transformational-generative (TG) theory of language, for example, is not practical, or pedagogically oriented. But unlike TG grammar, Pike's theory of tagmemic linguistics is not a general theory of language. Instead, Pike's is a "field theory," developed for use by linguists who were translating the Bible into languages that until then had never been written down. Tagmemics developed as a theory of discovery and then as a "slot theory" to aid translators in understanding the use—not the nature—of any unknown language.

First of all, what is a tagmeme? According to Pike, "a repeatable, relevant pattern of purposive activity is made up of a sequence of functional classes-in-slots. . . . This combination of slot-plus-class is called a tagmeme" (85). The essential nature of the tagmeme established it as the basic tool for translating unknown languages.

The slots that Pike mentions can be filled in by alternative units within classes. A simple example in linguistic terms would be the sentence

Mary *hit* Bill.

The slot between the subject, *Mary,* and the object, *Bill,* is filled by a class. In this case, the class is composed of verbs of a certain kind. Replace *hit* with another word in the class—say *kissed*—and the slot is filled.

Mary *kissed* Bill.

At the same time, the slot after the verb slot—the object of the sentence—can also be filled by a class, this time by nouns or pronouns.

Mary hit the *ball.*

Mary hit *him.*

The slot plus the class of alternative fillers is what Pike calls a tagmeme, and the tagmeme is the basis of his discovery-oriented theory of language. Tagmemics is a method of finding things out, of conceptualizing reality, and it is this method of conceptualization, rather than the tagmeme as an all-purpose tool, that Pike has brought to composition.

Tagmemic invention treats knowledge in terms of repeatable units and is concerned with the precise definition of these units. Sloppy rhetoric, according to Pike, is the result of sloppy methods of thought and inquiry; careful phrasing and definition are part of the answer. In *Rhetoric: Discovery and Change,* Richard E. Young, Alton L. Becker, and Pike argue that communication is a response to perceived misunderstanding or division. The authors articulate six maxims for resolving such misunderstandings; these maxims can help writers understand their own interpretations of the world, develop them, and present them to others.

First, "people conceive of the world in terms of repeatable units" (26), which are part of a larger system, for "units of experience are hierarchically structured systems" (29). At any level of focus, a unit "can be adequately understood only if three aspects of the unit are known: (1) its contrastive features, (2) its range of variation, and (3) its distribution in larger contexts" (56); hence, a unit of experience can be viewed "as particle, or as a wave, or as a field" (122). And "change between units can occur only over a bridge of shared features, the prerequisites for interaction and change" (172). Finally, however, all communication boils down to linguistic choices, which are made in "relation to a universe of discourse" (301), either consciously or unconsciously, a universe that constrains our linguistic choices. These maxims contain nearly all the aspects of that elegant inquiry machine, "the tagmemic heuristic," the final product of tagmemic theory.

Tagmemic Aspects of Definition

As Bruce Edwards, Jr. suggests, tagmemicists believe that "the composing *process* should be the focus of composition teaching and that, indeed, it is something which to some degree *can* be taught." For tagmemicists, invention is "essentially a problem-solving activity." If one can make this activity shareable, then one can "isolate and identify its features." And if this process is learned empirically, "then it may form the basis for a new rhetorical procedure which can be taught to the student" (15). Tagmemic invention sees problem solving as beginning with the careful definition of units—a good place to begin.

Contrastive features The first tagmemic mode of inquiry, an investigation of the contrastive features of a subject, starts by asking, "What features does a unit have that make it different from other similar things?" This is the simplest tagmemic mode to apply. Using the siege of Sarajevo, we might ask these questions.

> What features of the siege of Sarajevo make it different from other struggles of the Bosnian war?
>
> Of what sort are they?
>
> Do they form a pattern?

By identifying contrastive features, this mode brings out the most important definitive features of a subject, those elements that create its unique identity.

Range of variation The second tagmemic mode of inquiry concerns the subject's possible range of variation; it asks how the subject can be variously defined and still remain itself. Though it can be applied to any subject, this mode works best for concrete items and absolute abstracts. The classic examples used in the literature are "divan" and "democracy," both of which have an obvious range of variations: Is a love seat a divan? Can a divan have no arms? Can democracy exist without freedom of the press? Can there be a hereditary leader in a democracy? About "Political Correctness," we might ask the following questions:

Have all traditional liberal attitudes been labeled "politically correct"?

Is it "politically correct" to defend flag-burning? to denounce racism?

What sorts of people are called defenders of "political correctness"? What sorts are not?

Does Senator Kennedy ever use the term "politically correct?" Does Senator Dole?

In the hands of an imaginative questioner, the range-of-variation inquiry can be extremely flexible and useful, but it is often less fruitful than it might be. Key to this mode of inquiry is the idea of changing over time while maintaining the same identity—like the changes over time we undergo as we age. It is all very well to invent questions about the physical variations of a divan or the abstract variations of democracy, but in the uproar of inquiring about an actual subject, most important variations are chronological. Was the use of the term *political correctness* the same in 1988 as in 1995? Chronological or (diachronic) variations can be understandable and logical in ways that current (synchronic), abstract variations simply are not.

Distribution in larger contexts   The last tagmemic mode of inquiry in Pike's original system is made up of questions about the subject's distribution within larger systems. This mode is directly related to the definition of tagmeme as slot plus class; it asks, What place or slot does the unit occupy in a larger pattern? And it is extremely useful for nearly all subjects because it can locate a subject in physical patterns, chronological patterns, historical patterns or other abstract patterns—that is, in nearly any context.

Let's try running another common subject—deficit spending—through this mode in a number of different ways.

What part does deficit spending play in current fiscal policy?

When was deficit spending initiated, and why?

What is the relationship between deficit spending and stock prices?

Has deficit spending proved to be a valid government practice?

How is deficit spending related to the balance of trade?

What is the role of deficit spending in inflation?

The list is almost endless.

The range of questions implied by these three tagmemic modes is an inventive method in itself, one that can produce a wide range of subject matter. Questions from each mode can be rephrased in several different ways in order to get the most out of the mode. However, useful this method may be, tagmemic theory goes even further.

Further Development of Tagmemic Theory

Pike's rhetorical work first appeared in the mid-1960s and continued to be developed through the rest of that decade. Particularly valuable contributions were made by Pike's colleagues at the University of Michigan, Alton Becker, Richard Young, and Hubert English, Jr. English was largely responsible for the first testing of the "three-aspect" method discussed above. The theory was refined, and finally, in 1970, Young, Becker, and Pike produced their textbook *Rhetoric: Discovery and Change,* which codifies the work done on tagmemic invention in a form that the authors hoped composition teachers could use.

Rhetoric: Discovery and Change was widely reviewed, with most critics agreeing that the tagmemic approach to invention was both novel and important. However, the style of the text seemed too difficult for FY students, and the methods used to relate information appeared too complex to be grasped by any but the most intelligent students. As a result, *Rhetoric: Discovery and Change* has become known as a teachers' book and is not often assigned to classes. Another result, unfortunately, is that tagmemic invention is not as well known or as widely used as it deserves to be.

In their text, Young, Becker, and Pike take the invention technique as it was used by earlier experimenters—the three-aspect method investigated by English—and join it to Pike's *trimodal perspective* of particle, wave, and field (called *feature, manifestation,* and *distribution* until Pike noticed their similarity to physicists' theories about the form of light).

Throughout their discussion of these perspectives, the authors made it clear that they are not mutually exclusive. Any unit of experience can be discussed as a particle, as a wave, or as a field, but, they warn, "a unit is not *either* a particle *or* a wave *or* a field, but can rather be viewed as all these" (122). The *particle perspective* views units as essentially static; the *wave perspective,* as essentially dynamic; and the *field perspective,* as essentially a network of relationships or part of a larger network.

Particle perspective Particle perspective has these features.

1. It deals with static nature of a unit, ignoring changes in time.

2. It selects from a dynamic whole one "bit," usually the central bit, for presentation (the "snapshot" effect).

3. It arbitrarily specifies boundaries.

4. It isolates the unit from its surroundings.

The particle perspective on the siege of Sarajevo would deal with the siege in suspension, as having begun at a certain time and place, as having ended at a certain time and place, and as containing features A, B, C, D, and so forth. It would choose a single perspective on the siege and might present a single historical description of it. Particle perspective sees the subject as immovable, alone, and unrelated to physical or chronological continua.

Wave perspective   The wave perspective has these features.

1. It recognizes some dynamic function of the unit, noting spatial, chronological, or conceptual movement or flow.

2. It points out the central component of the unit.

3. It emphasizes the fusion, flow, or lack of distinct boundaries between the unit and other units.

The wave perspective on the siege of Sarajevo would deal with the different sorts of movement that the siege incorporated. It might discuss the siege as the central component of the movement of troops and the decisions by commanding officers in the weeks preceding the event, or it might look at the changing attitudes of the soldiers and the civilians on both sides as the hardships developed. It might follow the movements of troops on the mountains around the city or in the streets, or it might focus on the UN efforts to get supplies through and on the meaning of that movement to the outcome of the situation. Thus wave perspective emphasizes change and flow.

Field perspective   A unit viewed from the field perspective has two characteristics.

1. It is seen not as isolated but as occupying a place in a system of some kind.

2. It is seen as a system itself, composed of subsystems.

Field perspective of the siege might view the battle as part of the Yugoslavian civil war and deal with its meaning to the war, or it might view the siege in terms of its place in Milosevic's campaign for a Greater Serbia. This perspective could also place the event within a system of sieges or tactics and view it as part of the continuing evolution of warfare. Or it could see the siege as the reason for the downfall of Milosevic in the system of his political career.

If we view the siege as a system in itself, we can then detail its subsystems. We could follow the Serbian artillery through the siege or trace the movements of the UN forces on the outskirts of the city. We could follow the fortunes of one family or one person within the city or focus on one specific engagement within the larger siege, like the defense of the airport. Thus field perspective is concerned mainly with relationships among the whole and its parts.

Like the three tagmemic aspects, this trimodal perspective can be used alone as an invention heuristic. The best use of it currently is in Janice Lauer, Janet

Emig, and Andrea Lunsford's textbook, *Four Worlds of Writing*, which simplifies the perspectives for FY students, calling the particle perspective *static view*, the wave perspective *dynamic view*, and the field perspective *relative view* (31*ff*).

Using Tagmemic Invention in the Classroom

There have been several important classroom tests of tagmemic invention, notably by Hubert English, Richard Young and Frank Koen, and Lee Odell. Nearly unanimously these tests report mixed results. Composition teachers have also voiced serious criticisms of tagmemics. James Kinney, for instance, accuses tagmemicists of inflated claims, criticizes tagmemics in general as depending on an outmoded theory of linguistics, and contends that the heuristic is not really much different from the classical topics or other inventive procedures (141–43). How should teachers of composition respond to such criticism? Should we be discouraged from attempting to use tagmemic invention as a pedagogical tool?

No. As Lee Odell points out in his response to Kinney, systematic inquiry as represented by the tagmemic heuristic is important for our students. As long as there exists an "apparent gap between systematic inquiry and the art of writing," says Odell, our students will be able to use heuristics ("Another Look" 148). And contemporary rhetoricians, paying attention to criticisms of tagmemics, have worked to make the tagmemic heuristic more helpful in the classroom. A notable example of the revised tagmemic heuristic comes from Charles Kneupper and is shown in Example 7-3.

Whether you choose to use Kneupper's system or the original tagmemic heuristic, take note of some items concerning this highly structured system. The first is that students using tagmemic invention sometimes become absorbed in the elegance and sophistication of the system and concentrate on merely reeling off the information the system provides without attempting to arrange it in a coherent essay. Students who learn to manipulate the system can be so exhilarated by the informational possibilities tagmemics offers that they are loath to come back down to the linearity of arrangement. This fascination with the means rather than the end is to some degree a problem with any heuristic system, but tagmemics invites it particularly because the system is complex and novel—and fun. In your first explanation of the tagmemic system, therefore, you will want to stress that the invented material must ultimately be arranged coherently, that a mere listing of material does not guarantee successful arrangement.

To offset potential problems, some teachers stress that students should create a thesis before they tap the system for subject matter. Try this by asking students to create the list of questions, using a heuristic. Then ask them to choose several of the questions, the ones they feel most drawn to, and to answer them in one-sentence statements. Have them choose their favorite statement, which becomes a possible working thesis for the essay. Finally, students use the other questions they generated to provide support for the thesis.

The second pedagogical concern with tagmemic heuristics is that the method seems to work best when the teacher initially presents students with subjects

Example 7-3 THE REVISED TAGMEMIC HEURISTIC

	Unit in Contrast	*Unit as a System*	*Unit in a System*
S T A T I C	View the unit wholistically as an undifferentiated, isolated entity.	View the unit as composed of separable component parts.	View the unit as part in a larger system.
	What feature(s) serve to differentiate the unit from other similar things?	What are the components of the unit?	What are the other components in the larger system?
		How are the components organized in relation to each other?	How are these components organized in relation to each other?
		What is the structure of the system?	What is the structure of the system?

* *

D Y N A M I C	View the unit as a dynamic process, object, or event.	View the unit as composed of dynamic separable component parts.	View the unit as dynamic part of a larger dynamic system.
	What process of change occurred to create the unit?	How were the parts formed?	How was the larger system created?
	How is it changing currently?	What will happen to each in the future?	How is it currently changing?
	What will happen to it in the future?	Do different parts change at different rates?	What will happen to it in the future?
	What feature(s) serve to differentiate the unit from similar processes, objects, or events?	What does change in a particular part do to the overall system?	How does change in the larger system affect the unit?
		How is the structure of the system changing?	How does change in the unit affect the larger system?
			How is the structure changing?

and problems to run through the heuristic; otherwise, students may choose easy ones, problems about which they already know a good deal.

Finally, the heuristic must be used again and again; it must be applied to many different kinds of subjects until its use becomes almost unconscious. Once the use of the heuristic is established and students are familiar with what it can and cannot do, they can apply it to problems of their own choosing. Repetition and a movement from assigned to self-created subjects are the keys to teaching all inventive heuristics successfully and are particularly necessary for students learning to use tagmemic invention.

Classroom use of the tagmemic system proceeds in a manner similar to that advocated for the other invention systems described in this chapter. The teacher must first familiarize students with the terms and structure of the technique, usually by means of handouts and work on the blackboard, and then the students must be asked to manipulate the technique, at first in discrete pieces and later as a whole. Handouts with examples of the original three-element method and with the entire heuristic work well, but only when you take the time to explain thoroughly how the examples were derived. More than with most techniques, students need time and repetition to grasp the use of tagmemics. Do not become discouraged when your students still have trouble with the heuristic after a week's work on it. If you keep with it, eventually the work will pay off.

The subjects that you assign for practice should be carefully chosen. You might begin with relatively simple physical items: "your room" works well, as do "the pen" and "the divan." Slowly work up through general abstracts (like the South or socialism)—to what might be called specific abstracts—the siege of Sarajevo and unit-pricing laws—which make up so much of the world of writing assignments. Throughout this practice, you can ask students to generate lists of questions or lists of answers to questions, and at any point a list of answers can be developed into the germ of an essay. If you plan to concentrate each class day on the use of the system, both orally and in writing, it will begin to become an automatic response after about three weeks. Eventually you should be able to say, "Variation?" and hear from the back of the room, "Is prostitution a victimless crime?" or another question of the sort. Intuition of the system will come, but only with time and work.

Example 7-4 is a graduate student's rendition of "your room." First the student took her subject, which through the tagmemic grid of questioning she changed to "my office." Then, after reading over her piled-up information, she organized it into a coherent, sustained piece of discourse.

After the student read through her information, she thought about what information would best lend itself to an accurate description of her office. Her draft is shown in Example 7-5.

Example 7-4 STUDENT'S TAGMEMIC

My Office

<u>STATIC</u>

P
A
R
T
I
C
L
E

My office is pretty big yet cozy—a Hide-a-Bed, two walls of windows with bookshelves underneath. It's different from the other rooms because this is the messiest room in the house—papers and books piled high, Post-it notes stuck to the bookshelves. The shelves are especially nice because my husband built them. He thinks they're rough; I think they're perfect. When I finished them, *to polyurethane* became a verb. It's different from my school office because it's not cold; I can wear T-shirt and shorts. My daughter often sits down on the sofa and reads while I study at my desk. I can see out (not like my windowless office at school) to the beautiful Scott's Seed Company lawn across the street.

Home offices are pretty much the same except that someone actually works in this home office. They seem to be a yuppie 1980s concept, with a wet bar and built-in TV cabinet. But my office is a place to work. That's why we call it an office. It's still an office if we're all in there talking, yet it would not be an office if we watched TV or had lots of fun in there. It's a working office. It's hard for me to get things done in my school office. Lots of students might like to have an office like mine, a quiet place to work, a place to leave a mess.

The office is part of our downstairs, part of our house. It's at the front of the house. When we walk in the front door, we turn left immediately to get to the office. It's easy for ESL students to come here and study. In fact, they always like to come here. Its conceptual context is a place to work, much like our functional kitchen, which is two rooms away. Our living room and dining room are places to socialize, I guess. The dining room is directly opposite the office, also at the front of the house, on the other side of the living room.

Example 7-4 (continued)

DYNAMIC

The dynamism of this office is the work that is accomplished here. The energy field must be tremendous. Latin verbs are learned, thirty hours a week of Latin homework and studying are done here. Statements of (mis)understanding, journals, free-writing are all produced at my desk. I'm not always sure what's happening at the other energy fields: sometimes Anna sits on the sofa and does her too heavy load of homework; sometimes Dave sits at his desk and polishes up reports or works on that endless mess of stuff called income taxes. Late at night, after I've spent a long time at my desk, I sit on the couch and reread Shakespeare's plays. The room is electric with work being done, reading being devoured, masticated, and spat out on paper. I am a literary bulimic.

The office is changing in that Anna is working less in here. Although sometimes I used to think that she contaminated my personal space, I never said anything to her. Now I miss her. It's also changing in that my work schedule seems cyclical: I build up steam for each paper, and the room attracts more materials. After I've handed in a paper, I tidy up and wipe off the bookcase tops. Then my office looks like any other suburban office. But it continues to evolve into an even more alive place—books and papers breed on the shelves and in the drawers. The telephone is often shut off when the computer is turned on. I wonder how what used to be a tidy study will look after years of being a workplace.

The borders between the living room and the bathroom are clear-cut when the doors are closed. But when they're not, the same carpet rolls from the study to the living room to the dining room and seeps into the den/TV room, and the room draws people in. The kitchen and the bath both have beige flooring, so the downstairs is one big ocean of being—maybe it's more like the Gobi Desert. But when the doors are shut and the phone is off, the lines of demarcation are clear. Don't bother to bother me; I'm busy.

Example 7-4 (continued)

MULTIDIMENSIONAL

F
I
E
L
D

The parts of this office are the books and paper, the desks, the lights, the computer, and the telephone. From the books and papers, I get information that I need to deal with. At the desk, I deal with the information: I memorize, I analyze, I try to understand. The lights, of course, make my studying possible. At the computer, I transmit my ideas into legibility. Over the phone, I reach out for more information, keen insights, solace. The books litter the space as the fragments of information litter my brain. People invariably ask, "Have you read all those books?" Well, when you live forty minutes from school, you need a library. You need research materials. You need resources. The dimension obviously lacking in my office is *time*. I need some time to think, to gain intellectual calories. Right now, I seem to be burning them off too fast.

Sometimes the computer bombinates way into the night, stops for a bit of rest, then resumes its hum at the early hours of the morning. The lights, in winter, come on as early as 5:00 P.M.; now they're not lit until eight or so. the neighbors often comment that they see me sitting at my desk late at night or that when they arise in the morning—just to dash to the bathroom—they see the light in the office. Often they ask me what I'm going to do with all my education. I tell 'em, "I'm going to take it with me." After sitting at the desk for hours, my butt gets tired. I think of, and try to do, some work I can do while sitting on the couch. In the winter, I always sink down in the afghan Granny made. She made us an afghan for every room!

The office fits into a larger system—that of my life as a student and as a teacher. I suppose everyone manages to adapt to his/her environment. I know I need a place to spread out. I need surfaces to pile high with my orga-nized stacks. But most of all, I need to be alone to help balance out the craziness of the rest of my life—the daily commutes, the parking, the dashing between the English Department and the Latin Center, the stress of weekly Latin exams and weekly papers, of child care. The stress and noise of life are assuaged by the undervalued-by-most-people solitude of life in my office.

Example 7-5

My Office

The yuppie 1980s concept of a home office, complete with wet bar and built-in stereo, seems to deem all home offices as being of one type; but our home office is different—it's alive. It's the work accomplished in here that electrifies the room with an energy field that must be tremendous. Latin verbs are conjugated and memorized in here; thirty precious hours per week are sacrificed on the altar, which does double duty as my desk, to the Roman god of grades—good ones. Statements of understanding, freewriting, journals—all come to fruition at my desk. I'm not always sure of the magnetic fields elsewhere in the room: occasionally Anna works in here, scaling her mountain of homework; once in a while, Dave polishes up reports and works on that endless mess of stuff called income taxes, the symptom of capitalism (Marx's revenge?). After sitting at my desk for hours, I get tired. Each night I try to set aside some work to do while I sink into the couch in here, swathed in one of my granny's afghans. Tonight I'll slouch down and reread some plays by Shakespeare, preparation for this weekend's trip to Stratford, Ontario. This place lives off spent energy in work being done, reading being devoured, hardly masticated, and then spat out on paper. I am an academic bulimic.

The pieces of this office are more interesting separately than they are together, just as a finished jigsaw puzzle is a disappointment when compared with its thousand different pieces. As a whole, this is a sunny, book-lined, littered sort of office, filling my needs for a place to spread out, for surfaces to pile high with my organized stacks. As I build up steam for each paper, for each exam, the room's magnetic field sucks in more and more materials—like a black hole. The gobs and globs of information vanish into the darkness the day after I've handed in a paper. I tidy up and wipe off the tops of the bookcases. It looks like a yuppie office, for a while.

But this office, as though it has a life of its own, continues to evolve into a more dynamic place: books and papers in tangled masses fornicate on the shelves and in the drawers, giving multiple births to ideas. The telephone is often shut off when the computer is turned on. But most of all, the place fills my need for solitude. I need the solitude of my office to counterbalance the

stress and noise of the rest of my life—the daily commute,
the parking, the dash from the English Department to the
Latin Center, the stress of weekly Latin exams and weekly
papers for my English courses, child care, family life.
The noisy stress of daily life is assuaged by the solitude
and focus of life in my office.

Sometimes the computer clicks late into the night,
stops for a bit of rest, then resumes its hum in the early
morning hours. The neighbors tell me that they see me sitting at my desk late at night and that sometimes when they
stumble to the bathroom in the middle of the night, they
see my light. They ask me what I am going to do with all my
education. I tell them, "I'm going to take it with me."

Tagmemic invention is the Ferrari of inventive techniques: sleek, elegant,
and fast when well tuned. And like a Ferrari, it can break down—that is, if the
teacher doesn't understand how to keep it going. For this reason, some teachers claim that tagmemics should be reserved for upper-level students, yet
others have used it successfully with FY students. Most teachers agree, however, that if taught well, tagmemics can yield more information and information
presented more interestingly than any other system.

FREEWRITING

Freewriting, the technique central to this section, differs strikingly from the
other techniques discussed in this chapter. Unlike the other heuristic-type techniques of invention, freewriting is not a device through which experience can
be consciously processed, nor do freewriting exercises, in their pure form,
provide theses, arguments, or subject matter. Rather, freewriting is a ritual that
can elicit possible subjects, to which the conscious mind may not have easy
access. What freewriting does best is loosen the inhibitions of the inexperienced writer.

A number of writers over the past fifty years have developed freewriting
exercises as methods of getting potential writers used to the idea of writing.
Perhaps the first mention of freewriting-type exercises is in Dorothea Brande's
1934 *Becoming a Writer,* in which the author suggested freewriting as a way for
young would-be novelists to get in touch with their subconscious selves. Brande
advocated writing "when the unconscious is in the ascendent":

> The best way to do this is to rise half an hour, or a full hour, earlier than you
> customarily rise. Just as soon as you can—and without talking, without read-
> ing—begin to write. Write anything that comes to your head. Write any sort
> of early morning revery, rapidly and uncritically. The excellence or ultimate
> worth of what you write is of no importance yet. Forget that you have any
> critical faculty at all. (50-51)

Brande's technique, the ancestor of freewriting, was largely ignored by teachers
of expository writing until the 1950s, when Ken Macrorie, who had read *Becoming a Writer,* began to use an updated version of it in his composition classes.

He modified Brande's directions for use in general composition and told his students to "go home and write anything that comes to your mind. Don't stop. Write for ten minutes or till you've filled a full page." This exercise produced writing that was often incoherent but was also often striking in its transcendence of the dullness and clichéd thought we too often come to expect in English papers (*Uptaught* 20).

It was Macrorie who popularized the technique of freewriting with his books *Uptaught* and *Telling Writing,* but it was Peter Elbow who developed and refined freewriting, making it a well-known tool. In *Writing without Teachers* (which every writing teacher should read for the author's opinions on how to teach and learn writing) Elbow presented the most carefully wrought freewriting plan thus far.

Freewriting is a kind of structured brainstorming, a method of exploring a topic by writing about it—or whatever else it brings to mind—for a certain number of minutes without stopping. It consists of a series of exercises, conducted either in class or at home, during which students start with a blank piece of paper, think about their topic, and then simply let their minds wander while they write. For as long as their time limit, they write down everything that occurs to them (in complete sentences as much as possible). They must not stop for anything. If they can't think of what to write next, they can write "I can't think of what to write next" over and over until something else occurs to them. When their time is up, they can look at what they've written. They may find much that is unusable, irrelevant, or nonsensical. But they may also find important insights and ideas that they didn't know they had—freewriting has a way of jogging loose such ideas. As soon as a word or an idea appears on paper, it often triggers others.

The point of freewriting is to concentrate on writing, taking no time to worry about what others might think of it. When writers struggle to keep words—any words—flowing, they overload their "academic superego," which is usually concerned with content, criticism, spelling, grammar, and any of the other formal or content-based issues of correctness that so easily turn into writing blocks. In other words, they are writing—for five, ten, or fifteen minutes.

Here are Elbow's directions on freewriting:

> Don't stop for anything. Go quickly without rushing. Never stop to look back, to cross something out, to wonder how to spell something, to wonder what word or thought to use, to think about what you are doing. If you can't think of a word or a spelling, just use a squiggle or else write, "I can't think of it." Just put down something. The easiest thing is just to put down whatever is in your mind. If you get stuck, it's fine to write, "I can't think what to say" as many times as you want, or repeat the last word you wrote over and over again, or anything else. The only requirement is that you never stop. (*Writing without Teachers* 3)

This requirement that the pen never be lifted off the paper and that the writing continue even if nothing but gibberish is produced differentiates freewriting from brainstorming and other prewriting exercises. Other prewriting exercises are meant to tap certain unconscious processes, as is freewriting, but they do not produce the deliberate overload of the editing mechanism that freewriting does.

The requirement that the student never stop writing is matched by an equally powerful mandate to the teacher: never grade or evaluate freewriting exercises in any way. You can collect and read them—they are often fascinating illustrations of the working of the mind—but they must not be judged. To judge or grade freewriting would obviate the purpose of the exercise; this writing is *free*, not to be held accountable in the same way as other, more structured kinds of writing. The value of freewriting lies in its capacity to let students slip from the often self-imposed halter of societal expectations and roam without guilt in the pastures of their minds. If you grade or judge such productions, you will convey the message that this writing is not free.

Using Freewriting in the Classroom

Most teachers who use pure freewriting use it at the opening of each class, every day for at least four or five weeks of the term. A session or two of freewriting, though interesting, is insufficient. For long-term gains, students must freewrite constantly *and* regularly. Only then will the act of writing stop being the unnatural exercise that some students see it as and start being just a part of a writer's functioning arsenal. Regular freewriting in class has two particularly worthwhile effects, says William Irmscher: "It creates the expectation that writing classes are places where people come to write, and it makes writing habitual" (*Expository Writing* 82–83).

Students can also freewrite outside of class. You can assign freewriting as homework, grading it only according to whether or not it is done. One nice feature of freewriting is that it is grossly quantitative; students cannot pretend to substitute quality for quantity.

As students become more used to being pushed by a time constraint, their freewriting will become more coherent—the superego adapts and learns to work under pressure, although not with the deadly efficiency it once had. As this occurs, you can begin to intersperse directed writing assignments with the freewriting assignments. Or you may consider phasing out the pure freewriting exercises altogether.

Combined with brainstorming, freewriting can be used as an aid to writing longer pieces. But you won't want to try this combination of techniques until students are comfortable with each one individually. And this combination is most fruitful when students use it at home, since it requires an extended period of time.

To use this combination of techniques, give students a subject to write on, and then suggest the following pattern: (1) brainstorm for ten minutes; (2) make a list; (3) set a timer or an alarm clock for one hour, and write for that whole hour—don't stop and use only the brainstormed list as a basis for ideas.

Yes, students will grow tired during the hour. And yes, they will throw out much of what they write. But this piece of writing or maybe the next one will be the first draft of a paper that they can edit and you can grade.

This technique works best when you assign the topics a week or so before the papers are due. Successful topics are "the meaning of the funny papers" and "feminism"—topics even teenage students have lived with for many years.

Another possibility is for students to keep a journal of nothing but freewriting that they do outside of class. Such a journal is an efficient way for a teacher to monitor students' efforts because, once again, it can be evaluated quantitatively. The entries will improve over the course of the term, often because a freewriting journal is more personal than a conventional journal, but also because students can take writing risks and explorations.

Pure freewriting does not provide the neatness of heuristic systems nor even the coherent processes of prewriting techniques. What, then, is its use? The answer is bound up in the nature of FY students and their level of exposure to the writing process. Freewriting, so long as you explain its purpose and make certain that students don't see it as busywork, can do two things.

First, it can familiarize beginning writers with the physical act of writing. Mina Shaughnessy suggests that it is hard for some teachers to understand exactly how little experience many FY students have had in writing (14–15). Their penmanship is immature, and their command of sentence structure suffers because they cannot match their writing process with their thought process. Freewriting forces them to produce, without the conscious editorial mechanism making the writing process harder than it is. A full five or six weeks of directed freewriting and prewriting can make a difference.

Second, freewriting demystifies the writing process. After simply pouring out their thoughts in a freewriting exercise, students can no longer view the ability to write as a divine gift that has been denied them. They soon come to realize the difference between writing and editing, a difference crucial to their willingness and their ability to write. Freewriting primes the pump for more structured writing by demonstrating that a writer normally cannot produce a perfectly finished essay on the first try, that the process has many steps, and that the most seemingly unpromising gibberish can yield valuable material.

WORKS CITED

Berthoff, Ann. "The Problem of Problem Solving." *CCC* 22 (1971): 237–42.

Bilsky, Manuel, McCrae Hazlitt, Robert E. Streeter, and Richard M. Weaver. "Looking for an Argument." *CE* 14 (1953): 210–16.

Brande, Dorothea. *Becoming a Writer.* 1934. New York: Harcourt, 1970.

Burke, Kenneth. *Counter-Statement.* Los Altos, CA: Hermes, 1953.

——. *A Grammar of Motives.* Englewood Cliffs, NJ: Prentice, 1952.

——. *A Rhetoric of Motives.* Englewood Cliffs, NJ: Prentice, 1950.

Comley, Nancy R. "The Teaching Seminar: Writing Isn't Just Rhetoric." *Training the New Teacher of College Composition.* Ed. Charles W. Bridges. Urbana, IL: NCTE, 1986. 47–58.

Corbett, Edward P. J. *Classical Rhetoric for the Modern Student.* 3rd ed. New York: Oxford UP, 1990.

Daly, John. "The Effects of Writing Apprehension on Message Encoding." *Journalism Quarterly* 54 (1977): 566–72.

——. "Writing Apprehension and Writing Competency." *Journal of Educational Research* 72 (1978): 10–14.

Edwards, Bruce, Jr. *The Tagmemic Contribution to Composition Theory.* Manhattan: Kansas State, 1979.

Elbow, Peter. *Embracing Contraries*. New York: Oxford UP, 1986.

——. *Writing without Teachers*. New York: Oxford UP, 1973.

——. *Writing with Power*. New York: Oxford UP, 1981.

English, Hubert M., Jr. "Linguistic Theory as an Aid to Invention." *CCC* 15 (1964): 136-40.

Flower, Linda, and John Hayes. "Interpretive Acts: Cognition and the Construction of Discourse." *Poetics* 16 (1987).

——. "Uncovering Cognitive Processes in Writing: An Introduction to Protocol Analysis." *Research on Writing*. Ed. P. Mosenthal, S. Walmsley, and L. Tamor. London: Longmans, 1982. 207-20.

Gannett, Cinthia. *Gender and the Journal*. Albany: State U of New York, 1990.

Goswami, Dixie, and Lee Odell. "Naturalistic Studies of Nonacademic Writing." Paper delivered at the CCCC Convention, Washington, DC, March 1980.

Harrington, Elbert W. *Rhetoric and the Scientific Method of Inquiry: A Study of Invention*. Boulder: U. of Colorado, 1948.

Hughes, Richard P., and P. Albert Duhamel. *Rhetoric: Principles and Usage*. Englewood Cliffs, NJ: Prentice, 1967.

Irmscher, William F. *The Holt Guide to English*. New York: Holt, 1972.

——. *Teaching Expository Writing*. New York: Holt, 1979.

Kinney, James. "Tagmemic Rhetoric: A Reconsideration." *CCC* 29 (1978): 141-45.

Kneupper, Charles W. "Revising the Tagmemics Heuristic: Theoretical and Pedagogical Consideration." *CCC* 31 (1980): 161-67.

Lauer, Janice. "Heuristics and Composition." *CCC* 21 (1970): 396-404.

——. "Invention in Contemporary Rhetoric: Heuristic Procedures." Diss. U of Michigan, 1970.

——. "Response to Anne E. Berthoff, 'The Problem of Problem Solving.'" *CCC* 23 (1972): 208-10.

——. "Toward a Methodology of Heuristic Procedures." *CCC* 30 (1979): 268-69.

Lauer, Janice, Janet Emig, and Andrea A. Lunsford. *Four Worlds of Writing*. 4th ed. New York: HarperCollins, 1995.

Macrorie, Ken. *Telling Writing*. Rochelle Park, NJ: Hayden, 1970.

——. *Uptaught*. Rochelle Park, NJ: Hayden, 1970.

Odell, Lee. "Another Look at Tagmemic Theory: A Response to James Kinney." *CCC* 29 (1978): 146-52.

——. "Measuring the Effect of Instruction in Pre-Writing." *Research in the Teaching of English* 9 (1974): 228-40.

——. "Piaget, Problem-Solving, and Freshmen Composition." *CCC* 24 (1973): 36-42.

Osborne, Alex F. *Applied Imagination*. New York: Scribner, 1957.

Pike, Kenneth L. "A Linguistic Contribution to Composition." *CCC* 15 (1964): 82-88.

Rico, Gabriele Lusser. *Writing the Natural Way*. Los Angeles: Tarcher, 1983.

Rohman, D. Gordon. "Pre-Writing: The Stage of Discovery in the Writing Process." *CCC* 16 (1965): 106-12.

Rose, Mike. *Writer's Block: The Cognitive Dimension*. Carbondale, IL: Southern Illinois UP, 1984.

Rueckert, William. "The Rhetoric of Rebirth: A Study of the Literary Theory and Critical Practice of Kenneth Burke." Diss. U of Michigan, 1956.

Shaughnessy, Mina. *Errors & Expectations: A Guide for the Teacher of Basic Writing*. New York: Oxford UP, 1977.

Winterowd, W. Ross. *The Contemporary Writer*. New York: Harcourt, 1975.

Witte, Stephen. "Pre-Text and Composing." *CCC* 38 (1987): 397-425.

Young, Richard E. "Invention: A Topographical Survey." *Teaching Composition: Ten Bibliographic Essays*. Ed. Gary Tate. Fort Worth: Texas Christian UP, 1976. 1-44.

Young, Richard E., and Alton L. Becker. "Toward a Modern Theory of Rhetoric: A Tagmemic Contribution." *Harvard Education Review* 35 (1965): 50-68.

Young, Richard E., Alton L. Becker, and Kenneth L. Pike. *Rhetoric: Discovery and Change*. New York: Harcourt, 1970.

Young, Richard E., Frank Koen. *The Tagmemic Discovery Procedure: An Evaluation of Its Uses in the Teaching of Rhetoric*. Ann Arbor: U of Michigan, Department of Humanities, 1973.

8 TEACHING ARRANGEMENT AND FORM

One of the continuing criticisms of classical rhetoric concerns its seemingly arbitrary canonical divisions. Is there any essential reason, for example, for assuming that the process of generating discourse should be divided into the restrictive classifications of invention, arrangement, style, delivery, and memory? And if these divisions are arbitrary, having no real connection to the composing process, why use them in a book like this?

Controversial though they may be, the divisions of rhetoric are useful conventions. Were we to try to describe the composing process as the seamless interaction of form and content that it apparently is, our discussion would have to be considerably deeper and more theoretical than space allows here. Separating invention and arrangement is a convenient tool for discussing certain features of process composing even though the two operations are deeply interrelated and never carried out separately by practiced writers.

Experienced writers know that invention, arrangement, and style are inextricably intertwined, that no approach to one can ever ignore the others. Because of this intimate relationship between form and content, Richard Larson writes that "form in complete essays has not been the subject of much theoretical investigation" ("Structure" 45). Invention, with its many open-ended systems, has received much more recent attention, perhaps because of the expressive and romantic biases of our age, which militate against formal requirements in general and encourage self-ordered expression. Still, no one can claim that expectations about the characteristics of the different genres do not exist, and thus the demands of arrangement remain an integral part of rhetoric.

Specific internal arrangement of elements creates rhetorical form, which may be called genre, mode, or organization. Some teachers argue that preconceived arrangement (or formal structure) is artificial, that all organization should grow naturally out of the writer's purpose. Others see readily identifiable organization and form as the first step toward successful communication. Each teacher must gradually develop her own concept of forms and learn to strike a balance between form and content. This chapter can only suggest the various alternatives available, many of which have been used throughout the history of the teaching of rhetoric.

Forms and arrangements can sometimes be assigned and used artificially; therefore, when we discuss form with our students, we must remind them (and ourselves) of the relationships between structure and content: that purpose, the needs of the audience, and the subject should dictate arrangement—not

177

vice versa. We cannot, then, merely offer our students one or two prefabricated, all-purpose arrangements. Instead, we must regularly ask students to recognize the interconnections between form and content and between genre and intention, and we must work to assist them in the subtle task of creating forms that fit their ideas and emphases.

Whatever methods of arrangement or forms you choose to teach, you will want your students to realize that you are teaching them *conventions* to be adapted and changed as the writer specifies the needs of a particular subject and a particular audience. Methods of arrangement can provide a rough framework on which to build an essay, but they should neither limit the development of an essay nor demand sections that are clearly unnecessary.

The prescriptive forms in this chapter, then, should be thought of and taught only as stepping-stones—not as ends in themselves. You will want to teach your students to transcend them as well as to use them. Kenneth Burke gives us an immensely important message in telling us that "form is an arousing and fulfillment of desires, . . . correct in so far as it gratifies the needs which it creates" (*Counterstatement* 124). Form must grow from the human desires for both the familiar and the novel. If the prescriptive forms we give our students can help them realize this primary purpose, then we can offer the forms with the certainty that they will provide scaffolding only until the students can dismantle them and build on their own.

GENERAL PATTERNS OF ARRANGEMENT

The arrangement of material in an essay grows out of a complex blend of the author's purpose, her knowledge of the subject, and the formal expectations of the audience. In the course of ten or thirteen weeks, though, few teachers can present, and even fewer students can grasp, all of the intricacies in the marriage of form and content and all of the techniques used by experienced writers. Students can, however, begin to appreciate these intricacies in the material that is familiar to them. Try, for instance, asking them to examine the patterns of arrangement in articles and essays written by academicians in other fields of study and deducing their conventional formats wherever possible. You can also introduce students to the general conventional forms of arrangement covered here, which range from simple and short formats that can be adapted to nearly any subject matter to longer and more complex ones used specifically in argumentation. You can demonstrate and assign one, two, or all of these patterns of arrangement. But you and your students will want to remember that these patterns are not absolutes, should not be taught as absolutes, and must be seen as convenient devices, not as rigid structures.

The elements discussed as parts of each method of arrangement have no necessary correlation with paragraphs.[1] Some students are tempted to conceive of a "six-part" essay as a six-paragraph essay, but except for some minor and very prescriptive forms, such as the "five-paragraph theme," each element

---

[1] See Chapter 10.

in a discourse scheme consists of a minimum of a single paragraph. Thus a four-part essay might consist of a single paragraph for the introduction, three paragraphs for the statement of fact, four paragraphs for the argument, and a single paragraph for the conclusion. Each element can theoretically consist of an unlimited number of paragraphs, and you should beware of letting your students fall into the habit of perceiving each element as a single paragraph.

CLASSICALLY DESCENDED ARRANGEMENTS

The first theorists to propose generic forms for rhetoric were the Greeks, whose ideas were rendered more formally and more technically by the Roman rhetoricians. The first arrangement we have record of is from Aristotle, who may have been responding to the complicated, "improved" methods of arrangement retailed by his sophistic competition when he wrote, "A speech has two parts. You must state your case, and you must prove it. . . . The current division is absurd" (*Rhetoric* 1414b).[2] With the exception of the three-part essay, which has been generalized and modernized, all classical arrangements descend from Aristotle, and all are essentially argumentative in nature—like classical rhetoric itself. These arrangements, organized formally rather than according to content, rarely suit narrative or descriptive writing and can confuse students who try to use them for nonargumentative purposes. In *Classical Rhetoric for the Modern Student*, Edward P. J. Corbett points out that instead of being topically organized, classical arrangements are "determined by the functions of the various parts of a discourse" (282).

Three-Part Arrangement

"A whole," says Aristotle, "is that which has a beginning, a middle, and an end" (*Poetics* 24). Aristotle's observation—original, true, and now obvious—is the starting place for the most widely accepted method of rhetorical arrangement, the three-part arrangement. Like the dramatic works Aristotle was describing, a complete discourse, such as a successful essay, has three parts: an introduction, a body of some length, and a conclusion. From the simplest single-paragraph exercise to a forty-page research paper, every writing assignment is expected to contain these three parts.

The simplicity of this arrangement has positive and negative aspects. On the one hand, it is easy to teach and to demonstrate, it is not overly structured, and it is the one truly universal pattern of arrangement, workable for exposition and argumentation alike. On the other hand, it provides little actual guidance in structuring an essay, especially if the assignment calls for a response longer than five hundred words. With such longer essays, students often find that although they are able to write their introductions and conclusions, the bodies of their essays are amorphous. Nothing in the three-part essay provides interior structures that guide beginning writers in constructing the body of their essays,

---

[2] We will not discuss the two-part discourse here, for Aristotle relented in his next paragraph, allowing for four parts to a discourse, a pattern we do discuss.

nearly always the longest part. The three-part arrangement, then, is most suitable for assignments, under five hundred words. Each of the three parts can be taught separately.

The introduction   "The Introduction," writes Aristotle, "is the beginning of a speech, . . . paving the way . . . for what is to follow. . . . The writer should . . . begin with what best takes his fancy, and then strike up his theme and lead into it" (*Rhetoric* 1414b). In the three-part essay, the introduction has two main tasks. First, it must catch and hold the reader's attention with an opening "hook"—an introductory section that does not announce the thesis of the essay but instead begins to relate the as-yet-unannounced thesis in some brief, attention-catching way. The introduction can open with an anecdote, an aphorism, an argumentative observation, a quotation. Donald Hall calls such an opening strategy a "quiet zinger, . . . something exciting or intriguing and at the same time relevant to the material that follows" (38).

Second, the introduction must quickly focus the attention of the reader on the *thesis*. The thesis, or central informing principle of the essay, is determined by the writer's purpose, subject, and audience. It is usually found in the form of a single-sentence declarative statement near the end of the introduction. This *thesis statement* represents the essay-length equivalent of the topic sentence of a paragraph; it is general enough to announce what the following essay plans to do yet specific enough to suggest what the essay will not do. Sheridan Baker has made the controversial suggestion that the thesis statement is always the most specific sentence in the opening paragraph and should always come at the end of that paragraph, but although this is an easy-to-teach truism that may help students structure their introductions, critics have disputed how accurately it reflects the practice of experienced and published writers.

The body of the essay   According to Aristotle, the body of the essay is a middle, which follows something as some other thing follows it. In truth, little more can be said of the middle in terms of the theory of the three-part essay, but in practice, writers can choose from many organizational plans. Some teachers trail off into generalities when they discuss the body of the essay, talking about "shaping purpose," "order of development," and "correct use of transitions"—necessary considerations but of little help to students adrift between their first and last paragraphs.

The body of the three-part essay can take many shapes: writers can develop their essays according to the physical aspects, the chronology, or the logic of the subject matter, by illustrating points, defining terms, dividing and classifying, comparing and contrasting, analyzing causes and effects, or considering problems and solutions.[3] Whatever organizational plan writers choose, they will

[3] Some of the methods of structuring essays are described in Chapter 4 of *The St. Martin's Handbook*.

want to be sure that the main points of the body relate not only to the thesis but to one another.

The conclusion Like introductions, conclusions present special challenges, for a conclusion should indicate that a full discussion has taken place. Often a conclusion will begin with a restatement of the thesis and end with more general statements that grow out of it, reversing the common general-to-specific pattern of the introduction. This restatement is usually somewhat more complex than the original thesis statement, since now the writer assumes that the reader can marshal all of the facts of the situation as they have been presented in the body of the essay. A typical if obvious example of the opening of a conclusion might be "Thus, as we have seen," followed by the reworded thesis.

But besides reiterating the consequence and import of the thesis, the conclusion should include a graceful or memorable rhetorical note. Writers can draw on a number of techniques to conclude effectively and give their text a sense of ending: a provocative question, a quotation, a vivid image, a call for action, or a warning. Sheridan Baker writes that the successful conclusion satisfies the reader because it "conveys a sense of assurance and repose, of business completed" (22). William Zinsser, however, insists that

> the perfect ending should take the reader slightly by surprise and yet seem exactly right to him. He didn't expect the [piece] to end so soon, or so abruptly, or to say what it said. But he knows it when he sees it. (78–79)

Zinsser goes on to tell writers of nonfiction that when they are ready to stop, they should stop: "If you have presented all the facts and made the point that you want to make, look for the nearest exit" (79). Often, however, the best conclusions are those that answer the "so what?" of the thesis statement and overall argument.

Using the Three-Part Arrangement in the Classroom

Although it is applicable to many modes of discourse, the classical three-part arrangement simply does not provide enough internal structure to help students put together the middle sections of their essays. The three-part form is useful mainly as an introduction to the conventions of introductions and conclusions. The easiest way to consider the body of an essay is to teach patterns of other, more fully developed arrangements.

After introducing the basic three-part structure, you can discuss the importance of introductions and conclusions. Try to choose examples that put special emphasis on the structures of these parts, and ask students to respond to your examples. You might assign a series of short in-class essays on topics your students have chosen. So that students concentrate on recognizable introductions and conclusions, you might allow them to dispense with the writing of the body of each essay and to submit instead a rough outline or list of components.

This exercise is especially useful when the students work in writing groups. In the class after each short essay is written, convene the groups, and ask students to read over, and evaluate the success of, the introductions and conclusions of one another's essays. They might answer specific questions, such as these.

What does the opening of this essay accomplish?

How does it "hook" the reader?

Can you help the author improve the opening?

Does the essay end in a memorable way? Or does it seem to trail off into vagueness or end abruptly?

If you like the conclusion, what about it do you like?

Can you help the author improve the conclusion?

You may want to put the most effective introduction and conclusion on the blackboard so that the entire class can share them. After the students have conferred and improved one another's work and after the introductions and conclusions have been hammered into a final form, allow those students who have become intrigued by the ideas they've been working with to complete the essay for a grade. Several days of this kind of practice can give students a solid competence in beginning and ending essays.

Four-Part Arrangement

After blasting the hair-splitting pedagogues of his day and declaring that an oration has only two parts, Aristotle relented and admitted that as speakers actually practice rhetoric, a discourse generally has four parts: the *proem* or *introduction*, the *statement of fact*, the *confirmation,* or *argument*, and the *epilogue,* or *conclusion* (*Rhetoric* 200). Specifically an argumentative form, this four-part arrangement does not adapt well to narrative or description.

The introduction Called by Aristotle the *proem* (from the Greek word *proemium,* meaning "before the song") and the *exordium* (from the Latin weaving term for "beginning a web") by the author of the Roman handbook *Rhetorica ad herrenium,* the introduction to the four-part essay has two functions, one major and one minor. The major task is to inform the audience of the purpose or object of the essay; the minor task is to create a rapport, or relationship of trust, with the audience.

"The most essential function and distinctive property of the introduction," writes Aristotle, "[is] to show what the aim of the speech is" (*Rhetoric* 202). Corbett tells us that the introduction serves two important audience-centered functions: it orients the audience within the subject, and even more important, it seeks to convince readers that what is being introduced is worthy of their attention (283). In a fashion similar to the "quiet zinger" that opens the three-part essay, the four-part essay can catch the attention of the reader by using different devices. Richard Whately lists different types of introductions that can arouse the reader's interest (189–92). The usefulness of these types of introductions is of course not limited to the four-part essay, although they do complement argumentative subject matter.

Inquisitive shows that the subject in question is "important, curious, or otherwise interesting."

Paradoxical dwells on characteristics of the subject that seem improbable but are nonetheless real. This form of introduction searches for strange and curious perspectives on the subject.

Corrective shows that the subject has been "neglected, misunderstood, or misrepresented by others." As Whately says, this immediately removes the danger that the subject will be thought trite or hackneyed.

Preparatory explains peculiarities in the way the subject will be handled, warns against misconceptions about the subject, or apologizes for some deficiency in the presentation.

Narrative leads to the subject by narrating a story or anecdote.

These various introductions can accomplish the major task of acquainting the audience with the subject, and they often also accomplish the minor task of rendering the reader attentive and well-disposed toward the writer and her cause.

In rendering an audience benevolent, writers must be aware of certain elements concerning the rhetorical situation in which they find themselves. Corbett offers five questions that writers must ask themselves regarding their rhetorical situation before they can be certain of the conditions for their discourse.

1. What do I have to say?
2. To or before whom is it being said?
3. Under what circumstances?
4. What are the predispositions of the audience?
5. How much time or space do I have? (290)

The introduction is the best place to establish "bridges" between writer and reader by pointing to shared beliefs and attitudes—that is, by creating what Kenneth Burke calls *identification* of the writer with the audience and the audience with the writer.

The introduction to the four-part essay, then, performs functions similar to that of the three-part essay. It draws readers into the discourse with the promise of interesting information and informs them of the main purpose of the discourse while rendering them well-disposed toward the writer and the subject.

The statement of fact The Romans called the statement of fact the *narratio*, and it is sometimes today referred to as the *narration* or *background*. But Corbett's term *statement of fact* works well, especially since we now use *narration* to signify dramatized activities. This section of a discourse also presents more than just background. The statement of fact is a nonargumentative, expository presentation of the objective facts concerning the situation or problem—the subject—under discussion.

The statement of fact may contain circumstances, details, summaries, even narrative in the modern sense. It sets forth the background of the problem and very often explains the central point as well. Perhaps, the best general advice remains Quintilian's, who in the first century A.D., recommended that the statement of fact be *lucid, brief,* and *plausible.* Writers can order their statement of fact in a number of different ways: in chronological order, from general situation to specific details, from specific to general, or according to topics. The tone of the statement of fact should be neutral, calm, and matter-of-fact, free of overt stylistic mannerisms and obvious bias. Writers are best served by understatement, for readers will readily trust a writer they deem to be as striving for fairness.

Confirmation   Also called the *argument,* the confirmation is central to the four-part essay and is often the longest section. Corbett tells us that the confirmation is easily used in expository as well as argumentative prose; historically, it was used mainly in argumentation. Simply put, the confirmation is used to prove the writer's case. With the audience rendered attentive by the introduction and informed by the statement of fact, the writer is ready to show the reasons why her position concerning the facts should be accepted and believed. Most of the argumentative material discovered in the invention process is used in this section.

Of the three kinds of persuasive discourse—*deliberative, forensic,* and *epideictic*—the first two are truly argumentative. Aristotle theorizes that argumentative discourse deals with two different sorts of questions: deliberative, or political, oratory is always concerned with the future, and forensic, or judicial, oratory is always concerned with the past. (Epideictic, or ceremonial, oratory is concerned with the present.) If the question is about events in the past, the confirmation will try to prove

1. Whether an act was committed
2. Whether an act committed did harm
3. Whether the harm of the act is less or more than alleged
4. Whether a harmful act was justified.

If the question is about a course for the future, the confirmation will try to prove that

1. A certain thing can or cannot be done. If it can be done, then the confirmation tries to prove that
2. It is just or unjust
3. It will do harm or good
4. It has not the importance the opposition attaches to it.

After the writer has decided on a question and a position, she can move into the argument, choosing from definitions, demonstrations of cause or effect, analogies, authoritative testimony, maxims, personal experiences—evidence of all sorts—in order to prove her point.

Writers can build their arguments in different ways, but classical rhetoricians offer a rough plan. If there are, for instance, three specific lines of argument available to the writer, one strong, one moderately convincing, and one weak, they should be grouped thus: the moderate argument first, the weak argument second, and the strong argument last. This arrangement begins and ends the confirmation on notes of relative strength and prevents the writer's position from appearing initially weak or finally anticlimactic.

Conclusion   Called the *epilogue* by the Greeks and the *peroration* by the Romans (from *per-oratio*, a finishing off of the oration), the conclusion, according to Aristotle's *Rhetoric,* has four possible tasks.

1. It renders the audience once again well-disposed to the writer and ill-disposed toward the writer's opponent.
2. It magnifies the writer's points and minimizes those of the opposition.
3. It puts the audience in the proper mood.
4. It refreshes the memory of the audience by summarizing the main points of the argument.

Most conclusions do recapitulate the main points, or at least the central thesis, of the discourse. The other three possible tasks are less concrete. Although the conclusion tends to be the most obviously emotional of all the sections, the use of *pathos* (emotional appeal) in written assignments is a dangerous technique for beginners, in whose hands it can all too easily degenerate into *bathos* (laughable emotional appeal). The best conclusions restate or expand their main points and then sign off gracefully with a stylistic flourish that signals the end of the discourse.

Using the Four-Part Arrangement in the Classroom

Although the four-part arrangement gives more direction to an essay than does the three-part arrangement, it is not as adaptable to different sorts of discourse. The four-part pattern generally demands subject-directed, nonpersonal writing that can support an argumentative thesis. For an essay with such an arrangement, students usually need several days in which to conceptualize and investigate their subjects. They will also need to apply techniques of invention or do research on their subjects before writing their first drafts. Some teachers prefer to provide the subjects on which their students are to write four-part essays at least in the beginning, for this arrangement works best when applied to rigidly defined questions.

You may want to assign subjects that need little or no research and can support several different argumentative theses. You can decide whether to begin with a question involving actions in the past (a forensic question) or one involving future policy (a deliberative question). Some possible forensic topics might be these.

The conduct of the Alcohol, Tobacco, and Firearms (ATF) agents in the Branch Davidian disaster

Hillary Rodham Clinton's role in the Whitewater scandal

The fairness of the campus parking policy

Gangsta rap's role in the increase in urban violence

The First Amendment: safeguard of liberty or threat to women?

And deliberative topics might include these.

Should the federal government change hard-rock mining regulations?

Is mandatory recycling good for the state?

Should all undergraduates be required to have proficiency in a foreign language?

Should alcohol be banned at all Greek events? in all Greek houses?

Obviously, deliberative topics change as the issues of the day change. Current campus controversies make excellent topics.

While students can certainly master the forms in a week, that amount of time does not allow for a topic to be thoroughly researched. You may want to overlook the generalizations and the abstract, vague arguments your students make while they learn to apply the four parts of the arrangement. You can also give them some writing-group work that reinforces what they are learning about arrangement.

After your students have finished their first drafts of the four-part assignment, ask them to join their writing groups and read one another's drafts. Have them ask the following questions about each section of the essay:

Introduction

Do the first four sentences attract my interest?

Is the subject clearly defined in the introduction?

Is the introduction too long?

Does the introduction seem to be aimed at a specific audience? What is that audience?

Do I want to know more, to keep reading? Why?

Statement of fact

Does this section clearly explain the nature of the problem or the situation?

Is there anything not told that I need to know?

Does the problem or situation continue to interest me?

Confirmation

Is the argumentation convincing and believable?

Does the order of presentation seem reasonable?

Has any obvious argument been left out?

Has the opposing position been competently refuted?

Conclusion

Has the case been summarized well?

Do I feel well-disposed toward the writer? Why?

Does the ending seem graceful?

Many teachers like to drift among the writing groups as they work and remind students that any form must be adapted to its content. To help students adapt form to content, you may want to talk to each student individually while the groups are meeting.

After the groups have completed their discussions of the preceding questions and students have evaluated one another's drafts, ask each student for a typed copy of her essay. You may want to distribute copies of students' papers (without the authors' names) and review with the class the strengths and weaknesses of each argument. Often students will volunteer a draft of their paper if they know they can remain anonymous and receive the help and attention of the entire class.

The more that students know about the formal qualities of the form and what is successful in argument, the easier it will be for them to write their next papers.

Two More-Detailed Arrangements

The classical oration form used by Cicero and Quintilian was a four-part form, but the Latin rhetoricians went on to divide the third part, the confirmation, into *confirmatio* and *reprehensio*. Cicero said that "the aim of confirmation is to prove our own case and that of refutation (*reprehensio*) is to refute the case of our opponents" (337). Thus the classical oration is composed of five parts.

exordium, or introduction

narratio, or statement of facts

confirmatio, or proof of the case

reprehensio, or refutation of opposing arguments

peroratio, or conclusion

Setting off the refutation in its own section is not a meaningful change from the four-part arrangement, since the confirmation of the four-part essay can also be refutative. Still, a separate section of refutation makes the task of dealing with opposing arguments mandatory; hence, it can provide more structure for a discourse. Although the refutation does not always present the writer's own positive arguments, it usually does—that is, unless the opposing arguments are so powerful or so well accepted that the audience would not listen to an opposing confirmation without first being prepared by the refutation.

Corbett tells us that refutation is based on *appeal to reason*, on *emotional appeals*, on the *ethical or personal appeal of the writer*, or on *wit*. Refutation can usually be accomplished in one of two ways: (1) the writer denies the truth of one of the premises on which the opposing argument is built; or (2) the writer objects to the inferences drawn by the opposition from premises that cannot be broken down.

Most detailed of all the classically descended arrangements is the six-part arrangement recommended by Hugh Blair in his extremely influential *Lectures on Rhetoric and Belles-Lettres* of 1783. Blair's arrangement was largely influenced by the classical theorists, but Blair was also a practitioner of pulpit oratory. Hence, his arrangement shows both classical and sermonic elements. His model of a discourse was composed of these elements:

exordium, or introduction

statement and division of the subject

narration, or explication

reasoning, or arguments

pathetic or emotional part

conclusion. (341)

In this breakdown, the introduction captures the attention of the audience, renders the reader benevolent, and so on. Like some of the classical theorists, Blair distinguishes two sorts of introductions: the *principium*, a direct opening addressed to well-disposed audiences, and the *insinuatio*, a subtler method that prepares a hostile audience for arguments counter to their opinions. The *insinuatio* generally opens by first admitting the most powerful points made by the opposition, by showing how the writer holds the same views as the audience on general philosophical questions, or by dealing with ingrained audience prejudices. The *principium*, on the other hand, can proceed with the knowledge that the audience is sympathetic, going directly to the task of rendering readers attentive.

In Blair's arrangement, as in the three-part arrangement, the thesis is clearly stated at the end of the introduction, but here the thesis is immediately followed by the "division," or announcement of the plan of the essay, which is Blair's first large departure from the four-part essay. Both the proposition and the division should be short and succinct. According to Blair, the division should avoid "unnecessary multiplication of heads." In other words, it should contain as simple an outline as possible, presented in a natural, nonmechanistic fashion.

The next two sections, "narration" and "reasoning," correspond to the statement of fact and the confirmation in the four-part essay. Then, however, Blair proposes that a new division of arrangement, termed the *pathetic part*, follow the argumentation section. The word *pathetic* in this case refers to the pathetic or emotional appeal of classical rhetoric. Thus after presenting her argument, Blair's writer would appeal to the audience's feelings; in addition, she would begin to draw the discourse to a close.

Blair recommends using a formula remarkably similar to T. S. Eliot's "objective correlative" for arousing the emotions of the audience: the writer must connect the audience's emotions with a specific instance, object, or person. A writer arguing against nuclear power, for instance, might close her arguments with specific examples of nuclear harm—factory workers made sterile by isotope poisoning or workers killed in grisly fashion at Chernobyl, for example. A writer arguing for nuclear generation of electricity might paint a picture of poor people freezing to death because the cost of heating without nuclear power is too great for them to bear.

In the pathetic part, the writer should conclude her argumentation with a powerful emotional appeal, an appeal that will bring together the arguments, leading readers to act on their feelings. The pathetic appeal at the end of the arguments can be very effective.

The pathetic part should also be short, Blair says, and must not rely on any stylistic or oratorical flourishes; therefore, the language should be bold, ardent, and simple. And finally, Blair warns, writers should not attempt to create a pathetic effect if they themselves are not moved, for the result of such attempts will not only be ineffective and artificial but hypocritical as well.

Following the pathetic part of this six-part form is the conclusion, similar to the conclusion presented in the less-detailed arrangements.

Using the More-Detailed Arrangements in the Classroom

For the advanced or honors student, the more detailed forms are profitable. Based on the four-part essay, these forms are best taught as mere extensions of it. Teachers who provide their students with a more complex arrangement often find the students unwilling to go back to the less detailed structure and its larger burden of decision. Often teachers present both of the more-detailed forms, spending time on the four-part structure and then progressing to the classical oration and Blair's arrangement. Each successive structure subsumes those that precede it.

Because your students will probably need more time to think through and develop their argumentative essays than they will need for any other type of discourse, your choice for this assignment is of paramount importance. Even when they understand the argumentative arrangement, students cannot assemble their essays overnight. The forensic and deliberative topics mentioned earlier can be profitably applied to these arrangements. But by the time you have reached the stage of teaching these forms, it is often close to the end of the term, and students will be able to choose their own topics. Having been led through the four-part form, they know which topics can be well argued and which will present problems. Sometimes, however, the class will need to work together, coming up with and developing topics for stumped classmates.

Both the five- and the six-part forms provide specific sorts of practice, the five-part form in refutation, the six-part form in emotional appeals of a certain sort. Before they begin to write, students using the five-part form should be able to list at least two arguments their opposition would be likely to use; otherwise, their refutations could be too general, or indistinguishable from their confirmations. Students using the six-part form must keep in mind the difference between pathos and bathos and avoid embarrassing attempts to sway the emotions. The six-part form is best used by honors or upper-level students whose emotional perceptions are likely to be informed by the rational and calculating judgment necessary for effective pathetic appeal.

To familiarize your students with the soon-to-be-assigned form, you may want to hand out a model of the form. You will want to exemplify as well as introduce each element in a new argument. Some teachers elicit an argumentative subject from the class and then, with the class, outline the course of that argument on the board. Students often have strong ideas of how one specific form of arrangement best suits a particular argument. Working together this way is the best practice you can give your class.

During each stage of teaching these prescriptive arrangements, you'll want to illustrate the flexibility of the demands made by these forms. The more complex the pattern of arrangement, the greater the chance that one or more sections will be extraneous or actually harmful to the discourse. Students must learn to use common sense in deciding whether or to what degree the method of arrangement fits the needs of the writer and her audience.

NONCLASSICAL ARRANGEMENTS

Larson's Problem-Solving Form

"Problem-solving," says Richard Larson, is "the process by which one moves from identifying the need to accomplish a particular task (and discovering that the task is difficult) to finding a satisfactory means for accomplishing that task" ("Problem-Solving" 629). What this emphasis on action-based task definition means, of course, is that the problem-solving form is both exploratory and argumentative. It deals more successfully with situations in which a change needs to be accomplished than with narrative or purely expository writing. Defining a problem leads, as in the classical deliberative oration, to arguing for one specific answer. The novel and valuable aspect of Larson's method is that it uses the very process of arriving at an arguable position as the pattern of arrangement for the essay.

In "Problem-Solving, Composing, and Liberal Education," Larson identifies eight steps that must be accomplished in order to complete the process of identifying and solving a problem, steps that can be used as a pattern of arrangement.

1. *Definition of the problem.* After a short introduction, this section provides "a clear statement of exactly what is to be decided." This statement usually involves a choice among possible courses of action or the identification of an undesirable condition that can be corrected.

2. *Determination of why the problem is indeed a problem or a source of difficulty.* If a course of action is clear, as Larson points out, there can be no problem. This section clarifies the need for a decision on policy or an explanation of what is undesirable about the current situation. The explanation may demand a causal analysis of the present situation.

3. *An enumeration of the goals that must be served by whatever action is taken.* Sometimes the determination of the goals to be strived for is in itself a problem-solving situation, but most possible subjects for students' essays present readily identifiable goods as goals—world peace, equitable distribution of wealth, the best education, and so on.

4. *Determination of the goals that have the highest priority for the decision maker.* This step can be difficult. Usually there are several goals in any realistic solution, and if possible goals include mutually exclusive goals, such as "free trade" and "fair trade," for instance, some decision must be made on priority. This assigning of priorities may need to be argued for in itself, depending on the essay's projected audience.

5. *"Invention" of procedures that might be implemented to attain the stated goals.* If the question is one of choosing among several possible courses of action, no invention will be necessary unless some sort of compromise is proposed. If the problem solver must discover how to improve an undesirable situation, though, invention of possible methods will be necessary. For example, the problem of poor urban transit could be solved by creating more bus stops, by buying more buses, or by instituting peak-hour special runs. If choices are not immediately apparent, they must be created.

6. *Prediction of the results of each possible action.* This is the most difficult step, requiring careful study of evidence—conditions, precedents, laws of nature, history, past cause-and-effect sequences, and so on. This entire section must be based on intelligent appraisals of probability. Each possible action must be weighed against the good it would accomplish, its cost, and any unavoidable evil attached to it.

7. *Weighing of the predictions.* This part of the essay compares the possible actions and their projected outcomes, trying to gauge which action will be most likely to attain the chosen goals with the fewest unwanted side effects.

8. *Final evaluation of the choice that seems superior.* The essay closes with a determination of whether the chosen alternative does indeed solve the problem. Some modification of the chosen action may be seen as needed to minimize the bad effects or to maximize the good. (631–33)

Larson posits this method as both a pattern of arrangement and a system of invention. As mentioned at the beginning of this chapter, one canon implies the other; both canons of rhetoric—arrangement and invention—are inherent in problem solving. All patterns of arrangement contain aspects of invention.

Using Larson's Problem-Solving Form in the Classroom

The problem-solving technique has many uses for students outside English classes; thus it can be one of the most practical forms to teach. It is, for example, the primary report form used in technical and professional writing of all sorts, a tool that many students will be able to employ throughout their careers. It also provides a method for thinking situations through that may help remedy the easy assertions and corner-cutting thought processes that plague introductory English classes.

It is important, though, that Larson's method of arrangement—indeed, that *any* system of arrangement—*not* be used as a sterile formula. But, once you have introduced the eight steps of Larson's problem-solving process, you may find that students want to stick to them slavishly no matter how often you advise them to be flexible. The problem-solving form is a duplication of actual conceptual steps, so students' essays may seem formulaic to some degree. But as students discover the real demands of problems they face, their dependence on the form will decrease.

To introduce students to the problem-solving pattern of arrangement, hand out sheets that detail the eight steps. The example of this arrangement mentioned by Larson is Swift's "Modest Proposal," which is frequently anthologized. If you wish to expose your students to a more modern example, you might look through technical writing texts for models of the feasibility study, usually an important assignment in technical writing. You might also ask a colleague who teaches technical writing whether you may borrow and reproduce copies of students' essays using that form. The simpler the example, the better; too much technical detail can discourage FY students.

After you have explained and demonstrated the steps of the process, and when you feel your students are comfortable with and able to identify, the steps, ask them for a simple problem-solving outline—two or three sentences under each heading—on a campus-related topic: "Should the school newspaper be free, or should it be sold for a nominal sum?" "Should the library go to a closed-stack system?" The best problem-solving topics are deliberative, having to do with future policy. Students usually need several days to come up with this outline. On the day it is due, convene writing groups, and ask students to evaluate one another's work, examining each step of the outline for strengths and weaknesses. At this stage, they need to examine the logical structure of the outline, making certain that no important goal or prediction has been ignored or underplayed.

Students are now usually ready for a longer assignment. You can ask them to expand their outlines into full-length essays, or you may go directly to a full-length deliberative question and assign a problem-solving essay based on it. Any of the deliberative topics mentioned in connection with the classical forms will work here; others, on current political and cultural questions, will probably suggest themselves to you. It is a good idea to discuss the outline of this paper with your students before they commit themselves to a first draft or to ask them to review one another's outlines in their groups.

Larson's is not the only problem-solving technique available; it merely happens to be a good problem-solving heuristic that is adaptable as a method of arrangement and offers service as an invention technique as well. It is useful as an arrangement mainly because it is one of the most schematic of problem-solving heuristics.

Problem-solving offers the student writer a model for planning rigorous arguments on complex issues, and it is a technique by which students can investigate systems and draw intelligent, defensible conclusions. If you expose your students to Larson's system, you will be providing them not only with a rhetorical tool but also with a method of analysis that will leave them better able to handle the complex demands that contemporary culture makes on educated people.

D'Angelo's Paradigmatic Arrangements

Of all the contemporary rhetorical theorists, Frank J. D'Angelo of Arizona State University has probably given the most thought to problems of arrangement. In his numerous articles, in his theoretical treatise *A Conceptual Theory of Rhetoric*, and in his text *Process and Thought in Composition*, he has taken on some of the more persistent problems that arrangement presents for both teacher and student. He proposes in *Conceptual Theory*, and treats at length in his textbook, a theory of arrangement that he calls *paradigmatic analysis*. A paradigm, says D'Angelo, is "the core structure that represents the *principle of forward motion* in . . . writing" (56). Paradigmatic analysis, by investigating the core structures of various sorts of discourses, can isolate those that appear again and again and allow writers to use them as structures for arrangement. D'Angelo says:

> The purpose of this kind of analysis is not only to reveal the underlying principles that inform discourse, but also to make them generative (in the sense of actually producing discourse). The abstracted paradigm can be re-individuated in new content and can thus be used as the informing principle to generate new discourse. (*Conceptual Theory of Rhetoric* 86)

D'Angelo has isolated what he considers to be the ten most common paradigms of discourse, and he has presented each one in the form of a model or outline that students can use as the plan for essays of their own. D'Angelo says that these paradigmatic structures reflect the way our minds work when we write, and although his list of paradigms may not be all-inclusive, it does encompass most of the important methods of exposition.

Other rhetoricians have listed and dealt with some of these patterns of arrangement—indeed, insofar as they recapitulate the classical topics, they can be said to go back to Aristotle. And critics accuse D'Angelo of merely formalizing what textbooks have long called the "patterns of exposition," but D'Angelo's presentation is the most thorough we have today.[4] Paradigms as he discusses them, stresses D'Angelo, are not merely the arbitrary structures of abstract philosophy but formal extensions of the underlying thought patterns of the human mind.

---

[4] For more information on the "methods of exposition," see Connors.

Paradigms can take a number of different forms, but the useful form for arrangement is the outline paradigm, what D'Angelo calls *abstract paradigms*, those that are stripped to their most basic structures. For instance, an abstract paradigm for a cause-to-effect essay might look like this.

1. Introduction (stating the thesis)
2. Cause 1
3. Cause 2
4. Cause(s) (3, 4, 5, and so on)
5. Effect
6. Conclusion (restating the thesis, summarizing, and so forth)

In order to make it useful, this bare-bones outline must be given first a basic clothing of content in the form of simple declarative statements.

1. The war in Vietnam was the result of a number of historical forces at work all over the world.
2. The first was the awakened Vietnamese nationalism under the guerilla hero Ho Chi Minh.
3. The second was the Truman Doctrine of containment of communism by American forces.
4. The third was the reawakening, aided by the Soviet Union, of Chinese regional imperialism under Mao Tse-tung.
5. All of these factors met in Vietnam in 1965, producing the "dirty little war" that changed modern history.
6. Without all of these factors the Vietnam War would never have started or would have been over in a year.

While we don't propose this outline as the basis of a prize-winning essay, it is obvious that the paradigm allows the writer considerable flexibility while guiding the general direction of the essay. You will notice that the elements of the paradigm seem to transfer themselves to topic sentences of the paragraphs of the essay being created. This direct translation of paradigm element to paragraph topic is seldom seen, and usually each element of a paradigm needs more than a single paragraph to be developed fully. Once the outline statement of each element has been created, the writer must decide how many paragraphs will be needed to deal adequately with that element.

D'Angelo's Common Paradigms

D'Angelo has proposed certain paradigmatic forms as common enough in use to be worth teaching. They include the following:

Narration   Narration conceives of events chronologically in relation to one another. As a pattern of thought, writes D'Angelo, it "consists of the act of following a sequence of actions or events in time. It is a recounting of the facts or particulars of some occurrence" (*Process and Thought* 88). Its abstract paradigm is this.

Introduction (containing time, place, agent, and beginning of action)

Event 1 (or Incident 1)

Event 2 (or Incident 2)

Event 3 (or Incident 3)

Event 4 (or Incident 4)

Events 5, 6, 7 (or Incidents 5, 6, 7)

Conclusion (the falling action)

Process A "process" says D'Angelo, "is a series of actions, functions, steps, or operations that bring about a particular end or result" (101). The sequentially ordered, interlocking steps of a process focus on how something works or is done. Process suggests the concept of change through time, and its paradigm is this.

Introduction (the thesis—usually a simple one)

Step 1 (Phase 1)

Step 2 (Phase 2)

Step 3 (Phase 3)

Step 4 (Phase 4)

Steps 5, 6, 7 . . . (Phases 5, 6, 7 . . .)

Cause and effect Like the classical topic of consequence, this paradigm is concerned with the question of influence. A cause, says D'Angelo, is "an agency or operation responsible for bringing about an action, event, condition, or result," and an effect is "anything that has been caused; . . . the result of an action." Cause and effect are always related; "one always implies the other" (113-14). A cause-and-effect pattern is always concerned with the explanation of phenomena, and its paradigm in simplest form is this.

Introduction (including the thesis)

Cause

Effect

Conclusion (the summary and so forth)

In actual essays, though, the patterns are more complex. They can proceed either deductively, from effect to cause, or inductively, from cause to effect. There are many permutations, depending on the number of causes or effects to be explained. Here are some common cause-effect patterns.

Inductive

Introduction (including the thesis)		Introduction (including the thesis)
Cause 1		Cause
Cause 2		Effect 1
Cause 3		Effect 2
Causes 4, 5, 6	OR	Effect 3
Effect		Effects 4, 5, 6
Conclusion (the summary		Conclusion (the summary
and so forth)		and so forth)

Deductive

Introduction (including the thesis)		Introduction (including the thesis)
Effect		Effect 1
Cause 1		Effect 2
Cause 2	OR	Effect 3
Cause 3		Effects 4, 5, 6
Causes 4, 5, 6		Cause
Conclusion (the summary		Conclusion (the summary
and so forth)		and so forth)

Description Description, says D'Angelo, is "a way of picturing images verbally in speech or writing and of arranging those images in some kind of logical or associational pattern" (129). The central question to be dealt with in this kind of arrangement concerns that logical or associational pattern, and D'Angelo says that this grouping can be done in one of four ways, each representing a different form of the paradigm.

1. Vertical order (bottom to top, top to bottom)
2. Horizontal order (left to right, right to left)
3. Depth order (inside to outside or vice versa)
4. Circular order (clockwise, counterclockwise)

Thus a typical paradigmatic arrangement using vertical order might look like this.

Introduction (including the thesis)

Element 1 (upper part of object or scene)

Element 2 (middle part of object or scene)

Element 3 (bottom part of object or scene)

Conclusion (the summary and so forth)

This is obviously extremely simplistic, and there are certainly many other possible abstract paradigms available for use in descriptive writing. The element that each has in common, that all good descriptive writing must have, is a dominant perspective or impression of the subject that can serve as a thesis and inform all the details with meaning.

Definition "To define," says D'Angelo, "is to set bounds or limits to a thing, to state its essential nature" (147). There are a number of different sorts of shorter and more specific meanings of definition: logical definitions, lexical definitions, stipulative definitions. An essay-length definition, however, must be an extended version of a formal or logical definition, which is composed of three parts: *species*, *genus*, and *differentia*. The species, or term to be defined, is always a member of a larger class, or genus, and is set apart from other members of the genus by factors described by the differentia. For example,

Species	*Genus*	*Differentia*
Brazing is	a welding process	in which the filler metal is nonferrous.

A paradigmatic arrangement of an extended formal definition would look like this.

Introduction (including the logical definition)

Expansion of the genus

Expansion of the differentia (often more than one)

Conclusion (the summary or restatement)

Analysis Analysis is "the systematic separation of a whole into parts, pieces, or sections" (161), says D'Angelo. Analytic essays usually examine complex wholes and dissect them into understandable parts. A physical analysis breaks an object into its components, and a conceptual analysis divides an idea into other ideas. The paradigmatic structure of analysis is this.

Introduction (including the thesis)

Characteristic 1 (or Part 1)

Characteristic 2 (or Part 2)

Characteristics 3, 4, 5 (or Parts 3, 4, 5)

Conclusion (the summary, returning to the beginning)

Classification Classification is "the process of grouping similar ideas of objects, the systematic arrangement of things into classes on the basis of shared characteristics." Any group of people, objects, or ideas that possesses shared characteristics can be classified. D'Angelo points out that classification is differentiated from analysis by the fact that the object of analysis is always singular—"a painting, a movie, the human body"—while the subject of classification is always plural—"cars, jobs, popular songs" (174–75). The most important rule to keep in mind about classifying is that the classes created for the paradigm must be mutually exclusive. The paradigm is this.

Introduction (the thesis, including the basis of classification and a listing of the types or classes found)

Subclass 1

Subclass 2

Subclass 3

Conclusion (the summary or restatement)

Exemplification   "Exemplification," says D'Angelo, "is the process of illustrating a general principle, statement, or law by citing specific instances that illuminate the generalization" (186). Exemplification is perhaps the simplest and certainly one of the most common essay forms, especially for students. Its paradigm is this.

Introduction (including the generalization)

Example 1

Example 2

Examples 3, 4, 5

Conclusion

Comparison   Comparison is "the process of examining two or more things in order to establish their similarities or differences" (197-98). D'Angelo mentions three main paradigmatic structures, of which two are relatively common. He calls them the *half-and-half pattern* and the *characteristics pattern*.

The half-and-half pattern, which is also known as block or divided comparison, deals with the two objects to be compared as wholes and examines first one and then the other.

Introduction (including the thesis; sets up the comparison)

Subject 1

   Characteristic 1

   Characteristic 2

   Characteristic 3

   Characteristic 4

Subject 2

   Characteristic 1

   Characteristic 2

   Characteristic 3

   Characteristic 4

Conclusion (the summary, returning to the beginning)

The characteristics pattern, which is also called alternating comparison, treats the subjects alternately in terms of characteristics they share, examining each characteristic in relation to the corresponding characteristic.

Introduction (including the thesis; sets up the comparison)

Characteristic 1

    Subject 1

    Subject 2

Characteristic 2

    Subject 1

    Subject 2

Characteristic 3

    Subject 1

    Subject 2

Conclusion (the summary, returning to the beginning)

Analogy An analogy is an extended metaphor, "a kind of logical inference based on the premise that if two things resemble each other in some respects, they will probably be alike in other respects" (209). Analogy is a teaching technique in that it allows a writer to explain unfamiliar concepts by relating them to familiar concepts. The paradigmatic structure of analogy is similar to that of comparison.

Introduction (sets up the analogy)

Subject 1 is similar to Subject 2 in this respect.

Subject 1 is similar to Subject 2 in this respect.

Subject 1 is similar to Subject 2 in this respect.

Conclusion (Therefore, Subject 1 is similar to Subject 2 in some respect known of one but not known of the other.)

Using the Paradigmatic Arrangements in the Classroom

Although D'Angelo's paradigmatic arrangements have recently come under fire as being hardly more than extensions of the three-part essay, they still have a good deal of classroom usefulness.[5] Indeed, nearly every sort of essay can theoretically be written using one or more paradigms, but D'Angelo himself cautions that they should not merely be memorized as an artificial set of arrangements. "The idea," he says, "is to internalize the principles upon which the patterns are based so that when you use them they become intuitive rather than self-conscious" (79). In patterns of arrangement as in many other elements of the

[5] For a critique of the paradigmatic system, see Lunsford.

writing process, this shift from conscious to intuitive process is what teachers strive to instill in their students, but it is particularly difficult to accomplish in arrangement and formal work; in the time we have, about the best we can hope for is that our students apprehend a working knowledge of the paradigms.

You can introduce the outlines of the abstract paradigms in the same form in which they are reproduced here. But before you can expect your students to manipulate paradigmatic arrangement competently, they will need to practice two activities: the first is choosing which paradigms mesh best with which sorts of subjects, and the second is expanding the chosen abstract paradigm into a fuller outline-like form, which produces the essay's content and direction.

Practice in choosing paradigms that correspond to subjects can be done orally in class. After you have gone through the paradigmatic arrangements and explained what each one consists of, hand out a list of simple declarative, thesis-like statements that can be fitted into the various paradigms. You might begin the list with theses that fit obviously into one paradigm or another and gradually work down to theses that are more difficult to place. Here are some suggestions, from the beginning and the end of a list we have used.

There are three kinds of FY students at this university.

An incident in high school taught me the falsity of ethnic stereotypes.

The Toyota Tercel and the Nissan Altima look alike, but have many differences.

The eighties were called "the go-go decade," and the fads of those years reflect that name.

There is no obvious answer to the problem of pornography in the United States.

Ronald Reagan is responsible for the severity of the national debt.

My room is an accurate reflection of my personality.

Ask your students to try to place each statement into a paradigmatic context by running quickly through the listed elements of each paradigm to see whether that arrangement suits, or could be made to suit, the subject. Some theses, especially those near the bottom of the list, will be usable in several different arrangements. This practice in fitting form and content together is well worth extended class time. After oral discussion of each thesis and why it works with specific paradigms and not with others, you might ask each student to choose two of the examples—each thesis should now have a paradigm attached to it—and write out a somewhat abstract outline for each one in the form of key words.

This is the point at which practice in the second skill, that of developing an abstract paradigm into a sentence outline, begins. After a few minutes, most students will be able to produce a key-word outline from the abstract paradigm and the thesis. A typical key-word outline looks like this.

1. Introduction—three kinds of FY students
2. Classification 1: the granolas
3. Classification 2: the jocks
4. Classification 3: the preprofessionals
5. Conclusion—three kinds of FY students

From this rough (and seemingly unpromising) key-word outline, each idea can be expanded into a full sentence.

1. There are three types of FY students at this university.
2. The first is the granola, a child of the sixties who still thinks it is cool to listen to Led Zeppelin while smoking banana peels.
3. The second is the jock, who believes that hockey is life and has muscles everywhere, even between the ears.
4. The last kind is the serious preprofessional, who is here for an education and tolerates no nonsense.
5. Together these types make up the FY class at this university.

Expansion is most helpful when the work is read out loud or written on the blackboard. Do not fail to correct those who make mistakes in their expansions—gently, of course. Remember that those students who do not read their outlines aloud will be learning from those who do.

The final step, of course, is writing an essay from the expanded paradigm, and it is at this point that you need to stress the fact that each element of the paradigm does not automatically translate into a paragraph. Sometimes it does, of course, but often more than one paragraph will be needed to handle and exhaust each element.

When your students seem comfortable with the use of the paradigms applied to the theses and subject matter you supply, you can assign paradigms to be applied to theses and subject matter they invent. Asking for an abstract paradigmatic representation of the structure of an essay along with the essay itself is a good way to check the method of arrangement the student used—and of making sure the student used a method.

Despite the criticisms of D'Angelo's work, paradigmatic structures can help beginning students who need an informing principle around which to structure their writing. Whether or not the paradigms are genuine channels of thought, "dynamic organizational processes," students can learn to manipulate them consciously while internalizing their structures. At best, the paradigms can make available to them the intuitive formal sense of the mature writer, and even if they never internalize the intuition, they can use the paradigms as prescriptive patterns for their essays.

TECHNIQUES OF EDITING AND PLANNING

Thus far we have been discussing methods of arrangement that are "transcendent"; they prefigure the essays patterned on them. Some rhetoricians call these arrangements generative, on the theory that form can help to generate content. Although some of the prescriptive arrangements we have seen are fairly flexible, many teachers distrust the idea of prescriptive or transcendent arrangements. Rather than using preexisting arrangements, such teachers subscribe to the organic model of composition, one in which invention, arrangement, and style are informed by the writer's perceptions of her subject, purpose, and audience. Most mature writers do compose organically, but it can be argued that they do so because they have completely internalized prescriptive forms. In any case, teachers continue to offer students section-by-section prescriptive arrangements; otherwise, they may feel they have little more to offer than vague maxims: "Organize your points clearly,"; "Strive for unity, order, and coherence,"; "Don't ramble or digress."

Teachers can offer students sound advice without being prescriptive; and they can offer some of the following techniques of editing and rearranging sections.

Using the Outline in the Classroom

The outline, which has often been misused in writing classes, can be used successfully as an editorial technique. For the last hundred years, however, it has often been advanced as the primary tool available to students for generating and arranging material. Many teachers still hold to the sentiments of John F. Genung, whose 1893 textbook, *Outlines of Rhetoric*, states:

> It is strongly advisable, perhaps we had better say necessary, to draw up a careful plan of what you are going to write. . . . Even if a writer gets by experience the ability to make and follow a plan mentally, he must ordinarily have acquired that ability by planning much on paper. (239)

The "careful plan" is of course an outline of topics the essay would treat. Like a skeleton (a frequent analogy), it would give structure to the body of the essay. In composition courses, the idea of the outline became complex, with expectations of Roman and Arabic numerals, capital and lowercase letters—a full blueprint, in fact, of every topic, subtopic, and sub-subtopic in the proposed essay. The idea of outlining before writing became accepted practice in high schools and continues to be taught there and in many colleges.

As we are gradually learning, however, writing itself is an epistemological tool. Composition researchers are proving that, indeed, writing is a way of knowing. As the famous E. M. Forster quote goes, "How can I know what I think until I see what I say?"

Thus outlining before writing can be terribly inefficient. The full outline, with all its sets and subsets, is not a method that accurately reflects the mental processes by which writing is accomplished; often writers don't know what they are going to write about until they begin to write, or they use the context of their previous expression to decide where they should go next. Yet using a subset outline, the student must generate form and content simultaneously— and in an abstract context. To see just how difficult this process can be, try writing a full-blown subset outline before you write your own next essay.

Many successful writers draw up an ordered list of topics before they write, but the list is related more closely to prewriting note-taking than to a baroque outline. Full-scale outlines, written before writing, have little generative capacity. Hence, teachers are suggesting that their students turn to ordering lists or brainstorming lists for the generative part of the composing process; such lists are invaluable in helping to keep the general flow of ideas going.

What many teachers have discovered about the full-scale outline, however, is that it can be much more helpful to students in the editing stage of composition. To understand this use of outlining, let us look more closely at outlines themselves.

The two most common sorts of outlines that have been proposed for use in composition are the *topic outline* and its more complex sibling, the *topic-sentence outline*. The topic outline, as its name suggests, is a listing of the sections of the proposed essay, its topics and their subtopics, with a key word or a short clause attached to each letter or number as a designation of content. For the topic-sentence outline, the writer creates a topic sentence for each paragraph in the proposed essay and orders these topic sentences as the topics and subtopics of the essay; thus the major and minor ideas of the essay can be ranked according to their importance or the writer's purpose. As you may imagine, this sort of outline is extremely difficult to create beforehand.

Yet both these outlines can be turned around and written after the first draft of the essay has been completed. What were devices for creating frustration can become easily usable and illuminating tools for editing. Here is the way it works.

After your students have completed their first drafts, using one of the forms of arrangement already covered or proceeding intuitively, ask them to draw up an outline of the paragraphs in their drafts. Do not insist on sets and subsets at this point; merely suggest a numbered list, each number representing a paragraph. After each number, the student should write a short sentence summarizing the paragraph.

After each paragraph has been thus represented and charted, each student will have what is in essence a map of the argument of the essay. At this point, have the students meet in workshop groups or exchange lists with one another and discuss them for ten minutes or so. Questions to be asked about each list include the following:

1. Are there any paragraphs or topics that don't seem to relate well to the development of the subject?
2. Is there anything that should be cut?
3. Might one or several paragraphs work better in another position in the essay?
4. Is there any important part of the essay that seems to be missing?

After writing and discussing their post-factum outlines, students will have a much clearer idea of what changes need to be made in the paragraph arrangement of a rough draft. Generally, adding a few paragraphs, cutting a few, or rearranging a few will be the result, yielding a much more consciously organized final draft. The practice that the students will get in paragraph-level transitions is an extra bonus.

The same sort of after-the-fact outlining can also be done using the simpler topic outline, but the sentence outline produces clearer realizations about what it is the writer is saying as the argument proceeds.

Using Winterowd's "Grammar of Coherence" Technique in the Classroom

In "The Grammar of Coherence," W. Ross Winterowd argues that beyond the sentence level—that is, at the level of paragraphs and essay-units (what Willis Pitkin calls discourse blocs)—*transitions* control coherence (830). Form and coherence, says Winterowd, are synonymous at the paragraph and discourse-bloc level, and we perceive coherence as consistent relationships among transitions. Thus recognizing and controlling these transitional relationships are important skills for students, and the editorial technique that can promote them is implicit in Winterowd's discussion.

Winterowd has identified (and named) seven transitional relationships among parts of an essay, and the application of knowledge of these seven relationships can help students order the parts of their essays. The seven relationships are as follows:

Coordination: expressed by the terms *and, furthermore, too, in addition, also, again*

Obversativity: expressed by *but, yet, however, on the other hand*

Causativity: expressed by *for, because, as a result*

Conclusativity: expressed by *so, therefore, thus, for this reason*

Alternativity: expressed by *or*

Inclusativity: expressed by a colon

Sequentiality: expressed by *first . . . second . . . third, earlier . . . later,* and so forth

Winterowd suggests that this list of transitional relationships can be used for many generative and analytic purposes, but here it will be examined as a tool for maintaining coherence among the parts of an essay.

To thus use this list, first introduce your students to the transitional concepts, using illustrative handouts. Winterowd suggests that these concepts are much more easily illustrated than defined or explained, especially to beginning writers. A look through any of the common anthologies of essays will usually provide good material for examples. Choose blocks of two or three paragraphs—the shorter the better. After talking for a few minutes about the transitional relationships in the examples, ask students to do a short imitation exercise as homework, copying the transitional form of several of the examples while substituting their own content. The next step is to go directly to the anthology and work orally on the transitional links between paragraphs that are picked out at random. By this time, students should be able to manipulate the terms fairly confidently.

After the imitation exercise and class work have been completed, ask students to bring to class one of the essays they have already written and had evaluated.

Then ask them to go over the essay, marking each paragraph as it relates to the previous one. Each paragraph will be marked *alternativity, causativity*, and so forth. After the imitation practice, this task is not as hard as it sounds; most students will see most transitional relationships fairly easily. There will, of course, be the occasional mystery paragraph, which students can discuss with a friend or with the entire class. This exercise provides students with an immediate method for analyzing their papers for coherence and for learning to strike or regroup paragraphs that have no observable relation to those around them.

After having practiced it on finished papers, your students should be ready to use this analytic method on rough drafts of in-progress papers. Winterowd's system works well for checking arrangements already generated. You may want to ask your students to work in writing groups to check one another's papers for transitional relationships between the paragraphs. Although papers with clear transitions between paragraphs and between blocks of discourse may have other problems, they will generally be coherent. Continually using this method in class will help to ingrain in students intuitive grasp of transitions that will prove beneficial in the drafting process.

WORKS CITED

Aristotle. *Poetics*. Trans. S. H. Butcher. *Criticism: The Major Texts*. Ed. W. J. Bate. New York: Harcourt, 1970.

——. *Rhetoric*. Trans. Rhys Roberts. New York: Modern Library, 1954.

Baker, Sheridan. *The Practical Stylist*. 3rd ed. New York: Crowell, 1969.

Blair, Hugh. *Lectures on Rhetoric and Belles-Lettres*. 1783. Philadelphia: Zell, 1866.

Burke, Kenneth. *Counter-Statement*. Los Altos, CA: Hermes, 1953.

Cicero. *De Partitione Oratoria*. Trans. H. Rackham. London: Heinemann, 1960.

Connors, Robert J. "The Rhetoric of Explanation: Explanatory Rhetoric from 1850 to the Present." *Written Communication* 2 (1985): 49–72.

Corbett, Edward P. J. *Classical Rhetoric for the Modern Student*. 3rd ed. New York: Oxford UP, 1990.

D'Angelo, Frank J. *A Conceptual Theory of Rhetoric*. Cambridge, MA: Winthrop, 1975.

——. *Process and Thought in Composition*. Cambridge, MA: Winthrop, 1977.

Genung, John F. *Outlines of Rhetoric*. Boston: Ginn, 1893.

Hall, Donald. *Writing Well*. 2nd ed. Boston: Little Brown, 1976.

Larson, Richard L. "Problem-Solving, Composing, and Liberal Education." *CE* 33 (1972): 628–35.

——. "Structure and Form in Non-Fiction Prose." *Teaching Composition: Twelve Bibliographic Essays*. 2nd ed. Ed. Gary Tate. Fort Worth: Texas Christian UP, 1987. 39–82.

Lunsford, Andrea. "On D'Angelo's Conceptual Theory of Rhetoric." Paper delivered at the CCCC Convention, Washington, DC, March, 1980.

Pitkin, Willis. "Discourse Blocs." *CCC* 20 (1969): 138–48.

Whately, Richard. *Elements of Rhetoric*. 6th ed. London: Fellowes, 1841.

Winterowd, W. Ross. "The Grammar of Coherence." *CE* 31 (1970): 828–35.

Zinsser, William. *On Writing Well*. 3rd ed. New York: Harper, 1985.

CHAPTER

9 | TEACHING STYLE

Once considered little more than the study of schemes, tropes, and rhetorical flourishes, style is today one of the most important canons of rhetoric—at least, Edward P. J. Corbett tells us, if success is measured by the sheer number of works published ("Approaches" 73). Besides Corbett, who has written a classic work on stylistic analysis, other scholars have taken the study of style into the realms of personal and business writing. Style lurks behind much contemporary deconstructive and reader-response literary criticism, and cultural critics have considered the socioeconomic ramifications of style and revision, deepening our understanding of the connections among style, substance, and meaning along historical as well as contemporary continua.

Style, in other words, is not just "style." All composition teachers can benefit from a background in stylistics, and one of the easiest ways to obtain such a background is to borrow the duality that W. Ross Winterowd created in his *Contemporary Rhetoric*. Winterowd divides the study of style into two areas: *theoretical stylistics*, concerned primarily with the nature and existence of style, the application of stylistic criteria to literary studies, and the linguistic attributes of different styles; and *pedagogical stylistics*, which deals with the problem of teaching students to recognize and develop styles in their own writing (252). This chapter deals almost completely with works on pedagogic stylistics, far fewer in number than works in the fascinating but not always classroom practical field of theoretical stylistics.

Perhaps the central theoretical problem presented by the study of style is the question of whether style as an entity really exists. Is it, as some claim, "the totality of impressions which a literary work produces," or is it merely "sundry and ornamental linguistic devices" tacked on to a given content-meaning? (Chatman and Levin, *Literary Style*, 337-38). There is no agreement at all on this question among the foremost theorists of style in our time, yet every writing teacher must answer this question before she can decide on a teaching method. Three distinct views of the nature of style have emerged, says the eminent theoretician Louis T. Milic, who identifies and describes these views in his article "Theories of Style and Their Implications for the Teaching of Composition" (126).

The first of Milic's theories we'll discuss here is the one to which he gives the daunting name *Crocean aesthetic monism,* because it is based on the critical theories of Benedetto Croce. Milic writes that Crocean aesthetic monism, the most modern theory of style, is an organic view which denies the possibility of any separation between content and form. Any discussion of style in Croce's view is useless and irrelevant, for the work or art (the composition) is a unified whole, with no seam between meaning and style. ("Theories" 67)

To the Croceans, for instance, the sentences *John gave me the book* and *The book was given to me by John* have different semantic meanings as well as different syntactic forms.

The second theory is what Milic calls *individualist* or *psychological monism* and is best summed up by the famous aphorism of the French naturalist Georges de Buffon, *"Le style c'est l'homme même,"* usually translated as "Style is the man." Psychological monism holds that a writer cannot help writing the way she does for that is the dynamic expression of her personality. This theory claims that no writer can truly imitate another's style, for no two life experiences are the same; it further holds that the main formative influences on writers are their education and their reading ("Typology of Styles" 442). This theory and the Crocean theory are both monisms in that they perceive style and content as a unity, inseparable from each other, either because different locutions say different things or because an individual's style is her habitual and consistent selection from the expressive resources available in language, which is not consciously amendable to any great degree.

The third theory of style, and the one most applicable to teaching, is what Milic calls the *theory of ornate form, or rhetorical dualism.* The assumption behind rhetorical dualism is that "ideas exist wordlessly and can be dressed in a variety of outfits depending on the need or the occasion" ("Theories" 67). As the critic Michael Riffaterre puts it, "Style is understood as an emphasis (expressive, affective, or aesthetic) added to the information conveyed by the linguistic structure, without alteration of meaning." In other words, "language expresses and style stresses" (Riffaterre 443).

Milic points out that the two monisms make the teaching of style a rather hopeless enterprise, since for the Croceans, there is no "style" form and content being one; for the individualists, style is an expression of personality, and we cannot expect writers to change their personalities. These monisms leave teachers helpless and render all of the resources of rhetoric useless ("Theories" 69). In order to retain options, then, teachers must be dualists, at least to some degree. Although dualistic theory cannot be proved true empirically, it still seems to be the only approach we have to improving students' writing style. If we cannot tell a student that the struggle to find the best words in which to express an idea is a real struggle, then we cannot teach style at all.

A confessed individualist himself, Milic is aware that dualism must be adopted at least conditionally if we are to teach style. In an important essay, "Rhetorical Choice and Stylistic Option," he tries to resolve the division between his beliefs and the pedagogic options offered by dualism. He argues that most of what we call style is actually the production of a huge unconscious element that he calls the "language-generating mechanism." This mechanism, processing subconscious choices and operating at a speed that the conscious mind cannot possibly match, creates most of what we call style. After these decisions have been made, an editing process takes over that can make any stylistic changes the author consciously desires.

Milic distinguishes between *stylistic options,* decisions made unconsciously while the language-generating mechanism is proceeding, and *rhetorical choices,* decisions made consciously while the mechanism is at rest. Rhetorical choices, in other words, are an evaluation of what has been intuitively created by the "language-generating mechanism," an editorial element that can be practiced consciously and thus something we can teach our students. Of course, certain rhetorical choices can become habits of mind and thus stylistic options. The process of adding to the repertoire of the "language-generating mechanism" is what we hope to accomplish. Thus Milic seems to integrate successfully his roles as theorist and teacher.

This chapter, then, will be a discussion of rhetorical choices, since they are the only elements of style that can be handled consciously. In the realm of pedagogic stylistics, we must keep our discussion at a considerably lower level of abstraction than is characteristic of most of the works mentioned by Corbett in his bibliographic essay "Approaches to the Study of Style." The possibilities of our changing our students' styles in ten or thirteen weeks are limited, an opinion supported by Milic, who tells us that the process of learning to write takes a dozen years and must begin much earlier than at age eighteen. Style is the hardest canon to teach, linked as it is to reading. Only avid and accomplished readers can generate and perceive style, recognizing it in a contextual continuum. The more models and styles a writer knows or is aware of, the more raw data there are to feed the language-generating mechanism and the more informed are the choices that can be made both intuitively and consciously.

Let's examine what we can accomplish and some of the things we need to know in order to proceed. "Teaching Style: A Possible Anatomy," an excellent essay by Winston Weathers, mentions several obligatory tasks for those who would teach style in college. The first task is "making the teaching of style significant and relevant for our students" (144). Many beginning writers view the concept of style with suspicion, as if it were something that only effete snobs should be interested in. Thus, Weathers tells us, it is our task to justify the study of style on the grounds of better communication and as a proof of individuality. Style can be taught as a gesture of personal freedom or as a rebellion against rigid systems of conformist language, rather than as dainty humanism or mere aesthetic luxury. Students convinced that style is indeed a gesture of personal freedom will invest maximum effort in stylistic concerns.

The second task Weathers mentions is that of revealing style as a measurable and viable subject matter. Style seems vague and mysterious to many beginning writers because they have mostly been exposed to the metaphysical approach to style, in which arbitrarily chosen adjectives are used to identify different styles—the "abrupt," the "tense," the "fast-moving," the "leisurely," and the ever popular "flowing" styles. As a result of hearing styles described in these nebulous terms, students cannot see how such an amorphous entity might be

approached or changed. They need, then, to be exposed to the actual components, the nuts and bolts, of style—words, phrases, clauses, sentences, paragraphs—and to methods of analyzing them before they can begin to use them to
control their rhetorical options.

We do have important tools for explaining these stylistic features. In "A
Primer for Teaching Style," Richard Graves tells us that the following four explanatory methods are primary:

1. We can identify the technical name of a particular stylistic feature or
    concept.
2. We can give a definition or description of the feature.
3. We can provide a schematic description of the feature.
4. We can provide an example or illustration of the feature. (187)

The goals of these methods are recognition and then gradual mastery of the
different features. Explanations such as this one can be used in both stylistic
analyses and exercises in imitation, the central practical activities described
in this chapter. In addition to demonstrating discrete skills, though, every
paper a student writes must be informed by certain questions of style. Like the
other canons of rhetoric, style must be approached philosophically as well as
practically.

The study of style needs to be prefaced by a careful discussion of both the
purpose of each piece of writing a student does and a writer's need to be
aware of the interrelationships among author, subject, universe, and audience. M. H. Abrams presents a useful diagram of these elements in *The Mirror
and the Lamp* (8).

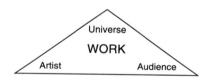

These four elements, based on the rhetorical theory of Aristotle, form a
central construct in modern communication theory. Composition teachers use
a version of this construct called the *communication triangle* to help students
formulate their concepts of the whole rhetorical situation in which they find
themselves.

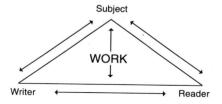

Each of these elements suggests a question every writer must face every time she sits down to write, and a significant factor in each question must necessarily be style. No one factor can predominate in a successful piece of writing, however, and Wayne Booth's famous essay, "The Rhetorical Stance," offers a well-expressed overview of this. The "rhetorical stance" he discusses

> depends on discovering and maintaining in any writing situation a proper balance among the three elements that are at work in any communicative effort: the available arguments about the subject itself, the interests and peculiarities of the audience, and voice, the implied character of the speaker. (74)

A "corruption" of the rhetorical stance, according to Booth, overemphasizes any one of the three elements of the communication triangle of author-audience-subject. Students' compositions are prone to all three sorts of corruptions or imbalances.

The first is the *pedant's stance*, which concentrates only on the subject while ignoring the author-audience relationship. This reliance on nothing but subject-based discourse makes the pedant's stance dry and uninteresting. It makes no concessions to a personal voice or to the reader's interest. It is the sort of depersonalized prose that students often think their teachers want to hear. Ken Macrorie's famous term for it is *Engfish,* and it is found in its purest form at a relatively high academic level—as "dissertation style."

The second sort of imbalance is the *advertiser's stance,* which concentrates on impressing the audience and underplays the subject. This imbalance is not so frequent as the first, mainly because only experienced writers will attempt it. Booth tells us that the "advertiser" overvalues pure effect. Student advertisers are likely to write directly to the teacher, attempting to charm her with candor, humor, or personal attention—often a novel experience for the teacher.

Related to the advertiser's stance is the *entertainer's stance,* which "sacrifices substance to personality and charm" (78). An imbalance in favor of the speaker's ethical appeal, this stance is the rarest corruption of the rhetorical stance found in students' essays. Most students are unaware of the methods used by writers to generate ethical appeal; hence, their imbalances are likely to tilt in other directions. Many FY writers were taught in high school never to use *I* in their writing—the key word of the entertainer's stance.

Booth's question of rhetorical balance is essential to an understanding of the methods available for the manipulation of stylistic choices. The question of the relationship between writer and subject is important, but more central to your students' understanding of style will be the question of their relationships as writers to their audience—an audience that, in the final analysis, will usually be composed only of you, their teacher. Obviously, students will attempt to choose a style that will suit their identified readership, and the voice they choose for a letter to a close friend will be very different from the one they choose for an essay to be read by their English teacher. But the danger of artificiality in the voice chosen for the essay is all too real.

Teachers and scholars have explored the problem of the teacher as the final audience for students' texts by trying to create other plausible audiences, with the most obvious sorts of such assignments being letters to the editor of a local newspaper, letters to the president of the United States or the university or the college. Some assignments have been created that specify a complex writing situation, complete with subject and audience; one example is the assignment that asks students to define and give examples of "conventional diction" to a group of ninth-grade French students who know basic English but who need more information about how Americans really use it.

The problem with these plausible or created audiences (not including ethical problems some teachers have with the artificial aspect of hypothetical audiences) stems from the fact that the students are always aware that behind the "editor" or the "French students" stands the teacher, who ultimately wields the power of the grade. This awareness makes the assignment even more complex. The student knows that in reality she is writing the way the teacher thinks one should write to the editor or for ninth-graders, not the way one really would write to them. In other words, a student must try to write for another person's concept of a fictional audience. It is no wonder that students often freeze solidly into take-no-chances dullness in such assignments.

The alternative, to specify no audience at all, leaves the student in a simpler— but no less difficult—situation. Most FY students, accustomed to the rich contextual responses of oral communication, find it difficult to conceptualize the abstract, fictionalized "universal audience" that the Belgian rhetorician Chaim Perelman says is the ultimate audience for written discourse (402). Many FY writers have trouble adjusting their styles, which may be sharp and skillful at the oral level, to what seem to them the difficult conventions of noncontextual written discourse. As a result, they tend to write pedantically, on the assumptions that stressing the subject is the safest thing to do and that, as college students, they may need to sound grown up. They cannot create a fictional audience easily, so they tend to write into the void.

The problem of audience is not easily answered, since both overspecification and underspecification of audience can have unfortunate consequences. Perhaps the best compromise is to admit that the teacher is the audience and to attempt to work accordingly. In *Teaching Expository Writing*, William Irmscher tells us,

> In the classroom it is difficult to escape the hard fact that the teacher is usually the only reader. The teacher is therefore the audience, and the style will no doubt be accommodated to the teacher. That's not all bad if the teacher is someone whom the student respects, feels comfortable with, and wants to write for. I have on occasion simply said to students in my classes that they should write for me, not so much me in the role of a professor who is going to give a grade, but me in the role of reader/critic or editor, who is going to make a professional judgment about their writing. (133-34)

Although students have a hard time seeing past their teacher as judge armed with red pen and grade book, to the coach who is honestly pulling for every student to get an A, this compromise is the best we have yet found.

Intimately related to the question of audience is the concept of different levels of style. Cicero mentions the high, middle, and low styles of oratory and suggests that each has its place and purpose. In the early days of teaching composition, however, this sort of liberalism was supplanted by prescriptive judgments about the different levels of style. Style was either Right or Wrong, Correct or Incorrect, and in general only an attempt to write in a high, "literary" style was acceptable. Gradually, this dichotomy between Good and Bad gave way to the three hierarchical levels of style that many of us were raised on: Formal, or Literary, Style; Informal, or Colloquial, Style; and Vulgar, or Illiterate, Style. Of the three, only the Formal was really proper for writing; the other two instead reflected the way we talk or the style of letters to friends. (The Vulgar style was how *they* talked, not how we talked.) Toward the middle of this century, this hierarchy was liberalized, becoming a continuum from which any stylistic form could be chosen (Marckwardt, viii).

Today many teachers accept another extension of this continuum, one developed by the language theorist Martin Joos, whose book *The Five Clocks* posits five major levels of style that run along a continuum. Perhaps the most important feature of Joos's theory is that it makes no judgments about stylistic validity. His most formal style is no more or less valid than his least formal, for Joos views the levels of style as alternatives available to all users of language for deployment in different situations. The following is a listing of Joos's five styles, the breadth of each, and the degree of responsibility each assumes for successful communication in any situation:

Style	Breadth	Responsibility
Frozen	genteel	best
Formal	puristic	better
Consultative	standard	good
Casual	provincial	fair
Intimate	popular	bad

According to Joos, the main element separating these levels of style is that of audience participation, the sender's reliance on the receiver for shared background and participation. Audience participation plays a major role in the Intimate style, and the background and participation of the audience are least expected in the Frozen style. Since the Intimate, Casual, and Consultative styles rely on a context of oral and visual signals, most expository writing takes place on the Formal or Frozen levels. Once again, this is not a negative judgment of the other styles.

> Good intimate style fuses two personalities. Good casual style integrates disparate personalities into a social group which is greater than the sum of its parts. . . . Good consultative style produces cooperation without the integration, profiting from the lack of it. Good formal style informs the individual separately, so that his future planning may be the more discriminate. Good frozen style, finally, lures him into educating himself. (Joos 111)

There are, in other words, reasons that are not merely arbitrary or conventional for telling your students to write according to certain formal standards. If Joos is correct, the nature of writing itself promotes using the Formal or Frozen style.

The main characteristic of Formal style, according to Joos, is that participation of the audience is lost. Without the immediate context provided by responses, Formal style has a "dominating character" and must be logical and organized. It demands planning in order to make all its points without reminders from the audience, and its hallmarks are detachment and cohesion. The Frozen style, even further removed from an audience, is, according to Joos, a style for print and declamation, a style for the most formal literary tasks and for oratory. This level of style is not useful for most students because it sacrifices much of its humanity through the enforced absence of intonation. Joos says that this is a style used between social strangers; thus it won't be usable in many classroom contexts.

The old correct-incorrect duality that teachers have for so long applied to style is not completely wrongheaded. Certain levels of stylistic formality really do correspond better than others to the needs and perceptions of readers of exposition. Certainly, some content can be expressed using any of Joos's styles, but other content can be best served by one or another. For this reason, we can teach the formal styles not as more correct but as more useful for writing. Formal style can be seen as a dialect like any other, teachable to those who feel that learning it is important.

To demonstrate the nature of the formal styles, you might ask your students to do a simple exercise. First, you will want to discuss and demonstrate Joos's last four styles (Intimate style, essentially private language, can be difficult to exemplify); then translate a few simple phrases from one style to another. And then ask your students to try to translate into Casual or Consultative style this passage by Richard Weaver, which is written in his own curious blend of Formal and Frozen styles.

> It will be useful to review here this flight toward periphery, or the centrifugal impulse of our culture. In the Middle Ages, when there obtained a comparatively clear perception of reality, the professor of highest learning was the philosophic doctor. He stood at the center of things because he had mastered principles. On a level far lower were those who had mastered only facts and skills. (*Ideas Have Consequences* 53)

After a student has made the brave beginning— "Now it will be cool to check out here this run toward the edge . . ." —and has realized that the sense of the thought is already lost before she has even tackled "the centrifugal impulse of our culture," she begins to see the point of the assignment. This exercise shows students that some content simply cannot be translated from level to level without seriously undermining its efficiency or meaning. Conversely, of course, there are messages that cannot be well served by the Formal or Frozen style, but the preceding exercise shows that the more formal styles are not merely empty conventions enforced by English teachers.

Styles grow organically out of the needs and nature of written exposition. Style is ubiquitous, a part of all canons of rhetoric. If invention and arrangement are indeed a seamless whole, then style provides the final tonal definition of that whole.[1]

In *Style: An Anti-Textbook*, Richard Lanham condemns the utilitarian prose and the "plain style" most commonly taught in FY writing classes, asserting that language as play should be the key concept in composition classes. "Style," says Lanham, "must be taught for and as what it is—a pleasure, a grace, a joy, a delight" (20). Given the limitations under which most writing teachers labor, you may not get that far. Students cannot learn to control style in three or four months, but if you provide them with methods of analysis and good models, they will become aware of style as a concrete, controllable entity. Winston Weathers's *An Alternate Style: Options in Composition* is perhaps the most accessible text for students interested in expanding their repertoire of stylistic options. Weathers writes that

> one of our major tasks as teachers of composition is to identify compositional options and teach students the mastery of the options and the liberating use of them. We must identify options in all areas of vocabulary, usage, sentence forms, dictional levels, paragraph types, ways of organizing material into whole compositions: options in all that we mean by style. Without options, there can be no rhetoric, for there can be no adjustment to the diversity of communication occasions that confront us in our various lives. (5)

Thus it ultimately rests with teachers to introduce students to their stylistic options. And once students stop viewing their styles as predestined and unchangeable and begin to perceive style as quantitative and plastic, they can begin to seek Lanham's "grace" and "delight" as they learn better and better how to control their rhetorical choices and their stylistic options.

ANALYSES OF STYLE

Most FY students declare that they *have* no writing style—that mysterious "extra" quality that only professional writers have. And no wonder our students feel this way: even if they have been introduced to style, the introduction was probably to literary style, that vague quality described by their teacher as "vigorous" or "curt" or "smooth," that quality found only in the writing of Hawthorne or Baldwin or Woolf. Style, nebulous and qualitative, is not to be found in students' writing—so they think.

Before you can make style understandable to your students and demonstrate that they, too, can develop their own style, you must make style measurable and describable. Teachers have to provide students with the necessary tools for

---

[1] The several sorts of activities that can help students improve their style are not limited to this chapter. Much of the material in Chapter 10 is devoted to working with style on the sentence and paragraph levels. Generative rhetoric and its exercises with sentences has been found to be a valuable stylistic tool, as have sentence-combining exercises. Tagmemic and generative-rhetorical paragraphing exercises also affect style; see Chapter 10 for details on sentence-combining and paragraphing theory.

dissecting and examining their own writing style; and the techniques of stylistic analysis can provide such tools.

Many different analyses of style can be performed; they have come a long way from the reliance on tropes and figures that once characterized such analysis. A *trope* (or "turn") involves a change or transference of a word's meaning from the literal to the imaginative in such devices as allegory, metaphor, and irony. The *figures* (or schemes) sometimes involve changes in meaning as well, but they are primarily concerned with the shape or physical structure of language, the placement of words in certain positions, their repetition in various patterns. To make an analogy with music, tropes exist in a vertical plane, like pitch or harmony; figures exist in a horizontal plane, like rhythm or other devices for denoting stress. For years, tropes and schemes were mechanically multiplied and given complex names. Students of style found themselves memorizing them all, a practice many upper-level graduate students continue to find useful, despite its difficulty.

But today stylistic analysis means more than simply analyzing tropes and schemes: it encompasses many of the elements of diction, usage, sentence construction, and paragraph treatment that writers use unconsciously. And today theoreticians of style can rely on the computer to do the bean counting while they concentrate on responding to, and analyzing, the style. In his bibliographic essay "Approaches to the Study of Style," Corbett tells us of two appropriate computer-software programs: HOMER and Writer's Workbench, both of which measure and display statistical (raw) data. HOMER offers the total number of words in the text, the number of sentences, and the number of *to be* forms, "shun" words, and "woolly" words (Lanham's terms). The Writer's Workbench, aimed at helping students analyze their own prose, provides information about the type and length of their sentences and the kinds of sentence openers they have used, as well as the percentages of abstract words, nominalizations, passive verb forms, and *to be* forms.

More recently, programs for analyzing style have become available on microcomputers. There are several smaller grammar- and style-checking programs, such as Grammatik and RightWriter, that run on PCs and Macintosh computers, but their compressed size makes them less flexible than Writer's Workbench, which is a large, complex program that runs on a mainframe computer. The comparative information that these programs provide tends to be mechanistic and to suggest that a simpler style is always better. Though the computer allows us to glean more information about style faster, unless we understand how to analyze that information, neither we nor the computer can help our students.[2]

Numerical analysis of style (with or without a computer) is relatively straightforward. It relies on the following teaching method:

1. Teachers introduce students to the terms and techniques of the method of analysis.

---

[2] See also Kiefer and Smith for more information on computer analysis of style.

2. Students apply the method to simple examples and practice it on familiar pieces of prose.
3. Students practice the method by analyzing the style of professional prose and discussing their findings in class.
4. Finally, students use the method to analyze their own prose, and they compare their findings with those for other sorts of prose.

As Weathers points out, "improvement in student style comes not by osmosis, but through exercises" ("Teaching Style" 146). More than anything else, stylistic analyses reveal to students the understandable basis of seemingly subjective labels on style. In addition, they reinforce the notion that no writer, not even a student writer, is the prisoner of her own unchangeable ways of writing.

CORBETT'S ANALYSIS OF PROSE STYLE

Developed in the early 1960s and refined throughout that decade, Edward P. J. Corbett's method of analyzing style remains a flexible teaching tool, offering a large number of stylistic features for analysis. It should be noted that many features of the aforementioned computer programs for analyzing prose are based on Corbett's own method. Teachers can choose from a few or the full range of features discussed by Corbett and assign them according to their students' abilities.

Counting is at the heart of Corbett's method (just as tabulating is at the heart of the computer programs). Corbett explains it in "A Method of Analyzing Prose Style with a Demonstration Analysis of Swift's *A Modest Proposal*" and presents it in a more finished form in his text *Classical Rhetoric for the Modern Student*. "Tedious counting and tabulating" are the necessary first steps, he says, the only way to obtain the raw data concerning the stylistic features of the prose work being examined—a time-consuming but fairly easy task. The next step, more challenging, is relating "what the statistics reveal to the rhetoric of the piece being analyzed" ("Method" 296). Corbett's method investigates three main areas of style: sentences, paragraphs, and diction. The prose to be analyzed should be at least five to six hundred words in length and no longer than a thousand words.

By using and filling in the following charts, students can begin to analyze prose and map out various stylistic elements. Of import is Corbett's definition of a sentence: "a group of words beginning with a capital letter and ending with some mark of end-punctuation" (*Classical Rhetoric* 415).

STYLISTIC STUDY—I
(SENTENCES AND PARAGRAPHS)

EVALUATION	Professional	Student
A. Total number of words in the piece studied	_____	_____
B. Total number of sentences in the piece studied	_____	_____

C. Longest sentence (in no. of words) _____ _____
D. Shortest sentence (in no. of words) _____ _____
E. Average sentence (in no. of words) _____ _____
F. Number of sentences that contain more
than 10 words over the average sentence _____ _____
G. Number of sentences that contain 5 words
or more below the average _____ _____
H. Percentage of sentences that contain more
than 10 words over the average _____ _____
I. Percentage of sentences that contain 5 words
or more below the average _____ _____
J. Paragraph length
longest paragraph (in no. of sentences) _____ _____
shortest paragraph (in no. of sentences) _____ _____
average paragraph (in no. of sentences) _____ _____

STYLISTIC STUDY—II
(GRAMMATICAL TYPES OF SENTENCE)

A simple sentence is a sentence beginning with a capital letter, containing one independent clause, and ending with terminal punctuation.
A compound sentence is a sentence beginning with a capital letter, containing two or more independent clauses, and ending with terminal punctuation.
A complex sentence is a sentence beginning with a capital letter, containing one independent clause and one or more dependent clauses, and ending with terminal punctuation.
A compound-complex sentence is a sentence beginning with a capital letter, containing two or more independent clauses and one or more dependent clauses, and ending with terminal punctuation.

Title of professional essay _____

Author _____

	Professional	Student
A. Total number of sentences in essay	_____	_____
B. Total number of simple sentences	_____	_____
C. Percentage of simple sentences	_____	_____
D. Total number of compound sentences	_____	_____
E. Percentage of compound sentences	_____	_____
F. Total number of complex sentences	_____	_____
G. Percentage of complex sentences	_____	_____
H. Total number of compound-complex sentences	_____	_____
I. Percentage of compound-complex sentences	_____	_____

STYLISTIC STUDY—III
(SENTENCE OPENERS)

Title of professional essay _____

Author _____

For this study use only *declarative* sentences. No interrogative or imperative sentences.

Total number of declarative sentences: Professional _____
                                        Student   _____

Sentences beginning with:	Professional No. %	Student No. %
A. Subject (e.g., *John broke the window. The high cost of living will offset . . .*)	— —	— —
B. Expletive (e.g., *It is plain that . . .*, *There are ten Indians.* Exclamations: *Alas, Oh*)	— —	— —
C. Coordinating conjunction (e.g., *And, But, Or, Nor, For, Yet, So*)	— —	— —
D. Adverb word (e.g., *First, Thus, Moreover, Nevertheless, Namely*)	— —	— —
E. Conjunctive phrase (e.g., *On the other hand, As a consequence*)	— —	— —
F. Prepositional phrase (e.g., *After the game, In the morning*)	— —	— —
G. Verbal phrase (e.g., participial, gerundive, or infinitive phrase)	— —	— —
H. Adjective phrase (e.g., *Tired but happy, we . . .*)	— —	— —
I. Absolute phrase (e.g., *The ship having arrived safely, we . . .*)	— —	— —
J. Adverb clause (e.g., *When the ship arrived safely, we . . .*)	— —	— —
K. Front-Shift (e.g., inverted word order: *The expense we could not bear. Gone was the wind. Happy were they to be alive.*)	— —	— —

STYLISTIC STUDY—IV
(DICTION)

Title of professional essay _____

Author _____

For this investigation, confine yourself to this range of paragraphs: paragraphs
____ through ____. For the investigation of your own prose, confine yourself to
a comparable number of paragraphs.

In A, B, and C below, count only substantive words—nouns, pronouns, verbs,
verbals, adjectives, and adverbs.

	Professional	Student
A. Total number of substantive words in the passage	_____	_____
B. Total number of monosyllabic substantive words	_____	_____
C. Percentage of monosyllabic substantive words	_____	_____
D. Total number of nouns and pronouns in the passage	_____	_____
E. Total number of concrete nouns and pronouns	_____	_____
F. Percentage of concrete nouns and pronouns	_____	_____
G. Total number of finite verbs in all dependent and independent clauses in the passage	_____	_____
H. What percentage does G represent of A?	_____	_____
I. Total number of linking verbs	_____	_____
J. Percentage of linking verbs (using A)	_____	_____
K. Total number of active verbs (do not count linking verbs)	_____	_____
L. Percentage of active verbs (using A)	_____	_____
M. Total number of passive verbs (do not count linking verbs)	_____	_____
N. Percentage of passive verbs (using A)	_____	_____
O. Total number of adjectives in the passage (do not count participles or articles)	_____	_____
P. Average number of adjectives per sentence (divide by the total number of sentences in the passage)	_____	_____

(*Classical Rhetoric* 415–24)

Using Corbett's Analysis of Style in the Classroom

Since Corbett's method was actually developed for use in the classroom, most
of our discussion of it will be in this practical-use section. As we mentioned,
the flexibility of this system allows it to be used profitably for nearly any analytic purpose.

To begin an assignment based on Corbett's analysis of style, you need to
choose the charts you wish your students to use. Chart I, dealing with the
length of sentences and paragraphs, is the simplest of the four and the only

chart that requires almost no preparatory teaching time. Chart II, dealing with the different grammatical types of sentences, requires more preparation by the teacher and the students. You will want to remind your students of the elements that make up a dependent clause. In order for the analysis to succeed, you must make certain before you begin that your students can recognize simple, compound, complex, and compound-complex sentences. Practice in sentence identification is really the only way to do this.

After defining the four kinds of sentences and giving examples on the board, pick out examples from your reader, and ask students to identify them and to discuss the different stylistic effects of sentence length and structure. With this sort of practice, students are usually conversant enough with grammatical classification to use Chart II. Just to be certain, though, Corbett includes definitions of the sentence types at the top of the chart, and it is a good idea to reproduce these along with the chart.

Although it does not call for the student to identify parts of speech and sentence structures that are difficult to recognize, Chart III seems to be the most complex chart, the first that teachers of less well-prepared students dispense with. Most FY students have trouble using this chart, for they usually have command of only three or four types of sentence openers. Nevertheless, study of sentence openers can be extremely revealing and profitable. If you do decide to use it, you will want to familiarize your students with its terms, just as you did for Chart II.

Chart IV looks complicated, but it is really nothing more than an analysis of monosyllables, nouns, verbs, and adjectives. In order to use it, you will undoubtedly have to give a short refresher course in grammatical nomenclature; but the terms are simple enough that this shouldn't take more than a class period. This chart can provide a great deal of interesting material and will well repay the time you spend teaching the terms.

You may want to advance under the assumption that upper-level students can use all four charts, advanced lower-level students can handily grasp Charts I, II, and sometimes IV, and BW students should probably be asked to do no analyses more complicated than those in Chart I. If students are asked to try to analyze stylistic elements that are difficult for them to grasp, the whole exercise becomes a prolonged and useless agony. You will find, if you are worried that the use of only a single chart will be unrevealing, that even one chart provides a great deal of material to consider.

The charts are the mechanical element in Corbett's analytic system, which his accompanying method brings to life. With most other methods of style analysis, the results are tabulated and commented on, and that's the end of it. The prose can be a professional essay or a student theme; the important activity is the analysis itself. Not so with Corbett's system. Though it can certainly be used to dissect discrete pieces of discourse—he uses it thus in "A Method of Analyzing Prose Style"—the pedagogical use of the more completely evolved method presented in *Classical Rhetoric* is much more productive: it is an assignment that asks students to analyze both professional prose and a sample of their own writing and then to write an essay that draws conclusions from the comparative analysis (415).

The essay Corbett used as the professional model in his assignment was F. L. Lucas's "What Is Style?" but almost any of the available readers has several essays that can serve as valuable reference points. Obviously, you will want to ask students to compare exposition with exposition or description with description, rather than argumentation with narration or exposition with description. Some teachers suggest that students choose a central section of around a thousand words from the essay rather than an opening or concluding section, because these extremities often have stylistic peculiarities that make them difficult to use as models. As for the sample of student writing to be used, it should be at least five to six hundred words long; if students can offer longer pieces, so much the better. You can ask FY students to use a paper written earlier in the course, but a long paper from their senior year of high school works better; students will approach such an essay with some detachment, which will make their analyses more objective. This assignment can be especially effective if students analyze, evaluate, and discuss the style of a professional piece and then wait a few weeks before they approach their own texts.

To complete the project, the student analyzes both writing samples—one at a time—and fills in the appropriate blanks on the assigned charts. You will want to devote several homework assignments to this time-consuming task. Students will undoubtedly use a calculator for the quantitative parts. When the assignments are due, devote a class to making certain that everyone has done the counting correctly, discussing and putting on the board the correct answers for the professional piece. If students have counted or see how to count the professional prose correctly, they will be able to count their own work correctly. You might then ask each student to write an essay that draws conclusions about her own style based on the comparative analysis.

When these essays are due—and your students will probably need two weeks for this assignment—ask that the data-filled charts be handed in as well for your reference. These essays, even on the FY level, are often extremely perceptive. Corbett calls them the "best themes" he has seen. By comparing their own writing with professional writing, students come to realizations that months of lecturing or nonpersonal analyses could never produce. For example, a first-semester student wrote this perceptive analysis.

> Sentence length is the area of greatest discrepancy between my writing and that of professional Anne Bernays. Bernays's longest sentence in words is 51, and her shortest is 4. This is a range of 47, a range that is quite extensive. On the other hand, my range is only 17 with a low of 11 and a high of 28. This, of course, is an extremely noticeable difference. This range difference shows that my current style of writing is rather "choppy." In other words, the length of sentences throughout the writing remains practically constant, creating a boring style. . . . The main problem in my present style is inexperience. I have not practiced the use of varied sentence openers and sentence structures as much as I should have practiced. A little more variety in a

number of aspects of my style should make a visible difference in my writing.

These are impressive insights from an FY student.

One warning about this assignment: it will make all other stylistic analyses seem anticlimactic. As John Fleischauer has suggested, after students have mastered statistical analysis, it quickly becomes a chore; and if Corbett's system is introduced completely and used carefully, it is complete and illuminating enough to make other systems superfluous (Fleischauer 100).

IMITATION

Different imitation techniques, whether they consist of direct copying, composition based on models, or controlled mutation of sentence structures, all have one thing in common: they lead students to internalize the structures of the piece being imitated. With those structures internalized, a student is free to make the informed choices that are the wellspring of creativity. William Gruber puts it succinctly when he suggests that imitation does not affect creativity but, rather, assists in design:

> Standing behind imitation as a teaching method is the simple assumption that an inability to write is an inability to design—an inability to shape effectively the thought of a sentence, a paragraph, or an essay. (493–94)

Imitation exercises provide students with practice in that "ability to design" that is the basis of a mature prose style.

Two Imitation Techniques

Perhaps more than any other contemporary rhetorician, Corbett is responsible for the resurgence in the popularity of imitation. His central statement on imitation and a large number of exercises in copying and creative imitation are to be found in *Classical Rhetoric for the Modern Student*. Corbett recommends several different sorts of exercises, the first and simplest of which involves "copying passages, word for word, from admired authors." This task is not quite as simple as it may seem, though; in order to derive benefit from this exercise, your students must follow these rules:

1. You must not spend more than fifteen or twenty minutes copying at any one time. If you extend this exercise much beyond twenty minutes at any one sitting, your attention will begin to wander, and you will find yourself merely copying words.
2. You must do this copying with a pencil or pen. [Keyboarding] is so fast and so mechanical that you can copy off whole passages without paying any attention to the features of an author's style. Copying by hand, you transcribe the passage at such a pace that you have time to observe the choice and disposition of words, the patterns of sentences, and the length and variety of sentences.
3. You must not spend too much time with any one author. If you concentrate on a single author's style, you may find yourself falling into the "servile imitation" that rhetoricians warned of. The aim of this exercise

is not to acquire someone else's style but to lay the groundwork for developing your own style by getting the "feel" of a variety of styles.

4.   You must read the entire passage before starting to copy it so that you can capture the thought and the manner of the passage as a whole. When you are copying, it is advisable to read each sentence through before transcribing it. After you have finished copying the passage, you should read your transcription so that you once again get a sense of the passage as a whole.

5.   You must copy the passage slowly and accurately. If you are going to dash through this exercise, you might as well not do it at all. A mechanical way of insuring accuracy . . . is to make your handwriting as legible as you can. (*Classical Rhetoric* 475)

Corbett provides a number of specimens for imitation in *Classical Rhetoric*, prose styles ranging from the King James Bible to Mary Wollstonecraft's *Vindication of the Rights of Women*.

For students who have spent some time copying passages, Corbett recommends a second kind of imitation exercise, *pattern practice*. In this, the student chooses or is given single sentences to use as patterns, after which she designs sentences of her own. "The aim of this exercise," says Corbett, "is not to achieve a word-for-word correspondence with the model but rather to achieve an awareness of the variety of sentence structure of which the English language is capable" (495). The model sentences need not be followed slavishly, but Corbett suggests that the student observe at least the same kind, number, and order of phrases and clauses. Here are a few of the model sentences and examples of imitations that Corbett gives.

MODEL SENTENCE: He went through the narrow alley of Temple Bar quickly, muttering to himself that they could all go to hell because he was going to have a good night of it. —James Joyce, "Counterparts"

IMITATION: They stood outside on the wet pavement of the terrace, pretending that they had not heard us when we called to them from the library.

MODEL SENTENCE: To regain the stage in its own character, not as a mere emulation of prose, poetry must find its own poetic way to the mastery the stage demands—the mastery of action. —Archibald MacLeish, "The Poet as Playwright"

IMITATION: To discover our own natures, not the personalities imposed on us by others, we must honestly assess the values we cherish—in short, our "philosophy of life." (*Classical Rhetoric* 498-99)

Another useful imitation technique is *controlled composition*. According to Edmund Miller, controlled composition is "the technique of having students copy a passage as they introduce some systematic change" ("Controlled Composition" 1). The changes that might be introduced can range from putting a third-person narrative into the first person to changing active to passive voice. Students are first given practice in copying the original model, making certain that every element of the copy is correct; they are then asked to rewrite it, making the stipulated changes. Here is an example of one of Miller's controlled composition assignments, from *Exercises in Style*.

Let's Hear It for Mickey Spillane

1. Watching television may be interesting and informative. 2. But reading a trashy novel is even more interesting and informative. 3. Even if you read two blood-and-guts thrillers a week, you can always count on finding them informative. 4. We learn not only from what is well written but also from what is poorly written. 5. Reading an inadequate book improves the reader's critical skills and also his general facility with reading. 6. Watching a mindless television show like "The New Treasure Hunt," "Gilligan's Island," or "Mork and Mindy" is considerably less informative. 7. This is because television is passive and aural, engaging the ear but only a small compartment of the mind. 8. Neither mind nor body gets challenged to do its best. 9. Reading, however, is always active and mental. 10. Body and mind help each other make reading even *Kiss Me, Deadly* or *The Erection Set* or *Me, Hood* an experience of an entirely different order from watching "The Mary Tyler Moore Show."

Directions:

I. Add the word *both* to each sentence, being careful to make all changes necessary for the proper use of the word but no other changes.

II. Leaving as much of the *original* sentence structure as possible, add the following *ideas* to the correspondingly numbered phrasing of the additions as necessary for good style:

1. Movie-going may be interesting and informative.
2. Reading a trashy novel gives us pleasure.
3. You can count on finding even some unforgettable Agatha Christie stories read to pass the time on a plane informative.
4. What is written indifferently also teaches.
5. We improve ourselves when we read great literature.
6. "The Dating Game" is a mindless television show.
7. Film too is a medium that requires our passivity.
8. Mind and body are working at less than full strength when we watch T.V.
9. Reading opens up our minds to new ideas.
10. A revival showing of Eisenstein's film classic "Ivan the Terrible, Part I," does not give us the same sort of experience that even a second-rate book does. (5-6)

Corbett's and Miller's exercises can serve to help students understand the context in which they create writing. Without knowledge of what has been done by others, there can be no profound originality. Speaking of his own instruction through the use of imitation, Winston Churchill said, "Thus I got into my bones the essential structure of the ordinary British sentence—which is a noble thing." If we can help our students get the structure of ordinary sentences "into their bones," the time and effort of imitation exercises will have been worthwhile.

Using Imitation Exercises in the Classroom

There are many ways to introduce imitation exercises into an FY class, and you can decide how you wish to approach them based on the amount of time you have available. Some kinds of imitation can be done as homework, but others really need the sort of encouragement that you can provide only in a classroom. One important point applies to all sorts of imitation, however: if you choose to use this technique, be prepared to work with it throughout the entire term if you want results from it. Like sentence combining (with which it shares other attributes), imitation has value only insofar as it leaves students with an intuitive sense of discourse patterns that they can apply to all their writing assignments. Donna Gorrell's *Copy/Write* and Winston Weathers's *Alternative Style* can provide you with additional ideas and exercises.

There are problems in teaching imitation. Students are initially suspicious of the method, seeing it as blocking their originality. They may balk at the rigidity of some of the exercises. And higher-level students sometimes see it as babyish, beneath their capacities (and obviously, for some students, it will be). In addition, you will see little improvement unless you work on the exercises regularly and expose your students to as many kinds of sentences as you can. You will have to keep reminding your students of the two criteria for successful imitation: the more removed the new content is from that of the original, the better the imitation will be, and the new content should coincide perfectly with the given rhetorical model.

Press on, and you will see a change. Imitation can liberate students by freeing them of enervating design decisions, at least temporarily. Paradoxically, through exercises that connote servitude, you will be promoting freedom.

WORKS CITED

Abrams, M. H. *The Mirror and the Lamp*. New York: Oxford UP, 1953.

Booth, Wayne. "The Rhetorical Stance." Winterowd 71–79.

Chatman, Seymour, and Samuel R. Levin., ed. *Literary Style: A Symposium*. London: Oxford UP, 1971.

——. *Essays on the Language of Literature*. Boston: Houghton, 1967.

Cohen, Michael E., and Charles R. Smith. "HOMER: Teaching Style with a Microcomputer." Wresch 83–90.

Corbett, Edward P. J. "A Method of Analyzing Prose Style with a Demonstration Analysis of Swift's *A Modest Proposal*." Tate 294–312.

——. "Approaches to the Study of Style." Tate 83–130.

——. *Classical Rhetoric for the Modern Student*. 3rd ed. New York: Oxford UP, 1989.

——. *Rhetorical Analyses of Literary Works*. New York: Oxford, 1969.

Fleischauer, John. "Teaching Prose Style Analysis." *Style* 9 (1975): 92–102.

Gorrell, Donna. *Copy/Write: Basic Writing through Controlled Composition*. Boston: Little, Brown 1982.

Graves, Richard. "A Primer for Teaching Style." *CCC* 25 (1974): 186–90.

Gruber, William. "'Servile Copying' and the Teaching of English." *CE* 39 (1977): 491–97.

Irmscher, William F. *Teaching Expository Writing*. New York: Holt, 1979.

Joos, Martin. *The Five Clocks*. New York: Harcourt, 1961.

Kiefer, Kathleen, and Charles R. Smith. "Improving Students' Revising and Editing: The Writer's Workbench." Wresch 62–82.

Lanham, Richard. *Style: An Anti-Textbook*. New Haven, CT: Yale UP, 1974.

Macrorie, Ken. *Uptaught*. Rochelle Park, N.J.: Hayden, 1970.

Marckwardt, Albert H. Introduction. *The Five Clocks*. Joos. i–x.

Milic, Louis T. "Against the Typology of Styles." Chatman and Levin 442–50.

——. "Rhetorical Choice and Stylistic Option: The Conscious and Unconscious Poles." Chatman and Levin 77–88.

——. "Theories of Style and Their Implications for the Teaching of Composition." *CCC* 16 (1965): 66–69, 126.

Miller, Edmund. "Controlled Composition and the Teaching of Style." Paper presented at CCCC 29, Denver, CO, 1978.

——. *Exercises in Style.* Normal: Illinois State, 1980.

Perelman, Chaim. "The New Rhetoric: A Theory of Practical Reasoning. " *The Rhetoric of Western Thought.* Ed. James L. Golden et al., Dubuque, IA: Kendall-Hunt, 1983. 403-23.

Riffaterre, Michael. "Criteria for Style Analysis." Chatman and Levin 442-50.

Tate, Gary, ed. *Teaching Composition: Twelve Bibliographic Essays.* 2nd ed. Fort Worth: Texas Christian UP, 1987.

Weathers, Winston. *An Alternate Style: Options in Composition.* Rochelle Park, NJ: Hayden, 1980.

——. "Teaching Style: A Possible Anatomy." *CCC* 21 (1970): 114-49.

Weaver, Richard. *Ideas Have Consequences.* Chicago: U of Chicago, 1948.

Winterowd, Ross, ed. *Contemporary Rhetoric: A Conceptual Background with Readings.* New York: Harcourt, 1975.

Wresch, William, ed. *The Computer in Composition Instruction.* Urbana, IL: NCTE, 1984.

10 TEACHING THE SENTENCE AND THE PARAGRAPH

TEACHING THE SENTENCE

A number of theories and methods of instruction in writing approach the writing process through practice in syntax: the writing of well-structured sentences. Imitation exercises can be considered a syntactic method because they ask students to practice sentence writing, but the best known and most completely tested syntactic methods are Francis Christensen's *generative rhetoric of the sentence* and *sentence combining* as evolved by John Mellon, Frank O'Hare, and William Strong. Developed to make students aware of the components of a good sentence and to provide practice in writing such sentences, these systems were influenced to some degree by Noam Chomsky's idea of transformational-generative grammar, which revolutionized linguistics in the late 1950s.

A key word in syntactic theory is *maturity,* the ability to compose sentences that compare favorably with those of more experienced writers. Francis Christensen called this goal *syntactic fluency* ("Rhetoric of the Sentence"); the term *syntactic maturity* was born only after Kellogg Hunt published *Grammatical Structures Written at Three Grade Levels,* revealing that intrasentence structures can be quantified according to the age and experience of the writer. Thereafter, sentence-combining theorists announced their goal of increasing students' syntactic maturity, of helping students build structures that reflect those of more advanced writers.

Syntactic maturity is not, of course, the same as overall quality of writing. Hunt, whose research lies behind the concept of syntactic maturity, never claimed that students who are more syntactically mature write better (Morenberg 3). Theoretically at least, syntactic maturity is an evaluation of elements completely separate from the overall quality of writing. Words per clause, clauses per sentence, and so forth do not and cannot measure tone, voice, organization, content—all qualitative factors that make up good writing. As John Mellon said after his sentence-combining study, "Syntactic maturity is only a statistical artifact" ("Issues" 4).

Nonetheless, important tests of syntactic methods found that as syntactic maturity increased in student writing, so did the overall quality of the writing as perceived by experienced English teachers.[1] The syntactic methods tested

---

[1] See Faigley; Kerek and Daiker.

were compared with traditional content-oriented methods and were found to produce writing that teachers judged better on average. Although they measure two different things, syntactic maturity and the quality of writing do in fact seem to be linked.

This development is not completely understood, even by supporters of syntactic methods. O'Hare, while carefully avoiding inflated claims for sentence combining, suggests that style may have a powerful immediate effect on the reader of an essay.

> This final choice made by every writer is . . . frequently a syntactic one.
> . . . The present study's findings strongly suggest that style, rather narrowly defined as the final syntactic choices habitually made from the writer's practical repertoire of syntactic alternatives, is an important dimension of what constitutes writing ability. (*Sentence-Combining* 74)

Syntactic methods are particularly valuable because they allow students to work on and practice many writing skills at once. They can assist students whose sentences frequently contain grammatical errors, such as fragments or run-ons. They are good, too, for students who need more familiarity with intrasentence punctuation, especially the use of commas. They give students control over the sentence and the options that the form of the sentence offers. They can, in fact, provide an entire lexicon of sentence sense concerning the way elements work together within a sentence.

Though it may seem to have been outdated by its more modern relatives, traditional sentence theory, too, can be a useful editorial tool for students, allowing them to check suspect areas of their syntax with a testing paradigm. It can give students a useful set of terms and help them identify flaws, reconstruct the purpose of the original sentence, and recast the sentence in a form that is correct yet reflects the meaning of the original. Traditional sentence theory can work hand-in-glove with syntactic practice to produce good sentences that are also correct sentences.

Much still lies outside our ken. As advanced as our understanding of syntactic units is, we still pay too little attention to the other levels on which sentences are structured: the semantic, the logical, and the rhythmic (Kane). Nonetheless, sentence theory can help students increase their syntactic fluency. Given the interactive relationship that exists between syntax and semantics, the task of helping students write syntactically fluent and mature sentences can hardly be overestimated.

Traditional Sentence Theory

Western rhetorical theories about the sentence date back to classical antiquity and have come to their present form through a long process of accretion. Because their roots are in Latin grammar and the oral rhetorical theories of the classical period, they strike many teachers today as outdated. Certainly, they are dated, yet this is, after all, the tradition that produced Burke, Madison, Melville, and Lincoln. Though traditional sentence theory must be filtered through present-day theories, it remains a highly effective way to teach sentence construction. Thus in this section, we will discuss the rhetorical components of traditional sentence theory and examine each individually.

Functional sentence types Along with the breakdown of sentences by grammatical types—simple, compound, complex, and compound-complex—the traditional classification of sentences is by function.

A *declarative sentence* is one that makes a statement, that formulates a single though sometimes complex proposition.

In 1945 the United Nations had fifty-one members.

Despite their physical similarities, the twins had somewhat different personalities, as Ray became a monk and Victor ended up directing Broadway plays.

An *imperative sentence* gives a command or makes a request. Unless it is a short command, the sentence seldom remains purely imperative. A purely imperative sentence might be

Please stop talking, and open your books.

An *imperative-declarative sentence* (mixing command with proposition) might be

Finish your dinner, and I'll let you have dessert.

An *interrogative sentence* asks a question. It always ends with a question mark.

Which book did you like most?

How did you live through last summer's heat?

An *exclamatory sentence* expresses strong feeling. It nearly always ends with an exclamation point.

Say, the study of grammar is fascinating!

Victor, that's the most brilliant play I've ever seen!

Traditional rhetorical classifications From the beginning of classical rhetorical theory, the sentence has been an object of study, and although rhetorical sentence classifications are not taught as often as they were, they can still be useful. There are several different types of rhetorical classifications, all relating to the traditional concept of a sentence as a single complete thought, suggesting, as John Genung puts it, that "it is requisite that . . . every part be subservient to one principal affirmation" (176).

The first traditional rhetorical division of sentences is into *short* and *long*. No quantitative definition of long or short sentences is possible, of course; as William Minto says in his *Manual of English Prose Literature*, "It would be absurd to prescribe a definite limit for the length of sentences, or even to say in what proportion long and short should be intermixed" (7). This unwillingness to be precise in numerical terms is representative of traditional rhetorical theory, but Genung, Minto, and other composition teachers of the past agreed that long and short sentences must be intermixed in order to produce a pleasing style. Short sentences are to be used to produce an effect of vigor and emphasis, and long sentences are to be used for detail and to create cadence and rhythm.

Beyond the injunction to mix sentences of different lengths, there is little to be done with the classification of sentences into long and short. Far more important is the traditional rhetorical classification of sentences into *loose, periodic*, and *balanced*. Of these three classes of sentences, by far the most important are the loose and the periodic, for taken together they represent a complete traditional taxonomy of the sentence. The balanced structure can be either loose or periodic and thus is not an equal or mutually exclusive class.

So far as we know, the division of sentences into loose and periodic is as old as the art of rhetoric itself. In his *Rhetoric*, Aristotle makes a distinction between "running" and "compact" sentences. "The style necessarily is either running, the whole made one only by a connecting word between part and part, . . . or compact, returning upon itself. . . . The compact is the style which is in periods" (202). As rhetoric developed through the classical age and the medieval era, the concept of loose and periodic styles remained a central doctrine of sentence construction, especially since Latin constructions in the periodic style are much more common than in most other languages.

We take up the story again in the second great age of rhetorical innovation, the eighteenth century, with the first truly modern statement of the doctrine, that of George Campbell in *The Philosophy of Rhetoric*. Following classical theory, Campbell claims that there are two kinds of sentences, periodic and loose. Campbell's description of periods and loose sentences has not been surpassed for clarity and ease of understanding.

> A period is a complex sentence, wherein the meaning remains suspended until the whole is finished. . . . The criterion of . . . loose sentences is as follows: There will always be found in them one place at least before the end, at which, if you make a stop, the construction of the preceding part will render it a complete sentence. (424-26)

Campbell provides examples of typical periodic and loose (today called *cumulative*) constructions that express the same thought.

> "At last, after much fatigue, through deep roads and bad weather, we came with no small difficulty to our journey's end."
>
> "We came to our journey's *end* at *last*, with no small *difficulty*, after much *fatigue*, through deep *roads*, and bad *weather*."

Notice that the second, loose (cumulative) sentence could be grammatically concluded after any of the italicized words, whereas the periodic sentence must continue to its termination.

Campbell's definitions of loose and periodic sentences were used throughout the nineteenth century with few changes, and the different stylistic natures of these two kinds of sentences were given close attention. Campbell had said of the periodic and loose constructions,

> The former savours more of artifice and design, the latter seems more the result of pure nature. The period is nevertheless more susceptible of vivacity and force; and the loose sentence is apt, as it were, to languish and grow tiresome. (426)

This concept of the drama of the periodic sentence and the naturalness of the cumulative sentence continued throughout the nineteenth century. Both sorts of sentences, of course, are always found in the practice of real writers, and the predominance of one or the other helps to classify the author's style. In the nineteenth century, the writings of Thomas De Quincey were said to typify the periodic style and those of Thomas Carlyle, the cumulative; more recently, we might point to the work of Henry James as exemplifying the periodic style and that of Ernest Hemingway, the cumulative.

In the practice of most writers in English, the cumulative sentence is far more common than the periodic. The history and nature of the language compel it, and we can even trace the decline of the periodic style in English as French and native influences won out over the Latinate and Germanic constructions that were common in Old English. For the most part, modern English demands a predominance of loose sentences over the periodic. This predominance is borne out by the problems inherent in the periodic style when it is pushed to extremes. The reader of a sentence in Henry James's later novels, for example, sometimes feels as if the author is working her very hard—too hard, in the minds of many. Too much reliance on the periodic sentence can exhaust the reader.

The cumulative and periodic structures are mutually exclusive, whereas the final traditional rhetorical classification, the *balanced,* or *antithetical,* sentence, can be either cumulative or periodic. The balanced sentence is a later development in rhetorical theory. Though the Greeks used it, it does not appear clearly in classical rhetoric, and once it does appear, it is for a while confused with antithesis. Campbell discusses antithesis as a sort of periodic sentence, but Richard Whately, in his 1828 *Elements of Rhetoric,* states that "antithesis has been sometimes reckoned as one form of the Period, but it is evident that . . . it has no necessary connexion with it" (356).

Gradually over the course of the nineteenth century, antithesis came to be associated with a single type of sentence. Alexander Bain stated in 1866 that "when the different clauses of a compound sentence are made similar in form, they are said to be Balanced" (302). John Genung makes the definition slightly more precise: "When the different elements of a compound sentence are made to answer to each other and set each other off by similarity of form, the sentence is said to be balanced" (191).

The writing of Samuel Johnson, perhaps more than that of any other author, gives examples of balanced sentences; for Johnson, they were habitual. "Contempt is the proper punishment of affectation, and detestation the just consequence of hypocrisy." "He remits his splendour, but retains his magnitude; and pleases more, though he dazzles less" (qtd. in Campbell 425-26). Balanced sentences can sound pompous and mechanical if overused, and for that reason, their use must always be limited. They can also present the reader with an "agreeable surprise," however, and enliven otherwise workaday prose with an element that can be oratorical and even poetic without calling attention to itself. As Genung later suggests, the balanced sentence can be used well for emphasis and for introducing paired concepts, but because of its tendency to become monotonous, writers should use care in determining the frequency of its appearance (191-92).

These three sentence types, then, represent the traditional rhetorical classification: the English-French-descended loose sentence, which makes up 70 to 80 percent of most English prose; the Latin- and German-descended periodic sentence, which makes up the other 20 to 30 percent, and the oratorical-sounding balanced sentence, which can be either loose or periodic. All have specific stylistic effects, and all are subject to corruptions, extremes, and overemphasis if not used carefully.

Using Traditional Sentence Theory in the Classroom

The traditional classifications are not a panacea for all writing ills, but they can be used successfully in the classroom. If you decide to teach them, remember that the balance between loose and periodic sentences in modern American prose favors the loose, or cumulative, sentence. You will want to familiarize students with cumulative and periodic constructions and with the stylistic and organizational differences between them, and you might suggest that the periodic construction not be overused or overextended.

Begin teaching with some simple blackboard exercises. Transpose a short, cumulative sentence to a periodic one without mentioning the names of the types: change, for example, *We went shopping to buy some sugar* to *To buy some sugar, we went shopping.* Discuss the difference between the two sentences, pointing out that the (unnamed) cumulative sentence can be ended after *shopping*, but the (unnamed) periodic sentence cannot. You may want to pass out examples and ask students to work for a while, both at the board and at their seats, with the transposition of similarly simple sentences from cumulative to periodic. Discuss some of the periodic structures students create and critique them. You can gradually work up to the more complex structures.

After the concepts of the two different sorts of sentences are established, you can name them and ask students to check the percentages of their occurrence in their own work, perhaps in an essay already completed. Many, of course, will find no periodic structures at all in their papers.

Finally, you may want to suggest that students make between 10 and 20 percent of the sentences in their essays periodic, none of which should be longer than three clauses. Yes, you may occasionally get stylistic monstrosities, but you will also get appealing and thoughtful periodic combinations as students attempt to widen their stylistic options.

As for balanced sentences, we know that our students, no Bacons or Johnsons, have little occasion to write them. Should you decide to teach the balanced sentence, however, you can use methods similar to those you used to teach cumulative and periodic sentences.

Christensen's Generative Rhetoric of the Sentence

In a series of essays written in the 1960s, Francis Christensen described a new way of viewing sentences and a pedagogic method that could be used to teach students to write longer, more mature, more varied, and more interesting sentences. Christensen considers the sentence the most important element in rhetoric because it is "a natural and isolable unit" ("Advanced Composition" 168). His theory of sentence composing articulates the following four principles:

Addition   The traditional formula for a good sentence has always been to use a concrete noun and an active verb, but Christensen's theory disputes this recipe. For Christensen, the composition of sentences is instead a process of adding different sorts of modifiers, some consisting of only a word, others consisting of a number of words or a clause.

Direction of modification   Writing moves in linear space: whenever a modifier is added to a sentence, it is added either before or after the word or clause it modifies. If the modifier is added before the noun, verb, or main clause being modified, the direction of modification can be indicated by an arrow pointing forward; if it is added after the unit being modified, the direction can be indicated by an arrow pointing backward.

With a rear fender torn loose, the battered *Trans-Am* slowly

limped, squeaking and grinding, to the curb.

You will notice two kinds of modifiers in this example. There are the *close,* or *bound,* modifiers of the noun and the verb—"battered" and "slowly." And there are the *free,* or *sentence,* modifiers—"with a rear fender torn loose," "squeaking and grinding," and "to the curb"—that modify the clause "Trans-Am limped." The difference between the two sorts of modifiers is simple: bound modifiers are generally fixed in position, and the only choice they call for is whether to use them at all. Free modifiers, on the other hand, can be placed in many different positions, thus creating different stylistic effects. Bound modifiers are usually said to be *embedded*, and free modifiers are said to be *added*.

Christensen claims that the overuse of bound modifiers is responsible for some of the worst excesses of teaching—what he calls the injunction that students "load the patterns" with bound modifiers. "Pattern practice" thus sets students to writing sentences like this: *The small boy on the red bicycle who lives with his happy parents on our shady street often coasts down the steep street until he comes to the city park.* The heavy use of single-word bound modifiers does not necessarily make for good prose.

Bound modifiers, then, have limitations in terms of helping students write varied and interesting sentences. Free modifiers, in contrast, offer a wider range of possibilities. Christensen considers sentences created through the use of free modifiers to be cumulative, the central sentence type used in modern prose. And since free modifiers sharpen, focus, and define the thought conveyed by the main clause of a cumulative sentence, "the mere form of the sentence generates ideas" ("Rhetoric of the Sentence" 156). The careful use of free modifiers compels writers to examine their thoughts and can thus be more than a merely descriptive tool.

Levels of generality   Addition and direction of modification are structural principles, but for Christensen, the structure has no meaning until a third principle is introduced, that of levels of generality, or levels of abstraction ("Rhetoric of the Sentence" 157). In terms of the cumulative sentence, if two clauses or modifiers are at the same level of generality, they can be called *coordinate;* if a modifier is at a lower level of generality than the clause or modifier adjacent to it, it can be called *subordinate.* Free modifiers are subordinate to the main idea of a sentence and thus function at a lower level of generality, as in this example: *The man sat silent, staring at his hands and his pipe, unable to still his trembling fingers.*

A cumulative sentence can be charted according to its levels of abstraction and each segment of the sentence assigned a number, a higher number indicating a lower level of generality (higher-numbered levels are more specific than lower-numbered levels).

1. He shook his hands,
2. a quick shake, [noun cluster]
3. fingers down, [absolute verb cluster]
4. like a pianist. [prepositional phrase] ("Rhetoric of the Sentence" 158)

Texture   This fourth principle provides an evaluative term that can be used when the first three principles are applied to prose. Christensen gives us a succinct definition of texture.

> If a writer adds to few of his nouns or verbs or main clauses, the texture may be said to be thin. The style will be plain or bare. . . . But if he adds frequently or much or both, then the texture may be said to be dense or rich. ("Rhetoric of the Sentence" 157)

The pedagogic end of Christensen's method is to introduce students to ways of increasing the density of their sentences and enriching the texture of their writing. Christensen's rhetoric does not follow the traditional canons; instead, it views all other skills in language as naturally following syntactic skills. For Christensen, you can probably be a good writer if you can learn to write a good cumulative sentence.

Using Christensen's Generative Rhetoric
of the Sentence in the Classroom

A good way to introduce Christensen's theory of the cumulative sentence is to discuss free modifiers versus bound modifiers. Put these two sentences on the blackboard.

> The old woman with the white hair who picks through the smelly trash in our crowded backyard gestured wildly and shrieked out joyfully.

> White-haired and beady-eyed, the old trash picker gestured wildly and shrieked out joyfully, her work-gloved hands beating the air, her thin voice rising and cracking, the smelly trash falling around her in our crowded backyard.

Discuss the differences between these two sentences. Ask students which is better, and why. Point out the *base clause* in both sentences: "the old woman/ trash picker gestured and shrieked out." Most students will choose the second sentence as better despite the fact that it contains no more propositional information than the first. Through this discussion, you can gradually come around to the question of bound and free modifiers and how they affect sentences.

At this point, explanation through example is the easiest course of action. Pass out a sheet of examples of two-level cumulative sentences (you can use examples from books or make up your own). These sentences should not have been broken down by level of abstraction—that activity will come later. Working at the board with some of these examples, you can introduce the principles of *addition* and *order of movement*. Show how each sentence has a base clause and how the free modifiers define or specify the material in that clause. Use arrows to show the direction of modification.

From this point onward, your students should begin to be able to write and manipulate cumulative sentences. You will need to continue to check their work, since they will have a tendency, especially at these early stages, to degenerate into "loading the patterns" with bound modifiers. Another problem to guard against is the tendency to create a dangling participle when attempting to write a free modifier. To keep an eye out for these problems, you might ask four or five students per day to prepare cumulative sentences and put them on the blackboard before class starts. The five minutes each day your class spends discussing these sentences can pay large dividends because this exercise gives students practice in both recognizing and writing cumulative sentences.

The actual instruction in writing cumulative sentences is not yet over, however. The third principle, that of *levels of generality,* must still be examined, even while students are studying two-level cumulative sentences. Only after some practice will students be able to grasp this principle and manipulate free modifiers in a really syntactically fluent way.

To illustrate how levels of generality work, distribute a handout showing the original sentences broken down and numbered according to their levels of generality. You will have to review the concept of the base clause as the center of the sentence and point out that this clause is isolated and assigned the number 1 and that the free modifiers are identified and assigned the number 2 because they are more specific than the base clauses. Although Christensen recommends that students use the grammatical names of the different kinds of free modifiers, you can choose whether or not you want to provide more than an initial introduction to this terminology.

One important factor that you will have to take into account when using cumulative-sentence practice in this generative way is the strong element of description and narration implied by the cumulative sentence. Cumulative sentences simply do not work as well with exposition or argumentation as they do with narration and description. What this means for the generation of sentences using Christensen's method is that the best exercises are based on immediate observation, for they push the student to use precise language.

The next stage of instruction is introducing the multilevel sentence, the cumulative sentence with more than one level of abstraction. This stage can get complicated, and you cannot expect quick results. To introduce the multilevel sentence, pass out examples of such sentences showing their levels of generality. Point out that some of the modifiers are on the same level and are thus called coordinate, and some are on lower levels—because they modify modifiers rather than the base clause—and are thus called subordinate. Go through the exercises as before, asking students first to chart the examples and then to generate sentences according to prescribed formulas. Here are a few of the multilevel sentence exercises that Francis and Bonniejean Christensen use in *A New Rhetoric*.

> Copy these sentences, using indentation and numbering to mark the levels. If your instructor so directs, mark the grammatical character of the levels added to the main clause.
>
> 1. Crane sat up straight, suddenly, smiling shyly, looking pleased, like a child who had just been given a present. /Irwin Shaw
> 2. For once, the students filed out silently, making a point, with youthful good manners, of not looking at Crane, bent over at his chair, pulling his books together. /Irwin Shaw
> 3. She was very old and small and she walked slowly in the dark pine shadows, moving a little from side to side in her steps, with the balanced heaviness and lightness of a pendulum in a grandfather clock. /Eudora Welty
> 4. As he walked into the club he noticed them, objectively and coldly, the headwaiter beckoning haughtily, head tilted, lips in a rigid arc reserved for those willing to pay the price of recognition and attention, the stiffly genteel crowd, eating their food in small bites, afraid of committing a breach of etiquette. (39)

Work with multilevel sentences completes the introduction to the cumulative sentence; the job now is getting students to use these sentences in their writing. If you want your students to remember and use Christensen's method, you must continue to emphasize the cumulative sentence.

At this point, it is appropriate to bring up Christensen's fourth principle, that of *texture*. The texture of most students' writing is thin, says Christensen, and the aim of his system is to help students generate texture—to become, as he says, weavers of dense prose and "sentence acrobats." To do this, create and hand out some examples of thin prose and some of dense prose that have similar patterns of content, juxtaposing the thin passages with the densely textured ones. Feel free to give a short "soapbox" speech about the advantages of dense texture and the usefulness of the cumulative sentence. This lecture will mark the end of the beginning of the study of Christensen's sentence theory.

From now on, at least two hours per week—generally as homework—must be devoted to the writing of cumulative sentences if anything is to be gained from the foregoing lessons. If the cumulative sentence does not become a writing habit, it will have no real value.

Practice can be set up in a number of ways: you can supply base clauses and ask students to modify them, or you can assign short observations using cumulative sentences. But you must make certain that students do this practice every week. Like sentence combining, work with cumulative sentences must be done often if students are to succeed with this method.

Since the best cumulative sentences are based on observation, students may initially have a hard time using such sentences with the more abstract modes of argumentation and exposition, even though these modes often do contain elements of narration and description. One way of helping students deal with this problem is to follow Christensen's sentence work immediately with his paragraph theory, an introduction to which is included in this chapter. The Christensen paragraph is based on expository paragraphs just as the sentence theory is based on narrative sentences, and the two theories balance each other out.

Finally, if you find Christensen's theories congenial, look at his original articles, and investigate the entire rhetorical program found in his and Bonniejean Christensen's *New Rhetoric*. This short overview cannot do justice to the delightfulness of Christensen's style. And although few teachers see the answers to all rhetorical problems in Christensen's syntactic work, his theories remain among the most interesting and suggestive weapons in our arsenal.

Sentence Combining

Sentence combining in its simplest form is the process of joining two or more short, simple sentences to make one longer sentence, using techniques of *embedding, deletion, subordination,* and *coordination.* Although its history stretches back to the *grammaticus* of classical Rome, not until recently has sentence combining been applied with any coherent scientific methodology or recognized as an important technique.

The theoretical base on which sentence combining was to be founded was established in 1957, when Noam Chomsky revolutionized grammatical theory with his book *Syntactic Structures.* This theoretical base was, of course, Chomskyan transformational-generative grammar, which caused immense excitement in the field of composition.[2] TG grammar, which swept aside both traditional and structural grammar, seemed to present the possibility of a new pedagogy based on the study of linguistic transformations.

In 1963, Donald Bateman and Frank J. Zidonis of Ohio State University conducted an experiment to determine whether teaching students TG grammar would reduce the incidence of errors in their writing. They found that students taught TG grammar indeed made fewer errors and also developed the ability to write more complex sentence structures. Despite some questionable features of their study, it did suggest that TG grammar has an effect on students' writing.

The Bateman and Zidonis study was published in 1964; that same year another study was published that was to have far more importance for sentence combining: Kellogg Hunt's *Grammatical Structures Written at Three Grade Levels.* Hunt's work provides the basis for most measurements of *syntactic maturity,* which has come to be seen as an important goal of sentence combining. Briefly, Hunt wished to find out which elements of writing changed as people matured and which structures seemed to be representative of mature writing. To this end, he studied the writing of average students at fourth-, eighth-, and twelfth-grade levels and expository articles in *Harper's* and the *Atlantic.* Hunt quickly realized that the tendency of younger writers to string together many short clauses with *and* means that sentence length is not a good indicator of maturity in writing ("Synopsis" 111). He then began studying clause length: "I became more and more interested in what I will describe as one main clause plus whatever subordinate clauses happen to be attached to or embedded within it" ("Synopsis" 111–12). This study lead him to express his most famous concept, the *minimal terminable unit,* or *T-unit.*

Each T-unit, says Hunt, is "minimal in length and each could be terminated grammatically between a capital and a period." He goes on:

> Here . . . is a simple theme written by a fourth-grader who punctuated it as a single 68-word sentence.
>
> I like the movie we saw about Moby Dick the white whale the captain said if you can kill the white whale Moby Dick I will give this gold to the one that can do it and it is worth sixteen dollars they tried and tried but while they were trying they killed a whale and used the oil for the lamps they almost caught the white whale.

That theme, cut into these unnamed units, appears below. A slant line now begins each clause. A period ends each unit, and a capital begins each one.

1. I like the movie/we saw about Moby Dick, the white whale.
2. The captain said/if you can kill the white whale, Moby Dick, /I will give this gold to the one/that can do it.
3. And it is worth sixteen dollars.

---

[2] Chomskyan thought has undergone some profound changes since TG grammar was first elaborated in 1957, and teachers new to Chomsky may want to look first at his more recent book, *Reflections on Language.*

4. They tried and tried.
5. But/while they were trying/they killed a whale and used the oil for the lamps.
6. They almost caught the white whale. ("Synopsis" 112)

The T-unit, Hunt found, is a much more reliable index of stylistic maturity than sentence length. Eventually he determined the best three indices of stylistic maturity: the average number of words per T-unit, the average number of clauses per T-unit, and the average number of words per clause. When they were applied to writing at different grade levels, he found that these numbers increased at a steady rate.

The study by Bateman and Zidonis and those by Hunt used no sentence combining at all, but they do represent the bases from which modern sentence-combining springs: the methodological linguistic base of TG grammar and the empirical evaluative base of Hunt's studies of syntactic maturity. These were brought together in the first important experiment involving sentence-combining exercises, by John Mellon. Reported in his *Transformational Sentence-Combining,* Mellon's was the first study to ask students to practice combining kernel sentences rather than merely to learn grammar. "Research," wrote Mellon, " . . . clearly shows that memorized principles of grammar, whether conventional or modern, clearly play a negligible role in helping students achieve 'correctness' in their written expression" (*Transformational Sentence-Combining* 2). What could help students do this, reasoned Mellon, was instruction in TG grammar plus practice in combining short sentences into longer, more complex sentences.

Despite his disclaimer of interest in teaching students to memorize grammar, Mellon actually asked the seventh-graders he used in the experiment to learn a rather complicated set of grammatical rules, including transformational terms like *T: rel, T: gerund.* The students were then asked to use these terms in signaled sentence-combining exercises with complex TG directions. Here is one of Mellon's exercises:

SOMETHING used to anger Grandfather no end. (T:exp)

SOMETHING should be so easy. (T:fact–T:exp)

The children recognized SOMETHING. (T:infin)

SOMETHING was only a preliminary to SOMETHING sometime. (T:wh)

He insisted SOMETHING. (T:gerund)

They had enough peppermints. (T:fact)

He gave them still another handful. (T:gerund) (*Transformational Sentence-Combining* 129)

Without going through the rules that Mellon asked his students to learn, we must simplify the explanation of how this exercise is to be done. Essentially, the transformational direction at the end of each kernel sentence shows how the sentence must be changed in order for it to fit into the combination, and the *something* shows where information from other kernels is to be included.

The sentence that Mellon's students were to create from the above set of kernels goes like this: "It used to anger Grandfather no end that it should be so easy for the children to recognize that his insisting that they had had enough peppermints was only a preliminary to his giving them still another handful."

This sort of sentence-combining exercise may seem initially difficult, but Mellon's experiment was a success. Using Hunt's data on normal growth in writing maturity, Mellon found that his experimental sentence-combining group showed from 2.1 to 3.5 years of syntactic growth, while his control group did not show even a year's growth. Sentence combining was thus established as an important tool in helping students write more mature sentences.

Further research on sentence combining left theoreticians doubtful as to its efficacy in improving student's writing.[3] In 1973, however, Frank O'Hare's *Sentence-Combining* showed beyond a doubt that sentence-combining exercises that do not include grammar instruction still help students achieve syntactic maturity. Again testing seventh-graders, O'Hare used sentence-combining exercises with his experimental group over a period of eight months without ever mentioning any of the formal rules of TG grammar. The amount of time spent on the exercises was considerable but not excessive; as O'Hare notes, "The sentence-combining treatment lasted an average of one hour and a quarter per week in class, and the students spent about half an hour per week on related homework assignments" (*Sentence-Combining* 42–43). The control group was not exposed to sentence combining at all.

The types of sentence-combining exercises used in the O'Hare study were related to Mellon's exercises, but O'Hare wanted to avoid the cumbersome TG nomenclature of Mellon's exercises. To achieve this goal and still give suggestions that would help students work the exercises, O'Hare devised a simpler, nongrammatical signaling system. Here is an example of one of his exercises.

SOMETHING led to SOMETHING.
James Watt discovered SOMETHING. ('s + DISCOVERY)
Steam is a powerful source of energy. (THAT)
Britain established an industrial society. ('s + ING) (*Sentence-Combining* 86)

In O'Hare's exercises, Mellon's transformational cues are replaced by easy-to-understand word-change and replacement directions, while the *something* still indicates where information from other kernels is to be placed. The student is asked to bring the term in parentheses to the front of the sentence it follows and to use it to change what must be changed in order to effect the combination. In the example above, the first kernel gives the general shape of the sentence to be created. Bringing each direction to the front of the sentence it follows and making the connection implied by the first kernel lead to the combined sentence that is the correct answer: "James Watt's discovery that steam is a powerful source of energy led to Britain's establishing an industrial society."

---

[3] See Miller and Ney for strictures on Mellon's work.

Some of O'Hare's later exercises completely do away with parenthesized cues and substitute a system of eliminating repeated words and underlining words to be kept.

The alleys <u>were littered with bottles and garbage.</u>
The alleys were <u>between the apartment buildings.</u>
The apartment buildings were <u>dismal.</u>
The bottles were <u>broken.</u>
The garbage was <u>rotting.</u>

This exercise specifies the words that will be needed in the final combined sentences by underlining them. By discarding the parts of the subsequent kernels that are not needed, we get the final combination: "The alleys between the dismal apartment buildings were littered with broken bottles and rotting garbage."

O'Hare's test measured six factors of syntactic maturity and found that significant growth had taken place in all six. His experimental group of seventh-graders, after eight months of sentence combining, wrote an average of 15.75 words per T-unit—more than Hunt had reported as the average for twelfth-graders. The other factors were similarly impressive. Just as important, though, were the results of a second hypothesis O'Hare was testing: whether the sentence-combining group's compositions would be judged better in overall quality than those of the control group. Eight experienced English teachers rated 240 experimental-group and control-group essays written after the eight-month test period; when asked to choose between matched pairs of essays, they chose an experimental-group essay 70 percent of the time. These results suggest that sentence-combining exercises not only improve syntactic maturity but also affect perceived quality of writing in general (*Sentence-Combining* 67–77).

Further research on sentence combining, most particularly an impressive study conducted by Donald Daiker and his colleagues at Miami University of Ohio, suggests that its positive effects on students' writing are also powerful at the college level but that they diminish over time.[4] Scholars continue to debate the issue; such intriguing controversy, can be safely ignored by new teachers of writing, who need know only that sentence combining offers a viable way to help students write clearly focused, grammatically correct, and thoughtfully worded sentences.

Using Sentence Combining in the Classroom

Two types of sentence-combining exercises, *cued* and *open,* can be used successfully in the classroom. Cued exercises have only one really "correct" answer, and they suggest it by using signals within or at the ends of certain kernel

---

[4] See Daiker, Kerek, and Morenberg, *Rhetorical Perspective,* "Syntactic Maturity," *Teaching of Writing,* and *Writer's Options;* Kerek, Daiker, and Morenberg, "College Composition" and "Effects"; and Morenberg, Daiker, and Kerek, "Experimental Study." For more criticism of sentence combining, see the works by Combs and by Ney.

sentences. Mellon's complex TG grammar signals are no longer used; instead, simple words and underlining instruct the student, as in this example from Frank O'Hare's *Sentencecraft* (81):

> The next letter comes from a viewer.
> The viewer doesn't understand <u>something.</u> (WHO)
> A polar bear would know <u>something somehow.</u> (HOW)
> A polar bear is <u>living in the arctic region.</u> (WHERE)
> <u>The sun never sets</u> in the arctic region. (WHERE)
> The bear is <u>to go to sleep sometime.</u> (WHEN TO)

The best solution to this example is the following sentence: "The next letter comes from a viewer who doesn't understand how a polar bear living in the arctic region, where the sun never sets, would know when to go to sleep."

Open exercises, on the other hand, merely present a series of kernel exercises and rely on students to use their intuition to create a grammatical sentence. Some open exercises are so simple that for all intents and purposes, they have only one correct answer, as in this example from William Strong's text *Sentence-Combining: A Composing Book* (109).

> The trout were blanketed.
>
> The trout were called rainbows.
>
> The blanketing was with ferns.
>
> The ferns were green.
>
> The ferns were sweet smelling.

The best solution to this exercise is "The rainbow trout were blanketed with green, sweet-smelling ferns." Other open exercises can be more complex and admit of a number of answers, as in this example from Daiker, Kerek, and Morenberg's *Writer's Options* (138):

> The vampire's existence may not appeal to many people.
>
> The appeal is conscious.
>
> But the all-important promise of life after death strikes a chord.
>
> The chord is deep in our unconscious.
>
> The chord is the powerful will to live.
>
> This is despite the cost.

Although there is no one right answer to the open exercises, the range of acceptable answers is limited, as you will see if you try to combine these kernels. They can be rewritten as "The vampire's existence may not appeal consciously to many people, but the all-important promise of life after death strikes a chord deep in our unconscious: the powerful will to live despite the cost." Another possibility is "The vampire's existence may not have conscious appeal to many people, but the all-important promise of life after death strikes a chord of the powerful will to live, despite the cost, that is deep in our unconscious." Other possibilities exist.

Both cued and open exercises are needed for most classes. Open exercises work well for students who have already acquired some degree of syntactic maturity, and cued exercises help students whose syntactic skills are still fairly undeveloped. Open problems keep up the interest of students who want some element of creativity, while cued problems push students to learn and practice particular structures in a given full-sentence configuration.

Once you have decided on an exercise format and on the book or books you wish to use,[5] the question of how to teach sentence combining still remains. You might want to begin with cued exercises. After explaining the sentence-combining process and how the cues work, assign six or eight problems per night as homework, using time during the following class to go over the answers. Ask students to read their answers or put them on the blackboard. Based on this sort of practice, you can gauge students' progress in cued combinations and determine when to go on to open exercises. You will want to hold class discussions of the different combinations possible for open problems; if you have access to an overhead projector, you can use projections to compare different combinations of the same kernels and discuss their stylistic effects.

These discussions and comparisons are of the utmost importance since sentence combining is much less useful if it is merely an at-home activity, haphazardly checked. Ask questions about style and why one version is more effective than another; talk about the placement of clauses and organizational techniques; and encourage students to share any versions they feel are better than those you have reproduced. Make certain they are aware of the option of *not* combining kernels should they have stylistic reasons not to. If you see problems or if some students seem to be struggling with the exercises, supplement the open exercises with cued problems, and spend some time nailing down basic additions, deletions, embeddings, transformations, and changes in punctuation.

The lesson of sentence combining is simple but extremely important: as Frank O'Hare says, "Writing behavior can be changed fairly rapidly and with relative ease" (*Sentence-Combining* 86). Sentence combining has fallen out of favor in some quarters, and it is not a panacea for all writing ills: it will not turn basic writers into high-level students overnight, and it should not be the only content of a writing class. But when used with care and patience, it is an effective part of a complete rhetorical program.

TEACHING THE PARAGRAPH

The paragraph began to appear in the seventeenth century as the craft of printing grew more polished. Initially, paragraphs were not indented, nor were they today's relatively small units. In manuscripts and incunabula, paragraphs were long stretches of discourse, sometimes covering several pages. Rather than being marked off by indention, they were divided by the familiar mark in the left

---

[5] Teachers interested in using a sentence-combining text in the classroom might consider the most recent edition of Daiker, Kerek, and Morenberg's *Writer's Options*, Memering and O'Hare's *Writer's Work*, or Strong's *Sentence-Combining*.

margin, indicating *paragraphos*, Greek for "mark outside." As printing matured, the exigencies of the process (the size of the printing plate, the construction of the form holding the lines of type) dictated a clean left-hand margin. Thus came about the present means of marking paragraphs—by indention. Gradually, too, the length of discourse marked by the indention stabilized (Lewis 37).

All of this happened more or less as circumstance dictated, for there was no classical theory of the paragraph. None of the neo-Ciceronian or Ramist rhetoricians of the seventeenth century mention the paragraph; the three great rhetorical theorists of the eighteenth century, Adam Smith, George Campbell, and Hugh Blair, pay it little mind. In 1866, however, in his *English Composition and Rhetoric,* the Scottish logician and educator Alexander Bain formulated rules for the production of correct paragraphs.[6]

Bain's "organic model" of the paragraph, in which every part contributes to the whole of the paragraph, became immensely influential within twenty years, especially in the United States. Every textbook used some version of it, and it took its place as the cornerstone of traditional paragraph theory. This theory remained unquestioned until the 1960s, when it was criticized as being reductive and prescriptive.

Though they deny the prescriptive importance of the paragraph, theorists Willis Pitkin and Paul Rodgers have established the groundwork for modern paragraph theory. They posit that discourse is not made up of either sentences or paragraphs; rather, it consists of segments that may sometimes be coterminous with paragraphs but often consist of several paragraphs. Pitkin calls these segments "discourse blocs," and Rodgers, "stadia of discourse"; they agree that these segments mark obvious ends and beginnings. The discourse bloc, according to Pitkin, is identified by *junctures,* "those moments in the meaningful continuum where we can say 'To this point we have been doing X; now we begin to do Y'" (139).

Rodgers agrees. "Paragraphs are not composed; they are discovered," he says; "to compose is to create; to indent is to interpret" ("Discourse-Centered Rhetoric" 4). These statements sum up Rodgers's beliefs about paragraphs, which are supported by our own awareness of how we write. Although formulas for the composition of paragraphs lay a measure of claim to being generative, the inductive study of paragraphs shows that these theories of paragraph construction cover only a few types of paragraphs. Insistence on topic sentences or levels of generality can be helpful tools in analyzing or discussing the makeup of a paragraph, but they do not locate or identify the true nature of the paragraph. Every deductive formula, in other words, is reductive as well.

What, then, is the use of trying to teach any paragraph theory? Few of our students are heavy readers; as a result, most have little experience to rely on. If they imagine a paragraph, it will probably be a newspaper paragraph or a paragraph in an advertisement. Although our students can generate discourse, they

---

[6] For a history of the organic paragraph, see Rodgers, "Alexander Bain."

often have problems ordering it and breaking it into parts. With our own paragraph intuition, informed by years of reading, we can generate paragraphs that need no revision. Our students, on the other hand, may have had little experience with the conventions of English prose.

This section will offer techniques for helping students order and revise rough-draft material that they generated without an awareness of paragraph theory. Throughout this section, we assume that the paragraph is a subject of revision, not prevision, and is formed by intuition. But if these theories about individual paragraphs are incomplete, if discourse is actually composed of "blocs" or "stadia" rather than paragraphs, why do we bother at all with paragraphing, intuitive or otherwise? The roots of the answer lie in cognitive psychology; in simple terms, we insist on paragraphing because readers expect it. That the paragraph as we know it is a relatively recent phenomenon does not cancel the fact that it spread immediately and until it had become universal, for the paragraph developed in response to the reader's need for breaks in written discourse. Although paragraph theories offer us ways to compose and analyze paragraphs, ultimately, paragraphs are for the reader's convenience—and we should teach them as such.[7]

Contending that the paragraph is mainly a device used to guide and aid readers is not to suggest that paragraphing is completely arbitrary or that the structural theorists have nothing to offer. That is far from the case. Readers have definite expectations about the content and form of paragraphs as well as about their length; the degree to which readers concur in dividing up an unbroken stretch of discourse shows that paragraph structure does play a large role in readers' expectations.[8]

Students who are uncertain about paragraphing usually show recurring problems in their paragraphing: paragraphs that are too short or thin in texture, that are too long and cover too much material, that are incoherent and mass together unrelated information. It is important to understand the student's faulty presuppositions about paragraphs before choosing a method for working with her.

Students who write paragraphs that are too short—that is, paragraphs that consistently contain only one to three normal-length sentences—are often unconsciously reproducing the models with which they are familiar: advertising copy and newspaper style, both of which use short paragraphs to move the reader rapidly through quickly digestible pieces of information. The paragraph structures of ads and newspapers are effective within their limited range but are bad models for expository prose. In the hands of students, short paragraphs become choppy, interruptive, and annoying in their continual insistence on a new start even when the material doesn't warrant it.

---

[7] See Chapter 6 of *The St. Martin's Handbook* for work that students can do on paragraphing.

[8] See Koen, Becker, and Young for an interesting study of this phenomenon. The issues of coherence and readers' expectations are also taken up in Halliday and Hasan; Witte and Faigley, "Coherence"; and Markels.

Christensen's work is most directly concerned with solving the problem of short paragraphs. A writer of short paragraphs needs to be told about levels of generality and density. In some cases, the problem is not one of underdeveloped paragraphs but of uninformed choices about where to begin new paragraphs. Students with such problems must learn to ask themselves, in Pitkin's terms, "Am I done showing the reader X, and am I ready to begin Y?" or "Does this indention serve a purpose? Why is it here?"

Writers of overly long paragraphs are usually completely unaware of the traditional uses of the paragraph, and they need to become acquainted with the paragraph as a structural and a conventional form. Such writers may underdifferentiate their paragraphs because they see their whole discourse as a rush in which they have to say something—anything. Students suffering from too-long paragraphs may need special help with other aspects of writing, particularly with invention and argumentation. If, in the essays your students write, paragraphing is one of the only problems, it is a problem that is easy to solve: showing students how to spot topic sentences or high levels of generality will help them differentiate the beginnings and ends of paragraphs within their own work. If there are larger organizational problems, however, settle in for a long, hard struggle to introduce the conventions of paragraphing.

Incoherence is fairly common among FY students: their paragraphs often skip from idea to idea, resulting in a jumbled mass of information. Presenting the traditional model paragraph with topic sentence and development is one way of dealing with this problem; it forces students to question the placement and purpose of each sentence in the paragraph. For those students who also have a difficult time with the "methods of development" central to the classical model, a perspective on paragraphing developed by Richard L. Larson in his article "Sentences in Action" may be helpful. The central point of Larson's article is that every sentence in a paragraph has a function. The most common roles are state, restate, expand, particularize, exemplify, define, describe, narrate, qualify, concede, support, refute, evaluate, identify a cause or result, compare or contrast, summarize, conclude. These roles are not, Larson points out, mutually exclusive (18). Teaching students to recognize these roles and to use them to check their sentences and paragraph development in first drafts can be a useful way to promote coherence. Larson suggests three questions to ask about each sentence in a paragraph:

1. Is the role of each sentence in the context of the surrounding sentences evident to the reader?
2. Do the words that connect the sentence to surrounding sentences accurately characterize that role?
3. Is the role useful? That is, would the paragraph do its work as effectively without the sentence as it does with the sentence? (21)

When students learn to question the role of each sentence, the extraneous sentences gradually get pared down, and transitions appear more frequently.

These, then, are the problems that the theories discussed below can help to solve. Yet all of the paragraph theories and models presented in this chapter are necessarily limited; we have not yet reached the paradigmatic stage of paragraph theory. And so how can we be prescriptive when we know that professional writers create paragraphs that ignore these models?

We can because despite the limits of these models, they do give students a structure with which to create coherent paragraphs. The paragraphs students create may not be professional, they may not be stylistically brilliant, but they will be understandable, and they will be solid bases on which to build.

As the early paragraph theorist Helen Thomas said about the placement of topic sentences, "The artist can afford to diverge from this rule. The mechanic cannot" (28). Our task is to teach mechanics who may someday be artists. Once the limiting rules are mastered, they can be transcended, but only those who know the law can afford to live without it. If you are honest with your students about the limitations of the rules you set, you need never apologize for being prescriptive.

Traditional Paragraph Theory

The paragraph as we know it today, with its qualities of consecutiveness and loose order of propositions, did not begin to emerge until the late seventeenth century and did not attain full codification until the eighteenth century. If there is a single ruling concept of the nature and construction of the paragraph, it is the legacy of the nineteenth-century rhetorician Alexander Bain, whose systematic formulation became our traditional paragraph structure: a *topic sentence* that announces the main idea of the paragraph and is followed by subsidiary sentences that *develop* or *illustrate* that main idea. The treatment of the idea presented in the topic sentence is marked by unity, coherence, and development. *Unity* means that the material in the paragraph does not stray from the main idea; *coherence* means that each sentence in the paragraph is related to those around it and to the topic sentence; *development* means that the elements of the main idea are treated at sufficient length.

The organic paragraph form that descended from Bain is often criticized because it is not easily made generative. It works well, however, as a tool for testing and revising material written intuitively. You can ask your students to generate individual paragraphs according to traditional theory, but if you try to teach this theory as a generative form for writing essays—as many teachers for many years have done, with little success—you run the risk of hopelessly frustrating your students. You want your students to develop an informed intuition about the revision process, and the traditional paragraph is just one tool they can use to check their "natural" groupings of ideas against a concrete model.

The notion that one sentence in every paragraph should announce the topic of that paragraph was derived from the fourth law of Alexander Bain's "seven laws" for creating paragraphs (91-134). Since Bain, the "topic sentence" has remained controversial in composition theory. Although most compositionists agree that every paragraph should have a unifying theme or purpose, not all agree that it should be announced by a topic sentence. On the one hand, in his study of professional writers, Richard Braddock found that topic sentences are used far less than we have traditionally believed; his research calls into question the value of teaching topic sentences (301). On the other hand, Frank D'Angelo argues that despite Braddock's findings, the use of topic sentences improves the readability of a paragraph; therefore, all writers—and especially beginning writers—should use topic sentences ("Topic Sentence"). Your beginning writers may want to heed D'Angelo's advice.

Students will need to know that the topic sentence, the master sentence of a paragraph, has three characteristics: it isolates and specifies the topic or idea of the entire paragraph; it acts as a general heading for all the other sentences; and it usually incorporates, at least implicitly, a transition from the paragraph that precedes it or to the one that follows it.

Often the topic sentence is the most obvious starting place for checking a traditional paragraph for its "wholeness." Unfortunately, however, the terminology used in the literature of paragraph theory to describe this wholeness can be confusing. For example, researchers often use the same terms (*unity, coherence, development*) to describe entire pieces of discourse as well as paragraphs; and some textbooks and articles suggest that *coherence* and *cohesion* are separate features, whereas others take them to mean the same thing. Therefore, you may want to introduce these elements to your students as separate entities: *unity* as a semantic concept—the paragraph's single topic; *development* as the movement in the paragraph; *coherence* as a stylistic concept that encompasses various methods for connecting the sentences of a paragraph; and *cohesion* as the whole-essay counterpart of unity.

Using Traditional Paragraph Theory in the Classroom

After supplying your students with a sample essay, you may want to ask them to identify the topic sentence of a paragraph and to specify relationships between the identified topic sentence and all of the other sentences in the paragraph. Either the other sentences contribute to the main idea, making for paragraph unity, or they deviate from it. You may want to offer students a sample of a disunified paragraph as well, perhaps from a student's essay.

The most common methods of paragraph development are *deductive*, general to specific, and *inductive*, specific to general. Traditionally, deductive reasoning has been the basis for paragraph development: the writer posits a sound general principle (a major premise) and then applies that principle to specific cases. Inductive development, on the other hand, is the movement from specific cases to sound general principle.

Most of us live according to inductive generalizations: we are aware of the probability that we will avoid heavy traffic if we take a particular route to school each day, that going to bed at a certain hour will guarantee our waking on time in the morning, that we can stay in the hot sun only so long without getting burned, that we must eat and exercise a specific amount if we are to maintain our desired shape, that contact with certain foods, animals, or plants causes us to itch or sneeze. But inductive and deductive reasoning almost always work together, for many of our deductions stem from inductive reasoning: morning traffic is heavy; a late night makes for a late morning; sun burns the skin; too many calories make one fat; poison ivy causes an itchy rash.

The easiest way to explain paragraph coherence is to demonstrate that every sentence must relate somehow, directly or indirectly, to the sentences that surround it. If these relationships are not respected, the result is a choppy and irritating prose that seems to proceed in fits and starts. Problems with incoherence can often be solved by attending to the composing process and by multiple-draft revisions.

A large number of devices can render paragraphs coherent; the single most easily taught device for promoting coherence is the use of transitions and transitional markers. Of course, such words and phrases cannot by themselves create ordered relationships among sentences where there are none. Most FY students, though, grasp the implications of these terms and thus can use them as reminders of the necessary relationships their sentences must have. You might stress that transitions are used for establishing the following:

1. The relationship between the topic sentence of a paragraph and the topic of the preceding paragraph
2. The relationship between the topic sentence and the sentences that develop the topic sentence
3. The relationship among the various sentences that develop the topic sentence

You might also want to list the various transitional markers.

To link related ideas from sentence to sentence or from paragraph to paragraph: and, also, likewise, and so, in like manner, first, second, again, besides, then, too, moreover, furthermore

To show unrelated or opposing ideas in adjacent sentences or paragraphs: but, or else, otherwise, but then, still, yet, only, nevertheless, at the same time, on the other hand, conversely, despite the fact

To conclude or wrap up a section or essay: in short, in a word, in conclusion, to sum up, as a result, in other words

But transitional markers are only one of the devices that writers use to achieve coherence; others include repetition (of key words and important groups of words), parallel structure, and pronoun reference.

To introduce the use of transitional markers, repetition, parallelism, or pronoun reference, you might want to distribute copies of three or four well-structured paragraphs that rely heavily on one or more of these devices. If you remove the transitions, ask your students to supply words or phrases that make the paragraph more coherent and less choppy. Then ask them to compare, and explain why they chose, the transitions they chose. If you provide a full essay, ask them to identify the elements that make it coherent.

The most illuminating classroom activity, however, will occur when students review some of their own essays, checking to see whether they used devices to achieve coherence. You will want to emphasize the importance of every sentence in relation to the sentences around it. If your students grow accustomed to this sentence-by-sentence testing procedure, they can improve their paragraphs.

Despite its limitations, the essential design of Bain's organic paragraph has served to introduce generations of students to some control element against which they can measure their efforts. The traditional paragraph paradigm contains enough truth about how we control segments of discourse to give students a good deal of the guidance they need.

Christensen's Generative Rhetoric of the Paragraph

Christensen's theory of the paragraph grew directly out of his work with cumulative sentences. After the success of his theory of sentences as containing differing levels of generality, each including a base clause and free modifiers, Christensen strove to apply a similar technique to his analysis of the paragraph. The result was "A Generative Rhetoric of the Paragraph," an important reevaluation of paragraph form and structure.

In the Christensen model and in the traditional model, the paragraph is a system of related sentences organized in some way by a master sentence, which usually appears at the beginning of the paragraph. The difference between the models lies in the nature of the relationships among the sentences within the paragraph. The traditional paragraph model claims that all the sentences must be *logically,* or *semantically,* related to one another, while Christensen says that the sentences in a paragraph can also be related *formally,* or *structurally,* by the concept of levels of generality.

The topic sentence in a traditional paragraph is also called the subject sentence, or the thesis sentence. It can appear in different places within the paragraph, but in strict Bainian theory, it announces the subject of the paragraph no matter where it is placed. In Christensen's model, the topic sentence is always the first sentence of the paragraph. It does not necessarily announce the subject, and it is defined only as the most general sentence in the paragraph. Christensen's topic sentence is analogous to the base clause of a cumulative sentence; it is "the sentence whose assertion is supported or whose meaning is explicated or whose parts are detailed by the sentences added to it" ("Rhetoric of the Paragraph").

Christensen's system is based entirely on the semantic and syntactic relationships among sentences, relationships that exist due to different levels of generality or abstraction. A paragraph, according to Christensen, is an expanded cumulative sentence whose components are related, as are those of the sentence, by coordinate and subordinate relationships. In "A Generative Rhetoric of the Paragraph," Christensen reduces his findings to four points, similar to those describing cumulative sentences, that define the unit as he sees it.

1. *No paragraphs are possible without addition.* In expository writing one sentence cannot, under normal circumstances, be an acceptable paragraph.

2. *When a supporting sentence is added, we must see the direction of modification or movement.* Assuming the first sentence of the paragraph to fulfill the same function as the base clause of a cumulative sentence, we have to be able to see what direction the modification of it takes—whether the level of generality of a sentence is the same as or lower than that of the one before it.

3. *When sentences are added, they are usually at a lower level of generality.* This is not an absolute rule, but is usually the case; as we saw in the classical paragraph, sentences that develop a topic are usually more specific in their relation to the topic than the topic sentence.

4. *The more sentences added, the denser the texture of the paragraph.* The paragraphs we see from students too often lack density—those one-sentence paragraphs are not as rare as they should be—and one of the greatest strengths of the Christensen method of paragraphing is to get students to see this thinness when they revise their work. (145)

The topic sentence For Christensen, "the topic sentence is nearly always the first sentence of the sequence" of structurally related sentences that make up the paragraph. It is the sentence from which the other sentences in the paragraph hang, so to speak, the sentence whose level of generality cannot be exceeded without starting a new paragraph. Unlike the thesis statement of traditional paragraph theory, Christensen's topic sentence often does not state the thesis of the paragraph clearly. It may only suggest it, or it may be nothing more than a "signal sentence" that moves up to a more general level of statement than that of the previous sentence, thus showing that a new chunk of discourse is about to begin. It may be a statement, a fragment, or a question. The only important thing about it is that the reader gets the signal "new level of generality—we're about to start something new."

The structure of the paragraph after the topic sentence, according to Christensen, can take a number of forms, all of which are marked by the relationships established by each sentence to the topic sentence and to the other sentences. Like the relationships between clauses that Christensen identified in his cumulative sentences, the relationships he sees between sentences in a paragraph are either coordinate or subordinate.

Christensen identifies two sorts of simple sentence sequences, *simple coordinate* and *simple subordinate,* and the most common sequence, the *mixed* sequence, in which both coordination and subordination are used. Coordinate sentences are equal in syntactic or semantic generality, and subordinate sentences are lower in generality—they are more specific or more concrete—than the sentences that precede them. Coordinate sentences emphasize and enumerate, while subordinate sentences clarify, exemplify, and comment.

The simple coordinate sequence The paragraph with a simple coordinate sequence has only two levels: that of the topic sentence and that of the other sentences, which are coordinate in terms of generality. It is the rarest and least used of all the sequence types, for it usually produces a repetitive effect more common in speeches than in expository writing. In the example below, taken from R. Emmett Tyrell's *Public Nuisances,* the numbers indicate levels of generality, with the lowest number equaling the highest levels of generality.

> [1] I prescribe ridicule. [2] It is an equitable response to the likes of Ralph Nader or Betty Friedan. [2] It is a soothing emollient for our peculiarly troubled national spirit. [2] Ridicule does not elevate nonsense to any higher level than that at which it is emitted. [2] It is entertaining and far more edifying to the public discourse than the facile dissimulations now rampant there. [2] Ridicule is the compliment lively intelligence pays jackassery. [2] It is a national treasure certified by Mark Twain, beloved by millions, and eschewed only at great peril.

The simple subordinate sequence   The simple subordinate sequence introduces multiple layers—in theory, an infinite number—of semantic or syntactic generality. The notable feature of the simple subordinate sequence is that it progresses from element to element and does not return to a higher level of generality. Once again, this sequence is not often found in nature, since it tends to introduce a large number of disparate ideas in one paragraph and does not stop to discourse on any one level. It is often found in the introductory sections of expository pieces, outlining the main ideas that will be covered, as in the following example:

> [1] *Why Johnny Can't Read.* [2] The title is instantly familiar to thousands, perhaps millions, of people who have never read Rudolf Flesch's 1955 book about reading pedagogy. [3] Most of those people don't know that the book is an extended argument for the "phonics first" method of reading instruction and against the "look and say" method. [4] Instead, the title has become a rallying cry for those who are interested in, or worried about, the supposed decline in the ability to read during the past two or three decades: a title like "What If Johnny Still Can't Read?" (from a Canadian business journal) illustrates the genre. [5] And it seems that as more people become worried about a "crisis" in literacy, the solutions proposed become simpler and simpler: witness the "back to basics" movement, which assumes, quite incorrectly, that the "basics" required and expected today are the same as those taught a generation or two ago. [6] This collection of essays is partially a response to the current interest in the question of literacy and illiteracy in the Western World; its aim is to provide the requisite background for informed and intelligent discussion of the many issues surrounding the question of literacy today. (Kintgen, Kroll, and Rose xi)

The mixed sequence   Simple paragraph sequences are not common; the simple coordinate sequence is particularly rare, and it is also rare to see a good paragraph move from element to element without returning to a previous level. Most paragraphs use some form that mixes coordination and subordination, that rises and falls in its levels. Look at the following mixed-sequence paragraph from an essay on Albert Goldman, John Lennon's controversial biographer:

[1] For years, Goldman felt like Schizoid Man, scissored down the middle between the academic drudge who taught freshman English and the cutup who engaged in comedy jam sessions with jazz-crazy characters every Saturday night at his Brooklyn pad. [2] For a time he considered becoming a professional comic. [3] "But I was just scared. [3] Many times in my life I've been defeated by my own fear. [3] I feel that's really been one of my single greatest problems. [3] What's held me back is diffidence, fear, self-doubt. [4] I didn't do it." [2] Instead he gravitated to criticism, where he found that words on the page are harder to budge than words in the air. [3] Yet he became adept. [3] He covered jazz and classical music for *The New Leader*, rock for *Life*. [3] A compilation of his riffing on rock, comedy, and jazz was briefly preserved in *Freakshow* (1971). [1] One of the best collections of pop criticism ever published, *Freakshow* showcases Goldman as that rare critic who can communicate a dizzy, complex thrill. [2] He opens up the full sensorium for Jimi Hendrix: [3] "I went home and put *The Jimi Hendrix Experience* on the turntable. [4] Tough, abrasive, brutally iterative, the uptake suggested the ironshod tracks of a bulldozer straining against a mountain of dirt. [4] Hendrix's program for the country blues was rural electrification. [4] The end products were futurist symphonies of industrial noise." [1] Unlike most books from rock's chesty youth, *Freakshow* hasn't faded into a dated piece of psychedelia. [2] Out of print, it may even be more apt today. [3] A doomed moonlit glamour still coats the memories of Hendrix, Joplin, Jim Morrison . . . the beautiful dead. (Wolcott 36)

Using Christensen's Generative Rhetoric of the Paragraph in the Classroom

Christensen's paragraph method is essentially descriptive, not generative. It is best used—as are all other theories of the paragraph—as an after-the-fact device for editing and testing paragraphs that have been generated intuitively.

If you have previously taught Christensen's sentence theory, that is a natural place to start; the parallels are obvious. If you have not, begin by handing out examples of cumulative sentences charted according to Christensen's levels of generality and paragraph structures using the same structures of coordination or subordination. Stick with relatively simple sequences at this point—nothing long or structurally hard to follow.

Start with a discussion of the concept of the topic sentence. You usually needn't stress the topic sentence; simply point out that it is always first in the sequence and that it is usually a fairly general statement. This should be sufficient for the time being because you have to establish its meaning contextually through an explanation of coordination and subordination before the ideal can come to life.

The best way to explain coordination in sentences is to stress the fact that coordinate sentences "put like things in like ways" and that all coordinate sentences in a paragraph have the same relationship to the topic sentence (Christensen, *Notes* 164). Your examples should include simple coordinate sequences that utilize parallel constructions, since parallelism is nearly always a sign of coordination; but make certain that you also demonstrate how coordination can work without parallelism. Point up the fact that coordinate sentences comment not on one another but on previous material.

Subordination is best explained in terms of clarification or exemplification. A subordinate sentence is usually more specific than the one that precedes it. In a subordinate sequence, as Christensen points out, each sentence is a comment on the sentence above it, and a mixed subordinate sequence is created by "any doubling or multiplying of examples, causes, reasons, or the like." You need not place too much stress on differentiating mixed coordinate sequences from mixed subordinate sequences, though; even Christensen admits that "it is of no great moment to settle whether a mixed sequence is coordinate or subordinate; these are just convenient terms to designate recurring configurations" (*Notes* 153).

After you have explained these terms, get right down to the analysis of paragraphs. You can choose paragraphs at random from a reader, but the best initial technique is to distribute copies of paragraphs that you have chosen—paragraphs that are not too difficult and that illustrate different sequences. Begin with a simple short sequence, and work up to more complex mixed sequences. Illustrate an analysis at the blackboard, and ask the class to help with it. Your instructions should be as simple as possible at this stage. Try the following approach:

1. Assume that the first sentence in the paragraph is the topic sentence. It may not state the thesis or the subject of the paragraph; just look at it as the signal sentence that announces a new level of generality and begins the paragraph. Write it at the left margin of a piece of paper, and number it *1*.

2. Now examine the second sentence. Does it continue the idea or structure of the first sentence, or does it comment on the idea or structure of the first sentence? If it continues the idea or structure of the first sentence, it is parallel or coordinate with the first sentence. In that case, write it directly beneath the first sentence, and label it *1*. If, as is usually the case, it comments on, refers to, or clarifies the idea or structure of the first sentence, it is subordinate to the first sentence. In that case, number it *2*, and indent it one-half inch when you write it down under the first sentence.

3. Look at the third sentence. Does it continue or comment on the first sentence? If it does not continue the idea or structure of the first sentence, compare it carefully with the second sentence. If it comments on the structure or ideas of the first sentence, ask yourself how it relates to the second sentence. If it continues the structure or ideas of the second sentence, it is coordinate with the second sentence. In that case, number it *2*, and write it directly under the second sentence. If, however, it comments on, refers to, or clarifies the structure or ideas of the second sentence, it is subordinate to that sentence, so indent it a full inch from the left-hand margin when you write it down, and number it *3*.

4. Continue this sort of analysis with the rest of the sentences in the paragraph. The essential test will always be the question of whether the next sentence continues or comments on the sentences above it. Remember that when you continue or comment on a level that is two or three sentences higher, you must return to that level. Don't be afraid of getting to level 5 and then returning to level 2. Paragraphs constantly rise and fall in levels of generality. Just make certain that you keep checking each new sentence against all the sentences that precede it.

This is a point in the course when oral discussion can help clarify students' understanding. There will be quite a few disagreements on the numbering of sentences at first, and if you can get students arguing with one another in favor of the levels they have assigned to sentences, the whole concept will become clear to them faster than if you lecture on it. Some sentences may be genuinely impossible to assign levels to with complete certainty. But as you go from simple to complex sequences, spend as much time on each one as your students need in order to be able to follow the discussion. They should gradually get over their initial distrust of the novel concept of levels of generality and feel more comfortable with the theory.

When they do, you can turn them loose with the reader, popular magazines, handouts—anything that contains more difficult sequences. Let them apply their analyses to exposition in the rough. Occasionally you will strike a paragraph with no topic sentence or one with introductory or transitional material in sentences at the beginning that are not part of the sequence, and then you will need to explain that the Christensen paragraph is a theoretical model, not an absolute rule.

Finally, your students should be ready to generate some paragraphs using the model. At first, suggest the paragraph sequences that they should follow by providing a list of directions.[9] Start with a coordinate sequence. You may want to suggest a topic sentence that contains a plural term, such as *reasons, causes, uses,* and so forth.

Write a topic sentence.

Add a sentence that supports it.

Add a second supporting sentence.

Add a third supporting sentence.

Conclude with a final supporting sentence.

As a sort of diagram, you can put this sequence on the board.

1. _____
  2. _____
  2. _____
  2. _____
  2. _____

[9] The paragraph-sequence exercises here are adapted from D'Angelo (243).

Then you can work up to a subordinate sequence.

Write a topic sentence.

Qualify that sentence. (Write a sentence that comments on the first sentence.)

Add a specific detail.

Add another detail.

Qualify that detail.

On the board, the subordinate sequence looks like this.

1. _____
  2. _____
    3. _____
    3. _____
      4. _____

Last, try mixed sequences. These are most difficult because they require planning and a ranking of concepts. Give your students a topic sentence to work with the first time through.

Write a topic sentence that has two components.

Qualify that sentence.

Add a specific detail.

Add another detail.

Qualify the topic sentence again.

Add a detail to this qualification.

Add another detail.

Qualify this detail.

This paragraph diagram looks like this.

1. _____
  2. _____
    3. _____
    3. _____
  2. _____
    3. _____
    3. _____
      4. _____

If your students have worked satisfactorily thus far, let them create their own sequences and write their own paragraphs. A good exercise for checking understanding is to ask each student to write out her paragraph in normal form and give it to a classmate to analyze. If the analysis differs from the original plan, the students can confer and try to find out where their perceptions diverge.

Using Christensen's Model to Revise Paragraphs

After you have reached the point at which your students are comfortable analyzing and generating discrete paragraphs—and reaching this point may take up to two weeks—you can concentrate on using Christensen's method in more realistic writing situations: to revise and edit intuitively generated paragraphs. The analyses allowed by the Christensen method are extremely useful for showing students how the sentences in their paragraphs work or do not work together. Although the progression from analysis to generation to revision of paragraphs may not be necessary for students to understand how to use Christensen's model of paragraphing as an editing technique, it does guarantee their familiarity with the analytic process that makes revision easier.

The application of Christensen's model to already generated paragraphs is not difficult. The single most important step is the actual dissection of each paragraph into coordinate or subordinate sequences. Direct your students to apply these three types of questions to the paragraphs they have written intuitively.

1. Is this sentence coordinate with or subordinate to the ones above it?
2. If it is coordinate,
   a. How does it relate to the topic sentence?
   b. How does it relate to the other sentences on its level?
   c. Does this concept need further explanation with a subordinate sequence?
3. If it is subordinate,
   a. How does it relate to the level above it?
   b. How does it relate to the other sentences on its level?
   c. Is it complete as it stands, or could it use further explanation in a coordinate or subordinate sentence?

Using these questions, students can pick through their intuitively generated paragraphs, weeding out sentences that are not related to the topic sentence or to coordinate sentences and deciding whether any given sequence is fully developed.

Tagmemic Paragraphing

Like tagmemic invention, tagmemic paragraph theory evolved from the linguistic work of Kenneth Pike, whose theories of tagmemic linguistics became the raw material for his theories of composition. Linguistics has always been primarily a descriptive discipline, devoted to the analysis of existing phenomena. This descriptive nature characterizes tagmemic paragraph theory as well; it was originally developed as a descriptive tool for use on "paragraph-level tagmemes." As a result, despite the fact that it can be used generatively for certain kinds of practice exercises, tagmemic paragraphing, like the other paragraph theories we have discussed, is primarily useful as an editing tool.

Tagmeme, as you will recall from Chapter 7, is the term that Pike invented to describe the central component of his linguistic theory. Simply put, a tagmeme equals a functional slot to be filled plus a class of possible fillers of that slot. Tagmemic paragraph analysis posits an expository paragraph as a series of slots, all of which can be filled by any one of a whole class of fillers. The position of each sentence in the paragraph indicates a slot, and tagmemic paragraph theory specifies both the slots that make up the paragraph and the kinds of sentences that make up the classes of fillers.

Alton L. Becker, who has done most of the work with tagmemic paragraph analysis, says that tagmemic analysis allows an examination of the relationship of the parts of a paragraph as well as a mere description of the parts themselves, which is the domain of traditional paragraph analysis. He cautions, though, that tagmemic analysis as it has evolved cannot describe all of the content-based aspects of paragraph structure; in addition, Becker has concentrated on expository paragraphs, excluding rigorous examination of other modes of discourse. With these caveats in mind, let us look at what tagmemic paragraph structures are.

Becker has found three major patterns in expository paragraphs, two of which are closely related.

T	Topic
R	Restriction
I	Illustration
P	Problem
S	Solution
Q	Question
A	Answer

According to Becker, students can derive these patterns inductively if they are given examples of expository paragraphs and asked to divide them into sections that seem significant. Becker found "a striking percentage of agreement" about the important divisions, "especially after students have partitioned enough paragraphs to recognize recurring patterns" (238). The three patterns, in different configurations, are found in most expository paragraphs in English.

The most common expository pattern that Becker's students found was composed of some version of TRI—*topic, restriction,* and *illustration.* None of these slots is absolutely limited to one sentence, but T is generally filled by a single sentence, and R is often also a single sentence. In its simplest form, TRI consists of a sentence that states the topic generally (T), a sentence that qualifies or restricts that general topic, narrowing its meaning (R), and a sentence or a group of sentences in which the restricted topic is illustrated or exemplified on a more specific level (I). The following paragraph is TRI:

[T] Progress toward the kind of future depicted in the science-fiction movies of twenty and thirty years ago has been getting difficult to detect lately, and it has begun to dawn on us that the year 2000 may not deliver on all the promises that used to be made for it: world government, the colonization of outer space, backpack jet transport for the masses, robots for every imaginable form of menial labor, and the rest. [R] Certain events of the summer of 1988, however, have been running eerily close to the plot of one science-fiction movie—a movie that came out in 1961. [I] In "The Day the Earth Caught Fire," the world is visited within the space of a few weeks by floods, earthquakes, dense fog stretching from England to India (it's an English movie), and a record-setting heat wave. [I] The experts at first refuse to acknowledge a common explanation for these quirks of nature, but then word gets out that, by chance, the Soviet Union and the United States chose the same moment for high-megaton nuclear tests, and the effect was to knock the earth out of its orbit and send it hurtling toward the sun. [I] The human species is given a life expectancy of four months. (Lardner 4)

As it is in Christensen's paragraph theory, the concept of levels of generality is important in tagmemic paragraphing since a shift from one slot to another in the TRI pattern is also usually a shift in levels of generality.

The second major pattern found by Becker is PS, *problem-solution,* of which QA, *question-answer,* is a subset. Unlike the TRI pattern, PS has only two slots: P, which states the problem to be solved or the effect to be explained, and S, which provides the solution or the causes of the effect. If the S slot is lengthy or complex, it is likely to be filled by a TRI pattern of some sort; the TRI structure is generally found in some form in every paragraph of any length. Here is an example of a paragraph that uses all of the slots.

[Q] It is not difficult to envision a network of private, unsubsidized and unregulated railroads and airplanes, but could there be a system of private roads? [Q] Could such a system be at all feasible? [A] One answer is that private roads have worked admirably in the past. [P] In England before the eighteenth century, for example, roads, invariably owned and operated by local governments, were badly constructed and even more badly maintained. [P] These public roads could never have supported the mighty Industrial Revolution that England experienced in the eighteenth century, the "revolution" that ushered in the modern age. [S][T] The vital task of improving the almost impassable English roads was performed by private turnpike companies, which, beginning in 1706, organized and established the great network of roads which made England the envy of the world. [R] The owners of these private turnpike companies were generally landowners, merchants, and industrialists in the area being served by the road, and they recouped their costs by charging tolls at selected tollgates. [I] Often the collection of tolls was leased out for a year or more to individuals selected by competitive bid at auction. [I] It was these private roads that developed an internal market in England, and that greatly lowered the costs of transport of coal and other bulky material. (Rothbard, *For a New Liberty*)

These, then, are the two major patterns into which expository paragraphs fall. The TRI pattern can also appear in inverted form, as IRT—an inductive form that proceeds from specific to general. (Becker makes the interesting observation that students who were asked to evaluate paragraphs out of context preferred IRT paragraphs to TRI paragraphs by a large margin. Perhaps this preference can be attributed to the desire for instant gratification—the examples of narration are dumped in readers' laps without their having to work through abstractions first.)

Using Tagmemic Paragraphing in the Classroom

Of the types of paragraphing discussed in this chapter, tagmemic paragraphing may be the easiest to teach because of the limited number of concepts it employs and because of the admittedly exploratory and unfinished nature of the theory itself. The result of the tentative nature of this theory is that it is both easy to absorb and incomplete.

As with any model, the first step is to familiarize your students with the terms of tagmemic paragraphing and their meaning. Make up handouts with at least three examples of each of the common paragraph patterns—different versions of simple TRI and PS/QA patterns. Go over the handouts, and analyze each example orally, explaining how each slot works and how all the slots work together. It is probably best to stay away from the vocabulary of technical tagmemic terms at this stage—you don't want your students more worried about terms than about substance. In particular, note the relationship between the T and R slots and the fact that the I slots follow not the T but the topic idea as it is restricted and defined in the R slot.

Analyzing the PS/QA patterns is easy, but make certain that your students understand that PS and QA are seldom found without some form of TRI embedded within them. Choose your examples of PS/QA carefully, making certain that they include both simple and embedded patterns.

The next examples you hand out should be carefully chosen paragraphs that are not marked or divided, and the exercise will be a controlled duplication of Becker's original experiment: your students should divide these paragraphs into TRIPSQA slots with a fair amount of consistency. Start with a simple TRI or PS pattern, then work into an embedded PSTRI pattern, and finish up with a $PST_1RI_1I_2S_2T_2RI$ or something equally complicated. If your students have trouble with this exercise, keep doing similar ones until they grasp the method; it is the key to all that comes after it.

Once students recognize the slots in "tame" paragraphs, set them loose on other material. You will have to screen the selections they choose, however, because some narrative and argumentative passages may be too difficult for them to dissect. Try assigning a page rather than a specific paragraph, and ask the students to work in groups. After the paragraphs have been analyzed, ask for a volunteer from each group to explain her group's analysis. This is a good point at which to initiate a discussion in which students can argue with one another about which slots sentences should fill. ("Look, it restricts that topic!" "No, it illustrates it. Look at the main idea." "It's a solution but also an illustration.") Argument about formal properties is not always easy to elicit, but this method allows categorizations simple and real enough to be involving.

At this stage, your students should be able to manipulate the patterns fairly well and are therefore ready to apply them to their own writing.

Using tagmemic paragraph generation in the classroom Asking for the generation of formally ordered paragraphs is not difficult. First, have students choose a subject or an idea on a general topic—apartment or dorm living, college requirements, nuclear energy; then ask them to work in groups and brainstorm for a minute or so. They should not need much time; explain that they have to generate only a simple proposition concerning the topic. The proposition generated will be the T slot of their paragraph.

After the T slot has been written, ask each group to write an R slot, reminding the class that the R slot can be one or two sentences and that it must narrow or define the general proposition advanced in T.

Finally, ask for sentences that illustrate or develop the restricted topic. Start with paragraphs with only one or two I slots and gradually work up to more I-slot sentences.

From this simple beginning, you can work up to generating a simple PS/QA paragraph, an embedded PSTRI pattern, and eventually more complex patterns. Remember, though, that encouraging complexity for its own sake can discourage students, especially those who fail to grasp the ideas it embodies. Our thought processes do obey formal rules; but if form is given too much precedence over content, it becomes sterile.

Using tagmemic paragraph revision in the classroom The paragraph methods we have discussed here are useful for editing the body of an essay but not the introductory or concluding paragraphs. Make clear, then, that the patterns tagmemic paragraphing describes are antithetical to the usual patterns of opening and closing paragraphs. Each body paragraph in the essays that your students write, on the other hand, should have some identifiable agglomeration of TRIPSQA that can be analyzed sentence by sentence and labeled accordingly.

Tagmemic paragraph revision assumes that students are familiar with the tagmemic terms. To introduce the revision process and acclimate students to it, assign a three-paragraph essay to be written in class. Ask students to choose a subject, and advise them not to worry about topics or restrictions as they write; they should merely draft an essay of about three paragraphs. The writing should take about half the class period. At the end of the period, collect the essays. You don't have to read them; just hang on to them. This forced disengagement from their drafts will give the students some objectivity, distancing them from the essays to a small degree. (This "cold storage" idea is used by many professional authors, over longer periods of time, of course.)

Next time the class meets—ideally the interval should include a weekend—return the essays. Ask students to number each sentence in their essay and then to analyze each paragraph using the TRIPSQA method. Ask them to mark on a separate sheet of paper the number of each sentence and the slot it fills. If they hit a sentence that seems to fill no slot, to be extraneous, or to be a part of another paragraph, it should be marked X. This process should take about fifteen minutes.

When all the students have completed their analyses, ask them to exchange essays and then to do the same tagmemic analysis on each paragraph in their classmate's essay. After they complete this task, the students should return the essays to their authors and compare the analysis of their own paper with that done by the classmate. Discussion between the two students who worked on each essay can take up the rest of the class period; there is usually a fair amount of disagreement and need for clarification.

The next step is to ask students to analyze the paragraphs in an older essay—the first one they wrote for this class is the best and most illuminating to use. When they have analyzed it for paragraph structure, you might offer them a chance to rewrite it for a better grade—if you feel up to reading it again; if not, merely ask them to mark each sentence. For students who choose to revise their essays, what you should insist on is not any specific pattern of slots but a coherent approach to whatever pattern is used. Warn against the TI pattern, for instance, which is common in primitive paragraphs. Insist that PS/QA paragraphs embed a TRI to increase their density. Remind students that the I slots must always refer to the T or R slots. And suggest that they eliminate the X sentences or rewrite them.

After you have taken the class through all these steps, your students are ready to perform tagmemic analyses on their rough drafts prior to printing them. This is the ultimate and the only really important use to be made of the TRIPSQA method. Whether you make this procedure a requirement for every subsequent essay is up to you. If you want to make sure it is being done, you can ask students to hand in the tagmemic analyses of their rough drafts along with their typescripts. (This is also a handy way to make certain that rough drafts are being produced.)

Once you have led your students through these steps, you should begin to see a real improvement in the structure of their paragraphs. Short, thin paragraphs should gradually fill out, incoherent paragraphs should tighten up, and disunified paragraphs should lose their dead limbs as what Becker calls "the organic nature of the paragraph" becomes clearer to your students.

Should you be uncomfortable with the prescriptive nature of any of the approaches in this chapter, you are not alone. We all may worry that in condensing writing to discrete, mechanical formulas, we are taking away more than we are giving. But be assured that with continued reading and practice in writing, your students should eventually transcend rigid, formal rules. In the final analysis, a grasp of the rules seldom holds anyone down and, when understood correctly, can help keep one up.

WORKS CITED

Aristotle. *Rhetoric.* Trans. Rhys Roberts. New York: Modern Library, 1954.
Bain, Alexander. *English Composition and Rhetoric.* 1866. London: Longman, 1877.

Bateman, Donald, and Frank J. Zidonis. *The Effect of a Study of Transformational Grammar on the Writing of 9th and 10th Graders.* Research Report 6. Urbana, IL: NCTE, 1966.

Becker, Alton L. "A Tagmemic Approach to Paragraph Analysis." *CCC* 16 (1965): 237–42.

Braddock, Richard. "The Frequency and Placement of Topic Sentences in Expository Prose." *Research in the Teaching of English* 8 (1972): 287–302.

Campbell, George. *The Philosophy of Rhetoric.* 1776. Boston: Ewer, 1823.

Chomsky, Noam. *Reflections on Language.* New York: Pantheon, 1975.

———. *Syntactic Structures.* The Hague: Mouton, 1957.

Christensen, Francis. "The Course in Advanced Composition for Teachers." *CCC* 24 (1973): 163–70.

———. "A Generative Rhetoric of the Paragraph." *CCC* 16 (1965): 146–56.

———. "A Generative Rhetoric of the Sentence." *CCC* 14 (1963): 155–61.

———. *Notes toward a New Rhetoric: Six Essays for Teachers.* New York: Harper, 1967.

Christensen, Francis, and Bonniejean Christensen. *A New Rhetoric.* New York: Harper, 1975.

Combs, Warren E. "Sentence-Combining Practice: Do Gains in Judgments of Writing 'Quality' Persist?" *Journal of Educational Research* 10 (1977).

Daiker, Donald, Andrew Kerek, and Max Morenberg. "Sentence-Combining and Syntactic Maturity in Freshman English." *CCC* 29 (1978): 36–41.

———. *The Writer's Options: College Sentence-Combining.* New York: Harper, 1979.

Daiker, Donald, Andrew Kerek, and Max Morenberg, eds. *Sentence-Combining: A Rhetorical Perspective.* Carbondale: Southern Illinois UP, 1985.

———. *Sentence-Combining and the Teaching of Writing.* Conway, AK: L&S, 1979.

D'Angelo, Frank. *Process and Thought in Composition.* Cambridge, MA: Winthrop, 1977.

———. "The Topic Sentence Revisited." *CE* 37 (1986): 431–41.

Faigley, Lester. "Problems in Analyzing Maturity in College and Adult Writing." *Sentence-Combining and the Teaching of Writing.* Ed. Donald Daiker, Andrew Kerek, and Max Morenberg. 94–100.

Genung, John F. *The Practical Elements of Rhetoric.* Boston: Ginn, 1886.

Halliday, M. A. K., and Ruquaiya Hasan. *Cohesion in English.* London: Longman, 1976.

Hunt, Kellog g W. "Anybody Can Teach English." *Sentence-Combining and the Teaching of Writing.* Ed. Donald Daiker, Andrew Kerek, and Max Morenberg. 149–56.

———. *Grammatical Structures Written at Three Grade Levels.* Urbana, IL: NCTE, 1965.

———. "A Synopsis of Clause-to-Sentence Length Factors." *Rhetoric and Composition: A Sourcebook for Teachers.* Ed. Richard L. Graves. Rochelle Park, NJ: Hayden, 1976.

Kane, Thomas S. "The Shape and Ring of Sentences: A Neglected Aspect of Composition." *CCC* 28 (1977): 38–42.

Kerek, Andrew, Donald A. Daiker, and Max Morenberg. "The Effects of Intensive Sentence-Combining on the Writing Ability of College Freshmen." *The Territory of Language.* Ed. Donald McQuade. Carbondale: Southern Illinois UP, 1986.

———. "Sentence-Combining and College Composition." *Perceptual and Motor Skills* 51 (1980): 1059–1157.

Kintgen, Eugene, Barry M. Kroll, and Michael Rose. *Perspectives on Literacy.* Carbondale: Southern Illinois UP, 1988.

Koen, Frank, Alton L. Becker, and Richard Young. "The Psychological Reality of the Paragraph." *Journal of Verbal Learning and Verbal Behavior* 8 (1969): 49–53.

Lardner, James. "Notes and Comments." *New Yorker* 29 Aug. 1988.

Larson, Richard. "Sentences in Action: A Technique for Analyzing Paragraphs." *CCC* 8 (1967): 16–22.

Lewis, Edwin H. *A History of the English Paragraph.* Chicago: U of Chicago, 1894.

Markels, Robin B. *A New Perspective on Cohesion in Expository Paragraphs.* Carbondale: Southern Illinois UP, 1984.

Mellon, John. "Issues in the Theory and Practice of Sentence-Combining: A Twenty-Year Perspective." *Sentence-Combining and the Teaching of Writing.* Ed. Donald Daiker, Andrew Kerek, and Max Morenberg. 1–38.

——. *Transformational Sentence-Combining: A Method for Enhancing the Development of Syntactic Fluency in English Composition.* Urbana, IL: NCTE, 1969.

Memering, Dean, and Frank O'Hare. *The Writer's Work.* Englewood Cliffs, NJ: Prentice, 1980.

Miller, B. D., and J. W. Ney. "The Effect of Systematic Oral Exercises on the Writing of Fourth-Grade Students." *Research in the Training of English* 1 (1968): 44–61.

Minto, William. *A Manual of English Prose Literature.* Boston: Ginn, 1892.

Morenberg, Max, Donald A. Daiker, and Andrew Kerek. "Sentence-Combining at the College Level: An Experimental Study." *Research in the Teaching of English* 12 (1978): 245–56.

Ney, James. "The Hazards of the Course: Sentence-Combining in Freshman English." *English Record* 27 (1976): 70–77.

O'Hare, Frank. *Sentence-Combining: Improving Student Writing without Formal Grammar Instruction.* Urbana, IL: NCTE 1973.

——. *Sentencecraft: A Course in Sentence-Combining.* Lexington, MA: Ginn, 1985.

Pike, Kenneth L. "A Linguistic Contribution to Composition." *CCC* 15 (1965): 237–42.

Pitkin, Willis L., Jr. "Discourse Blocs." *CCC* 20 (1966): 138–48.

Rodgers, Paul C., Jr. "Alexander Bain and the Rise of the 'Organic Paragraph.' " *Quarterly Journal of Speech* 51 (1965): 399–408.

——. "A Discourse-Centered Rhetoric of the Paragraph." *CCC* 17 (1966): 2–11.

Strong, William. *Sentence-Combining: A Composing Book.* New York: Random, 1973.

——. *Sentence-Combining and Paragraph Building.* New York: Random, 1981.

Thomas, Helen. *A Study of the Paragraph.* New York: American, 1912.

Whately, Richard. *Elements of Rhetoric.* 1828 London: Fellowes, 1841.

Witte, Stephen P., and Lester Faigley. "Coherence, Cohesion, and Writing Quality." *CCC* 32 (1981): 189–204.

Wolcott, James. "The Lives of Albert Goldman." *Vanity Fair* Oct. 1988: 36.

INVITATION TO FURTHER STUDY

If theory is tested when we put it into practice, the reverse holds true as well. All classroom practices need to be reexamined continually in the light of contemporary scholarly discussions. Beginning teachers are often interested in finding out why certain theories translate well into practice whereas others, seemingly worthwhile and sensible, refuse such adaptation. And after a year in the classroom, though they recognize certain successes, teachers cannot explain them in terms of their theoretical base. Fortunately for those interested in the theory and practice of composition, scholarly discussions are not hard to find.

In particular, professional organizations—such as the Conference on College Composition and Communication (CCCC), the Modern Language Association (MLA), the Rhetoric Society of America (RSA), the International Society for the History of Rhetoric (ISHR), the National Council of Teachers of English (NCTE), Teachers of English to Speakers of Other Languages (TESOL), Writing Program Administrators (WPA), and state and local organizations—offer a wide arena for activity and stimulation. Many teachers of writing feel that attendance at one of these national or state meetings every year provides the excitement of learning and sharing that sustains them through a hard year of work.

The NCTE is the most broad based of these organizations, for its membership comprises teachers of language arts, literature, and writing from prekindergarten through college. For college-level writing teachers, perhaps the most stimulating and useful of professional meetings is the CCCC, held annually in March. Over a four-day period, the CCCC offers over 250 sessions that balance pedagogy, theory, and research. And like most other organizations, it offers graduate students special membership and conference rates.

Some of these organizations have their own journals—*College Composition and Communication (CCC), College English (CE), English Journal (EJ), Teaching English in the Two-Year College (TETYC), TESOL Journal, Writing Program Administration (WPA), Research in the Teaching of English (RTE), Rhetoric Society Quarterly (RSQ), Rhetorica*—subscriptions to which can be included in the price of membership. *College English* is the most widely read journal of postsecondary pedagogy in English, and *CCC* remains the showcase for contemporary lines of research, theoretical debates, and reexamination of composition theory and praxis. In the last two decades, however, a number of new journals devoted to scholarship in rhetoric and composition have appeared: *Rhetoric Review (RR), The Writing Instructor (TWI), Dialogue,* and *Written Communication.* Taken together, these journals provide ample opportunity for publication in the field as well as a means of keeping up with the latest issues and concerns. New voices are particularly welcome at *TWI*, *Journal of Advanced Composition* (*JAC*), *Pre/ Text*, *Composition Studies*, *Journal of Teaching Writing* (*JTW*), *Journal of Basic Writing* (*JBW*), *Computers and Composition* (*C&C*), *Focuses*, and *Writing on the Edge*. *TWI*, published by the rhetoric and composition graduate students at the University of Southern California, is especially interested in featuring the work of other graduate students.

NCTE also sponsors (and the University of Southern Illinois Press publishes) expressly for CCCC a series of moderately priced monographs, "Studies in Writing and Rhetoric," the latest work by the best researchers in our field. The University of Pittsburgh Press, Southern Methodist University Press, and Southern Illinois University Press are all involved in producing respected series of books on composition issues. And in response to a call for collaboration between colleges and secondary schools, the State University of New York Press (Albany) has launched *Essays on the Teaching of English in the Secondary School*, edited by Gail Hawisher and Anna Soter. What you will soon realize in entering these conversations is the comfortable give-and-take between each organization and its publications—and between authors and subscribers.

What are the issues that most concern theorists and practitioners today? Of the many we might cite, three seem particularly crucial. The first, a difficult question that runs across all levels of education, is that of evaluation. Whom are we testing, and for whose purposes? While we as a nation seem completely devoted to assessing and testing, the reasons for doing so are far from clear. Even more troubling is the fact that our theory of testing (like most of the tests themselves) rests on a questionable epistemology, one that views knowledge as quantitative, externalizable, and statistically verifiable. Such a view has been under attack for most of the century in almost every field, but it still underlies our entire testing effort. Because tests are so important to our students' lives, we must take the lead in developing a more contemporary and complex theory of testing and then apply that theory in our testing practices.

Most pressing for the classroom teacher of composition is the question of how best to measure the success of students' writing. Gone are the days when a C+ at the top of a student's paper would speak for itself; today most teachers want to help, not merely evaluate, their students. Yet we find ourselves sensitive to and critical of the less-than-ideal aspects—shortcomings in content, organization, mechanics—of our students' papers. We are all English majors, educated in reading the most difficult, the most tortuous, the vaguest of prose, who feel satisfied and smug after we have wrung the meaning from an especially runic passage of *Ulysses* or a soliloquy in *Hamlet* or a creative spelling in a medieval manuscript. Why is it, then, that we are miffed if we stumble over a misuse of correlative conjunctions in any of our students' papers?

Several composition theorists are working toward tentative answers to questions of responding to students' papers. In "Students' Rights to Their Own Texts: A Model for Teacher Response," Lillian Brannon and C. H. Knoblauch argue that although we are willing to give experienced writers authority over their texts, we are unwilling to give student writers the same courtesy:

> In classroom writing situations, the reader assumes primary control of the choices that writers make, feeling perfectly free to "correct" those choices any time an apprentice deviates from the teacher-reader's conception of what the developing text ought to look like or ought to be doing. (158)

Brannon, Knoblauch, and Nancy Sommers express concern that in our attempt to tell writers how to do a better job, we in effect "appropriate the writers' texts" (Sommers 149-51). In addition, their research has shown that although our purpose is to help student writers communicate their ideas successfully, our theory falls short of its mark. Our own research on teachers' commentary shows that most teachers feel they must constantly criticize students' writing if they are to do their jobs. Ideally, we comment on students' papers to dramatize the presence of a reader, to help writers become that questioning reader themselves, and to create a motive for revising. But our comments will be especially useless if we read and mark only a single draft, the final product, with the expectation that our students will write better next time.

Recent theorists have provided us with several alternatives to the traditional approach to responding to our students' writing; pervasive in all these alternatives is the idea that supportive response to students' writing need not be limited to writing comments on it. In *Learning by Teaching,* Donald Murray tells us that we can listen to our students instead. The listening teacher waits, reads, and listens (152). In Murray's portfolio method of evaluation, students submit only their best work when they are ready to have it evaluated. Peter Elbow offers other alternatives to the traditional method of responding to students' writing. In *Writing without Teachers,* he tells us how to move the responsibility for responding from the teacher to the students as a group. In the process of learning how to respond to the writing of their peers, students also develop the ability to respond to their own texts. Elbow's *Writing with Power* shows us how to use collaboration; he spurs writers to take responsibility for seeking out collaborators who will provide two kinds of feedback: criterion based and reader based.

The best answer to the evaluation puzzle, as we suggest in Chapter 5, may be holistic rating, but many programs are simply not set up to allow its use. That is unfortunate because holistic grading answers many of the charges made against rating writers: it can be both valid and collaborative. Perhaps the most comprehensive yet easily understandable coverage of holistic grading is in Edward M. White's *Teaching and Assessing Writing.* White suggests that holistic evaluation creates an "interpretive community" of readers in which evaluation is properly categorized, and he goes on to offer much common-sense advice on testing, organizing holistic tests, and using testing and evaluation in teaching. It's a book well worth owning.

Evaluation is an important issue not only for students but for writing programs as well. In this age of accountability, teachers are often interested in measuring the success of their entire writing program. Fortunately, there are several good sources for such a quest. In *Evaluating College Writing Programs,* Stephen

P. Witte and Lester Faigley tell us that outside evaluators often confuse description with evaluation and that the quantitative approach to evaluation often rests on faulty assumptions about the goals or administrative structure of a writing program. Charles Cooper has edited *Evaluating Writing* and *The Nature and Measurement of Competency in English,* a collection that is particularly useful for administrators and their assistants and includes Cooper's own essay on the political and cultural implications of state-mandated testing.

A second major issue confronting scholars of composition, as we point out in Chapter 6, is the relationship between individual cognition and social ways of knowing. As that chapter shows, researchers have recently begun to pay close attention to what the writer does while writing, and this work is probably the most important ongoing research in composition studies. The work of contemporary researchers attempts to answer this twofold question: where do a writer's ideas come from, and how are such ideas formulated into writing? Such a question demands a new focus on *invention,* discussed in works by Janice Lauer, Richard Larson, Richard Young, Linda Flower, John Hayes, Stephen Witte, John Daly, and Mike Rose, many of which are cited in Chapter 6. This renewed interest in student writers has led in another powerful direction as well, notably in the work of Ken Macrorie (*Telling Writing*), Donald Murray, and most pervasively, Peter Elbow. Elbow is interested in how writers establish unique voices and realize individual selves in discourse, and his work with students presents dramatic evidence of such activity.

This relationship between individual cognition and social ways of knowing is being explored in many fields, particularly psychology, as researchers seek to understand the ways language mediates between self and society. In rhetoric and composition, the largest body of work on cognitive processes has traditionally concentrated on individual writers, seeking to map the ways in which they represent tasks, make plans, and choose strategies that will lead to text.

Kenneth Bruffee is probably the best-known composition theorist who argues that knowledge is constructed socially, and his work is related to a large body of research on collaborative writing, reading, and learning ("Brooklyn Plan," "Practical Models," and " 'Conversation of Mankind' "). Tori Haring-Smith bases arguments for writing-across-the-curriculum efforts on such a collaborative foundation. More recently, a group of researchers at Purdue University (Meg Morgan, Nancy Allen, Teresa Moore, Dianne Atkinson, and Craig Snow) has studied collaborative reading, writing, and learning in a number of settings, using differing research methodologies; they are attempting to understand the ways in which knowledge—and even texts—are constructed socially. In addition, the work of Andrea Lunsford and Lisa Ede ("Collaborative Learning: Lessons from the World of Work"; "Let Them Write—Together"; and *Singular Texts, Plural Authors*) demonstrates that this contextual element—collaboration—characterizes a great deal of writing and reading done on the job. Thus far, however, these two important strands of research have not been systematically linked—or approved—in theory or in practice. Such a link holds the promise of much exciting theoretical and practical work.

A final issue is of great concern to teachers and researchers of composition everywhere. That is, in what ways are issues of gender, race, and class related to success or failure in writing, to the dynamics of the classroom, to ways of knowing in general? Here we are at the earliest stages of investigation and understanding. Recent publications span the entire range of questions: Elizabeth Abel's *Writing and Sexual Difference;* Elizabeth Flynn and Patrocinio Schweickart's *Gender and Reading;* Liam Hudson and Bernadine Jacot's *The Way Men Think;* Cynthia Caywood and Gillian Overing's *Teaching Writing: Pedagogy, Gender, and Equity;* Deborah Tannen's *You Just Don't Understand;* Donnalee Rubin's *Gender Influences;* Richard Bullock, John Trimbur, and Charles Schuster's *Politics of Writing Instruction;* and *Women's Ways of Knowing* by Mary Field Belenky et al. These questions have been articulated clearly and persuasively in David Bleich's *The Double Perspective: Language, Literacy, and Social Relations.* Bleich argues for recognizing and implementing the "double perspective" that comes from acknowledging the simultaneous presence and interaction of biology, psychology, society, and culture with the way we use language to read, write, think, and react.

What lesson can we learn from the recent and compelling work of Abel, Hudson and Jacot, Bullock, Tannen, Flynn and Schweickart, Rubin, Caywood and Overing, Belenky et al., and Bleich? It should not be surprising that the lesson we learn from these books is a grammatical one, for structures of hierarchy and power are inscribed in our language in the ways we talk about gender, race, class, and clan, in the ways we read, write, think, and respond. Language study is part of a complex grammatical structure. Unless we learn this lesson, we may have listened in class and read the books to no avail. The time has come for us to respect the differences in our classroom and make them part of our pedagogy.

These three areas of study are only the three largest. The teaching of writing is still marked by huge areas that on old maps would be called "Terra Incognita." We have only begun, over the last few decades, to ask the questions about language and learning whose answers will shape the discourse of education in the twenty-first century. Unlike some other areas of English studies, which have been intensively examined for centuries, composition studies offers many areas in which the surface has hardly been scratched. The work is there, if you find yourself drawn to it. We hope that this book has helped you settle into teaching, and we also hope that it has raised some questions that you may want to continue to pursue as both teacher and scholar. Maybe someday we'll see you in the hall.

WORKS CITED

Abel, Elizabeth. *Writing and Sexual Difference.* Chicago: U of Chicago, 1982.

Belenky, Mary Field, et al. *Women's Ways of Knowing.* New York: Basic, 1986.

Bleich, David. *The Double Perspective: Language, Literacy, and Social Relations.* New York: Oxford UP, 1988.

Brannon, Lillian, and C. H. Knoblauch. "Students' Rights to Their Own Texts: A Model for Teacher Response." *CCC* 33 (1982): 157–66.

Bruffee, Kenneth. "The Brooklyn Plan: Attaining Intellectual Growth through Peer-Group Tutoring." *Liberal Education* 64 (1978): 447-69.

——. "Collaborative Learning: Some Practical Models." *CE* 34 (1973): 634-43.

——. "Collaborative Learning and the 'Conversation of Mankind.' " *CE* 46 (1984): 635-52.

Bullock, Richard, John Trimbur, and Charles Schuster, eds. *The Politics of Writing Instruction: Postsecondary.* Portsmouth, NH: Boynton/Cook, 1992.

Caywood, Cynthia, and Gillian Overing. *Teaching Writing: Pedagogy, Gender, and Equity.* Albany: State U of New York, 1987.

Cooper, Charles R., ed. *The Nature and Measurement of Competency in English.* Urbana, IL: NCTE, 1981.

Cooper, Charles R., and Lee Odell, eds. *Evaluating Writing: Describing, Measuring, Judging.* Urbana, IL: NCTE, 1977.

Elbow, Peter. *Writing without Teachers.* New York: Oxford UP, 1973.

——. *Writing with Power.* New York: Oxford UP, 1981.

Flynn, Elizabeth, and Patrocinio Schweickart. *Gender and Reading.* Baltimore: Johns Hopkins UP, 1986.

Haring-Smith, Tori, ed. *A Guide to Writing Programs, Writing Centers, Peer Tutoring Programs, and Writing Across the Curriculum.* Glenview, IL: Scott, 1985.

Hawisher, Gail, and Anna Soter, eds. *Essays on the Teaching of English in the Secondary School.* Albany: State U of New York, 1989.

Hudson, Liam, and Bernadine Jacot. *The Way Men Think: Intellect, Intimacy, and the Erotic Imagination.* New Haven, CT: Yale UP, 1991.

Lunsford, Andrea, and Lisa Ede. "Collaborative Learning: Lessons from the World of Work." *Writing Program Administration* 9 (1986): 17-26.

——. "Let Them Write—Together." *English Quarterly* 18 (1985): 119-27.

——. *Singular Texts/Plural Authors.* Carbondale: Southern Illinois UP, 1990.

Macrorie, Ken. *Telling Writing.* Rochelle Park, NJ: Hayden, 1970.

Morgan, Meg, Nancy Allen, Teresa Moore, Diane Atkinson, and Craig Snow. "Collaborative Writing in the Classroom." *The American Business Communication Asociation Bulletin* Sept. 1987: 20-26.

Murray, Donald. *Learning By Teaching.* Upper Montclair, NJ: Boynton/Cook, 1982.

Rubin, Donnalee. *Gender Influences: Reading Student Texts.* Carbondale: Southern Illinois UP, 1993.

Sommers, Nancy. "Responding to Student Writing." *CCC* 33 (1982): 149-51.

Tannen, Deborah. *You Just Don't Understand: Women and Men in Conversation.* New York: Morrow, 1990.

White, Edward M. *Teaching and Assessing Writing.* 2nd ed. San Francisco: Jossey-Bass, 1994.

Witte, Stephen P., and Lester Faigley. *Evaluating College Writing Programs.* Carbondale: Southern Illinois UP, 1983.

SUGGESTED READINGS FOR COMPOSITION TEACHERS

Bibliographies

Bizzell, Patricia, and Bruce Herzberg. *The Bedford Bibliography for Teachers of Writing.* Boston: Bedford, 1990.

Braddock, Richard, Richard Lloyd-Jones, and Lowell Schoer. *Research in Written Composition.* Urbana, IL: NCTE, 1963.

Cooper, Charles R., and Lee Odell, eds. *Research on Composing: Points of Departure.* Urbana, IL: NCTE, 1978.

Hillocks, George C. *Research on Written Composition: New Directions for Teaching.* Urbana, IL: NCRE, 1986.

Lindemann, Erika. *Longman Bibliography of Composition and Rhetoric.* New York: Longman, 1984-85, 1986.

——. *CCCC Bibliography of Composition and Rhetoric.* Carbondale: Southern Illinois UP, 1987 present.

Moran, Michael G., and Ronald F. Lunsford. *Research in Composition and Rhetoric: A Bibliographic Sourcebook*. Westport, CT: Greenwood, 1984.

Tate, Gary, ed. *Teaching Composition: Twelve Bibliographical Essays*. Fort Worth: Texas Christian UP, 1987.

Collections

Beach, Richard, and Lillian S. Bridwell, eds. *New Directions in Composition Research*. New York: Guilford, 1984.

Bizzell, Patricia, and Bruce Herzberg. *The Rhetorical Tradition*. Boston: Bedford, 1990.

Connors, Robert J., Lisa S. Ede, and Andrea A. Lunsford, eds. *Essays on Classical Rhetoric and Modern Discourse*. Carbondale: Southern Illinois UP, 1984.

Corbett, Edward P. J., James L. Golden, and Goodwin F. Berquist. *Essays on the Rhetoric of the Western World*. Dubuque, IA: Kendall/Hunt, 1990. 91-109.

Donovan, Timothy R., and Ben W. McClelland. *Eight Approaches to Teaching Composition*. Urbana, IL: NCTE, 1980.

Enos, Theresa, ed. *A Sourcebook for Basic Writing Teachers*. New York: Random, 1987.

Graves, Richard, ed. *Rhetoric and Composition*. 3rd ed. Portsmouth, NH: Boynton/Cook, 1990.

Kirsch, Gesa, and Patricia Sullivan. *Methods and Methodology in Composition Research*. Carbondale: Southern Illinois UP, 1992.

Lindemann, Erika, and Gary Tate, eds. *An Introduction to Composition Studies*. New York: Oxford UP, 1991.

McClelland, Ben W., and Timothy Donovan, eds. *Perspectives on Research and Scholarship in Composition*. New York: MLA, 1985.

McQuade, Donald A., ed. *The Territory of Language*. Carbondale: Southern Illinois UP, 1986.

Newkirk, Thomas, ed. *Only Connect*. Upper Montclair, NJ: Boynton/Cook, 1986.

Rose, Mike, ed. *When a Writer Can't Write*. New York: Guilford, 1985.

Tate, Gary, and Edward P. J. Corbett, eds. *The Writing Teacher's Sourcebook*. 2nd ed. New York: Oxford UP, 1988.

Winterowd, W. Ross. *Contemporary Rhetoric: A Conceptual Background with Readings*. New York: Harcourt, 1975.

Witte, Stephen P., Neil Nakadate, and Roger D. Cherry. *A Rhetoric of Doing*. Carbondale: Southern Illinois UP, 1992.

Books

Applebee, Arthur, et al. *A Study of Writing in the Secondary Schools*. Urbana, IL: NCTE, 1974.

Bartholomae, David, and Anthony Petrosky. *Facts, Artifacts, and Counterfacts*. Upper Montclair, NJ: Boynton/Cook, 1986.

Beale, Walter. *A Pragmatic Theory of Rhetoric*. Carbondale: Southern Illinois UP, 1987.

Berlin, James. *Rhetoric and Reality: Writing Instruction in American Colleges, 1900-1985*. Carbondale: Southern Illinois UP (NCTE/CCCC), 1987.

——. *Writing Instructions in Nineteenth Century American Colleges*. Carbondale: Southern Illinois UP (NCTE/CCCC), 1984.

Berthoff, Ann E. *The Making of Meaning*. Upper Montclair, NJ: Boynton/Cook, 1987.

Brannon, Lillian, Melinda Knight, and Vara Neverow-Turk. *Writers Writing*. Upper Montclair, NJ: Boynton/Cook, 1983.

Britton, James, et al. *The Development of Writing Abilities, 11-18*. London: Macmillan, 1975.

Bruner, Jerome. *The Process of Education*. New York: Vintage, 1960.

Cooper, Charles, and Lee Odell, eds. *Evaluating Writing: Describing, Measuring, and Judging*. Urbana, IL: NCTE, 1977.

Corbett, Edward P. J. *Selected Essays*. Ed. Robert J. Connors. Dallas: Southern Methodist UP, 1989.

Elbow, Peter. *Embracing Contraries*. New York: Oxford UP, 1986.

——. *Writing with Power.* New York: Oxford UP, 1981.

——. *Writing without Teachers.* New York: Oxford UP, 1973.

Emig, Janet. *The Composing Process of Twelfth Graders. Research Report* 13. Urbana, IL: NCTE, 1971.

——. *The Web of Meaning.* Upper Montclair, NJ: Boynton/Cook, 1983.

Gere, Anne Ruggles. *Writing Groups: History, Theory, and Implications.* Carbondale: Southern Illinois UP, 1987.

Halliday, M. A. K., and R. Hasan. *Cohesion in English.* White Plains, NY: Longman, 1976.

Heath, Shirley Brice. *Ways with Words.* Cambridge: Cambridge UP, 1983.

Hirsch, E. D. *The Philosophy of Composition.* Chicago: U of Chicago, 1977.

Hunt, Kellogg. *Grammatical Structures Written at Three Grade Levels.* Urbana, IL: NCTE, 1965.

Kinneavy, James L. *A Theory of Discourse.* Englewood Cliffs, NJ: Prentice, 1971. New York: Norton, 1980.

Kitzhaber, Albert R. *Rhetoric in American Colleges 1850–1900.* Dallas: Southern Methodist UP, 1991.

——. *Themes, Theories, and Therapy: The Teaching of Writing in College.* New York: McGraw, 1963.

Knoblauch, C. H., and Lillian Brannon. *Rhetorical Traditions and the Teaching of Writing.* Portsmouth, NH: Boynton/Cook, 1984.

Labov, William. *The Study of Nonstandard English.* Urbana, IL: NCTE, 1970.

Lanham, Richard A. *Literacy and the Survival of Humanism.* New Haven, CT: Yale UP, 1983.

Lauer, Janice, and William Asher. *Composition Research: Empirical Designs.* New York: Oxford UP, 1988.

LeFevre, Karen Burke. *Invention as a Social Act.* Carbondale: Southern Illinois UP, 1987.

Lindemann, Erika. *A Rhetoric for Writing Teachers.* 2nd ed. New York: Oxford UP, 1987.

Loban, Walter. *Language Development: Kindergarten through Grade Twelve.* Urbana, IL: NCTE, 1976.

Macrorie, Ken. *Telling Writing.* Rochelle Park, NJ: Hayden, 1970.

——. *Uptaught.* Rochelle Park, NJ: Hayden, 1970.

Mellon, John C. *Transformational Sentence-Combining.* Urbana, IL: NCTE, 1967.

Miller, Susan. *Textual Carnivals: The Politics of Composition.* Carbondale: Southern Illinois UP, 1991.

Moffett, James. *Coming on Center.* Upper Montclair, NJ: Boynton/Cook, 1981.

——. *A Student-Centered Language Arts and Reading, K–13.* Boston: Houghton, 1968.

——. *Teaching the Universe of Discourse.* Boston: Houghton, 1968.

Murray, Donald. *A Writer Teaches Writing.* 2nd ed. Boston: Houghton, 1985.

Neel, Jasper. *Plato, Derrida, and Writing.* Carbondale: Southern Illinois UP, 1988.

North, Stephen. *The Making of Knowledge in Composition.* Portsmouth, NH: Boynton/Cook, 1987.

Odell, Lee, and Dixie Goswami. *Writing in Non-Academic Settings.* New York: Guilford, 1985.

O'Hare, Frank. *Sentence-Combining: Improving Student Writing without Formal Grammar Instruction.* Urbana, IL: NCTE, 1973.

Rose, Mike. *Lives on the Boundary: The Struggles and Achievements of America's Underprepared.* New York: Free Press, 1989.

——. *Writer's Block: The Cognitive Dimension.* Carbondale: Southern Illinois UP, 1984.

Shaughnessy, Mina. *Errors & Expectations.* New York: Oxford UP, 1977.

Smith, Frank. *Understanding Reading.* 2nd ed. New York: Holt, 1978.

Vygotsky, L. S. *Mind and Society.* Cambridge, MA: Harvard UP, 1978.

——. *Thought and Language.* Trans. Eugenia Hanfman and Gertrude Vakar. Boston: MIT, 1962.

Weaver, Richard. *Language Is Sermonic.* Baton Rouge, Louisiana State UP, 1970.

White, Edward. *Teaching and Assessing Writing.* 2nd ed. San Francisco: Jossey-Bass, 1994.

Winterowd, Ross. *Contemporary Rhetoric.* New York: Harcourt, 1975.

Witte, Stephen, and Lester Faigley. *Evaluating College Writing Programs.* Carbondale: Southern Illinois UP, 1983.

Young, Richard E., Alton L. Becker, and Kenneth L. Pike. *Rhetoric: Discovery and Change*. New York: Harcourt, 1970.

Articles

Modern Rhetorical Theory

Connors, Robert. "Composition Studies and Science." *CE* 45 (1983): 1-20.

Emig, Janet. "Writing as a Mode of Learning." *CCC* 33 (1977): 122-28.

Hairston, Maxine. "The Winds of Change: Thomas Kuhn and the Revolution in the Teaching of Writing." *CCC* 33 (1982): 76-86. Rpt. Richard Graves, ed. *Rhetoric and Composition*. 2nd ed. Portsmouth, NH: Boynton/Cook, 1984. 3-15.

Kinneavy, James. "The Basic Aims of Discourse." *CCC* 20 (1969): 297-304.

Lunsford, Andrea A. "Composing Ourselves: Politics, Commitment, and the Teaching of Writing." *CCC* 41 (1990): 71-82.

McCrimmon, James. "Writing as a Way of Knowing." The Promise of English: NCTE 1970 Distinguished Lectures. Carbondale, IL: NCTE, 1970. Rpt. Richard Graves, ed. *Rhetoric and Composition*. 2nd ed. Portsmouth, NH: Boynton/Cook, 1984.

The Composing Process

Flower, Linda. "Interpretive Acts: Cognition and the Construction of Discourse." *Poetics* 16 (1987).

Graves, Donald. "An Examination of the Writing Process of Seven-Year-Old Children." *Research in the Teaching of English* 9 (1975): 227-41.

Macrorie, Ken. "To Be Read." *English Journal* 57 (1968): 686-92. Rpt. Richard Graves, ed. *Rhetoric and Composition.* 2nd ed. Portsmouth, NH: Boynton/Cook, 1984.

Murray, Donald. "Teach Writing as a Process, not Product." *Leaflet* Nov. 1972: 11-14. Rpt. Richard Graves, ed. *Rhetoric and Composition*. 2nd ed. Portsmouth, NH: Boynton/Cook, 1984. 89-92.

Perl, Sondra. "The Composing Process of Unskilled College Writers." *Research in the Teaching of English* 13 (1979): 317-36.

———. "Understanding Composing." *CCC* 31 (1980): 363-69. Rpt. Richard Graves, ed. *Rhetoric and Composition*. 2nd ed. Portsmouth, NH: Boynton/Cook, 1984. 304-11.

Pianko, Sharon. "A Description of the Composing Process of College Freshman Writers." *Research in the Teaching of English* 13 (1979): 5-22.

Stallard, Charles. "An Analysis of the Writing Behavior of Good Student Writers." *Research in the Teaching of English* 8 (1974): 206-18.

Voss, Ralph. "Janet Emig's *The Composing Process of Twelfth Graders*: A Reassessment." *CCC* 34 (1983): 278-83.

Witte, Stephen. "Pre-Text and Composing." *CCC* 38 (1987): 397-425.

Revision

Berthoff, Ann E. "Recognition, Representation, and Revision." *Journal of Basic Writing* 3 (1981): 19-32.

Faigley, Lester, and Stephen Witte. "Analyzing Revision." *CCC* 34 (1981): 400-14.

Flower, Linda. "Writer-Based Prose: A Cognitive Basis for Problems in Writing." *CE* 41 (1979): 19-37.

Huff, Roland. "Teaching Revision: A Model of the Drafting Process." *CE* 45 (1983): 800-16.

Sommers, Nancy. "Revision Strategies of Student Writers and Experienced Adult Writers." *CCC* 31 (1980): 378-88. Rpt. Richard Graves, ed. *Rhetoric and Composition*. 2nd ed. Portsmouth, NH: Boynton/Cook, 1984. 328-37.

Witte, Stephen. "Topical Structure and Revision: An Exploratory Study." *CCC* 34 (1983): 313-41.

Basic Writing

Bartholomae, David. "The Study of Error." *CCC* 31 (1980): 253-69.

Bizzell, Patricia. "What Happens When Basic Writers Come to College?" *CCC* 37 (1986): 294-301.

Lunsford, Andrea. "Cognitive Development and the Basic Writer." *CE* 41 (1979): 38-46.

——. "The Content of Basic Writers' Essays." *CCC* 31 (1980): 278-90.

Rose, Mike. "The Language of Exclusion: Writing Instruction at the University." *CE* 47 (1985): 341-59.

An Anthology of Essays

We hope that the first two parts of this book have helped you organize, plan, and make choices about the writing course you teach. Our central purpose has been to focus on the practical concerns of real writing teachers in real classrooms, and we've tried to keep that purpose in sight. But we also realize that the concerns of teachers are often theoretical as well as practical.

This part, an anthology of readings from the recent history of composition studies, should help address your theoretical concerns. Like the first two parts, this one is included to help you be the most effective and the most informed teacher you can be. In addition, however, we hope that this collection of journal articles (some of the best we know) will serve to reinforce our invitation to you to join the field of composition studies. We'd like you to become a reader of, as well as a contributor to, the ongoing conversation in the field. Teaching writing is the ground for almost everything else that goes on in composition studies, but in the last forty years, the field has become an established scholarly discipline as well—one that we hope will interest you.

The articles reprinted here discuss composition theory and practice; after all, that's what our field is all about. And these discussions serve as the basis for much of what we do in the classroom—the theories we choose to build on, the traditions and wisdoms we challenge, and the speculations we deem most promising. Parts I and II suggest that in its own way, every teaching practice is theoretical. So we hope that Part III will demonstrate just how intimately related theory and practice are. Rhetorical theory is neither arcane nor archaic knowledge nor is it merely desirable knowledge for a writing teacher to possess. Rhetorical theory is the very stuff that makes a writing teacher effective. A great deal of this theoretical background may be intuitive—learned through practice, simple listening, common-sense awareness of life and human interactions. But some theory becomes more useful when it is foregrounded and contextualized. For this reason, we have chosen the articles that follow. To put these articles in context, we have provided original publication information in a footnote at the end of each essay.

Our theories, the ideas we evolve to explain what has happened and to predict on that basis what will happen, arise in our classrooms, in our studies, or in our library carrels. They are shared in hallway conversations, meetings, workshops, and journal articles. And from there, they are carried back into the world of action—for us, back to our classrooms through our teaching and the textbooks we write and use. The best textbook is simply the best teaching on a much larger scale—a repository of successful ideas and techniques available to other teachers and their students.

Our own research and the research available to us help keep us current in the ongoing discussion about writing and the teaching of writing. But this conversation is not a recent one: it has been going on in different forms for over twenty-five hundred years, and it will continue long after we are gone. The late Kenneth Burke, in one of his most famous passages, likens such ongoing conversation to a parlor that we all may visit for a while.

> Imagine you enter a parlor. You come late. When you arrive, others have long preceded you, and they are engaged in a heated discussion, a discussion too heated for them to pause and tell you exactly what it is about. In fact, the discussion had already begun long before any of them got there, so that no one present is qualified to retrace for you all the steps that had gone before. You listen for a while, until you decide that you have caught the tenor of the argument; then you put in your oar. Someone answers; you answer him; another comes to your defense; another aligns himself against you, to either the embarrassment or gratification of your opponent, depending upon the quality of your ally's assistance. However, the discussion is interminable. The hour grows late, you must depart. And you do depart, with the discussion still vigorously in progress. (110-11)

Of course, some good teachers have never entered this conversation. But from our own experiences, we can testify to the excitement, the usefulness, and even the inspiration that can come from joining a national community of people who are all working on the same questions and the same issues. And besides addressing the basic issues surrounding students' writing and teaching students to write, our conversation now addresses issues of working with students whose strongest language or dialect is not standard academic English or Edited American English.

Therefore, the articles we have included here speak not only to established concerns of basic writers, process writing, teachers' responses, and grammar but also to the recent concerns of literate practices, language variation, the reading and writing relationship, and genre. Whatever the article, whether we wrote it or someone else did, we have chosen those articles that have been the most practically helpful to us, especially when we were looking to understand our own teaching. And that, for us, is the bottom line: the scholarship and theory collected here returns to our teaching and to our students' learning. We in composition studies have never lived in any ivory tower; on a weekly or daily basis, most of us are called back to the place that is really important to us, our writing classes. We hope you find this conversation as useful as we do—and we hope you'll join it.

WORK CITED

Burke, Kenneth. *The Philosophy of Literary Form.* Berkeley: U of California P, 1941.

Linda Flower

WRITER-BASED PROSE: A COGNITIVE BASIS FOR PROBLEMS IN WRITING

If writing is simply the act of "expressing what you think" or "saying what you mean," why is writing often such a difficult thing to do? And why do papers that do express what the writer meant (to his or her own satisfaction) often fail to communicate the same meaning to a reader? Although we often equate writing with the straightforward act of "saying what we mean," the mental struggles writers go through and the misinterpretation readers still make suggest that we need a better model of this process. Modern communication theory and practical experience agree; writing prose that actually communicates what we mean to another person demands more than a simple act of self-expression. What communication theory does not tell us is how writers do it.

An alternative to the "think it/say it" model is to say that effective writers do not simply *express* thought but *transform* it in certain complex but describable ways for the needs of a reader. Conversely, we may find that ineffective writers are indeed merely "expressing" themselves by offering up an unretouched and underprocessed version of their own thought. Writer-Based prose, the subject of this paper, is a description of this undertransformed mode of verbal expression.

As both a style of writing and a style of thought, Writer-Based prose is natural and adequate for a writer writing to himself or herself. However, it is the source of some of the most common and pervasive problems in academic and professional writing. The symptoms can range from a mere missing referent or an underdeveloped idea to an unfocused and apparently pointless discussion. The symptoms are diverse but the source can often be traced to the writer's underlying strategy for composing and to his or her failure to transform private thought into a public, Reader-Based expression.

In *function,* Writer-Based prose is a verbal expression written by a writer to himself and for himself. It is the record and the working of his own verbal thought. In its *structure,* Writer-Based prose reflects the associative, narrative path of the writer's own confrontation with her subject. In its *language,* it reveals her use of privately loaded terms and shifting but unexpressed contexts for her statements.

In contrast, Reader-Based prose is a deliberate attempt to communicate something to a reader. To do that, it creates a shared language and shared context between writer and reader. It also offers the reader an issue-centered rhetorical structure rather than a replay of the writer's discovery process. In its language

277

and structure, Reader-Based prose tends to reflect its *process*. Good writing, therefore, is often the cognitively demanding transformation of the natural but private expressions of Writer-Based thought into a structure and style adapted to the reader.

This analysis of Writer-Based prose style and the transformations that create Reader-Based prose will explore two hypotheses:

1. Writer-Based prose represents a major and familiar mode of expression which we all use from time to time. While no piece of writing is a pure example, Writer-Based prose can be identified by features of structure, function, and style. Furthermore, it shares many of these features with the modes of inner and egocentric speech described by Vygotsky and Piaget. This paper will explore that relationship and look at newer research in an effort to describe Writer-Based prose as a verbal style which in turn reflects an underlying cognitive process.

2. Writer-Based prose is a workable concept which can help us teach writing. As a way to intervene in the thinking process, it taps intuitive communication strategies writers already have, but are not adequately using. As a teaching technique, the notion of transforming one's own Writer-Based style has proved to be a powerful idea with a built-in method. It helps writers attack this demanding cognitive task with some of the thoroughness and confidence that comes from an increased and self-conscious control of the process.

My plan for this paper is to explore Writer-Based prose from a number of perspectives. Therefore, the next section, which considers the psychological theory of egocentrism and inner speech, is followed by a case study of Writer-Based prose. I will then pull these practical and theoretical issues together to define the critical features of Writer-Based prose. The final section will look ahead to the implications of this description of Writer-Based prose for writers and teachers.

INNER SPEECH AND EGOCENTRISM

In studying the developing thought of the child, Jean Piaget and Lev Vygotsky both observed a mode of speech which seemed to have little social or communicative function. Absorbed in play, children would carry on spirited elliptical monologues which they seemed to assume others understood, but which in fact made no concessions to the needs of the listener. According to Piaget, in Vygotsky's synopsis, "In egocentric speech, the child talks only about himself, takes no interest in his interlocutor, does not try to communicate, expects no answers, and often does not even care whether anyone listens to him. It is similar to a monologue in a play: The child is thinking aloud, keeping up a running accompaniment, as it were, to whatever he may be doing."[1] In the seven-year-olds Piaget studied, nearly fifty percent of their recorded talk was egocentric in

[1] Lev Vygotsky, *Thought and Language,* ed. and trans. Eugenia Hanfmann and Gertrude Vakar (Cambridge, Mass.: M.I.T. Press, 1962), p. 15.

nature.[2] According to Piaget, the child's "non-communicative" or egocentric speech is a reflection, not of selfishness, but of the child's limited ability to "assume the point of view of the listener: [the child] talks of himself, to himself, and by himself."[3] In a sense, the child's cognitive capacity has locked her in her own monologue.

When Vygotsky observed a similar phenomenon in children he called it "inner speech" because he saw it as a forerunner of the private verbal thought adults carry on. Furthermore, Vygotsky argued, this speech is not simply a by-product of play; it is the tool children use to plan, organize, and control their activities. He put the case quite strongly: "We have seen that egocentric speech is not suspended in a void but is directly related to the child's practical dealings with the real world . . . it enters as a constituent part into the process of rational activity" (*Thought and Language,* p. 22).

The egocentric talk of the child and the mental, inner speech of the adult share three important features in common. First, they are highly elliptical. In talking to oneself, the psychological subject of discourse (the old information to which we are adding new predicates) is always known. Therefore, explicit subjects and referents disappear. Five people straining to glimpse the bus need only say, "Coming!" Secondly, inner speech frequently deals in the sense of words, not their more specific or limited public meanings. Words become "saturated with sense" in much the way a key word in a poem can come to represent its entire, complex web of meaning. But unlike the word in the poem, the accrued sense of the word in inner speech may be quite personal, even idiosyncratic; it is, as Vygotsky writes, "the sum of all the psychological events aroused in our consciousness by the word" (*Thought and Language,* p. 146).

Finally, a third feature of egocentric/inner speech is the absence of logical and causal relations. In experiments with children's use of logical, causal connectives such as *because, therefore,* and *although,* Piaget found that children have difficulty managing such relationships and in spontaneous speech will substitute a non-logical, non-causal connective such as *then.* Piaget described this strategy for relating things as *juxtaposition*: "the cognitive tendency simply to link (juxtapose) one thought element to another, rather than to tie them together by some causal or logical relationship."[4]

One way to diagnose this problem with sophisticated relationships is to say, as Vygotsky did, that young children often think in *complexes* instead of concepts.[5] When people think in complexes they unite objects into families that

---

[2] Jean Piaget, *The Language and Thought of the Child,* trans. Marjorie Gabin (New York: Harcourt, Brace, 1932), p. 49.

[3] Herbert Ginsberg and Sylvia Opper, *Piaget's Theory of Intellectual Development* (Englewood Cliffs, N.J.: Prentice-Hall, 1969), p. 89.

[4] John Flavell, *The Developmental Psychology of Jean Piaget* (New York: D. Van Nostrand, 1963), p. 275. For these studies see the last chapter of Piaget's *Language and Thought of the Child* and *Judgment and Reasoning in the Child,* trans. M. Warden (New York: Harcourt, Brace, 1926).

[5] *Thought and Language,* p. 75. See also the paper by Gary Woditsch which places this question in the context of curriculum design, "Developing Generic Skills: A Model for a Competency-Based General Education," available from CUE Center, Bowling Green State University.

really do share common bonds, but the bonds are concrete and factual rather than abstract or logical. For example, the notion of "college student" would be a complex if it were based, for the thinker, on facts such as college students live in dorms, go to classes, and do homework.

Complexes are very functional formations, and it may be that many people do most of their day-to-day thinking without feeling the need to form more demanding complex concepts. *Complexes* collect related objects; *concepts,* however, must express abstract, logical relations. And it is just this sort of abstract, synthetic thinking that writing typically demands. In a child's early years, the ability to form complex concepts may depend mostly on developing cognitive capacity. In adults this ability appears also to be a skill developed by training and a tendency fostered by one's background and intellectual experience. But whatever its source, the ability to move from the complexes of egocentric speech to the more formal relations of conceptual thought is critical to most expository writing.

Piaget and Vygotsky disagreed on the source, exact function, and teleology of egocentric speech, but they did agree on the features of this distinctive phenomenon, which they felt revealed the underlying logic of the child's thought. For our case, that may be enough. The hypothesis on which this paper rests is not a developmental one. Egocentric speech, or rather its adult written analogue, Writer-Based prose, is not necessarily a stage through which a writer must develop or one at which some writers are arrested. But for adults it does represent an available mode of expression on which to fall back. If Vygotsky is right, it may even be closely related to normal verbal thought. It is clearly a natural, less cognitively demanding mode of thought and one which explains why people who can express themselves in complex and highly intelligible modes are often obscure. Egocentric expression happens to the best of us; it comes naturally.

The work of Piaget and Vygotsky, then, suggests a source for the cognitive patterns that underlie Writer-Based prose, and it points to some of the major features such a prose style would possess. Let us now turn to a more detailed analysis of such writing as a verbal style inadequately suited for the needs of the reader.

WRITER-BASED PROSE:
A CASE STUDY OF A TRANSFORMATION

As an introduction to the main features of Writer-Based prose and its transformations, let us look at two drafts of a progress report written by students in an organizational psychology class. Working as consulting analysts to a local organization, the writers needed to show progress to their instructor and to present an analysis with causes and conclusions to the client. Both readers—academic and professional—were less concerned with what the students did or saw than with *why* they did it and *what* they made of their observations.

To gauge the Reader-Based effectiveness of this report, skim quickly over Draft 1 and imagine the response of the instructor of the course, who needed to answer these questions: As analysts, what assumptions and decisions did my students make? Why did they make them? At what stage in the project are they now? Or, play the role of the client-reader who wants to know: How did they define my problem, and what did they conclude? As either reader, can you quickly extract the information the report should be giving you? Next, try the same test on Draft 2.

DRAFT 1: GROUP REPORT

(1) Work began on our project with the initial group decision to evaluate the Oskaloosa Brewing Company. Oskaloosa Brewing Company is a regionally located brewery manufacturing several different types of beer, notably River City and Brough Cream Ale. This beer is marketed under various names in Pennsylvania and other neighboring states. As a group, we decided to analyze this organization because two of our group members had had frequent customer contact with the sales department. Also, we were aware that Oskaloosa Brewing had been losing money for the past five years and we felt we might be able to find some obvious problems in their organizational structure.

(2) Our first meeting, held February 17th, was with the head of the sales department, Jim Tucker. Generally, he gave us an outline of the organization from president to worker, and discussed the various departments that we might ultimately decide to analyze. The two that seemed the most promising and most applicable to the project were the sales and production departments. After a few group meetings and discussions with the personnel manager, Susan Harris, and our advisor Professor Charns, we felt it best suited our needs and the Oskaloosa Brewing's to evaluate their bottling department.

(3) During the next week we had a discussion with the superintendent of production, Harry Holt, and made plans for interviewing the supervisors and line workers. Also, we had a tour of the bottling department which gave us a first hand look into the production process. Before beginning our interviewing, our group met several times to formulate appropriate questions to use in interviewing, for both the supervisors and workers. We also had a meeting with Professor Charns to discuss this matter.

(3a) The next step was the actual interviewing process. During the weeks of March 14–18 and March 21–25, our group met several times at Oskaloosa Brewing and interviewed ten supervisors and twelve workers. Finally during this past week, we have had several group meetings to discuss our findings and the potential problem areas within the bottling department. Also, we have spent time organizing the writing of our progress report.

(4) The bottling and packaging division is located in a separate building, adjacent to the brewery, where the beer is actually manufactured. From the brewery the beer is piped into one of five lines (four bottling lines and one canning line) in the bottling house where the bottles are filled, crowned, pasteurized, labeled, packaged in cases, and either shipped out or stored in the warehouse. The head of this operation, and others, is

production manager Phil Smith. Next in line under him in direct control of the bottling house is the superintendent of bottling and packaging, Henry Holt. In addition, there are a total of ten supervisors who report directly to Henry Holt and who oversee the daily operations and coordinate and direct the twenty to thirty union workers who operate the lines.

(5) During production, each supervisor fills out a data sheet to explain what was actually produced during each hour. This form also includes the exact time when a breakdown occurred, what it was caused by, and when production was resumed. Some supervisors' positions are production staff oriented. One takes care of supplying the raw material (bottles, caps, labels, and boxes) for production. Another is responsible for the union workers' assignment each day.

These workers are not all permanently assigned to a production line position. Men called "floaters" are used filling in for a sick worker, or helping out after a breakdown.

(6) The union employees are generally older than 35, some in their late fifties. Most have been with the company many years and are accustomed to having more workers per a slower moving line. They are resentful to what they declare "unnecessary" production changes. Oska-Brewery also employs mechanics who normally work on the production line, and assume a mechanic's job only when a breakdown occurs. Most of these men are not skilled.

DRAFT 2: MEMORANDUM

TO: Professor Martin Charns

FROM: Nancy Lowenberg, Tod Scott, Rosemary Nisson, Larry Vollen

DATE: March 31, 1977

RE: *Progress Report: The Oskaloosa Brewing Company*

WHY OSKALOOSA BREWING?

(1) Oskaloosa Brewing Company is a regionally located brewery manufacturing several different types of beer, notably River City and Brough Cream Ale. As a group, we decided to analyze this organization because two of our group members have frequent contact with the sales department. Also, we were aware that Oskaloosa Brewing had been losing money for the past five years and we felt we might be able to find some obvious problems in their organizational structure.

INITIAL STEPS: WHERE TO CONCENTRATE?

(2) Through several interviews with top management and group discussion, we felt it best suited our needs, and Oskaloosa Brewing's, to evaluate the production department. Our first meeting, held February 17, was with the head of the sales department, Jim Tucker. He gave us an outline of the organization and described the two major departments, sales and production. He indicated that there were more obvious problems in the pro-

duction department, a belief also implied by Susan Harris, personnel manager.

NEXT STEP

(3) The next step involved a familiarization of the plant and its employees. First, we toured the plant to gain an understanding of the brewing and bottling process. Next, during the weeks of March 14–18 and March 21–25, we interviewed ten supervisors and twelve workers. Finally, during the past week we had group meetings to exchange information and discuss potential problems.

THE PRODUCTION PROCESS

(4) Knowledge of the actual production process is imperative in understanding the effects of various problems on efficient production; therefore, we have included a brief summary of this process.

The bottling and packaging division is located in a separate building, adjacent to the brewery, where the beer is actually manufactured. From the brewery the beer is piped into one of five lines (four bottling lines and one canning line) in the bottling house where the bottles are filled, crowned, pasteurized, labeled, packaged in cases, and either shipped out or stored in the warehouse.

PEOPLE BEHIND THE PROCESS

(5) The head of this operation is production manager Phil Smith. Next in line under him in direct control of the bottling house is the superintendent of bottling and packaging, Henry Holt. He has authority over ten supervisors who each have two major responsibilities: (1) to fill out production data sheets that show the amount produced/hour, and information about any breakdowns—time, cause, etc., and (2) to oversee the daily operations and coordinate and direct the twenty to thirty union workers who operate the lines. These workers are not all permanently assigned to a production line position. Men called "floaters" are used to fill in for a sick worker or to help out after a breakdown.

(6) The union employees are a highly diversified group in both age and experience. They are generally older than 35, some in their late fifties. Most have been with the company many years and are accustomed to having more workers per a slower moving line. They are resentful to what they feel are unnecessary production changes. Oskaloosa Brewing also employees mechanics who normally work on the production line, and assume a mechanic's job only when a breakdown occurs. Most of these men are not skilled.

PROBLEMS

Through extensive interviews with supervisors and union employees, we have recognized four apparent problems within the bottle house operations. First, the employees' goals do not match those of the company. This is especially apparent in the union employees whose loyalty lies with the union instead of the company. This attitude is well-founded as the union ensures them of job security and benefits. . . .

In its tedious misdirection, Draft 1 is typical of Writer-Based prose in student papers and professional reports. The reader is forced to do most of the thinking, sorting the wheat from the chaff and drawing ideas out of details. And yet, although this presentation fails to fulfill our needs, it does have an inner logic of its own. The logic which organizes Writer-Based prose often rests on three principles: its underlying focus is egocentric, and it uses either a narrative framework or a survey form to order ideas.

The *narrative framework* of this discussion is established by the opposing announcement: "Work began . . ." In paragraphs 1–3 facts and ideas are presented in terms of when they were discovered, rather than in terms of their implications or logical connections. The writers recount what happened when; the reader, on the other hand, asks "Why?" and "So what?" Whether he or she likes it or not, the reader is in for a blow-by-blow account of the writer's discovery process.

Although a rudimentary chronology is reasonable for a progress report, a narrative framework is often a substitute for analytic thinking. By burying ideas within the events that precipitated them, a narrative obscures the more important logical and hierarchical relations between ideas. Of course, such a narrative could read like an intellectual detective story, because, like other forms of drama, it creates interest by withholding closure. Unfortunately, most academic and professional readers seem unwilling to sit through these home movies of the writer's mind at work. Narratives can also operate as a cognitive "frame" which itself generates ideas.[6] The temporal pattern, once invoked, opens up a series of empty slots waiting to be filled with the details of what happened next, even though those details may be irrelevant. As the revision of Draft 2 shows, our writers' initial narrative framework led them to generate a shaggy project story, instead of a streamlined logical analysis.

The second salient feature of this prose is its focus on the discovery process of the writers: the "I did/I thought/I felt" focus. Of the fourteen sentences in the first three paragraphs, ten are grammatically focused on the writers' thoughts and actions rather than on issues: "Work began," "We decided," "Also, we were aware . . . and we felt. . . ."

In the fourth paragraph the writers shift attention from their discovery process to the facts discovered. In doing so they illustrate a third feature of Writer-Based prose: its idea structure simply copies the structure of the perceived information. A problem arises when the internal structure of the data is not already adapted to the needs of the reader or the intentions of the writer. Paragraph 5, for example, appears to be a free-floating description of "What happens during production." Yet the client-reader already knows this and the instructor probably does not care. Lured by the fascination of facts, these Writer-

---

[6] The seminal paper on frames is M. Minsky's "A Framework for Representing Knowledge" in P. Winston, ed., *The Psychology of Computer Vision* (New York: McGraw Hill, 1973). For a more recent discussion of how they work see B. Kuipers, "A Frame for Frames" in D. Bowbow and A. Collins, eds., *Representation and Understanding: Studies in Cognitive Science* (New York: Academic Press, 1975), pp. 151–184.

Based writers recite a litany of perceived information under the illusion they have produced a rhetorical structure. The resulting structure could as well be a neat hierarchy as a list. The point is that the writers' organizing principle is dictated by their information, not by their intention.

The second version of this report is not so much a "rewrite" (i.e., a new report) as it is a transformation of the old one. The writers had to step back from their experience and information in order to turn facts into concepts. Pinpointing the telling details was not enough: they had to articulate the meaning they saw in the data. Secondly, the writers had to build a rhetorical structure which acknowledged the function these ideas had for their reader. In the second version, the headings, topic sentences, and even some of the subjects and verbs reflect a new functional structure, focused on Process, People, and Problems. The report offers a hierarchical organization of the facts in which the hierarchy itself is based on issues both writer and reader agree are important. I think it likely that such transformations frequently go on in the early stages of the composing process for skilled writers. But for some writers the under-transformed Writer-Based prose of Draft 1 is also the final product and the starting point for our work as teachers.

In the remainder of this paper I will look at the features of Writer-Based prose and the ways it functions for the writer. Clearly, we need to know about Reader-Based prose in order to teach it. But it is also clear that writers already possess a great deal of intuitive knowledge about writing for audiences when they are stimulated to use it. As the case study shows, the concept of trying to transform Writer-Based prose for a reader is by itself a powerful tool. It helps writers identify the lineaments of a problem many can start to solve once they recognize it as a definable problem.

WRITER-BASED PROSE: FUNCTION, STRUCTURE, AND STYLE

While Writer-Based prose may be inadequately structured for a reader, it does possess a logic and structure of its own. Furthermore, that structure serves some important functions for the writer in his or her effort to think about a subject. It represents a practical strategy for dealing with information. If we could see Writer-Based prose as a *functional system*—not a set of random errors known only to English teachers—we would be better able to teach writing as a part of any discipline that asks people to express complex ideas.

According to Vygotsky, "the inner speech of the adult represents his 'thinking for himself' rather than social adaptation [communication to others]: i.e., it has the same function that egocentric speech has in the child" (*Language and Thought*, p. 18). It helps him solve problems. Vygotsky found that when a child who is trying to draw encounters an obstacle (no pencils) or a problem (what shall I call it?), the incidence of egocentric speech can double.

If we look at an analogous situation—an adult caught up in the complex mental process of composing—we can see that much of the adult's output is not well adapted for public consumption either. In studies of cognitive processes of

writers as they composed, J. R. Hayes and I observed much of the writer's
verbal output to be an attempt to manipulate stored information into some
acceptable pattern of meaning.[7] To do that, the writer generates a variety of
alternative relationships and trial formulations of the information she has in
mind. Many of these trial networks will be discarded; most will be significantly
altered through recombination and elaboration during the composing process.
In those cases in which the writer's first pass at articulating knowledge was also
the final draft—when she wrote it just as she thought it—the result was often a
series of semi-independent, juxtaposed networks, each with its own focus.

Whether such expression occurs in an experimental protocol or a written
draft, it reflects the working of the writer's mind upon his material. Because
dealing with one's material is a formidable enough task in itself, a writer may
allow himself to ignore the additional problem of accommodating a reader.
Writer-Based prose, then, functions as a medium for thinking. It offers the writer
the luxury of one less constraint. As we shall see, its typical structure and style
are simply paths left by the movement of the writer's mind.

The *structure* of Writer-Based prose reflects an economical strategy we have
for coping with information. Readers generally expect writers to produce complex concepts—to collect data and details under larger guiding ideas and place
those ideas in an integrated network. But as both Vygotsky and Piaget observed,
forming such complex concepts is a demanding cognitive task; if no one minds,
it is a lot easier to just list the parts. Nor is it surprising that in children two of
the hallmarks of egocentric speech are the absence of expressed causal relations and the tendency to express ideas without proof or development. Adults
too avoid the task of building complex concepts buttressed by development
and proof, by structuring their information in two distinctive ways: as a narrative of their own discovery process or as a survey of the data before them.

As we saw in the Oskaloosa Brewing Case Study, a *narrative* structured around
one's own discovery process may seem the most natural way to write. For this
reason it can sometimes be the best way as well, if a writer is trying to express a
complex network of information but is not yet sure how all the parts are related.
For example, my notes show that early fragments of this paper started out with
a narrative, list-like structure focused on my own experience: "Writer-Based
prose is a working hypothesis because it works in the classroom. In fact, when
I first started teaching the concept. . . . In fact, it was my students' intuitive
recognition of the difference between Writer-Based and Reader-Based style in
their own thought and writing. . . . It was their ability to use even a sketchy
version of the distinction to transform their own writing that led me to pursue
the idea more thoroughly."

The final version of this sketch (the paragraph numbered 2 on [p. 282]) keeps
the reference to teaching experience, but subordinates it to the more central

---

[7] L. Flower and J. Hayes, "Plans That Guide the Composing Process," in C. Frederikson, M.
Whiteman, and J. Dominic, eds., *Writing: The Nature, Development and Teaching of Written
Communication* (Hillsdale, N.J.: Lawrence Erlbaum, 1981).

issue of why the concept works. This transformation illustrates how a writer's major propositions can, on first appearance, emerge embedded in a narrative of the events or thoughts which spawned the proposition. In this example, the Writer-Based early version recorded the raw material of observations; the final draft formed them into concepts and conclusions.

This transformation process may take place regularly when a writer is trying to express complicated information which is not yet fully conceptualized. Although much of this mental work normally precedes actual writing, a first draft may simply reflect the writer's current place in the process. When this happens, rewriting and editing are vital operations. Far from being a simple matter of correcting errors, editing a first draft is often the act of transforming a narrative network of information into a more fully hierarchical set of propositions.

A second source of pre-fabricated structure for writers is the internal structure of the information itself. Writers use a *survey* strategy to compose because it is a powerful procedure for retrieving and organizing information. Unfortunately, the original organization of the data itself (e.g., the production process at Oskaloosa Brewing) rarely fits the most effective plan for any given piece of focused analytical writing.

The prose that results from such a survey can, of course, take as many forms as the data. It can range from a highly structured piece of discourse (the writer repeats a textbook exposition) to an unfocused printout of the writer's memories and thoughts on the subject. The form is merely a symptom, because the governing force is the writer's mental strategy: namely, to compose by surveying the available contents of memory without adapting them to a current purpose. The internal structure of the data dictates the rhetorical structure of the discourse, much as the proceedings of Congress organize the *Congressional Record*. As an information processor, the writer is performing what computer scientists would call a "memory dump": dutifully printing out memory in exactly the form in which it is stored.

A survey strategy offers the writer a useful way into the composing process in two ways. First, it eliminates many of the constraints normally imposed by a speech act, particularly the contract between reader and writer for mutually useful discourse. Secondly, a survey of one's own stored knowledge, marching along like a textbook or flowing with the tide of association, is far easier to write than a fresh or refocused conceptualization would be.

But clearly most of the advantages here accrue to the writer. One of the tacit assumptions of the Writer-Based writer is that, once the relevant information is presented, the reader will then do the work of abstracting the essential features, building a conceptual hierarchy, and transforming the whole discussion into a functional network of ideas.

Although Writer-Based prose often fails for readers and tends to preclude further concept formation, it may be a useful road into the creative process for some writers. The structures which fail to work for readers may be powerful strategies for retrieving information from memory and for exploring one's own knowledge network. This is illustrated in Linde and Labov's well-known New

York apartment tour experiment.[8] Interested in the strategies people use for retrieving information from memory and planning a discourse, Linde and Labov asked one hundred New Yorkers to "tell me the layout of your apartment" as a part of a "sociological survey." Only 3% of the subjects responded with a map which gave an overview and then filled in the details; for example, "I'd say it's laid out in a huge square pattern, broken down into 4 units." The overwhelming majority (97%) all solved the problem by describing a tour: "You walk in the front door. There was a narrow hallway. To the left, etc." Furthermore, they had a common set of rules for how to conduct the tour (e.g., you don't "walk into" a small room with no outlet, such as a pantry; you just say, "on the left is . . ."). Clearly the tour structure is so widely used because it is a remarkably efficient strategy for recovering all of the relevant information about one's apartment, yet without repeating any of it. For example, one rule for "touring" is that when you dead-end after walking through two rooms, you don't "walk" back but suddenly appear back in the hall.

For us, the revealing sidenote to this experiment is that although the tour strategy was intuitively selected by the overwhelming majority of the speakers, the resulting description was generally very difficult for the listener to follow and almost impossible to reproduce. The tour strategy is like the narrative and textbook structure in prose—it is a masterful method for searching memory but a dud for communicating that information to anyone else.

Finally, the *style* of Writer-Based prose also has its own logic. Its two main stylistic features grow out of the private nature of interior monologue, that is, of writing which is primarily a record or expression of the writer's flow of thought. The first feature is that in such monologues the organization of sentences and paragraphs reflects the shifting focus of the writer's attention. However, the psychological subject on which the writer is focused may not be reflected in the grammatical subject of the sentence or made explicit in the discussion at all. Secondly, the writer may depend on code words to carry his or her meaning. That is, the language may be "saturated with sense" and able to evoke—for the writer—a complex but unexpressed context.

Writers of formal written discourse have two goals for style which we can usefully distinguish from one another. One goal might be described as stylistic control, that is, the ability to choose a more embedded or more elegant transformation from variations which are roughly equivalent in meaning. The second goal is to create a completely autonomous text, that is, a text that does not need context, gestures, or audible effects to convey its meaning.

It is easy to see how the limits of short-term memory can affect a writer's stylistic control. For an inexperienced writer, the complex transformation of a periodic sentence—which would require remembering and relating a variety of elements and optional structures such as this sentence contains—can be a difficult juggling act. After all, the ability to form parallel constructions is not

---

[8] C. Linde and W. Labov, "Spatial Networks as a Site for the Study of Language and Thought," *Language*, 51 (1975), 924–939.

innate. Yet with practice many of these skills can become more automatic and require less conscious attention.

The second goal of formal written discourse—the complete autonomy of the text—leads to even more complex problems. According to David Olson, the history of written language has been the progressive creation of an instrument which could convey complete and explicit meanings in a text. The history of writing is the transformation of language from utterance to text—from oral meaning created within a shared context of a speaker and listener to a written meaning fully represented in an autonomous text.[9]

In contrast to this goal of autonomy, Writer-Based prose is writing whose meaning is still to an important degree in the writer's head. The culprit here is often the unstated psychological subject. The work of the "remedial" student is a good place to examine the phenomenon because it often reveals first thoughts more clearly than the reworked prose of a more experienced writer who edits as he or she writes. In the most imaginative, comprehensive and practical book to be written on the basic writer, Mina Shaughnessy has studied the linguistic strategies which lie behind the "errors" of many otherwise able young adults who have failed to master the written code. As we might predict, the ambiguous referent is ubiquitous in basic writing: *he*'s, *she*'s, and *it*'s are sprinkled through the prose without visible means of support. *It* frequently works as a code word for the subject the writer has in mind but not on the page. As Professor Shaughnessy says, *it* "frequently becomes a free-floating substitute for thoughts that the writer neglects to articulate and that the reader must usually strain to reach if he can."[10]

> With all the jobs available, he will have to know more of *it* because there is a great demand for *it*.

For the writer of the above sentence, the pronoun was probably not ambiguous at all; *it* no doubt referred to the psychological subject of his sentence. Psychologically, the subject of an utterance is the old information, the object you are looking at, the idea on which your attention has been focused. The predicate is the new information you are adding. This means that the psychological subject and grammatical subject of a sentence may not be the same at all. In our example, "college knowledge" was the writer's psychological subject—the topic he had been thinking about. The sentence itself is simply a psychological predicate. The pronoun *it* refers quite reasonably to the unstated but obvious subject in the writer's mind.

The subject is even more likely to be missing when a sentence refers to the writer herself or to "one" in her position. In the following examples, again from *Errors and Expectations,* the "unnecessary" subject is a person (like the writer) who has a chance to go to college.

[9] David R. Olson, "From Utterance to Text: The Bias of Language in Speech and Writing," *Harvard Educational Review,* 47 (1977), 257–281.

[10] Mina Shaughnessy, *Errors and Expectations* (New York: Oxford University Press, 1977), p. 69.

Even if a person graduated from high school who is going on to college to obtain a specific position in his career [   ] should first know how much in demand his possible future job really is.

[he]

If he doesn't because the U.S. Labor Department say's their wouldn't be enough jobs opened [   ] is a waste to society and a "cop-out" to humanity.

[he]

Unstated subjects can produce a variety of minor problems from ambiguous referents to amusing dangling modifiers (e.g., "driving around the mountain, a bear came into view"). Although prescriptive stylists are quite hard on such "errors," they are often cleared up by context or common sense. However, the controlling but unstated presence of a psychological subject can lead to some stylistic "errors" that do seriously disrupt communication. Sentence fragments are a good example.

One feature of an explicit, fully autonomous text is that the grammatical subject is usually a precise entity, often a word. By contrast, the psychological subject to which a writer wished to refer may be a complex event or entire network of information. Here written language is often rather intransigent; it is hard to refer to an entire clause or discussion unless one can produce a summary noun. Grammar, for example, normally forces us to select a specific referent for a pronoun or modifier: it wants referents and relations spelled out.[11] This specificity is, of course, its strength as a vehicle for precise reasoning and abstract thought. Errors arise when a writer uses one clause to announce his topic or psychological subject and a second clause to record a psychological predicate, a response to that old information. For example:

The jobs that are listed in the paper, I feel you need a college degree.

The job that my mother has, I know I could never be satisfied with it.

The preceding sentences are in error because they have failed to specify the grammatical relationship between their two elements. However, for anyone from the Bronx, each statement would be perfectly effective because it fits a familiar formula. It is an example of topicalization or Y-movement and fits a conventionalized, Yiddish-influenced intonation pattern much like the one in "Spinach— you can have it!" The sentences depend heavily on certain conventions of oral speech, and insofar as they invoke those patterns for the reader, they communicate effectively.[12]

However, most fragments do not succeed for the reader. And they fail, ironically enough, for the same reason—they too invoke intonation patterns in the reader which turn out to be misleading. The lack of punctuation gives off incorrect cues about how to segment the sentence. Set off on an incorrect intonation

---

[11] "Pronouns like *this, that, which* and *it* should not vaguely refer to an entire sentence or clause," and "Make a pronoun refer clearly to one antecedent, not uncertainly to two." Floyd Watkins, et al., *Practical English Handbook* (Boston: Houghton Mifflin, 1974), p. 30.

[12] I am greatly indebted here to Thomas Huckin for his insightful comments on style and to his work in linguistics on how intonation patterns affect writers and readers.

pattern, the thwarted reader must stop, reread and reinterpret the sentence. The following examples are from Maxine Hairston's *A Contemporary Rhetoric* (Boston: Houghton Mifflin, 1974):

> The authorities did not approve of their acts. These acts being considered detrimental to society. (society, they . . .)
>
> Young people need to be on their own. To show their parents that they are reliable. (reliable, young people . . .)

(p. 322)

Fragments are easy to avoid; they require only minimal tinkering to correct. Then why is the error so persistent? One possible reason is that for the writer the fragment is a fresh predicate intended to modify the entire preceding psychological subject. The writer wants to carry out a verbal trick easily managed in speech. For the reader, however, this minor grammatical oversight is significant. It sets up and violates both intonation patterns and strong structural expectations, such as those in the last example where we expect a pause and a noun phrase to follow "reliable." The fragment, which actually refers backward, is posing as an introductory clause.

The problem with fragments is that they are perfectly adequate for the writer. In speech they may even be an effective way to express a new idea which is predicated on the entire preceding unit thought. But in a written text, fragments are errors because they do not take the needs of the reader into consideration. Looked at this way, the "goodness" of a stylistic technique or grammatical rule such as parallelism, clear antecedents, or agreement is that it is geared to the habits, expectations, and needs of the reader as well as to the demands of textual autonomy.

Vygotsky noticed how the language of children and inner speech was often "saturated with sense." Similarly, the words a writer chooses can also operate as code words, condensing a wealth of meaning in an apparently innocuous word. The following examples come from an exercise which asks writers to identify and transform some of their own pieces of mental shorthand.

The students were asked to circle any code words or loaded expressions they found in their first drafts of a summer internship application. That is, they tried to identify those expressions that might convey only a general or vague meaning to a reader, but which represented a large body of facts, experiences, or ideas for them. They then treated this code word as one would any intuition—pushing it for its buried connections and turning those into a communicable idea. The results are not unlike those brilliant explications one often hears from students who tell you what their paper really meant. This example also shows how much detailed and perceptive thought can be lying behind a vague and conventional word:

> First Draft: "By having these two jobs, I was able to see the business in an entirely (different perspective.)" (Circle indicates a loaded expression marked by the writer.)
>
> Second Draft with explanation of what she actually had in mind in using the circled phrase: "By having these two jobs, I was able to see the true rela-

tionship and relative importance of the various departments in the company. I could see their mutual dependence and how an event in one part of the firm can have an important effect on another."

The tendency to think in code words is a fact of life for the writer. Yet the following example shows how much work can go into exploring our own saturated language. Like any intuition, such language is only a source of potential meanings, much as Aristotle's topics are places for finding potential arguments. In this extended example, the writer first explores her expression itself, laying out all the thoughts which were loosely connected under its name. This process of pushing our own language to give up its buried meanings forces us to make these loose connections explicit and, in the process, allows us to examine them critically. For the writer in our example, pushing her own key words leads to an important set of new ideas in the paper.

EXCERPT FROM AN APPLICATION FOR THE
NATIONAL INSTITUTE OF HEALTH INTERNSHIP PROGRAM

First Draft: "I want a career that will help other people while at the same time be challenging scientifically. I had the opportunity to do a biochemical assay for a neuropsychopharmacologist at X — Clinic in Chicago. Besides learning the scientific procedures and techniques that are used, I realized some of the (organizational, financial and people problems) which are encountered in research. This internship program would let me pursue further my interest in research, while concurrently exposing me to (relevant and diverse) areas of bioengineering."

EXCERPT FROM WRITER'S NOTES WORKING ON THE CIRCLED PHRASES

How did research of Sleep Center tie into overall program of X — Clinic? Not everyone within dept. knew what the others were doing, could not see overall picture of efforts.

Brainstorm

Dr. O—dept. head—trained for lab yet did 38-40 hrs. paperwork. Couldn't set up test assay in Sleep Center because needed equip. from biochem.

Difficulties in getting equipment

1. Politics between administrators
   Photometer at U. of —— even though Clinic had bought it.
2. Ordering time, not sufficient inventory, had to hunt through boxes for chemicals.
3. Had to schedule use by personal contact on borrowing equipment— done at time of use and no previous planning.

No definite guidelines had been given to biochem. people as to what was "going on" with assay. Partner who was supposed to learn assay was on vacation. Two people were learning, one was on vac.

No money from state for equipment or research grants.
Departments stealing from each other.
Lobbying, politics, included.

My supervisor from India, felt prejudices on job. Couldn't advance, told me life story and difficulties in obtaining jobs at Univ. Not interested in research at Clinic per se, looking for better opportunities, studying for Vet boards.

REVISION (ADDITIONS IN ITALICS)

"As a biomedical researcher, I would fulfill my goal of a career that will help other people while at the same time be challenging scientifically. I had exposure to research while doing a biochemical assay for a neuropsychophar-macologist at X —— Clinic in Chicago. Besides learning the scientific procedures and techniques that are used, I realized some of the organizational, financial and people problems which are encountered in research. *These problems included a lack of funds and equipment, disagreements among research staff, and the extensive amounts of time, paperwork and steps required for testing a hypothesis which was only one very small but necessary part of the overall project. But besides knowing some of the frustrations, I also know that many medical advancements, such as the cardiac pacemaker, artificial limbs and cures for diseases, exist and benefit many people because of the efforts of researchers.* Therefore I would like to pursue my interest in research by participating in the NIH Internship Program. The exposure to many *diverse projects, designed to better understand and improve the body's functioning,* would help me to decide which *areas of biomedical engineering to pursue.*"

We could sum up this analysis of style by noting two points. At times a Writer-Based prose style is simply an interior monologue in which some necessary information (such as intonation pattern or a psychological subject) is not expressed in the text. The solution to the reader's problem is relatively trivial in that it involves adding information that the writer already possesses. At other times, a style may be Writer-Based because the writer is thinking in code words at the level of intuited but unarticulated connections. Turning such saturated language into communicable ideas can require the writer to bring the entire composing process into play.

IMPLICATIONS FOR WRITERS AND TEACHERS

From an educational perspective, Writer-Based prose is one of the "problems" composition courses are designed to correct. It is a major cause of that notorious "breakdown" of communication between writer and reader. However, if we step back and look at it in the broader context of cognitive operations involved, we see that it represents a major, functional stage in the composing process and a powerful strategy well fitted to a part of the job of writing.

In the best of all possible worlds, good writers strive for Reader-Based prose from the very beginning: they retrieve and organize information within the framework of a reader/writer contract. Their top goal or initial question is not, "What do I know about physics, and in particular the physics of wind resistance?" but, "What does a model plane builder need to know?" Many times a writer can do this. For a physics teacher this particular writing problem would be a trivial one. However, for a person ten years out of Physics 101, simply retrieving any relevant information would be a full-time processing job. The reader would simply have to wait. For the inexperienced writer, trying to put complex thought into written language may also be task enough. In that case, the reader is an extra constraint that must wait its turn. A Reader-Based strategy which includes the reader in the entire thinking process is clearly the best way to write, but it is not always possible. When it is very difficult or impossible to write for a reader from the beginning, writing and then transforming Writer-Based prose is a practical alternative which breaks this complex process down into manageable parts. When transforming is a practiced skill, it enters naturally into the pulse of the composing process as a writer's constant, steady effort to test and adapt his or her thought to a reader's needs. Transforming Writer-Based prose is, then, not only a necessary procedure for all writers at times, but a useful place to start teaching intellectually significant writing skills.

In this final section, I will try to account for the peculiar virtues of Writer-Based prose and suggest ways that teachers of writing—in any field—can take advantage of them. Seen in the context of memory retrieval, Writer-Based thinking appears to be a tapline to the rich sources of episodic memory. In the context of the composing process, Writer-Based prose is a way to deal with the overload that writing often imposes on short-term memory. By teaching writers to use this transformation process, we can foster the peculiar strengths of Writer-Based thought and still alert writers to the next transformation that many simply fail to attempt.

One way to account for why Writer-Based prose seems to "come naturally" to most of us from time to time is to recognize its ties to our episodic as opposed to semantic memory. As Tulving describes it, "episodic memory is a more or less faithful record of a person's experiences." A statement drawn from episodic memory "refers to a personal experience that is remembered in its temporal-spatial relation to other such experiences. The remembered episodes are . . . autobiographical events, describable in terms of their perceptible dimensions or attributes."[13]

Semantic memory, by contrast, "is the memory necessary for the use of language. It is a mental thesaurus, organized knowledge a person possesses about words and other verbal symbols, their meaning and referents, about relations among them, and about rules, formulas, and algorithms for the manipulation of these symbols, concepts, and relations." Although we know that table salt is NaCl and that motivation is a mental state, we probably do not remember learning the fact or the first time we thought of that concept. In semantic memory, facts and concepts stand as the nexus for other words and symbols, but shorn of their temporal and autobiographical roots. If we ex-

---

[13] Edel Tulving, "Episodic and Semantic Memory," in Edel Tulving and Wayne Donaldson, eds., *Organization of Memory* (New York: Academic Press, 1972), p. 387.

plored the notion of "writing" in the semantic memory of someone we might produce a network such as this:

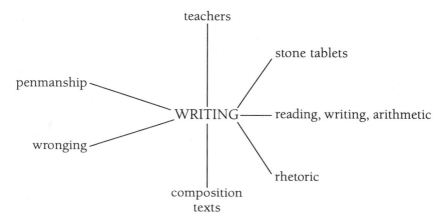

In an effort to retrieve what she or he knew about stone tablets, for example, this same person might turn to episodic memory: "I once heard a lecture on the Rosetta Stone, over in Maynard Hall. The woman, as I recall, said that . . . and I remember wondering if. . . ."

Writers obviously use both kinds of memory. The problem only arises when they confuse a fertile source of ideas in episodic memory with a final product. In fact, a study by Russo and Wisher argues that we sometimes store our ideas or images (the symbols of thought) with the mental operations we performed to produce these symbols.[14] Furthermore, it is easier to recall the symbols (that fleeting idea, perhaps) when we bring back the original operation. In other words, our own thinking acts can serve as memory cues, and the easiest way to recover some item from memory may be to *reprocess* it, to reconstruct the original thought process in which it appeared. Much Writer-Based prose appears to be doing just this—reprocessing an earlier thinking experience as a way to recover what one knows.

Writing is one of those activities that places an enormous burden on short-term or working memory. As George Miller put it, "The most glaring result [of numerous experiments] has been to highlight man's inadequacy as a communication channel. As the amount of input information is increased, the amount of information that the man transmits increases at first but then runs into a ceiling. . . . That ceiling is always very low. Indeed, it is an act of charity to call man a channel at all. Compared to telephone or television channels, man is better characterized as a bottleneck."[15]

The short-term memory is the active central processor of the mind, that is, it is the sum of all the information we can hold in conscious attention at one time.

[14] J. Russo and R. Wisher, "Reprocessing as a Recognition Cue," *Memory and Cognition,* 4 (1976), 683-689.

[15] George Miller, *The Psychology of Communication* (New York: Basic Books, 1967), p. 48.

We notice its capacity most acutely when we try to learn a new task, such as driving a car or playing bridge. Its limited capacity means that when faced with a complex problem—such as writing a college paper—we can hold and compare only a few alternative relationships in mind at once.

Trying to evaluate, elaborate, and relate all that we know on a given topic can easily overload the capacity of our working memory. Trying to compose even a single sentence can have the same effect, as we try to juggle grammatical and syntactic alternatives plus all the possibilities of tone, nuance, and rhythm even a simple sentence offers. Composing, then, is a cognitive activity that constantly threatens to overload short-term memory. For two reasons, Writer-Based prose is a highly effective strategy for dealing with this problem.

1. Because the characteristic structure of Writer-Based prose is often a list (either of mental events or the features of the topic) it temporarily suspends the additional problem of forming complex concepts. If that task is suspended indefinitely, the result will fail to be good analytic writing or serious thought, but as a first stage in the process of the list-structure has real value. It allows the writer freedom to generate a breadth of information and a variety of alternative relationships before locking himself or herself into a premature formulation. Furthermore, by allowing the writer to temporarily separate the two complex but somewhat different tasks of generating information and forming networks, each task may be performed more consciously and effectively.

2. Taking the perspective of another mind is also a demanding cognitive operation. It means holding not only your own knowledge network but someone else's in conscious attention and comparing them. Young children simply can't do it.[16] Adults choose not to do it when their central processing is already overloaded with the effort to generate and structure their own ideas. Writer-Based prose simply eliminates this constraint by temporarily dropping the reader out of the writer's deliberations.[17]

My own research suggests that good writers take advantage of their strategies in their composing process. They use scenarios, generate lists, and ignore the reader, but only for a while. Their composing process, unlike that of less effective writers, is marked by constant re-examination of their growing product and an attempt to refine, elaborate, or test its relationships, plus an attempt to anticipate the response of a reader. Everyone uses the strategies of Writer-Based prose; good writers go a step further to transform the writing these strategies produce.

---

[16] Marlene Scardamalia, "How Children Cope with the Cognitive Demands of Writing," in C. Frederikson, M. Whiteman, and J. Dominic, eds., *Writing: The Nature, Development and Teaching of Written Communication.*

[17] Linda Flower and John R. Hayes, "The Dynamics of Composing: Making and Juggling Constraints," in Lee Gregg and Irwin Steinberg, eds., *Cognitive Processes in Writing: An Interdisciplinary Approach* (Hillsdale, N.J.: Lawrence Erlbaum, 1979).

But what about the writers who fail to make this transformation or (like all of us) fail to do it adequately in places? This is the problem faced by all teachers who assign papers. I think this study has two main and quite happy implications for us as teachers and writers.

The first is that Writer-Based prose is not a composite of errors or a mistake that should be scrapped. Instead, it is a half-way place for many writers and often represents the results of an extensive search and selection process. As a stage in the composing process, it may be a rich compilation of significant thoughts which cohere *for the writer* into a network she or he has not yet fully articulated. Writer-Based prose is the writer's homework, and so long as the writer is also the audience, it may even be a well-thought-out communication.

The second happy implication is that writing Reader-Based prose is often simply the task of transforming the groundwork laid in the first stage of the process.[18] Good analytic writing is not different in kind from the Writer-Based thought that seems to come naturally. It is an extension of our communication with ourselves transformed in certain predictable ways to meet the needs of the reader. The most general transformation is simply to try to take into account the reader's purpose in reading. Most people have well-developed strategies for doing this when they talk. For a variety of reasons—from cognitive effort to the illusion of the omniscient teacher/reader—many people simply do not consider the reader when they write.

More specifically, the transformations that produce Reader-Based writing include these:

Selecting a focus of mutual interest to both reader and writer (e.g., moving from the Writer-Based focus of "How did I go about my research or reading of the assignment and what did I see?" to a focus on "What significant conclusions can be drawn and why?").

Moving from facts, scenarios, and details to concepts.

Transforming a narrative or textbook structure into a rhetorical structure built on the logical and hierarchical relationships between ideas and organized around the purpose for writing, rather than the writer's process.

Teaching writers to recognize their own Writer-Based writing and transform it has a number of advantages. It places a strong positive value on writing that represents an effort and achievement for the writer even though it fails to communicate to the reader. This legitimate recognition of the uncommunicated content of Writer-Based prose can give anyone, but especially inexperienced writers, the confidence and motivation to go on. By defining writing as a multi-stage process (instead of a holistic act of "expression"), we provide a rationale

---

[18] For a study of heuristics and teaching techniques for this transformation process see L. Flower and J. Hayes, "Problem-Solving Strategies and the Writing Process, *College English,* 39 (1977), 449–461.

for editing and alert many writers to a problem they could handle once it is set apart from other problems and they deliberately set out to tackle it. By recognizing transformation as a special skill and task, we give writers a greater degree of self-conscious control over the abilities they already have and a more precise introduction to some skills they may yet develop.

This article is reprinted from *College English* 41 (September 1979): 19-37. —Ed.

Janet Emig

WRITING AS A MODE OF LEARNING

Writing represents a unique mode of learning—not merely valuable, not merely special, but unique. That will be my contention in this paper. The thesis is straightforward. Writing serves learning uniquely because writing as process-and-product possesses a cluster of attributes that correspond uniquely to certain powerful learning strategies.

Although the notion is clearly debatable, it is scarcely a private belief. Some of the most distinguished contemporary psychologists have at least implied such a role for writing as heuristic. Lev Vygotsky, A. R. Luria, and Jerome Bruner, for example, have all pointed out that higher cognitive functions, such as analysis and synthesis, seem to develop most fully only with the support system of verbal language—particularly, it seems, of written language.[1] Some of their arguments and evidence will be incorporated here.

Here I have a prior purpose: to describe as tellingly as possible *how* writing uniquely corresponds to certain powerful learning strategies. Making such a case for the uniqueness of writing should logically and theoretically involve establishing many contrasts, distinctions between (1) writing and all other verbal language processes—listening, reading, and especially talking; (2) writing and all other forms of composing, such as composing a painting, a symphony, a dance, a film, a building; and (3) composing in words and composing in the two other major graphic symbol systems of mathematical equations and scientific formulae. For the purpose of this paper, the task is simpler, since most students are not permitted by most curricula to discover the values of composing, say, in dance, or even in film; and most students are not sophisticated enough to create, to originate formulations, using the highly abstruse symbol system of equations and formulae. Verbal language represents the most *available* medium for composing; in fact, the significance of sheer availability in its selection as a mode for learning can probably not be overstressed. But the uniqueness of writing among the verbal languaging processes does need to be established and supported if only because so many curricula and courses in English still consist almost exclusively of reading and listening.

WRITING AS A UNIQUE LANGUAGING PROCESS

Traditionally, the four languaging processes of listening, talking, reading, and writing are paired in either of two ways. The more informative seems to be the division many linguists make between first-order and second-order

---

[1] Lev S. Vygotsky, *Thought and Language*, trans. Eugenia Hanfmann and Gertrude Vakar (Cambridge: The M. I. T. Press, 1962); A. R. Luria and F. Ia. Yudovich, *Speech and the Development of Mental Processes in the Child*, ed. Joan Simon (Baltimore: Penguin, 1971); Jerome S. Bruner, *The Relevance of Education* (New York: W. W. Norton and Co., 1971).

299

processes, with talking and listening characterized as first-order processes; reading and writing, as second-order. First-order processes are acquired without formal or systematic instruction; the second-order processes of reading and writing tend to be learned initially only with the aid of formal and systematic instruction.

The less useful distinction is that between listening and reading as receptive functions and talking and writing as productive functions. Critics of these terms like Louise Rosenblatt rightfully point out that the connotation of passivity too often accompanies the notion of receptivity when reading, like listening, is a vital, construing act.

An additional distinction, so simple it may have been previously overlooked, resides in two criteria: the matters of origination and of graphic recording. Writing is originating and creating a unique verbal construct that is graphically recorded. Reading is creating or re-creating *but not* originating a verbal construct that is graphically recorded. Listening is creating or re-creating but not originating a verbal construct that is *not* graphically recorded. Talking is creating *and* originating a verbal construct that is *not* graphically recorded (except for the circuitous routing of a transcribed tape). Note that a distinction is being made between creating and originating, separable processes.

For talking, the nearest languaging process, additional distinctions should probably be made. (What follows is not a denigration of talk as a valuable mode of learning.) A silent classroom or one filled only with the teacher's voice is anathema to learning. For evidence of the cognitive value of talk, one can look to some of the persuasive monographs coming from the London Schools Council project on writing: *From Information to Understanding* by Nancy Martin or *From Talking to Writing* by Peter Medway.[2] We also know that for some of us, talking is a valuable, even necessary, form of pre-writing. In his curriculum, James Moffett makes the value of such talk quite explicit.

But to say that talking is a valuable form of pre-writing is not to say that writing is talk recorded, an inaccuracy appearing in far too many composition texts. Rather, a number of contemporary trans-disciplinary sources suggest that talking and writing may emanate from different organic sources and represent quite different, possibly distinct, language functions. In *Thought and Language*, Vygotsky notes that "written speech is a separate linguistic function, differing from oral speech in both structure and mode of functioning."[3] The sociolinguist Dell Hymes, in a valuable issue of *Daedalus*, "Language as a Human Problem," makes a comparable point: "That speech and writing are not simply interchangeable, and have developed historically in ways at least partly autonomous, is obvious."[4] At the first session of

---

[2] Nancy Martin, *From Information to Understanding* (London: Schools Council Project Writing across the Curriculum, 11–13, 1973); Peter Medway, *From Talking to Writing* (London: Schools Council Project Writing across the Curriculum, 11–13, 1973).

[3] Vygotsky, p. 98.

[4] Dell Hymes, "On the Origins and Foundations of Inequality among Speakers," *Daedalus*, 102 (Summer, 1973), 69.

the Buffalo Conference on Researching Composition (4-5 October 1975), the first point of unanimity among the participant-speakers with interests in developmental psychology, media, dreams and aphasia was that talking and writing were markedly different functions.[5] Some of us who work rather steadily with writing research agree. We also believe that there are hazards, conceptually and pedagogically, in creating too complete an analogy between talking and writing, in blurring the very real differences between the two.

What are these differences?

1. Writing is learned behavior; talking is natural, even irrepressible, behavior.
2. Writing then is an artificial process; talking is not.
3. Writing is a technological device—not the wheel, but early enough to qualify as primary technology; talking is organic, natural, earlier.
4. Most writing is slower than most talking.
5. Writing is stark, barren, even naked as a medium; talking is rich, luxuriant, inherently redundant.
6. Talk leans on the environment; writing must provide its own context.
7. With writing, the audience is usually absent; with talking, the listener is usually present.
8. Writing usually results in a visible graphic product; talking usually does not.
9. Perhaps because there is a product involved, writing tends to be a more responsible and committed act than talking.
10. It can be said that throughout history, an aura, an ambience, a mystique has usually encircled the written word; the spoken word has for the most part proved ephemeral and [been] treated mundanely (ignore, please, our recent national history).
11. Because writing is often our representation of the world made visible, embodying both process and product, writing is more readily a form and source of learning than talking.

UNIQUE CORRESPONDENCES BETWEEN LEARNING AND WRITING

What then are some *unique* correspondences between learning and writing? To begin with some definitions: Learning can be defined in many ways, according to one's predilections and training, with all statements about learning of course hypothetical. Definitions range from the chemophysiological ("Learning is changed patterns of protein synthesis in relevant portions of the cortex")[6] to transactive views drawn from both

---

[5] Participant-speakers were Loren Barrett, University of Michigan; Gerald O'Grady, SUNY/Buffalo; Hollis Frampton, SUNY/Buffalo; and Janet Emig, Rutgers.

[6] George Steiner, *After Babel: Aspects of Language and Translation* (New York: Oxford University Press, 1975), p. 287.

philosophy and psychology (John Dewey, Jean Piaget) that learning is the re-organization or confirmation of a cognitive scheme in light of an experience.[7] What the speculations seem to share is consensus about certain features and strategies that characterize successful learning. These include the importance of the classic attributes of reinforcement and feedback. In most hypotheses, successful learning is also connective and selective. Additionally, it makes use of propositions, hypotheses, and other elegant summarizers. Finally, it is active, engaged, personal—more specifically, self-rhythmed—in nature.

Jerome Bruner, like Jean Piaget, through a comparable set of categories, posits three major ways in which we represent and deal with actuality: (1) enactive—we learn "by doing"; (2) iconic—we learn "by depiction in an image"; and (3) representational or symbolic—we learn "by restatement in words."[8] To overstate the matter, in enactive learning, the hand predominates; in iconic, the eye; and in symbolic, the brain.

What is striking about writing as a process is that, by its very nature, all three ways of dealing with actuality are simultaneously or almost simultaneously deployed. That is, the symbolic transformation of experience through the specific symbol system of verbal language is shaped into an icon, the graphic product by the enactive hand. If the most efficacious learning occurs when learning is reinforced, then writing through its inherent reinforcing cycle involving hand, eye, and brain marks a uniquely powerful multirepresentational mode for learning.

Writing is also integrative in perhaps the most basic possible sense: the organic, the functional. Writing involves the fullest possible functioning of the brain, which entails the active participation in the process of both the left and right hemispheres. Writing is markedly bispheral, although in some popular accounts, writing is inaccurately presented as a chiefly left-hemisphere activity, perhaps because the linear written product is somehow regarded as analogue for the process that created it; and the left hemisphere seems to process material linearly.

The right hemisphere, however, seems to make at least three, perhaps four, major contributions to the writing process—probably, to the creative process generically. First, several researchers, such as Geschwind and Snyder of Harvard and Zaidal of Cal Tech, through markedly different experiments, have very tentatively suggested that the right hemisphere is the sphere, even the *seat*, of emotions.[9] Second—or perhaps as an illustration of the first—Howard Gardner, in his important study of the brain-damaged, notes that our sense of emotional appropriateness in discourse may reside in the right sphere:

[7] John Dewey, *Experience and Education* (New York: Macmillan, 1938); Jean Piaget, *Biology and Knowledge: An Essay on the Relations between Organic Regulations and Cognitive Processes* (Chicago: University of Chicago Press, 1971).

[8] Bruner, pp. 7-8.

[9] Boyce Rensberger, "Language Ability Found in Right Side of Brain," *New York Times,* 1 August 1975, p. 14.

Emotional appropriateness, in sum—being related not only to *what* is said, but to how it is said and to what is *not* said, as well—is crucially dependent on right hemisphere intactness.[10]

Third, the right hemisphere seems to be the source of intuition, of sudden gestalts, of flashes of images, of abstractions occurring as visual or spatial wholes, as the initiating metaphors in the creative process. A familiar example: William Faulkner noted in his *Paris Review* interview that *The Sound and the Fury* began as the image of a little girl's muddy drawers as she sat in a tree watching her grandmother's funeral.[11]

Also, a unique form of feedback, as well as reinforcement, exists with writing, because information from the *process* is immediately and visibly available as that portion of the *product* already written. The importance for learning of a product in a familiar and available medium for immediate, literal (that is, visual) re-scanning and review cannot perhaps be overstated. In his remarkable study of purportedly blind sculptors, Géza Révész found that without sight, persons cannot move beyond a literal transcription of elements into any manner of symbolic transformation—by definition, the central requirement for reformulation and re-interpretation, i.e., revision, that most aptly named process.[12]

As noted in the second paragraph, Vygotsky and Luria, like Bruner, have written importantly about the connections between learning and writing. In his essay "The Psychobiology of Psychology," Bruner lists as one of six axioms regarding learning: "We are connective."[13] Another correspondence then between learning and writing: in *Thought and Language*, Vygotsky notes that writing makes a unique demand in that the writer must engage in "deliberate semantics"—in Vygotsky's elegant phrase, "deliberate structuring of the web of meaning."[14] Such structuring is required because, for Vygotsky, writing centrally represents an expansion of inner speech, that mode whereby we talk to ourselves, which is "maximally compact" and "almost entirely predicative"; written speech is a mode which is "maximally detailed" and which requires explicitly supplied subjects and topics. The medium then of written verbal language requires the establishment of systematic connections and relationships. Clear writing by definition is that writing which signals without ambiguity the nature of conceptual relationships, whether they be coordinate, subordinate, superordinate, causal, or something other.

Successful learning is also engaged, committed, personal learning. Indeed, impersonal learning may be an anomalous concept, like the very notion of objectivism itself. As Michael Polanyi states simply at the beginning of *Personal*

[10] Howard Gardner, *The Shattered Mind: The Person after Brain Damage* (New York: Alfred A. Knopf, 1975), p. 372.

[11] William Faulkner, *Writers at Work: The Paris Review Interviews*, ed. Malcolm Cowley (New York: The Viking Press, 1959), p. 130.

[12] Géza Révész, *Psychology and Art of the Blind*, trans. H. A. Wolff (London: Longmans-Green, 1950).

[13] Bruner, p. 126.

[14] Vygotsky, p. 100.

Knowledge: "the ideal of strict objectivism is absurd." (How many courses and curricula in English, science, and all else does that one sentence reduce to rubble?) Indeed, the theme of *Personal Knowledge* is that

> into every act of knowing there enters a passionate contribution of the person knowing what is being known, ... this coefficient is no mere imperfection but a vital component of his knowledge.[15]

In *Zen and the Art of Motorcycle Maintenance*, Robert Pirsig states a comparable theme:

> The Quality which creates the world emerges as *a relationship* between man and his experience. He is a *participant* in the creation of all things.[16]

Finally, the psychologist George Kelly has as the central notion in his subtle and compelling theory of personal constructs man as a scientist steadily and actively engaged in making and re-making his hypotheses about the nature of the universe.[17]

We are acquiring as well some empirical confirmation about the importance of engagement in, as well as self-selection of, a subject for the student learning to write and writing to learn. The recent Sanders and Littlefield study, reported in *Research in the Teaching of English*, is persuasive evidence on this point, as well as being a model for a certain type of research.[18]

As Luria implies in the quotation [below], writing is self-rhythmed. One writes best as one learns best, at one's own pace. Or to connect the two processes, writing can sponsor learning because it can match its pace. Support for the importance of self-pacing to learning can be found in Benjamin Bloom's important study "Time and Learning."[19] Evidence for the significance of self-pacing to writing can be found in the reason Jean-Paul Sartre gave last summer for not using the tape-recorder when he announced that blindness in his second eye had forced him to give up writing:

> I think there is an enormous difference between speaking and writing. One rereads what one rewrites. But one can read slowly or quickly: in other words, you do not know how long you will have to take deliberating over a sentence. ... If I listen to a tape recorder, the listening speed is determined by the speed at which the tape turns and not by my own needs. Therefore I will always be either lagging behind or running ahead of the machine.[20]

---

[15] Michael Polanyi, *Personal Knowledge: Toward a Post-Critical Philosophy* (Chicago: University of Chicago Press, 1958), p. viii.

[16] Robert Pirsig, *Zen and the Art of Motorcycle Maintenance* (New York: William Morrow and Co., Inc., 1974), p. 212.

[17] George Kelly, *A Theory of Personality: The Psychology of Personal Constructs* (New York, W. W. Norton and Co., 1963).

[18] Sara E. Sanders and John H. Littlefield, "Perhaps Test Essays Can Reflect Significant Improvement in Freshman Composition: Report on a Successful Attempt," *RTE*, 9 (Fall, 1975), 145-153.

[19] Benjamin Bloom, "Time and Learning," *American Psychologist*, 29 (September, 1974), 682-688.

[20] Jean-Paul Sartre, "Sartre at Seventy: An Interview," with Michael Contat, *New York Review of Books*, 7 August 1975.

Writing is connective as a process in a more subtle and perhaps more significant way, as Luria points out in what may be the most powerful paragraph of rationale ever supplied for writing as a heuristic:

> Written speech is bound up with the inhibition of immediate synpractical connections. It assumes a much slower, repeated mediating process of analysis and synthesis, which makes it possible not only to develop the required thought, but even to revert to its earlier stages, thus transforming the sequential chain of connections in a simultaneous, self-reviewing structure. Written speech thus represents a new and powerful instrument of thought.[21]

But first to explicate: writing inhibits "immediate synpractical connections." Luria defines *synpraxis* as "concrete-active" situations in which language does not exist independently but as a "fragment" of an ongoing action "outside of which it is incomprehensible."[22] In *Language and Learning*, James Britton defines it succinctly as "speech-cum-action."[23] Writing, unlike talking, restrains dependence upon the actual situation. Writing as a mode is inherently more

---

FIGURE 1. Unique cluster of correspondences between certain learning strategies and certain attributes of writing

Selected characteristics of successful learning strategies	Selected attributes of writing, process and product
(1) Profits from multi-representational and integrative reinforcement	(1) Represents process [as] uniquely multirepresentational and integrative
(2) Seeks self-provided feedback:	(2) Represents powerful instance of self-provided feedback:
(a) immediate	(a) provides product uniquely available for *immediate* feedback (review and re-evaluation)
(b) long-term	(b) provides record of evolution of thought since writing is epigenetic as process-and-product
(3) Is connective:	(3) Provides connections:
(a) makes generative conceptual groupings, synthetic and analytic	(a) establishes explicit and systematic conceptual groupings through lexical, syntactic, and rhetorical devices
(b) proceeds from propositions, hypotheses, and other elegant summarizers	(b) represents most available means (verbal language) for economic recording of abstract formulations
(4) Is active, engaged, personal—notably, self-rhythmed	(4) Is active, engaged, personal—notably, self-rhythmed

---

[21] Luria, p. 118.

[22] Luria, p. 50.

[23] James Britton, *Language and Learning* (Baltimore: Penguin, 1971), pp. 10–11.

self-reliant than speaking. Moreover, as Bruner states in explicating Vygotsky, "Writing virtually forces a remoteness of reference on the language user."[24]

Luria notes what has already been noted above: that writing, typically, is a "much slower" process than talking. But then he points out the relation of this slower pace to learning: this slower pace allows for—indeed encourages—the shuttling among past, present, and future. Writing, in other words, connects the three major tenses of our experience to make meaning. And the two major modes by which these three aspects are united are the processes of analysis and synthesis: analysis, the breaking of entities into their constituent parts; and synthesis, combining or fusing these, often into fresh arrangements or amalgams.

Finally, writing is epigenetic, with the complex evolutionary development of thought steadily and graphically visible and available throughout as a record of the journey, from jottings and notes to full discursive formulations.

For a summary of the correspondence stressed here between certain learning strategies and certain attributes of writing see Figure 1.

This essay represents a first effort to make a certain kind of case for writing—specifically, to show its unique value for learning. It is at once over-elaborate and under-specific. Too much of the formulation is in the off-putting jargon of the learning theorist, when my own predilection would have been to emulate George Kelly and to avoid terms like *reinforcement* and *feedback* since their use implies that I live inside a certain paradigm about learning I don't truly inhabit. Yet I hope that the essay will start a crucial line of inquiry; for unless the losses to learners of not writing are compellingly described and substantiated by experimental and speculative research, writing itself as a central academic process may not long endure.

---

[24] Bruner, p. 47.

This article is reprinted from *College Composition and Communication* 28 (May 1977): 122–28. —Ed.

Nancy Sommers

RESPONDING TO
STUDENT WRITING

More than any other enterprise in the teaching of writing, responding to and commenting on student writing consumes the largest proportion of our time. Most teachers estimate that it takes them at least 20 to 40 minutes to comment on an individual student paper, and those 20 to 40 minutes times 20 students per class, times 8 papers, more or less, during the course of a semester add up to an enormous amount of time. With so much time and energy directed to a single activity, it is important for us to understand the nature of the enterprise. For it seems, paradoxically enough, that although commenting on student writing is the most widely used method for responding to student writing, it is the least understood. We do not know in any definitive way what constitutes thoughtful commentary or what effect, if any, our comments have on helping our students become more effective writers.

Theoretically, at least, we know that we comment on our students' writing for the same reasons professional editors comment on the work of professional writers or for the same reasons we ask our colleagues to read and respond to our own writing. As writers we need and want thoughtful commentary to show us when we have communicated our ideas and when not, raising questions from a reader's point of view that may not have occurred to us as writers. We want to know if our writing has communicated our intended meaning and, if not, what questions or discrepancies our reader sees that we, as writers, are blind to.

In commenting on our students' writing, however, we have an additional pedagogical purpose. As teachers, we know that most students find it difficult to imagine a reader's response in advance, and to use such responses as a guide in composing. Thus, we comment on student writing to dramatize the presence of a reader, to help our students to become that questioning reader themselves, because, ultimately, we believe that becoming such a reader will help them to evaluate what they have written and develop control over their writing.[1]

Even more specifically, however, we comment on student writing because we believe that it is necessary for us to offer assistance to student writers when they are in the process of composing a text, rather than after the text has been completed. Comments create the motive for doing something different in the next draft; thoughtful comments create the motive for revising. Without comments from their teachers or from their peers, student writers will revise in a consistently narrow and predictable way. Without comments from readers, students assume that their writing has communicated their meaning and perceive no need for revising the substance of their text.[2]

Yet as much as we as informed professionals believe in the soundness of this approach to responding to student writing, we also realize that we don't know how our theory squares with teachers' actual practice—do teachers comment and students revise as the theory predicts they should? For the past year my colleagues Lil Brannon, Cyril Knoblach, and I have been researching this problem, attempting to discover not only what messages teachers give their students through their comments, but also what determines which of these comments the students choose to use or to ignore when revising. Our research has been entirely focused on comments teachers write to motivate revisions. We have studied the commenting styles of thirty-five teachers at New York University and the University of Oklahoma, studying the comments these teachers wrote on first and second drafts, and interviewing a representative number of these teachers and their students. All teachers also commented on the same set of three student essays. As an additional reference point one of the student essays was typed into the computer that had been programmed with the "Writer's Workbench," a package of twenty-three programs developed by Bell Laboratories to help computers and writers work together to improve a text rapidly. Within a few minutes, the computer delivered editorial comments on the student's text, identifying all spelling and punctuation errors, isolating problems with wordy or misused phrases, and suggesting alternatives, offering stylistic analysis of sentence types, sentence beginnings, and sentence lengths, and finally, giving our freshman essay a Kincaid readability score of eighth-grade which, as the computer program informed us, "is a low score for this type of document." The sharp contrast between the teachers' comments and those of the computer highlighted how arbitrary and idiosyncratic most of our teachers' comments are. Besides, the calm, reasonable language of the computer provided quite a contrast to the hostility and mean-spiritedness of most of the teachers' comments.

The first finding from our research on styles of commenting is that *teachers' comments can take students' attention away from their own purposes in writing a particular text and focus that attention on the teachers' purpose in commenting.* The teacher appropriates the text from the student by confusing the student's purpose in writing the text with her own purpose in commenting. Students make the changes the teacher wants rather than those that the student perceives are necessary, since the teachers' concerns imposed on the text create the reasons for the subsequent changes. We have all heard our perplexed students say to us when confused by our comments: "I don't understand how you want me to change this" or "Tell me what you want me to do." In the beginning of the process there was the writer, her words, and her desire to communicate her ideas. But after the comments of the teacher are imposed on the first or second draft, the student's attention dramatically shifts from "This is what I want to say" to "This is what *you* the teacher are asking me to do."

This appropriation of the text by the teacher happens particularly when teachers identify errors in usage, diction, and style in a first draft and ask students to correct these errors when they revise; such comments give the student an impression of the importance of these errors that is all out of proportion to how they should view these errors at this point in the process. The comments create the concern that these "accidents of discourse" need to be attended to before the meaning of the text is attended to.

It would not be so bad if students were only commanded to correct errors, but, more often than not, students are given contradictory messages; they are commanded to edit a sentence to avoid an error or to condense a sentence to achieve greater brevity of style, and then told in the margins that the particular paragraph needs to be more specific or to be developed more. An example of this problem can be seen in the following student paragraph:

> *wordy – be precise*   *which Sunday?*   *comma needed*
> Every year [on one Sunday in the middle of January]
>   *word choice*
> tens of millions of people cancel all events, plans
>
> or work to watch the Super Bowl. This audience in-
>   *wordy*
> cludes [little boys and girls, old people, and house-
>   *Be specific – what reasons?*
> wives and men.] Many reasons have been given to ex-
>   *and why*
> plain why the Super Bowl has become so popular that
>   *what spots?*
> commercial spots/cost up to $100,000.00. One explana-
> *awkward*
> tion is that people like to take sides and root for a
>   *another what?*   *spelling*
> team. Another is that some people like the pagentry
>
> and excitement of the event. These reasons alone,
>   *too*
>   *colloquial*
> however, do not explain a happening as big as the
>
> Super Bowl.

(left margin: You need to do more research.)

(right margin: This paragraph needs to be expanded in order to be more interesting to the reader.)

In commenting on this draft, the teacher has shown the student how to edit the sentences, but then commands the student to expand the paragraph in order to make it more interesting to a reader. The interlinear comments and the marginal comments represent two separate tasks for this student; the interlinear comments encourage the student to see the text as a fixed piece, frozen in time, that just needs some editing. The marginal comments, however, suggest that the meaning of the text is not fixed, but rather that the student still needs to develop the meaning by doing some more research. Students are commanded to edit and develop at the same time; the remarkable contradiction of developing a paragraph after editing the sentences in it represents the confusion we encountered in our teachers' commenting styles. These different signals given to students, to edit and develop, to condense and elaborate, represent also the failure of teachers' comments to direct genuine revision of a text as a whole.

Moreover, the comments are worded in such a way that it is difficult for students to know what is the most important problem in the text and what problems are of lesser importance. No scale of concerns is offered to a student with the result that a comment about spelling or a comment about an awkward sentence is given weight equal to a comment about organization or logic. The comment that seemed to represent this problem best was one teacher's command to his student: "Check your commas and semicolons and think more about what you are thinking about." The language of the comments makes it difficult for a student to sort out and decide what is most important and what is least important.

When the teacher appropriates the text for the student in this way, students are encouraged to see their writing as a series of parts—words, sentences, paragraphs—and not as a whole discourse. The comments encourage the students to believe that their first drafts are finished drafts, not invention drafts, and that all they need to do is patch and polish their writing. That is, teachers' comments do not provide their students with an inherent reason for revising the structure and meaning of their texts, since the comments suggest to students that the meaning of their text is already there, finished, produced, and all that is necessary is a better word or phrase. The processes of revising, editing, and proofreading are collapsed and reduced to a single trivial activity, and the students' misunderstanding of the revision process as a rewording activity is reinforced by their teachers' comments.

It is possible, and it quite often happens, that students follow every comment and fix their texts appropriately as requested, but their texts are not improved substantially, or, even worse, their revised drafts are inferior to their previous drafts. Since the teachers' comments take the students' attention away from their own original purposes, students concentrate more, as I have noted, on what the teachers commanded them to do than on what they are trying to say. Sometimes students do not understand the purpose behind their teachers' comments and take these comments very literally. At other times students understand the comments, but the teacher has misread the text and the comments, unfortunately, are not applicable. For instance, we repeatedly saw comments in which teachers commanded students to reduce and condense what was written, when in fact what the text really needed at this stage was to be expanded in conception and scope.

The process of revising always involves a risk. But, too often revision becomes a balancing act for students in which they make the changes that are requested but do not take the risk of changing anything that was not commented on, even if the students sense that other changes are needed. A more effective text does not often evolve from such changes alone, yet the student does not want to take the chance of reducing a finished, albeit inadequate, paragraph to chaos—to fragments—in order to rebuild it, if such changes have not been requested by the teacher.

The second finding from our study is that *most teachers' comments are not text-specific and could be interchanged, rubber-stamped, from text to text*. The comments are not anchored in the particulars of the students' texts, but rather are a series of vague directives that are not text-specific. Students are commanded to "think more about [their] audience, avoid colloquial language, avoid the passive, avoid prepositions at the end of sentences or conjunctions at the beginning of sentences, be clear, be specific, be precise, but above all, think more about what [they] are thinking about." The comments on the following student paragraph illustrate this problem:

Begin by telling your reader what you are going to write about

In the sixties it was drugs, in the seventies it was

avoid "one of the"

rock and roll. Now in the eighties, <u>one of the</u> most

controversial subjects is nuclear power. The United

elaborate

States is <u>in great need of its own</u> source of power.

Because of environmentalists, coal is not an accept-

able source of energy. [Solar and wind power have not

be specific

yet received the technology necessary to use them.] It

avoid "it seems"

<u>seems</u> that nuclear power is the only feasible means

right now for obtaining self-sufficient power. How-

ever, too large a percentage of the population are

against nuclear power claiming it is unsafe. With as

be precise

many <u>problems</u> as the United States is having concern-

ing energy, it seems a shame that the public is so

quick to "can" a very feasible means of power. Nuclear

energy should not be given up on, but rather, more

nuclear plants should be built.

think more about your reader

Thesis sentence needed.

One could easily remove all the comments from this paragraph and rubber-stamp them on another student text, and they would make as much or as little sense on the second text as they do here.

We have observed an overwhelming similarity in the generalities and abstract commands given to students. There seems to be among teachers an accepted, albeit unwritten canon for commenting on student texts. This uniform code of commands, requests, and pleadings demonstrates that the teacher holds a license for vagueness while the student is commanded to be specific. The students we interviewed admitted to having a great difficulty with these vague directives. The students stated that when a teacher writes in the margins or as an end comment, "choose precise language," or "think more about your audience," revising becomes a guessing game. In effect, the teacher is saying to the student, "Somewhere in this paper is imprecise language or lack of awareness of an audience and you must find it." The problem presented by these vague commands is compounded for the students when they are not offered any strategies for carrying out these commands. Students are told that they have done something wrong and that there is something in their text that needs to be fixed before the text is acceptable. But to tell students that they have done something wrong is not to tell them what to do about it. In order to offer a useful revision strategy to a student, the teacher must anchor that strategy in the specifics of the student's text. For instance, to tell our student, the author of the above paragraph, "to be specific," or "to elaborate," does not show our student what questions the reader has about the meaning of the text, or what breaks in the logic exist, that could be resolved if the writer supplied information; nor is the student shown how to achieve the desired specificity.

Instead of offering strategies, the teachers offer what is interpreted by students as rules for composing; the comments suggest to students that writing is just a matter of following rules. Indeed, the teachers seem to impose a series of abstract rules about written products even when some of them are not appropriate for the specific text the student is creating.[3] For instance, the student author of our sample paragraph presented above is commanded to follow the conventional rules for writing a five-paragraph essay—to begin the introductory paragraph by telling his reader what he is going to say and to end the paragraph with a thesis sentence. Somehow these abstract rules about what five-paragraph products should look like do not seem applicable to the problems this student must confront when revising, nor are the rules specific strategies he could use when revising. There are many inchoate ideas ready to be exploited in this paragraph, but the rules do not help the student to take stock of his (or her) ideas and use the opportunity he has, during revision, to develop those ideas.

The problem here is a confusion of process and product; what one has to say about the process is different from what one has to say about the product. Teachers who use this method of commenting are formulating their comments as if these drafts were finished drafts and were not going to be revised. Their commenting vocabularies have not been adapted to revision and they comment on first drafts as if they were justifying a grade or as if the first draft were the final draft.

Our summary finding, therefore, from this research on styles of commenting is that the news from the classroom is not good. For the most part, teachers do not respond to student writing with the kind of thoughtful commentary which will help students to engage with the issues they are writing about or which will help them think about their purposes and goals in writing a specific text. In defense of our teachers, however, they told us that responding to student writing was rarely stressed in their teacher-training or in writing workshops; they had been trained in various prewriting techniques, in constructing assignments, and in evaluating papers for grades, but rarely in the process of reading a student text for meaning or in offering commentary to motivate revision. The problem is that most of us as teachers of writing have been trained to read and interpret literary texts for meaning, but, unfortunately, we have not been trained to act upon the same set of assumptions in reading student texts as we follow in reading literary texts.[4] Thus, we read student texts with biases about what the writer should have said or about what he or she should have written, and our biases determine how we will comprehend the text. We read with our preconceptions and preoccupations, expecting to find errors, and the result is that we find errors and misread our students' texts.[5] We find what we look for; instead of reading and responding to the meaning of a text, we correct our students' writing. We need to reverse this approach. Instead of finding errors or showing students how to patch up parts of their texts, we need to sabotage our students' conviction that the drafts they have written are complete and coherent. Our comments need to offer student revision tasks of a different order of complexity and sophistication from the ones that they themselves identify, by forcing students back into the chaos, back to the point where they are shaping and restructuring their meaning.[6]

For if the content of a text is lacking in substance and meaning, if the order of the parts must be rearranged significantly in the next draft, if paragraphs must be restructured for logic and clarity, then many sentences are likely to be changed or deleted anyway. There seems to be no point in having students correct usage errors or condense sentences that are likely to disappear before the next draft is completed. In fact, to identify such problems in a text at this early first draft stage, when such problems are likely to abound, can give a student a disproportionate sense of their importance at this stage in the writing process.[7] In responding to our students' writing, we should be guided by the recognition that it is not spelling or usage problems that we as writers first worry about when drafting and revising our texts.

We need to develop an appropriate level of response for commenting on a first draft, and to differentiate that from the level suitable to a second or third draft. Our comments need to be suited to the draft we are reading. In a first or second draft, we need to respond as any reader would, registering questions, reflecting befuddlement, and noting places where we are puzzled about the meaning of the text. Comments should point to breaks in logic, disruptions in meaning, or missing information. Our goal in commenting on early drafts should be to engage students with the issues they are considering and help them clarify their purposes and reasons in writing their specific text.

For instance, the major rhetorical problem of the essay written by the student who wrote the first paragraph (the paragraph on nuclear power) quoted above was that the student had two principal arguments running through his text, each of which brought the other into question. On the one hand, he argued that we must use nuclear power, unpleasant as it is, because we have nothing else to use; though nuclear energy is a problematic source of energy, it is the best of a bad lot. On the other hand, he also argued that nuclear energy is really quite safe and therefore should be our primary resource. Comments on this student's first draft need to point out this break in logic and show the student that if we accept his first argument, then his second argument sounds fishy. But if we accept his second argument, his first argument sounds contradictory. The teacher's comments need to engage this student writer with this basic rhetorical and conceptual problem in his first draft rather than impose a series of abstract commands and rules upon his text.

Written comments need to be viewed not as an end in themselves—a way for teachers to satisfy themselves that they have done their jobs—but rather as a means for helping students to become more effective writers. As a means for helping students, they have limitations; they are, in fact, disembodied remarks— one absent writer responding to another absent writer. The key to successful commenting is to have what is said in the comments and what is done in the classroom mutually reinforce and enrich each other. Commenting on papers assists the writing course in achieving its purpose; classroom activities and the comments we write to our students need to be connected. Written comments need to be an extension of the teacher's voice—an extension of the teacher as reader. Exercises in such activities as revising a whole text or individual paragraphs together in class, noting how the sense of the whole dictates the smaller changes, looking at options, evaluating actual choices, and then discussing the effect of these changes on revised drafts—such exercises need to be designed to take students through the cycles of revising and to help them overcome their anxiety about revising: that anxiety we all feel at reducing what looks like a finished draft into fragments and chaos.

The challenge we face as teachers is to develop comments which will provide an inherent reason for students to revise; it is a sense of revision as discovery, as a repeated process of beginning again, as starting out new, that our students have not learned. We need to show our students how to seek, in the possibility of revision, the dissonances of discovery—to show them through our comments why new choices would positively change their texts, and thus to show them the potential for development implicit in their own writing.

NOTES

[1] C. H. Knoblauch and Lil Brannon, "Teacher Commentary on Student Writing: The State of the Art," *Freshman English News*, 10 (Fall 1981), 1-3.

[2] For an extended discussion of revision strategies of student writers see Nancy Sommers, "Revision Strategies of Student Writers and Experienced Adult Writers," *College Composition and Communication*, 31 (December 1980), 378-388.

[3] Nancy Sommers and Ronald Schleifer, "Means and Ends: Some Assumptions of Student Writers," *Composition and Teaching*, 2 (December 1980), 69-76.

[4] Janet Emig and Robert P. Parker, Jr., "Responding to Student Writing: Building a Theory of the Evaluating Process," unpublished paper, Rutgers University.

[5] For an extended discussion of this problem see Joseph Williams, "The Phenomenology of Error," *College Composition and Communication*, 32 (May 1981), 152-168.

[6] Ann Berthoff, *The Making of Meaning* (Montclair, N.J.: Boynton/Cook Publishers, 1981).

[7] W. U. McDonald, "The Revising Process and the Marking of Student Papers," *College Composition and Communication*, 24 (May 1978), 167-170.

This article is reprinted from *College Composition and Communication* 33 (May 1982): 148-56. —Ed.

William G. Clark

THE ESL STUDENT IN THE FRESHMAN COMPOSITION CLASS

Students for whom English is a second language are present in many freshman composition classes in both two- and four-year colleges. Sometimes they are sufficiently fluent in English to be able to perform well; sometimes they are not. Sometimes their instructors are familiar with ESL students and find them valuable additions to their classes; frequently they are not and do not. Many instructors have not had the experience which teaches them how to work with a class containing ESL students.

For those instructors who lack experience with ESL students, information about the process of acquiring a second language can make the difference between a pleasant, profitable class and an uncomfortable, unprofitable class. Obviously, I do not refer here to the problems of teaching beginning ESL students who know little English; those students belong with specialists in ESL instruction. The information I offer does apply, however, to ESL students with moderate competence in English—students, for example, who score 550 or above on the standardized Test of English as a Foreign Language (TOEFL).

Helping ESL students succeed in the conventional composition class requires not only the cooperation of the ESL students, but also the cooperation of English as a Native Language (ENL) students and the willingness of the instructor to take the steps necessary for success. The ESL student is usually quite willing to cooperate, the ENL student is usually ready to take a cue from the instructor, and the instructor can easily understand the pedagogical steps involved.

Assuming the cooperation of both ESL and ENL students, what the instructor should know can be divided into three categories:

1. The general process of second-language learning.
2. Factors which interfere with second-language learning.
3. Factors which facilitate second-language learning.

THE PROCESS OF SECOND-LANGUAGE LEARNING

Human beings learn language through the tacit internalization of patterns and principles that are acquired "through extensive exposure to and practical experience with the use of language in actual, natural contexts and situations" (Falk 440). Language learning follows the familiar process of generalizing a set of experiences into a principle and then applying the principle to new situations. The unexpected feature of this generalizing is that the process works only when the mastery is by *tacit internalization*. That is, we cannot "teach" sets of rules and then expect students to consciously apply the rules. Students do not learn through examining the rules nor by memorizing them; such conscious activity is merely learning about language, not learning language. The process of "language acquisition is, by its very nature, an unconscious process" (440).

The crucial feature, and to most of us the deceptive feature, of language learning is that language acquisition comes about through tacit internalization of patterns. The learner's mind, like that of a child's learning her first language, fits together related features of the language and makes decisions about when to use which words and what forms and sequence of those words to use; but neither the child nor the second-language learner fits the features together and makes decisions about using them by conscious act: the mind performs these operations at a separate, unconscious level. In the process of learning, the learner will, at times, make conscious choices, but once the learning is complete, that happens infrequently.

Second-language learning often takes place without formal instruction. If the learner feels the need to acquire a second language and is in frequent contact with native speakers who can serve as models, the learner will begin to acquire skills in the second language. Indeed, given enough time, enough motivation, and enough contact with native speakers, the learner becomes fluent.

The ESL student taught by a specialist will learn more rapidly and acquire fluency sooner. Even though the specialist provides situations and activities which expedite the learning process, it is still the student who does the learning. "We must realize that the student must do the job for himself, . . . that [although] we can struggle with him in his task of learning the second language, . . . we can provide little more than encouragement and a certain, but not unimportant amount of help" (Wardhaugh 111).

For those of us who are not specialists in ESL, understanding language acquisition is of considerable importance. It tells us, for example, that we do our ESL student no favor by providing them with grammar drills or vocabulary exercises; such activities only take time away from useful activities.

Two other facts about second-language learning may also be helpful in working with ESL students:

1. When individuals are learning two languages simultaneously, they progress more rapidly in the language they use most. The significance of this fact is that the more ESL students practice English, the sooner they achieve fluency.
2. ESL students understand considerably more English than they can produce. A corollary here is that ESL students' writing and speaking are not valid measures of their understanding of English.

Our own experiences with foreign languages should remind us of the truth of the second statement; it is far easier for us to understand the written or spoken language than to speak or write it. When we listen or read, the hard work is done for us; someone else generates the vocabulary or chooses the correct form or assembles the words in the proper sequence. When we write and speak, we have to do that complicated work ourselves, and it is quite different from processing the communications which someone else has assembled. This fact reminds us that we must not judge ESL students' understanding of English by reading their writing and hearing their speech.

These two facts about second-language learning help us to understand what our ESL students do not need and to recognize that what we can see and hear of their use of English may be misleading.

FACTORS WHICH INTERFERE WITH SECOND-LANGUAGE LEARNING

We also need to know those factors which interfere with ESL learning, for they tell us behaviors to avoid and behaviors over which we have no control.

Limited Motivation

Student motivation has considerable bearing on how much English students will learn and how well they will learn it. Some students are not interested in learning any more English than is absolutely essential to achieve their immediate goals. When motivation is limited, the students can spend hours in the classroom doing all that is required of them and still learn little.

John Schumann tells of an adult student with minimal motivation who studied seven months with a skilled ESL specialist on the use of negatives in English. At the end of the seven months, the man's knowledge of negatives in test situations improved significantly. However, his spontaneous use of negatives remained unaltered; he did not transfer the learning to his self-generated use of English. Evidently, he was not interested in mastering elements of English which were, to him, frills (267–68).

For students whose interest in English extends only to short-term goals that require no more than rudimentary control of English, the chances are slight of helping them write or speak appreciably better than they do at the outset. The chances that we can alter their motivation are equally slight. However, we should not be dissuaded from encouraging and otherwise seeking to motivate our ESL students, but we should also know why some of them won't respond to the motivation.

First, we should ensure a classroom atmosphere that is nonthreatening. We should be supportive and make certain that the student's limited progress is not the result of shyness or fear. And we must be content to help students with low motivation learn only enough English to achieve their short-term goals without disparaging their limited goals. Of course, we must accurately reflect in our evaluations the learning which does not take place. If we provide the appropriate setting, encouragement, and instruction, we've done what we can for the marginally motivated student.

Performance Inhibition

When we consider the difficulty that many capable native speakers of English experience when called upon to speak in public, we get some idea of the difficulty that some ESL students experience when faced with the need to communicate, formally or informally, with native speakers of English. Although many ESL students are reasonably fluent in English, their "shyness, perfectionism, and other factors . . . mask knowledge of the second language by performance inhibition" (Erwin-Tripp 113). For these students, we must make a special effort to ease tension and to help them take the risk which performance in English poses for them. Once over the hurdle these particular ESL students will show far more fluency than in their previous communication.

Inaccurate Assessment of ESL Students' Fluency

Teachers who are misled by surface features of ESL students' language often conclude that the students are incapable of learning at the class level to which they have been assigned. Such misinterpretation can be devastating.

As instructors, we must be cautious in assessing the fluency of ESL students. It is particularly important that those of us not familiar with the writing and speaking of ESL students reserve judgment until the students have provided a detailed set of examples of their writing and speaking skills. Often our initial reaction to ESL communications is one of shock, but that shock frequently gives way in a short time to recognition of the students' comparatively fluent grasp of the basics of English grammar and syntax.

If that initial reaction does not change, we should seek advice from a more experienced composition instructor or an ESL instructor, and we should always bear in mind that the student's apparent lack of skill may be really our own lack of familiarity with the performance of ESL students.

To become familiar with that performance, we need to spend time consciously looking behind the variant spellings or the unusual syntax to find the basic elements of the communication. We should look for a limited controlling idea and for detailed and relevant support; we should look for organizational guidance which indicates awareness of audience and a desire to help the audience to follow the movement of the communication. As we become more familiar with the process of reading through the haze of the surface features, we will begin to see that many ESL students handle the important elements of communication with as much skill as the ENL students display.

Observe, for example, in the following journal entry of Chinese student Wen-Ling Tsai the skillful structure and movement of the explanation and the effective supporting detail. Observe, too, the enthusiastic tone and the light-hearted self-deprecation which easily come through the surface features. Then imagine the impact on this woman of a flood of revisions of her language and a paragraph or two of instructor comments on her grammar, syntax, and diction. Finally, guess what the next journal or theme would be like.

> From the first time I went to the supermarket, I crazily like all kinds of food storage containers. I like any shape of them, round, square, rectangular, cylinder, cube or rectangular solid, and any material of them: plastic, glass or acrylic.

If I go to the supermarket, I will stand in front of the shelf of kitchen utensils for a while, or if I go to the shopping more, I will spend a lot of time on kitchen-ware store or a lot of time on the home center of department store. I look all the containers, touch their smooth surface and image what stuff can put inside. I like the picture on the stickers, too. That might be heaps of fresh, red strawberry put on a round, glass containers or green beans and corns on a square plastic containers, or varied small cookies on the yellow lip cylinder container. I like all of them and I think I can store my food like that way. They are beautiful, keep food fresh, and I just like them.

At first my husband let me buy what I want, but after several times, he just allow me to watch and touch but not buy it. He will say, "We already have another square set." "But they are plastic" I might reply. However, we seldom buy food storage containers recently. Because we have only two persons in our house. We don't buy many food a week, and I cook adequate quantity every day; therefore we don't need many containers for store our food. Besides, we don't have plenty space to put more containers.

But, stop to buy is one thing; I like it is another thing. I still spend much time on watching the containers, and touching them at the stores. Or if I have time at home, I will collect all the containers I have, examine how many I have, or how many shape, how many color I have.

I can't explain my habitual inclination. Actually, in my country, we don't use container very often and we don't have various containers. I "think" the reasons are: we seldom store food because we go to the market everyday, we eat fresh meat and vegetable every meal, and if we need to store food, we have many bowls—this is totally the reasons, I guess. Bowls are our major dinner set; just like American's dishes, we have many kind and many size bowls; therefore, we can use bowls instead of using the real food storage containers. But the first time I saw varied containers here, I was simply like it. I like their shapes and their lips. Specially, I like the sound when I seal the lip. That makes me feel I keep anything food fresh.

My husband said I am childish in loving this tiny things, but I don't care. I enjoy my hobby and I will keep it.

When we can move behind the unusual surface features to see the substance of the writing in terms of the controlling idea, the organization and organizational guidance, and the support, we can appreciate the real communication ability which the student displays and recognize the problems with mechanics and expression as interference rather than as the nature of the communication itself.

As we progress with our task of learning about ESL communications, we learn how to facilitate the learning of the ESL students. As we shift our attention from surface features to substantive features, we can in the process shift the attention of the ESL students from undue preoccupation with the surface features to a more rewarding preoccupation with the central communication elements. This is a desirable focus for the ESL students' attention because not only does it engage them in important learning, it moves them into an area where they can progress more rapidly and more productively.

FACTORS WHICH FACILITATE
SECOND-LANGUAGE LEARNING

Sentence Combining

Naturally, ESL students need to continue the long battle to achieve a close approximation to native diction, grammar, and syntax, but such close approximation cannot come quickly; it must follow the route of being internalized in order to be mastered. A limited emphasis on linguistic skills and primary emphasis on rhetorical skills will often ensure steady progress in language learning and rapid improvement in other communication skills.

For instructors who wish to devote time to language learning that will benefit both ESL and ENL students, one helpful activity is the use of sentence-combining exercises twice each week for a semester. Doing these exercises once or twice will do the students little good, but doing 10 or 15 or more each Monday and Wednesday for 18 weeks does help many students. They pay attention to the language elements which they are called upon to manipulate, and they gradually make the various syntactic patterns a part of their internalized understanding of how to use English. Using sentence combining, both ESL and ENL students should improve the syntactic maturity of their writing by the end of the semester.

Freewriting

Another useful way to help students to improve their fluency in English is to require weekly freewriting journals of 400 or 500 words each. These journals are graded on quantity only and are not to be rewritten or carefully planned as coherent productions. The teacher's response to these journals is that of an interested reader who provides occasional marginal notes such as "I would have found that frightening" or "I remember coming home late one night when I was a child and finding my grandfather waiting up with a shotgun to save me from God knows what threat" or "That must have made you feel ten feet tall!"

Letting the students write without worrying about mechanics, grammar, vocabulary, or coherence frees them to experiment with English and to stretch their writing muscles a bit. It is useful practice for any student who has not been writing regularly.

A Period of Benign Neglect

Another technique which works well is for the instructor to refrain entirely from commenting on mechanical matters or expression during the first third (or even half) of the semester. The focus of the instructor's attention during that time is entirely on thesis, support, and organization, which should help all students make more than usual progress in those categories. A surprising number of ENL students will show improvement in mechanics and expression as well, probably just from exercising their composition muscles. The ESL students will show some of this improvement, too, and it will probably be about as much as they would have been able to make with thorough criticism of syntax, spelling, and other mechanical matters. (For the ESL student who solicits help with mechanics, circling or underlining some of the more noticeable departures from the American idiom will provide enough data for the student to begin practicing with.)

Motivation and Minimal Self-Consciousness

The two factors which do much to help ESL students in the composition class—motivation and lack of self-consciousness—are attributes which the students, in varying degrees, bring to class as potential assets. The potential will be realized only if the in-class experience permits it to be realized.

Strong motivation comes from the students' desire to learn English because they see a long-term need to be able to use it. Minimal self-consciousness is the ability to undergo the experience of learning without feeling painful emotional bruises from the process. This condition equates to being able to laugh at oneself or to being able to learn from making errors without being ashamed or troubled.

Obviously, we rarely find students who are so motivated that they never lose interest or students so free of self-consciousness that they can tolerate devastating criticism without pain or diminished learning ability. However, we will find many who can work in any circumstances which let them feel that they are making progress and are not threatened with failure or ridicule. The primary way in which instructors can facilitate the learning of the ESL students is to provide them with the supportive and encouraging atmosphere which will make the most of the students' potential.

When there is enough interaction among the students in a class to permit the ESL students to get to know the ENL students, both groups will be able to relax and to feel less pressure from the classroom situation and will be able to progress rapidly. The instructor's effort to create an unthreatening atmosphere for all the students provides them with the assurance that their learning is the goal of the course. They are then able to make the most of the opportunity to learn.

Grading

The troublesome issue of grading I leave to last because its role must be seen in the context of the ESL students' complex language-acquisition circumstance. Since our primary concern with students is to provide them with the knowledge, activities, and feedback which will do most to help them to learn, we must consider what impact our grading will have on their learning. If our conventional grading system (whatever it may be) interferes with their learning, we need to consider altering the system.

For the good of the ESL students, an alteration which places minimal emphasis on grading of expression and mechanics doubtless helps them to make more progress with their learning to communicate in English than would heavy emphasis on these features of composition.

For the good of the ENL students in the class, the same emphasis will probably lead to more progress with their learning to communicate. They, too, make changes in their expression and mechanics at a slower rate than changes in focus, organization, and support; a grading system which places less emphasis on expression and mechanics will show them, too, that they can make meaningful progress in their writing when they can spend less time worrying about matters which they can change only gradually.

For the good of both ESL and ENL students, limited emphasis on expression and mechanics means maintaining a low-key but consistent identification of problems in those areas. Students must continue to be aware of the need for *some* attention to their syntax, grammar, spelling, and diction. Limited emphasis on expression and mechanics also means that both comments about student communications and the grades which those communications receive should suggest that aspects other than expression and mechanics are important.

Naturally, such a change in grading needs to be explained carefully to the students. Once they understand that the system does not ask them to ignore syntax, diction, punctuation, and spelling, does not discard standards, does not proclaim "Anything goes!" they will be able to accept the opportunities the system offers them to improve the substance of their writing at a reasonably rapid rate and to improve the surface features of their writing at the slower rate which is best for that kind of learning.

SUMMING UP

Helping the ESL students in the composition class entails, first, understanding the nature of the process by which they acquire their new language. The key knowledge is that the acquisition is by internalization of the rules of the new language; the process is slow and cannot be significantly speeded up, except by the concentrated efforts of specialists. Becoming fluent in the new language requires many years, and we cannot hope to assist ESL students with very many linguistic matters in the short time we have. What we can do is to provide frequent writing assignments and situations that require the use of either oral or written English. The combination will give students opportunity to improve both their rhetorical and their linguistic skills.

A second important fact about working with ESL students is that we should not let the surface features of ESL students' writing and speaking mislead us into believing that their control of English is much weaker than it really is. If we do, we are inclined to misjudge the quality of ESL performance. We should not work with surface features first, but with rhetorical features.

A third important fact is that the ESL students will be able to perform at their best when they feel secure. Improving both their writing and speaking skills depends on a comfortable learning environment; such an environment gives free rein to their motivation and to their willingness to take the chance of making mistakes in order to learn.

WORKS CITED

Erwin-Tripp, Susan M. "Is Second Language Learning Like the First?" *TESOL Quarterly* 8 (1974): 111-27.

Falk, Julia S. "Language Acquisition and the Teaching and Learning of English." *College English* 41 (1979): 436-47.

Schumann, John. "Second-Language Acquisition: The Pidginization Process." *Second Language Acquisition.* Ed. Evelyn Hatch. Rowley, MA: Newbury, 1978. 256-71.

Wardhaugh, Ronald. "Current Problems and Classroom Practices." *TESOL Quarterly* 3 (1969): 105-14.

This article is reprinted from *Teaching English in the Two-Year College* (February 1986): 12-19. —Ed.

Roger H. Garrison

ONE-TO-ONE: TUTORIAL INSTRUCTION IN FRESHMAN COMPOSITION

Twenty-five years of frustration with the usual methods of teaching freshman composition were quite enough. I was fed up, as most English teachers are, with endless stacks of mediocre papers piling up relentlessly every week, every month, all year; with minimum student improvement, despite my efforts; and with the increasingly defeated sense that a slob culture's effect on student language habits was much too strong for a mere school effort to combat.

I had been a professional writer before I became a school teacher. I knew that school, even a fine liberal arts college and graduate study on top of that, hadn't taught me how to write. (Indeed, graduate school had a negative influence.) So, when I had an opportunity at a small college, with perfectly ordinary, pleasant, unmotivated students, I determined to try to teach them how to write in much the same ways that I had finally learned—in ways that most professionals learn: by self-instruction, with the guidance and help of an editor.

What is described in the rest of this article is a highly individualized, flexible approach to writing instruction. It can be developed within traditional class and schedule patterns. It can also be adapted by any teacher to suit his personal-professional stance. The suggested teaching pattern derives from a series of premises and assumptions about writing and how it is done.

Traditional methods of freshman composition instruction are teacher-oriented and text-oriented, and are grossly inefficient. (If the writing of the typical college graduate is any measure, the methods are also ineffective.) The teacher designs the assignments, guides the reading, conducts the class, grades the papers; and, if he is conscientious, laboriously handwrites comments, admonitions, and instructions on returned papers. Typically, class time is spent talking about readings assigned as examples of good writing; talking about forms and styles and devices of writing; or discussing good points and bad points of student papers. All the while the talking is going on, the students are not learning how to write.

Students may be learning (a) how others have written, (b) what techniques have (apparently) been used by professionals to achieve certain effects, (c) what grammatical errors to avoid, (d) how to respond to the questions at the end of each segment of a "College Reader," and (e) not

least, how to write for the demands, quirks, prejudices, and tastes of a particular instructor (how to pass the course). But busy as all this may keep a
freshman it will be largely irrelevant to the business of learning to write.

The plain fact is that writing is learned while writing—and rewriting—and
in no other way. All professional writers know this.

So, the problem in teaching writing is to find ways to keep students
writing nearly all the time and to provide constant and almost immediate
feedback for each student as he wrestles with a problem of expression. Further, students need to learn how to diagnose their own writing difficulties
and how to resolve them with less and less dependence on the instructor.
Indeed, the primary job of a teacher of writing is to do himself out of a job
as quickly and efficiently as he can.

Two other important realities:

First, given the probable tightness of most college budgets, now and in
the future, the productivity of instruction has to increase significantly. "Productivity" may be a dirty word to teacher unions, but the facts of academic
life are plain: each teacher has to learn how to teach *more* students *better*
than he is now doing. Despite the policy recommendations of the Conference on College Composition and Communication (1968) that a college
composition class section should not exceed twenty-five and that a writing
teacher's load ought to be fifty students (and at the most, seventy-five), it is
possible with the methods described in this article for individual instructors to handle class sections of up to thirty-five students and give individual
attention to a total of one hundred students.

Second, at least 50 percent of college freshmen, especially in community
colleges, need some kind of remedial work on writing, and this is probably
a conservative estimate. Remedial instruction should be as nearly as possible on a one-to-one basis. Some of the methods described here suggest
ways for teachers to come close to this tutorial situation, even with increased
numbers of students.

A sensible response to these administrative-instruction realities, if it is to
be practical, has to have several elements:

- It has to be workable within a college's regular scheduling framework
  and adaptable to the requirements of the college calendar. (Innovations which call for the total disruption of the status quo are easy
  to invent but relatively impossible to apply, save in isolated circumstances.)
- It has to be flexible enough to allow modification by *each* instructor,
  according to his personal-professional needs and strengths. (One man's
  method may be another person's mistake.)
- It has to be inexpensive. Some colleges have "communications laboratories" with tens of thousands of dollars worth of capital investment in
  hardware. But evidence is not at all conclusive that the applied technology has significantly improved students' writing ability—though it may
  have encouraged certain healthy changes in teaching approaches.

- It has to be systematic and capable of being divided into "modules" or "units" of almost any length and complexity (or brevity and simplicity) to suit the needs of individual students.
- As nearly as it can be managed in an academic setting, it has to provide some elements of the learning-to-write experiences that every professional knows, from his own work, taught *him* how to write.

So, the response cannot be self-persuasive; that is, it can't simply assume that "good reading" might favorably affect a student's writing or that "indirect learnings" might take place from class discussion. It has to show results: unmistakable improvement in the writing of most students that other departments in the college could recognize. Freshman composition is a *service* course. Students *should* write better for other courses. Other instructors *should* see the effects of more efficient instruction. The only valid measure of a student's real learning in a writing course is his actual performance.

ASSUMPTIONS ABOUT TEACHING WRITING—MOSTLY SOUND AND DEFENSIBLE

Premise: To teach others to learn to write you need to know—clearly and in detail—what the act of writing is and how a writer works.

Premise: A writer is any person who successfully communicates thoughts, information, ideas, feelings, or any material from experience, in writing to others.

The following assumptions complement the foregoing premises.

—Writing is a craft, a skill which can be acquired through diligent and systematic practice. (Writing can also be an art. But almost any craft can become an art: it depends on the genius of the craftsman. Craftsmanship comes first.)

—There is no right or wrong in writing. There is only what communicates and what does not communicate.

—A group (a class) has no writing problems; there are only individuals who have problems saying what they mean.

—A writing teacher is a good listener, a fast reader, a good diagnostician: in short, an editor-on-the-spot.

—The major training device in learning how to write is *rewriting*.

—The attempt to write often generates much of what you want to say.

ASSUMPTIONS ABOUT TEACHING WRITING—MOSTLY MISTAKEN

In most colleges, writing is still taught in almost the same ways it was thirty or more years ago. Basic textbooks haven't changed much, either. In typography and layout, they are certainly more attractive and sophisticated. But whether they are readers or manuals for grammar and style, they are simply updated versions of the old rhetoric-essay books and grammar-usage workbooks.

The books and the teaching are based on assumptions about how people learn to write. These assumptions are largely or entirely mistaken. The proof that they are mistaken is simple: the students who have "studied writing" in a course based on these assumptions generally write just about as badly when they have finished the course as when they began it. What is worse, they don't usually recognize how poorly they write; and even if they did, they don't know how to improve themselves. It seems fair, then, to say that their writing course taught them nothing useful about writing.

Here, in approximate order of fallacy, are the major assumptions about writing instruction that still dominate current practices in most colleges.

Classes. A class of twenty-five to thirty-five students and a teacher make up An Administrative Convenience. Their very organization and scheduling require that they have group meetings and involve themselves in group efforts. This means a lot of talking. Writing is not learned by talking about it. Writing is not learned by talking about essays read for "homework" and by responding to questions about the essays. Writing is not learned by discussing forms and techniques. The student learns writing when he is writing. Period.

Smaller classes, even the yearned-for ideal of some teachers of the intimate seminar of ten, do not improve the writing instruction: they simply tend to concentrate the futility.

Reading. Publishers annually spend hundreds of thousands of dollars on "readers" for freshmen composition courses. These readers are collections of writings, often first-rate, usually clustered around a theme or arranged according to forms (essays and news stories, for example). In recent years, the readers have strained mightily to be *relevant*, and their contents have bravely dealt with current abrasions on the social body, such as drugs, sex (the bad kind—somebody else's), dissent (the civil liberties of head-breaking), and assorted panderings to what the academic compilers of these readers believe are current youthful interests or preoccupations.

Generally, these readers have a triple purpose. (a) They intend to *motivate* the student; that is, to interest him enough in a subject supposedly close to his heart or his experience that he will feel impelled to write something about that subject himself. ("What I Think of Pot Smoking.") (b) They provide *models* for the student to think about, analyze, maybe write about, and possibly emulate. (See the inevitable questions at the end of each piece: "Why did the author use irony in the third and fourth paragraphs?" and so on.) (c) They supply the *content* of a course which, without the reader, would seem to have no content.

But writing about reading is secondhand. It is words about words. It is, of course, respectably academic. As Alfred North Whitehead said, "What the learned world tends to offer is one second-hand scrap of information illustrating ideas derived from another second-hand scrap of information. The second-handedness of the learned world is the secret of its mediocrity."

Real writing, even by amateurs, is always from first hand. The content in a writing course is in each student's head, in each student's experience, in each student's written attempts to pin down that personal material in the quicksilver of words.

Forms of Writing. To teach forms of writing (essay, feature article, report, and the like) as subjects for the student's attention and study is like trying to teach concepts of Beauty or Goodness in the abstract, without immediate reference to and immersion in objects or situations which may be considered beautiful. The form of a piece of writing is a compound of the writer's subject, his intentions, his audience, and his own personal quirks. Form is what a piece of writing finally becomes. As in the world of nature, form follows function. Since writing is essentially artificial (*arti* + *ficium* = a thing made), form also depends on the nature of the subject matter, the person of the maker-writer, and the aim he has in writing anything in the first place.

To teach a student the forms of writing is to get him to think about the end product when his real problems are with the *process of making* the product. Thus, to teach "forms" is literally to inhibit and to confuse.

Correctness. For which, read *grammar, spelling, usage,* and all that. Like the forms of writing, grammar is an *ex post facto* description of certain traditional writing habits, or rules-of-the-written-road. Certainly, no reasonably literate person likes to hear or read "between you and I," or "them guys ought to have went earlier." The question is not *whether* to teach grammar but *when* to teach it so that it is truly, functionally learned. This is a matter of choosing priorities— what to teach first. "Correctness" is considerably down the priority ladder. Attempts to teach correct writing to students who have nothing to say is of the same order as making silk purses out of sows' ears. In effect, too much emphasis on the grammar-spelling business tells the student: *what* you say is less important than saying it correctly.

Also, correction by the teacher of student inabilities is a questionable practice. When is the student going to learn to correct himself?

Assignments. The assignment is a crutch both for the student and for the instructor. To tell the student what to write, even within broad limits, does much of his work for him. It directs what he says and suggests how he will say it.

But the truth is that to write you have to have something to say; and conversely, the way to have something to say is to try to write what you want or need to say, either for yourself or to someone else. Since all students have genuine interests, though not necessarily those attached to school, the exploration of those interests can be the source of writing projects. Or, for the increasing number of career-oriented students, there are clear writing demands inherent in any line of work. There is no reason why you cannot help a student learn to write by involving him in the kinds of writing which are typically required by his future job or profession.

Long Papers. The folklore of English teachers says that extended papers are good discipline in organization of material. This sounds as though it ought to be true, but it isn't. For most freshmen, any paper over six or seven paragraphs is an exercise in padding out to a required word limit, or a cut-and-paste paraphrase job, on the edge of plagiarism. The average undergraduate "research" paper (in fact, many a Ph.D. thesis) is, in Ambrose Bierce's words, "merely the transfer of tombstones from one graveyard to another." The usual rationalization for assigning a long paper is that it will give the student experience in developing a subject in depth. Most experienced English teachers will testify, however, that long papers simply test most students' capacities for spinning out a subject which wasn't worth more than two or three good tight paragraphs to begin with.

Vocabulary. It seems incredible that vocabulary lists and "word power" exercises are still used by teachers—at any level. A working vocabulary (the only kind that counts) is literally a function of what one is working at. When you learn to sail a boat, you learn the words that go with the job. When you ski, you use the terms of the sport. When you tear the guts out of a car engine, your vocabulary is at your greasy finger ends and in the parts manuals you use to order clutch plates or generator brushes. Learning words in a vacuum—in a nonuse context—is a waste of attention.

The student writer's vocabulary is built when he is trying to communicate to someone else something important to himself. He fumbles, digs, flounders, asks for, looks up the words he must have. In so doing, he builds a vocabulary.

ORDER OF PRIORITIES

Premise: The content of a writing course is what a student is writing, has written. The teaching method in such a course is the professional response of the instructor to how the student is working and what he has produced.

The single objective of a writing course for college freshmen should be to teach them to write clear, simple, vigorous expository prose. The mastery of such a skill is no small achievement. It is ample work for a full year course and intensive work for a semester course. Any shorter period is usually not enough, unless the student can concentrate his time on little else.

Writing is a developmental craft. It is a performance made up of a series of lesser skills, one built upon another. In some respects, learning to write is like learning to play a musical instrument. The novice learns certain operational skills, beginning with the most basic and gradually developing to the complex coordination of several skills. An "operational" skill is one which, when it is mastered, permits the person to learn further. (An example is the young woman who is learning to be a dental hygienist. The most basic operational skill she must learn in the clinic is the use of the dental mirror. Until she can use the mirror with reasonable facility, she cannot learn the proper use of the explorers, curettes, and other instruments which are used in the mouth.)

There are priorities in the teaching of the needed operational skills for writing. These priorities derive from the basic assumptions an instructor makes about how writing is done. The priorities then become the basic outline of the writing course: the successive steps or skills that the student needs to *master*—one at a time.

(The trouble with traditional writing instruction is twofold: it talks about writing before the student actually writes; and it "corrects" the end-product after the student has written. But rarely does writing instruction systematically break the process down into a logical progression of lesser skills. Even more rarely does the teaching intervene—the word is deliberate—helpfully as the student is actually trying to put a piece of writing together. *Helpful intervention* in an ongoing process or experience is a useful definition of the verb "teach.") The successive skills of putting it together are not academic (artificial) separations: they conform pretty closely to what almost all experienced writers actually do, both in their heads and on paper.

Before taking the successive steps in writing a piece, a student must be helped to general answers to two basic questions: What do I want to say (my subject)? and To whom do I want to say it (my audience)? The answers may be so broad as to be spongy, but they will serve temporarily to get the student writer started. He will quickly learn, as he works on the first two operational skills, that he may have bitten off more subject than he can digest, or that perhaps his audience was too wide-ranging. The very act of composing—getting a piece of writing together—will force a refinement of subject and a sharper definition of audience. If, for example, a student wants to write about drugs and says that his audience is middle-aged people like his parents, he will discover immediately that "drugs" is too big a subject and "middle-aged people" are too diffuse an audience. He will discover these things *because the steps he will take in trying to write about the subject will force him to that conclusion.*

OPERATIONAL SKILLS

Learning to Be Specific. Good writing is explicit. It deals with facts, comparisons, sights, sounds, and evidence (Aristotle termed it "witnesses and documents"). It is usually *show* rather than *tell*. Good writing is as forthright as a punch on the nose.

One of the most difficult things for beginning writing students to learn is how to derive specific facts from a subject. Their tendency is to generalize, to make vague assertions. Merely to identify the vagueness and the generality is not enough; nor is it enough to scrawl "Be specific" across the limp sentences or paragraphs. Many students even need to be taught what "specific" means. Most of them need to be taught *how* to be specific and why being specific is necessary to clear, forceful writing.

Until a student can demonstrate that he knows how to approach a subject and from it to dig, pull, infer, create, and accumulate a mass of specifics, there is little point in suggesting that he is ready to write anything worth reading. Indeed, most teachers are not fully enough aware of the crucial importance of this first operational skill and of the student's need to master it before he is permitted—or simply thoughtlessly "assigned"—a piece of writing to accomplish. The student should not try to write much of anything consecutive — even short paragraphs may be too much—until he can show that he knows how to provide a list of specifics, the raw material from which the writing is composed.

What students have to learn first is that content is more important than form, that what they have to say will shape how they say it. Students also must learn what seems to contradict this: that the way to *have* something to write is to go ahead and write. Every professional writer knows that as you batter words onto blank paper, you are simultaneously digging, discovering, and revealing material about your subject.

But simply "go ahead and write" does not mean necessarily scrawling out sentence after sentence. Writing begins with thinking, and thinking results in a lot of work before a single sentence is written. Many teachers call this *prewriting*. The most useful kind of prewriting is making lists of facts, feelings, statements, keeping the items as closely related as possible to the subject to be written about. The writer should make his list quickly, paying no attention to logical order but simply putting down as single words or phrases as much material about the subject as he can think of. (He should sometimes have as much as ten times the material he will actually use.) Suppose, for instance, he wants to describe a plain, wooden pencil. His fact list would include this sort of thing: length, diameter, shape (hexagonal, cylindrical), number of parts (four: eraser, metal band, wooden casing, lead-graphite core), color, and so on.

Making the list is already writing.

An analogy from sculpture is useful here. Suppose a sculptor wishes to make a small clay figure of a man with upraised arms and feet-apart stance. This figure is his subject. He will make an armature, a kind of stick figure, of heavy wire, as a skeletal outline of the figure in the position, roughly, that he wants. Then he will scoop handfuls of wet clay from a crock and press these roughly around the armature. (The wet clay is analogous to the writer's fact-list.) Then he will scrape off excess clay and press and shape the remaining clay until it begins to conform to his inner vision of the figure. (The writer selects from his specifics and organizes his selections.)

It is while the student is learning to master this crucial first operational skill that the writing instructor can most quickly and accurately help him to identify his strengths and weaknesses. It is in this prewriting stage that you can see most clearly whether a student knows what he is talking about or whether he simply makes one vague assertion after another. It is in working over his lists with him that you can best *show* him what "specific" means, as compared to "vague" or "general." You have something to point to, something to ask questions about.

I cannot stress too strongly the importance of this first skill. Keep the student at it for as long as it takes him to learn, unequivocally, how to do it. The effort will pay off for him eventually: if his learning is slow at the beginning, the mastery of *this* skill will permit him to learn faster later on.

Organizing Specifics. When the student has mastered the first skill—at least to the point where both you and he feel comfortable with his ability—you should then ask him to make brief statements about his list of specifics. The student should respond to such questions as: What do these facts say? What do I want to say about these facts? Do the facts add up to anything? Are there several generalizations which will cover or explain the facts? In what logical framework, in short, am I going to organize these facts?

As the student works at these statements, he will find himself writing lead sentences or brief lead paragraphs: "topic" sentences or the opening statements of a longer piece in which the scope, tone, and direction of the finished writing may be suggested. The student learns organizing principles as he tries to shape actual material that he has created himself. You haven't taught him "organization" or "forms," as such; you haven't tried to instruct him to apply a prefabricated logic to material, like a cookie cutter to a mass of dough. Any piece of writing develops from the inherent logic embedded in the facts which the writer assembles; from his own slant or bias; from his objective in writing—that is, what he wants the piece of writing to *do*.

In the process of finding a logical beginning, middle, and end to his list of specifics, the student will also find out for himself the need to select some material and reject some other. Probably he will discover, too, that he hasn't enough material from which to draw. Most students *under*develop paragraphs at first.

Up to this point, the student has been doing groundwork. If he has tried any consecutive writing—anything more than three or four paragraphs—you should encourage him to circle back, in effect, for *more* list-making, *more* organizing attempts, and third, fourth, fifth, and more drafts of whatever consecutive writing he has tried. This persistent prewriting and rough drafting is time well spent.

Point of View. Point of view is the writer's stance, his angle of vision toward his material. The stance should be consistent (in the grammar books this would be called coherence) and not jump from a let-me-explain-it-to-you tone to an I'm-telling-you tone. It should be the student's own individual view; at this point in the instruction you can begin to show him how to develop his own personal voice. ("Style" is a bit too complex a word for a beginning writer.)

Now is the time for the student to write short (three or four paragraphs at the most), unified pieces, and then begin learning how to revise by asking these three questions:

(a) Am I writing specifically? (That is, am I saying anything?)
(b) Does each part of this piece lead naturally to the next? (Is it logically organized according to my own premises—according to my own lead sentences or paragraph?)

(c) Is my tone of voice, point of view, consistent and appropriate to my subject?

At this first-draft, second-draft stage the student also needs to ask: Are the proportions right? Is each part of the piece developed enough, or too little or too much? (In the grammar manuals, this would be called *emphasis*.) Does the piece, in fact, have a beginning, a middle, and an end? (Aristotle's questions are still valid.)

Sentences. When a student's draft (it may be the third draft or the tenth) reasonably satisfies the requirements of the first three steps, he can start to work with individual sentences. Is he using long, complicated sentences to state simple facts or ideas? Is he trapped in relative clauses (*which, that, whom,* and so on)? Is each sentence clear on its own?

Here, finally, grammar—correctness—becomes a functional consideration. A run-on sentence is bad not because it is ungrammatical but because it is usually misleading. Disagreement of subject and verb may be confusing. Mixture of the active and passive voice will muddy meaning. Poor grammar is almost always lack of precision.

The time for a student to learn (study, understand) grammar is when he needs its precision and verbal logic. Most student grammar errors are simple. Ninety per cent of them are *sentence fragments* (incomplete sentences), *run-on sentences* (comma splice), *nonagreement of verb and subject* (he—do, instead of does), or *incorrect object* (between he and I). These grammatical misusages are not difficult for even reluctant or slow students to understand, especially if they can be assured that these will be all the grammar rules they need to master. (The rest of the dozens of rules and conventions are largely trivial.)

Many students find that this fourth operational skill—the flexible, sensitive molding of sentences—becomes genuine fun. Mastery of the first three skills usually gives a student, often for the first time, a sense that he is beginning to have language under real control, that writing is indeed something he can *do.* So when at last, perhaps after many weeks or even months, he discovers he can put together pieces of rough writing which are interesting (have real content) and which genuinely communicate with others (with you, his instructor, and with his fellow students), he will see that polishing and honing sentences can be a real reward.

Diction. Many writers feel that tinkering with individual words—diction—is the real fun of revising, since words have so many shades of meaning and suggestion. If the student writer has mastered the skills to this point, he too may begin to sense this pleasure, even though he may be a "nonverbal type." As Mark Twain put it, "The difference between the right word and the almost right word is the difference between the lightning and the lightning bug." (And also, getting to be good at something has its own built-in rewards.)

It is important to encourage the student, from the beginning, to use the vocabulary *he* has under genuine control at the moment of writing. (For instance, the thesaurus is a devil's instrument for a beginning writer: it seduces him into using words for their own sake and tempts him away from the words he is sure of.) Many students try to use "school" (academic) vocabularies because they think the teacher likes high-toned words.

Your encouragement, always, should be given to directness and honesty. Has the student written what he knows or believes, as honestly as he can? Honest writing tends to be simple, while forced writing is usually wordy, awkward, often in the passive voice, pretentious and overblown.

Not only do these five priorities represent the sequence of steps most writers take in making a piece of writing, they are also basic skills which build one on the other. Obviously, in practice they overlap and are not separated in as clear-cut a way as they have been presented here. The separation is mainly to indicate the sequence and the emphasis of instruction. Also, you cannot teach these operational skills to a student in any direct sense. Just telling him about them, as I have had to do here, is not the way he learns them. In fact, he teaches himself by his very attempts to put down what he wants to say and by your responses to what he has put down. These steps simply allow the student to get the most mileage out of his efforts. Your role is to help him limit and focus his efforts; to react specifically, with suggestions (*not* directives), to what the student has done; to help the student see and understand his *strengths*, and by indirection let him identify and work on his own weaknesses.

Some notion of the difficulty and sophistication of the kind of learning the student must do even to learn to write with modest clarity and grace is in an analogy originally used by Elizabeth Bowen:

> Imagine the writer, perched like Humpty Dumpty on the top of a wall. On one side of the wall, imagine a great heap of all the material he wants to write about: facts, happenings, feelings, ideas. On the other side of the wall, facing it, is a reader. He cannot see what the writer sees; he can see only the wall. The writer's job is to select from the welter of material on the opposite side of the wall what he wants the reader to know and understand, shape this selection into sequence and sense, translate the sequence into words and sentences and paragraphs, and finally post these on the reader's side of the wall. These written symbols are all that the reader has to make some sort of contact with the material the writer has tried to communicate from the wall's other side.

MANAGING TIME AND WORK

Premise: Students need instruction to the degree that they are unable to learn for themselves.

Premise: Quality of time spent is more important than quantity of time. Students profit most from intensity.

Premise: It is better for a student to be an apprentice at your side for five minutes than a disciple at your feet for five months.

The management of your time and your students' time and work is especially important in a skill course. Some students need a lot of help continuously. Others need much help at the beginning of a course and then rapidly less and less. Still others require sporadic help for special problems. A few (the self-directed learners) are best served when you make a few suggestions and then get out of their way. In any class group, these four patterns of student need will be typical. The teaching problem for you is how best to respond to these varied necessities.

The *least* effective method is the regular class meeting. Whether you act as moderator or dictator, lecturer or "facilitator," class conductor or class participant, makes little difference. Whether students should have a discussion as a class group, or break into smaller groups, or take notes on what you say, doesn't matter much. The fact is that in these group circumstances no writing is being done, and therefore *learning* writing is not taking place.

The *most* effective teaching method is one-to-one: tutorial, or editor-to-writer. The student brings his work-in-progress to the face-to-face session; and you, the teacher-editor, bring analytical reading, judgment, diagnosis, and suggestions for further action by the student. This kind of teaching is creative intervention in the student's work process, at times and in ways that can be most immediately useful to his understanding of what he is doing.

Your time-management dilemma is how to use the scheduled class hours in such a way that group discussions or lectures are at a minimum and one-to-one sessions become your common teaching practice. (There is no reason to call for a revolution in traditional scheduling to accomplish this. True innovations are actually steady, *conservative* adaptations.)

Traditional Time Management. Most composition classes in most colleges still meet three times a week for fifty minutes. In a thirty-week academic year, they spend ninety hours in class. The student is usually expected to do two hours of work outside of class for every hour in class, which adds one hundred eighty hours in a year. Total regular expectation of student: about two hundred and seventy hours.

You, the instructor, need time for preparation. Assume, optimistically, one hour per class for this—or another ninety hours, for a total of one hundred eighty hours per year. Then assume you have one hundred students, each of whom writes the standard one theme per week for thirty weeks. At the most optimistic rate of ten minutes per paper, reading and correcting three thousand papers adds five hundred hours to the annual load you carry. So the relative time commitment looks like this:

Student . . . 270 hours.

Teacher . . . 680 hours.

The bare arithmetic shows how ridiculous the traditional pattern is. You spend two and a half times the hours that the student does—and yet he is supposed to be the learner. (As most English instructors will testify, this arithmetic is conservative. The time ratio is probably closer to four-to-one than two-to-one.)

More than time and energy are inappropriately directed in the traditional pattern: the impact of instruction is almost wholly misdirected, too. For example, assume that a class section of thirty-five students meets on a Monday, having been given an assignment the previous Friday to read and "prepare for discussion." For fifty minutes in Monday's class, the group does, indeed, have a discussion, led by the instructor. For charity's sake, we might assume that the discussion was sharp, vivid, focused, and interesting. Then the instructor asks the class to write "about five hundred words" of interpretation of this reading assignment, the paper to be due on the following Monday. In the intervening two classes (Wednesday and Friday) the instructor presents "several ways to go about writing" the paper. The following Monday, the instructor receives thirty-five papers, all more or less within the five-hundred-word range required. He takes them home to "correct" and grade. If he is conscientious, he will return them to his students the following Monday—a full week or more after they were written. Meantime, of course, another reading assignment will have been given, more discussion will take place, and yet another paper will be in the works and will have fallen due.

The returned papers will have errors meticulously identified. The instructor's comments, cautions, scoldings, and suggestions will vignette the page margins. (He is a conscientious instructor.) But the student, typically, will look only at the grade. If it is a good grade, he probably will not read the marginal comments or pay much attention to the identified errors of grammar or spelling. If it is a poor grade, he will likely use the marginal comments as debating points to argue with the instructor. ("What do you mean, *really*, by this comment?" And the like.)

There are at least seven major teaching errors (or misdirections) in the traditional process just described:

(1) The group of thirty-five students is treated as a block. They are asked to read the same assignment, write the same kind of paper (of the same approximate length), meet the same deadline—despite the obvious fact that thirty-five people can be presumed to have thirty-five different sets of interests, thirty-five different rates of learning speed, thirty-five different varieties of problems in expression. There are, in short, thirty-five *individuals*.

(2) The instructor in this example apparently assumes that discussing the reading assignment helps the students write about it. But the certainty is that he gets only *spoken* feedback from *some* students on the subject of the reading. (In any class group of thirty-five, at least half the students won't open their mouths in a discussion, even if they are directly called upon.)

(3) The instructor tries to teach writing approaches or forms which "fit" the assignment. (It is the rare student who even begins to write the five hundred words before the weekend; and thus it is only the rare student who has even *tried* to discover for himself the appropriate form of his own response.)

(4) The instructor has no idea, when he collects the papers, whether they are first drafts (highly likely) or whether they have been worked over several times (most unusual). After all, "ways to write about the assign-

ment" were discussed both Wednesday and Friday—and the papers were due Monday.

(5) The instructor does not see any of his students' work in progress. He does not, in short, actually watch them learning to write. He sees only the end product of a process which he can only guess at.

(6) The student receives no editorial feedback on his piece of writing until a week or more after he completes it, and meantime, he has to write another paper. For the most part, the feedback tells him mostly what he did wrong, not right; and it does not, usually, tell him thoroughly enough *how* to change his mistakes or improve his shortcomings.

(7) If, as is usual, the instructor "goes over" a set of papers in class, he is apt to point out what students did inappropriately or "wrong"; or he reads, with approval (or shows on an opaque projector), some *good* student writing; or he reads, or refers to, examples of how some professionals solved a similar writing problem and suggests that the students "study" these solutions.

Very rarely does an instructor give individual, step-by-step guidance to *each* student for that student's major problems of expression in any paper. "There just isn't time enough for that," instructors say. And indeed there is not enough time in the traditional procedure just described.

Better Time and Work Management. There's a better way to do it. Limit your fifty-minute, all-class sessions to the first two or three weeks (six to nine meetings) at the beginning of the course. Use these to find out what kinds of students you have. Help them get oriented to what is expected of *them* and how your role will be different from their ordinary expectations. And make sure that you are all using the same kind of vocabulary about writing. They ought to know, for instance, what you mean when you say "a first draft" or "prewriting" or what standard editing symbols are.

But after the first few weeks of preliminaries, convene all-class meetings rarely, and then only to discuss some special situation which seems common to the whole class group. Such single-agenda meetings should take up no more than five or ten minutes of class. (Have you ever thought what *good* things can happen when a teacher vows not to talk more than five minutes?) Spend the rest of class time in one-to-one sessions with those students who need to see you for editorial advice or suggestions.

The mechanical operation of this time scheduling is fairly simple. Assuming a standard class attendance policy, with a "cut" system allowing three unexcused absences, the expectation will be that most of the students will be physically in class on any given day. Students come into the classroom at the beginning of the hour and immediately settle down to their writing. If a student wants to see you (you are at your desk in the corner of the room, or if you're lucky, in a special office next to the room), he simply picks up a numbered card from a holder by the door and keeps on working until you call his number.

As both you and your students become both skilled and comfortable with this quick-conference method, you will find that you can manage eighteen to twenty individual conferences within the fifty minutes of class time. In fact, three-minute, two-minute, and even one-minute "conferences" can be productive. There are two basic reasons why even such brief encounters can be satisfactory:

First, you have a chance to see a piece of student writing from its inception (prewriting) through its final draft—or as many as five times, corresponding to the sequence of the five operational skills described earlier. (With some students, of course, even more conferences are needed and with some, fewer.)

Second, both you and the student are looking for, and coping with, only one problem at a time (specifics, organization, diction, or whatever). Your function at first is to help the student identify his most important problem (or strength, perhaps) and then prescribe or suggest what he might do to solve that problem or build on that strength. *It is the student's job to do all the writing work—all of it.*

As a student becomes more sophisticated, you more and more become simply an editorial reflector, responding to his writing as a skilled reader, letting him increasingly identify for himself where and how a piece of writing can be improved, strengthened, made more interesting.

Though the formal expectation may be that students will attend all scheduled class sessions, you need not waste time taking attendance, unless your college policy requires it. A writing course is where the *product* and its improvement are what count. ("Performance-oriented" is the jargon.) If you have your students follow the developmental sequence I have suggested, you will see individual papers as they evolve through successive drafts. This will give you a number of checkpoints to use to assess each student's product and the effective work being done (or not being done). In this way, you can quickly identify the delinquent and/or nonattending students. Every college has routine administrative devices for at least trying to help such students learn the self-discipline and self-responsibility of regular attendance, and you can use these devices almost automatically. Similarly, if a student's writing production falls too far below the minimum standard you set for the course, you should use any or all of the discipline options open to you.

With this one-to-one brief conference pattern, you will find that each class hour is intense and exhausting. When you work directly with one student after another, scanning their work swiftly and fairly to make an assessment, your attention has to be taut and unremitting—yet outwardly casual. You cannot relax into small talk or digressions, as you so easily can in a longer lecture or discussion. But you will find, to your pleasure, that as you become more skilled in this situation, your students, too, will respond with attention more sharply honed; and the quality—the intensity—of your short minutes will more than justify the brevity. Also, happily, you will not be collecting one set of papers after another to be read and corrected later, at home or in your office time. You will be familiar enough with each student's writing that you can comment on the spot, directly to him; and grade on the spot, too, if necessary.

The Instructor's "Homework." The immediate result of your person-to-person work with students will be the need to develop dozens of different specific writing projects or assignments, literally tailor-made for individuals. (This kind of provision for your students' learning is a far more creative use of your "homework" time than ploughing through endless stacks of papers.) These projects can be duplicated and put into a resource file in the Writing Room. Over a period of time, such a resource file becomes a small library of dozens of folders. Some of these folders contain brief descriptions of ways to handle typical writing problems, such as how to write an effective memorandum, or simple ways to explain complex subjects. Or, for example, dental hygiene students, who have a course in Dental Hygiene Health, will have special communication problems: How to Explain Plaque and Cavities to Public School Children; How to Set Up a General Dental Education Program in a High School; and so on. For such students, these are real situations, not simulated ones. You can devise special writing projects for each one of them, capitalizing on their immediate, practical need to communicate medical-dental terms and concepts to laymen of all ages and backgrounds. Similar applications can be made for students in any career program. The best of these projects are those which you and individual students design together, to meet needs which they identify.

Creating appropriate learning sequences for each of your students is the most efficient use of your out-of-class homework time, for the simple and compelling reason that it produces the most immediate, relevant work for your students to accomplish. Immediacy, relevance, and practicality are strong motivators. Motivated students learn more quickly than their apathetic fellows. Thus, the kind of individualizing described is efficient and productive—obviously and measurably so.

Premise: "The best education is to be found in gaining the utmost information from the simplest apparatus. The provision of elaborate instruments is greatly deprecated."

—A. N. Whitehead

The term "workshop" expresses an idea more than it describes an actual, specially equipped place. Essentially, the workshop is where students come regularly to work at their writing, to get editorial advice from you, and sometimes to share their ideas with other students. The place can be simply a regular classroom with the usual equipment: desk-arm chairs, blackboard, and the teacher's desk up front. This can be transformed into a workshop for writing by turning most of the chairs to face the walls, putting the teacher's desk in one corner with an extra chair by its side, and adding a table (or bookcase) for a small library of grammar manuals, dictionaries, magazines, a clipping file, a project file, selected books of various kinds of prose, and a file of examples of student writing.

If your college's resources and facilities permit, a more flexible and less cramped arrangement is to use two adjoining classrooms (preferably with an interior connecting doorway, as well as outside ones). One room is set up as a regular classroom for group discussion, lecture, audio-visual presentation, and so on. The other room has a small office built into one corner. This is your editorial office—and it can be your regular office, too, for that matter. It need not be elaborate; only head-high partitions need to separate it from the rest of the room. Then, in the remaining large space, set up to make maximum use of the square footage, can be twenty or more individual carrels; a large table for conferences or for spreading out work; a duplicating corner, with ditto machine, supplies, and two or three typewriters.

However the workshop is arranged, it should be large enough for a class of up to thirty-five students, since this is about the maximum number that you will handle with any real effectiveness in any single class period.

Note especially: The most important fact for you to establish with your students, and as early in the course as possible, is that the workshop *is*, in fact, a place where they are expected to come regularly and to work, without urging, on their current writing project. *This expectation of self-directed work is a major behavioral objective of the course.*

The workshop is, in fact, simply a specially created environment to encourage *self*-instruction.

SELF-PACED, SELF-MANAGED LEARNING

Premise: The complexity of learning is precisely the complexity of the individual in relation to his experience. To "learn" is to be creatively active in the presence of the thing to be learned. No one can manage this activity for another: it must be self-motivated and self-managed. It can, however, be guided.

One of your major teaching objectives should be to help each student reach a point where he takes the chief responsibility for managing his own time and work and where he helps you to define some clear minimum and maximum standards of performance. This performance measure is seen as both practical and fair by most students. When it comes to grading students—and most situations still demand grades—your mutual understanding as to what constitutes good work will take at least some of the tension and adversary feeling out of the necessary judgments.

Also, a student's ability to improve his own writing depends on the growth in him of editorial judgment—of the sense and "feel" of good writing. Neither skill nor judgment can be taught, that is, imposed or injected from the outside. You can only guide their development by pointing out to the student what he does well, by encouraging his "ear for the specific" and for the little, vivid details that *show*—and communicate. But the student himself must do the work: he must pace himself and manage himself.

The objectives and apparatus of such a self-paced course have to be developed to match the kind of students you have, your college calendar, the expectations of your department, and other realities.

BEGINNING THE COURSE

Premise: Especially in basic courses, the way a student is brought to a subject is far more important than the subject itself.

Starting a course—the manner, pace, attitude, focus of the beginning—is far more important than most teachers recognize. Like a good feature article lead, the course beginning sets the tone, direction, and realistic expectations for all the rest of it. So you need to think through with great care what you want the start of the course to accomplish. Here are brief suggestions for an appropriate beginning for the freshman writing course.

Diagnostic Assignments. Before you can effectively teach a student, you need to find out what he knows or doesn't know and what he can do or can't do. It can be taken as a truism that all freshmen have writing problems. But what problems? Are they really all the same, or do they just seem so? What problems of expression seem common to a whole class? (There are fewer than you think.) What are each person's basic writing difficulties?

You can quickly find adequate beginning answers by giving diagnostic assignments immediately. These assignments should:

(a) be brief,
(b) reveal major problems (such as overgeneralizing, disorganization, awkward or incoherent sentences), and
(c) have some relationship to each student's major interest(s). It is useful to plan on giving at least two—and better, three—short diagnostic assignments right away: one for each of the first three classes. Read these immediately, before the next meeting of the class, so that you can determine both group problems and individual ones. Keep a brief record of *each* student's apparent difficulties.

Find out as soon as possible (in the first class, if you can) what the students' individual career or other major interests are and what vocational, professional, or general program each student is enrolled in at the college. This can be done with a single questionnaire, for instance, that can be answered in five minutes.

Part of your preclass work is to prepare at least a dozen or more different diagnostic assignments, suited to a variety of student interests or career commitments. These should be duplicated and ready to distribute to your class as their first take-home assignment—for return by the next class meeting; or, even better, if you have a full half hour left in the first class, ask the students to write the assignment immediately, or as much of it as they can. *No writing should be more than one paragraph.* That's plenty for initial diagnostic purposes.

This kind of assignment needs to have three basic characteristics: it should require specific (factual, substantive) statements. (An impression, opinion, or interpretation will too often lead a student to generalize or make unsupported assertions.) It should be simple enough in content to need only a straightforward logic in its organization. It should be *brief*—under two hundred words, and hopefully only *one* developed paragraph. (If a student doesn't know how to be specific and how to organize a series of simple factual statements, a brief paragraph will make this abundantly clear. Further, the likelihood is that any student with these two major deficiencies will also be ungrammatical and a bad speller.)

Here is an example of a particular class section and the diagnostic assignments provided for the students in it.

Class group:

    34 students, all women. They are divided.

    10 secretarial majors, average age 18–19.

    4 medical technology students (4-year course, heavily scientific in first year), average age 21.

    9 nursing students, average age 24; 3 married (1 divorced, two with small children), one 54-year-old widow.

    11 liberal arts students (transfer), average age 18–19.

Assignments:

    For secretarial majors: "You are the instructor's secretary. He has been asked by Dean John Doe, of Exxine College, to act as a consultant for that college's English department, in a two-day workshop about three months from now. Dates are still relatively open. You have the instructor's appointments calendar. Write a brief note to Dean Doe offering three alternate dates within a two-week period." (Further information is supplied to the student in a random list of facts.)

    For medical technology students: "Describe two specific influences (or reasons) which caused you to choose this career program."

    For nursing students: "Describe specifically two or three (no more) of the most important personal qualities you think a nurse should have."

    For liberal arts students: "Write a specific description of an ordinary steel thumbtack (or a newly sharpened wooden pencil.)"

When a student has done three assignments like these, his writing strengths and weaknesses ought to be clear enough so that you can begin to prescribe specific work for him to do.

Individually Designed Work. After diagnosis comes prescription; now you can begin to design each student's work for his particular needs. This sounds excessively time-consuming, but in practice it is not, especially as time goes on, for the student should be increasingly engaged in designing his own work. (Later in the course, he ought to be designing 95 percent of it.) The most important rule of thumb is that every piece of writing the student attempts should relate as directly as possible to his *immediate experience* and his *genuine interests.* These may be career interests, personal enthusiasms, current preoccupations with social issues, or whatever. But unless there is an immediate relationship or a real involvement, the subject becomes "academic"— that is, secondhand, merely verbal, the-kind-of-thing-they-make-you-do-in-school: in brief, irrelevant.

For example, take the case of an inner-city community college student in an automotive mechanics program. His past schooling record is dismal; he is functionally illiterate; he "hates" English, reads with difficulty, and resists writing anything more than his own name. But he is genuinely interested in becoming a skilled mechanic. Get him to talk about the problems of a balky engine or transmission. Ask him how he uses a parts manual. Suggest that he write a brief letter to a parts wholesaler, ordering certain parts. If he agrees that this is a realistic thing for a mechanic to have to do, then you and he have designed a useful *writing* assignment for him.

Or, for a contrasting example, take the bright, spoiled, lazy girl who is in liberal arts because she has no special interest, and in college because "what else is there to do?" She professes no strong interests—or, more typically, she has a list of lukewarm disinterests. But on the fourth finger of her left hand there is a tiny engagement ring. Engaged? Like the ring? Oh, *yes!* O.K., describe it: accurately, thoroughly. (And, for a later and more detailed writing project, get her to describe how she got the ring.) Here again is a genuine interest, tapped for a writing problem to be solved. (*It doesn't matter one bit whether you think the student's interest is dull or insignificant: the only necessity is that the interest is genuine.*)

The writing work for each person needs to be carefully orchestrated in difficulty. Early projects should be kept simple and sharply focused. Problems in description or factual summary are good ones to use initially. But as the student masters the crucial operating skills of finding specifics and organization, encourage him to tackle more sophisticated challenges of critical or interpretive pieces. Wherever possible, too, give students every incentive to explore career interests and do the kinds of writing appropriate to their special vocational or professional courses. (English teachers have both a natural bias toward literature and training in it, and the constant temptation is to ask students to write about "literary" subjects—poems, short stories, essays, and the like. This bias should be strictly curbed, *strictly*, except when a student is genuinely interested in such [subjects].) It can be taken as a truism that real skill can only follow real interest. This should be the major guideline for designing student writing projects.

Designing Individual Projects. Productive writing projects are limited only by your ingenuity and your students' abilities. The basic suggestion here is that no project should be too long. It is the rare freshman who will get much profit from a paper over fifteen hundred words long (a little more than five typed, double-spaced pages). Rather, shorter projects which require various kinds of thinking are the ones that help students most.

For example, a student who has trouble organizing material with a coherent point of view might profit from analyzing a photo-story in one of the picture journals or analyzing the prose-and-pictures of a particularly effective advertisement. One device which students have reported as helpful is to create a montage of cut-out pictures on a large poster board. The montage should illustrate (focus on) a single generalized word: joy, frustration, contentment, and so on. From the selection of pictures and the layout on the poster board, the student can begin to *see* a pattern of organization. Then he can try to turn his own montage into words.

Or, for another example, many students have told of the value of trying to write a one-paragraph description in words of one syllable. This is an instructive exercise, especially for those who are wordy.

The more a student learns to design his own appropriate assignments, the faster he will develop editorial judgment and thus the capacity to teach himself—which is what your major objective has been all along.

"CORRECTING" AND GRADING PAPERS

Premise: Students usually learn best when they can work from a position of strength. But first they have to discover what that strength is.

Premise: Students should be evaluated, and often. The real questions are *when* and *how* and *why*.

Premise: The only valid measure of a student's learning in a writing course is his actual performance. What a student "knows" about writing technique is almost wholly irrelevant.

Veteran teachers of freshman English can look back over years—even decades—at a nightmare vista of stacks and stacks of paper, thousands of them, red-spattered, margin-marked (*sp, gr, coh, awk, ref, punct*), pocked with outraged mini-essays of advice, admonition, or analysis in the blank space after the final offending sentence, and labeled with grades ranging from savage D-minus-minus-minus to an occasional lyrical A and "well done." We can look back and recognize, if we are ruthlessly honest, that all the red ink and all that creative outrage didn't actually teach students much. It may have scared a few, temporarily. But what students may have learned either from red ink or fright usually had to do with passing the course, not necessarily with learning to write.

Why so? Because the real work was done by the wrong people. Who made the rewriting suggestions? We did. Who identified the errors? We did. Who spotted the incoherence, the lack of logic, the stumblefooted sentences? We did. But ultimately, if the student is to learn to write, it is he who must correct the paper—many times. It is he who must rewrite and edit, and not merely accept passively our editing. It is he who must batter the resistant words and sentences and paragraphs on the stubborn anvil of thought until meaning begins to ring from them.

Your job is to:

(1) help the student see what he is doing right and get him to build on that,

(2) point out the interesting and communicative facts that may be hidden, like raisins, in the student's pudding-prose,

(3) recognize the occasional deft phrase or evocative image, and show the student how it might be used to rescue a spongy paragraph from acute dullness, and

(4) identify good work, suggest solutions for difficulties, encourage the student to rewrite, rewrite, rewrite. Help him to work from strength, not from error.

A practical warning. It takes constant alertness and real courage (literally) *not* to correct a paper, *not* to check, circle, or underline grammatical or spelling errors, *not* to write in a more felicitous phrase than a student's barbaric one. Rather, make up your mind long before you see a student paper what the priorities to be corrected are; and then deal with these, one at a time. For example, if a student's paper is too general and poorly organized, if it jumps from one point of view to another, and if it is marred with bad grammar and many misspellings, the student's first job is to attack the spongy generalizing. Until he licks that problem, he shouldn't even be asked to handle the others—and you shouldn't waste time or energy even identifying them. *One problem at a time, and the most important problem first,* is the proper correcting motto.

It is useful for you to know that if problems are worked at systematically in this way, many of the lesser problems begin to solve themselves. They are only added symptoms of the larger problems anyway. For instance, the vague generalizer usually doesn't know for sure what he is talking about. (And he may not care much, either.) If he doesn't know (or care) what he is talking about, he won't have a clear principle of organization in his mind. If he has neither specific knowledge nor organization, he is likely to jump around in his points of view and be incoherent. Further, his vocabulary will be inaccurate because his knowledge is inaccurate; and hence, his spelling will be bad. "For want of a nail, the shoe was lost/For want of a shoe, the horse was lost. . ." and so on.

Grading. To the extent that your college's administrative requirements allow you, keep grading to a minimum, especially at the beginning of the course. In fact, for the first six or seven weeks, don't grade a single paper unless a student presses you to do so; and then, don't record the grade. Writing skill is a slow, hard development, and the fewer punitive elements you can put between the student and his work-and-growth, the better. When grading is required, you might ask students to submit one or two samples of what they consider their best work to date; and give them time to polish or rewrite these as much as they wish to. You are grading a student's skill as it is at the time of evaluating, not as it was weeks ago. (For this reason, you should never average grades. Why punish a student who may be doing excellent work now for his past inabilities? Yet that's what "averaging" is.)

Don't ask students to grade themselves. This is just playing games with evaluating. The purpose of a grade, if it is to have meaning, is to give the student a professional evaluation of his work. You're the professional; he is not. If your students understand very clearly the basis on which grades are given, they are usually surprisingly cooperative. You should, for example, tell your students at the start of the course exactly what is expected of them in quantity or writing: number of finished papers by the end of a grading period. Express this in a range: for instance, for a semester the minimum quantity is seven finished papers, for no more than a D or D-plus; and the maximum may be twelve for the B-plus or A range. Within the range, specify the quality elements which will also be part of the grading. These quality elements may be expressed in brief descriptive terms, such as: use of detail; organization; word use; control of grammar; and the like.

BRIEF SUMMARY

The secret of learning, as Whitehead pointed out nearly half a century ago, is *pace*. Today, the jargon is "individualized learning." Each person's learning pace is indeed different from another's. To fail to recognize this in our teaching is to guarantee unnecessary waste of time, energy, and interest—of students *and* teachers. The teaching scheme set out in these pages is the barest outline, consistent with clarity, of a practical way to allow for individual pace and to permit you to teach with greatest impact: on a one-to-one basis.

The suggestions made here are just that—ideas and methods for your consideration. The principles of instruction in this outline are surprisingly flexible, and they can be adapted in whole or in part to suit the realities of your teaching situation and the kinds of students you have.

No learning takes place smoothly or steadily. There are fits and starts; arid periods and creative periods; long frustrations and brief insights. The learning graph for each of us begins at a different place and moves in different jumps and to different plateaus. Perhaps the most useful visual analogy is a spiral, which keeps swinging back on itself, though further outward and upward each swing; and some swings are flatter than others, yet they always turn back on themselves. If you can help each of your students find his own spiral, his own rhythm of learning the difficult craft of writing, then you are teaching well, and he will be learning efficiently. *His* learning is the only real reason for your teaching.

This article is reprinted from *New Directions for Community Colleges* 5 (1974): 55–84. —Ed.

Beverly J. Moss and Keith Walters

RETHINKING DIVERSITY: AXES OF DIFFERENCE IN THE WRITING CLASSROOM

Few issues on campus in recent memory have sparked the debate, argument, and some would contend uncivil behavior by students and faculty that have accompanied the topic of diversity. From our perspective, the topic represents the latest attempt to deal with long-standing issues—many would say problems—in the academy and the larger society. Yet given the social, economic, and political contexts in which the topic has been raised, it represents far more than a trendy relabeling of another problem that simply will not go away. As citizens and educators, we are faced with the fact that large numbers of students—mostly African Americans, Hispanics, Native Americans, Appalachians, and other poor Americans of European roots—are not succeeding in our schools and universities or in the workplace. At the same time, these institutions have begun to confront a major demographic shift in the populations they serve, the ultimate result of which is that no single ethnic group will constitute the majority of Americans: instead, the majority will soon be composed of various groups of ethnic minorities that have traditionally been underrepresented in these same institutions.

Although many would reduce discussions of diversity to questions of the changing demographics of this society and issues of ethnicity and social class, we contend that a serious analysis of diversity in American writing classrooms encompasses far more—especially in higher education.

DIVERSITY AND HOW WE TEACH

One can approach teaching from many perspectives. One can see it as transferring information, coaching (or something akin to it), or assuming the role of master craftsperson in a process of apprenticeship. Similarly, but perhaps less obviously, one can think about teaching as a speech event, an activity or aspects of an activity "directly governed by rules or norms for the use of speech" (Hymes 52). From this sociolinguistic perspective, teaching involves participants—minimally, a teacher and students, although assistants, observers, or visitors may be part of the event. Likewise, it involves rules for speaking or remaining silent as well as norms for evaluating both linguistic and nonlinguistic behavior. As is usually the case with social phenomena, the rules and norms usually go unstated: they are assumed to be shared and are noted only when violated.

*This article has been excerpted with the kind permission of the authors.

From this perspective, the focus of teaching, even the teaching of writing, becomes spoken language and the ways in which spoken language is used for a host of purposes. Thus, a discussion of how we teach focuses our attention on the very complex, unfolding world of the pedagogical conversation,[1] whether in the classroom, the office, the hallway, or some other setting, in which we can never be sure that our norms or motives for interacting will automatically be shared by our interlocutors. Increasingly, we are learning to ask questions about misunderstandings between teachers and students and coming to realize that many axes of difference can interfere with what at one level seems like such a simple task: helping students develop the skills they already have in order to progress as writers and thinkers.

Last year, Keith had a problem involving a Pakistani-American student who clearly had different rules from those that Keith expected for asking questions of the teacher. For instance, in class discussion, the student sometimes asked what he believed to be an information question and received what Keith believed to be an adequate reply. Then, when asking a follow-up question, the student began by restating the assumption that led to the original question as if to reconstruct his position and perhaps to rehearse all of the steps of argumentation in whatever was being discussed. Perceiving that the student had ignored (or at least failed to acknowledge) the answer that he had just given the student, Keith believed that his authority was being baldly challenged. From discussions with the student, Keith knew that the student perceived his own behavior to be neither overly insistent nor rude, yet given Keith's own assumptions about questions and how they should be asked in the classroom, Keith perceived the behavior to be rude and even belligerent. Did the student have a problem because Keith and some of his other professors perceived that he challenged them to an excessive degree in class? Did Keith have a problem because his assumptions were not shared by all of his students? Or did the student and his teachers share a problem because they seem to be operating with different assumptions about the rules and norms for the use of speech in classroom settings? What are the consequences of assigning the "problem" to the student or teacher alone, or to the student and his teachers?

Similar questions arise for Beverly and other teachers with respect to issues of age difference in the classroom. Although many teachers lament that they and their eighteen- and nineteen-year-old undergraduates inhabit different worlds, we rarely examine seriously the role of age differences as a source of misunderstanding in the classroom. Beverly, because she looks as young as some of her undergraduates and is younger than many of her graduate students, finds herself in the position of dealing with possible conflicts resulting from age differences. She frequently finds herself questioning how she deals with older students who, Beverly feels, at times seem to challenge her authority in the classroom. Yet these older students appear to think they treat her the way they treat all of their professors. Are there assumptions that members of our culture make about cross-age face-to-face interaction that might lead to misunderstandings between a younger professor and an older student or an older professor and a younger student? The sorts of misunderstandings related to assumptions about language and language use extend far beyond students' asking questions in what teachers might feel are inappropriate ways or differences of age between teacher and student.

For example, Sarah Michaels and Susan Philips have examined the nature of misunderstandings that can occur between teachers and students from different cultural and linguistic backgrounds. In the first-grade class that she studied, Michaels found that the black children were more likely to be interrupted and "corrected" by the white teacher than were the white children during sharing-time (sometimes referred to as "Show and Tell," when first graders shared stories with their classmates while all sat on a rug at the front of the classroom). An analysis of the discourse patterns used by black and white children during sharing-time revealed that the white children's discourse patterns, labeled topic-centered, more closely matched those of the white teacher and more closely resembled an academic notion of a narrative than did those of the black children. Yet the black children's discourse patterns—moving from one event to another and assuming that context or listeners' knowledge would establish connections among these events—were the norm in their home communities, where to be explicit about the links between episodes of a narrative is to insult the listener by assuming that he or she is not intelligent or interested enough to deduce the connections. The well-meaning teacher assumed that the black children did not know how to tell stories properly and sought to "help" them by interjecting questions as they talked. At least some of the black students, however, perceived these questions as frustrating interruptions. As Michaels clearly demonstrates, sharing-time is not just about telling stories—the characterization that both teacher and students might initially offer; rather, it is really about a student's co-narrating a story with the teacher, who, through questions and comments, creates a scaffolding of sorts that the student, through responses, fills in. When teacher and student share this schema for storytelling and for teacher/student interaction, the stories are acceptable to the teacher—and by extension the academy. But when teacher and student begin with different notions of what a good story is or how one co-narrates a story with a social superior, the mismatch may well have grave repercussions for not only sharing-time but later instruction and achievement in speaking and writing as well.[2]

Working in the Warm Springs Indian community, Philips found that the cultural expectations brought into the classroom by Anglos were very often in direct conflict with rules for communicative behavior native to the reservation community. Like others who have worked in Native American communities, she found that the preferred response patterns of the Indian children did not match the patterns of white, middle-class students and were often unacceptable to the non-Indian teachers. Because, for example, the Native American children would not respond to direct questions and sought to avoid going to the blackboard, the Anglo teachers perceived the students to be uncooperative or unintelligent. As Philips pointed out, what the teachers did not understand (and therefore could not appreciate) was that in this Native American community, as in many, direct questions are rarely posed because the person who tries to answer but answers incorrectly loses face. Similarly, individuals in this community are rarely forced into public situations—like going to the blackboard—in which they could fail before their peers and superiors or in which they might be forced as individuals to excel, thereby distinguishing themselves from other members of the group. Rather than seeking to demonstrate individual competence or mastery—so much a goal of mainstream schooling—these students were much happier working in groups with no appointed leader or "helping" the teacher solve a problem. Thus, Philips concluded that "in the structuring of attention, and in the regulation of talk, there are differences between Anglos and Warm Springs Indians that result in miscommunication between students and teacher in the Indian classrooms" (127). Certainly, research such as that of Michaels and Philips has encouraged us to see that no methodology or pedagogy is culture free or culture neutral.

Traditionally, teachers at the college and university level have favored the lecture method as a teaching tool, and those who teach large classes may feel they need to rely on a classroom format that involves the teacher holding the floor and speaking all (or nearly all) of the time. In such cases, the goal is transmitting a body of knowledge organized and presented (some might say broadcast) by the teacher. Writing teachers, however, have long held such methods in disdain, arguing instead for small-group activities or discussions that students participated in or led. Of course, organizing classroom time so that students talk to the teacher or to one another represents a shift in goal: the focus is no longer the monologic transmission of knowledge but creating (or, more accurately, cocreating) it through dialogue or polylogue. These methods are not without controversy. They are not value free; rather, they entail assumptions about using spoken and written language that may not be shared by everyone who enters the classroom door.

As demonstrated in the following sections, "Diversity and What We Teach" and "Diversity and Whom We Teach," teachers of writing, like all educators, find themselves in a fix. Unhappy with the lecture method that informed most of our own educations and all too acquainted with its limitations for many students, we seek alternative methods of teaching and interacting with students. Yet we understand little about the ways in which various teaching techniques or methods constrain or shape students' possibilities for displaying knowledge (cf. Freeman; Janda; Sperling; and Walters "'It's Like Playing Password'"). In his research on classroom interaction, Hugh Mehan has pointed out that the competent student must not only possess the requisite information, but he or she must also display it in an acceptable fashion. With respect to diversity, it is this issue of display, the complex problem of finding acceptable packaging, that we believe to be especially crucial. In a very important sense, each display of knowledge is a possible locus—a point in real time and social space—at which diversity may play itself out before our eyes.

Our goal here is to point out that if we are committed to broadening our repertoire of pedagogical strategies and widening our methods of sampling and evaluating student ability, knowledge, and achievement, we can begin in our own classrooms, usually without waiting for administratively sanctioned curricular change.

From our perspective, how we teach—our assumptions as well as our actions—reflect the extent to which we accommodate diversity, whether we use it as an integral part of learning, merely acknowledge it, or, perhaps, at worst, teach to an ideal student who may bear little resemblance to those who actually occupy the seats in our classrooms.

DIVERSITY AND WHAT WE TEACH

Teachers of writing at the college and university level are teachers of language and of advanced literacy skills. In this section, we deal with a basic part of what we teach, language and, more particularly, Standard English as it relates to other varieties of English. In a very real sense, our discussion of what we teach spills over into the next section, "Diversity and Whom We Teach," in which we consider the related but broader topic of home literacies and language use as they sometimes contrast with what Ron Scollon and Suzanne Scollon term the *essayist literacy* of the academy. Although the topics of language and literacy are closely related, we have chosen to separate them in order to highlight the constellations of issues surrounding each. As noted in the introduction, we see the topic of language as a very important one because our assumptions about language ultimately influence nearly everything we say and do. Certainly, nearly all of the spoken or written language that is produced in the context of writing classes is in some sense language about how to use written language effectively. Equally important, because writing teachers insist that students use Standard English, it is important for teachers to have as rich as possible an understanding of that variety and the nature of standard languages in general.

If asked to define what Standard English is, most students and many teachers would reply that it is "good grammar" or "correct language that doesn't break any rules"—characterizations they learned from teachers and textbooks. There would be no comment about where this variety of language came from, who makes up the rules, or where we might find them.

In fact, defining what the standard is and is not constitutes a very complex task because we are dealing with several notions of the standard at once. In one instance, we might think of the *descriptive standard,* the variety of American English that corresponds to the definitions of standard languages that most sociolinguists and language planners might give. Such definitions usually note that a standard variety is the one used by people with social, political, and economic power and influence—"a dialect with an army and a navy," as some put it. It is also the variety taught to native and nonnative speakers of the language and used in the various media in its spoken and written forms.

Such a descriptive standard is much broader than the *prescriptive standard,* which corresponds to the written variety the rules of which are inscribed in handbooks of the sort that are used in writing classes. Most of the marks that are made in the margins of student papers—frag, dm, split inf., diction—represent efforts to get students to respect, use, and internalize the rules of this prescriptive standard. Of course, handbooks differ, and pronouncements about usage change. Most important, careful readers frequently find "violations" of these prescriptive rules in the speaking of the socially, politically, and economically powerful and in such written texts as *The New York Times,* textbooks, and professional journals. In other words, teachers of writing ultimately must acknowledge that these speakers and writers do not seem to be following the sets of rules inscribed in the handbooks used in our classes. Additionally, those of us with prescriptivist tendencies should acknowledge that many of the students who currently suffer our marginal comments are soon likely to wield far more economic, social, or political power than we ever will; consequently, their speaking and writing will help determine the descriptive standard for the coming generation. In earlier periods when our profession sought to acknowledge and deal with linguistic diversity, considerations such as these were frequently marshaled by those trained in linguistics in order to argue against the existence of something called Standard English. For example, these sorts of arguments favored prominently in the discussions and debates surrounding the "Students' Right to Their Own Language" statement issued in 1976.

In addition to the descriptive and prescriptive standards, we also find what we might term the *perceived standard,* that is, what speakers and writers believe Standard English to be. Here, we find such myths as "Never start a sentence with *and,*" and "Never end a sentence with a preposition," as well as patterns of conscious analysis that lead writers to mispunctuate dependent clauses beginning with "whereas" or "which is to say" as if they were sentences. Thus, the perceived standard is what language users, whether students, graduates, or teachers, ultimately invoke when evaluating their own language and that of others or when called upon to justify their judgments or behaviors. And for many speakers, this perceived standard contains inconsistencies or logical contradictions.

Because a component of the *perceived standard* involves judging the behavior of the self and the other, whatever is different from one's own behavior becomes part of that "everything else." There, unsavory things like regional, social, and ethnic dialects exist along with all of the "ill's," "un's," and "non's," of the society: illiteracy, illegitimacy, unemployment, underachievement, and nonstandard language. In these cases, "different from the standard" really means "inferior" because what is being judged is not simply language but a host of personal and cultural attributes that members of the society associate with varieties of language and, by extension, their users. It is not acceptable for most Americans to label someone inferior because of his or her skin color; far more acceptable, however, is the sort of claim made by a white American on *The Oprah Winfrey Show* during a discussion of Black English when he asserted that the use of "good English," which he assumed he spoke and wrote, to be a question of self-discipline. In his eyes, speakers of Black English simply lacked self-discipline—because their speech did not resemble his. This speaker, like most, clearly associates the use of what he perceives to be Standard English with particular moral virtues. His comments remind us that the issues involved in discussions of standard language extend far beyond the question of the nature of Standard English as a linguistic variety.

As our discussion has demonstrated, there is variability even within what is usually termed *Standard English*. More specifically, it in no way represents the fact that educated Americans are far more tolerant of a speaker's maintaining his or her native regional accent while speaking Standard English than they are of his or her retaining grammatical features of a regional dialect when speaking or writing. It is fine to sound like a Southerner, a New Yorker, or a Californian, as long as one sounds educated—that is, as long as one's "grammar" stays within the range acceptable to speakers of Standard English. Equally important, the figure does not capture other observations that any speaker of English who has lived in this country for any length of time realizes: as one goes up the social ladder, one finds less variation among dialects. In other words, it is from lesser-educated individuals that one most frequently hears forms labeled non-standard. In contrast, the more that people become educated, the more likely they are to have learned to bleach their speech and writing of markers that reveal their native regional and social dialect, especially if these dialects are considered nonstandard by society at large. Such a commonsense observation is, of course, an admission that access to Standard English is related to issues of social class and social mobility.

Speakers of stigmatized regional and social dialects have, literally, a longer way to go as they move from their native variety to Standard English. Of course, the same is true for speakers of Black English. Their ability to style-shift from African-American English toward Standard English will depend on their life circumstances. Speakers who live, work, and relax in communities where African-American English is the most commonly used variety of American English will probably be most comfortable using that variety. On the other hand, African Americans who live, work, and relax in communities where Black English is rarely or never used may not even be able to speak Black English. Their native variety of American English may be one that is close to the regional and social variety of the community in which they live, work, and relax. Most African Americans will find themselves somewhere between these two extremes.

Interestingly, a number of African-American students at the University of Texas at Austin who come from racially integrated, middle-class communities and who attended public high schools in Texas report that they are exposed to and use Black English more now that they are at UT than at any previous time in their lives. Because African Americans constitute a very small minority at UT and because they perceive that the university is hostile to their presence, they turn to other African Americans for support and hence spend a great deal of time in the presence of African Americans from a variety of social backgrounds. Thus, some African-American students who grew up not speaking Black English make a conscious effort to acquire and use it while at UT in order to be accepted as members of the African-American community there. These are the kinds of forces that are likely to influence the linguistic behavior of speakers of highly stigmatized social or regional dialects across their lifetimes.

Writing teachers talk about language and its use a great deal of the time, and most of their comments on student papers represent efforts to persuade students to develop certain kinds of strategies for using written language in particular ways in particular contexts. All of this talk about writing is based on some sort of model—however implicit, however inchoate, however unexamined—of language and the relationship of the standard to other varieties. And the less accurate and less rich the model of language that informs a teacher's comments and commentary, the more likely his or her students will not reach everyone's goal: mastery of Standard English for use when it is appropriate. Talking about "correct" or "incorrect," for example, assumes one model of language; talking about "appropriate" and "inappropriate" in this or that context assumes a very different model. Over the years, Keith has discovered in his own teaching that replacing a model of language based on correctness with one based on appropriateness is a very challenging task because it forces him to think constantly about *why* a particular usage should be labeled inappropriate or appropriate in a given context. Marking things "wrong" is much simpler than thinking seriously about context and appropriateness, but the consequences of the former view seem to be overwhelmingly negative. Certainly if writing teachers talked about language as if diversity were an integral part of it—if we admitted that the standard language itself continues to change and that the notion of standard is itself problematic—we would have to move away from the view of language correctness and spend more time examining our own linguistic assumptions and educating ourselves about the actual nature of language.

In this section, we have tried to outline productive ways of thinking about one of the major things that we teach—language and specifically the standard language. Rejecting the society's ideology about the nature of Standard English, we have provided alternative ways of representing the relationship between the standard variety and other varieties of English. For us, a view of language and human behavior—one that attempts to describe what speakers and writers do as they use language strategically to create and maintain individual and group identities—is far more likely to help us value and appreciate linguistic diversity in its many forms than a view of language that *ab initio* labels some varieties and users of language deficient.

DIVERSITY AND WHOM WE TEACH

At least since the time of Aristotle, teachers of rhetoric have taught their students that one persuades different audiences in different ways and that the successful rhetor knows a great deal about the characteristics of his or her listeners. As our student audience becomes increasingly diverse, we as writing teachers need to consider the possible axes of difference we may encounter in our classroom and our potential responses to these kinds of difference. In this section, we look at several axes of difference that our experience has led us to conclude influence the ways various segments of our increasingly diverse student population respond in the writing class. These variables include language and literacy practices of the home community, first language, age, sex or gender, and sexual orientation.

Home Literacies and Language Use

Although thinkers like E. D. Hirsch, Jr., argue for a monolithic approach to issues of literacy, language, and knowledge (cf. Walters, "Whose Culture?"), we find such an approach seriously lacking when we consider the challenges we face in the classroom or the challenges our students face during their lives as they become part of an increasingly interdependent world economy. At the heart of this monolithic approach is the notion that only one kind of literacy—academic literacy—exists. In contrast, we argue that academic literacy is but one of many literacies, albeit a powerful and important one. Associated with this literacy (as with all others) is a particular belief system, which includes beliefs about how language—oral and written—should be learned and used. Even though the notion of academic literacy has been most closely associated with school literacy, it has also become the standard for judging literacy and language practices outside of school.

It is easy to see why schools in this culture and around the world succeed admirably in the task of educating children from middle-class backgrounds: they arrive at school bringing with them the very assumptions about using language and literacy that the school seeks to inculcate and most frequently rewards. The greater challenge—and one we have yet to meet in this country—involves those who arrive with expectations that are no less rational, no less systematic, no less grounded in social practice, but that differ from those assumed by the school. Thus far, however, schools have had little room for difference, preferring a pedagogy that has often guaranteed near exclusion for many of the very groups most in need of assistance.

One of the many ways to help us rethink our traditional ways of thinking about language and literacy is to consider work in such fields as anthropology, sociolinguistics, and education about linguistically and culturally diverse populations. Although a quick survey of a few of these studies provides teachers with information about the linguistic and cultural backgrounds of particular groups of students, it more importantly suggests the kinds of issues teachers might begin considering when thinking about issues of diversity in the classroom.

Probably the best-known research in home literacy and language practices is Shirley Brice Heath's work, which has challenged many teachers to ask questions about the literacy and language practices in the home communities of their students. From Heath, we learn about functions and uses of literacy in three Piedmont Carolina communities in the late 1970s. Heath concludes that

> the patterns of language use of the children of Roadville [a blue-collar white community] and Trackton [a blue-collar black community] before they go to school stand in sharp contrast to each other and to those of the youngsters from [middle-class] townspeople families. Though parents in all three communities want to "get ahead," their constructions of the social activities the children must engage in for access to language, oral or written, vary greatly. The sequence of habits Trackton children develop in learning language, telling stories, making metaphors, and seeing patterns across items and events

do not fit the developmental patterns of either linguistic or cognitive growth reported in the research literature on mainstream children. Roadville children, on the other hand, seem to have developed many of the cognitive and linguistic patterns equated with readiness for school, yet they seem not to move outward from these basics to the integrative types of skills necessary for sustained academic success. (343)

Like Heath, Scollon and Scollon also point out differences between the practices of a non-mainstream group, the Athabaskan, a group of Alaskan Native Americans, and mainstream practices. For example, as they grow up, Athabaskan children are taught not to take the initiative in speaking to a person they do not know. Scollon and Scollon note that "where the relationship of the communicants is unknown [in face-to-face interaction] . . . the Athabaskan prefer silence" (*Narrative* 53). Yet, in mainstream schools, these students are expected to write to an unknown audience on a consistent basis, a practice that conflicts with the norms governing interaction in their home community. Using examples like this one, Scollon and Scollon conclude that "where the interethnic communication patterns produce social conflict between [Athabaskan and non-Athabaskan] speakers, these same patterns produce internal conflict for an Athabaskan writer." Continuing, they contend that "it is this internal conflict that explains much of the problem of native literacy programs as well as problems with English literacy in the public school systems of Alaska and Canada" (53). The examples from the work of Heath and that of Scollon and Scollon should remind us of the potential for conflict between home community patterns for using language and literacy and those of the school. Although some students may be relatively successful in moving between the two, that success often comes at a great price as these students seek to create identities that will allow them to belong to the communities of both home and school. Traditionally, however, school has set up a false dichotomy, forcing non-mainstream students to choose one—the "correctness" of the school and its practices—or the other—the "ignorance" of native and natural ways of using language and literacy (Walters, "Whose Culture").

Among the barriers we as teachers face in understanding, learning about, and then building upon the growing diversity in our classrooms is a lack of information about groups to which we do not natively belong. Important complicating factors are the myths and false information—which we often treat as fact—that we have about the practices of those who are different from the mainstream "ideal" student. As the passage from Heath cited above makes unequivocally clear, the shared goal of families in many communities—ensuring a better life for their children—does not entail using spoken or written language in ways that the school expects, supports, encourages, or rewards or in ways familiar to many of us. From our perspective, ethnographic research about the patterns of language and literacy use across communities can become the basis for building bridges between home communities and schools, a necessary step if educators are to move from being merely curious about linguistic and cultural diversity to using such diversity as a resource.[3]

Beverly's own research (Moss 1988), an ethnographically oriented study of literacy in African-American worship services in Chicago, grew out of her desire to build such bridges between the academic and home communities of African-American students. From her own experience, she knew that a great deal of literate behavior took place in black churches among the very people who were often labeled illiterate by schools and other institutions and that schools seemed to be unable to capitalize on the kinds of literacy and literate behavior used in black churches and black homes. In conducting her fieldwork, Beverly learned a great deal about the kinds of texts and literacy people are exposed to as they grow up in this community; she also observed that the nature of the major literacy events in this community differ markedly from that of the major literacy events in school. Additionally, although she found some literacy practices that are similar to those in the academy, the function and uses of these events and the values attached to those practices are complicated and probably unique to the African-American church. One of the more interesting and complex literate texts, for example, was the church bulletin. In most churches, bulletins include the order of service and a few church-related announcements. Generally, they are printed on two to three 8-1/2-by-11-inch sheets folded in half to comprise four to six pages of information. In the largest church that Beverly observed, however, the Sunday bulletin averaged fifteen letter-sized pages with print on both the front and back of each sheet. In addition to the traditional order of worship and church-related announcements, the bulletin of this church also included advertisements for apartments and jobs, information about upcoming plays and concerts, community-related news, as well as statements, memos, and essays from the minister. The texts written by the minister covered a range of topics, but their general function was protest. For example, one memo called for a boycott of Colgate-Palmolive products because the company was marketing a new product, Sambo toothpaste, the name of which carried negative connotations for African Americans. Another piece stated the minister's position against apartheid and P. W. Botha. A third memo railed against a local Chicago politician.

Clearly, this text fulfills the traditional roles of church bulletins in that it provides information about the day's service and related announcements. We can safely assume that the creators of such a large bulletin believe that members of the congregation have certain kinds of literacy skills that lead them to do far more than merely receive information. In fact, the text is used to connect the congregation to the church community, the local African-American community, the city, the nation, and the world. It is also a text that introduces people to and engages them in political debates. It is sometimes a document of protest. Finally, this voluminous text, read from front to back by most congregants, signals to us that print literacy is an integral part of what has traditionally been mislabeled and reduced to an oral culture. Many of our African-American students have probably been exposed to this type of multi-functional literate text. Yet, because we know little about the language and literacy practices of students from home communities like these, we remain ignorant about this complex use of a written text, the skills they might bring to our classrooms, or the ways in which we might be able to build upon their knowledge and skills.[4]

If we understand that African-American churches have historically been the community institution that African Americans have looked to not only for spiritual guidance but also for information and for models of how to use language, then we begin to appreciate the influence of this institution on language use in the community. We can recognize that the participant structures—the interweaving of text and talk during the service, the dialogic quality of the sermon, the seamlessness of the service—are the norm for interaction in the African-American community. Yet, the behaviors that are appropriate in this community setting are usually anything but appropriate outside this setting, largely because outsiders know so little about what goes on in this community that they devalue its practices. Hence, a potential resource in the classroom is lost.

In our discussion of home language and literacy practices, we have sought to demonstrate the ways in which the culture the student brings to the classroom may have a profound influence on his or her behavior there. If teachers of writing are to do any more than scratch our heads and comment "Well, the problem must have something to do with the kid's background," that is, if we are to build any sorts of bridges between the kinds of knowledge about language and literacy students bring to the classroom and the expectations of the academy, a necessary first step is learning a great deal about those kinds of knowledge. Perhaps the best way to learn about those kinds of knowledge is to examine available ethnographic research on literacy across communities (e.g., Moss, *Literacy Across Communities*). Such research can provide important information about particular communities, but more important, it can help us as teachers develop a healthy respect for differences in this area and a useful perspective for considering the problems experienced by our own students.

First Language

Certainly, a major change in writing classrooms across the country over the last few decades has been the decrease in the number of classrooms made up uniquely of native speakers of English. Consequently, teachers, even those with extensive training and experience in teaching composition to native speakers, find themselves faced with new kinds of problems at many levels. Although a growing body of research deals with many of these issues, we have little understanding of the range of topics that are relevant. A tendency of many teachers is to belabor the point that speakers of certain languages have special problems with articles or the use of the perfect tenses. We do not wish to minimize the importance of mastering the code itself; however, from our perspective, focusing on patterns of fossilized errors may not be a teacher's or student's best use of time or energy. Our concerns here are those that relate to issues of rhetoric: how to develop and arrange arguments in order to persuade readers; how to select and organize material to support arguments; how to use logical, ethical, and pathetic appeals appropriately.

From his own study of Arabic, his experience teaching speakers of Arabic, and his reading of available research on the Arabic rhetorical tradition and the problems speakers of Arabic have when learning to write in English, Keith has learned some of the ways that Arabs and Americans are likely to differ when they construct, for example, an argumentative text. A native speaker of Arabic reared in an Arab country and trained in the tradition of Arab rhetoric is likely to provide far more background information than an English-speaking American reared in the United States probably would. Often, the Arab will begin at a far more abstract level of generalization than the American is likely to. Keith remembers one Arab student's essay on families that began "All over the world and in many places, we find families." In addition to what seems to be the unnecessarily obvious generalization to the American academic reader, the pair of prepositional phrases in this opening sentence illustrates the extent to which repetition with variation is highly valued among speakers and writers of Arabic, at least partly because of the ways in which the morphology and semantics of the Arabic language interact, thereby providing linguistic resources simply not available to the English-language writer. Perhaps most important, however, might be the general notion that whereas persuasion in this country is ostensibly based on carefully amassing logical arguments for a position not already held by the hearer or reader, in the Arab tradition, persuasion is based on reminding the hearer or reader of some truth that he or she already shares with the speaker or writer, making way for a view of persuasion requiring logical, ethical, and pathetic appeals.[5]

Particularly important in discussions of these issues are the observations that cross-cultural and cross-linguistic differences exist and that they can create problems for members of either group who are trying to use the other language to persuade. For example, when Keith has attempted to write something in Arabic, he has had to work very hard to keep from falling back on what seemed like his perfectly good American strategies, which do not get him very far. What seemed like such an obvious, straight line to him was evaluated as being far too short and dotted by his Arab readers in much the same way that their English-language texts represent lines that are far too long, doubling back on themselves far too often. Thus, other cultures have conventionalized ways of selecting, organizing, and presenting information; even if we as researchers or classroom teachers have a very incomplete grasp of what those ways may be, we can begin to acknowledge the existence of differences and to realize that our preferred ways of structuring texts are themselves conventional, standing at the intersection of English as a linguistic system, the Western rhetorical tradition, the teaching of writing in American schools, and a host of other influences. Such a rethinking of our own position, such a decentering, reminds us again of the limitations of our own knowledge of our tradition and the traditions of others; it also demonstrates the need for models of teaching and learning based on mutual respect through collaboration and cooperation.

Age

In addition to the increase in the number of students from diverse ethnic backgrounds who will attend college in the coming years, the average age of students attending college will continue to rise, a tendency already clear in many schools. Consequently, no longer can we expect our first-year writing courses to be made up of eighteen- and nineteen-year-old students fresh out of high school. Our older students may include wives, husbands, single parents, military veterans, full-time workers, and part-timers of many sorts. These "non-traditional" older students bring life and work experiences into our classes that affect the way they value school and many of its practices. With these experiences come knowledge, expectations, and skills that we might not normally associate with the typical eighteen-year-old first-year student who may be away from home for the first time. Although we know of no research concerning the ways in which the presence of this population might affect the writing classroom, we know from personal experience that these students have different kinds of goals and different strategies for reaching them than their younger classmates. Beverly has noticed, for example, that older women returning to school often prefer to rely on their own life experiences and those of their friends rather than simply citing secondary sources when arguing a point. Beverly welcomes this source for authority and the concomitant personal narratives that are woven into otherwise academic papers, but she also recognizes that the academy traditionally values citations from scholarly works far more highly than it values narratives of personal experience. She has also observed that these older women's classmates are sometimes enthralled by the women's argumentative strategies; other times, however, they are baffled by them.

And because many of these students are older than we are, patterns of face-to-face interaction shift as we find ourselves speaking with people who are our elders even though we may be their teachers and vested with the authority to evaluate their work and assign them grades. Additionally, for these students, responsibilities outside school often have to take priority over schoolwork. Therefore, helping older students balance their schoolwork and personal lives will bring us new challenges. While we view the different perspectives that older students bring as resources, teaching them well will likely require that we rethink our notion of whom we teach and our assumptions about them. Having older students may ultimately affect our assignment-making, class discussions, and dynamics inside and outside the classroom just as having students from a variety of linguistic and ethnic backgrounds often does.

Sex/Gender

The last two decades have seen a great deal of research devoted to male and female differences in language use. With rare exception, researchers have assigned subject to categories according to biological sex (or, more accurately, apparent or reported biological sex), although their real interest has been gender, the complex set of cultural beliefs, norms, and behaviors associated with appropriate behavior for males and females or assumptions about the nature of masculinity and femininity. Even distinguishing between sex and gender in this fashion does not automatically make the relationship between sex, gender, and language transparent in any way. When researchers discuss sex- or gender-related patterns of language use in English, they are usually concerned with what Sally McConnell-Ginet in "Language and Gender" terms *gender markers,* ways of using language associated with, but by no means exclusive to, members of one sex or the other (80–81), although they often seem to rely heavily and unreflectively on gender stereotypes or gender norms, even in discussion and interpretation of empirical data.[6]

Among the most important findings to emerge from the research on sex- or gender-related patterns of language use in this society is the observation that males and females may well use language in different ways because they have different sorts of interactional goals (e.g., Tannen, *You Just Don't Understand*) and because they were socialized in different ways as children (e.g., Maltz and Borker). Male children tend to grow up playing in hierarchical groups, whereas female children seem to prefer to have a "best friend" who may change frequently. Researchers such as Penelope Eckert, who conducted ethnographic fieldwork in a Detroit high school as part of a study of linguistic variation and language change in progress, points out that the reputation of male adolescents seems to depend on what they do, but the reputation of female adolescents seems to depend on "the whole woman": "Girls in high school are more socially constrained than boys. Not only do they monitor their own behavior and that of others more closely, but they maintain more rigid social boundaries" ("The Whole Woman" 258).

Given these differences in life experience and perception of the self and the Other (as well as the self in contrast to the Other), should we be surprised that females and males might use language in different ways to different ends? Females, it appears, are often concerned with watching the group interaction and paying attention to both what is said and how it is said—the affective dimensions of the interaction. Borrowing Eckert's language, in general, females seem to monitor carefully the interactions in which they are involved in ways that most males do not. Based on these sorts of observations, Pamela Fishman has contended that most, if not all, of the "shitwork" in interactions falls to females. Males, on the other hand, appear to be less attuned to the affective aspects of messages. As Deborah Tannen ("Teachers' Classroom Strategies") points out, in class discussions, for example, males may feel it is their responsibility to contribute by speaking, even if they seem to dominate, whereas females may see their responsibility as being sure that they do not speak too often lest others not have the opportunity. Similar situations occur and recur in our classrooms. Not surprisingly, researchers investigating language and sex or gender frequently talk about issues of power.

In "Teachers' Classroom Strategies Should Recognize That Men and Women Use Language Differently," Tannen reminds university professors that such differences in using language have implications for what happens in the classroom. Professors who rely uniquely on one style of interaction should not be surprised to find that males or females as a group may be uncomfortable—or perhaps even alienated—by what occurs or fails to occur. Because large-group discussions are in many ways "public" forums, males may feel more comfortable contributing to them than females; similarly, males may be more comfortable than females with interactions that resemble debate or argument. Yet, as earlier research (Hall and Sandler as well as references cited in Kramerae et al.) reminds us, both male and female teachers tend to give male students more eye contact and verbal feedback than their female counterparts; similarly, teachers tend to reward uses of language that resemble "essayist literacy" as discussed above, practices that some have associated with male ways of using language (cf. Tannen's discussion of Ong's *Fighting for Life* in "Teachers' Classroom Strategies").

Such studies and observations are sometimes seen as indictments of the particular teacher whose behavior is analyzed or evidence of a societal conspiracy to silence females or to eradicate certain styles of interaction. Yet, as researchers such as Tannen remind us, sex and gender interact with culturally influenced conversational style and individual personality in complex ways. Our point in discussing this body of research is to remind ourselves and our readers that sex or, perhaps more accurately, interactional styles traditionally associated with male and female socialization in this culture constitute one additional axis of diversity that is likely to manifest itself in the classroom. Related work such as that of Cynthia Selfe and Paul Meyer, on the one hand, and Elizabeth Flynn, on the other, on the behavior of female writers and readers reminds us again of how much we have to learn about the ways that sex and gender may influence the production or comprehension of written language.

Sexual Orientation

We know very little about the ways in which sexual orientation can be an issue in educational settings or more specifically writing classes. First, as Sarah Sloane, in "Invisible Diversity: Gay and Lesbian Students Writing Our Way into the Academy," reminds us, "the gay and lesbian community . . . comprises a unique minority because, to a large extent, members can choose whether or not to reveal their minority status." Because of societal homophobia and the fear it inspires in individual lesbians, gay males, and bisexuals, few should be surprised that many members of this group choose not to reveal their sexual orientation, especially when one considers the possible negative consequences of doing so. Additionally, we must acknowledge that there is little encouragement for students to be honest about these issues in the classroom. Certainly, any bisexual, lesbian, or gay student can attest to the absence of representation (except perhaps negative ones) of his or her life experience in the reading assigned for most courses. Yet teachers who have been influenced even marginally by reader-response or feminist theories of reading or by social constructionist epistemologies must logically acknowledge that because the life experiences of lesbian, bisexual, or gay students differ in significant ways from those of their strictly heterosexual classmates, their responses to the texts they are asked to read or construct may differ. Investigating these differences is made all the more complex because college represents a time when many students are first dealing with these issues for themselves and because various institutions of our society including the university are being challenged to rethink their public and private stances on these issues.

Despite these difficulties, we can point to the findings of some research and speculate about other potential areas of interest. Sloane interviewed several gay and lesbian students at a large Midwestern university. On the basis of her research, she reminds teachers that assignments in writing classes, especially highly personal writing assignments, can put lesbian and gay students in a difficult position, leading them to engage in what she terms "omission," the silencing of parts of experience that they fear may not be safe to reveal, and "transformation," which might include such strategies as "pronoun laundering" to disguise the sex of the participants involved in an event. Deciding how to respond honestly to such assignments for gay, lesbian, and bisexual students is likely to be a different sort of choice than it is for heterosexual students, something that most professors probably have not considered.

Similarly, if teachers want bisexual, lesbian, or gay students in their classrooms to feel comfortable talking about issues related to their life experience—and we acknowledge that many teachers do not—those who do will have to let these students know that it is safe to do so.

In our discussion of whom we teach, we have considered a number of particular axes of difference for several reasons. Obviously, the easily labeled variables we have discussed do not show up in disembodied form in our classrooms. Instead, we teach individuals who may differ from their teacher along several of these axes at once. These variables are in no sense additive: to be a first-generation Asian-American lesbian is not to be merely "native language other than English + Asian-American + female + lesbian." It represents a particular way of being in the world—in this society at this time—that is similar to and different from the ways of being in the world of others who are different. Similarly, although understanding the cultural and linguistic backgrounds of our students provides teachers with great insight, we must constantly recognize that not all students from a particular cultural background are alike. Not all African Americans are alike. Not all women or Native Americans are alike. Not all bisexual, lesbian, or gay students are alike just as not all straight white males—dead or alive—are alike. Assuming that we should treat all members of a particular group the same is just as dangerous as not recognizing the differences between groups. Teachers and students who are similar in some way because society has labeled them different will often negotiate their response to such labeling in complex, contrasting ways.

Many times what emerges from efforts to deal with diversity is a well-meaning but, we believe, errant notion that recognizing and building upon diversity means developing separate pedagogies for each group—the "right" way to teach African-American students, Native Americans, women, and so on. We find such a move troubling. For example, following the work of Sarah Michaels on what she has characterized as ethnic differences in narrative style, many educators seem now tempted to assume that all (and only) African-American children use a topic-associative discourse style and that all (and only) white children use a topic-centered discourse style. We fear the day may have already arrived when students in education programs are given charts contrasting these two ways of constructing and using narratives with one column labeled black and the other labeled white. If so, the black or white child coming into a classroom for the first time will not be an individual; instead, regardless of social class background or prior life or school experience, he or she will be labeled a "topic associator" or a "topic centerer" before uttering a word. For us, the desire or need to put students into fixed categories or to lock them into our neat little boxes based on ethnicity, sex, age, first language, sexual orientation, or some other sociodemographic variable is as irresponsible as denying that diversity exists in our classrooms.

DIVERSITY AND WHO WE ARE: RETHINKING AUTHORITY IN OUR CLASSROOMS

Thus far, we have concentrated on diversity among students, who they are, what they know, and what they bring to the classroom. Yet, no discussion of diversity would be complete without a consideration of the teacher, who, we contend, is always more than simply a conduit of information. Every teacher who reads this text is an individual of a particular social class, age, sex, sexual orientation, and ethnic and social background. It is our belief that these axes of difference matter in the classroom and that they influence how all of us have learned and how we now teach in ways we can probably never understand. When we seek to understand the significance of these kinds of difference, we find ourselves confronting issues of authority, its origin, and its manifestations in the classroom.

Sometimes, the significance of one or more of these axes of difference in relation to authority is both evident and salient. Most of us, for example, would be surprised to find a male teaching a course entitled "Introduction to Women's Studies," a reaction that should remind us of our assumptions about who is mostly likely or most suited to teach certain subjects. When, for example, Keith began teaching an undergraduate course about the structure, history, and use of Black English, he was immediately faced with issues of authority. A few minutes into the course on the first day of class the first time he taught the course, a Hispanic female asked about his "background." Certain facts—that he is a sociolinguist familiar with the relevant research literature, that he had grown up in the South and taught in sub-Saharan Africa, that he had worked with many African-American students—were not obvious in the way that his ethnicity is.

Certainly, Beverly faces different issues than does Keith. Almost every time that she walks into an undergraduate English course (other than one with "African-American" in the title), students are surprised to see her, an African-American woman, stand before the class. Because she teaches at a university that attracts large numbers of white students from rural or suburban areas, many of her students, especially the first-quarter freshmen, have never had or even seen an African-American teacher. Most of what they know or think they know about

African Americans comes from the media, and much of that is negative. Once many of these students get over the shock of finding out that she is the professor, many of them start to question her authority. She is asked many times if she has a PhD, where she went to school, and how old she is. And often she is challenged by students in ways that she doubts a white male or even a white female would be.[7] She remembers the day that someone observed her Freshman Honors Composition class and commented afterwards that the all-white class seemed uncomfortable with a black teacher. She also recalls that in one of the evaluations of an introductory literature and composition class, a student complained that Beverly had focused too much on "that minority literature" when actually less than twenty percent of the writers read in the course were people of color, a percentage Beverly sees as low when one considers the demographics of the English-speaking world. She wonders if the student would have complained about the syllabus had the teacher not been a woman of color. Many times when Beverly attempts to design a class in which she and the students negotiate or share authority, the students never perceive her as having any authority to begin with. She sees part of her task as teacher as helping students see that her being an African-American woman adds a positive dimension to their classroom experience as their presence contributes to her life experience. Yet she knows that students must be educated to rethink their views on diversity in the classroom (including diversity in front of the class) in the same way that teachers must be.

We contend, however, that issues of power and authority are inherent in all acts of teaching and learning and that they manifest themselves in myriad ways in all classrooms. We likewise believe that all of us need to continue thinking about these issues with respect to the teaching we do. At the same time, we do not believe we can or should tell others how to negotiate issues of authority in their classrooms. We can only point to our current understanding of our experiences, share what we think we have learned from them, and challenge others to do the same.

Traditionally, the notion of teaching culturally and linguistically diverse populations within one institution, one classroom, has often resulted in the question, "What am I supposed to do with them?" (The "them," of course, refers to those who have not been represented in large numbers in our university writing classes, and the "I" is someone whose ancestors hail most recently from Europe.) This panicked approach has traditionally been dealt with by the scholarly community through a growing number of conferences and publications on the topic. A similar attitude prevailed in the 1960s, when the advent of open admissions served as impetus for such work as Shaughnessy's *Errors and Expectations* and sometime later David Bartholomae's "Inventing the University." What this body of scholarship and most of our teaching experience have encouraged us to do is to rethink our definition of "student." We now acknowledge that there is no monolithic student; there are students who come to the classroom from various communities and bring with them much of the baggage, positive and negative, of those communities as well as their own individual idiosyncrasies and agendas. They also bring into the classroom their own discourse patterns, reflecting community values and world views. Sometimes these patterns and values match those of the teacher and others in the academic institutions; sometimes they do not. The mismatches and the ways in which teachers and those who design curricula respond to them call attention to how sensitive or insensitive we are to issues of linguistic and cultural diversity. Because we have operated for so long with an "ideal student" mentality that has not only failed to acknowledge difference but also been philosophically and ideologically opposed to building upon whatever difference might have grudgingly been acknowledged, reeducating ourselves to serve our diverse student populations represents a major task.

It is easy to see why we as teachers, even teachers of writing, have long wished to ignore diversity. Acknowledging difference, examining it, and finding creative ways to build upon it—to make it the cornerstone of individual and corporate philosophies of educational theory and classroom practice—require that we see ourselves, our beliefs, and even our actions, from a new perspective, one that forces us, as Clifford Geertz has put it, to see ourselves among others. Our preferred way of using language and of being literate becomes a way among ways rather than the single, correct way; it is appropriate in some contexts and useless in others. What seem like natural or logical ways of presenting information or evaluating knowledge no longer stand alone as the only possible alternatives or even the most expedient ones.

We have come to realize that dealing with diversity has led us to change not only how we teach but also our understanding of what constitutes "those things which are to be understood" in the first place (Augustine 7). Throughout this process, we find ourselves having to rethink—that is, renegotiate—our authority and, consequently, our role and our practice in the classroom and in the larger professional arena. We have come to see these sites as places where we should assume far less common ground than we traditionally have and where we realize we probably have more to learn than we do to teach or at least a great deal to learn as we teach. These are lessons all good teachers no doubt know. The need to relearn them and to think about them in new and deeper ways constitutes, we believe, a challenge of tremendous proportion, one that, if met, has the potential of changing what it means to teach and learn in this society in important, positive ways.

NOTES

[1] We use "conversation" metaphorically to include, as implied above, a variety of teacher/student interactions ranging from classroom lectures during which a teacher may speak to a group of students, receiving little direct verbal feedback, to conversations between student and teacher on the telephone or in the office to electronic exchanges between two or more parties, one of whom is the teacher. To varying degrees, all of these kinds of interactions are based on patterns associated with face-to-face two-party conversations; as the literature on language in the classroom reminds us, these categories of interactions also differ crucially from one another and from "everyday conversation" in ways that are not at all transparent.

[2] Michaels's work clearly shows that the black students are quite aware of the differences between their narrative style and that of the teacher. In "Deena's Story: The Discourse of the

Other," Beth Daniell argues that Deena's refusal to adopt the teacher's preferred strategies lest she forfeit her own identity and autonomy constitutes an act of resistance. Deena's refusal can also be read in light of the work of Le Page and Tabouret-Keller.

[3] For an especially interesting exchange on the possible limits of ethnographic research in effecting educational change, see the paper by Cazden ("Can Ethnographic Research Go Beyond the Status Quo?"), Kleinfeld's response ("First Do No Harm"), and the comments on this exchange by Amsbury, Barnhardt, Bishop, Chandler, Greenbaum and Greenbaum, Grubis, Harrison, and Stearns as well as the final statements of Kleinfeld ("Some of My Best Friends") and Cazden ("Response").

[4] Valerie Balester's unpublished dissertation examines some of the ways in which the rhetorical practices of the African-American community and especially the African-American church influence the writing of students familiar with these traditions.

[5] Of course, exceptions to this generalization are plentiful. Advertising in this country rarely focuses uniquely on logical appeals alone; in fact, Keith would contend that an interesting part of Western rhetoric (or at least Western rhetoric as instantiated in most freshman texts) is its pretending that only logical appeals matter. In some ways, the task of the Arab rhetor might be compared to that of many Christian ministers, especially Fundamentalist ones, who, even in their efforts to save souls, often do so by reminding the lost ones of the Truth that, at some level, they are assumed already to know. Many of these issues are treated in a book by Barbara Johnstone and an unpublished manuscript by Keith ("On Written Persuasive Discourse").

[6] A major intellectual problem for this field of research—like all fields involving axes of difference—is determining the extent to which its findings represent actual accounts or explanations of phenomena rather than reifications of cultural categories, stereotypes, or norms.

[7] Interestingly, in his course about Black English, Keith wonders if his students—African-American and non-African-American—do not question the data he presents in class (often from published research) in ways they might not if he were black.

WORKS CITED

Amsbury, Clifton. "The Problem of Simplicity." *Anthropology and Education Quarterly* 15 (1984): 168-69.

Augustine, Saint. *On Christian Doctrine.* Trans. D. W. Robertson, Jr. Indianapolis: Bobbs-Merrill, 1978.

Balester, Valerie M. "The Social Construction of *Ethos:* A Study of the Spoken and Written Discourse of Two Black College Students." Diss. U of Texas at Austin, 1989.

Barnhardt, Ray. "Anthropology Needs No Apology." *Anthropology and Education Quarterly* 15 (1984): 179-80.

Bartholomae, David. "Inventing the University." *When a Writer Can't Write.* Ed. Mike Rose. New York: Guilford, 1985. 134-65.

Bishop, Ralph J. "Educational Failure and the Status Quo." *Anthropology and Education Quarterly* 15 (1984): 167-68.

Cazden, Courtney. "Can Ethnographic Research Go Beyond the Status Quo?" *Anthropology and Education Quarterly* 14 (1983): 33-41.

———. "Response." *Anthropology and Education Quarterly* 15 (1984): 184-85.

Chandler, Joan M. "Education Equals Change." *Anthropology and Education Quarterly* 15 (1984): 176-78.

Daniell, Beth "Deena's Story: The Discourse of the Other." *Gender, Composition, and the Academy.* Ed. Deborah H. Holdstein. New York: MLA, in press.

Eckert, Penelope. "The Whole Woman: Sex and Gender Differences in Variation." *Language Variation and Change* 1 (1989): 245-67.

Fishman, Pamela M. "Interaction: The Work Women Do." Thorne, Kramerae, and Henley 89-101.

Flynn, Elizabeth. "Gender and Reading." *Gender and Reading: Essays on Readers, Texts, and Contexts.* Ed. Elizabeth Flynn and Patrocinio Schwieckart. Baltimore: Johns Hopkins UP, 1986. 267-88.

Freeman, Sarah, ed. *The Acquisition of Written Language: Revision and Response.* Norwood, NJ: Ablex.

Geertz, Clifford. *Local Knowledge: Further Essays in the Interpretive Anthropology.* New York: Basic Books, 1983.

Greenbaum, Susan D., and Paul E. Greenbaum. "Integrating Ethnographic and Quantitative Research: A Reply to Kleinfeld with Implications for American Indian Self-Determination." *Anthropology and Education Quarterly* 15 (1984): 171-73.

Grubis, Steve. "A Teacher Perspective." *Anthropology and Education Quarterly* 15 (1984): 178-79.

Hall, Roberta M., and Bernice R. Sandler. "A Chilly Climate in the Classroom." *Beyond Sex Roles.* 2nd ed. Ed. Alice G. Sargent. St. Paul, MN: West Publishing, 1985. 503-10.

Harrison, Barbara. "Training for Cross-Cultural Teaching." *Anthropology and Education Quarterly* 15 (1984): 169-70.

Heath, Shirley Brice. *Ways with Words: Language, Life and Work in Communities and Classrooms.* Cambridge: Cambridge UP, 1983.

Hirsch, E. D., Jr., *Cultural Literacy: What Every American Needs to Know.* Boston: Houghton, 1987.

Hymes, Dell. "Models of the Interaction of Language and Social Life." *Directions in Socio-Linguistics: The Ethnography of Communication.* Ed. John G. Gumperz and Dell Hymes. New York: Holt, 1972. 35-71.

Janda, Mary Ann. "Collaboration in a Traditional Classroom Environment." *Written Communication* 7 (1990): 291-315.

Johnstone, Barbara. *Repetition in Arabic Discourse: Paradigms, Syntagms, and the Ecology of Language.* Amsterdam: John Benjamins, 1991.

Kleinfeld, Judith. "First Do No Harm: A Reply to Courtney Cazden." *Anthropology and Education Quarterly* 14 (1983): 282-87.

———. "Some of My Best Friends Are Anthropologists." *Anthropology and Education Quarterly* 15 (1984): 180-84.

Kramerae, Cheris, Barrie Thorne, and Nancy Henley. "Sex Similarities and Differences in Language, Speech, and Nonverbal Communication: An Annotated Bibliography." Thorne, Kramerae, and Henley. 151-331.

Le Page, R. B., and Andrée Tabouret-Keller. *Acts of Identity: Creole-Based Approaches to Language and Ethnicity.* Cambridge: Cambridge UP, 1985.

McConnell-Ginet, Sally. "Language and Gender." Newmeyer 75-99.

Maltz, Daniel, and Ruth Borker. "A Cultural Approach to Male-Female Miscommunication." *Language and Social Identity.* Ed. John J. Gumperz. Cambridge: Cambridge UP, 1982. 196-216.

Mehan, Hugh. "The Competent Student." *Working Paper #69.* Austin, TX: Southwest Educational Development Laboratory, 1979.

Michaels, Sarah. "Sharing Time: Children's Narrative Styles and Differential Access to Literacy." *Language in Society* 10 (1981): 423-42.

Moss, Beverly J. "The Black Sermon as a Literacy Event." Diss. U of Illinois at Chicago, 1988.

———. ed. *Literacy Across Communities.* Cresskill, NJ: Hampton Press, in press.

Newmeyer, Frederick, ed. *Language: The Socio-Cultural Matrix.* Vol. 4 of *Linguistics: The Cambridge Survey.* Cambridge: Cambridge UP, 1988.

Ong, Walter. *Fighting for Life: Contest, Sexuality, and Consciousness.* Ithaca, NY: Cornell UP, 1981.

The Oprah Winfrey Show. Exec. prod. Debra DiMaio. Dir. Jim McPharlin. With Bernadette Anderson, Ronnie Carter, Gary D., Thomas Kochman, Geneva Smitherman, and Bonnie Thompson. NBC. WXAN, Austin, TX. 19 Nov. 1987.

Philips, Susan U. *The Invisible Culture: Communication in Classroom and Community on the Warm Springs Indian Reservation.* New York: Longman, 1983.

Scollon, Ron, and Suzanne B. K. Scollon. "Literacy as Focused Interaction." *Quarterly Newsletter of the Laboratory of Comparative Human Cognition* 2.2 (1986): 26-29.

——. *Narrative, Literacy and Face in Interethnic Communication*. Norwood, NJ: Ablex, 1981.

Selfe, Cynthia, and Paul Meyer. "Testing Claims for On-Line Conferences." *Written Communication* 8 (1991): 163-92.

Shaughnessy, Mina. *Errors and Expectations*. New York: Oxford UP, 1977.

Sloane, Sarah. "Invisible Diversity: Gay and Lesbian Students Writing Our Way into the Academy." *Writing Ourselves into the Story*. Ed. Laura Fontaine and Susan Hunter. Southern Illinois UP, 1993.

Sperling, Melanie. "Dialogues of Deliberation: Conversation in the Teacher-Student Writing Conference." *Written Communication* 8 (1991): 131-62.

Stearns, Robert D. "Beyond an Emic View of Anthropologists and Anthropology: An Alaskan Perspective." *Anthropology and Education Quarterly* 15 (1984): 174-76.

Students' Right to Their Own Language. Urbana, IL: NCTE, 1976.

Tannen, Deborah. "Teachers' Classroom Strategies Should Recognize That Men and Women Use Language Differently." *Chronicle of Higher Education* 19 June 1991: B1, B3.

——. *You Just Don't Understand: Women and Men in Conversation*. New York: Morrow, 1990.

Thorne, Barrie, Cheris Kramerae, and Nancy Henley, eds. *Language, Gender and Society*. Cambridge, MA: Newbury, 1975.

Walters, Keith. " 'It's Like Playing Password, Right?': Socratic Questioning and Questioning at School." *Texas Linguistics Forum* 24 (1984): 157-88.

——. "Language, Logic, and Literacy." *The Right to Literacy*. Ed. Andrea A. Lunsford, Helene Moglen, and James Slevin. New York: MLA, 1990. 173-88.

——. "On Written Persuasive Discourse in Arabic and English." Unpublished essay, University of Texas at Austin, 1987.

——. "Whose Culture? Whose Literacy?" *Diversity as Resource in the Classroom: Redefining Cultural Literacy*. Ed. Denise Murray. Alexandria, VA: TESOL, 1992.

This article is excerpted from *Theory and Practice in the Teaching of Writing: Rethinking the Discipline*. Ed. Lee Odell. Carbondale: Southern Illinois UP, 1993. —Ed.

Patrick Hartwell

GRAMMAR, GRAMMARS, AND THE TEACHING OF GRAMMAR

For me the grammar issue was settled at least twenty years ago with the conclusion offered by Richard Braddock, Richard Lloyd-Jones, and Lowell Schoer in 1963.

> In view of the widespread agreement of research studies based upon many types of students and teachers, the conclusion can be stated in strong and unqualified terms: the teaching of formal grammar has a negligible or, because it usually displaces some instruction and practice in composition, even a harmful effect on improvement in writing.[1]

Indeed, I would agree with Janet Emig that the grammar issue is a prime example of "magical thinking": the assumption that students will learn only what we teach and only because we teach.[2]

But the grammar issue, as we will see, is a complicated one. And, perhaps surprisingly, it remains controversial with the regular appearance of papers defending the teaching of formal grammar or attacking it.[3] Thus Janice Neuleib, writing on "The Relation of Formal Grammar to Composition" in *College Composition and Communication* (23 [1977], 247-250), is tempted "to sputter on paper" at reading the quotation above (p. 248), and Martha Kolln,

[1] *Research in Written Composition* (Urbana, Ill.: National Council of Teachers of English, 1963), pp. 37-38.

[2] "Non-magical Thinking: Presenting Writing Developmentally in Schools," in *Writing Process, Development and Communication,* Vol. II of *Writing: The Nature, Development and Teaching of Written Communication,* ed. Charles H. Frederiksen and Joseph F. Dominic (Hillsdale, N.J.: Lawrence Erlbaum, 1980), pp. 21-30.

[3] For arguments in favor of formal grammar teaching, see Patrick F. Basset, "Grammar—Can We Afford Not to Teach It?" *NASSP Bulletin,* 64, No. 10 (1980), 55-63; Mary Epes et al., "The COMP-LAB Project: Assessing the Effectiveness of a Laboratory-Centered Basic Writing Course on the College Level" (Jamaica, N.Y.: York College, CUNY, 1979) ERIC 194 908; June B. Evans, "The Analogous Ounce: The Analgesic for Relief," *English Journal,* 70, No. 2 (1981), 38-39; Sydney Greenbaum, "What Is Grammar and Why Teach It?" (a paper presented at the meeting of the National Council of Teachers of English, Boston, Nov. 1982) ERIC 222 917; Marjorie Smelstor, *A Guide to the Role of Grammar in Teaching Writing* (Madison: University of Wisconsin School of Education, 1978) ERIC 176 323; and A. M. Tibbetts, *Working Papers: A Teacher's Observations on Composition* (Glenview, Ill.: Scott, Foresman, 1982).

For attacks on formal grammar teaching, see Harvey A. Daniels, *Famous Last Words: The American Language Crisis Reconsidered* (Carbondale: Southern Illinois University Press, 1983); Suzette Haden Elgin, *Never Mind the Trees: What the English Teacher Really Needs to Know about Linguistics* (Berkeley: University of California College of Education, Bay Area Writing Project Occasional Paper No. 2, 1980) ERIC 198 536; Mike Rose, "Remedial Writing Courses: A Critique and a Proposal." *College English,* 45 (1983), 109-128; and Ron Shook, "Response to Martha Kolln," *College Composition and Communication,* 34 (1983), 491-495.

writing in the same journal three years later ("Closing the Books on Alchemy," *CCC*, 32 [1981], 139-151), labels people like me "alchemists" for our perverse beliefs. Neuleib reviews five experimental studies, most of them concluding that formal grammar instruction has no effect on the quality of students' writing nor on their ability to avoid error. Yet she renders in effect a Scots verdict of "Not proven" and calls for more research on the issue. Similarly, Kolln reviews six experimental studies that arrive at similar conclusions, only one of them overlapping with the studies cited by Neuleib. She calls for more careful definition of the word *grammar*—her definition being "the internalized system that native speakers of a language share" (p. 140)—and she concludes with a stirring call to place grammar instruction at the center of the composition curriculum: "our goal should be to help students understand the system they know unconsciously as native speakers, to teach them the necessary categories and labels that will enable them to think about and talk about their language" (p. 150). Certainly our textbooks and our pedagogies—though they vary widely in what they see as "necessary categories and labels"—continue to emphasize mastery of formal grammar, and popular discussions of a presumed literacy crisis are almost unanimous in their call for a renewed emphasis on the teaching of formal grammar, seen as basic for success in writing.[4]

AN INSTRUCTIVE EXAMPLE

It is worth noting at the outset that both sides in this dispute—the grammarians and the anti-grammarians—articulate the issue in the same positivistic terms: what does experimental research tell us about the value of teaching formal grammar? But seventy-five years of experimental research has for all practical purposes told us nothing. The two sides are unable to agree on how to interpret such research. Studies are interpreted in terms of one's prior assumptions about the value of teaching grammar: their results seem not to change those assumptions. Thus the basis of the discussion, a basis shared by Kolln and Neuleib and by Braddock and his colleagues—"what does educational research tell us?"—seems designed to perpetuate, not to resolve, the issue. A single example will be instructive. In 1976 and then at greater length in 1979, W. B. Elley, I. H. Barham, H. Lamb, and M. Wyllie reported on a three-year experiment in New Zealand, comparing the relative effectiveness at the high school level of instruction in transformational grammar, instruction in traditional grammar, and no grammar instruction.[5] They concluded that the

---

[4] See, for example, Clifton Fadiman and James Howard, *Empty Pages: A Search for Writing Competence in School and Society* (Belmont, Cal.: Fearon Pitman, 1979); Edwin Newman, *A Civil Tongue* (Indianapolis, Ind.: Bobbs-Merrill, 1976); and *Strictly Speaking* (New York: Warner Books, 1974); John Simons, *Paradigms Lost* (New York: Clarkson N. Potter, 1980); A. M. Tibbets and Charlene Tibbets, *What's Happening to American English?* (New York: Scribner's, 1978); and "Why Johnny Can't Write," *Newsweek*, 8 Dec. 1975, pp. 58–63.

[5] "The Role of Grammar in a Secondary School English Curriculum." *Research in the Teaching of English*, 10 (1976), 5-21; *The Role of Grammar in a Secondary School Curriculum* (Wellington: New Zealand Council of Teachers of English, 1979).

formal study of grammar, whether transformational or traditional, improved neither writing quality nor control over surface correctness.

> After two years, no differences were detected in writing performance or language competence; after three years small differences appeared in some minor conventions favoring the TG [transformational grammar] group, but these were more than offset by the less positive attitudes they showed towards their English studies. (p. 18)

Anthony Petrosky, in a review of research ("Grammar Instruction: What We Know," *English Journal,* 66, No. 9 [1977], 86–88), agreed with this conclusion, finding the study to be carefully designed, "representative of the best kind of educational research" (p. 86), its validity "unquestionable" (p. 88). Yet Janice Neuleib in her essay found the same conclusions to be "startling" and questioned whether the findings could be generalized beyond the target population, New Zealand high school students. Martha Kolln, when her attention is drawn to the study ("Reply to Ron Shook," *CCC,* 32 [1981], 139–151), thinks the whole experiment "suspicious." And John Mellon has been willing to use the study to defend the teaching of grammar; the study of Elley and his colleagues, he has argued, shows that teaching grammar does no harm.[6]

It would seem unlikely, therefore, that further experimental research, in and of itself, will resolve the grammar issue. Any experimental design can be nitpicked, any experimental population can be criticized, and any experimental conclusion can be questioned or, more often, ignored. In fact, it may well be that the grammar question is not open to resolution by experimental research, that, as Noam Chomsky has argued in *Reflections on Language* (New York: Pantheon, 1975), criticizing the trivialization of human learning by behavioral psychologists, the issue is simply misdefined.

> There will be "good experiments" only in domains that lie outside the organism's cognitive capacity. For example, there will be no "good experiments" in the study of human learning.
>
> This discipline . . . will, of necessity, avoid those domains in which an organism is specially designed to acquire rich cognitive structures that enter into its life in an intimate fashion. The discipline will be of virtually no intellectual interest, it seems to me, since it is restricting itself in principle to those questions that are guaranteed to tell us little about the nature of organisms. (p. 36)

ASKING THE RIGHT QUESTIONS

As a result, though I will look briefly at the tradition of experimental research, my primary goal in this essay is to articulate the grammar issue in different and, I would hope, more productive terms. Specifically, I want to ask four questions:

---

[6] "A Taxonomy of Compositional Competencies," in *Perspectives on Literacy,* ed. Richard Beach and P. David Pearson (Minneapolis: University of Minnesota College of Education, 1979), pp. 247–272.

1. Why is the grammar issue so important? Why has it been the dominant focus of composition research for the last seventy-five years?
2. What definitions of the word *grammar* are needed to articulate the grammar issue intelligibly?
3. What do findings in cognate disciplines suggest about the value of formal grammar instruction?
4. What is our theory of language, and what does it predict about the value of formal grammar instruction? (This question—"What does our theory of language predict?"—seems a much more powerful question than "what does educational research tell us?")

In exploring these questions I will attempt to be fully explicit about issues, terms, and assumptions. I hope that both proponents and opponents of formal grammar instruction would agree that these are useful as shared points of reference: care in definition, full examination of the evidence, reference to relevant work in cognate disciplines, and explicit analysis of the theoretical bases of the issue.

But even with that gesture of harmony it will be difficult to articulate the issue in a balanced way, one that will be acceptable to both sides. After all, we are dealing with a professional dispute in which one side accuses the other of "magical thinking," and in turn that side responds by charging the other as "alchemists." Thus we might suspect that the grammar issue is itself embedded in larger models of the transmission of literacy, part of quite different assumptions about the teaching of composition.

Those of us who dismiss the teaching of formal grammar have a model of composition instruction that makes the grammar issue "uninteresting" in a scientific sense. Our model predicts a rich and complex interaction of learner and environment in mastering literacy, an interaction that has little to do with sequences of skills instruction as such. Those who defend the teaching of grammar tend to have a model of composition instruction that is rigidly skills-centered and rigidly sequential: the formal teaching of grammar, as the first step in that sequence, is the cornerstone or linchpin. Grammar teaching is thus supremely interesting, naturally a dominant focus for educational research. The controversy over the value of grammar instruction, then, is inseparable from two other issues: the issues of sequence in the teaching of composition and of the role of the composition teacher. Consider, for example, the force of these two issues in Janice Neuleib's conclusion: after calling for yet more experimental research on the value of teaching grammar, she ends with an absolute (and unsupported) claim about sequences and teacher roles in composition.

> We do know, however, that some things must be taught at different levels. Insistence on adherence to usage norms by composition teachers does improve usage. Students can learn to organize their papers if teachers do not accept papers that are disorganized. Perhaps composition teachers can teach those two abilities before they begin the more difficult tasks of developing syntactic sophistication and a winning style. ("The Relation of Formal Grammar to Composition," p. 250)

(One might want to ask, in passing, whether "usage norms" exist in the monolithic fashion the phrase suggests and whether refusing to accept disorganized papers is our best available pedagogy for teaching arrangement.)[7]

But I want to focus on the notion of sequence that makes the grammar issue so important: first grammar, then usage, then some absolute model of organization, all controlled by the teacher at the center of the learning process, with other matters, those of rhetorical weight—"syntactic sophistication and a winning style"—pushed off to the future. It is not surprising that we call each other names: those of us who question the value of teaching grammar are in fact shaking the whole elaborate edifice of traditional composition instruction.

THE FIVE MEANINGS OF "GRAMMAR"

Given its centrality to a well-established way of teaching composition, I need to go about the business of defining grammar rather carefully, particularly in view of Kolln's criticism of the lack of care in earlier discussions. Therefore I will build upon a seminal discussion of the word *grammar* offered a generation ago, in 1954, by W. Nelson Francis, often excerpted as "The Three Meanings of Grammar."[8] It is worth reprinting at length, if only to re-establish it as a reference point for future discussions.

> The first thing we mean by "grammar" is "the set of formal patterns in which the words of a language are arranged in order to convey larger meanings." It is not necessary that we be able to discuss these patterns self-consciously in order to be able to use them. In fact, all speakers of a language above the age of five or six know how to use its complex forms of organization with considerable skill; in this sense of the word—call it "Grammar 1"—they are thoroughly familiar with its grammar.
>
> The second meaning of "grammar"—call it "Grammar 2"—is "the branch of linguistic science which is concerned with the description, analysis, and formulization of formal language patterns." Just as gravity was in full operation before Newton's apple fell, so grammar in the first sense was in full operation before anyone formulated the first rule that began the history of grammar as a study.
>
> The third sense in which people use the word "grammar" is "linguistic etiquette." This we may call "Grammar 3." The word in this sense is often coupled with a derogatory adjective: we say that the expression "he ain't here" is "bad grammar." . . .
>
> As has already been suggested, much confusion arises from mixing these meanings. One hears a good deal of criticism of teachers of English couched in such terms as "they don't teach grammar any more." Criticism of this sort is based on the wholly unproven assumption that teaching Grammar 2 will improve the student's proficiency in Grammar 1 or improve his manners in Grammar 3. Actually, the form of Grammar 2 which is usually taught is a very

---

[7] On usage norms, see Edward Finegan, *Attitudes toward English Usage: The History of a War of Words* (New York: Teachers College Press, 1980), and Jim Quinn, *American Tongue in Cheek: A Populist Guide to Language* (New York: Pantheon, 1980); on arrangement, see Patrick Hartwell, "Teaching Arrangement: A Pedagogy," *CE*, 40 (1979), 548–554.

[8] "Revolution in Grammar," *Quarterly Journal of Speech*, 40 (1954), 299–312.

inaccurate and misleading analysis of the facts of Grammar 1; and it therefore is of highly questionable value in improving a person's ability to handle the structural patterns of his language. (pp. 300–301)

Francis' Grammar 3 is, of course, not grammar at all, but usage. One would like to assume that Joseph Williams' recent discussion of usage ("The Phenomenology of Error," *CCC*, 32 [1981], 152–168), along with his references, has placed those shibboleths in a proper perspective. But I doubt it, and I suspect that popular discussions of the grammar issue will be as flawed by the intrusion of usage issues as past discussions have been. At any rate I will make only passing reference to Grammar 3—usage—naively assuming that this issue has been discussed elsewhere and that my readers are familiar with those discussions.

We need also to make further discriminations about Francis' Grammar 2, given that the purpose of his 1954 article was to substitute for one form of Grammar 2, that "inaccurate and misleading" form "which is usually taught," another form, that of American structuralist grammar. Here we can make use of a still earlier discussion, one going back to the days when *PMLA* was willing to publish articles on rhetoric and linguistics, to a 1927 article by Charles Carpenter Fries, "The Rules of the Common School Grammars" (42 [1927], 221–237). Fries there distinguished between the scientific tradition of language study (to which we will now delimit Francis' Grammar 2, scientific grammar) and the separate tradition of "the common school grammars," developed unscientifically, largely based on two inadequate principles—appeals to "logical principles," like "two negatives make a positive," and analogy to Latin grammar; thus, Charlton Laird's characterization, "the grammar of Latin, ingeniously warped to suggest English" (*Language in America* [New York: World, 1970], p. 294). There is, of course, a direct link between the "common school grammars" that Fries criticized in 1927 and the grammar-based texts of today, and thus it seems wise, as Karl W. Dykema suggests ("Where Our Grammar Came From," *CE*, 22 [1961], 455–465), to separate Grammar 2, "scientific grammar," from Grammar 4, "school grammar," the latter meaning, quite literally, "the grammars used in the schools."

Further, since Martha Kolln points to the adaptation of Christensen's sentence rhetoric in a recent sentence-combining text as an example of the proper emphasis on "grammar" ("Closing the Books on Alchemy," p. 140), it is worth separating out, as still another meaning of *grammar,* Grammar 5, "stylistic grammar," defined as "grammatical terms used in the interest of teaching prose style." And, since stylistic grammars abound, with widely variant terms and emphases, we might appropriately speak parenthetically of specific forms of Grammar 5— Grammar 5 (Lanham): Grammar 5 (Strunk and White); Grammar 5 (Williams, *Style*); even Grammar 5 (Christensen, as adapted by Daiker, Kerek, and Morenberg).[9]

---

[9] Richard A. Lanham, *Revising Prose* (New York: Scribner's, 1979); William Strunk and E. B. White, *The Elements of Style,* 3rd ed. (New York: Macmillan, 1979); Joseph Williams, *Style: Ten Lessons in Clarity and Grace* (Glenview, Ill.: Scott, Foresman, 1981); Christensen, "A Generative Rhetoric of the Sentence," *CCC*, 14 (1963), 155–161; Donald A. Daiker, Andrew Kerek, and Max Morenberg, *The Writer's Options: Combining to Composing,* 2nd ed. (New York: Harper & Row, 1982).

THE GRAMMAR IN OUR HEADS

With these definitions in mind, let us return to Francis' Grammar 1, admirably defined by Kolln as "the internalized system of rules that speakers of a language share" ("Closing the Books on Alchemy," p. 140), or, to put it more simply, the grammar in our heads. Three features of Grammar 1 need to be stressed: first, its special status as an "internalized system of rules," as tacit and unconscious knowledge; second, the abstract, even counterintuitive, nature of these rules, insofar as we are able to approximate them indirectly as Grammar 2 statements; and third, the way in which the form of one's Grammar 1 seems profoundly affected by the acquisition of literacy. This sort of review is designed to firm up our theory of language, so that we can ask what it predicts about the value of teaching formal grammar.

A simple thought experiment will isolate the special status of Grammar 1 knowledge. I have asked members of a number of different groups—from sixth graders to college freshmen to high-school teachers—to give me the rule for ordering adjectives of nationality, age, and number in English. The response is always the same: "We don't know the rule." Yet when I ask these groups to perform an active language task, they show productive control over the rule they have denied knowing. I ask them to arrange the following words in a natural order:

French   the   young   girls   four

I have never seen a native speaker of English who did not immediately produce the natural order, "the four young French girls." The rule is that in English the order of adjectives is first, number, second, age, and third, nationality. Native speakers can create analogous phrases using the rule—"the seventy-three aged Scandinavian lechers"; and the drive for meaning is so great that they will create contexts to make sense out of violations of the rule, as in foregrounding for emphasis: "I want to talk to the French four young girls." (I immediately envision a large room, perhaps a banquet hall, filled with tables at which are seated groups of four young girls, each group of a different nationality.) So Grammar 1 is eminently usable knowledge—the way we make our life through language—but it is not accessible knowledge; in a profound sense, we do not know that we have it. Thus neurolinguist Z. N. Pylyshyn speaks of Grammar 1 as "autonomous," separate from common-sense reasoning, and as "cognitively impenetrable," not available for direct examination.[10] In philosophy and linguistics, the distinction is made between formal, conscious, "knowing about" knowledge (like Grammar 2 knowledge) and tacit, unconscious, "knowing how" knowledge (like Grammar 1 knowledge). The importance of this distinction for the teaching of composition—it provides a powerful theoretical justification for

---

[10] "A Psychological Approach," in *Psychobiology of Language,* ed. M. Studdert-Kennedy (Cambridge, Mass.: MIT Press, 1983), pp. 16–19. See also Noam Chomsky, "Language and Unconscious Knowledge," in *Psychoanalysis and Language: Psychiatry and the Humanities,* Vol. III, ed. Joseph H. Smith (New Haven, Conn.: Yale University Press, 1978), pp. 3–44.

mistrusting the ability of Grammar 2 (or Grammar 4) knowledge to affect Grammar 1 performance—was pointed out in this journal by Martin Steinmann, Jr. in 1966 ("Rhetorical Research," *CE*, 27 [1966], 278-285).

Further, the more we learn about Grammar 1—and most linguists would agree that we know surprisingly little about it—the more abstract and implicit it seems. This abstractness can be illustrated with an experiment, devised by Lise Menn and reported by Morris Halle, about our rule for forming plurals in speech. It is obvious that we do indeed have a "rule" for forming plurals, for we do not memorize the plural of each noun separately. You will demonstrate productive control over that rule by forming the spoken plurals of the nonsense words below:

> thole   flitch   plast

Halle offers two ways of formalizing a Grammar 2 equivalent of this Grammar 1 ability. One form of the rule is the following, stated in terms of speech sounds:

    a. If the noun ends in /s z š ž č ǰ/, add /ɨz/;
    b. otherwise, if the noun ends in /p t k f Ø/, add /s/;
    c. otherwise, add /z/.[11]

This rule comes close to what we literate adults consider to be an adequate rule for plurals in writing, like the rules, for example, taken from a recent "common school grammar," Eric Gould's *Reading into Writing: A Rhetoric, Reader, and Handbook* (Boston: Houghton Mifflin, 1983):

> *Plurals* can be tricky. If you are unsure of a plural, then check it in the dictionary. The general rules are
> Add *s* to the singular: *girls, tables*
> Add *es* to nouns ending in *ch, sh, x* or *s: churches, boxes, wishes*
> Add *es* to nouns ending in *y* and preceded by a vowel once you have changed *y* to *i: monies, companies.* (p. 666)

(But note the persistent inadequacy of such Grammar 4 rules: here, as I read it, the rule is inadequate to explain the plurals of *ray* and *tray,* even to explain the collective noun *monies,* not a plural at all, formed from the mass noun *money* and offered as an example.) A second form of the rule would make use of much more abstract entities, sound features:

    a. If the noun ends with a sound that is [coronal, strident], add /ɨz/;
    b. otherwise, if the noun ends with a sound that is [non-voiced], add /s/;
    c. otherwise, add /z/.

(The notion of "sound features" is itself rather abstract, perhaps new to readers not trained in linguistics. But such readers should be able to recognize that the spoken plurals of *lip* and *duck,* the sound [s], differ from the spoken plurals of

---

[11] Morris Halle, "Knowledge Unlearned and Untaught: What Speakers Know about the Sounds of Their Language," in *Linguistic Theory and Psychological Reality,* ed. Halle, Joan Bresnan, and George A. Miller (Cambridge, Mass.: MIT Press, 1978), pp. 135-140.

sea and *gnu,* the sound [z], only in that the sounds of the latter are "voiced"—one's vocal cords vibrate—while the sounds of the former are "non-voiced.")

To test the psychologically operative rule, the Grammar 1 rule, native speakers of English were asked to form the plural of the last name of the composer Johann Sebastian *Bach,* a sound [x], unique in American (though not in Scottish) English. If speakers follow the first rule above, using word endings, they would reject a) and b), then apply c), producing the plural as /baxz/, with word-final /z/. (If writers were to follow the rule of the common school grammar, they would produce the written plural *Baches,* apparently, given the form of the rule, on analogy with *churches.*) If speakers follow the second rule, they would have to analyze the sound [x] as [non-labial, non-coronal, dorsal, non-voiced, and non-strident], producing the plural as /baxs/, with word-final /s/. Native speakers of American English overwhelmingly produce the plural as /baxs/. They use knowledge that Halle characterizes as "unlearned and untaught" (p. 140).

Now such a conclusion is counterintuitive—certainly it departs maximally from Grammar 4 rules for forming plurals. It seems that native speakers of English behave as if they have productive control, as Grammar 1 knowledge, of abstract sound features (± coronal, ± strident, and so on) which are available as conscious, Grammar 2 knowledge only to trained linguists—and, indeed, formally available only within the last hundred years or so. ("Behave as if," in that last sentence, is a necessary hedge, to underscore the difficulty of "knowing about" Grammar 1.)

Moreover, as the example of plural rules suggests, the form of the Grammar 1 in the heads of literate adults seems profoundly affected by the acquisition of literacy. Obviously, literate adults have access to different morphological codes: the abstract print -s underlying the predictable /s/ and /z/ plurals, the abstract print -ed underlying the spoken past tense markers /t/, as in "walked," /əd/, as in "surrounded," /d/, as in "scored," and the symbol /∅/ for no surface realization, as in the relaxed standard pronunciation of "I walked to the store." Literate adults also have access to distinctions preserved only in the code of print (for example, the distinction between "a good sailer" and "a good sailor" that Mark Aranoff points out in "An English Spelling Convention," *Linguistic Inquiry,* 9 [1978], 299–303). More significantly, Irene Moscowitz speculates that the ability of third graders to form abstract nouns on analogy with pairs like *divine: :divinity* and *serene: :serenity,* where the spoken vowel changes but the spelling preserves meaning, is a factor of knowing how to read. Carol Chomsky finds a three-stage developmental sequence in the grammatical performance of seven-year-olds, related to measures of kind and variety of reading; and Rita S. Brause finds a nine-stage development sequence in the ability to understand semantic ambiguity, extending from fourth graders to graduate students.[12] John Mills and

[12] Moscowitz, "On the Status of Vowel Shift in English," in *Cognitive Development and the Acquisition of Language,* ed. T. E. Moore (New York: Academic Press, 1973), pp. 223–260; Chomsky, "Stages in Language Development and Reading Exposure," *Harvard Educational Review,* 42 (1972), 1–33; and Brause, "Developmental Aspects of the Ability to Understand Semantic Ambiguity, with Implications for Teachers," *RTE,* 11 (1977), 39–48.

Gordon Hemsley find that level of education, and presumably level of literacy, influence judgments of grammaticality, concluding that literacy changes the deep structure of one's internal grammar; Jean Whyte finds that oral language functions develop differently in readers and non-readers; José Morais, Jésus Alegria, and Paul Bertelson find that illiterate adults are unable to add or delete sounds at the beginning of nonsense words, suggesting that awareness of speech as a series of phones is provided by learning to read an alphabetic code. Two experiments—one conducted by Charles A. Ferguson, the other by Mary E. Hamilton and David Barton—find that adults' ability to recognize segmentation in speech is related to degree of literacy, not to amount of schooling or general ability.[13]

It is worth noting that none of these investigators would suggest that the developmental sequences they have uncovered be isolated and taught as discrete skills. They are natural concomitants of literacy, and they seem best characterized not as isolated rules but as developing schemata, broad strategies for approaching written language.

GRAMMAR 2

We can, of course, attempt to approximate the rules or schemata of Grammar 1 by writing fully explicit descriptions that model the competence of a native speaker. Such rules, like the rules for pluralizing nouns or ordering adjectives discussed above, are the goal of the science of linguistics, that is, Grammar 2. There are a number of scientific grammars—an older structuralist model and several versions within a generative-transformational paradigm, not to mention isolated schools like tagmemic grammar, Montague grammar, and the like. In fact, we cannot think of Grammar 2 as a stable entity, for its form changes with each new issue of each linguistics journal, as new "rules of grammar" are proposed and debated. Thus Grammar 2, though of great theoretical interest to the composition teacher, is of little practical use in the classroom, as Constance Weaver has pointed out (*Grammar for Teachers* [Urbana, Ill.: NCTE, 1979], pp. 3-6). Indeed Grammar 2 is a scientific model of Grammar 1, not a description of it, so that questions of psychological reality, while important, are less important than other, more theoretical factors, such as the elegance of formulation or the global power of rules. We might, for example, wish to replace the rule for ordering adjectives of age, number, and nationality cited above with a more general rule—what linguists call a "fuzzy" rule—that adjectives in English are ordered by their abstract quality of "nouniness": adjectives that are very much like nouns, like *French* or *Scandina-*

[13] Mills and Hemsley, "The Effect of Levels of Education on Judgments of Grammatical Acceptability," *Language and Speech*, 19 (1976), 324-342; Whyte, "Levels of Language Competence and Reading Ability : An Exploratory Investigation," *Journal of Research in Reading*, 5 (1982), 123-132; Morais et al., "Does Awareness of Speech as a Series of Phones Arise Spontaneously?" *Cognition*, 7 (1979), 323-331; Ferguson, *Cognitive Effects of Literacy: Linguistic Awareness in Adult Non-readers* (Washington, D.C.: National Institute of Education Final Report, 1981) ERIC 222 857; Hamilton and Barton, "A Word Is a Word: Metalinguistic Skills in Adults of Varying Literacy Levels" (Stanford, Cal.: Stanford University Department of Linguistics, 1980) ERIC 222 859.

vian, come physically closer to nouns than do adjectives that are less "nouny," like *four* or *aged.* But our motivation for accepting the broader rule would be its global power, not its psychological reality.[14]

I try to consider a hostile reader, one committed to the teaching of grammar, and I try to think of ways to hammer in the central point of this distinction, that the rules of Grammar 2 are simply unconnected to productive control over Grammar 1. I can argue from authority: Noam Chomsky has touched on this point whenever he has concerned himself with the implications of linguistics for language teaching, and years ago transformationalist Mark Lester stated unequivocally, "there simply appears to be no correlation between a writer's study of language and his ability to write."[15] I can cite analogies offered by others: Francis Christensen's analogy in an essay originally published in 1962 that formal grammar study would be "to invite a centipede to attend to the sequence of his legs in motion,"[16] or James Britton's analogy, offered informally after a conference presentation, that grammar study would be like forcing starving people to master the use of a knife and fork before allowing them to eat. I can offer analogies of my own, contemplating the wisdom of asking a pool player to master the physics of momentum before taking up a cue or of making a prospective driver get a degree in automotive engineering before engaging the clutch. I consider a hypothetical argument, that if Grammar 2 knowledge affected Grammar 1 performance, then linguists would be our best writers. (I can certify that they are, on the whole, not.) Such a position, after all, is only in accord with other domains of science: the formula for catching a fly ball in baseball ("Playing It by Ear," *Scientific American,* 248, No. 4 [1983], 76) is of such complexity that it is beyond my understanding—and, I would suspect, that of many workaday centerfielders. But perhaps I can best hammer in this claim—that Grammar 2 knowledge has no effect on Grammar 1 performance—by offering a demonstration.

The diagram on the next page is an attempt by Thomas N. Huckin and Leslie A. Olsen (*English for Science and Technology* [New York: McGraw-Hill, 1983]) to offer, for students of English as a second language, a fully explicit formulation of what is, for native speakers, a trivial rule of the language—the choice of definite article, indefinite article, or no definite article. There are obvious limits to such a formulation, for article choice in English is less a matter of rule than of idiom ("I went to college" versus "I went to a university" versus British "I went to univer-

---

[14] On the question of the psychological reality of Grammar 2 descriptions, see Maria Black and Shulamith Chiat, "Psycholinguistics without 'Psychological Reality,'" *Linguistics,* 19 (1981), 37–61; Joan Bresnan, ed., *The Mental Representation of Grammatical Relations* (Cambridge, Mass.: MIT Press, 1982); and Michael H. Long, "Inside the 'Black Box': Methodological Issues in Classroom Research on Language Learning," *Language Learning,* 30 (1980), 1–42.

[15] Chomsky, "The Current Scene in Linguistics, *CE,* 27 (1966), 587–595; and "Linguistic Theory," in *Language Teaching: Broader Contexts,* ed. Robert C. Meade, Jr. (New York: Modern Language Association, 1966), pp. 43–49; Mark Lester, "The Value of Transformational Grammar in Teaching Composition," *CCC,* 16 (1967), 228.

[16] Christensen, "Between Two Worlds," in *Notes toward a New Rhetoric: Nine Essays for Teachers,* rev. ed., ed. Bonniejean Christensen (New York: Harper & Row, 1978), pp. 1–22.

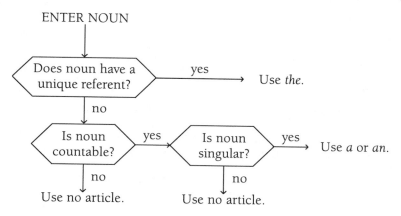

sity"), real-world knowledge (using indefinite "I went into a house" instantiates definite "I looked at the ceiling," and indefinite "I visited a university" instantiates definite "I talked with the professors"), and stylistic choice (the last sentence above might alternatively end with "the choice of the definite article, the indefinite article, or no article"). Huckin and Olsen invite non-native speakers to use the rule consciously to justify article choice in technical prose, such as the passage below from P. F. Brandwein (*Matter: An Earth Science* [New York: Harcourt Brace Jovanovich, 1975]). I invite you to spend a couple of minutes doing the same thing, with the understanding that this exercise is a test case: you are using a very explicit rule to justify a fairly straightforward issue of grammatical choice.

> Imagine a cannon on top of _____ highest mountain on earth. It is firing _____ cannonballs horizontally. _____ first cannonball fired follows its path. As _____ cannonball moves, _____ gravity pulls it down, and it soon hits _____ ground. Now _____ velocity with which each succeeding cannonball is fired is increased. Thus, _____ cannonball goes farther each time. Cannonball 2 goes farther than _____ cannonball 1 although each is being pulled by _____ gravity toward the earth all _____ time. _____ last cannonball is fired with such tremendous velocity that it goes completely around _____ earth. It returns to _____ mountaintop and continues around the earth again and again. _____ cannonball's inertia causes it to continue in motion indefinitely in _____ orbit around earth. In such a situation, we could consider _____ cannonball to be _____ artificial satellite, just like _____ weather satellites launched by _____ U. S. Weather Service. (p. 209)

Most native speakers of English who have attempted this exercise report a great deal of frustration, a curious sense of working against, rather than with, the rule. The rule, however valuable it may be for non-native speakers, is, for the most part, simply unusable for native speakers of the language.

COGNATE AREAS OF RESEARCH

We can corroborate this demonstration by turning to research in two cognate areas, studies of the induction of rules of artificial languages and studies of the role of formal rules in second language acquisition. Psychologists have studied the ability of subjects to learn artificial languages, usually constructed of nonsense syllables or letter strings. Such languages can be described by phrase structure rules:

S ⇒ VX
X ⇒ MX

More clearly, they can be presented as flow diagrams, as below:

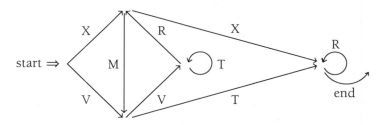

This diagram produces "sentences" like the following:

VVTRXRR.	XMVTTRX.	XXRR.
XMVRMT.	VVTTRMT.	XMTRRR.

The following "sentences" would be "ungrammatical" in this language:

*VMXTT.	*RTXVVT.	*TRVXXVVM.

Arthur S. Reber, in a classic 1967 experiment, demonstrated that mere exposure to grammatical sentences produced tacit learning: subjects who copied several grammatical sentences performed far above chance in judging the grammaticality of other letter strings. Further experiments have shown that providing subjects with formal rules—giving them the flow diagram above, for example—remarkably degrades performance: subjects given the "rules of the language" do much less well in acquiring the rules than do subjects not given the rules. Indeed, even telling subjects that they are to induce the rules of an artificial language degrades performance. Such laboratory experiments are admittedly contrived, but they confirm predictions that our theory of language would make about the value of formal rules in language learning.[17]

The thrust of recent research in second language learning similarly works to constrain the value of formal grammar rules. The most explicit statement of the value of formal rules is that of Stephen D. Krashen's monitor model.[18] Krashen

[17] Reber, "Implicit Learning of Artificial Grammars," *Journal of Verbal Learning and Verbal Behavior,* 6 (1967), 855–863; "Implicit Learning of Synthetic Languages: The Role of Instructional Set," *Journal of Experimental Psychology: Human Learning and Memory,* 2 (1976), 889–894; and Reber, Saul M. Kassin, Selma Lewis, and Gary Cantor, "On the Relationship between Implicit and Explicit Modes in the Learning of a Complex Rule Structure," *Journal of Experimental Psychology: Human Learning and Memory,* 6 (1980), 492–502.

[18] "Individual Variation in the Use of the Monitor," in *Principles of Second Language Learning,* ed. W. Richie (New York: Academic Press, 1978), pp. 175–185.

divides second language mastery into *acquisition*—tacit, informal mastery, akin to first language acquisition—and *formal learning*—conscious application of Grammar 2 rules, which he calls "monitoring" output. In another essay Krashen uses his model to predict a highly individual use of the monitor and a highly constrained role for formal rules:

> Some adults (and very few children) are able to use conscious rules to increase the grammatical accuracy of their output, and even for these people, very strict conditions need to be met before the conscious grammar can be applied.[19]

In *Principles and Practice in Second Language Acquisition* (New York: Pergamon, 1982) Krashen outlines these conditions by means of a series of concentric circles, beginning with a large circle denoting the rules of English and a smaller circle denoting the subset of those rules described by formal linguists (adding that most linguists would protest that the size of this circle is much too large):

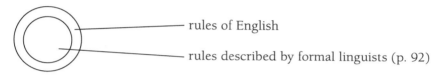

rules of English

rules described by formal linguists (p. 92)

Krashen then adds smaller circles, as shown below—a subset of the rules described by formal linguists that would be known to applied linguists, a subset of those rules that would be available to the best teachers, and then a subset of those rules that teachers might choose to present to second language learners:

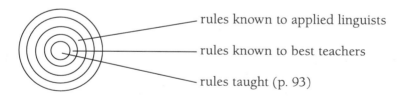

rules known to applied linguists

rules known to best teachers

rules taught (p. 93)

Of course, as Krashen notes, not all the rules taught will be learned, and not all those learned will be available, as what he calls "mental baggage" (p. 94), for conscious use.

An experiment by Ellen Bialystock, asking English speakers learning French to judge the grammaticality of taped sentences, complicates this issue, for reaction time data suggest that learners first make an intuitive judgment of grammaticality, using implicit or Grammar 1 knowledge, and only then search

---

[19] "Applications of Psycholinguistic Research to the Classroom," in *Practical Applications of Research in Foreign Language Teaching,* ed. D. J. James (Lincolnwood, Ill.: National Textbook, 1983), p. 61.

for formal explanations, using explicit or Grammar 2 knowledge.[20] This distinction would suggest that Grammar 2 knowledge is of use to second language learners only after the principle has already been mastered as tacit Grammar 1 knowledge. In the terms of Krashen's model, learning never becomes acquisition (*Principles,* p. 86).

An ingenious experiment by Herbert W. Seliger complicates the issue yet further ("On the Nature and Function of Language Rules in Language Learning," *TESOL Quarterly,* 13 [1979], 359–369). Seliger asked native and non-native speakers of English to orally identify pictures of objects (e.g., "an apple," "a pear," "a book," "an umbrella"), noting whether they used the correct form of the indefinite articles *a* and *an.* He then asked each speaker to state the rule for choosing between *a* and *an.* He found no correlation between the ability to state the rule and the ability to apply it correctly, either with native or non-native speakers. Indeed, three of four adult non-native speakers in his sample produced a correct form of the rule, but they did not apply it in speaking. A strong conclusion from this experiment would be that formal rules of grammar seem to have no value whatsoever. Seliger, however, suggests a more paradoxical interpretation. Rules are of no use, he agrees, but some people think they are, and for these people, assuming that they have internalized the rules, even inadequate rules are of heuristic value, for they allow them to access the internal rules they actually use.

THE INCANTATIONS OF THE "COMMON SCHOOL GRAMMARS"

Such a paradox may explain the fascination we have as teachers with "rules of grammar" of the Grammar 4 variety, the "rules" of the "common school grammars." Again and again such rules are inadequate to the facts of written language; you will recall that we have known this since [Fries's] 1927 study. R. Scott Baldwin and James M. Coady, studying how readers respond to punctuation signals ("Psycholinguistic Approaches to a Theory of Punctuation," *Journal of Reading Behavior,* 10 [1978], 363–383), conclude that conventional rules of punctuation are "a complete sham" (p. 375). My own favorite is the Grammar 4 rule for showing possession, always expressed in terms of adding -'s or -s' to nouns, while our internal grammar, if you think about it, adds possession to noun phrases, albeit under severe stylistic constraints: "the horses of the Queen of England" are "the Queen of England's horses" and "the feathers of the duck over there" are "the duck over there's feathers." Suzette Haden Elgin refers to the "rules" of Grammar 4 as "incantations" (*Never Mind the Trees,* p. 9: see footnote 3).

It may simply be that as hyperliterate adults we are conscious of "using rules" when we are in fact doing something else, something far more complex, access-

---

[20] "Some Evidence for the Integrity and Interaction of Two Knowledge Sources," in *New Dimensions in Second Language Acquisition Research,* ed. Roger W. Andersen (Rowley, Mass.: Newbury House, 1981), pp. 62–74.

ing tacit heuristics honed by print literacy itself. We can clarify this notion by reaching for an acronym coined by technical writers to explain the readability of complex prose—COIK: "clear only if known." The rules of Grammar 4—no, we can at this point be more honest—the incantations of Grammar 4 are COIK. If you know how to signal possession in the code of print, then the advice to add -'s to nouns makes perfect sense, just as the collective noun *monies* is a fine example of changing -*y* to -*i* and adding -*es* to form the plural. But if you have not grasped, tacitly, the abstract representation of possession in print, such incantations can only be opaque.

Worse yet, the advice given in "the common school grammars" is unconnected with anything remotely resembling literate adult behavior. Consider, as an example, the rule for not writing a sentence fragment as the rule is described in the best-selling college grammar text, John C. Hodges and Mary S. Whitten's *Harbrace College Handbook,* 9th ed. (New York: Harcourt Brace Jovanovich, 1982). In order to get to the advice, "as a rule, do not write a sentence fragment" (p. 25), the student must master the following learning tasks:

Recognizing verbs.
Recognizing subjects and verbs.
Recognizing all parts of speech. (*Harbrace* lists eight.)
Recognizing phrases and subordinate clauses. (*Harbrace* lists six types of phrases, and it offers incomplete lists of eight relative pronouns and eighteen subordinating conjunctions.)
Recognizing main clauses and types of sentences.

These learning tasks completed, the student is given the rule above, offered a page of exceptions, and then given the following advice (or is it an incantation?):

> Before handing in a composition, . . . proofread each word group written as a sentence. Test each one for completeness. First, be sure that it has at least one subject and one predicate. Next, be sure that the word group is not a dependent clause beginning with a subordinating conjunction or a relative clause. (p. 27)

The school grammar approach defines a sentence fragment as a conceptual error—as not having conscious knowledge of the school grammar definition of *sentence.* It demands heavy emphasis on rote memory, and it asks students to behave in ways patently removed from the behaviors of mature writers. (I have never in my life tested a sentence for completeness, and I am a better writer—and probably a better person—as a consequence.) It may be, of course, that some developing writers, at some points in their development, may benefit from such advice—or, more to the point, may think that they benefit—but, as Thomas Friedman points out in "Teaching Error, Nurturing Confusion" (*CE,* 45 [1983], 390–399), our theory of language tells us that such advice is, at the best, COIK. As the Maine joke has it, about a tourist asking directions from a farmer, "you can't get there from here."

REDEFINING ERROR

In the specific case of sentence fragments, Mina P. Shaughnessy (*Errors and Expectations* [New York: Oxford University Press, 1977]) argues that such errors are not conceptual failures at all, but performance errors—mistakes in punctuation. Muriel Harris's error counts support this view ("Mending the Fragmented Free Modifier," *CCC*, 32 [1981], 175-182). Case studies show example after example of errors that occur *because of* instruction—one thinks, for example, of David Bartholomae's student explaining that he added an *-s* to *children* "because it's a plural" ("The Study of Error," *CCC*, 31 [1980], 262). Surveys, such as that by Muriel Harris ("Contradictory Perceptions of the Rules of Writing," *CCC*, 30 [1979], 218-220), and our own observations suggest that students consistently misunderstand such Grammar 4 explanations (COIK, you will recall). For example, from Patrick Hartwell and Robert H. Bentley and from Mike Rose, we have two separate anecdotal accounts of students, cited for punctuating a *because*-clause as a sentence, who have decided to avoid using *because*. More generally, Collette A. Daiute's analysis of errors made by college students shows that errors tend to appear at clause boundaries, suggesting short-term memory load and not conceptual deficiency as a cause of error.[21]

Thus, if you think seriously about error and its relationship to the worship of formal grammar study, we need to attempt some massive dislocation of our traditional thinking, to shuck off our hyperliterate perception of the value of formal rules, and to regain the confidence in the tacit power of unconscious knowledge that our theory of language gives us. Most students, reading their writing aloud, will correct in essence all errors of spelling, grammar, and, by intonation, punctuation, but usually without noticing that what they read departs from what they wrote.[22] And Richard H. Haswell ("Minimal Marking," *CE*, 45 [1983], 600-604) notes that his students correct 61.1% of their errors when they are identified with a simple mark in the margin rather than by error type. Such findings suggest that we need to redefine error, to see it not as a cognitive or linguistic problem, a problem of not knowing a "rule of grammar" (whatever that may mean), but rather, following the insight of Robert J. Bracewell ("Writing as a Cognitive Activity," *Visible Language,* 14 [1980], 400-422), as a problem of metacognition and metalinguistic awareness, a matter of accessing knowledges that, to be of any use, learners must have already internalized by means of exposure to the code. (Usage issues—Grammar 3—probably represent a different order of problem. Both Joseph Emonds and Jeffrey Jochnowitz estab-

---

[21] Hartwell and Bentley, *Some Suggestions for Using Open to Language* (New York: Oxford University Press, 1982), p. 73; Rose, *Writer's Block: The Cognitive Dimension* (Carbondale: Southern Illinois University Press, 1983), p. 99; Daiute, "Psycholinguistic Foundations of the Writing Process," *RTE,* 15 (1981), 5-22.

[22] See Bartholmae, "The Study of Error"; Patrick Hartwell, "The Writing Center and the Paradoxes of Written-Down Speech," in *Writing Centers: Theory and Administration,* ed. Gary Olson (Urbana, Ill.: NCTE, 1984), pp. 48-61; and Sondra Perl, "A Look at Basic Writers in the Process of Composing," in *Basic Writing: A Collection of Essays for Teachers, Researchers, and Administrators* (Urbana, Ill.: NCTE, 1980), pp. 13-32.

lish that the usage issues we worry most about are linguistically unnatural, departures from the grammar in our heads.)[23]

The notion of metalinguistic awareness seems crucial. The sentence below, created by Douglas R. Hofstadter ("Metamagical Themas," *Scientific American,* 235, No. 1 [1981], 22–32), is offered to clarify that notion; you are invited to examine it for a moment or two before continuing.

Their is four errors in this sentence. Can you find them?

Three errors announce themselves plainly enough, the misspellings of *there* and *sentence* and the use of *is* instead of *are.* (And, just to illustrate the perils of hyperliteracy, let it be noted that, through three years of drafts, I referred to the choice of *is* and *are* as a matter of "subject-verb agreement.") The fourth error resists detection, until one assesses the truth value of the sentence itself—the fourth error is that there are not four errors, only three. Such a sentence (Hofstadter calls it a "self-referencing sentence") asks you to look at it in two ways, simultaneously as statement and as linguistic artifact—in other words, to exercise metalinguistic awareness.

A broad range of cross-cultural studies suggests that metalinguistic awareness is a defining feature of print literacy. Thus Sylvia Scribner and Michael Cole, working with the triliterate Vai of Liberia (variously literate in English, through schooling; in Arabic, for religious purposes; and in an indigenous Vai script, used for personal affairs), find that metalinguistic awareness, broadly conceived, is the only cognitive skill underlying each of the three literacies. The one statistically significant skill shared by literate Vai was the recognition of word boundaries. Moreover, literate Vai tended to answer "yes" when asked (in Vai), "Can you call the sun the moon and the moon the sun?" while illiterate Vai tended to have grave doubts about such metalinguistic play. And in the United States Henry and Lila R. Gleitman report quite different responses by clerical workers and PhD candidates asked to interpret nonsense compounds like "house-bird glass": clerical workers focused on meaning and plausibility (for example, "a house-bird made of glass"), while PhD candidates focused on syntax (for example, "a very small drinking cup for canaries" or "a glass that protects house-birds").[24] More general research findings suggest a clear relationship between measures of metalinguistic awareness and measures of literacy level.[25] William

---

[23] Emonds, *Adjacency in Grammar: The Theory of Language-Particular Rules* (New York: Academic Press, 1983); and Jochnowitz, "Everybody Likes Pizza, Doesn't He or She?" *American Speech,* 57 (1982), 198–203.

[24] Scribner and Cole, *Psychology of Literacy* (Cambridge, Mass.: Harvard University Press, 1981); Gleitman and Gleitman, "Language Use and Language Judgment," in *Individual Differences in Language Ability and Language Behavior,* ed. Charles J. Fillmore, Daniel Kemper, and William S. Y. Wang (New York: Academic Press, 1979), pp. 103–126.

[25] There are several recent reviews of this developing body of research in psychology and child development: Irene Athey, "Language Development Factors Related to Reading Development," *Journal of Educational Research,* 76 (1983), 197–203; James Flood and Paula Menyuk, "Metalinguistic Development and Reading/Writing Achievement," *Claremont Reading Conference Yearbook,* 46 (1982), 122–132; and the following four essays: David T. Hakes, "The Development of Metalinguistic Abilities: What Develops?," pp. 162–210; Stan A. Kuczaj II

Labov, speculating on literacy acquisition in inner-city ghettoes, contrasts "stimulus-bound" and "language-bound" individuals, suggesting that the latter seem to master literacy more easily.[26] The analysis here suggests that the causal relationship works the other way, that it is the mastery of written language that increases one's awareness of language as language.

This analysis has two implications. First, it makes the question of socially nonstandard dialects, always implicit in discussions of teaching formal grammar, into a non-issue.[27] Native speakers of English, regardless of dialect, show tacit mastery of the conventions of Standard English, and that mastery seems to transfer into abstract orthographic knowledge through interaction with print.[28] Developing writers show the same patterning of errors, regardless of dialect.[29] Studies of reading and of writing suggest that surface features of spoken dialect are simply irrelevant to mastering print literacy.[30] Print is a complex cultural code—or better yet, a system of codes—and my bet is that, regardless of instruction, one masters those codes from the top down, from pragmatic questions of voice, tone, audience, register,

and Brooke Harbaugh, "What Children Think about the Speaking Capabilities of Other Persons and Things," pp. 211-227; Karen Saywitz and Louise Cherry Wilkinson, "Age-Related Differences in Metalinguistic Awareness," pp. 229-250; and Harriet Salatas Waters and Virginia S. Tinsley, "The Development of Verbal Self-Regulation: Relationships between Language, Cognition, and Behavior," pp. 251-277; all in *Language, Thought, and Culture*, Vol. II of *Language Development*, ed. Stan Kuczaj, Jr. (Hillsdale, N.J.: Lawrence Erlbaum, 1982). See also Joanne R. Nurss, "Research in Review: Linguistic Awareness and Learning to Read," *Young Children*, 35, No. 3 (1980), 57-66.

[26] "Competing Value Systems in Inner City Schools," in *Children In and Out of School: Ethnography and Education*, ed. Perry Gilmore and Allan A. Glatthorn (Washington, D.C.: Center for Applied Linguistics, 1982), pp. 148-171; and "Locating the Frontier between Social and Psychological Factors in Linguistic Structure," in *Individual Differences in Language Ability and Language Behavior*, ed. Fillmore, Kemper, and Wang, pp. 327-340.

[27] See, for example, Thomas Farrell, "IQ and Standard English," *CCC*, 34 (1983), 470-484; and the responses by Karen L. Greenberg and Patrick Hartwell, *CCC*, [35, Dec. 1984].

[28] Jane W. Torrey, "Teaching Standard English to Speakers of Other Dialects," in *Applications of Linguistics: Selected Papers of the Second International Conference of Applied Linguistics*, ed. G. E. Perren and J. L. M. Trim (Cambridge University Press, 1971), pp. 423-428; James W. Beers and Edmund H. Henderson, "A Study of the Developing Orthographic Concepts among First Graders," *RTE*, 11 (1977), 133-148.

[29] See the error counts of Samuel A. Kirschner and G. Howard Poteet, "Non-Standard English Usage in the Writing of Black, White, and Hispanic Remedial English Students in an Urban Community College," *RTE*, 7 (1973), 351-355; and Marilyn Sternglass, "Close Similarities in Dialect Features of Black and White College Students in Remedial Composition Classes," *TESOL Quarterly*, 8 (1974), 271-283.

[30] For reading, see the massive study by Kenneth S. Goodman and Yetta M. Goodman, *Reading of American Children Whose Language Is a Stable Rural Dialect of English or a Language Other Than English* (Washington, D.C.: National Institute of Education Final Report, 1978) ERIC 175 754; and the overview by Rudine Sims, "Dialect and Reading: Toward Redefining the Issues," in *Reader Meets Author/Bridging the Gap: A Psycholinguistic Approach*, ed. Judith A. Langer and M. Tricia Smith-Burke (Newark, Del.: International Reading Association, 1982), pp. 222-232. For writing, see Patrick Hartwell, "Dialect Interference in Writing: A Critical View," *RTE*, 14 (1980), 101-118; and the anthology edited by Barry M. Kroll and Roberta J. Vann, *Exploring Speaking-Writing Relationships: Connections and Contrasts* (Urbana, Ill.: NCTE, 1981).

and rhetorical strategy, not from the bottom up, from grammar to usage to fixed forms of organization.

Second, this analysis forces us to posit multiple literacies, used for multiple purposes, rather than a single static literacy, engraved in "rules of grammar." These multiple literacies are evident in cross-cultural studies.[31] They are equally evident when we inquire into the uses of literacy in American communities.[32] Further, given that students, at all levels, show widely variant interactions with print literacy, there would seem to be little to do with grammar—with Grammar 2 or with Grammar 4—that we could isolate as a basis for formal instruction.[33]

GRAMMAR 5: STYLISTIC GRAMMAR

Similarly, when we turn to Grammar 5, "grammatical terms used in the interest of teaching prose style," so central to Martha Kolln's argument for teaching formal grammar, we find that the grammar issue is simply beside the point. There are two fully-articulated positions about "stylistic grammar," which I will label "romantic" and "classic," following Richard Lloyd-Jones and Richard E. Young.[34] The romantic position is that stylistic grammars, though perhaps useful for teachers, have little place in the teaching of composition, for students must struggle with and through language toward meaning. This position rests on a theory of language ultimately philosophical rather than linguistic (witness, for example, the contempt for linguists in Ann Berthoff's *The Making of Meaning: Metaphors, Models, and Maxims for Writing Teachers* [Montclair, N.J.: Boynton/ Cook, 1981]); it is articulated as a theory of style by Donald A. Murray and, on somewhat different grounds (that stylistic grammars encourage overuse of the

---

[31] See, for example, Eric A. Havelock, *The Literary Revolution in Greece and Its Cultural Consequences* (Princeton, N.J.: Princeton University Press, 1982); Lesley Milroy on literacy in Dublin, *Language and Social Networks* (Oxford: Basil Blackwell, 1980); Ron Scollon and Suzanne B. K. Scollon on literacy in central Alaska, *Interethnic Communication: An Athabascan Case* (Austin, Tex.: Southwest Educational Development Laboratory Working Papers in Sociolinguistics, No. 59, 1979) ERIC 175 276; and Scribner and Cole on literacy in Liberia, *Psychology of Literacy* (see footnote 24).

[32] See, for example, the anthology edited by Deborah Tannen, *Spoken and Written Language: Exploring Orality and Literacy* (Norwood, N.J.: Ablex, 1982); and Shirley Brice Heath's continuing work: "Protean Shapes in Literacy Events: Ever-Shifting Oral and Literate Traditions," in *Spoken and Written Language*, pp. 91–117; *Ways with Words: Language, Life and Work in Communities and Classrooms* (New York: Cambridge University Press, 1983); and "What No Bedtime Story Means," *Language in Society*, 11 (1982), 49–76.

[33] For studies at the elementary level, see Dell H. Hymes et al., eds., *Ethnographic Monitoring of Children's Acquisition of Reading/Language Arts Skills In and Out of the Classroom* (Washington, D.C.: National Institute of Education Final Report, 1981) ERIC 208 096. For studies at the secondary level, see James L. Collins and Michael M. Williamson, "Spoken Language and Semantic Abbreviation in Writing," *RTE*, 15 (1981), 23–36. And for studies at the college level, see Patrick Hartwell and Gene LoPresti, "Sentence Combining as Kid-Watching," in *Sentence Combining: Toward a Rhetorical Perspective*, ed. Donald A. Daiker, Andrew Kerek, and Max Morenberg (Carbondale: Southern Illinois University Press, [1985, pp. 107–126]).

[34] Lloyd-Jones, "Romantic Revels—I Am Not You," *CCC*, 23 (1972), 251–271; and Young, "Concepts of Art and the Teaching of Writing," in *The Rhetorical Tradition and Modern Writing*, ed. James J. Murphy (New York: Modern Language Association, 1982), pp. 130–141.

monitor), by Ian Pringle. The classic position, on the other hand, is that we can
find ways to offer developing writers helpful suggestions about prose style,
suggestions such as Francis Christensen's emphasis on the cumulative
sentence, developed by observing the practice of skilled writers, and Joseph
Williams' advice about predication, developed by psycholinguistic studies of
comprehension.[35] James A. Berlin's recent survey of composition theory (*CE*, 45
[1982], 765-777) probably understates the gulf between these two positions
and the radically different conceptions of language that underlie them, but it
does establish that they share an overriding assumption in common: that one
learns to control the language of print by manipulating language in meaningful
contexts, not by learning about language in isolation, as by the study of formal
grammar. Thus even classic theorists, who choose to present a vocabulary of
style to students, do so only as a vehicle for encouraging productive control of
communicative structures.

We might put the matter in the following terms. Writers need to develop
skills at two levels. One, broadly rhetorical, involves communication in meaningful contexts (the strategies, registers, and procedures of discourse across a
range of modes, audiences, contexts, and purposes). The other, broadly
metalinguistic rather than linguistic, involves active manipulation of language
with conscious attention to surface form. This second level may be developed
tacitly, as a natural adjunct to developing rhetorical competencies—I take this to
be the position of romantic theorists. It may be developed formally, by manipulating language for stylistic effect, and such manipulation may involve, for pedagogical continuity, a vocabulary of style. But it is primarily developed by any
kind of language activity that enhances the awareness of language as language.[36]
David T. Hakes, summarizing the research on metalinguistic awareness, notes
how far we are from understanding this process:

> the optimal conditions for becoming metalinguistically competent involve grow-
> ing up in a literate environment with adult models who are themselves
> metalinguistically competent and who foster the growth of that competence in
> a variety of ways as yet little understood. ("The Development of Metalinguistic
> Abilities," p. 205; see footnote 25)

---

[35] For the romantic position, see Ann E. Berthoff, "Tolstoy, Vygotsky, and the Making of Mean-
ing," *CCC*, 29 (1978), 249-255; Kenneth Dowst, "The Epistemic Approach," in *Eight
Approaches to Teaching Composition,* ed. Timothy Donovan and Ben G. McClellan (Urbana,
Ill.: NCTE, 1980), pp. 65-85; Peter Elbow, "The Challenge for Sentence Combining"; and
Donald Murray, "Following Language toward Meaning," both in *Sentence Combining: Toward
a Rhetorical Perspective* (see footnote 33); and Ian Pringle, "Why Teach Style? A Review-
Essay," *CCC*, 34 (1983), 91-98.

   For the classic position, see Christensen's "A Generative Rhetoric of the Sentence"; and
Joseph Williams' "Defining Complexity," *CE,* 41 (1979), 595-609; and his *Style: Ten Lessons in
Clarity and Grace* (see footnote 9).

[36] Courtney B. Cazden and David K. Dickinson, "Language and Education: Standardization
versus Cultural Pluralism," in *Language in the USA,* ed. Charles A. Ferguson and Shirley
Brice Heath (New York: Cambridge University Press, 1981), pp. 446-468; and Carol Chomsky,
"Developing Facility with Language Structure," in *Discovering Language with Children,* ed.
Gay Su Pinnell (Urbana, Ill.: NCTE, 1980), pp. 56-59.

Such a model places language, at all levels, at the center of the curriculum, but not as "necessary categories and labels" (Kolln, "Closing the Books on Alchemy," p. 150), but as literal stuff, verbal clay, to be molded and probed, shaped and reshaped, and, above all, enjoyed.

THE TRADITION OF EXPERIMENTAL RESEARCH

Thus, when we turn back to experimental research on the value of formal grammar instruction, we do so with firm predictions given us by our theory of language. Our theory would predict that formal grammar instruction, whether instruction in scientific grammar or instruction in "the common school grammar," would have little to do with control over surface correctness nor with quality of writing. It would predict that any form of active involvement with language would be preferable to instruction in rules or definitions (or incantations). In essence, this is what the research tells us. In 1893, the Committee of Ten (*Report of the Committee of Ten on Secondary School Studies* [Washington, D.C.: U.S. Government Printing Office, 1893]) put grammar at the center of the English curriculum, and its report established the rigidly sequential mode of instruction common for the last century. But the committee explicitly noted that grammar instruction did not aid correctness, arguing instead that it improved the ability to think logically (an argument developed from the role of the "grammarian" in the classical rhetorical tradition, essentially a teacher of literature—see, for example, the etymology of *grammar* in the *Oxford English Dictionary*).

But Franklin S. Hoyt, in a 1906 experiment, found no relationship between the study of grammar and the ability to think logically; his research led him to conclude what I am constrained to argue more than seventy-five years later, that there is no "relationship between a knowledge of technical grammar and the ability to use English and to interpret language" ("The Place of Grammar in the Elementary Curriculum," *Teachers College Record,* 7 [1906], 483-484). Later studies, through the 1920s, focused on the relationship of knowledge of grammar and ability to recognize error; experiments reported by James Boraas in 1917 and by William Asker in 1923 are typical of those that reported no correlation. In the 1930s, with the development of the functional grammar movement, it was common to compare the study of formal grammar with one form or another of active manipulation of language; experiments by I. O. Ash in 1935 and Ellen Frogner in 1939 are typical of studies showing the superiority of active involvement with language.[37] In a 1959 article, "Grammar in Language Teaching" (*Elementary English,* 36 [1959], 412-421), John J. DeBoer noted the consistency of these findings.

---

[37] Boraas, "Formal English Grammar and the Practical Mastery of English." Diss. University of Illinois, 1917; Asker, "Does Knowledge of Grammar Function?" *School and Society,* 17 (27 January 1923), 109-111; Ash, "An Experimental Evaluation of the Stylistic Approach in Teaching Composition in the Junior High School," *Journal of Experimental Education,* 4 (1935), 54-62; and Frogner, "A Study of the Relative Efficacy of a Grammatical and a Thought Approach to the Improvement of Sentence Structure in Grades Nine and Eleven," *School Review,* 47 (1939), 663-675.

The impressive fact is . . . that in all these studies, carried out in places and at times far removed from each other, often by highly experienced and disinterested investigators, the results have been consistently negative so far as the value of grammar in the improvement of language expression is concerned. (p. 417)

In 1960 Ingrid M. Strom, reviewing more than fifty experimental studies, came to a similarly strong and unqualified conclusion:

direct methods of instruction, focusing on writing activities and the structuring of ideas, are more efficient in teaching sentence structure, usage, punctuation, and other related factors than are such methods as nomenclature drill, diagramming, and rote memorization of grammatical rules.[38]

In 1963 two research reviews appeared, one by Braddock, Lloyd-Jones, and Schoer, cited at the beginning of this paper, and one by Henry C. Meckel, whose conclusions, though more guarded, are in essential agreement.[39] In 1969 J. Stephen Sherwin devoted one-fourth of his *Four Problems in Teaching English: A Critique of Research* (Scranton, Penn.: International Textbook, 1969) to the grammar issue, concluding that "instruction in formal grammar is an ineffective way to help students achieve proficiency in writing" (p. 135). Some early experiments in sentence combining, such as those by Donald R. Bateman and Frank J. Zidonnis and by John C. Mellon, showed improvement in measures of syntactic complexity with instruction in transformational grammar keyed to sentence-combining practice. But a later study by Frank O'Hare achieved the same gains with no grammar instruction, suggesting to Sandra L. Stotsky and to Richard Van de Veghe that active manipulation of language, not the grammar unit, explained the earlier results.[40] More recent summaries of research—by Elizabeth I. Haynes, Hilary Taylor Holbrook, and Marcia Farr Whiteman—support similar conclusions. Indirect evidence for this position is provided by surveys reported by Betty Bamberg in 1978 and 1981, showing that time spent in grammar instruction in high school is the least important factor, of eight factors examined, in separating regular from remedial writers at the college level.[41]

[38] "Research on Grammar and Usage and Its Implications for Teaching Writing," *Bulletin of the School of Education,* Indiana University, 36 (1960), pp. 13-14.

[39] Meckel, "Research on Teaching Composition and Literature," in *Handbook of Research on Teaching,* ed. N. L. Gage (Chicago: Rand McNally, 1963), pp. 966-1006.

[40] Bateman and Zidonnis, *The Effect of a Study of Transformational Grammar on the Writing of Ninth and Tenth Graders* (Urbana, Ill.: NCTE, 1966); Mellon, *Transformational Sentence Combining: A Method for Enhancing the Development of Fluency in English Composition* (Urbana, Ill.: NCTE, 1969); O'Hare, *Sentence-Combining: Improving Student Writing without Formal Grammar Instruction* (Urbana, Ill.: NCTE, 1971); Stotsky, "Sentence-Combining as a Curricular Activity: Its Effect on Written Language Development," *RTE,* 9 (1975), 30-72; and Van de Veghe, "Research in Written Composition: Fifteen Years of Investigation," ERIC 157 095.

[41] Haynes, "Using Research in Preparing to Teach Writing," *English Journal,* 69, No. 1 (1978), 82-88; Holbrook, "ERIC/RCS Report: Whither (Wither) Grammar," *Language Arts,* 60 (1983), 259-263; Whiteman, "What We Can Learn from Writing Research," *Theory into Practice,* 19 (1980), 150-156; Bamberg, "Composition in the Secondary English Curriculum: Some Current Trends and Directions for the Eighties," *RTE,* 15 (1981), 257-266; and "Composition Instruction Does Make a Difference: A Comparison of the High School Preparation of College Freshmen in Regular and Remedial English Classes," *RTE,* 12 (1978), 47-59.

More generally, Patrick Scott and Bruce Castner, in "Reference Sources for Composition Research: A Practical Survey" (*CE*, 45 [1983], 756–768), note that much current research is not informed by an awareness of the past. Put simply, we are constrained to reinvent the wheel. My concern here has been with a far more serious problem: that too often the wheel we reinvent is square.

It is, after all, a question of power. Janet Emig, developing a consensus from composition research, and Aaron S. Carton and Lawrence V. Castiglione, developing the implications of language theory for education, come to the same conclusion: that the thrust of current research and theory is to take power from the teacher and to give that power to the learner.[42] At no point in the English curriculum is the question of power more blatantly posed than in the issue of formal grammar instruction. It is time that we, as teachers, formulate theories of language and literacy and let those theories guide our teaching, and it is time that we, as researchers, move on to more interesting areas of inquiry.

---

[42] Emig, "Inquiry Paradigms and Writing," *CCC*, 33 (1982), 64-75; Carton and Castiglione, "Educational Linguistics: Defining the Domain," in *Psycholinguistic Research: Implications and Applications*, ed. Doris Aaronson and Robert W. Rieber (Hillsdale, N.J.: Lawrence Erlbaum, 1979), pp. 497-520.

This article is reprinted from *College English* 47 (February 1985): 105-27. —Ed.

Andrea A. Lunsford and Cheryl Glenn

RHETORICAL THEORY AND THE TEACHING OF WRITING

RHETORIC AND THE DYNAMIC ELEMENTS OF WRITTEN COMMUNICATION*

For some 2,500 years, speakers and writers have relied—often unknowingly—on rhetorical theory to achieve successful persuasion and communication or to gain cooperation. "Rhetorical theory?"—it sounds formidable, perhaps even beside the point. Yet every teacher and every student works out of rhetorical theory, a conceptual framework that guides us in the dynamic process of making meaning, sustains our classroom writing practices, and informs our textbooks.

Long the staple of communication theory, the *"communication triangle,"* comprising *sender, receiver,* and *message,* has expanded to incorporate *universe* (or *context*), the fourth component of this rhetorical set of interrelationships. These

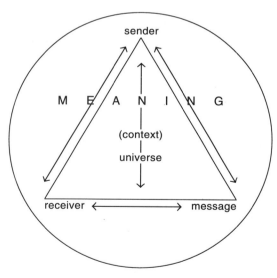

Figure 1

*We thank Gerald Nelms for helping with the citations and bibliography. We are also grateful to Jon Olson and Jamie Barlowe, whose sensible suggestions and supportive criticism helped us rewrite parts of the manuscript.

394

four elements of meaning not only guide teachers in their teaching choices but also guide writers in their writing choices, choices based on (1) their own values; (2) those of their receivers; (3) the possible range of messages; and (4) the nature of the universe, of reality.

Aristotle may have been the first to separate the rhetorical elements (the persuasive appeals) of communication when he wrote that the true constituents of the art of rhetoric are *ethos,* the appeals exerted by the speaker (the sender); *pathos,* the appeals to the emotions or values of the audience (the receiver); and *logos,* the appeals to reason of the message itself—with all appeals reflecting or affecting the *universe* (*Rhetoric,* I.2.1356c). And his definition of *rhetoric* as "the faculty of observing in any given case the available means of persuasion" (I.2.1355b) has undergirded all rhetorical theory thenceforth, providing scholars, critics, and rhetoricians a dependable and expandable base for their own contributions to rhetorical theory and practice.

In his landmark *Theory of Discourse* (1971), James Kinneavy relates Aristotle's rhetorical triangle to fields other than rhetoric (such as literary theory, anthropology, communication, and semiotics), showing, in each case, just how *any* communication can emphasize one particular element of the triangle. Like Aristotle, who demonstrates three purposeful discourses, Kinneavy locates the variable aims of discourse in its emphatic triangulation of author, audience, universe, or in its reflexive emphasis on itself, the text.

Kinneavy refers to the work of literary theorist M. H. Abrams (310–48), whose *The Mirror and the Lamp* posits the four elements in the total situation of a work of art: the *work,* the artistic product itself; the *artist,* who produced the work; the *universe,* the subject of the work itself or from which the work is derived; and the *audience* to whom the work is addressed or made available (6–7). Although a work of artistic literature itself always implicitly assumes an author, an audience, a universe, the four coordinates of the work vary in significance according to the theory in which they occur: mimetic theories emphasize art's imitation of the *universe;* pragmatic theories propound art's effect on the *audience,* on getting things done; expressive theories center on the *artist* as cause and criterion of art; and objective theories deal with the *work of art* itself, in parts and in the mutual relations of its parts.

Kinneavy also refers to the work of anthropological linguists, who, like the literary theorists, evaluate language in terms of its aims: as verbal gesture, *interjectional;* as imitation of reality, *representational;* as a pragmatic symbol for getting things done, *utilitarian;* and as expression of the sender, poetic or *play* (51–52). The communication theorists, too, refer to language aims: informative, exploratory, instrumental, and emotive—aims that stress the importance of one rhetorical element (53–54). Communication theorists call the elements *encoder, decoder, signal,* and *reality,* and they connect informative communication with the signal or text; exploratory with reality or the universe; instrumental with the decoder or the audience; and emotive with the encoder or the author.

Eminent rhetorician Kenneth Burke extended the grammar of rhetoric to encompass five elements, expanding the rhetorical triangle to a pentad: agent (who?), action (what?), scene (where and when?), purpose (why?), and agency (how?) (*A Grammar of Motives*). Not intended as a heuristic, an aid to discovery or invention, Burke's pentad, nonetheless, supplies writers and readers with a method for establishing the focus of a written or spoken text. His theory of dramatism, focusing as it does on the ratios between the elements in the pentad, calls attention to the ways these representative terms are linked. Dramatism is a theory of action that breathes life into a text, humanizing the action. When a person's acts are to be interpreted in terms of the scene in which she is acting (as in *Robinson Crusoe, Lord of the Flies,* or *Riddley Walker,* for example), her behavior falls under the heading of a "scene-act ratio." In *Lord of the Flies,* both Ralph and Jack, leaders of opposing factions, "act" in reaction to the "scene": they are stranded on a desert island without the traditional protection of society. Yet, within the scene-act ratio falls a range of behavior that must again be evaluated according to the "agent-act ratio"—what is the correspondence between a person's character and action and between the action and the circumstances? Well-adjusted, optimistic, and athletic Ralph "naturally" acts out the desire for civilization, while Jack, the cruel and ugly bully, acts out the feral desire for mastery by intimidation and violence. Other dynamic relationships, other ratios, disclose still other features of human relations, behavior, and motives. Yet no matter how we look at texts, no matter which theorist's game we play, we always seem to swing around the poles of the original rhetorical triangle.

Like Burke, Wayne Booth also expands the notion of the rhetorical triangle. Burke uses his pentad retrospectively to analyze the motives of language (human) actions—texts or speeches—while Booth stresses the persuasive potential of his triangulated proofs: *ethos,* which is situated in the sender; *pathos,* in the receiver; and *logos,* in the text itself (*Modern Dogma and the Rhetoric of Assent* 144-64). Both their analytic frameworks can be used two ways: (1) as systems or frames on which to build a text; and (2) as systems of analysis for already-completed texts. Booth's rhetorical triangle provides a framework that can be used to analyze a text, for it is the dynamic interaction of *ethos, pathos,* and *logos* that creates that text. To understand the *meaning* of an already-completed text, however, Booth would examine the content, analyze the audience that is implied in the text, and recover the attitudes expressed by the implied author. The total act of communication must be examined in order to recover the ethos/character of the speaker, authorial attitude and intention, and voice—vital elements, resonant with attitude, that create a text. Burke, too, realized the importance of "attitude" and often talked of adding it to his dramatistic pentad (thereby transforming it into a hexad).

In "The Rhetorical Stance," Booth's message to teachers, he posits a concept of rhetoric that can support an undergraduate curriculum:

> The common ingredient that I find in all of the writing I admire . . . is something that I shall reluctantly call the rhetorical stance, a stance which depends on discovering and maintaining in any writing situation a proper balance among the three elements that are at work in any communicative effort: the available

arguments about the subject itself, the interests and peculiarities of the audience, and the voice, the implied character, of the speaker. (27)

Like Aristotle, Booth posits a carefully balanced tripartite division of rhetorical appeals. Ever mindful of the audience being addressed, Booth would have us—as writers—strike such a balance to have a clear relationship with our reader(s) and our texts. As readers, Booth would have us keep this triangulation in mind, too, searching for and analyzing ethical, emotional, and logical appeals as we read. Otherwise, he warns, our reading of the text will be at best insensitive, at worst inaccurate. In *Lord of the Flies,* we analyze Ralph's and Jack's speeches for persuasive appeals, just as we analyze the appeals imbricating the omniscient author's narrative. Similar to Aristotle, who believed the ethical appeal to be the most effective, Booth wants speakers and writers—teachers and students alike—to examine their assumptions and to inspect the reasons for their strong commitments. Booth would like to reintroduce into education a strong concept of *ethos,* the dynamic start of persuasive communication: in balancing these three elements, the *logos* may determine how far we extend our *ethos* or what *ethos* we use or how much *pathos.* Booth goes on to say that "it is this balance, this rhetorical stance, difficult as it is to describe, that is our main goal as teachers of rhetoric" (27).

The traditional, stable, tricornered dynamics of written communication have been recently expanded. Gone is the notion of one speaker, one listener, one message—one voice. Instead, such univocal discourse has been replaced with many speakers, many listeners, many messages. In most communications, people are both speakers *and* listeners, or there is a multitude of listeners for one speaker; and the message is constantly affected by and adjusted to both speakers and listeners. To complicate communication even further, each listener interprets each speaker differently, even if only one speaker exists. Thus, just as the speaker and listener cannot be univocal, neither can the interpretation. Although the resulting icon is no longer the "rhetorical triangle," the triangular dynamics remain, for the figure becomes one of equilateral triangles with varying but concentric orientations. The familiar triangle has been embellished, but the original three key terms—speaker, listener, subject—remain.

WHAT RESEARCH TELLS US ABOUT THE ELEMENTS OF WRITTEN COMMUNICATION

The revival of rhetorical theory witnessed during the last twenty-five years has reacquainted teachers with the primary elements of the rhetorical tradition—ethos/audience; logos/text—and with the way those elements have been played out in the canon of rhetoric. Although they might not be familiar with the actual names, most teachers are familiar with concepts forming the canons of rhetoric: invention, arrangement, style, memory, and delivery. While this formulation is in some sense reductive, it nevertheless provides a useful framework for investigating the recent contributions of rhetorical theory to the teaching of writing. Close attention to the *writer* during this time has resulted in much important work that attempts essentially to answer this twofold question: where do a writer's ideas come from and how are such ideas formulated into writing? Such a question demands a new focus on *invention,* the first canon of rhetoric, and has led in two provocative and profitable directions. The first, represented in the work of Richard Young, Janice Lauer, and Richard Larson (to name only a very few) aims at deriving heuristic procedures or systematic strategies that will aid students in discovering and generating ideas about which they might write. Such strategies may be as simple as prompting students to generate ideas about a subject by asking—who, what, when, where, why, and how—the traditional "journalistic formula" mentioned above. Or they can be as complex as the nine-cell matrix presented in Young, Becker, and Pike's *Rhetoric: Discovery and Change.* Essentially, this heuristic asks student writers to look at any subject from nine different perspectives. For example, a student writing about a campus strike might look at it first as a "happening" frozen in time and space, or as the result of a complex set of causes, or as a *cause* of some other effects, or as one tiny part of a larger economic pattern. Looking at the subject in such different ways "loosens up" mental muscles and jogs writers out of unidimensional or tunnel-vision views of a subject.

We see this interest in procedural heuristics as related theoretically to the work of researchers interested in cognition. Linda Flower and coauthor John Hayes are best known for their studies of writers' talk-aloud protocols, tape-recorded documents that catch a writer's *thoughts* about writing while the writing is actually in progress. As any methodology is bound to be, such methodology is flawed, but it *has* provided a fascinating "window on writers' minds," to use Flower's descriptive phrase. Stephen Witte has recently built on the work of Flower and Hayes in order to study what he calls a writer's "pretext," a writer's "trial locution that is produced in the mind, stored in the writer's memory, and sometimes manipulated mentally prior to being transcribed as written text" (397). Other researchers have attempted to map the relationship of affective factors to a writer's "invention": John Daly, in terms of writing apprehension, and Mike Rose, in terms of writer's block. All of this research aims to help teachers understand the rich, diverse, complex, and largely *invisible* processes student writers go through in writing.

But a renewed interest in student writers has led in another powerful direction as well, notably in the work of Ken Macrorie and, more pervasively, of Peter Elbow. Elbow is interested in how writers establish unique voices, in how they realize individual selves in discourse, and his work with students presents dramatic evidence of such activity. In a series of very influential books (*Writing without Teachers, Writing with Power, Embracing Contraries*), Elbow has focused on how writers come to know themselves—and then share those selves with others.

The researchers and teachers we have been surveying here differ in many ways, but their work is all aimed primarily at that point of the rhetorical triangle that focuses on the writer and her powers of invention. They want to know what makes writers tick—and how teachers can help writers "tick" most effectively.

If we shift the focus of our discussion from writer to *text*, we also find that rhetorical theory has much to offer the teacher of writing. Students are often puzzled when teachers do not "get the meaning" they intend. Rhetorical theory helps us explain why such miscommunication takes place and suggests powerful ways to avoid it. One of the simplest to use with students is I. A. Richard's own version of the rhetorical triangle:

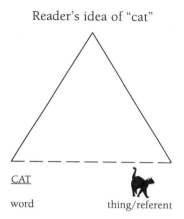

Reader's idea of "cat"

CAT
word   thing/referent

Figure 2

Richards argues that no direct relationship exists between a word—a set of black marks on a page—and its referent in the world (Ogden and Richards *The Meaning of Meaning* 10-13). That is to say, the meaning of *cat* is not inherent in the little squiggles we call letters nor in the furry, purry pet we might have. Rather, meaning arises in the perceivers—in people—as they filter the linguistic signal *cat* through all their experience with both word and thing. So *cat* might well mean one thing to someone who adores cats and something quite different to someone who was, as a child, badly scratched by a cat.

Richards uses another principle to help us understand how we derive meaning from texts. He calls this principle *interinanimation of words*, which simply means that any one word is strongly affected by other words around it (*Philosophy of Rhetoric* 47-66). The word *love*, for instance, suggests one meaning when connected to the words *grandparent* and *grandchild*, another when connected to *husband* and *wife*, and yet another when connected to a business tycoon and her self-image. Students can put Richard's principle to use by examining a text closely for the ways its words interinanimate one another. And teachers can use the principle of interinanimation to show students that we are all very much *what we say*, that our words work together (interinanimate) to create the people we are, with our individual values, prejudices, and so on.

Three other concepts used by modern rhetorical theorists may help students and teachers get inside the intricacies of any text. Richard Weaver provides one set, what he calls *ultimate* or *God terms* and *Devil terms*, to indicate those words or concepts that represent something we will make sacrifices for (87-112). In the 1950s, Weaver hypothesized that *Americanism, progress,* and *science* served as God terms, large concepts that most people held very dear. He went on to suggest that God or Devil terms establish hierarchical relationships in texts—that is, that many other related terms usually clustered under them. Identifying such central terms and then mapping related clusters of terms can help students get at complex meanings in texts.

Burke suggests that we look at a text (or any discourse, spoken or written) as a *terministic screen* (LSA "Terministic Screens" 59 ff). If we think of a text as a very fine-meshed screen, with every point connected to every other point, what Burke has in mind becomes apparent. The "screen" of the text directs our attention in certain ways, selecting some points for emphasis, deflecting others. And the screen is made up not of wire, but of words or *terms.* Burke challenges us to trace all the minute interstitial connections among terms in any text/screen as a means of constructing meaning.

One other key principle deserves our attention in discussing rhetorical theory and texts: *intertextuality,* which refers to a principle very similar to those we have been discussing. Most simply, intertextuality denotes the great conversation among texts, the way texts refer or allude to one another, build on or parody one another, revolve around one another. The Mel Brooks movie *Young Frankenstein,* for instance, is part of an elaborate and extensive conversation stretching back through countless other movies to Mary Shelley's novel (with its subtitle *The Modern Prometheus*) to many poems and plays and mythical accounts of Prometheus, to the creation of Adam in the Bible—or *forward* to the contemporary debate over genetic engineering and our ability to create life. Introducing students to this principle of intertextuality allows them to enter this great conversation and provides them with an effective method for probing textual meaning.

The theorists we have been discussing offer ways to see the "big picture" of a text; they deal with the macrostructure element of the second canon of rhetoric, the *arrangement* of argument. But rhetorical theory offers help on the microstructures of the "little picture" as well. This tradition of research, which focuses on organization, on the relationship between form and function, is extensive and complex. Here we will cite two rhetoricians whose work seems most helpful for the teaching of writing. Many readers of this book already might be familiar with the first, Francis Christensen. In a series of essays, Christensen demonstrated a way to map sentences and paragraphs according to levels of generality and modification. *Periodic* sentences and paragraphs are those that delay or postpone announcing the general main clause/topic until the very end, leading into the topic with supporting or modifying details ("A Generative Rhetoric of the Sentence" 155-56). This kind of structure forces a reader to hold the subject in mind until the very end and keeps syntactic tension high. In the hands of skilled writers, periodic structures can keep readers alert for what is to come and make the main idea, when it finally does appear, all the more impressive.

Although structures using various degrees of periodicity can be very effective in challenging and interesting readers, they do not constitute the most frequently used pattern in modern English. Rather, the *cumulative* structure, which adds details after the main clause or announcement of the topic, is the more dominant. Christensen writes: "The main clause, which may or may not have a sentence modifier before it, advances the discussion; but the additions move backwards, as in this clause, to modify the statement of the main clause or more often to explicate it or exemplify it, so that the sentence has a flowing and ebbing movement, advancing to a new position and then pausing to consolidate it, leaping and lingering as the popular ballad does" (156). Because the main clause/topic is presented at or near the beginning of the sentence/ paragraph, cumulative structures do not require readers to hold the subject in suspense until the end. In one sense, then, these structures may be easier to read than periodic ones, yet the skillful writer can position the most important piece of information at the end. Like all sentence patterns, however, the cumulative sentence can be used effectively or, as in the following example, ineffectively: "The cumulative sentence in unskilled hands is unsteady, allowing a writer to ramble on, adding modifier after modifier, until the reader is almost overwhelmed, because the writer's central idea is lost."

Using exclusively periodic or cumulative structures, of course, would be monotonous. And so the best writers mingle structures—short and long, periodic and cumulative—although never forgetting that the most important ideas naturally deserve the most prominent positions. Our own students can easily test the structures of others' as well as their own texts, relating purpose to structure, and can learn to balance their own prose with purposeful and effective movement between general and specific information.

More recently, Richard Coe has elaborated and extended the work of Christensen, moving toward what he calls a *grammar of passages*. In his monograph by the same name, Coe takes the traditional syntactic relationships between form and function—coordinate, subordinate, and superordinate—and subdivides them further: (1) coordination: contrasting, contradicting, conjoining, and repeating on the same level of generality; (2) subordination: defining, exemplifying, giving reasons, deducing (deductive conclusion), explaining (making plain by restating more specifically), qualifying; and (3) superordination: drawing conclusions, generalizing (making an inductive inference), commenting on a previously stated proposition (32–33). Then Coe goes on to develop a system of mapping these relationships. This syntactical system has been tested extensively with student writers, in classes ranging from ESL to technical writing, to basic writing, to advanced composition, with dramatic results. Students learn to "map" their own texts and thereby have a means of deciding whether those texts are coherent, whether they "make sense."

But what of the third angle of the rhetorical triangle—that pointing to *audience* and *context*? Does rhetorical theory offer any insights into these crucial elements in communication? Of course. As a discipline, rhetoric has always been intensely interested in the effects a writer's intentions, words, texts, have *on people* in varying situations. That is to say, taking a "rhetorical stance" always places us in a full context. In this regard, rhetorical theory has helped us learn about the psychology of readers (or listeners, interpreters, responders), from Aristotle's discussion of how different types of people react to different subjects and Plato's elegant oration on souls, to contemporary persuasion theorists (Petty, Ostrom, and Brock) on the one hand and reader-oriented researchers and critics (Rosenblatt, Bleich, and Iser) on the other.

What this research tells us as teachers of writing is simply this: the processes of reading and responding to texts are at least as complex as those of writing a text; that all readers build up frameworks (called schemata), which they use to make sense as they read; that such frameworks are affected both by everything we already know and by what we are (gender, for example, exerts powerful influence on patterns of interpretation and response). As teachers, we must help students understand and theorize about their own such patterns. Doing so leads to the second major point we want to make here. That is, we can often understand our own patterns of response by seeing them *in context*, as related to others' responses and as part of a large social process aimed at negotiating and constructing meaning. If intertextuality is a coin, this is its flip side— interreaderability—the fully contextualized, multiple voices out of which we forge an understanding of texts.

PEDAGOGICAL IMPLICATIONS OF A WRITTEN COMMUNICATION

A rhetoric of written communication demands a dynamic balancing of speaker, listener, subject (of *ethos, pathos, logos*). And when a teacher introduces these elements into the writing classroom, she can expect learning to emerge. The interdependency of these elements creates galvanic tension, in terms not only of the rhetorical elements themselves, but also of the students, teacher, and texts.

The pedagogical implications for teachers are manifold, most prominent being that they must learn to share authority, thereby enabling students to experience, create, and evaluate their own and others' texts. One of the best ways teachers can share responsibility for learning is to provide "demonstrations," occasions for active learning for their students. In the terms of education researcher Frank Smith, demonstrations provide students with opportunities to become so engaged that they really teach themselves; they forget that they are learning and take an active role in their own learning.

In fact, writing teachers can most easily provide students with demonstrations by adjusting writing assignments, making them (to use an overused term) "relevant" to the students' lives. Often, meaningful writing assignments are merely those that provide students with information on their intended audience, their purpose for writing, and the context of the communication—information that encourages students to harness the dynamics of the rhetorical triangle. Other teachers provide demonstrations by building their syllabi on a theme, such as "education" (cf. Bartholomae and Petrosky; Lunsford). A teacher in an open admissions college provided his students with demonstrations by building a syllabus on "work." Urging his students to meet in small groups, to speak out, to read and respond to one another's writing, to expect concrete details and supporting observations, this teacher watched as his class of low-paid, blue-collar manual workers reinvented their daily lives, sharing their experiences, critically analyzing their situations, and writing persuasively and feelingly about their lives. No longer was learning the retrieval and transmission of static information—from the teacher's head to the students'. Rather, learning became the dynamic interactions of the students, a demonstration of their abilities to discover and create, construe and communicate their own knowledge. Once they realized their own rhetorical stance, the values and attitudes of their intended audience, and the importance of their message, their rhetorical triangles were balanced. In this case, choice of writing assignments indicated the teacher's willingness to share responsibility for classroom learning.

Hence, such a classroom transforms itself from uni- to polyvocal. The original rhetorical triangle, weighted fully on the teacher/speaker side, becomes a series of phase-shift rotations, rhetorical triangles that constantly achieve, lose, and reestablish rhetorical balance. Each shift, a fusion of rhetoric and dialectic, is determined by whose paper is being featured, who is serving as author, who is serving as audience, and how the in-draft text is being affected and effected by the speaker and audience. And ultimately, that original triangle, in recreating itself, begins to round out and resemble an expanded circular universe of discourse.

To make the polyvocal, rhetorical classroom "work," students, too, must learn to share responsibility for their learning, and to rely no longer solely on their teacher for grades, knowledge, approval, or ego gratification. What might be initially perceived as instability will soon be seen for what it is—dynamics. Once students begin to take advantage of these classroom dynamics—teacher and students alike working as sharers and evaluators—they will realize the potential for their own written communication. No longer will they be content to serve as repositories for their teacher's knowledge, to write *for* and *to* only their teachers, to remain silent. Yet often and understandably, just transferring their allegiance from their teacher to their peers is difficult, accustomed as they are to years of passive learning. Accustomed as teachers are to years of one-way teaching and nearly total responsibility for learning (and teaching), many find relief in newly shared allegiance. Students need to know that in the rhetorical classroom, their teachers are willing to share their work, their responsibility, even their authority.

In the rhetorical writing classroom, students broaden their intended audience from the teacher-evaluator to include their peers, carefully considering the responses and evaluations of those peers, perhaps more than they did those of their teachers. Many students choose to respond orally and in writing to classroom, in-draft texts and to participate in the final evaluation of themselves and their peers. Peers create an actual audience and often a reason for writing, for they provide response—what Elbow calls "the main experience that makes people want to write more" (130). In *Writing without Teachers,* Elbow writes about one student's thrill of working with her peers: "Her words got through to the readers. She sent words out into the darkness and heard someone shout back. This made her want to do it again, and this is probably the most powerful thing that makes people improve their writing" (130).

When students are involved in one another's writings, serving as senders and receivers of communication, as questioners of purpose, as judges of *ethos, pathos,* and *logos,* as refiners of style and tone, when they are respectfully attentive of one another's *author*-ity, when students have the opportunity to question responses to their drafts *as they draft,* when they coach as they are being coached, then they are indeed sharing the responsibility for their own learning and incorporating in their learning the dynamics of rhetorical theory.

The implications for a rhetoric of written communication go beyond those for the teacher and students, however, to affect the very physical structure of the classroom itself. Always, or so it seems, students have sat in neat rows of nailed-down desks, discouraged from making so much as eye contact with their peers, asked to write in solitude. But as teachers and students begin to use rhetorical theory, begin to see that senders need the responses of receivers, that the universe, the "out there," plays an integral part in communication, and that messages are colored by all the elements in the rhetorical triangle, they will be unable to work in the traditional classroom environment. They will want tables or moveable desks so they can sit and work together. They will want to talk on the phone or through their computers both during and after school. They need to be together. And they need time.

Gone should be the days when students are asked to complete their writing in forty-eight minutes or to evaluate the work of their groups in forty-eight minutes. Gone should be the days when one draft—the first and final—is handed in for an unchangeable grade. Many schools, in fact, are moving toward the portfolio method of evaluation, which encourages students to gather their best revisions for one end-of-the-term grade.[1] Thoughtful writing and thoughtful responding take time, time for planning, thinking, drafting, responding, revising, and polishing. Hence, classrooms themselves must be designed in response to the evolution of classroom practices as well as classroom schedules.

ISSUES RAISED BY A RHETORIC
OF WRITTEN COMMUNICATION

Teachers and students committed to examining the dynamic relationship among writers, audiences, texts, and contexts will face a number of important issues, foremost among them the complex question of ethics and language use. If we are not so much what we *eat* as what we say or write, if as Jacques Derrida claims, we don't write language so much as language *writes us,* then words can never be "mere" words again. Instead words are, to use Burke's term, symbolic *acts* (*LSA*); as Weaver says, a speaker's words have *consequences,* and these consequences affect other people, texts, and contexts (221 ff). As language users, we thus must be responsible for our words, must take the responsibility for examining our own and others' language and seeing how well, how truly, it represents the speaker. We can do so playfully, through parody or spoofing, or we can do so most seriously, as in an analysis of the consequences of political doublespeak. But we—teachers and students alike—must carry out such analyses consistently and rigorously.

Once students grasp this principle of analytic responsibility, they become rhetors. They see writing and reading not as boring school-bound drills or as ways of packaging static information, but as ways of creating and recreating themselves through and with others, as a student reported during a recent evaluation of one of our courses:

> When we first started this class, I couldn't *imagine* what you meant by our being rhetoricians, getting rhetorical stances of our own. What's all this, I thought? You're the teacher. You know a whole lot of stuff, and you better just *tell* it to us. Now I know that you really do know a lot of stuff, more even than I thought. But that's not what matters. What matters is what I know. And now I know that I'm making what I know in language, forming, transforming, and reforming myself with other people. What I know is we are all of us learners in progress. Even you! So—*wish me luck.*

Teachers, of course, are the ones who develop and nurture such an atmosphere, who set the terms within which an ethos of the classroom emerges. Building such an atmosphere implies that the teacher becomes a member/participant of the class, providing questions, tasks, and situations that will allow the class to experience what it means not to *reveal* knowledge but to *construct* it, to be learners-in-progress. This role is a demanding one, far more so than traditional teacherly roles have been.

In the final analysis, a rhetorical perspective on the teaching of writing pushes us outside our private selves, beyond our solitary teacherly or writerly desks, to a realization of the ways in which we all use language to create—or destroy—communities, societies, worlds. The writing classroom is one such world. Rhetorical theory provides us, together with our students, with the means of making that world, one that is rich in diversity, complex in meaning, and full of all the life our blended voices can give it.

NOTE

[1] The portfolio method of assessment has been most thoroughly documented and argued for by Peter Elbow of University of Massachusetts—Amherst. The largest school with plans to adopt a portfolio method of assessment is University of Minnesota, which, beginning in 1990, plans to use portfolios for evaluation in introductory composition as well as for promotion.

WORKS CITED

Abrams, M. H. *The Mirror and the Lamp: Romantic Theory and the Critical Tradition.* New York: Oxford UP, 1953.

Aristotle. *The Rhetoric and the Poetics of Aristotle.* Trans. W. Rhys Roberts. New York: Modern Library, 1984.

Bartholomae, David, and Anthony Petrosky. *Facts, Artifacts, and Counterfacts: Theory and Method for a Reading and Writing Course.* Upper Montclair, NJ: Boynton/Cook, 1986.

Bleich, David. *Subjective Criticism.* Baltimore, MD: Johns Hopkins UP, 1978.

——. *Readings and Feelings: An Introduction to Subjective Criticism.* Urbana, IL: National Council of Teachers of English, 1975.

——. "The Subjective Character of Critical Interpretation." *College English* 36 (1975): 739–55.

Booth, Wayne C. *Modern Dogma and the Rhetoric of Assent.* Chicago: U of Chicago P, 1974.

——. "The Rhetorical Stance." *Now Don't Try to Reason with Me: Essays and Ironics for a Credulous Age.* Chicago: U of Chicago P, 1970.

——. "The Brooklyn Plan: Attaining Intellectual Growth through Peer-Group Tutoring." *Liberal Education* 64 (1978): 447–69.

——. "Collaborative Learning: Some Practical Models." *College English* 34 (1973): 634–43.

Burke, Kenneth. *A Grammar of Motives.* Cleveland: World, 1962.

——. *A Rhetoric of Motives.* Cleveland: World, 1962.

——. "Terministic Screens." *Language as Symbolic Action.* Berkeley: U of California P, 1966.

Christensen, Francis, "A Generative Rhetoric of the Sentence." *College Composition and Communication* 14 (1963): 155–61.

——. "A Generative Rhetoric of the Paragraph." *College Composition and Communication* 16 (1968): 144–56.

Coe, Richard. *A Grammar of Passages.* Carbondale: Southern Illinois UP, 1987.

Daly, John. "The Effects of Writing Apprehension on Message Encoding." *Journalism Quarterly* 54 (1977): 566–72.

——. "Writing Apprehension and Writing Competency." *Journal of Educational Research* 72 (1978): 10–14.

Derrida, Jacques. *Of Grammatology.* Trans. Gayatri Chakrovorty Spivak. Baltimore, Md.: Johns Hopkins UP, 1974.

Elbow, Peter. *Embracing Contraries.* New York: Oxford UP, 1986.

——. *Writing with Power.* New York: Oxford UP, 1981.

——. *Writing without Teachers.* New York: Oxford UP, 1973.

Flower, Linda, and John R. Hayes. "Uncovering Cognitive Processes in Writing: An Introduction to Protocol Analysis." *Research on Writing.* Ed. P. Mosenthal, S. Walmsley, and L. Tamor. London: Longmans, 1982. 207–20.

Iser, Wolfgang. *The Act of Reading: A Theory of Aesthetic Response.* Baltimore, MD: Johns Hopkins UP, 1974.

——. *The Implied Reader.* Baltimore, MD: Johns Hopkins UP, 1975.

Kinneavy, James L. *A Theory of Discourse.* New York: Norton, 1971.

Larson, Richard L. "Discovery through Questioning: A Plan for Teaching Rhetorical Invention." *College English* 30 (1968): 126–34.

Lauer, Janice. "Heuristics and Composition." *College Composition and Communication* 21 (1970): 396–404.

Lunsford, Andrea A. "Assignments for Basic Writers: Unresolved Issues and Needed Research." *Journal of Basic Writing* 5 (1986): 87–99.

Ogden, C. K., and I. A. Richards. *The Meaning of Meaning: A Study of the Influences of Language upon Thought and of the Science of Symbolism.* New York: Harcourt, 1936.

Petty, Richard E., Thomas M. Ostrom, and Timothy Brock, eds. *Cognitive Responses in Persuasion.* Hillsdale, NJ: Erlbaum, 1981.

Richards, I. A. *The Philosophy of Rhetoric.* New York: Oxford UP, 1936.

Rose, Mike. *Writer's Block: The Cognitive Dimension.* Carbondale: Southern Illinois UP, 1984.

Rosenblatt, Louise. *Literature as Exploration.* 3d ed. New York: Barnes and Noble, 1976.

——. *The Reader, the Text, the Poem: The Transactional Theory of the Literary Work.* Carbondale: Southern Illinois UP, 1978.

Smith, Frank. "Research Update: Demonstrations, Engagements, and Sensitivity—A Revised Approach to Language Learning." *Language Arts* 68 (1981): 103–12.

Weaver, Richard M. *Language Is Sermonic: Richard M. Weaver on the Nature of Rhetoric.* Ed. Richard L. Johannesen, Rennard Strickland, and Ralph T. Eubanks. Baton Rouge: Louisiana State UP, 1970.

Witte, Stephen. "Pre-Test and Composing." *College Composition and Communication* 38 (1987): 397–425.

Young, Richard E., Alton L. Becker, and Kenneth L. Pike. *Rhetoric: Discovery and Change.* New York: Harcourt, 1970.

This article is reprinted from *On Literacy and Its Teaching.* Ed. Gail Hawisher and Anna Soter. Albany: SUNY P, 1990. 174–89. —Ed.

David Bartholomae

INVENTING THE UNIVERSITY

> Education may well be, as of right, the instrument whereby every individual, in a society like our own, can gain access to any kind of discourse. But we well know that in its distribution, in what it permits and in what it prevents, it follows the well-trodden battle-lines of social conflict. Every educational system is a political means of maintaining or of modifying the appropriation of discourse with the knowledge and the powers it carries with it.
>
> —Foucault, "The Discourse on Language"

Every time a student sits down to write for us, he has to invent the university for the occasion—invent the university, that is, or a branch of it, like History or Anthropology or Economics or English. He has to learn to speak our language, to speak as we do, to try on the peculiar ways of knowing, selecting, evaluating, reporting, concluding, and arguing that define the discourse of our community. Or perhaps I should say the *various* discourses of our community, since it is in the nature of a liberal arts education that a student, after the first year or two, must learn to try on a variety of voices and interpretive schemes—to write, for example, as a literary critic one day and an experimental psychologist the next, to work within fields where the rules governing the presentation of examples or the development of an argument are both distinct and, even to a professional, mysterious.

The students have to appropriate (or be appropriated by) a specialized discourse, and they have to do this as though they were easily and comfortably one with their audience, as though they were members of the academy, or historians or anthropologists or economists; they have to invent the university by assembling and mimicking its language, finding some compromise between idiosyncrasy, a personal history, and the requirements of convention, the history of a discipline. They must learn to speak our language. Or they must dare to speak it, or to carry off the bluff, since speaking and writing will most certainly be required long before the skill is "learned." And this, understandably, causes problems.

Let me look quickly at an example. Here is an essay written by a college freshman, a basic writer:

> In the past time I thought that an incident was creative was when I had to make a clay model of the earth, but not of the classical or your everyday model of the earth which consists of the two cores, the mantle and the crust. I thought of these things in a dimension of which it would be unique, but easy to comprehend. Of course, your materials to work with were basic and limited at the same time, but thought help to put this limit into a right attitude or frame of mind to work with the clay.

408

In the beginning of the clay model, I had to research and learn the different dimensions of the earth (in magnitude, quantity, state of matter, etc.). After this, I learned how to put this into the clay and come up with something different than any other person in my class at the time. In my opinion color coordination and shape was the key to my creativity of the clay model of the earth.

Creativity is the venture of the mind at work with the mechanics relay to the limbs from the cranium, which stores and triggers this action. It can be a burst of energy released at a precise time a thought is being transmitted. This can cause a frenzy of the human body, but it depends of the characteristics of the individual and how they can relay the message clearly enough through mechanics of the body to us as an observer. Then we must determine if it is creative or a learned process varied by the individual's thought process. Creativity is indeed a tool which has to exist, or our world will not succeed into the future and progress like it should.

I am continually impressed by the patience and good will of our students. This student was writing a placement essay during freshman orientation. (The problem set to him was "Describe a time when you did something you felt to be creative. Then, on the basis of the incident you have described, go on to draw some general conclusions about 'creativity.'") He knew that university faculty would be reading and evaluating his essay, and so he wrote for them.

In some ways it is a remarkable performance. He is trying on the discourse even though he doesn't have the knowledge that makes the discourse more than a routine, a set of conventional rituals and gestures. And he does this, I think, even though he *knows* he doesn't have the knowledge that makes the discourse more than a routine. He defines himself as a researcher, working systematically, and not as a kid in a high school class: "I thought of these things in a dimension of . . ."; "had to research and learn the different dimensions of the earth (in magnitude, quantity, state of matter, etc.)." He moves quickly into a specialized language (his approximation of our jargon) and draws both a general, textbook-like conclusion ("Creativity is the venture of the mind at work . . .") and a resounding peroration ("Creativity is indeed a tool which has to exist, or our world will not succeed into the future and progress like it should"). The writer has even, with that "indeed" and with the qualifications and the parenthetical expressions of the opening paragraphs, picked up the rhythm of our prose. And through it all he speaks with an impressive air of authority.

There is an elaborate but, I will argue, a necessary and enabling fiction at work here as the student dramatizes his experience in a "setting"—the setting required by the discourse—where he can speak to us as a companion, a fellow researcher. As I read the essay, there is only one moment when the fiction is broken, when we are addressed differently. The student says, "Of course, your materials to work with were basic and limited at the same time, but thought help to put this limit into a right attitude or frame of mind to work with the clay." At this point, I think, we become students and he the teacher, giving us a lesson (as in, "You take your pencil in your right hand and put your paper in front of you"). This is, however, one of the most characteristic slips of basic writers. It is very hard for them to take on the role—the voice, the person—of an authority whose authority is rooted in scholarship, analysis, or research. They slip, then, into the more immediately available and realizable voice of authority, the voice of a teacher giving a lesson or the voice of a parent lecturing at the dinner table. They offer advice or homilies rather than "academic" conclusions. There is a similar break in the final paragraph, where the conclusion that pushes for a definition ("Creativity is the venture of the mind at work with the mechanics relay to the limbs from the cranium . . .") is replaced by a conclusion which speaks in the voice of an Elder ("Creativity is indeed a tool which has to exist, or our world will not succeed into the future and progress like it should").

It is not uncommon, then, to find such breaks in the concluding sections of essays written by basic writers. Here is the concluding section of an essay written by a student about his work as a mechanic. He had been asked to generalize about "work" after reviewing an on-the-job experience or incident that "stuck in his mind" as somehow significant: "How could two repairmen miss a leak? Lack of pride? No incentive? Lazy? I don't know." At this point the writer is in a perfect position to speculate, to move from the problem to an analysis of the problem. Here is how the paragraph continues, however (and notice the change in pronoun reference):

> From this point on, I take my time, do it right, and don't let customers get under your skin. If they have a complaint, tell them to call your boss and he'll be more than glad to handle it. Most important, worry about yourself, and keep a clear eye on everyone, for there's always someone trying to take advantage of you, anytime and anyplace.

We get neither a technical discussion nor an "academic" discussion but a Lesson on Life.[1] This is the language he uses to address the general question "How could two repairmen miss a leak?" The other brand of conclusion, the more academic one, would have required him to speak of his experience in our terms; it would, that is, have required a special vocabulary, a special system of presentation, and an interpretive scheme (or a set of commonplaces) he could use to identify and talk about the mystery of human error. The writer certainly had access to the range of acceptable commonplaces for such an explanation: "lack of pride," "no incentive," "lazy." Each would dictate its own set of phrases, examples, and conclusions, and we, his teachers, would know how to write out each argument, just as we would know how to write out more specialized arguments of our own. A "commonplace," then, is a culturally or institutionally authorized concept or statement that carries with it its own necessary elaboration. We all use commonplaces to orient ourselves in the world; they provide a point of reference and a set of "prearticulated" explanations that are readily available to organize and interpret experience. The phrase "lack of pride" carries with it its own account for the repairman's error just as, at another point in time, a reference to "original sin" would provide an explanation, or just as, in a certain university classroom, a reference to "alienation" would enable a writer to continue and complete the discussion. While there is a way in which these terms are interchangeable, they are not all permissible. A student in a composition class would most likely be turned away from a discussion of original sin. Commonplaces are the "controlling ideas" of our composition textbooks, textbooks that not only insist upon a set form for expository writing but a set view of public life.[2]

When the student above says, "I don't know," he is not saying, then, that he has nothing to say. He is saying that he is not in a position to carry on this discussion. And so we are addressed as apprentices rather than as teachers or scholars. To speak to us as a person of status or privilege, the writer can either speak to us in our terms—in the privileged language of university discourse—or, in default (or in defiance), he can speak to us as though we were children, offering us the wisdom of experience.

I think it is possible to say that the language of the "Clay Model" paper has come through the writer and not from the writer. The writer has located himself (he has located the self that is represented by the *I* on the page) in a context that is, finally, beyond him, not his own and not available to his immediate procedures for inventing and arranging text. I would not, that is, call this essay an example of "writer-based" prose. I would not say that it is egocentric or that it represents the "interior monologue of a writer thinking and talking to himself" (Flower 63). It is, rather, the record of a writer who has lost himself in the discourse of his readers. There is a context beyond the reader that is not the world but a way of talking about the world, a way of talking that determines the use of examples, the possible conclusions, the acceptable commonplaces, and the key words of an essay on the construction of a clay model of the earth. This writer has entered the discourse without successfully approximating it.

Linda Flower has argued that the difficulty inexperienced writers have with writing can be understood as a difficulty in negotiating the transition between writer-based and reader-based prose. Expert writers, in other words, can better imagine how a reader will respond to a text and can transform or restructure what they have to say around a goal shared with a reader. Teaching students to revise for readers, then, will better prepare them to write initially with a reader in mind. The success of this pedagogy depends upon the degree to which a writer can imagine and conform to a reader's goals. The difficulty of this act of imagination, and the burden of such conformity, are so much at the heart of the problem that a teacher must pause and take stock before offering revision as a solution. Students like the student who wrote the "Clay Model" paper are not so much trapped in a private language as they are shut out from one of the privileged languages of public life, a language they are aware of but cannot control.

Our students, I've said, have to appropriate (or be appropriated by) a specialized discourse, and they have to do this as though they were easily or comfortably one with their audience. If you look at the situation this way, suddenly the problem of audience awareness becomes enormously complicated. One of the common assumptions of both composition research and composition teaching is that at some "stage" in the process of composing an essay a writer's ideas or his motives must be tailored to the needs and expectations of his audience. A writer has to "build bridges" between his point of view and his readers'. He has to anticipate and acknowledge his readers' assumptions and biases. He must begin with "common points of departure" before introducing new or controversial arguments. There is a version of the pastoral at work here. It is assumed that a person of low status (like a shepherd) can speak to a person of power (like a courtier), but only (at least so far as the language is concerned) if he is not a shepherd at all, but actually a member of the court out in the field in disguise.

Writers who can successfully manipulate an audience (or, to use a less pointed language, writers who can accommodate their motives to their readers' expectations) are writers who can both imagine and write from a position of privilege. They must, that is, see themselves within a privileged discourse, one that already includes and excludes groups of readers. They must be either equal to or more powerful than those they would address. The writing, then, must somehow transform the political and social relationships between basic writing students and their teachers.

If my students are going to write for me by knowing who I am—and if this means more than knowing my prejudices, psyching me out—it means knowing what I know; it means having the knowledge of a professor of English. They have, then, to know what I know and how I know what I know (the interpretive schemes that define the way I would work out the problems I set for them); they have to learn to write what I would write, or to offer up some approximation of that discourse. The problem of audience awareness, then, is a problem of power and finesse. It cannot be addressed, as it is in most classroom exercises, by giving students privilege and denying the situation of the classroom, by having students write to an outsider, someone excluded from their privileged circle: "Write about 'To His Coy Mistress,' not for your teacher, but for the students in your class"; "Describe Pittsburgh to someone who has never been there"; "Explain to a high school senior how best to prepare for college"; "Describe baseball to a Martian."

Exercises such as these allow students to imagine the needs and goals of a reader, and they bring those needs and goals forward as a dominant constraint in the construction of an essay. And they argue, implicitly, what is generally true about writing—that it is an act of aggression disguised as an act of charity. What they fail to address is the central problem of academic writing, where students must assume the right of speaking to someone who knows Pittsburgh or "To His Coy Mistress" better than they do, a reader for whom the general commonplaces and the readily available utterances about a subject are inadequate. It should be clear that when I say that I know Pittsburgh better than my basic writing students, I am talking about a way of knowing that is also a way of writing. There may be much that they know that I don't know, but in the setting of the university classroom, I have a way of talking about the town that is "better" (and for arbitrary reasons) than theirs.

I think that all writers, in order to write, must imagine for themselves the privilege of being "insiders"—that is, of being both inside an established and powerful discourse, and of being granted a special right to speak. And I think that right to speak is seldom conferred upon us—upon any of us, teachers or students—by virtue of the fact that we have invented or discovered an original idea. Leading students to believe that they are responsible for something new or original, unless they understand what those words mean with regard to writing, is a dangerous and counterproductive practice. We do have the right to expect students to be active and engaged, but that is more a matter of being continually and stylistically working against the inevitable presence of conventional language; it is not a matter of inventing a language that is new.

When students are writing for a teacher, writing becomes more problematic than it is for the students who are describing baseball to a Martian. The students, in effect, have to assume privilege without having any. And since students assume privilege by locating themselves within the discourse of a particular community—within a set of specifically acceptable gestures and commonplaces—learning, at least as it is defined in the liberal arts curriculum, becomes more a matter of imitation or parody than a matter of invention and discovery.

What our beginning students need to learn is to extend themselves into the commonplaces, set phrases, rituals, gestures, habits of mind, tricks of persuasion, obligatory conclusions, and necessary connections that determine the "what might be said" and constitute knowledge within the various branches of our academic community. The course of instruction that would make this possible would be based on a sequence of illustrated assignments and would allow for successive approximations of academic or "disciplinary" discourse. Students will not take on our peculiar ways of reading, writing, speaking, and thinking all at once. Nor will the command of a subject like sociology, at least as that command is represented by the successful completion of a multiple choice exam, enable students to write sociology. Our colleges and universities, by and large, have failed to involve basic writing students in scholarly projects, projects that would allow them to act as though they were colleagues in an academic enterprise. Much of the written work students do is test-taking, report or summary, work that places them outside the working discourse of the academic community, where they are expected to admire and report on what we do, rather than inside that discourse, where they can do its work and participate in a common enterprise.[3] This is a failure of teachers and curriculum designers who, even if they speak of writing as a mode of learning, all too often represent writing as a "tool" to be used by [an] educated mind.

Pat Bizzell is one of the most important scholars writing now on basic writers and on the special requirements of academic discourse.[4] In a recent essay, "Cognition, Convention, and Certainty: What We Need to Know about Writing," she argues that the problems of basic writers might be

> better understood in terms of their unfamiliarity with the academic discourse community, combined, perhaps, with such limited experience outside their native discourse communities that they are unaware that there is such a thing as a discourse community with conventions to be mastered. What is underdeveloped is their knowledge both of the ways experience is constituted and

interpreted in the academic discourse community and of the fact that all discourse communities constitute and interpret experience. (230)

One response to the problems of basic writers, then, would be to determine just what the community's conventions are, so that those conventions can be written out, "demystified," and taught in our classrooms. Teachers, as a result, could be more precise and helpful when they ask students to "think," "argue," "describe," or "define." Another response would be to examine the essays written by basic writers—their approximations of academic discourse—to determine more clearly where the problems lie. If we look at their writing, and if we look at it in the context of other student writing, we can better see the points of discord when students try to write their way into the university.

The purpose of the remainder of this paper will be to examine some of the most striking and characteristic problems as they are presented in the expository essays of basic writers. I will be concerned, then, with university discourse in its most generalized form—that is, as represented by introductory courses—and not with the special conventions required by advanced work in the various disciplines. And I will be concerned with the difficult, and often violent, accommodations that occur when students locate themselves in a discourse that is not "naturally" or immediately theirs.

I have reviewed five hundred essays written in response to the "creativity" question used during one of our placement exams. (The essay cited at the opening of this paper was one of that group.) Some of the essays were written by basic writers (or, more properly, those essays led readers to identify the writers as "basic writers"); some were written by students who "passed" (who were granted immediate access to the community of writers at the university). As I read these essays, I was looking to determine the stylistic resources that enabled writers to locate themselves within an "academic" discourse. My bias as a reader should be clear by now. I was not looking to see how the writer might represent the skills demanded by a neutral language (a language whose key features were paragraphs, topic sentences, transitions, and the like—features of a clear and orderly mind). I was looking to see what happened when a writer entered into a language to locate himself (a textual self) and his subject, and I was looking to see how once entered, that language made or unmade a writer.

Here is one essay. Its writer was classified as a basic writer. Since the essay is relatively free of sentence level errors, that decision must have been rooted in some perceived failure of the discourse itself.

> I am very interested in music, and I try to be creative in my interpretation of music. While in high school, I was a member of a jazz ensemble. The members of the ensemble were given chances to improvise and be creative in various songs. I feel that this was a great experience for me, as well as the other members. I was proud to know that I could use my imagination and feelings to create music other than what was written.
>
> Creativity to me, means being free to express yourself in a way that is unique to you, not having to conform to certain rules and guidelines. Music is only one of the many areas in which people are given opportunities to show their

creativity. Sculpting, carving, building, art, and acting are just a few more areas where people can show their creativity.

Through my music I conveyed feelings and thoughts which were important to me. Music was my means of showing creativity. In whatever form creativity takes, whether it be music, art, or science, it is an important aspect of our lives because it enables us to be individuals.

Notice, in this essay, the key gesture, one that appears in all but a few of the essays I read. The student defines as his own that which is a commonplace. "Creativity, to *me,* means being free to express yourself in a way that is unique to you, not having to conform to certain rules and guidelines." This act of appropriation constitutes his authority; it constitutes his authority as a writer and not just as a musician (that is, as someone with a story to tell). There were many essays in the set that told only a story, where the writer's established presence was as a musician or a skier or someone who painted designs on a van, but not as a person removed from that experience interpreting it, treating it as a metaphor for something else (creativity). Unless those stories were long, detailed, and very well told (unless the writer was doing more than saying, "I am a skier or a musician or a van-painter"), those writers were all given low ratings.

Notice also that the writer of the jazz paper locates himself and his experience in relation to the commonplace (creativity is unique expression; it is not having to conform to rules or guidelines) regardless of whether it is true or not. Anyone who improvises "knows" that improvisation follows rules and guidelines. It is the power of the commonplace (its truth as a recognizable, and, the writer believes, as a final statement) that justifies the example and completes the essay. The example, in other words, has value because it stands within the field of the commonplace. It is not the occasion for what one might call an "objective" analysis or a "close" reading. It could also be said that the essay stops with the articulation of the commonplace. The following sections speak only to the power of that statement. The reference to "sculpting, carving, building, art, and acting" attest to the universal of the commonplace (and it attests to the writer's nervousness with the status he has appropriated for himself—he is saying, "Now, I'm not the only one here who's done something unique"). The commonplace stands by itself. For this writer, it does not need to be elaborated. By virtue of having written it, he has completed the essay and established the contract by which we may be spoken to as equals: "In whatever form creativity takes, whether it be music, art, or science, it is an important aspect of *our lives* because it enables *us* to be individuals." (For me to break that contract, to argue that *my* life is not represented in that essay, is one way for me to begin as a teacher with that student in that essay.)

I said that the writer of the jazz paper offered up a commonplace regardless of whether it was "true" or not, and this, I said, was an example of the power of a commonplace to determine the meaning of an example. A commonplace determines a system of interpretation that can be used to "place" an example within a standard system of belief. You can see a similar process at work in this essay.

During the football season, the team was supposed to wear the same type of cleats and the same type socks, I figured that I would change this a little by wearing my white shoes instead of black and to cover up the team socks with a pair of my own white ones. I thought that this looked better than what we were wearing, and I told a few of the other people on the team to change too. They agreed that it did look better and they changed there combination to go along with mine. After the game people came up to us and said that it looked very good the way we wore our socks, and they wanted to know why we changed from the rest of the team.

I feel that creativity comes from when a person lets his imagination come up with ideas and he is not afraid to express them. Once you create something to do it will be original and unique because it came about from your own imagination and if any one else tries to copy it, it won't be the same because you thought of it first from your own ideas.

This is not an elegant paper, but it seems seamless, tidy. If the paper on the clay model of the earth showed an ill-fit between the writer and his project, here the discourse seems natural, smooth. You could reproduce this paper and hand it out to a class, and it would take a lot of prompting before the students sense something fishy and one of the more aggressive ones might say, "Sure he came up with the idea of wearing white shoes and white socks. Him and Bill White-shoes Johnson. Come on. He copied the very thing he said was his own idea, 'original and unique.'"

The "I" of this text, the "I" who "figured," "thought," and "felt" is located in a conventional rhetoric of the self that turns imagination into origination (I made it), that argues an ethic of production (I made it and it is mine), and that argues a tight scheme of intention (I made it because I decided to make it). The rhetoric seems invisible because it is so common. This "I" (the maker) is also located in a version of history that dominates classroom accounts of history. It is an example of the "Great Man" theory, where history is rolling along—the English novel is dominated by a central, intrusive narrative presence; America is in the throes of a great depression; during football season the team was supposed to wear the same kind of cleats and socks—until a figure appears, one who can shape history—Henry James, FDR, the writer of the football paper—and everything is changed. In the argument of the football paper, "I figured," "I thought," "I told," "they agreed," and, as a consequence, "I feel that creativity *comes from* when a person lets his imagination come up with ideas and he is not afraid to express them." The story of appropriation becomes a narrative of courage and conquest. The writer was able to write that story when he was able to imagine himself in that discourse. Getting him out of it will be a difficult matter indeed.

There are ways, I think, that a writer can shape history in the very act of writing it. Some students are able to enter into a discourse, but, by stylistic maneuvers, to take possession of it at the same time. They don't originate a discourse, but they locate themselves within it aggressively, self-consciously.

Here is one particularly successful essay. Notice the specialized vocabulary, but also the way in which the text continually refers to its own language and to the language of others.

Throughout my life, I have been interested and intrigued by music. My mother has often told me of the times, before I went to school, when I would "conduct" the orchestra on her records. I continued to listen to music and eventually started to play the guitar and the clarinet. Finally, at about the age of twelve, I started to sit down and to try to write songs. Even though my instrumental skills were far from my own high standards, I would spend much of my spare time during the day with a guitar around my neck, trying to produce a piece of music.

Each of these sessions, as I remember them, had a rather set format. I would sit in my bedroom, strumming different combinations of the five or six chords I could play, until I heard a series which sounded particularly good to me. After this, I set the music to a suitable rhythm, (usually dependent on the mood at the time), and ran through the tune until I could play it fairly easily. Only after this section was complete did I go on to writing lyrics, which generally followed along the lines of the current popular songs on the radio.

At the time of the writing, I felt that my songs were, in themselves, an original creation of my own; that is, I, alone, made them. However, I now see that, in this sense of the word, I was not creative. The songs themselves seem to be an oversimplified form of the music I listened to at the time.

In a more fitting sense, however, I *was* being creative. Since I did not purposely copy my favorite songs, I was, effectively, originating my songs from my own "process of creativity." To achieve my goal, I needed what a composer would call "inspiration" for my piece. In this case the inspiration was the current hit on the radio. Perhaps with my present point of view, I feel that I used too much "inspiration" in my songs, but, at that time, I did not.

Creativity, therefore, is a process which, in my case, involved a certain series of "small creations" if you like. As well, it is something, the appreciation of which varies with one's point of view, that point of view being set by the person's experience, tastes, and his own personal view of creativity. The less experienced tend to allow for less originality, while the more experienced demand real originality to classify something a "creation." Either way, a term as abstract as this is perfectly correct, and open to interpretation.

This writer is consistent and dramatically conscious of herself forming something to say out of what has been said *and* out of what she has been saying in the act of writing this paper. "Creativity" begins, in this paper, as "original creation." What she thought was "creativity," however, she now calls "imitation," and, as she says, "in this sense of the word" she was not "creative." In another sense, however, she says that she *was* creative since she didn't purposefully copy the songs but used them as "inspiration."

The writing in this piece (that is, the work of the writer within the essay) goes on in spite of, or against, the language that keeps pressing to give another name to her experience as a song writer and to bring the discussion to closure. (Think of the quick closure of the football shoes paper in comparison.) Its style is difficult, highly qualified. It relies on quotation marks and parody to set off the language and attitudes that belong to the discourse (or the discourses) it would reject, that it would not take as its own proper location.[5]

In the papers I've examined in this essay, the writers have shown a varied awareness of the codes—or the competing codes—that operate within a discourse. To speak with authority student writers have not only to speak in another's voice but through another's "code"; and they not only have to do this, they have to speak in the voice and through the codes of those of us with power and wisdom; and they not only have to do this, they have to do it before they know what they are doing, before they have a project to participate in and before, at least in terms of our disciplines, they have anything to say. Our students may be able to enter into a conventional discourse and speak, not as themselves, but through the voice of the community. The university, however, is the place where "common" wisdom is only of negative value; it is something to work against. The movement toward a more specialized discourse begins (or perhaps, best begins) when a student can both define a position of privilege, a position that sets him against a "common" discourse, and when he can work self-consciously, critically, against not only the "common" code but his own.

The stages of development that I've suggested are not necessarily marked by corresponding levels in the type or frequency of error, at least not by the type or frequency of sentence level errors. I am arguing, then, that a basic writer is not necessarily a writer who makes a lot of mistakes. In fact, one of the problems with curricula designed to aid basic writers is that they too often begin with the assumption that the key distinguishing feature of a basic writer is the presence of sentence level error. Students are placed in courses because their placement essays show a high frequency of such errors and those courses are designed with the goal of making those errors go away. This approach to the problems of the basic writer ignores the degree to which error is not a constant feature but a marker in the development of a writer. Students who can write reasonably correct narratives may fall to pieces when faced with more unfamiliar assignments. More importantly, however, such courses fail to serve the rest of the curriculum. On every campus there is a significant number of college freshmen who require a course to introduce them to the kinds of writing that are required for a university education. Some of these students can write correct sentences and some cannot, but as a group they lack the facility other freshmen possess when they are faced with an academic writing task.

The "White Shoes" essay, for example, shows fewer sentence level errors than the "Clay Model" paper. This may well be due to the fact, however, that the writer of that paper stayed well within the safety of familiar territory. He kept himself out of trouble by doing what he could easily do. The tortuous syntax of the more advanced papers on my list is a syntax that represents a writer's struggle with a difficult and unfamiliar language, and it is a syntax that can quickly lead an inexperienced writer into trouble. The syntax and punctuation of the "Composing Songs" essay, for example, show the effort that is required when a writer works against the pressure of conventional discourse. If the prose is inelegant (although I'll confess I admire those dense sentences), it is still correct. This writer has a command of the linguistic and stylistic resources (the highly embedded sentences, the use of parentheses and quotation marks) required to complete the act of writing. It is easy to imagine the possible pitfalls for a writer working without this facility.

There was no camera trained on the "Clay Model" writer while he was writing, and I have no protocol of what was going through his mind, but it is possible to speculate that the syntactic difficulties of sentences like the following are the result of an attempt to use an unusual vocabulary and to extend his sentences beyond the boundaries that would be "normal" in his speech or writing:

> In the past time I thought that an incident was creative was when I had to make a clay model of the earth, but not of the classical or your everyday model of the earth which consists of the two cores, the mantle and the crust. I thought of these things in a dimension of which it would be unique, but easy to comprehend.

There is reason to believe, that is, that the problem is with this kind of sentence, in this context. If the problem of the last sentence is a problem of holding together these units—"I thought," "dimension," "unique," and "easy to comprehend"—then the linguistic problem is not a simple matter of sentence construction.

I am arguing, then, that such sentences fall apart not because the writer lacks the necessary syntax to glue the pieces together but because he lacks the full statement within which these key words are already operating. While writing, and in the thrust of his need to complete the sentence, he has the key words but not the utterance. (And to recover the utterance, I suspect, he will need to do more than revise the sentence.) The invisible conventions, the prepared phrases remain too distant for the statement to be completed. The writer must get inside of a discourse he can only partially imagine. The act of constructing a sentence, then, becomes something like an act of transcription, where the voice on the tape unexpectedly fades away and becomes inaudible.

Mina Shaughnessy speaks of the advanced writer as a writer with a more facile but still incomplete possession of this prior discourse. In the case of the advanced writer, the evidence of a problem is the presence of dissonant, redundant, or imprecise language, as in a sentence such as this: "No education can be *total,* it must be *continuous.*" Such a student, Shaughnessy says, could be said to hear the "melody of formal English" while still unable to make precise or exact distinctions. And, she says, the prepackaging feature of language, the possibility of taking over phrases and whole sentences without much thought about them, threatens the writer now as before. The writer, as we have said, inherits the language out of which he must fabricate his own messages. He is therefore in a constant tangle with the language, obliged to recognize its public, communal nature and yet driven to invent out of this language his own statements (19).

For the unskilled writer, the problem is different in degree and not in kind. The inexperienced writer is left with a more fragmentary record of the comings and goings of academic discourse. Or, as I said above, he often has the key words without the complete statements within which they are already operating.

It may very well be that some students will need to learn to crudely mimic the "distinctive register" of academic discourse before they are prepared to actually and legitimately do the work of the discourse, and before they are sophisticated enough with the refinements of tone and texture to do it with grace or elegance. To say this, however, is to say that our students must be our students. Their initial progress will be marked by their abilities to take on the role of privilege, by their abilities to establish authority. From this point of view, the student who wrote about constructing the clay model of the earth is better prepared for his education than the student who wrote about playing football in white shoes, even though the "White Shoes" paper was relatively error-free and the "Clay Model" paper was not. It will be hard to pry the writer of the "White Shoes" paper loose from the tidy, pat discourse that allows him to dispose of the question of creativity in such a quick and efficient manner. He will have to be convinced that it is better to write sentences he might not so easily control, and he will have to be convinced that it is better to write muddier and more confusing prose (in order that it may sound like ours), and this will be harder than convincing the "Clay Model" writer to continue what he has begun.[6]

NOTES

[1] David Olson has made a similar observation about school-related problems of language learning in younger children. Here is his conclusion: "Depending upon whether children assumed language was primarily suitable for making assertions and conjectures or primarily for making direct or indirect commands, they will either find school texts easy or difficult" (107).

[2] For Aristotle there were both general and specific commonplaces. A speaker, says Aristotle, has a "stock of arguments to which he may turn for a particular need."

> If he knows the *topic* (regions, places, lines of argument)—and a skilled speaker will know them—he will know where to find what he wants for a special case. The general topics, or *common*places, are regions containing arguments that are common to all branches of knowledge. . . . But there are also special topics (regions, places, *loci*) in which one looks for arguments appertaining to particular branches of knowledge, special sciences, such as ethics or politics. (154-55)

And, he says "The topics or places, then, may be indifferently thought of as in the science that is concerned, or in the mind of the speaker." But the question of location is "indifferent" *only* if the mind of the speaker is in line with set opinion, general assumption. For the speaker (or writer) who is not situated so comfortably in the privileged public realm, this is indeed not an indifferent matter at all. If he does not have the commonplace at hand, he will not, in Aristotle's terms, know where to go at all.

[3] See especially Bartholomae and Rose for articles on curricula designed to move students into university discourse. The movement to extend writing "across the curriculum" is evidence of a general concern for locating students within the work of the university: see especially Bizzell or Maimon et al. For longer works directed specifically at basic writing, see Ponsot and Deen, and Shaughnessy. For a book describing a course for more advanced students, see Coles.

[4] See especially Bizzell, and Bizzell and Herzberg. My debt to Bizzell's work should be evident everywhere in this essay.

[5] In support of my argument that this is the kind of writing that does the work of the academy, let me offer the following excerpt from a recent essay by Wayne Booth ("The Company We Keep: Self-Making in Imaginative Art, Old and New"):

> I can remember making up songs of my own, no doubt borrowed from favorites like "Hello, Central, Give Me Heaven," "You Can't Holler Down My Rain Barrel," and one

about the ancient story of a sweet little "babe in the woods" who lay down and died, with her brother.

I asked my mother, in a burst of creative egotism, why nobody ever learned to sing my songs, since after all I was more than willing to learn *theirs*. I can't remember her answer, and I can barely remember snatches of two of "my" songs. But I can remember dozens of theirs, and when I sing them, even now, I sometimes feel again the emotions, and see the images, that they aroused then. Thus who I am now—the very shape of my soul—was to a surprising degree molded by the works of "art" that came my way.

I set "art" in quotation marks, because much that I experienced in those early books and songs would not be classed as art according to most definitions. But for the purposes of appraising the effects of "art" on "life" or "culture," and especially for the purposes of thinking about the effects of the "media," we surely must include every kind of artificial experience that we provide for one another. . . .

In this sense of the word, all of us are from the earliest years fed a steady diet of art. . . . (58-59)

While there are similarities in the paraphrasable content of Booth's arguments and my student's, what I am interested in is each writer's method. Both appropriate terms from a common discourse (about *art* and *inspiration*) in order to push against an established way of talking (about tradition and the individual). This effort of opposition clears a space for each writer's argument and enables the writers to establish their own "sense" of the key words in the discourse.

[6] Preparation of this manuscript was supported by the Learning Research and Development Center of the University of Pittsburgh, which is supported in part by the National Institute of Education. I am grateful also to Mike Rose, who pushed and pulled at this paper at a time when it needed it.

WORKS CITED

Aristotle. *The Rhetoric of Aristotle*. Trans. L. Cooper, Englewood Cliffs: Prentice, 1932.

Bartholomae, D. "Writing Assignments: Where Writing Begins." *Forum*. Ed. P. Stock. Montclair: Boynton/Cook, 1983. 300-12.

Bizzell, P. "The Ethos of Academic Discourse." *College Composition and Communication* 29 (1978): 351-55.

———. "Cognition, Convention, and Certainty: What We Need to Know about Writing." *Pre/text* 3 (1982): 213-44.

———. "College Composition: Initiation into the Academic Discourse Community." *Curriculum Inquiry* 12 (1982): 191-207.

Bizzell, P., and B. Herzberg. "'Inherent' Ideology, 'Universal' History, 'Empirical' Evidence, and 'Context-Free' Writing: Some Problems with E. D. Hirsch's *The Philosophy of Composition*." *Modern Language Notes* 95 (1980): 1181-1202.

Coles, W. E., Jr. *The Plural I*. New York: Holt, 1978.

Flower, Linda S. "Revising Writer-Based Prose." *Journal of Basic Writing* 3 (1981): 62-74.

Maimon, E. P., G. L. Belcher, G. W. Hearn, B. F. Nodine, and F. X. O'Connor. *Writing in the Arts and Sciences*. Cambridge: Winthrop, 1981.

Olson, D. R. "Writing: The Divorce of the Author from the Text." *Exploring Speaking-Writing Relationships: Connections and Contrasts*. Ed. B. M. Kroll and R. J. Vann. Urbana: National Council of Teachers of English, 1981.

Ponsot, M., and R. Deen. *Beat Not the Poor Desk*. Montclair: Boynton/Cook, 1982.

Rose, M. "Remedial Writing Courses: A Critique and a Proposal." *College English* 45 (1983): 109-28.

Shaughnessy, Mina. *Errors and Expectations*. New York: Oxford UP, 1977.

This article is reprinted from *When a Writer Can't Write: Studies in Writer's Block and Other Composing Process Problems*. Ed. Mike Rose. New York: Guilford, 1985. 273-85. —Ed.

Elisabeth McPherson

WHERE WERE WE, WHERE ARE WE AS COMMUNITY COLLEGE ENGLISH TEACHERS?

It may be presumptuous of me to talk about both the past and present of two-year college English. I know a good deal more about where we were than where we are. I'm not the expert on the present. The only classes I've taught in the last five years are for people as far out of it as I am. The classes are part of a program called Focus on Mature Learning, but that fancy title merely means that anybody who looks old enough can, for two dollars, spend ten hours scattered over five weeks, in a loose kind of seminar on practically anything. No papers, no tests, no grades, and though reading suggestions are made in those groups, nobody does the reading unless they jolly well feel like it—a far cry from the conditions real teachers face every day.

The last time I talked to a two-year regional conference, in St. Louis exactly three years ago, I gave what I thought was an inspirational speech, full of advice as to what good English teachers ought to do, and when it was over, a man I'd known for a long time—a man still immersed in the harsh realities of community college teaching—came up and said, "You sound like the sixties; I could feel my hair growing!" I didn't know whether or not that was a compliment (I still don't) but I'm a bit relieved that most of my job today is to take myself back to the sixties and early seventies where my friend thought I belonged. I'll try to go back to those early days and see where we were, what we worried about, and discover if possible what we, or at least what I, learned from them.

GROWTH AND OPTIMISM

For community colleges those early years were a period of enormous optimism. Undoubtedly higher education showed some symptoms that needed treating, but all we had to do was find the right cure—and it looked like two-year colleges might provide that cure. The Carnegie Commission on Higher Education had reported in the 1960s that the United States didn't need a single new institution granting doctor's degrees but it did need a lot more urban community colleges, and the country was quick to respond. In 1962 there were just over four hundred two-year colleges. In 1969 the PMLA Directory listed 1013. It was fashionable to say that a new junior college opened somewhere every week. Some of them were free, a few of them—fashionable finishing school types—were very expensive. Some enrolled 200 students, some 20,000. Some were little more than pale copies of what was offered during the first two years at the nearest state university, with a secretarial course or two thrown in to justify the term "comprehensive." Some were ex-technical schools, with a course in humanities added so they could call themselves "community colleges." The public relations directors, writing copy for the college catalogs, were given to saying that their college was "dedicated to the educational needs of the whole community," that it "accepts every student where he is and takes him as far as he can go," that it "recognizes a variety of abilities and objectives and tries to meet all of them."

Some of that sounds as dated as an old photograph album. No self-respecting PR person would write "student/he" these days, and if more than one new community college opens a year, I'd be very astonished. If there are any that don't charge tuition, I'd be equally astonished. I hope some of the old PR boasts remain accurate, at least the part about recognizing a variety of abilities and objectives and trying to meet all of them.

In those early days most of us thought that if we couldn't completely reform the educational world, we could certainly identify some of the problems and suggest some of the remedies.

GAINING RECOGNITION

From our point of view, one symptom of what was wrong was the way we thought the rest of the higher education establishment looked at junior college English teachers: second rate at best, refugees from the high schools who might be improved with a little help. One of the earliest conferences I ever attended, in the midfifties, was at the prestigious university in my state. A few representatives of the university English department sat us down in a room, 40 or 50 of us from all over the state, and condescendingly explained to us what college English was supposed to be. They asked us no questions and they didn't let us ask any. We didn't go home inspired; we went home angry.

Ten years later that same university was not condescending to us; it was coaxing us to send it our transfer students. Their enrollments were dropping; ours were going up. The change in attitude may not have indicated more respect; I think it indicated a concern for dollars and cents.

Meantime, we'd gotten a clearer notion of what it meant to teach English at a two-year college. We knew, most of us, that we were probably going to teach some kind of composition, and very little but composition, for the rest of our professional lives. We also knew that composition teaching at prestige schools was not very high on the hierarchy if indeed it was taught by regular faculty at all. We turned that around and made a virtue of it, boasting with considerable accuracy in those years that students at community colleges took their composition from full-time professionals, not graduate students earning their way through school by a little temporary slave labor.

Not very many community colleges can make that boast any more. Too many of them have turned half the comp classes over to part-timers at less than half the pay, sometimes about a quarter of what a full-time teacher gets for the same work. If TAs are still the slave labor of the universities, part-timers have become the slave labor of the community colleges.

WORK LOAD

Another serious symptom 20 years ago was the work load under which the majority of community college teachers labored. That heavy load was unhealthy both for the educational well-being of our students and the physical and emotional well-being of ourselves. In 1969 more than half the country's junior college English teachers were meeting classes for 13 to 15 hours a week, and nearly a quarter of them had more than a hundred composition students. That load is not abnormal today.

The prescription was a work-load statement issued jointly by NCTE and the National Junior College Committee, as it was known in those days. The prescription was for nine hours a week, limited to fifty composition students. Looked at from today's perspective, those recommendations sound like pipe dreams, pie-in-the-sky, an excursion to never-never land. They were widely circulated, but if they were realized anywhere, I never heard about it. The only teacher with a work load of nine hours a week, the only teacher meeting a mere fifty writing students, is likely to be a part-timer, paid at part-time wages.

SEXISM IN LANGUAGE

In other areas, too, not so directly concerned with our own welfare, we recognized the symptoms of disease, and CCCC and NCTE, of which we had become an integral and important part, were there to offer prescriptions.

We knew there was sexism in language, and some of us realized that the usage habits we were teaching contributed to it. In the early seventies, we got help from NCTE's guidelines for avoiding sexist language. The guidelines haven't reformed the world, but they have, I think, made some difference. The catalogs no longer talk as though all students were male. Conference sessions are no longer headed by "chairmen." Knowledgeable teachers are no longer self-conscious about saying, "Will everybody please turn *their* papers in before *they* leave." We've realized that a statement like "Everybody clapped *his* hands" is pretty silly.

Sexism in language has not completely disappeared, of course. Ingrained language habits are hard to change. I listen to people trying to explain their lapses, to justify saying "men of good will" instead of "people of good will." They protest that using "men" when they mean both men and women is a lifetime habit; they explain that they feel so self-conscious when they try to shift that they forget what they meant to say. These aren't the people who think the attempt to change is silly. They're *people* of good will and good intentions. English teachers, especially, have trouble changing their ingrained habits, and in the light of another problem we tried to cure, I find their difficulties very interesting.

STUDENTS' RIGHT STATEMENT

We knew that many of our students were being shut out of education because they didn't talk right, according to middle-class notions. And we knew, some of us, that the way we were letting them in wasn't doing much for them—calling them "remedial," hiding them in labs or bonehead sections (I apologize for that dated term; I should at least be saying developmental or learning centers) until they managed to exchange their ingrained habits for the language of power and prestige, thus demonstrating that they were ready for some "real college."

The prescription for that problem was the famous (or infamous, depending on your point of view) statement on the Students' Right to Their Own Language. Adopted in 1974, it was intended to recognize the value of dialects as part of the American heritage, to convince both teachers and the general public that a missing comma is not a crime, that missing *ed*'s and *s*'s are a good deal less important than missing ideas, that misspelled words are not an inevitable cause of misunderstanding. It pointed out that the notion of a single standard English is a myth, but the booklet that accompanied it was careful to say that Edited American English is not a myth—that when people write something they think is worth saying, of course they go back and edit it, with the help of a dictionary, a friend, or a manuscript editor, if the writing's going to be published.

We're still trying to attack the same problem the Students' Right to Their Own Language was attacking. And in spite of the hullabaloo that statement created, it was an honest statement, and still is, even if we had to wait until three years ago for National Public Television to concede, in its documentary, "The Story of English," that dialects are fascinating and worth preserving.

TEACHER TRAINING

The final sentence of the Students' Right statement pointed to another serious symptom: a lot of teachers were woefully ignorant about the language we were trying to teach. Community college teachers were not alone; that ignorance was characteristic of university professors, too, unless they were members of the linguistics department, and that department was not held in high regard by the English department.

We were ignorant because nobody had taught us. Most of us got to be English teachers because we liked to read, and we walked into classes where almost none of the students read anything for pleasure. Or we majored in English because we wanted to be writers, another fairly common reason, but we certainly didn't mean we wanted to write 500-word themes. Most of us had taken the required freshman composition course ourselves, quite awhile ago, and probably had never taken anything else related to writing. Our own college practice had been limited to term papers and maybe a dissertation. Then we walked into classes and fumbled with teaching other people how to write. We didn't know anything about the nature of language or how human beings acquire it and not much about dialects except that Mark Twain and Thomas Hardy wrote them pretty well. We were innocent of grammatical theory except for a hazy recollection of some eighth grade grammar, all of it based on Latin. We didn't know much about urban sociology or urban poverty, either practical or theoretical.

Again the prescription was a set of guidelines, this time for training junior college English teachers. The requirements outlined early in the seventies are still valid not only for training junior college English teachers but for training anybody who is going to teach freshman composition in any open admissions college or, for that matter, in any high school.

Two or three universities I know of did start training programs based on the guidelines, but I'm not sure any of those programs exist any more. It would be nice to think the programs disappeared because the things they called for are now requirements for all English majors: courses in the nature of language, the appreciation of dialects, the sociology of urban ghettos, the process of learning to compose. It's probably true that more people who now emerge with nice fresh master's degrees can answer the question "What's your field?" by saying "Language and composition" instead of "Minor lyric poets of the early seventeenth century." I've nothing against lyric poets, minor or major, but I'm a little nervous about their value in helping beginning writers learn to express themselves clearly.

RACISM AND BIAS

We knew that another serious symptom of society's sickness was racism, and we knew that the schools were at least somewhat responsible for it. In that minority students were a majority of the people being discriminated against because of their language—the dialects of their nurture in which they found their identity and style—the Students' Right to Their Own Language was an indirect attack on racism.

But belittling students because of dialect difference was only one part of discrimination; we showed our contempt by the materials we gave them to study. Another prescription for the malady of racism, this one offered mainly by NCTE, was called *Searching for America,* a little book that insisted texts shouldn't be labelled "American" unless they included the work of all Americans, not just or even primarily white males. Textbooks, especially anthologies, the Racism and Bias Committee said, should include black writers and Chicanos, native Americans and Orientals. Those guidelines affected our textbooks for a while, particularly the anthologies. Some of us refused to adopt books unless they made *some* gestures toward including minority writers, and the books got a little better, perhaps because some of them were written by community college teachers—a phenomenon completely unheard of 30 years ago.

CREATION OF SLATE

Another symptom of misunderstanding was the back-to-basics movement. In the early seventies the public—or the pundits who are never tired of telling us what's wrong with the educational system and the media which obligingly make headlines from those pronouncements—was much upset about literacy, that is, what they saw as the lack of it, and there was a big back-to-basics movement. The outcry was mainly about the public schools, but a lot of the misinformation rubbed off on us too. That was the period when NCTE created SLATE, an organization within the council, whose acronym meant Support for the Learning and Teaching of English. It wasn't primarily a community college organization, but we were a part of it. The idea was to lobby state legislatures, write to the local newspapers, get out short position papers that would educate parents and ourselves about good English teaching, to act instead of reacting. A lot of community college English teachers did act. They used the skills they were supposed to be teaching—writing, talking, listening, convincing—in an attempt to change public notions of what English is and how it can be taught.

Another attempt to change public attitudes and also as usual to change the attitudes of some diehard English teachers was the publication in 1969 of a little pamphlet called "Essentials of English," which emphasized that learning to write meant learning to think clearly and pointed out that mechanics—punctuation, capitalization, spelling, and the like—are only one part of the effectiveness of finished writing, a matter of polishing a final draft.

USAGE TESTS

In spite of such attempts to explain what good writing is, the media furor persisted. We were directly affected when Educational Testing Service put a usage test back into the SAT because, they said, there was so much demand for it. Our prescription for that malady was a resolution or a lot of resolutions pointing out that usage tests reward students whose language habits are those of the ruling class and penalize those whose habits are different; that usage tests don't measure the ability to write well unless our definition of good writing is very superficial indeed; that usage tests do measure geography and economic status and ancestry; and that we didn't like it.

DOUBLESPEAK

One final symptom and I have done listing the maladies that beset us. We certainly knew that a lot of the language out there in the real world was used deliberately to deceive in advertising and, more seriously, in news reports and political speeches. You could hardly miss it in those days when "pacification" meant "bombing," when we destroyed a Vietnamese village in order to "save" it, when a weapon that could blow up a big piece of the world was called a "peacekeeper."

The prescription was the Doublespeak Committee with its annual awards for the most outrageous examples of language intended to deceive. I haven't noticed that public discourse has improved much, witness the name-calling and deception of the last political campaigns, especially the slant and innuendo of "card-carrying ACLU members" with its implications of un-Americanism. Half the people who voted in that election could remember when "card-carrying," all by itself, meant "communist." Doublespeak awards may not have changed language behavior much, but they did, and do, get some good publicity.

OTHER PROBLEMS

In this quick and incomplete survey of where we were in the first decade after the two-year college regionals were born in 1965, I've left out a lot of things we worried about: accreditation; articulation; behavioral objectives; performance objectives; competency testing, not of students but of teachers; sporadic attempts to legislate course content; talk about cost effectiveness and student outputs. We even produced a booklet on how to give a conference.

We saw problems and we tried to find solutions. If the result of our efforts seems only the accumulation of a huge heap of paper—well, after all writing and persuading are our business, the only weapons we have to fight with. Some of that paper has disappeared, and some of it you can still find if you look hard enough. *Search for America* is out of print, but *Students' Right to Their Own Language* is still available for 75 cents. "Essentials of English" and "Guidelines for Nonsexist Use of Language in NCTE Publications" can both be had from NCTE, both of them free, but the guidelines statement for the workload of junior college English teachers has drifted back into the never-never land from whence it came. Actually, I think community college teachers are included in the 1978 "Guidelines for the Workload of the College English Teacher," where naturally they belong—we've convinced the profession that we *are* college teachers—but we're kidding ourselves if we think we'll get the kind of workload enjoyed in the universities. What happened to "How to Give a Conference," I don't know. SLATE is still among the living, and both the Doublespeak Committee and unfortunately doublespeak itself are still flourishing. Resolutions of protest, of course, are decently interred in the record of organizational proceedings.

You've noticed, I hope, that I've carefully refrained from giving a sermon. I've not offered you McPherson's short course in linguistics. I've not lectured you on the three meanings of "wrong" as in $2 + 2 = 5$—a question of accuracy; as in murder is wrong—a question of ethics; as in "She don't" is wrong—a question of conventional usage. I've tried to provide a more or less objective review of where we were, with only some of my prejudices showing, and let you be the judges of where we are now.

TWENTY YEARS AGO

But I'm not sure I've captured the flavor, the feel, of those early days, so I'm going to end with a short excerpt from a speech I made to another regional exactly 20 years ago. You can decide for yourselves whether you feel your hair growing.

Some of you will remember that one of the early junior college buzz words was "innovation"; I think there was even a high-powered organization of college presidents devoted to it called The League for Innovation. But I wasn't at all sure their definition of innovation was the same as mine. I undertook the task of setting English teachers, if not college presidents, straight on what innovation ought to mean.

> Innovation means being willing to try something really new; it means taking a chance on an experiment that may not work, even though you think it will. It means going around with your neck stuck permanently out. Innovation, however, doesn't mean just reshuffling the same old ideas and calling them new. It

doesn't mean just changing the labels, or the seating arrangements, or the titles of the courses. It doesn't even mean substituting a machine for a human being, if all you train the machine to do is the same old thing, more mechanically this time because it's in the nature of machines to behave mechanically. The notion of innovation is one of the junior college clichés we either have to do something about or scrap. So what can English teachers do about it? If the innovations I'm going to suggest strike you as radical, they're intended to be.

Let's throw out the sectioning tests. It may be a lot of work to read the diagnostic papers on which more honest advice could be given but the work can be done, and should be.

Let's throw out all arbitrary tracking based on those discriminatory sectioning tests. We can't afford damaging assumptions about the relative worth of students. We can continue to offer a variety of courses on a variety of levels, if it turns out we really need them, but let's make them all elective. If we describe them honestly and clearly, if we're prepared to offer individual students advice on which courses they would probably get the most out of, we just might be able to depend on students showing that maturity we talk so much about.

Let's throw out the rigid subject matter with which we encumber the courses and let some fresh air and freedom in. Let's put the emphasis back where it belongs, on what the students need. Let's bring English back to the real world.

Let's throw out textbooks whenever they make inaccurate and unfounded assumptions about student needs.

Let's throw out curriculum outlines because they assume, first of all, that all teachers are alike, and worst of all, that all students, or even all classes, are alike. A curriculum outline pretends that it's possible to predict, in January, where students will be in May. That simply isn't so.

Let's throw out grades—that arrogant assumption that we can categorize, in five narrow slots, what students know, what they have learned, what they can do, what they understand, what will seem valuable to them next week or next year. Grades are primarily a measurement of how well the students have learned to please us, their willingness to say "yes" to our own tastes and prejudices. If we can believe the theologians, even God on the judgment day grades only pass or fail. There's no report that St. Peter has ever given a C-.

Finally, let's throw out teachers—not ourselves but our vision of ourselves as authority figures who know best, by definition. We can become listening moderators instead, useful if we happen to have read the right books, watched the right TV programs, subscribed to the right newspapers and read the right articles, lived in the right neighborhoods and endured the right troubles. If we haven't done these things, we might have a try at letting the students teach us. Teachers need to be replaced by coadventurers in learning.

That's what I said in 1969. As for whether any of it could be a cure for today's different symptoms, you can mark it "all of the above," "some of the above," "none of the above."

This article is reprinted from *Teaching English in the Two-Year College* (May 1990): 92–99. —Ed.

Robert J. Connors and Andrea A. Lunsford

FREQUENCY OF FORMAL ERRORS IN CURRENT COLLEGE WRITING, OR MA AND PA KETTLE DO RESEARCH

PROEM: IN WHICH THE CHARACTERS ARE INTRODUCED

The labyrinthine project of which this research is a part represents an ongoing activity for us, something we engage in because we like to work together, have a long friendship, and share many interests. As we worked on this error research together, however, we started somewhere along the line to feel less and less like the white-coated Researchers of our dreams and more and more like characters we called Ma and Pa Kettle—good-hearted bumblers striving to understand a world whose complexity was more than a little daunting. Being fans of classical rhetoric, *prosopopoeia, letteraturizzazione,* and the like, as well as enthusiasts for intertextuality, *plaisir de texte, differance,* etc., we offer this account of our travails—with apologies to Margorie Main and Percy Kilbride.

EXORDIUM: THE KETTLES SMELL A PROBLEM

Marking and judging formal and mechanical errors in student papers is one area in which composition studies seems to have a multiple-personality disorder. On the one hand, our mellow, student-centered, process-based selves tend to condemn marking formal errors at all. Doing it represents the Bad Old Days. Ms. Fidditch and Mr. Flutesnoot with sharpened red pencils, spilling innocent blood across the page. Useless detail work. Inhumane, perfectionist standards, making our students feel stupid, wrong, trivial, misunderstood. Joseph Williams has pointed out how arbitrary and context-bound our judgments of formal error are. And certainly our noting of errors on student papers gives no one any great joy; as Peter Elbow says, English is most often associated *either* with grammar or with high literature—"two things designed to make folks feel most out of it."

Nevertheless, very few of us can deny that an outright comma splice, its/it's error, or misspelled common word distracts us. So our more traditional pedagogical selves feel a touch guilty when we ignore student error patterns altogether, even in the sacrosanct drafting stage of composing. Not even the most liberal of process-oriented teachers completely ignores the problem of mechanical and formal errors. As Mina Shaughnessy put it, errors are "uninten-

430

tional and unprofitable intrusions upon the consciousness of the reader. . . . They demand energy without giving back any return in meaning" (12). Errors are not merely mechanical, therefore, but rhetorical as well. The world judges a writer by her mastery of conventions, and we all know it. Students, parents, university colleagues, and administrators expect us to deal somehow with those unmet rhetorical expectations, and, like it or not, pointing out errors seems to most of us part of what we do.

Of course, every teacher has his or her ideas of what errors are common and important, but testing those intuitive ideas is something else again. We became interested in error-frequency research as a result of our historical studies, when we realized that no major nationwide analysis of actual college essays had been conducted, to our knowledge, since the late 1930s. As part of the background for a text we were writing and because the research seemed fascinating, we determined to collect a large number of college student essays from the 1980s, analyze them, and determine what the major patterns of formal and mechanical error in current student writing might be.

NARRATIO: MA AND PA VISIT THE LIBRARY

Coming to this research as historians rather than as trained experimenters has given us a humility based on several different sources. Since we are not formally trained in research design, we have constantly relied on help from more expert friends and colleagues. Creating a sense of our limitations even more keenly, however, have been our historical studies. No one looking into the history of research on composition errors in this country can emerge very confident about definitions, terms, and preconceptions. In almost no other pedagogical area we have studied do the investigators and writers seem so time-bound, so shackled by their ideas of what errors *are*, so blinkered by the definitions and demarcations that are part of their historical scene. And, ineluctably, we must see ourselves and our study as history-bound as well. Thus we write not as the torchbearers of some new truth, but as two more in the long line of people applying their contemporary perspectives to a numbering and ordering system and hoping for something of use from it.

The tradition of research into error patterns is as old as composition teaching, of course, but before the growth of the social-science model in education it was carried on informally. Teachers had "the list" of serious and common errors in their heads, and their lists were probably substantially similar (although "serious" and "common" were not necessarily overlapping categories).[1] Beginning around 1910, however, teachers and educational researchers began trying to taxonomize errors and chart their frequency. The great heyday of error-frequency seems to have occurred between 1915 and 1935. During those two decades, no fewer than thirty studies of error frequency were conducted.[2] Unfortunately, most of these studies were flawed in some way: too small a data sample, too regional a data sample, different definitions of errors, faulty methodologies (Harap 440). Most early error research is hard to understand today because the researchers used terms widely understood at the time but now incomprehensible or at best strange. Some of the studies were very seriously conducted, however, and deserve further discussion later in this paper.

After the middle 1930s, error-frequency research waned as the progressive-education movement gained strength and the "experience curriculum" in English replaced older correctness-based methods. Our historical research indicates that the last large-scale research into student patterns of formal error was conducted in 1938–39 by John C. Hodges, author of the *Harbrace College Handbook*. Hodges collected 20,000 student papers that had been marked by sixteen different teachers, mainly from the University of Tennessee at Knoxville. He analyzed these papers and created a taxonomy of errors, using his findings to inform the thirty-four-part organization of his *Harbrace Handbook*, a text which quickly became and remains today the most popular college handbook of writing.

However Hodges may have constructed his study, his results fifty years later seem problematic at best. Small-scale studies of changes in student writing over the past thirty years have shown that formal error patterns have shifted radically ever since the 1950s. The kinds and quantities of formal errors revealed in Mina Shaughnessy's work with basic writers in the 1970s were new and shocking to many teachers of writing. We sensed that the time had come for a study that would attempt to answer two questions: (1) what are the most common patterns of student writing errors being made in the 1980s in the United States? and (2) which of these patterns are marked most consistently by American teachers?

CONFIRMATIO I: THE KETTLES GET CRACKING

The first task we faced was gathering data. We needed teacher-marked papers from American college freshmen and sophomores in a representative range of different kinds of schools and a representative range of geographic areas. We did not want to try to gather the isolated sample of timed examination-style writing that is often studied, although such a sample would probably have been easier to obtain than the actual marked papers we sought. We wanted "themes in the raw," the actual commerce of writing courses all across America. We wanted papers that had been personally marked or graded, filled with every uncontrolled and uncontrollable sign of both student and teacher personalities.

Gathering these papers presented a number of obstacles. In terms of ideal methodology, the data-gathering would be untouched by self-selection among teachers, and we could randomly choose our sources. After worrying about this problem, we finally could conceive of no way to gather upwards of 20,000 papers (the number of papers Hodges had looked at) without appealing to teachers who had marked them. We could think of no way to go directly to students, and, though some departments stockpile student themes, we did not wish to weight our study toward any one school or department. We had to ask composition teachers for help.

And help us they did. In response to a direct mail appeal to more than 1,500 teachers who had used or expressed interest in handbooks, we had received by September 1985 more than 21,500 papers from 300 teachers all across America.[3]

To say that the variety in the papers we were sent was striking is a serious understatement. They ranged in length from a partial page to over twenty pages. About 30% were typed, the rest handwritten. Some were annotated marginally until they looked like the Book of Kells, while others merely sported a few scrawled words and a grade. Some were pathologically neat, and others looked dashed off on the jog between classes. Some were formally perfect, while others approximated Mina Shaughnessy's more extreme examples of basic writing. Altogether, the 21,500+ papers, each one carefully stamped by paper number and batch number, filled approximately thirty feet of hastily-installed shelving. It was an imposing mass.

We had originally been enthusiastic (and naive) enough to believe that with help we might somehow look over and analyze 20,000 papers. Wrong. Examining an average paper even for mechanical lapses, we soon realized, took at the very least ten busy minutes; to examine all of them would require over 3,000 Ma-and-Pa-hours. We simply could not do it. But we could analyze a carefully stratified sample of 3,000 randomly chosen papers. Such an analysis would give us data that were very reliable. Relieved that we would not have to try to look at 20,000 papers, we went to work on the stratification.[4] After stratifying our batches of papers by region, size of school, and type of school, we used the table of random numbers and the numbers that had been stamped on each paper as it came in to pull 3,000 papers from our tonnage of papers. Thus we had our randomized, stratified sample, ready for analysis.

CONFUTATIO: MA AND PA SUCK EGGS

But—analyzed using what? From very early on in the research, we realized that trying to introduce strict "scientific" definitions into an area so essentially values-driven as formal error marking would be a foolhardy mistake. We accepted Williams' contention that it is "necessary to shift our attention from error treated strictly as an isolated item on a page, to error perceived as a flawed verbal transaction between a writer and a reader" (153). Williams' thoughtful article on "The Phenomenology of Error" had, in fact, persuaded us that some sort of reader-response treatment of errors would be far more useful than an attempt to standardize error patterns in a pseudo-scientific fashion based on Hodges' or any other handbook.

We were made even more distrustful of any absolutist claims by our further examination of previous error-frequency research. Looking into the history of this kind of research showed us clearly how teachers' ideas about error definition and classification have always been absolute products of their times and cultures. What seem to us the most common and permanent of terms and definitions are likely to be newer and far more transient than we know. Errors like "stringy sentences" and "use of *would* for simple past tense forms" seemed obvious and serious to teachers in 1925 or 1917 but obscure to us today.[5]

While phenomena and adaptable definitions do continue from decade to decade, we knew that any system we might adopt, however defensible or linguistically sound it might seem to us, would someday represent one more historical curiosity. "Comma splice?" some researcher in the future will murmur, "What a strange term for Connors and Lunsford to use. Where could it have come from?"[6] Teachers have always marked different phenomena as errors, called them different things, given them different weights. Error-pattern study is essentially the examination of an ever-shifting pattern of skills judged by an ever-shifting pattern of prejudices. We wanted to try looking at this situation as it existed in the 1980s, but clearly the instrument we needed could not be algorithmic and would not be historically stable.

We settled, finally, on several general understandings. First, examining what teachers had marked on these papers was as important as trying to ascertain what was "really there" in terms of formal error patterns. Second, we could only analyze for a limited number of error patterns—perhaps twenty in all. And finally, we had no taxonomy of errors we felt we could trust. We would have to generate our own, then, using our own culture- and time-bound definitions and perceptions as best we could.

CONFIRMATIO II: MA AND PA HIT THE ROAD

Producing that taxonomy meant looking closely at the papers. Using the random number tables again, we pulled 300 papers from the remaining piles. Each of us took 150, and we set out inductively to note every formal error pattern we could discover in the two piles of papers. During this incredibly boring part of the study, we tried to ignore any elements of paper content or organization except as they were necessary to identify errors. Every error marked by teachers was included in our listing, of course, but we found many that had not been marked at all, and some that were not even easily definable. What follows is the list of errors and the numbers of errors we discovered in that first careful scrutiny of 300 papers:

Error or Error Pattern	No. in 300 Papers
Spelling	450
No comma after introductory element	138
Comma splice	124
Wrong word	102
Lack of possessive apostrophe	99
Vague pronoun reference	90
No comma in compound sentence	87
Pronoun agreement	83
Sentence fragment	82
No comma in non-restrictive phrase	75
Subject-verb agreement	59
Unnecessary comma with restrictive phrase	50
Unnecessary words/style rewrite	49

Wrong tense	46
Dangling or misplaced modifier	42
Run-on sentence	39
Wrong or missing preposition	38
Lack of comma in series	35
Its/it's error	34
Tense shift	31
Pronoun shift/point of view shift	31
Wrong/missing inflected endings	31
Comma with quotation marks error	28
Missing words	27
Capitalization	24
"Which/that" for "who/whom"	21
Unidiomatic word use	17
Comma between subject and verb	14
Unnecessary apostrophe after "s"	11
Unnecessary comma in complex sentence	11
Hyphenation errors	9
Comma before direct object	6
Unidiomatic sentence pattern	6
Title underlining	6
Garbled sentence	4
Adjectival for adverbial form—"ly"	4

In addition, the following errors appeared fewer than 4 times in 300 papers:

Wrong pronoun
Wrong use of dashes
Confusion of a/an
Missing articles (the)
Missing question mark
Wrong verb form
Lack of transition
Missing/incorrect quotation marks
Incorrect comma use with parentheses
Use of comma instead of "that"
Missing comma before "etc."
Incorrect semicolon use
Repetition of words
Unclear gerund modifier
Double negative
Missing apostrophe in contraction
Colon misuse
Lack of parallelism

As expected, many old favorites appear on these lists. To our surprise, however, some errors we were used to thinking of as very common and serious proved to be at least not so common as we had thought. Others, which were not thought of as serious (or even, in some cases, as actual errors), seemed very common.

Our next step was to calibrate our readings, making certain we were both counting apples as apples, and to determine the cutoff point in this list, the errors we would actually count in the 3,000 papers. Since spelling errors predominated by a factor of 300% (which in itself was a surprising margin), we chose not to deal further with spelling in this analysis, but to develop a separate line of research on spelling. Below spelling, we decided to go arbitrarily with the top twenty error patterns, cutting off below "wrong inflected ending." These were the twenty error patterns we would train our analysts to tote up.

Now we had a sample and we had an instrument, however rough. Next we needed to gather a group of representative teachers who could do the actual analysis. Fifty teaching assistants, instructors, and professors from the Ohio State University English Department volunteered to help us with the analysis. The usual question of inter-rater reliability did not seem pressing to us, because what we were looking for seemed so essentially charged with social conditioning and personal predilection. Since we did not think that we could always "scientifically" determine what was real error and what was style or usage variation, our best idea was to rationalize the arbitrariness inherent in the project by spreading out the analytical decisions.

On a Friday afternoon in January 1986 we worked with the fifty raters, going over the definitions and examples we had come up with for the "top twenty," as we were by then calling them. It was a grueling Friday and Saturday. We trained raters to recognize error patterns all Friday afternoon in the dusty, stuffy old English Library at OSU—the air of which Thurber must have breathed, and probably the very same air, considering how hard the windows were to open. On returning to our hotel that night, we found it occupied by the Ohio chapter of the Pentecostal Youth, who had been given permission to run around the hotel giggling and shouting until 3:30 a.m. In despair, we turned our TV volumes all the way up on the white-noise stations that had gone off the air. They sounded like the Reichenbach Falls and almost drowned out the hoo-raw in the hallway. After 3:30 it did indeed quiet down some, and we fell into troublous sleep. The next day the Pentecostal Youth had vanished, and Ma & Pa had research to do.

AMPLIFICATIO: MA AND PA HUNKER DOWN

The following day, rating began at 9:00 a.m. and, with a short lunch break, we had completed the last paper by 5:00 p.m. We paused occasionally to calibrate our ratings, to redefine some term, or to share some irresistible piece of student prose. (Top prize went to the notorious "One Night," one student's response to an assignment asking for "analysis." This essay's abstract announced it as "an analysis of the realm of different feelings experienced in one night by a man and wife in love.") The rating sheets and papers were reordered and bundled up, and we all went out for dinner.[7]

The results of this exercise became real for us when we totaled up the numbers on all of the raters' sheets. Here was the information we had been seeking, what all our efforts had been directed toward. It was exciting to finally see in black and white what we had been wondering about. What we found appears in Table 1.

PERORATIO: THE KETTLES SAY, "AW, SHUCKS"

The results of this research by no means represent a final word on any question involving formal errors or teacher marking patterns. We can, however, draw several intriguing, if tentative, generalizations.

First, teachers' ideas about what constitutes a serious, markable error vary widely. As most of us may have expected, some teachers pounce on every "very unique" as a pet peeve, some rail at "Every student . . . their. . . ." The most prevalent "error," failure to place a comma after an introductory word or phrase, was a *bête noire* for some teachers but was ignored by many more. Papers marked by the same teacher might at different times evince different patterns of formal marking. Teachers' reasons for marking specific errors and patterns of error in their students' papers are complex, and in many cases they are no doubt guided by the perceived needs of the student writing the paper and by the stage of the composing process the paper has achieved.

Second, teachers do not seem to mark as many errors as we often think they do. On average, college English teachers mark only 43% of the most serious errors in the papers they evaluate. In contrast to the popular picture of English teachers mad to mark up every error, our results show that even the most-often marked errors are only marked two-thirds of the time. The less-marked patterns (and remember, these are the Top Twenty error patterns overall) are marked only once for every four times they appear. The number of errors found compared to the number of errors marked suggests a fascinating possibility for future research: detailed observation of teacher marking, accompanied by talk-aloud protocols. Such research seems to us a natural follow-up to the findings presented here.[8]

Third, the reasons teachers mark any given error seem to result from a complex formula that takes into account at least two factors: how serious or annoying the error is perceived to be at a given time for both teacher and student, and how difficult it is to mark or explain. As Table 1 shows, the errors marked by the original teachers on our papers produce a different (although not completely dissimilar) ranking of errors than the formal count we asked our raters to do. Some of the lesser-marked errors we studied are clearly felt to be more stylistic than substantive. Certain of the comma errors seem simply not to bother teachers very much. Others, like wrong words or missing inflections, are much more frequently marked, and might be said to have a high "response quotient" for teachers. In addition, we sensed that in many cases errors went unmarked not because the teacher failed to see them, but because they were not germane to the lessons at hand. A teacher working very hard to help a student master subject-verb agreement with third-person singular nouns, for instance, might well ignore most other errors in a given paper.

Table 1

Error or Error Pattern	No. Found in 3,000 Papers	% of Total Errors	No. Found Marked by Teacher	% Marked by Teacher	Rank by No. of Errors Marked by Teacher
1. No comma after introductory element	3,299	11.5%	995	30%	2
2. Vague pronoun reference	2,809	9.8%	892	32%	4
3. No comma in compound sentence	2,446	8.6%	719	29%	7
4. Wrong word	2,217	7.8%	1,114	50%	1
5. No comma in non-restrictive element	1,864	6.5%	580	31%	10
6. Wrong/missing inflected endings	1,679	5.9%	857	51%	5
7. Wrong or missing preposition	1,580	5.5%	679	43%	8
8. Comma splice	1,565	5.5%	850	54%	6
9. Possessive apostrophe error	1,458	5.1%	906	62%	3
10. Tense shift	1,453	5.1%	484	33%	12
11. Unnecessary shift in person	1,347	4.7%	410	30%	14
12. Sentence fragment	1,217	4.2%	671	55%	9
13. Wrong tense or verb form	952	3.3%	465	49%	13
14. Subject-verb agreement	909	3.2%	534	58%	11
15. Lack of comma in series	781	2.7%	184	24%	19
16. Pronoun agreement error	752	2.6%	365	48%	15
17. Unnecessary comma with restrictive element	693	2.4%	239	34%	17
18. Run-on or fused sentence	681	2.4%	308	45%	16
19. Dangling or misplaced modifier	577	2.0%	167	29%	20
20. Its/it's error	292	1.0%	188	64%	18

Teachers' perceptions of the seriousness of a given error pattern seem, however, to be only part of the reason for marking an error. The sheer difficulty of explanation presented by some error patterns is another factor. Jotting "WW" in the margin to tip a student off to a diction problem is one thing; explaining a subtle shift in point of view in that same marginal space is quite another. Sentence fragments, comma splices, and wrong tenses, to name three classic "serious" errors, are all marked less often than possessive apostrophes. This is, we think, not due to teachers' perception that apostrophe errors are worse than sentence-boundary or tense problems, but to their quickness and ease of indication. The its/it's error and the possessive apostrophe, the two highest-marked patterns, are also two of the easiest errors to mark. This is, of course, not laziness; many composition teachers are so chronically overworked that we should not wonder that the errors most marked are those most quickly indicated.

Fourth, error patterns in student writing are shifting in certain ways, at least partially as a result of changing media trends within the culture. Conclusions must be especially tentative here, because the time-bound nature of studies of error makes comparisons difficult and definitions of errors counted in earlier research are hard to correlate. Our research turned up several earlier lists of serious errors in freshman composition, however, whose order is rather different from the order we discovered.

Roy Ivan Johnson, writing in 1917, reported on 198 papers written by 66 freshmen, and his list of the top-ten error patterns in his study is as follows (wherever possible, we have translated his terms into ours):

1. Spelling
2. Capitalization
3. Punctuation (mostly comma errors)
4. Careless omission or repetition
5. Apostrophe errors
6. Pronoun agreement
7. Verb tense errors and agreement
8. Ungrammatical sentence structure (fragments and run-ons)
9. Mistakes in the use of adjectives and adverbs
10. Mistakes in the use of prepositions and conjunctions

In 1930, Paul Witty and Roberta Green analyzed 170 papers written in a timed situation by freshmen. Here is their top-ten list, translated into our terms where possible:

1. Faulty connectives
2. Vague pronoun reference
3. Use of "would" for simple past tense forms
4. Confusion of forms from similarity of sound or meaning
5. Misplaced modifiers
6. Pronoun agreement
7. Fragments
8. Unclassified errors

9. Dangling modifier
10. Wrong tense

As we mentioned earlier, the largest-scale analysis of errors was done by John C. Hodges in the late 1930s. Unfortunately, we know very little about Hodges' research. He never published any results in contemporary journals, and thus it is difficult to know his methods or even very much about his findings, because we can see them only as they are reflected in the *Harbrace Handbook,* which today still uses the exact arrangement that Hodges gave it in its first edition in 1941. In the "To the Instructor" preface of his first edition, Hodges says that his 20,000 themes "have been tabulated according to the corrections marked by sixteen instructors," which suggests that his raters looked only for teacher-marked errors (Hodges iii). In a footnote on the same page, Hodges gives the only published version of his top-ten list.

1. Comma
2. Spelling
3. Exactness
4. Agreement
5. Superfluous commas
6. Reference of pronouns
7. Apostrophe
8. Omission of words
9. Wordiness
10. Good use

That is all we know of Hodges' findings, but it does not seem unreasonable to assume that he reports them in order of frequency.

In terms of how patterns of error have changed, our findings are, of course, extremely tentative. Assuming that Hodges' *Harbrace* list constitutes some version of the error patterns he found in 1939, however, we note some distinct changes. In general, our list shows a proliferation of error patterns that seem to suggest declining familiarity with the visual look of a written page. Most strikingly, spelling errors have gone from second on the list to first by a factor of three. Spelling is the most obvious example of this lack of visual memory of printed pages seen, but the growth of other error patterns supports it as well.[9]

Some of the error patterns that seem to suggest this visual-memory problem were not found or listed in earlier studies but have come to light in ours. The many wrong word errors, the missing inflected endings, the wrong prepositions, even the its/it's errors—all suggest that students today may be less familiar with the visible aspects of written forms. These findings confirm the contrastive analysis between 2,000 papers from the 1950s and 2,000 papers from the 1970s that was carried out by Gary Sloan in 1979. Sloan determined that many elements of formal writing convention broke down severely between the fifties and seventies, including spelling, homophones, sentence structure elements, inflected endings, and others (157–59). Sloan notes that the effects of an oral—and we would stress, an *electronic*—culture on literacy skills are subversive. Students who do not read the "texts" of our culture will continue to come to school without the tacit visual knowledge of written conventions that "text-wise" writers carry with them effortlessly. Such changes in literate behavior have and will continue to affect us in multiple ways, including the ways we perceive, categorize, and judge "errors."

Finally, we feel we can report some good news. One very telling fact emerging from our research is our realization that college students are *not* making more formal errors in writing than they used to. The numbers of errors made by students in earlier studies and the numbers we found in the 1980s agree remarkably. Our findings chart out as follows:[10]

Study	Year	Average Paper Length	Errors per Paper	Errors per 100 words
Johnson	1917	162 words	3.42	2.11
Witty & Green	1930	231 words	5.18	2.24
Ma & Pa	1986	422 words	9.52	2.26

The consistency of these numbers seems to us extraordinary. It suggests that although the length of the average paper demanded in freshman composition has been steadily rising, the formal skills of students have not declined precipitously.

In the light of the "Johnny Can't Write" furor of the 1970s and the sometimes hysterical claims of educational decline oft heard today, these results are strik-ing—and heartening. They suggest that in some ways we *are* doing a better job than we might have known. The number of errors has not gone down, but neither has it risen in the past five decades. In spite of open admissions, in spite of radical shifts in the demographics of college students, in spite of the huge escalation in the population percentage as well as in the sheer numbers of people attending American colleges, freshmen are still committing approximately the same number of formal errors per 100 words they were before World War I. In this case, not losing means that we are winning.

EPILOGOS

Our foray into the highways of research and the byways of the Pentecostal Youth are over for a time, and we are back on the farm. From our vantage point here on the porch, we can see that this labor has raised more questions than it has answered. Where, for instance, *do* our specific notions of error come from? Can we identify more precisely the relationship among error patterns in written student discourse and other forms of discourse, especially the mass media? Could we identify regional or other variations in error patterns? How might certain error patterns correlate with other patterns—say age, gender, habits of reading, etc.? How might they correlate with measures of writing apprehension, or the "ethos," the ideology of a specific curriculum? Most provocatively, could we derive a contemporary theory of error which would account for the written behaviors of all our students as well as the marking behavior of teachers? These are a few of the problems we'd like to fret over if and when we decide to take to the research road again.

NOTES

[1] As an example of shifting perceptions of student error patterns, it is worth noting that Charles T. Copeland and Henry M. Rideout, writing in 1901, identified the most serious and common grammatical error in Harvard freshman papers as a confusion of the rules for use of "shall" and "will" to express futurity (71n).

[2] For a list of most of these studies, see Harap 444–46.

[3] We wish here to express our gratitude to the College Division of St. Martin's Press, which graciously offered respondents a choice from the St. Martin's trade book list in exchange for thirty or more teacher-marked student papers or Xeroxes of student papers. We are especially grateful to Nancy Perry, Marilyn Moller, and Susan Manning, without whose help this research could never have been accomplished. From assistance with mailings to the considerable tasks of paper stacking, stamping, sorting, and filing, they made the task possible. Their support, both institutional and personal, is deeply appreciated.

The demographics of the papers we were sent were interesting, as we found when examining them for our stratified sample. After pulling all the papers that were illegible, or were not undergraduate papers, were too short to be useful, or were clearly papers from ESL courses, we were left with 19,615 papers. We divided up the U.S. into seven fairly standard geographical regions: (1) Northeast, (2) Southeast, (3) Midwest, (4) Mid-South, (5) Plains States, (6) Southwest (including Hawaii), (7) Northwest (including Alaska). Here are the raw numbers of how the papers were distributed as they came in to us:

Region	1	2	3	4	5	6	7	Total
Total number of papers	3,652	3,478	3,099	4,974	1,229	2,292	891	19,615
Total number of teachers	61	51	54	55	18	47	14	300
Total number of 4-year schools	47	35	40	39	14	24	7	206
Total number of 2-year schools	14	16	14	16	4	23	7	94
Total number of state schools	44	49	48	48	18	44	13	264
Total number of private schools	17	2	6	7	0	3	1	36
Number of schools with total enrollment under 1,000	2	2	0	1	1	1	1	8
Enrollment 1–3,000	9	13	7	11	3	5	4	52
Enrollment 3,000–5,000	13	5	5	14	2	7	2	48
Enrollment 5,000–10,000	19	9	16	10	6	7	4	71
Enrollment 10,000–20,000	14	9	13	13	1	15	2	67
Enrollment over 20,000	4	13	13	6	5	12	1	54

[4] We wanted to find out whether the sample of papers we had received mirrored the demographic realities of American higher education. If it did not, we would have to adjust it to represent the student and teacher populations that were really out there.

When we looked at *The Digest of Education Statistics*, we found that some of our numbers approximated educational statistics closely enough not to need adjustment. The breakdown between 4-year colleges and 2-year colleges, for instance, is 71%/29% in the statistical tables and 69%/31% in our sample. The state schools/private schools ratio is statistically 79%/21%, while our sample ratio was 88%/12%, but the over-representation of state schools did not seem serious enough to worry about for our purposes. In terms of enrollment, we found middle-sized schools slightly over-represented and very small and very large schools slightly under-represented, but in no case was the deviation more than 7% either way:

	% of students nationally	% in sample
Number of schools with total enrollment under 1,000	4	2
Enrollment 1–3,000	11	17
Enrollment 3,000–5,000	13	16
Enrollment 5,000–10,000	21	24
Enrollment 10,000–20,000	25	22
Enrollment over 20,000	25	18

We found the most serious discrepancies in the regional stratification, with some regions over- and others under-represented.

Region	1	2	3	4	5	6	7
% of students nationally	23	12	23	15	4	19	4
% of students in sample	19	18	15	25	6	12	5

On the basis of the regional discrepancy we found, we decided to stratify the sample papers regionally but not in any other way.

For help with the methodological problems we faced, and for advice on establishing a random stratified sample of 3,000 papers, many thanks to Charles Cooper. When the going gets tough, the tough go ask Charles for advice.

5 These two examples of old-time error patterns are cited in Pressey and in Johnson.

6 The term "comma fault" was by far the most popular term to describe this error pattern until the ubiquitous *Harbrace* seeded the clouds with its terms in 1941, advancing "comma splice," previously a term of tertiary choice, into a primary position by 1960.

7 In addition to the error-rating sheets, on which the raters kept track of errors found and errors marked, we asked them to write down on a separate list every misspelled word in every paper they saw. This spelling research is only partially tabulated and will be presented in another study.

8 We were also intrigued to find that of the 3,000 papers examined, only 276 had been marked using the letter-number system of any handbook. Handbooks may be widely used, but fewer than 10% of our papers relied on their systems. The rest had been marked using the common symbols and interlinear notes.

9 With our spelling research partially tabulated at this point, we are struck by the prevalence of homophone errors in the list of the most commonly misspelled words. The growth of *too/ to* and *their/there/they're* error patterns strongly suggests the sort of problem with visual familiarity suggested by our list of non-spelling errors.

10 These comparisons are not absolutely exact, of course. Johnson counted spelling errors, while Witty and Green and we did not. The numbers in the chart for Johnson's research were derived by subtracting all spelling errors from his final error total.

WORKS CITED

Copeland, Charles T., and Henry M. Rideout. *Freshman English and Theme-Correcting at Harvard College.* Boston: Silver, Burdett, 1901.

Elbow, Peter. Unpublished document. English Coalition Conference. July 1987.

Harap, Henry. "The Most Common Grammatical Errors." *English Journal* 19 (June 1930): 440–46.

Hodges, John C. *Harbrace Handbook of English.* New York: Harcourt, Brace, 1941.

Johnson, Roy Ivan. "The Persistency of Error in English Composition." *School Review* 25 (Oct. 1917): 555–80.

Pressey, S. L. "A Statistical Study of Children's Errors in Sentence-Structures." *English Journal* 14 (Sept. 1925): 528–35.

Shaughnessy, Mina P. *Errors & Expectations*. New York: Oxford UP, 1977.

Sloan, Gary. "The Subversive Effects of an Oral Culture on Student Writing." *College Composition and Communication* 30 (May 1979): 156–60.

Snyder, Thomas D. *Digest of Education Statistics 1987*. Washington: Center for Education Statistics, 1987.

Williams, Joseph. "The Phenomenology of Error." *College Composition and Communication* 32 (May 1981): 152–68.

Witty, Paul A., and Roberta La Brant Green. "Composition Errors of College Students." *English Journal* 19 (May 1930): 388–93.

This article is reprinted from *College Composition and Communication* 39 (December 1988): 395–409. —Ed.

Robert J. Connors and Andrea A. Lunsford

TEACHERS' RHETORICAL COMMENTS ON STUDENT PAPERS

As far back as we can trace student papers, we can see the attempts of teachers to squeeze their reactions into a few pithy phrases, to roll all their strength and all their sweetness up into one ball for student delectation. Every teacher of composition has shared in this struggle to address students, and writing helpful comments is one of the skills most teachers wish to develop toward that end. Given that writing evaluative commentary is one of the great tasks we share, one might think it would have been one of the central areas of examination in composition studies.

Indeed, a number of thoughtful examinations of written teacher commentaries exist, most of them measuring empirically the comments of a relatively small teacher and student population. No studies we could find, however, have ever looked at large numbers of papers commented on by large numbers of teachers. We do not have, in other words, any large-scale knowledge of the ways that North American teachers and students tend to interact through written assessments. There are clear logistical reasons for this lack of large-scale studies; the gathering and analysis of a large data base are daunting tasks, and evaluating rhetorical (as opposed to formal) commentary is a challenge. But we had the data base gathered from previous research, and in the great tradition of fools rushing in where wise number-crunchers fear to tread, we thought we'd take a look at this question of teacher commentary.

As inveterate historical kibbitzers, we naturally started research by asking what sorts of comments teachers had made on student papers in the past. Have teacher comments become more or less prescriptive, longer or shorter, more positive or more negative? We headed for the stacks to try to find out. Rather to our amazement, we discovered that what we were proposing to look at— teachers' rhetorical comments on student papers—was a relatively recent phenomenon in general composition teaching.

THE HISTORICAL TRAIL

Evidence of widespread acceptance of teachers acting as rhetorical audiences for their first-year students simply does not exist much farther back than the early 1950s.[1] Before that time, the most widely accepted idea was that teachers' jobs were to correct, perhaps edit, and then grade student papers. Now and then someone attacked this approach, but it seems to have held sway through the first half of this century. As Walter Barnes put it in 1913, writing students live

> in an absolute monarchy, in which they are the subjects, the teacher the king (more often, the queen), and the red-ink pen the royal scepter. . . . Theme correction is an unintelligent process. . . . In our efforts to train our children, we turn into martinets and discipline the recruits into a company of stupid, stolid soldierkins—prompt to obey orders, it may be, but utterly devoid of initiative. (158-59)

The teacher who "pounces on the verbal mistake, who ferrets out the buried grammatical blunder, who scents from afar a colloquialism or a bit of slang" (159) seemed to Barnes a weak writing teacher, but by far the most common kind.

The idea that the teacher's most important job was to rate rather than to respond rhetorically to themes seems to have been well-nigh universal from the 1880s onward, perhaps as a result of the much-cried-up "illiteracy crisis" of the 1880s and 1890s. Those who have examined older college themes preserved in archives at Harvard and Baylor have noted that teacher "comments" overwhelmingly comprised formal and mechanical corrections (for example, see Copeland and Rideout). College programs, in fact, very early came up with "correction cards," editing sheets, and symbol systems that were meant to allow teachers numerically to assess students' adherence to conventional rules, and it seemed reasonable to extrapolate that approach to issues of content, organization, and style. Thus were born during the first decade of this century, the various "rating scales" that represented the first systematic attempt we know of to deal with the issue of rhetorical effectiveness in student writing.

This is not the place for a complete history of the rise of rating scales, the various purposes they covered, the arguments they engendered, or the epistemological assumptions that fostered their development. Suffice it to say that between 1900 and 1925 a number of scales were proposed for rating composition. It's probably fair to say that these scales evolved from the rising status of scientific method and statistics and from writing teachers' uncomfortable awareness of exactly how "subjective" their grading of papers was (James). Teachers wished for a defensible rating instrument, and, beginning with the Hillegas Scale in 1912, educational theorists proposed to give them one. Many developments and variations of Hillegas's scale followed: the Thorndike Extension, the Trabue Scale, the Hudelson Scale, the Harvard-Newton Scale, the Breed-Frostic and Willing Scales, and others (Hudelson 164-67).

We don't want to suggest that these composition scales were entirely devoted to formal and mechanical ratings; their interest for us, in fact, lies primarily in their attempts to evolve an early holistic-style set of standards by which the more qualitative elements of composition could be "reliably" judged. This pedagogically interesting attempt found a supporter in no less than Sterling Leonard, much of whose early work in composition involved his attempt to build more rhetorical awareness into rating scales he felt were too much weighted toward formal aspects (Leonard 760-61). Interest in the perfect rating scale, however, eventually waned, doubtless because rating rhetorical elements was simply too complex and multi-layered a task for any scale. As two scale-using researchers admitted in 1917, after having been through a complex study using a variant of the Harvard-Newton Scale, "This study raises more questions than it answers. In fact, it cannot be said to have settled any question satisfactorily" (Brown and Hagerty 527).

The fact that rating scales usually served as instruments for administrative judgment rather than for student improvement also led to their gradual abandonment by many teachers. Fred Newton Scott, with his customary sagacity, identified this problem early on, noting in 1913 that "whenever a piece of scientific machinery is allowed to take the place of teaching—which is in essence but an attempt to reveal to the pupil the unifying principle of life—the result will be to artificialize the course of instruction" (4). Scott drew a strong distinction between a system which grades a composition for administrative purposes and that which evaluates it as a stage in the pupil's progress. Hillegas's Scale clearly served the former purpose, and thus Scott ended his discussion of it with this Parthian shot:

> I leave this problem with you, then, with the seemingly paradoxical conclusion that we ought in every way to encourage Professor Thorndike and Dr. Hillegas in their attempts to provide us with a scale for the measurement of English compositions, but that when the scale is ready, we had better refrain from using it. If this sounds like the famous recipe for a salad which closes with the words "throw the entire mixture out the window," you will not, I am sure, if you have followed me thus far, be under any misapprehension as to my meaning. (5)

The liberal wing of the profession (including most of Scott's PhD students) followed this line, and the controversy over rating scales lasted for better than a dozen years.

By the mid-1920s, the excitement over rating scales died down as teachers began discussing the most effective ways of "criticizing a theme" outside of the question of grading it. Various kinds of advice were advanced: raise the standards as the course advances; don't be too severe; always include a bit of praise; don't point out every error.[2] All good advice, but the attitude of these authors toward the job of the teacher was almost universally in support of critical/judgmental rather than editorial/interventionist relations with students. "Correction" of papers was always uppermost, even to "liberal" teachers and writers. James Bowman, whose "The Marking of English Themes" of 1920 provides a sensible discussion of teacher marking, devotes only one short paragraph to the whole issue of teacher comments: "The comments are of far greater importance than the mark which is given the theme. These should be stern and yet kindly. While they should overlook no error, they should, in addition, be constructive and optimistic. It is necessary, above all, for the teacher to enter intimately and sympathetically into the problems of the student" (242–43). No one would argue with these ideas, but, even if well-intentioned, they are immensely general. Against that one paragraph, the rest of the article discussed correction of errors and assignment of grades.

This ratio held sway in most quarters. Oh, there were the forward-looking articles that always surprise first-time readers of old volumes of the *English*

Journal—such as Allan Gilbert's "What Shall We Do with Freshman Themes?" which proposes a socially-constructed and process-oriented regimen of peer review and group conferencing.[3] But for every Gilbert or Leonard or Scott or Gertrude Buck there were ten Hilda Jane Holleys, for whom "Interest and originality" was but one of ten areas rated (and third from the bottom of her chart, too, way after "Grammar" and "Vocabulary") and Louise Griswold, proposing to reread each graded theme and change the grade to F if every formal error had not been corrected.

Such formal-error correction characterized teacher response through the twenties, thirties, and early forties, and the centrality of the correction approach was not widely questioned until the advent of the communications movement during the late forties. Then, the concept of teachers best serving students by "correcting" their papers, like many other accepted traditions in writing pedagogy, began to come under sustained fire from a new generation of writing teachers.[4] Jeffrey Fleece in 1952 made what seemed to many a novel suggestion: that teachers actually consider themselves as students' real audiences and respond to their essays accordingly. Since "purpose" was the watchword of the communications movement, said Fleece, why not stop pretending that the teacher was not the only final and actual audience for students, and make use of that relationship? On papers with a real purpose, said Fleece, "the teacher should react to the content in some way, to guarantee the student's continued confidence in his interest" (273).

Fleece's view hardly seems radical today, but at the time it was received as a startling suggestion about the relations that students and teachers in writing might have. Even students were unused to having what they *said* in papers taken seriously. In an essay called "Conversing in the Margins," Harold Collins reported in 1953 that:

> When I return the themes, hands go up over pained faces, and injured innocence makes itself heard.
>
> "Aren't you supposed to stick to the grammar and punctuation and that sort of thing and not bother about what we say, the—er—content of our themes?"
>
> "I had only one error in spelling and three in punctuation. What do you mark on?" (He means, "Why didn't I get an A or a B?")
>
> "Do we have to agree with you? That doesn't seem . . ."
>
> I must justify my extensive commentary, explain why I have seen fit to stray from such textbook concerns as diction, spelling, punctuation, sentence structure, and organization. With some warmth, I protest that I am not a theme-reading machine, a new marvel of electronics grading for grammar. Though it may be hard to credit, I am a real human being, and so I am naturally interested in what my students say in their themes. . . . (465)

Between 1900 and 1940, the concept that most students could have anything to "say" in their writing that would *really* interest the teacher was hardly imagined except by a few rare teachers.[5]

By the middle fifties, however, educators were more and more expected to try to address their students' essays as "real" audiences and to write long personal comments. "It requires extra time and care on the teacher's part," admitted Delmer Rodabaugh. "Perhaps it is not strictly his job to go to so much trouble, but trouble turns to pleasure when he begins to get results" (37). Rodabaugh admitted that what he proposed was not new, but was "a deliberate and persistent attempt to extend what we all do." This new effort, based on the idea that students should get full-scale rhetorical comments both in margins and at the end of papers, was very much in place by the end of the 1950s, and new teachers after that time who gave no rhetorical advice along with their formal corrections did their work with a certain guilt.

But what, exactly, did that work really come to? The attitudes that first appeared during the heyday of the communications movement still control much of what is presumed today about written teacher responses to student writing. Since the 1950s the field of composition studies has waxed, and its attitude toward teacher response to student writing has remained marked by the essential assumption that the teacher must and should engage the student in rhetorical dialogue. Around this assumption lies a large literature, which began to burgeon in the middle 1960s, hit a peak in the early 1980s, and has recently come up for discussion again in an excellent collection of essays edited by Chris Anson.[6]

We won't review this literature here, since so many people in the Anson collection have already done that better than we could. But we did notice, as we looked through the many thoughtful essays about teacher response, how few of them have studied the subject in numerical depth. Many discussions about response are inspiring, but most are either prescriptive, idealistic, or theoretical. Now and then a discouraging word had been heard—Albert Kitzhaber's flinty assessment of how few Dartmouth teachers actually wrote any comments on papers in the early 1960s, Cy Knoblauch and Lil Brannon's glum assertion in 1981 that no kind of written comment from teachers did much good or harm or had much attention paid to it, or Nancy Sommers's study of 35 teachers responding at Oklahoma and NYU, which concluded that "the news from the classroom is not good," that teachers were not responding to students in ways that would help them engage with issues, purposes, or goals (154). But most of the rest of the college-level literature is largely exploratory. No really large-scale study of the sorts of comments teachers were actually making on student papers existed, at least none that we knew of. We thought we'd give it a try.

THE SAMPLE AND THE METHODOLOGY

In 1986, we had collected 21,000 teacher-marked student essays for a national study of patterns of formal error. After identifying a randomized, stratified sample of 3,000 papers, we asked 50 analyzers to find examples of the top twenty error patterns in the writing of contemporary college students. The results of that study were published in 1988 as "Frequency of Formal Errors in Current College Writing."[7] As we sat through the long day of analysis and talked afterwards about what we'd seen that was interesting, everyone agreed that the whole issue of the ways in which the teachers responded to the student writing was something we ought to study. Not, of course, the ways in which teachers marked up the formal and mechanical errors, which nearly always tended to be done using either handbook numbers or the standard set of mysterious phatic grunts: "awk," "ww," "comma," etc. No, what we wanted to try to look at was a sometimes vague entity that we called "global comments" by the teachers. What were teachers saying in response to the *content* of the paper, or to the specifically *rhetorical* aspects of its organization, sentence structure, etc.? What kinds of teacher-student relationships did the comments reflect?

We had a data base that we could use. Back in 1985, when we had been soliciting papers from teachers nationally, we had specifically asked that we be sent only papers that had been marked by teachers; some of the papers had very minimal markings, but each one had been evaluated in some way, had passed under the eye and been judged by the pen of a teacher. Our original request letter asked only for student papers "to which teachers have responded with interlinear, marginal, or terminal comments." The Methodology Police would probably bust us for the way the sample was gathered; the 300 teachers who sent us papers were a self-selected group who responded to an initial mailing (offering books from the St. Martin's Press trade list in exchange for commented papers) that went to over 8,000 teachers. We can't be sure why these folks were the ones who came forward, but even though the paper sample itself is randomized and nationally stratified by region, size and type of college, and so on, the teachers themselves were self-selected. Though it would be more satisfying to be able to say we had papers from 3,000 teachers who were chosen randomly from some giant national bingo drum, getting such a sample is simply beyond us. As it stands, we have a larger sample, and a better national distribution, than any previous study. Nothing, as one of our students once wrote, is extremely perfect.[8]

Okay, the data base was in hand. Now, as before, we faced the question of what instrument we would use to try to understand what we might find in the 3,000-paper sample.

We figured that we might as well work as inductively as we could, so we again selected 300 random papers, 150 for Andrea and 150 for Bob. We then looked carefully at these 300 papers, trying to note any important patterns we could see of teacher response to global rhetorical issues. Each of us came up with a list, and then we compared lists. We found that we had both noted some responses based on individual comments and some that were based in the *forms* and *genres* of teacher comments. We melded our lists and came up with a checklist form that we hoped would capture a substantial number of the different kinds of global comments our readers might see.

With lots of help from Eric Walborn, Heather Graves, and Carrie Lèverenz in the Ohio State graduate program, one Saturday morning in May 1991 we assembled a group of 26 experienced writing teachers and eager readers. Lured by the prospect of a promised twelve feet of high-quality submarine sandwiches, these champions of the proletariat plunged into a learning curve and then into large stacks of papers, looking only at the teacher comments on each paper, and searching for a number of specific elements to record.[9]

We were specifically interested in what we called "global comments" by teachers, general evaluative comments found at the end or the beginning of papers. Such comments may be quite long or as short as a single word, or they may take the form of marginal or interlinear comments in the body of the paper which are rhetorically oriented and not related to formal or mechanical problems. Global comments by teachers are meant to address global issues in students' writing: issues of rhetoric, structure, general success, longitudinal writing development, mastery of conventional generic knowledge, and other large-scale issues.

In other words, we asked our readers to ignore any comments on the level of formal error, grammar, punctuation, spelling, syntax, etc., unless those comments were couched in a specifically rhetorical way, i.e., "Your audience will think harshly of you if they see lots of comma splices." What we wanted to try to get at were the ways in which teachers judge the rhetorical effectiveness of their students' writing, and the sorts of teacher-student relationships reflected in the comments that teachers give. The following table summarizes what we found.

Table 1
Numerical Results: Global Commentary Research

Total number of papers examined: 3,000

	# of 3,000	Percentage
Number of papers with global or rhetorical comments	2,297	77% of all Ps
Papers without global or rhetorical comments	703	23%
Numbers of papers graded	2,241	75%
Number of papers with initial or terminal comments	1,934	64%
Number of initial comments	318	16% of Ps with I or T comments
Number of terminal comments	1,616	84% of Ps with I or T comments
Purpose of comments:		
To give feedback on draft in process	242	11% of Ps with I or T comments
To justify grades	1,355	59%
Global comments in general:		
Comments that are all essentially positive	172	9% of Ps with I or T comments
Comments that are all essentially negative	451	23%
Comments that begin positively and then go to negative	808	42%
Comments that begin negatively and then go to positive	217	11%

Table (Continued)

	# of 3,000	Percentage
Global Comments in General (continued)		
Comments that lead with rhetorical issues	692	36%
Comments that lead with mechanical issues	357	18%
Very short comments—fewer than 10 words	460	24%
Very long comments—more than 100 words	101	5%
Comments focused exclusively on rhetorical issues	472	24%
Comments focused exclusively on formal/mechanical issues	435	22%
Comments that argue with content points made in paper	478	24%
Comments that indicate use of mechanical criteria as gate criteria ("The comma splices force me to give this an F despite....")	150	8%
Comments that give general reader response ("like/dislike")	322	17%
Comments evaluating specific rhetorical elements:		
Supporting evidence, examples, details	1,296	56% of all Ps with comments
Organization	643	28%
Purpose	240	11%
Response to assignment	246	11%
Audience	137	6%
Overall progress, beyond commentary on paper	176	8%
Comments that deal with specific formal elements:		
Sentence structure	767	33% of all Ps with comments
Paragraph structure	417	18%
Documentation	154	7%
Quotations	142	6%
Source materials	133	6%
Paper format	372	16%

GRADES AND PATTERNS OF COMMENTARY

We looked at 3,000 papers. Of that number, 2,297 (77%) contained global comments. We had asked in our letter only for teacher-marked student papers, not for specifically "global" comments, so this percentage seems heartening. In fact, the 77% of teachers who took the time and effort to write even minimal global comments on student papers seem to us rather to diminish the claim sometimes heard that teachers do nothing with student papers except bleed upon errors. Of our sample, more than three-quarters dealt in some way with larger issues of rhetorical effectiveness.

The number of papers bearing some sort of grade was 2,241, or 75% of the total. These grades did not, we hasten to say, always appear on papers with global comments; in fact, our readers noted with some amazement how many of the graded papers contained no other form of commentary on them. The overwhelming impression our readers were left with was that grades were implicitly—or often explicitly—overwhelming impediments both for teachers and for students. If papers had no other markings, they had grades or evaluative symbols.[10]

The grades themselves took an extraordinary variety of forms, ranging from standard letter grades, with pluses and minuses; to standard 100-point number grades; to cryptic systems of numbers, fractions, decimals; and finally to symbolic systems of different kinds, including varieties of stars, moons, checks, check-pluses and -minuses. We had meant to attempt an average of these grades, but the different systems they used and the different contexts out of which they came made such an attempt seem silly; we had no idea how to average notations such as ***, 94/130, 3.1, +, F+, and ☺. So we desisted.

Of the 3,000 papers, 1,934 (64%) had identifiable terminal or initial comments on them. Such comments, appearing at the end or the beginning of a paper, serve as the teacher's most general and usually final comment on the work of the paper as a whole, and so we paid very close attention to them. Of the two styles, the terminal comments were by far the most common. We found that only 318 papers (16% of all the papers with overview-style comments), placed that general overview at the beginning of the paper; the other 84% of teachers using these comments placed them at the end of the paper, usually along with the grade. There are probably simple reasons for this phenomenon. Terminal comments, especially those with grades to justify, are written on the last page of the essay, seeming to result from the reading process more naturally. They flow when the teacher's memory is freshest, at the point when she has just stopped reading. Their being buried in a later page allows them to be more private and even secret, unlike initial comments, which announce the teacher's judgment to the world in public fashion. But some teachers seem to prefer initial overall comments, perhaps because they hope to engage the student in thinking about central issues *before* looking at the rest of the commentary.

As we looked over the patterns of general commentary our readers found, we were reminded of how much rhetorical *forms* can tell us about the purposes and attitudes of those using them. Every intellectual field might be said to have its announced public values and its secret soul. Most composition teachers know what the field *says* is important—our public "tropes," so to speak. We talk and write often of purpose, of audience, of organization, of proof, of process and invention and revision and so on. These words fill our journals, our professional books, our conferences, and especially our textbooks. But do we really follow through? Do comments on papers show us acting on these public tropes, giving them more than lip service? Or do we have more genuine and less overt agendas? That was one of our major questions as we looked at these longer comments. As we examined the longer comments, we began to find patterns, and we came more and more to see our findings as a sort of exploration of the tropics of teacher commentary. Teachers, we found, tend to return to well-understood topoi as well as to familiar terms, phrases, and locutions as they make their judgments on student writing. These topoi and tropes of commentary have several origins: they are public and private, conscious and habitual, social and individualistic. They are powerful tacit genres, and we were particularly interested in how these patterns of commentary reflected the beliefs of the field of composition studies.

Initial and terminal comments in particular have, we discovered, certain patterns and genres that they tend to fall into. The rarest of these tropes is the comment consisting of nothing else except praise and positive evaluation. Of the papers with global comments, only 9% exhibited this pattern of totally positive commentary. These figures correlate with Daiker's Miami of Ohio study and illustrate how American teachers tend to be trained in finding and isolating problems in writing (104). Rarely can teachers keep themselves to completely positive commentary. As our readers noted, these positive comments tended to be the shortest of all the global comments found, as well as the friendliest. They were nearly all found next to A-level grades, and the teachers seem commonly to have felt that such good grades needed little explanation or commentary. Interestingly, our readers mentioned that completely positive global comments were the most personal comments, and were even commonly signed with the teacher's initials—a phenomenon not noted in mixed or negative global comments. "Very well done," "Your usual careful job," and "Superb!" were all examples of this pattern, which by its rarity and the sometimes surprising intensity of the praises rendered probably indicates how starved teachers feel for work they can wholeheartedly praise.

The next most common pattern we found consisted of comments that began by critiquing some aspect of the student's writing—very often a formal or mechanical aspect—and then moved into a positive commentary on the effective aspects of the papers. That pattern was still rather rare, with only 11% of the comments falling into the class.

More than twice as common was the comment consisting of nothing except negative judgments. Of our commented papers, 23% fell into this category, and they usually accompanied the worst grades. These completely critical comments ranged from savagely indignant to sadly resigned, but all gave the message that the teacher was seriously disappointed with this effort and was not equal to the task of finding anything about the paper to like. On a paper about the writer's feelings after being called to an accident scene where a sixteen-year-old girl had died, the comment was, "Learn to use subordination. You might have given us more on the drunken driver and your subsequent thoughts about him. You are still making comma splices! You must eliminate this error once and for all. Is it because you aren't able to recognize an independent clause?" George Hillocks, reviewing studies relating to teacher comments in his *Research on Written Composition*, found that although negative comments did not have any definitive effect on the quality of students' writing, they did strongly affect students' attitudes toward writing (160-68).

The most common trope in global comments proved to be the comment that began positively, with some praise of some element of a paper, and then turned negative toward the end. "Jodie—You describe much of Rodriguez's dilemma well. I'd like to see some of your own ideas expanded—they deserve more attention! And be careful of those apostrophes!" A full 42% of all terminal and initial comments—almost half—fell into this category. The reasons for its popularity probably derive from the by-now traditional wisdom about always trying to find something to praise in each student's work. Seeing that many teachers do conscientiously try to find at least one good point to comment on in a paper was heartening.[11]

In terms of the order of presentation of materials in the terminal and initial comments, the most common order was *global/local*, leading with rhetorical comments, followed up by comments on mechanical or formal issues. Twice as many comments—36%—began with rhetorical comments as with formal comments, and this order ties in with the positive-negative duality; the single most common kind of comment we found consisted of a positive rhetorical comment followed by complaints and suggestions of different sorts, often concerning mechanical elements in the paper: "Paul, you've organized the paragraphs here well to support your thesis, but your sentences are all still short and simple, and you really need to check the comma rules."

The lengths of terminal and initial comments ranged widely. The longest comment we found was over 250 words long, but long comments were far less common than short. The average comment length throughout the run of papers was around 31 words, but this is not a very meaningful figure. Very short comments—fewer than ten words—were much more common than longer comments. A full 24% of all global comments had ten words or fewer; of these, many were a very few words, or one word—"Organization" or "No thesis" or "Handwriting—learn to type!" or "Tense!" Conversely, only 5% of comments exceeded 100 words. The portrait of teacher-student interchange painted by these numbers is one in which overworked teachers dash down a few words which very often tell students little about how or why their papers succeed or fail. The rarity of longer comments seemed to our readers to indicate not so much that teachers had nothing to say as that they had little time or energy to say it and little faith that what they had to say would be heard.

We found that only 22% of the longer comments were concerned exclusively with formal issues, indicating that 78% of all the longer global comments made by teachers took cognizance of rhetorical issues in the paper. (This number corresponds to the very small number of papers whose comments indicated that formal or mechanical criteria had been used as "gate criteria," without success in which a passing grade was impossible. Only 8% of the comments indicated uses of gates such as "The comma splices force me to give this paper an F despite. . . .") Some comments (24%) were focused exclusively on rhetorical issues and never went into any detail about mechanics, but the most common tropes of teacher comment took *both* rhetorical and mechanical elements of the paper into consideration. In general, teachers seem determined to respond to what their students are saying as well as to how they say it, which is interesting news to those critics of contemporary teaching who claim that writing teachers are obsessed only with errors.

TROPES WITHIN COMMENTARY

One section of our tally sheets was devoted to recording numbers for how often teachers commented on some of the more common rhetorical elements that are a staple of freshman textbooks and teaching. What we found was instructive, and somewhat surprising. From the comments counted by our readers—and here we counted all global comments, not just terminal and initial comments— teachers comment in large numbers only on two general areas: supporting details and overall paper organization. A full 56% of *all* papers with global comments contained comments on the effectiveness—or more commonly, the lack—of supporting details, evidence, or examples. The next most commonly discussed rhetorical element, at 28%, was overall paper organization, especially issues of introductory sections and issues of conclusion and ending, and thematic coherence.

Since most textbooks, and many teachers, put considerable stress on the two large issues of purpose and audience, we might expect that teacher comments would similarly emphasize these issues. We were surprised, then, to find that very few teacher comments discussed them. Only 11% of the papers we examined had comments that could, even with liberal interpretation, be considered to be about purpose in the essay. Even rarer were comments about the writer's approach toward audience, with only 6% of papers mentioning anything about audience considerations such as tone or voice. According to our readers, the impression left by reading most teacher comments was that the audience for the writing was clearly the teacher, only the teacher, and nothing but the teacher, and thus most comments on audience outside of those parameters seemed redundant.

We also found that 11% of the papers contained comments concerned with how successfully the paper responded to the assignment. Many of these papers were clearly written either to formal assignments ("comparison/contrast paper," "narrative essay," "research paper," etc.) or to full content-based assignments ("Give me a synopsis of the Orwell essay followed by your own examples of doublespeak," etc.). Many of these papers did not contain comments specifically directed toward the assignment in spite of their clear nature as assignment-driven, but very often when the writer chose an incorrect genre or failed to take some specific instruction into proper consideration, the teacher would call it out as a serious failure. "This really is not a process analysis at all," complains one teacher about an essay called "What Are Friends For?" "You haven't given instructions to follow in performing or achieving something." The paper, which seemed acceptable to our readers except for failing to meet these generic expectations, received a D+.

Finally, we asked our readers to look at comments that went beyond the paper at hand to relate this piece of work to other work the teacher had seen the student accomplish. "Jennifer, I've enjoyed having you in class, and we've really seen some improvement. Good luck! I hope that next quarter you find more people that you fit in with." Here, again, we found that such commentary was thin on the ground; only 8% of the papers displayed any comments that dealt with the writer's work as a developing system. The other 92% dealt only with the individual work at hand, making no comments on progress or development. Various reasons may account for this lack of longitudinal commentary. Our most immediate hypothesis is that teachers simply have too many students and too many papers to have time to look for the "big picture" of any one student's development.

While this research was meant to deal with global or rhetorical comments rather than mechanical elements in student writing, we couldn't separate those two factors absolutely. The formal and the mechanical are always rhetorical as well, and we wanted to try to look at the ways in which teachers commented on the rhetorical effectiveness of formal decisions student writers had made. Here we found that the most widely noted formal feature was sentence structure, with 33% of the commented papers mentioning it. (These were not merely syntactic or grammatical complaints or corrections, but longer comments on the effectiveness of sentences.) Paragraph structure was also mentioned in 18% of the commented papers, which was a bit of a surprise, since textbooks bear down so hard on paragraphs as organic units. General paper format—margins, spacing, neatness, cover sheets, etc.—elicited response on 16% of the commented papers.[12]

Finally, we examined the terminal and initial comments for their purpose. It was not always possible to divide comments into clear categories, of course, but we wanted to see what we could tell about the writing processes encouraged in the classrooms of the teachers whose comments we had. We found that the majority of the comments at the beginning or end of the papers served one purpose: to justify and explain final grades. Over 59% of the initial and terminal comments were grade justifications, "autopsies" representing a full stop rather than any medial stage in the writing process. In contrast, only 11% of the papers with such comments exhibited commentary clearly meant to advise the student about the paper as an ongoing project. It's probable that our process of paper-gathering specifically solicited papers at the final stage of the writing process, [that is,] papers which had already been revised and which had been submitted for final grading. Nevertheless, this study suggests that consistent and widespread use of multiple drafts and revisions may hold more in theory than it does in practice.

READER IMPRESSIONS

We worked on recording numerical information for about five hours, at which point we broke to munch subs and talk about what we'd seen in the teacher comments on the papers and about our impressions. These impressionistic responses are, of course, just that—and therefore are not generalizable. We nevertheless found them fascinating, because they emerged immediately from the people who read through all those 3,000 papers. Because numbers tell only one story, we want to include our readers' voices here.

The primary emotion that they felt as they read through these teacher comments, our readers told us, was a sort of chagrin: these papers and comments revealed to them a world of teaching writing that was harder and sadder than they wanted it to be—a world very different from the theoretical world of composition studies most readers hoped to inhabit. It was a world, many said, whose most obvious nature was seen in the exhaustion on the parts of the teachers marking these papers. Many of the more disturbing aspects of the teacher-student interaction revealed by these comments could be traced to overwork. A teacher with too many students, too many papers to grade, can pay only small attention to each one, and small attention indeed is what many of these papers got. A quarter of them had no personal comments at all, a third of them had no real rhetorical responses, and only 5% of them had lengthy, engaged comments of more than 100 words.

Just as students invent the university every time they write, teachers invent not only a student writer but a responder every time they comment. One characteristic of the responder that many teachers construct, our readers said, was its nature as a general and objective judge. Many of the comments seemed to speak to the student from empyrean heights, delivering judgments in an apparently disinterested way. Very few teachers, for instance, allowed themselves the subjective stance implicit in telling students simply whether they liked or disliked a piece of writing. This kind of reader-response stance was found in 17% of the global comments; the other 83% of comments pronounced on the paper in a distanced tone, like reified personifications of Perelman's Universal Audience. "You've structured the paper well in the block format," "You have a suitable opening paragraph with thesis statement," or "There are some lapses in style that need attention" were much more common than comments like "Don't get discouraged. Good writing takes years."

Similarly, teachers seemed unwilling to engage powerfully with content-based student assertions or to pass anything except "professional" judgments on the student writing they were examining. Only 24% of the comments made any move toward arguing or refuting any content points made in the paper, and many of these "refutations" were actually formal comments on weak argumentative strategies. In some way, then, teachers seem conditioned *not* to engage with student writing in personal or polemical ways. What we found, in short, was that most teachers in this sample give evidence of reading student papers in ways antithetical to the reading strategies currently being explored by many critical theorists.[13] (It's our guess that even the most devoted reader-response critics, by the way, tend to produce similar disinterested commentary on student papers.) For whatever reasons, our readers found evidence to support the contention of Robert Schwegler that "professional practices and assumptions have encouraged composition instructors to suppress value-laden responses to student writing and ignore the political dimensions of their reading and teaching practices" (205). Schwegler's conclusion that "the language of marginal and summative commentary . . . is predominantly formalist and implicitly authoritarian" is one our study clearly supports (222).

The authoritarian attitude came through most clearly in the insensitivity our readers felt some of the teacher comments evinced. They sensed, they said, not only exhaustion but a kind of disappointment on the parts of many teachers, and, as a result, patience was often in short supply. "Do over, and pick one subject for development. This is just silly." "Throw away!" "You apparently do not understand thing one about what a research paper is." At times the harshness, which might be justified in particular contexts, even segued into a downright punitive state of mind; one teacher wrote at the end of a paper, "Brian, this is much too short, as I'm sure you know. You've not fulfilled the requirements of the course. Besides receiving an F for the paper, I'm lowering another grade 20 points. You should have consulted with me." Another teacher wrote:

> I refuse to read this research paper. You have not done adequate research, you have not narrowed the topic as directed, you have not followed the format described, *and you have not been directed by my comments during the research assignment.* (emphasis added)

Here is disappointment brimming over into accusation and acrimony.

Some teachers were disturbed when students seemed not to have a grasp of materials that teachers expected them to have mastered. This disappointment, our readers said, seemed to stem from a disjunction between what teachers thought they taught and what they then evaluated. "Ken, you know better than to create comma splices at this point in the semester!" wrote a teacher in rueful disappointment, but Ken obviously did not know. In assuming that Ken purposefully had "created" some comma splices after no doubt being taught that such creations were to be avoided, the teacher showed a dissociation between *her* knowledge as she assumed it was disseminated into the class and *Ken's* grasp of some fairly complex and experience-based conventions.

Our readers also told us that the large number of short, careless, exhausted, or insensitive comments really made them notice and appreciate comments that reflected commitment to students and to learning. They noted lengthy comments from teachers who seemed really to care, not only about students' writing, but also about the students themselves:

> Elly—this is not a good essay, but you'd have to be superhuman to write a good essay on this topic, given how important and immediate it is for you. I *feel* for your situation—I know what it is like to feel like a different person in a different place, and however much people tell you it is possible to change anywhere,

it surely is MUCH harder in some places than others. (Run away to NYC!) Unfortunately, my job is not to encourage you to run away, but to write a good essay. Let's make it a short but specific one: tell me *one* incident that will show how you used to put yourself down, and *one* incident during your visit to NYC that shows how you didn't put yourself down or were even proud of yourself.

Some might complain that this teacher is being too directive, telling the student exactly how to revise, but after looking at many papers with no evidence that a revision option had ever existed and no evidence that the teacher cared much for the student or her situation, this kind of comment really captured our readers' attention.

Another trait our readers admired was the skill of careful marginal comments. Teachers who use marginal comments and a revision option were praised by our readers for their thoroughness and the care they took in calling all sorts of rhetorical elements—not just very large-scale ones—to students' attention. One teacher particularly won raves from the readers; his marginal questions were dense—questions like "When did she do this?" and "You didn't know how to steer?" were interspersed with shorter notes like "Paragraph"—and the whole was followed up with a half-page typed response to the paper, giving comments and suggestions for the next draft. At the same time we admired this teacher's work and care, however, we also wondered, as one reader put it, "When does this guy ever sleep?"

It was also good to discover teachers experimenting with different systems to help students revise. Although, as we suggested, many teachers seemed to see revision as merely editing out of formal errors, other teachers clearly encouraged revision for content issues. One teacher had even invented a "contract" form for revision, which was a sort of written proposal of the changes the student would make in a draft, and a promise from the teacher—signed and dated—of what grade would be given the paper if the changes were successfully carried out.

Many of the teachers commenting in our study did seem to use the concept of teaching the writing process in their responses to students, but all too often the process reflected a rigid stage model. Some students were asked to attach their outlines or invention materials to the draft handed in, leading to comments like "This is terrible prewriting!" Our readers saw few attempts to discuss any recursive model of writing, and although prewriting was sometimes mentioned, revision had very little place in the comments we read. With only 11% of the papers showing any evidence of a revision policy (and we deliberately asked our readers to use the most liberal definition of "draft in process" possible, even to the extent of defining a graded paper as a draft if it gave evidence of being the final product of another draft process), and many of the "revisions" suggested being the editing and correction of errors, the practices mirrored by these comments are still governed by the older form of "one-shot writing."

Although we had not meant to look at formal or mechanical comments, our readers told us that it had been impossible for them to ignore the editing and corrections they saw. There was, they said, a pervasive tendency to isolate problems and errors individually and "correct" them, without any corresponding attempt to analyze error patterns in any larger way, as is recommended by Mina

Shaughnessy and the entire tradition that follows her. The "job" that teachers felt they were supposed to do was, it seemed, overwhelmingly a job of looking at papers rather than students; our readers found very little readerly response and very little response to content. Most teachers, if our sample is representative, continue to feel that a major task is to "correct" and edit papers, primarily for formal errors but also for deviation from algorithmic and often rigid "rhetorical" rules as well. The editing was often heavy-handed and primarily apodictic, concerned more with ridding the paper of problems than with helping the student learn how to avoid them in the future.

In spite of what we know about how grading works against our goals, our readers saw evidence everywhere that much teacher commentary was grade-driven. A large number of teachers used some form of dittoed or xeroxed "grading sheet" clipped or stapled to the student's essay. These sheets, which varied in format, were sometimes obviously departmental in origin, but a number of them were individual. They were great boons to grading, because teachers could circle a few words or phrases, rate several different elements in the paper independently and easily, and go on to the next paper with hardly any personal commentary on the paper. These rating sheets also allowed teachers to pass hierarchical judgments on rhetorical matters; one teacher used an editing sheet that gave checks and points for the quality of the prewriting. Our readers discerned a relationship between use of these grading sheets and lower grades on papers, which they ascribed to the atomistic division of the paper such sheets encourage and the teacher's resulting difficulty in seeing the piece of writing holistically or with much affect. Some teachers had a set of "penalty points" criteria which produced an automatic F if a certain number of types of error was found. "I stopped here," wrote one teacher in the middle of a research paper. "You've already messed this up to the point of failure."

One notable subset of these rating sheets were the "correction sheets," sometimes found in labeled "correction folders." Correction sheets were not merely reactive, but prophylactic as well. Some contained written instructions demanding that students examine their teacher-marked paper, then list the error symbol, the error name, the rule that the error had broken, and the rewritten sentence in which the error originally had appeared. This technique, which appeared in a number of papers, did not always use a separate sheet; very often, students were asked to rewrite elements with formal errors as part of the *post-grading* work on the paper. In one case, in fact, we found a teacher who, after each error marking, placed a row of numbers—1, 2, 3, 4, 5—on succeeding lines in the margin. The student's task, as far as we can reconstruct it, was to identify the error and then write the correct word or phrase out five times in the margin so as to really "get it through her head."

But even those teachers not using grading sheets often gave few reasons why they approved of or condemned some aspect of a paper. The judgments expressed in writing by teachers often seemed to come out of some privately held set of ideals about what good writing should look like, norms that students may have been taught but were certainly expected to know. One of our readers called this tacit assumption the problem of "writer-based teacher response," and it was as pervasive among our teachers as writer-based prose is among students.

The reactions of our readers made us realize anew how difficult the situations of many teachers remain today. Behind the abstractions we push about as counters in our scholarly game, there exist real persons facing real and sometimes grim circumstances. We have a long road ahead of us if we are to make real and useful so much of what we confidently discuss in our journals and our conference talks. So the news we bring back from the Tropics of Commentary is both good and bad. The good news is that teachers are genuinely involved in trying to help their students with rhetorical issues in their writing. Counter to the popular image of the writing teacher as error-obsessed and concerned only with mechanical issues, the teachers whose work we looked at clearly cared about how their students were planning and ordering writing. The classical canons invoked in more than three-quarters of the papers we examined were invention and arrangement, not merely style. Similarly, more comments were made on the traditional rhetorical issues of supporting details/examples and general organization than were made on smaller-scale issues. Very few comments were entirely negative, and very few showed use of formal and mechanical standards as completely dominating standards of content. Grading standards have softened up a little in the last 70 years, but not as much as many people may have thought.

The bad news is that many teachers seem still to be facing classroom situations, loads, and levels of training that keep them from communicating their rhetorical evaluations effectively. Even given the nature of our sample, there was not much reflection in these papers of revision options, or of contemporary views of the composing process. The teachers whose comments we studied seem often to have been trained to judge student writing by rhetorical formulae that are almost as restricting as mechanical formulas. The emphasis still seems to be on finding and pointing out problems and deficits in the individual paper, not on envisioning patterns in student writing habits or prompts that could go beyond such analysis. As D. Gordon Rohman put it as long ago as 1965, merely pointing out errors or praising good rhetorical choices is based on a fundamental misconception, the idea that

> if we train students how to recognize an example of good prose ("the rhetoric of the finished word"), we haven't given them a basis on which to build their own writing abilities. All we have done, in fact, is to give them standards to judge the goodness or badness of their finished effort. *We haven't really taught them how to make that effort.* (106)

For reasons of overwork, or incomplete training, or curricular demand, many of the teachers whose comments we looked at are still not going beyond giving students standards by which to judge finished writing.

It may be, in addition, that to some degree teachers perceive that their comments *don't count*—that students ignore them, that the discursive system at work in institutional grading won't allow for any communication *not* algorithmic and grade-based. As our readers, with their admirable idealism, told us, many of the comments they saw seemed to be part of a web of institutional constraints that made teacherly "voice" in commentary a rare thing. If we're accurate in this perception, it is the entire industry and institution of rank ordering, hyper-competition, and grading that is culpable, and teachers are as much victims of it as students.

Janet Auten's recent claim that we need a rhetorical context for every disruption we make in a student text is certainly compelling, and her suggestions that teachers become aware of their separate roles as readers, coaches, and editors are helpful (11–12). What we would like to see are future studies that would build such awareness by describing *in detail* the topography we have only sketched in here, perhaps in "thick descriptions" of teacher-responders at work, in their full context. Ethnographies of response would certainly provide a starting point for analyses of instructional constraints, for the ideologies of teacher response, and for the ethos of this particular teacher-student interaction. But in addition to knowing more about the complex act of response, we have to work at seeing that what we know *now* is enacted in writing programs. We need to start putting into programmatic practice what we've learned about effective teacher commentary from scholars like Nancy Sommers, Lil Brannon, and Chris Anson. Doing so might best begin, for each of us, at home—by cataloguing and studying our own tropics of commentary. By determining those genres and tropes of response we tend to privilege, perhaps we can begin to learn how our students "read" these teacherly tropes, which seem so obvious and helpful to us but may not be so easily deciphered by those still striving to enter the community we take for granted.

NOTES

[1] During the nineteenth century, of course, when most writing courses were taught at the sophomore level and above, teachers at the better colleges often engaged with their students' essays at some length in commentary. This practice of serious and lengthy engagement died out quickly, however, after the first freshman writing courses began to evolve with their drastic teacher overwork and underprepared students. By 1900 the practice of engagement with the content of the student essays was the rare exception to the rule.

[2] Those who thought this piece of advice was relatively new will be surprised to learn that it can be dated with certainty back to 1921, and we have no doubt that, traced truly, it predates Quintilian. Each generation seems to feel that truly humanistic pedagogy began only a decade or two ago. See Bowman, 249–53, Hewitt, 85–87, and Daiker, 105.

[3] Gilbert, writing in 1922, is a startlingly "modern" voice who often sounds a lot like David Bartholomae or Ann Berthoff. Listen:

> The course in freshman rhetoric—without plenty of reading—is an attempt to make bricks out of straw only. . . . The teacher of Freshman English must deserve his right to stand on the same level as any other teacher of Freshmen, and must deal with big things, ideas, and books that hit the intelligence of the students. This does more to improve slovenly sentences, than does constant worrying of details. The mint, anise, and cumin must be tithed, but the teacher of Freshmen who gives himself to trivial things and neglects the weightier matters of good literature does not make his course a power for literacy. (400)

Gilbert goes on to recommend literature as a springboard for students' own choices of what to write, then suggests that students read their papers before the class because to do so "gives the writer an audience," after which comes group criticism, then personal conferences with the teacher, then group conferences. Sadly, Gilbert was a rather lonely voice in his time.

[4] For more information on the importance of this generation to composition pedagogy, see the "Introduction" to *Selected Essays of Edward P. J. Corbett*.

[5] Fred Newton Scott had been encouraging teachers to read their students' essays rhetorically, of course, but although we admire Scott today, his influence (and that of his students) was not enough to change composition pedagogy in general.

[6] For an overview of the work done during the seventies and early eighties, see Griffin. For good discussions of contemporary ideas and attitudes, see the essays in Anson, several of which have very complete bibliographies.

[7] Those who want to know the details about how the 3,000 randomized and stratified papers were selected for this study are referred to the long footnotes in our 1988 study. These papers are not the same ones, but they were pulled from the pile of 21,000 using exactly the same methodology.

[8] One of our *CCC* referees made the irrefutable point that the self-selected nature of our sample meant that this study could make no claim of reflecting all of the possible kinds of student-teacher interaction:

> For instance, if I had received the request to send in a set of papers, and the set I had currently at hand were papers I mark in preparation for personal conferences, to discuss how the paper should be revised for a further draft, then indeed I would become one of the 7,700 who declined, simply because my commenting on that type of draft is extremely minimal. . . . I wouldn't send the set in because I am sure the researchers would be able to make little out of it, and yet the very kind of conferencing and push toward revision and treatment of writing as an act in progress and not as a completed copy is the kind of teacher commentary that the authors complain they found little of in the "database."

This observation is very accurate, and it is a prime reason why we make no attempt to claim that our sample represents all teachers, or to derive percentages about teachers using revision, etc. What we wanted to try to analyze here was specifically *written* commentary, the rhetorical interaction that goes between teachers and students via the traditional marginal and terminal commentary. We make no claims at all about the various other sorts of student-teacher interaction possible; indeed, there is no way we can know any more than what is suggested by the papers we studied. Nonetheless, we can't agree with Lil Brannon's assessment, given at a panel on this research at the 1992 CCCC, that "we do not learn very much from this kind of study." For many teachers and students, written commentary remains the primary interchange they have, and understanding it better cannot be unimportant.

[9] The ratings of our 26 readers were not checked for traditional kinds of inter-rater reliability either by us or by repeated ratings. Because of the "slippery" nature of rhetorical possibility, such tight controls were simply not realistic. We counted on the number of readers and their level of expertise to give our study the only kind of reliability we thought practical. We have little doubt that 26 other readers looking at 3,000 other papers would come up with slightly different numbers, but we would be surprised if those numbers led to substantially different inferences.

[10] As our readers looked at these papers, they had the impression that the grading curve on them was lower than their own, and while we could not, as we said, complete a serious statistical analysis of the grades because we had no context for many of them, a very rough analysis of the first 350 pure-letter grades on our sheets turned up the following, which, for the sake of interest, we contrast with similar information gleaned from Bowman (248) on grades at the University of Missouri in 1920:

	1915–1920	1980–1985
A-range grades	4%	9%
B-range grades	21%	39%
C-range grades	52%	37%
D-range grades	16%	12%
F grades	7%	3%

Sue Carter Simmon's research with Barrett Wendell's gradebook provides an interesting corroboration of those early figures. His English A grades at Harvard between 1887 and 1890 were in these ranges: A-4%, B-16%, C-46%, D-30%, and F-4% (178–79). Our findings are very speculative, and concentrating only on the pure letter grades clearly skews the results in this rough comparison, but certainly we see some grade inflation, especially at the B-range level. At many schools today, grade inflation has turned the old "gentleman's C" into the "partier's B," thus putting a crack in the classic bell curve, but these numbers do not seem to us to be completely out of line with grading expectations from our own teaching.

[11] Of course, these sorts of comments can easily become mechanically formulaic, as was early recognized. For a funny (and early) view of these and other rhetorical commentary formulas, see Eble.

[12] In this same section of the study we also asked our readers to look for comments aimed at uses of quotations, use of source materials, and use of documentation and citation forms; all three of these elements elicited comments from between 6% and 7% of all commented papers. The conclusion we draw from these numbers is simply that between 6% and 7% of the papers examined were generic "research papers," and could thus be expected to contain quotations, sources, and cites, all of which are likely to be commented on by teachers. Quotations were seldom found outside of research papers and literary analyses; students, it seems, rarely use sources or citations unless pushed to do so by specific assignments.

[13] This whole question of how teachers engage as readers of student writing has tantalizing implications about men's and women's ways of knowing and about gendered response and teacher-student interaction. In this study, we did not build in any systematic ways of identifying the gender of either teachers or students. Given our data base, it could have been done, but it would have made what we did do immensely more complex. That piece of research remains in the future, but we do hope to take it up.

WORKS CITED

Anson, Chris M., ed. *Writing and Response: Theory, Practice, and Research.* Urbana: NCTE, 1989.

Auten, Janet Gebhart. "A Rhetoric of Teacher Commentary: The Complexity of Response to Student Writing." *Focuses* 4 (1991): 3–18.

Barnes, Walter. "The Reign of Red Ink." *English Journal* 2 (Mar. 1913): 158–65.

Bowman, James C. "The Marking of English Themes." *English Journal* 9 (May 1920): 245–54.

Brannon, Lil. "Response." Conference on College Composition and Communication. Cincinnati, 20 Mar. 1992.

Brown, Marion D., and M. E. Hagerty. "The Measurement of Improvement in English Composition." *English Journal* 6 (Oct. 1917): 515–27.

Collins, Harold R. "Conversing in the Margins." *College English* 15 (May 1954): 465–66.

Connors, Robert J., and Andrea A. Lunsford. "Frequency of Formal Errors in Current College Writing, or, Ma and Pa Kettle Do Research." *College Composition and Communication* 39 (Dec. 1988): 395–409.

Copeland, Charles T., and H. M. Rideout. *Freshman English and Theme Correcting at Harvard College.* New York: Silver-Burdett, 1901.

Corbett, Edward P. J. *Selected Essays of Edward P. J. Corbett.* Ed. Robert J. Connors. Dallas: Southern Methodist UP, 1989.

Daiker, Donald A. "Learning to Praise." Anson 103–13.

Eble, Kenneth E. "Everyman's Handbook of Final Comments on Freshman Themes." *College English* 19 (Dec. 1957): 126–27.

Fleece, Jeffrey. "Teacher as Audience." *College English* 13 (Feb. 1952): 272-75.

Gilbert, Allan H. "What Shall We Do with Freshman Themes?" *English Journal* 11 (Sep. 1922): 392-403.

Griffin, C. W. "Theory of Responding to Student Writing: The State of the Art." *College Composition and Communication* 33 (Oct. 1982): 296-301.

Griswold, Louise. "Getting Results from Theme-Correction." *English Journal* 18 (Mar. 1929): 245-47.

Hewitt, Charles C. "Criticism—Getting It Over." *English Journal* 10 (Feb. 1921): 85-88.

Hillocks, George Jr. *Research on Written Composition: New Directions for Teaching.* Urbana: NCRE, 1986.

Holley, Hilda. "Correcting and Grading Themes." *English Journal* 13 (Jan. 1924): 29-34.

Hudelson, Earl. "The Development and Comparative Values of Composition Scales." *English Journal* 12 (Mar. 1923): 163-68.

James, H. W. "A National Survey of the Grading of College Freshman Composition." *English Journal* 12 (Oct. 1926): 579-87.

Kitzhaber, Albert R. *Themes, Theories, and Therapy: The Teaching of Writing in College.* New York: McGraw-Hill, 1963.

Knoblauch, C. H., and Lil Brannon. "Teacher Commentary on Student Writing: The State of the Art." *Freshman English News* 10 (Fall 1981): 1-4.

Leonard, Sterling A. "Building a Scale of Purely Composition Quality." *English Journal* 14 (Dec. 1925): 760-75.

Phelps, Louise W. "Images of Student Writing: The Deep Structure of Teacher Response." Anson 37-67.

Rodabaugh, Delmer. "Assigning and Commenting on Themes." *College English* 16 (Oct. 1954): 33-37.

Rohman, D. Gordon. "Pre-Writing: The Stage of Discovery in the Writing Process." *College Composition and Communication* 16 (May 1965): 106-12.

Schwegler, Robert. "The Politics of Reading Student Papers." *The Politics of Writing Instruction: Postsecondary.* Ed. Richard Bullock and John Trimbur. Portsmouth: Boynton/Cook, 1991, 203-26.

Simmons, Sue Carter. "A Critique of the Stereotypes of Current-Traditional Rhetoric: Invention and Writing Instruction at Harvard, 1875-1900." Diss. U of Texas at Austin, 1991.

Sommers, Nancy I. "Responding to Student Writing." *College Composition and Communication* 33 (May 1982): 148-56.

Scott, Fred Newton. "Our Problems." *English Journal* 2 (Jan. 1913): 1-10.

This article is reprinted from *College Composition and Communication* 44 (May 1993): 200-24. —Ed.

Acknowledgments (continued from copyright page)

"Rethinking Diversity: Axes of Difference in the Writing Classroom," Beverly J. Moss and Keith Walters from *Theory and Practice in the Teaching of Writing: Rethinking the Discipline.* Ed. Lee Odell. Carbondale: Southern Illinois University Press, 1993.

"Revising the Tagmemic Heuristic: Theoretical and Pedagogical Considerations," Charles Kneupper. *College Composition and Communication,* May 1980. Copyright 1980 by the National Council of Teachers of English. Reprinted with permission.

"Rhetorical Theory and the Teaching of Writing," Andrea A. Lunsford and Cheryl Glenn. *On Literacy and Its Teaching: Issues in English Education.* Ed. Gail E. Hawisher and Anna O. Soter. 1990. Reprinted with permission of the authors and the State University of New York Press.

"Teachers' Rhetorical Comments on Student Papers," Robert J. Connors and Andrea A. Lunsford. *College Composition and Communication.* May 1993. Copyright 1993 by the National Council of Teachers of English. Reprinted with permission.

"Where Were We, Where Are We as Community College English Teachers?" Elisabeth McPherson. *Teaching English in the Two-Year College.* May 1990. Copyright 1990 by the National Council of Teachers of English. Reprinted with permission.

"Writer-Based Prose: A Cognitive Basis for Problems in Writing," Linda Flower. *College English.* September 1979. Copyright 1979 by the National Council of Teachers of English. Reprinted with permission.

"Writing as a Mode of Learning," Janet Emig. *College Composition and Communication.* May 1977. Copyright 1977 by the National Council of Teachers of English. Reprinted with permission.

Writing the Natural Way, Gabriele Lusser Rico. From pages 11, 12, 36, 37. Reprinted by permission of The Putnam Publishing Group/Jeremy P. Tarcher, Inc. Copyright © 1983 by Gabriele Lusser Rico.

467

INDEX